ARCHAEOLOGY

ORIGINAL READINGS IN METHOD AND PRACTICE

Edited by

Peter N. Peregrine
Lawrence University

Carol R. Ember
Human Relations Area Files

Melvin Ember
Human Relations Area Files

Prentice
Hall

UPPER SADDLE RIVER, NEW JERSEY 07458

Library of Congress Cataloging-in-Publication Data

Archaeology: original readings in method and practice/edited by Peter N. Peregrine,
Carol R. Ember, Melvin Ember.
   p. cm.
   Includes bibliographical references.
   ISBN 0-13-093978-1
     1. Archaeology—Methodology. 2. Archaeology—Research. 3. Archaeology—Case studies.
I. Peregrine, Peter N. (Peter Neal). II. Ember, Carol R. III. Ember, Melvin.

CC75 .A658 2001
930.1'028—dc21   2001052332

AVP, Publisher: Nancy Roberts
Editorial assistant: Lee Peterson
Marketing manager: Chris Barker
Editorial/production supervision: Kari Callaghan Mazzola
Prepress and manufacturing buyer: Ben Smith
Electronic page makeup: Kari Callaghan Mazzola and John P. Mazzola
Interior design: John P. Mazzola
Cover director: Jayne Conte

This book was set in 10/12 Palatino by Big Sky Composition
and was printed and bound by Von Hoffman Graphics.
The cover was printed by Phoenix Color Corp.

 © 2002 by Pearson Education, Inc.
Upper Saddle River, New Jersey 07458

Printed in the United States of America
10 9 8 7 6 5 4 3 2 1

ISBN 0-13-093978-1

Pearson Education LTD., London
Pearson Education Australia PTY, Limited, Sydney
Pearson Education Singapore, Pte. Ltd
Pearson Education North Asia Ltd, Hong Kong
Pearson Education Canada, Ltd., Toronto
Pearson Educación de Mexico, S.A. de C.V.
Pearson Education—Japan, Tokyo
Pearson Education Malaysia, Pte. Ltd
Pearson Education, Upper Saddle River, New Jersey

CONTENTS

end
notes
important

our focus

iii

PART IV   ARCHAEOLOGISTS AT WORK

PREFACE

Which would you rather read: (A) "The stratigraphic profile was partially obscured due to the extremely arid conditions," or (B) "The dust rising from the strong desert wind made it hard for me to see the stratigraphy"? If you answered B, then this book is for you. Most collections of articles that are used in undergraduate courses are made up of works patched together from material written by archaeologists for other archaeologists or, in some cases, for a popular audience. Rarely are works included that were written explicitly for college students. This is a problem, for works written for scholars are too detailed and jargon-laden for students to digest easily, while works written for a popular audience contain little information that would be new to students who have already been exposed to archaeology. This book, on the other hand, is composed of chapters written explicitly for college students. The chapters are not reprints of articles published elsewhere, but were composed for you, a student of archaeology, to help you appreciate the methods, practices, and experiences of some of the top archaeologists working today.

How do the chapters in this book differ from those in other collections? Usually when we read an article or book chapter about a piece of research, we find out about the results—what the researchers think they have discovered, what they think they know. Rarely do we get to understand the process. Where do ideas come from? How does an idea get transformed into a research project? What was exciting about the research? What was disappointing? What is the person behind the process like? These questions are rarely addressed in scholarly writing, and they are often absent even in popular accounts of research. Here these questions are central, for the archaeologists who wrote the chapters in this collection wanted to help you understand the process of archaeological discovery. They wanted you to understand not only what they found, but also how they went about finding it, and what the experience was like. Most of all, they wanted to excite you about archaeology—not only about the findings in archaeology, but also about the process of doing archaeology itself.

The purpose of this collection is to make research more alive for students like you who are just beginning to get to know archaeology. Part I, "Archaeological Methods," focuses on the way archaeologists find and recover data from archaeological sites and materials. Rather than being dry "by-the-numbers" instructions for doing research, each chapter brings the experiences and insights of an active archaeologist to the practical matters of doing archaeological research. The authors all provide examples from their own research to give you a better sense of how archaeological methods are actually employed in the field and laboratory.

Part II, "Issues and Controversies in Contemporary Archaeology," also tries to convey a feeling for the research process, but each chapter is focused on a particular issue or controversy rather than a method. Here the authors deal with some of the following kinds of questions: "What are the different theories or opinions in this controversy?" "What is the evidence, if any, for each side?" "What kinds of research might be brought to bear on this issue to help resolve it?" "What rethinking might be necessary?" By focusing on issues and controversies where there is no obvious agreement in the archaeological community, the authors convey a feeling for the dynamics of research and the excitement of debate.

The dynamics of research are further explored in Part III, "Archaeological Case Studies." Here the authors illustrate how they applied archaeological methods to particular cases of interest to them—from the origins of complex polities in sub-Saharan Africa to gender roles in the Inka empire. As in Part II, the authors in Part III deal with a set of related questions: "What made you interested in this particular case?" "What data did you need to examine this case?" "What methods did you use to collect the data?" "What did you discover and what new questions did your research raise?" The purpose of Part III is to illustrate the variety of questions asked by archaeologists and the diverse methods they use to answer them.

Finally, Part IV, "Archaeologists at Work," includes two autobiographical articles. We left it up to the archaeologists to choose what they wanted to write about. After all, we want you to get a feeling for how archaeological researchers vary, not just how archaeological research varies. In these ways, we hope you will come to appreciate that archaeology is not just an unemotional set of methods and data, but rather a bunch of hard-working, insightful people who employ those methods to answer particular questions about the past.

ACKNOWLEDGMENTS

The chapters collected here were composed between 1995 and 2000 by a diverse group of scholars who set aside their research projects and teaching loads to take the time to write these engaging pieces. The task was easy for some, difficult for others, but enjoyable for all. We want to thank all the authors for their efforts in producing these fine works for undergraduate students. We also want to thank the people at Prentice Hall, particularly Nancy Roberts and Sharon Chambliss, who have been tremendously supportive and helpful throughout the process of getting this work into print. Before appearing here many of the chapters were part of the *Research Frontiers in Anthropology* series, published by Simon & Schuster Custom Publishing, and our thanks go to Pat Naturale, Stephanie Mathiessen, and Kari Callaghan Mazzola for their help in the initial production of these works. Finally, we want to thank you, the reader, for taking the time to explore the product of our collective efforts.

Peter N. Peregrine
Carol R. Ember
Melvin Ember

THE DISCOVERY
OF ARCHAEOLOGICAL SITES

STEPHEN BALL

Archaeologists seek to reconstruct the lifeways of past cultures through the analysis of material remains people in the past have left behind. The locations where these artifacts are recovered are called sites and they represent the areas where people lived, worked, ate, died, and, perhaps most significantly, produced trash. The information gleaned from the excavation of sites, and the recovery of this "trash"—which archaeologists call artifacts—provides us with a deeper understanding of when, where, and how past human groups lived.

The identification of archaeological sites constitutes an essential part of any archaeologist's training. My first discovery of a site remains a vivid memory. It was during my first year of graduate research. I was an instructor in the Indiana University archaeological fieldschool, and I had been assigned the task of locating an area for a prospective surface survey. After participating in archaeological excavations and surveys for four years in the Boston area and in northern Kenya, I had yet to discover a site. My previous experience consisted of being led by others to areas where sites were known to be and then instructed to search (or excavate) for them. Now, however, as an experienced archaeologist, I was expected to be able to find sites on my own.

SURFACE SURVEYS

Having arrived in Indiana only eight months before, I was now in unfamiliar territory: the lower Ohio River Valley just south of Evansville, Indiana. My ignorance of the region was a serious impediment to my search. Fortunately, I had a companion in my quest. Shawn French was a native of Evansville and an undergraduate student assisting in our excavation. As a hobby, he had collected arrowheads from the surface of farmers' fields in the floodplain below Evansville for most of his life and was familiar with the area.

Initially, Shawn and I narrowed our search to the cultivated fields in the floodplain where site visibility would be high. Surface surveys, a form of systematic artifact collection, are more likely to be successful if they are directed toward areas where erosion brings buried cultural remains to the surface. A favorite location for such surveys are farm fields. The annual plowing brings buried artifacts to the surface and increases the rate of soil erosion. In time, this erosion exposes more archaeological sites that had been concealed below the surface.

Unfortunately for us, it had been a dry spring and most of the farmers had already planted their crops. Overall, farmers are a congenial group, but they do not appreciate college students systematically trampling their freshly sown seeds. We were thus unable to secure permission to walk many of the fields in which we were interested.

As we drove up and down the county roads searching for a survey location, we repeatedly drove by a farmhouse that stood on a large earthen mound. Rising in striking contrast to the otherwise flat floodplain, the mound had no geological explanation and was obviously artificial. We suspected that it was of modern construction because many of the contemporary residents of the floodplain build their houses on mounds to keep their basements dry during the spring floods. However, there was the possibility that it was prehistoric since there are also many prehistoric earthen mounds on the floodplains of southwest Indiana. Each time we drove by the mound we stopped, looked at it for a few seconds, looked at each other, shrugged, and then drove off to continue our search. After six fruitless hours of searching we decided to stop and examine the mound more closely. It was then that we noticed that the field directly in front of the house was unplanted! We walked up to the house to ask about the mound and whether we could walk on the field. The man who answered the door said that he only rented the place and did not know the mound's origin, but we were welcome to walk the field.

We began our survey by casually looking over the field, but our anticipation soon grew. We observed large quantities of potsherds (broken pottery vessels) and fragments from stone tools, but soon other, more exotic items began to command our attention. A piece of a clay figurine, worked turtle shell, cut mica, finely crafted stone blades, and a galena crystal were among our finds. Not only had we found a site, but we had located a significant Hopewellian site!

Hopewellian societies were characterized by extensive trade networks, large burial mounds, geometric earthworks, and a marked increase in mortuary ceremonialism. At our feet lay the debris from a Hopewellian settlement that prospered between 1,500 and 2,000 years ago. The only trace now left of these people was this scatter of artifacts and the nearby earthen mound in which they had buried their dead.

Having succeeded in our search, we tracked down the landowner and received permission to conduct a surface survey. Surface surveys, also referred to as field surveys, come in many styles; ours followed one of the most basic formats. We lined up the students on one end of the field, supplied them with plastic yellow pin flags, spaced them 1.5 meters apart, and had them walk across the field in a straight line. Whenever they came across an artifact they marked the location with a yellow flag. At the end of their survey line, called a transect, we would shift them over to an unsurveyed part of the field and repeat the exercise. By the end of the day two distinct clusters of yellow flags were apparent. The larger of the two clusters was the Hopewellian site Shawn and I had discovered, the second cluster was a Late Archaic site (circa 1500 B.C.), as indicated by the style of the projectile points recovered there. We had failed to notice it in our cursory examination but the more systematic survey had revealed its location. The two sites were then mapped and the artifacts collected.

Surface surveys are the oldest and most common method of finding archaeological sites. A knowledge of a region's landscapes and the type of landforms common to it are critical to an archaeologist. Through this knowledge the archaeologist can detect geographical features that seem odd or out of place, as in the case of the earthen mound. However, most sites are not so obvious and require more rigorous surveys, such as the one that detected the Archaic site. Archaeologists have sought to develop methods that allow them to systematically find sites. These methods range from simple surface surveys and local interviews to the use of satellite digital imagery and geophysical instruments.

GENERAL SURFACE SURVEYS

Surface surveys can be subdivided into two broad categories; general surface surveys and directed surface surveys. General surface surveys seek to identify all archaeological sites within a survey area. There are several initial steps in the design of a general surface survey for a region. The first step involves a review of records to determine if previous archaeological surveys have been done in the area; these survey records are usually kept by the local government. This is followed by a document search in which local histories, maps, and accounts from early travelers are examined for any information pertaining to archaeological sites. In my own experience of working in the American Midwest, one of the most important aspects of any survey are interviews with the local inhabitants. It will be the local people, with an intimate knowledge of the land, who will be aware of localities that produce artifacts. In countries where oral traditions still survive, ethnohistorical research may produce clues that can direct the archaeologist to prehistoric sites. Such sensitive use of indigenous oral tradition has been used, for example, by Peter Schmidt to uncover Iron Age smelting sites in Africa.[1]

DIRECTED SURFACE SURVEYS

Directed surface surveys, also known as "predictive" surveys, are aimed toward the discovery of specific types of sites within the survey area. The classification of the site type may be based on its cultural affiliation (for example, Roman settlements), function (hunting camps), or age (Medieval). Directed surface surveys are, by their nature, based on some knowledge of the selection criteria by which the site location was chosen. There are many factors that people take into consideration when deciding where they want to live. By identifying some of these choices the survey area can be narrowed to those site locations preferred in the past.

Environmental variables strongly influence the location of human settlements. All societies, including our own, live under ecological constraints, which limit the areas favorable to them. In extreme environmental situations certain ecological factors are so important that they dominate all other considerations. In desert regions, proximity to water is one such limiting factor. In most cases, however, the environment is not so demanding and there usually is an assortment of ecological parameters that will influence site location. While we may never know all the reasons that were involved in selecting a site, we can deduce some of the factors from an analysis of the locations of known sites of a similar type.

When developing a directed survey plan for the location of Angel phase sites (A.D. 1100–1400) in the lower Ohio Valley, I had a large body of knowledge to draw from to optimize the survey. The Angel phase is part of a more widespread archaeological complex called the Middle Mississippian. The Mississippians were primarily maize horticulturists, and previous surveys in the lower Ohio Valley had indicated that they focused on a relatively limited number of ecological parameters in their selection of settlement locations. Their farmsteads would typically be located on floodplain ridges in close proximity to wetland resources. The favored ridges were situated above the annual flood level and contained a minimum amount of fertile, easily tilled silt loam soils.[2]

I was able to identify the tracts of land within the survey area that fulfilled these ecological requirements fairly quickly, thanks to a new analytical tool, a Geographic Information System (GIS). A GIS is a computer program designed to store, display, and manipulate geographically referenced data. Within the GIS I had already developed map layers containing information on wetland resources, elevation, soil types, slope, aspect, and distance to water for the region of the lower Ohio Valley. The data for the map layers were derived from U.S. government sources.

Each map layer in the GIS consisted of a grid of geographically referenced cells containing values representing the ecological variables. In other words, each cell in the grid is represented by three numbers, the x and y coordinates specifying its location in the grid, and a z value, which is the value of the cell itself. On the elevation map layer, each cell's z value would be the number of feet above sea level at that particular location. The slope layer cells would contain the slope value in degrees. Each separate map layer represented the same geographical area, the lower Ohio Valley. A query could then be posed to the program, asking it to isolate the cells on each layer that met the ecological requirements that were important in locating Middle Mississippian sites. The GIS would compare the results from the search of each data layer and create a new data layer consisting of only those areas where all the requirements had been met. I was able to identify all tracts of land within the survey area that met the specified requirements with a single query to the GIS.

I do not wish to leave the impression that ecological factors are the only ones that guide site location. Economic, political, ideological, and historically contingent factors all enter into human decisions on site location. For example, the Chinese would traditionally plan their towns and buildings according to the tenets of *Feng Shui* (wind and water), a system of knowledge that would seek to locate structures so that they would be in harmony with the natural forces of the world.[3] Economic factors favor the location of trade centers along major transportation routes, and administrative centers are usually placed in the center of an administrative region.[4] Other groups whose cosmologies, economies, and political structures are known to us require far more complex models of site location than the example I presented earlier for the Angel phase.

As a general rule in any directed survey plan, the older the site you are looking for the more important will be the impact of geological process. Problems of environmental reconstruction become of great importance when the modern environment is radically different from the ancient one. For example, in the lower Mississippi Valley the active nature of the Mississippi River in carving new channels and meandering across its floodplain will govern where you would look for sites belonging to a certain time period. It would be a waste of resources and time to survey for Middle Woodland sites (200 B.C. to A.D. 500) on a floodplain ridge that formed less than 500 years ago.[5]

An excellent example of a directed survey governed by geological concerns is the search for early human sites. While taking part in hominid surveys at Koobi Fora on the east side of Lake Turkana in Kenya, I realized how dependent archaeologists are on their geology skills, or more often the skills of the full-time geologist involved in the survey. The Rift Valley of East Africa is a favorite haunt of paleoanthropologists due to the geological characteristics of the area. Hominids (the ancestors of modern humans) lived in various areas of the tropical Old World during the Pliocene and Pleistocene time periods (5.3 million to 30,000 years ago). Over time, these hominid sites were buried by natural geological processes. It is only with the reexposure of these geological levels that these sites can be located.

The spreading apart of the earth's crust in the Rift Valley of East Africa has exposed these Plio-Pleistocene sediments, from which early human fossils and artifacts have been recovered. This geological situation makes Kenya and

Ethiopia the target of many hominid surveys. On the other hand, the Badlands of Montana, rather than Kenya, are where researchers interested in dinosaur fossils go. The sediments being exposed in the Rift Valley are far younger (by millions of years!) than the Mesozoic deposits, which contain dinosaur fossils, being exposed in the Badlands. The key, then, is to select areas in which the geological strata from the appropriate time period are exposed and accessible.

A major weakness to surface surveys is that most archaeological sites are not visible from the ground; they are too deeply buried. Archaeologists often make use of test pits to locate these subsurface archaeological deposits. Test pits can come in a range of sizes and techniques, but they are basically holes dug into the ground in the hope of finding a site. You can imagine the amount of time and effort that this entails and the potential damage to sites. Therefore, archaeologists have sought more efficient and less destructive methods of subsurface site location. These nondestructive, noninvasive methods are grouped under the category of remote sensing.

REMOTE SENSING

Remote sensing techniques are used to identify subsurface archaeological sites by measuring various qualities of the physical environment that are changed due to the effects of human habitation and other activities. Remote sensing surveys can be divided into two broad categories: geophysical and airborne remote sensing. Geophysical remote sensing employs instruments on or near the surface of the ground. Airborne remote sensing, as the name implies, utilizes measurements taken from the air or even from space. The results from remote sensing surveys are not as easy to interpret as those from surface surveys. Interpretation of these results must be based on some understanding of the physical properties being measured.

NOT SITE DISCOVERY TECHNIQUES

GEOPHYSICAL REMOTE SENSING

Magnetic surveys detect small changes in the earth's magnetic field near the surface of the ground. An instrument known as a magnetometer is used to record the intensity of the earth's magnetic field over the survey area. A magnetic survey conducted over an area with a homogenous soil would reveal a uniform magnetic field—there would be no variation in the readings. A magnetic survey over an area with subsurface concentrations of burned soil, fire-cracked rocks, ceramics, or iron would reveal the location of these features as anomalous magnetic readings. These anomalous readings are due to the enhanced magnetic susceptibility of these materials. Magnetic susceptibility is the natural ability of an object or material to produce a magnetic field when exposed to an external magnetic field, in this case that of the earth.

Human behavior will often enhance a material's magnetic susceptibility. One of the primary agents in enhancing an object's magnetic susceptibility is heating. Human activities such as the production of metal, ceramics, or the heating of earth under a hearth all produce materials with a residual magnetism called thermoremanent magnetism. The presence of this thermoremanent magnetism dramatically increases a material's magnetic susceptibility. Such materials, when buried, provide a strong magnetic contrast to the surrounding soil matrix.

Magnetic surveys are conducted by establishing a grid of points or a series of transects over a survey area and recording the magnetic intensity at selected points. During the survey, the readings can be recorded by the instruments' on-board data logger, or the old-fashioned way, by hand, and loaded into a computer program that will map the magnetic values. Two popular forms of maps used to display magnetic data are dot density and contour (isoline) maps. Dot-density maps indicate the intensity of the magnetic field through the density of dots per inch, while contour maps use lines to connect values of a similar intensity. An example of each is shown in Figure 1-1 on page 8.

The maps in Figure 1-1 are the results of an actual magnetic survey and indicate the presence of a buried Angel phase house (the square three-sided anomaly). The high magnetic susceptibility of at least three of the house walls is the result of its construction technique and the manner in which it was destroyed. It provides a good illustration of the value of magnetic surveys. Angel phase houses were constructed of wattle and daub, consisting of a wicker-work frame (wattle) over which was smeared a thick layer of clay (the daub). The roofs of the houses were thatched. In the normal course of events this structure would decay over time and the daub would erode back into the soil. However, if the building burned down, which was not uncommon for thatched roof cabins, the daub would be fired to a hard ceramic, which is quite durable and has an enhanced magnetic susceptibility. The magnetic survey detected concentrations of this fired daub deposited at the base of the burned house walls.

The enhanced magnetic susceptibility of fired clay is due to the iron oxides that occur naturally in most clays. These iron oxide particles have their own individual magnetic fields (magnetic domains), but the particles within the clay tend to be randomly aligned, so their magnetic domains usually cancel one another out. When a clay is heated to a high temperature (around 700° C), as during ceramic production, the magnetic domains of the iron particles enter a state of flux and line up preferentially with an external magnetic field, in this case that of the earth. This preferential alignment is maintained after the material cools, resulting in a material with a permanent thermoremanent magnetism and a far higher magnetic susceptibility than the clay from which it was formed.

Resistivity surveys focus on different physical properties of sites than magnetic surveys. Resistivity surveys measure the resistance of a volume of

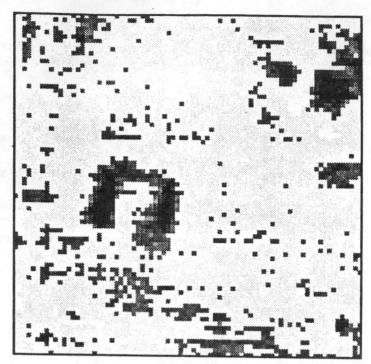

FIGURE 1-1
Top: Dot-Density Map; Bottom: Contour Map

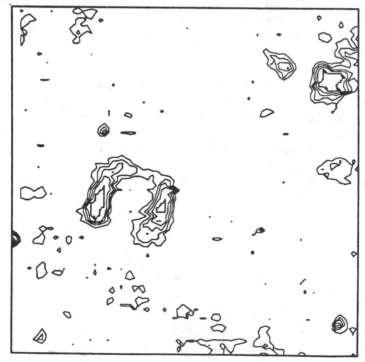

soil to the passage of an electrical current. Resistivity surveys come in a variety of forms, but they share a basic configuration. An electrical current is introduced into the ground by external probes while the measurements are made over selected points by a resistivity meter.

A variant of resistivity surveys are conductivity surveys, sometimes referred to as electromagnetic (EM) surveys. Both methods measure the same property (the ability of a volume of soil to conduct an electrical current), but they go about it in different ways. Conductivity meters generally contain two coils, one of which sends a radio wave into the ground, which induces a current in the soil. The other coil is located at the opposite end of the instrument and acts as a receiver for the signal produced by the induced current. The induced current will be modified by the nature of the soil through which it passes.

Many variables affect the ability of a soil to conduct an electrical current, but the primary factor is the ability of a soil to retain water. This ability can be augmented or decreased by human action. Let us return to the example of an Angel phase house (Figure 1-2). The posts that supported the wattle and daub walls were placed in the ground using a construction technique known as a wall trench. First, a shallow trench was dug into the subsoil and the postholes were excavated in the trench. Wooden posts were set in the postholes and the trench was then backfilled around the posts to provide a more stable footing for the walls. An inadvertent result of this process was the mixing of the more organic topsoil with the subsoil within the wall trench. After the house had been torn down or decayed naturally, the wall trench remained as a slightly more organic soil feature. It is more organic than the surrounding soil due to the mixing of the topsoil with the subsoil during the backfilling of the trench and the decay of the wooden posts within the trench itself. The trench will retain water better than the surrounding soil, resulting in a low resistivity reading (Figure 1-2).

Legend

▨ wall trench
▦ posthole
▩ hearth
▨ house floor

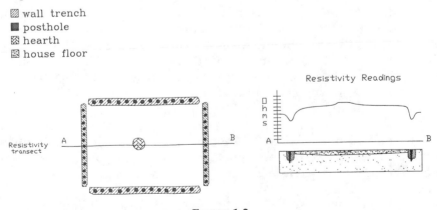

FIGURE 1-2
Left: Plan View; Right: Cross-Section

Conversely, the dirt floor of the house, under normal conditions, will register a high resistivity reading. This high resistivity is due to the compression of the dirt floor by foot traffic, which reduces the pore size of the soil. The compressed soil of the house floor will retain less water than the surrounding soil (Figure 1-2). In a similar manner, a buried stone wall will be highly resistive, given the nonporous nature of most stone building materials, while a subsurface trash pit would be less resistive due to the decomposition of organic materials within it. As in magnetic surveys, it is the contrast between archaeological features and the natural soil matrix that is most important.

Ground Penetrating Radar (GPR) is a remote sensing technique of great promise. Though in use since the 1970s, the technique has only recently begun to be applied extensively to archaeological sites. GPR operates in a manner similar to that of above ground radar. Pulses of electromagnetic radiation are sent into the earth and the return signals are analyzed for the location of subsurface features. The method responds to discontinuities in the electrical properties of soils, as do resistivity surveys. The refraction of these radio waves, due to marked differences in soil boundaries, are recorded by the radar receiver. An important advantage of GPR is the ability to control the range of the signal (the depth to which the instrument will read) and the ability to determine the depth of the detected feature by measuring the return times of the reflected signals. This technique works best on features that have very distinct boundaries in contrast to the surrounding soil.

The effectiveness of most geophysical techniques depends on the existence of discrete features (pits, houses, hearths) that provide a contrast with the surrounding soil matrix. There are some geophysical methods that can detect human occupation even when there are no longer intact features present. Magnetic susceptibility surveys are one of these methods. Magnetic susceptibility surveys focus on the magnetic properties of the topsoil rather than on sub-surface features. The magnetic susceptibility of a topsoil can be changed dramatically by the effects of human habitation. Enhanced magnetic susceptibility can be traced to the human use of fire and the resulting production of slightly magnetic forms of iron oxides, such as maghaemite. Soils that have been magnetically enhanced by human habitation will retain these characteristics even after hundreds of years of weathering and plowing.[6] It is possible through this method to detect an area that had been a village, even if all the material traces of village life had been plowed away. A magnetic susceptibility survey can be conducted in the field like a magnetometer survey, or alternatively, soil samples can be collected from selected points and brought back to the laboratory for analysis.

Geochemical surveys, like magnetic susceptibility surveys, focus on the effects of human habitation on the topsoil. The most common of these techniques is phosphate detection. Humans absorb phosphates through the ingestion of plants and animals, and the phosphate is then concentrated in their bodies and eventually in their excreta. Human site occupation can dramatically increase the amount of phosphate being deposited in the soil. These phosphates then bind to the clay particles within the soil and are quite durable. Phosphate analysis can be quite useful when searching for sites of sedentary groups, but it can also be used in the detection of more ephemeral pastoralist encampments. Pastoralists, groups who subsist primarily on the products of domestic animals, do not generally erect substantial housing and they seldom stay in one place throughout the year. The concentration of these domestic animals, especially in holding pens or kraals, will leave a distinct phosphate signature on the soil. The phosphate levels are retained within the topsoil and can give indications as to the size of the site. Phosphate surveys usually consist of taking soil samples from the survey area and measuring the soil phosphate level in a laboratory.

AIRBORNE REMOTE SENSING

One of the oldest remote sensing techniques used in archaeology is that of aerial photography. The use of oblique aerial photography to locate prehistoric sites was first widely applied in Great Britain after World War I.[7] It had been noticed during Royal Air Force (R.A.F.) training missions that certain features of prehistoric sites were visible from the air but invisible on the ground. Buried archaeological sites were often distinguished by shadows, soil color, moisture marks, or the differential growth of vegetation. A high vantage point made these extensive patterns visible to the observer. Aerial photography provides the capability of systematically examining entire regions for traces of cultural site locations that are not apparent to an observer on the ground.

The visual indicators of sites detected from the air are often quite ephemeral, only appearing under certain environmental conditions. Shadow sites are formed by buried archaeological structures, part of which are still above ground. Undetectable from the surface, these sites are revealed by the slight shadows they cast in the early morning and late afternoon, the result of the low angle of the sun's rays. Soil sites are formed by differences in soil color usually associated with differential moisture retention. Such soil stains are often the result of buried ditches, whose contents provide a marked contrast with their soil matrix, or buried stone structures that retain less water than the surrounding soils. These are basically the same phenomena measured by resistivity surveys. Soil sites are especially apparent after a rainstorm or during an extended drought. Crop sites occur due to the effect that differences in the nature of the underlying soils have on vegetative growth. Buried archaeological features will affect the development of crops growing above them (see Figure 1-3 on page 12).

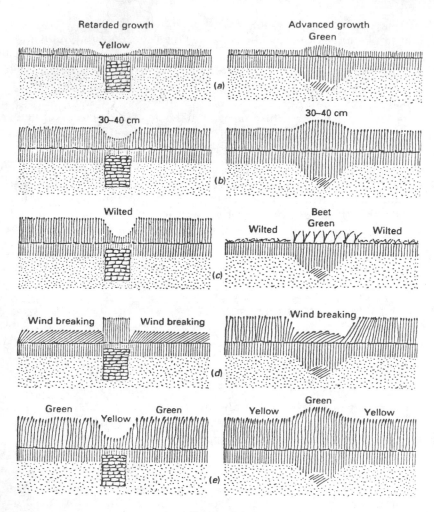

FIGURE 1-3

The effect of a buried structure on an overlying crop—retardation or normal growth: (a) the spring; (b) the appearance; (c) and (d) fixing; and (e) ripening.

Thermal sensing can also be done from the air. In this method the phenomenon being detected is the tendency of some materials to retain heat better than others. By mapping the variation in the surface temperature of the ground, usually with an airborne radiometer, subsurface structures can be detected. A buried Roman road can be detected due to the ability of the road rock to retain solar heat better than the surrounding soils. A "poor man's" thermal survey can be accomplished by aerial surveys of a region after a light snowfall. The differential melting can reveal the locations of archaeological sites. Thermal surveys are best undertaken over bare soil to avoid the masking effects of vegetation. Farm fields after harvesting are usually the best choice. On the other hand, thermal surveys using cameras loaded with near-infrared film focus on the thermal properties of the overlying vegetation, which is dependent on the plants' health. This in turn is highly dependent on the nature of the underlying soil and will be affected by subsurface archaeological features.

Satellite remote sensing incorporates many of the advantages of aerial photography but from an even higher vantage point. The satellites measure the spectral properties of vegetation and soils across the electromagnetic spectrum. These properties can be used to determine the health of the vegetation, its biomass, species type, moisture level, and soil types. The data are recorded electronically as digital images. Each of the images is a matrix of cells, similar to a map layer in a GIS, referred to as pixels. Just as the individual grains of a color photograph represent a color, each pixel making up the digital image has a numerical value, which represents the reflectance of a section of the earth's surface. This digital image can be converted to visual images or manipulated statistically in its original form.

Present uses of satellite data by archaeologists are quite varied. The chief use of satellite digital imagery in archaeology is its incorporation into models of archaeological site location. Satellite data are used to better define the environmental characteristics of areas where archaeological sites have been found and then to identify unsurveyed areas with the same characteristics, in other words, to identify areas that have a high potential for sites. It has been used to detect ancient caravan routes in the Middle East. The soils of the caravan routes had been modified by the impact of donkey and camel hooves. This soil modification was not detectable in visible light but was quite obvious in the near-infrared portion of the electromagnetic spectrum. A new microwave radar has been developed that can actually penetrate some soils up to thirteen feet deep. It has been used on the space shuttle to detect ancient rivers buried by the Sahara Desert. This information will be used to direct the search for buried sites located along these ancient rivers.

The techniques of archaeological site surveying have been enriched by the technological developments of the past thirty years. However, archaeologists have not forgotten the basic principles of surface surveying to embrace what is the new and technically sophisticated. Rather, they have continued to improve the methodological basis of traditional site surveying while incorporating new techniques into their overall survey plans.

NOTES

1. Peter Schmidt, *Historical Archaeology: A Structural Approach to an African Culture* (Westport, CT: Greenwood Press, 1978).
2. Jon Muller, *Archaeology of the Lower Ohio River Valley* (New York: Academic Press, 1986).
3. Paul Wheatley, *The Pivot of the Four Quarters: A Preliminary Enquiry into the Origins and Character of the Ancient Chinese City* (Chicago: Aldine, 1971).
4. Joyce Marcus, *Emblem and State in the Classic Maya Lowlands: An Epigraphic Approach to Territorial Organization* (Washington, D.C.: Dumbarton Oaks, 1986).
5. Roger T. Saucier, "Quaternary Geology of the Lower Mississippi Valley," *Arkansas Archaeological Survey Research Series* 6 (1974).
6. Anthony Clark, *Seeing Beneath the Soil: Prospecting Methods in Archaeology* (London: B.T. Batsford Ltd., 1990).
7. O. G. S. Crawford, "Air Survey and Archaeology," *Ordnance Survey Professional Papers*, New Series 7 (London: Ordnance Survey, 1924).

SUGGESTED READINGS

Clark, Anthony. *Seeing Beneath the Soil: Prospecting Methods in Archaeology*. London: B.T. Batsford Ltd., 1990. A very good introduction to the subject by one of the pioneers in geophysical remote sensing.

Flannery, Kent V., ed. *The Early Mesoamerican Village*. New York: Academic Press, 1976. An edited volume that discusses some of the more important issues in archaeological surveying. Well-written and at times humorous.

Gaffney, Vincent, and Zoran Stancic. *GIS Approaches to Regional Analysis: A Case Study of the Island of Hvar*. Ljubljana: Znanstveni institut Filozofoske fakultete, 1991. This book may be difficult to find but it is one of the few basic and approachable works on the use of GIS in archaeology.

Scollar, Irwin, A. Tabbagh, A. Hesse, and I. Herzog. *Archaeological Prospecting and Remote Sensing*. Cambridge: Cambridge University Press, 1990. This book is at times quite technical but it is one of the best sources on the use of geophysical remote sensing and aerial photography in archaeology.

Thomas, David Hurst. *Archaeology*. New York: Holt, Rinehart & Winston, 1989. My most highly recommended book. Thomas is able to discuss some of the more sophisticated theories on sampling in archaeological surveys in a clear and approachable manner.

seriation + exercise

DATING ARCHAEOLOGICAL MATERIALS

R. E. TAYLOR

A colleague asked my laboratory to undertake the radiocarbon dating of a bone from a human skeleton recovered near the town of Kennewick, Washington. This skeleton exhibited some very interesting features. Upon initial examination of the physical characteristics of the skull and other bones, the first impression was that it was the skeleton of an early European settler in the Pacific Northwest. Europeans had first arrived in that region at the earliest only in the late 1700s. However, on closer inspection, a stone projectile point that in other contexts had been dated as old as 8,000 years in this area was found imbedded in the pelvis of the skeleton. How could an ancient artifact be found in a skeleton that appeared at most to be only several hundred years old? A radiocarbon date would provide the answer as to the age.

When the date was obtained, it turned out that the skeleton dated to the ninth millennium B.C. This result catapulted the Kennewick skeleton into both the popular press and subjected it to close scientific scrutiny. What were the implications of having a skeleton that did not appear to be Native American in appearance present in the New World at such an early time period? Could a group from Eurasia distinct from the people whose descendants are the modern Native Americans have entered the New World very early?

"How old is it?" is one of the most frequent questions that visitors to museums ask when viewing archaeological objects. When newspapers report on the discovery of a supposed new fossil ancestor of our species, almost inevitably the suggested age of the fossil is mentioned in the first paragraph of the story. When results from an excavation at an archaeological site are discussed, the question of "how old?" is almost always one of the first questions posed. The interested public are most curious about how long ago a fossil lived or an artifact was used. Professional archaeologists and paleoanthropologists are also concerned with the age of archaeological materials. This is because one of the purposes of archaeological research is to examine the evolution of human cultures over relatively long periods of time.[1]

CHRONOLOGICAL FRAMEWORKS

Chronology orders the sequential relationship of physical events by associating these events with some type of time scale. Depending on the types of materials for which temporal placement is required, different types of time scales have been developed. Geochronological (geological) time temporally relates elements of the physical structures of the earth's solid surface and buried features, documenting a 4.5 to 5.0 billion year period. The paleontological time scale orders the physical remains (fossils) of once living organisms and thus must cover at least the last 500 to 600 million years.

The paleoanthropological time scale involves the fossil record over about the last 5 to 6 million year period documenting the evolution of the *Hominidae* (hominids), the group of bipedal primates of which we (anatomically modern *Homo sapiens*) are the only extant species—all others having become extinct. The archaeological time scale temporally orders the physical remains (artifacts) and features reflecting hominid behavior over at least the last 2 million years. Finally, the historical time scale involves a period of time—not more than about the last 5,000 years—during which a few human societies have documented their activities with textual (written) data whose meanings, at least in part, can be deciphered.

Different historic and scientific disciplines require and utilize chronologies using vastly different time scales. However, a fundamental distinction of particular significance in archaeology involves relative ordering or *relative dating* in contrast to chronometric dating. Relative ordering places events in a temporal sequence—namely, earlier than or later than—without specifying any temporal scale that specifies how much earlier or how much later. Chronometric dating applies a specific time scale utilizing some fixed-rate mechanism the defined time is based on, for example, observable recurring natural phenomenon (e.g., earth rotation [day] or revolution [year]) or physical principle (e.g., radioactive decay) in the case of a physical dating method.

The primary basis of chronology building in most historic or text-aided archaeological contexts is dependent on the recovery of various types of documentary or inscriptional data or materials. Such text-based data is used to provide chronologically significant information such as sequential listing of rulers or officials, sometimes in association with the interpretation of notations of a calendar system or in relationship to some astronomical event that can be securely dated on the basis of modern calculations.

The scholarship required to undertake the study of textual source data most directly involves the ability to decipher the symbols used to record the language and assign meaning to these symbols. Although there are notable exceptions, in most cases, the principal purpose of archaeological excavation within such contexts is to recover complementary evidence or supplementary textual data reflecting a society whose cultural and political history have already been documented in existing texts at least in broad outline.

In contrast, the principal basis of chronology building for text-less or pre-historic societies is the artifact record itself together with associated materials reflecting the depositional and environmental contexts of the material culture of these societies. Primary chronologies are constructed based on analysis of the artifacts, the geological or paleoenvironmental contexts from which the artifacts are recovered, and the application of various instrument-based chronometric methods, such as radiocarbon dating.[2]

CHRONOLOGY IN ARCHAEOLOGY

One of the major advancements in scientific understanding of the natural world has been the progressive unfolding over the last two centuries of an understanding of the geological history of our planet including the most recent geological periods during which our species (*Homo sapiens*) came to occupy a dominant position in the natural world.

With few exceptions, until the early nineteenth century, traditional Western concepts of time and thus chronology were tightly constrained by the cosmological world view reflected in the Judaeo-Christian Bible as interpreted by theologians and scholars of the medieval and early modern Christian Church. In the absence of a knowledge of any other data thought to be relevant, the Hebrew Creation and Noahian flood narratives along with the genealogical data contained in Genesis were considered chronologically authoritative and capable of providing reliable chronological data that could be employed in tracing human history back to "the beginning." In this sense, within such a framework, for the Western world until less than 300 years ago, the entire period of human presence on earth was conceived of as being historically documented.[3]

Literary scholarship linked the chronological data contained in the Biblical narratives with post- and extra-Biblical historical sources to create a traditional Western historical chronological framework ranging over some 6,000 to 7,000 years since the assumed original Creation. In the English speaking world, the best known example of such a traditional chronological synthesis was that developed by the seventeenth-century English scholar and churchman, the Anglo-Irish Archbishop of Armagh, James Ussher. His dates for important traditional events in Hebrew history (e.g., the Creation, Flood, and Exodus) were included in the margins of the Biblical text, beginning with a 1650 reprint of the original text of the 1611 "Authorized" or King James translation of the English Bible. His calculations set the Creation event at 4,004 B.C.[4]

Developments beginning in early nineteenth-century geology and paleontology were largely responsible for the profound transformation of Western consciousness concerning the temporal dimensions of both earth and human history. By the middle of the nineteenth century, with the creation of a sense of "deep time" for earth history, geological chronology or geochronology was now conceived in units of hundreds of millions of years. The most recent geological periods were associated with the development of humankind, in part due to the first evidence of human fossils (e.g., Neanderthals) and the association of what were assumed to be artifacts with fossils of a number of extinct animals. By the middle of the nineteenth century, *prehistory* had emerged as an area of concern for a type of archaeologist who took up the task of providing chronological frameworks for this uncharted period. The strategies and approaches that were employed were, in large part, directly borrowed from what had been developed by geologists and paleontologists, rather than from the views and perspectives of literary and historical scholarship.[5]

Almost two centuries of geological field studies combined with a wide ranging array of analytical data available over the last few decades have created a detailed chronological framework for the earth sciences, paleontology, oceanography—and archaeology. A number of specialized areas of scientific study have especially contributed to the progressive development of chronological frameworks documenting the period of time that human populations have been a part of the natural environment on earth.

Only the last few percent of the geological column is chronologically relevant to the period of time spent on earth by our species (*Homo sapiens*) and our immediate biological and cultural ancestors (earlier members of genus *Homo*, such as *Homo erectus*, and the various species of *Australopithicus*, and a possible ancestral hominid, *Kenyanthropus platyops*) (Figure 2-1). In geological terms, this involves, at most, the last 4 to 5 million years: the period of the late Tertiary followed by the Quaternary period, which is divided into the Pleistocene, popularly referred to as the Ice Ages, and the Holocene (recent) epoch, which began about 10,000 years ago.

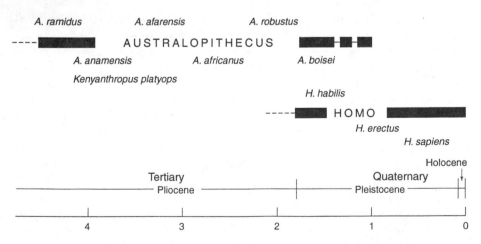

FIGURE 2-1   CHRONOLOGICAL RELATIONSHIPS OF HOMINID SPECIES
IN THE LATE TERTIARY AND QUATERNARY PERIODS

In the last half of the twentieth century, a number of different strategies were developed to provide a chronological framework for the geological periods encompassing the biological and cultural evolution of the hominids. These include the earth's magnetic polarity time scale, oxygen isotope series from the Pliocene and Pleistocene and the central European loess sequence. Other major indicators of chronological subdivisions of the Quaternary include the terrestrial *climatostratigraphic* units built up from studies of changes in worldwide (eustatic) sea level, successions of plant communities, biostratigraphic markers involved in fossil mammalian successions, and the examination of varves (successive stratified layers of sediment) in lakes adjacent to melting glaciers, and the study of solar insolation variations, namely, changes in the amount of energy from the sun received on earth over geologic time due to the "wobble" of the earth's axis in its orbit around the sun. The various analytical or instrument-based dating methods—utilizing radioactivity or other physio-chemical processes as "clocks"—have come, within the last half century, to provide increasingly accurate and precise chronometric age estimates.[6]

The original divisions of the Quaternary were based on observations of sediments in the European Alps interpreted as reflecting the advance and retreat of the major glaciers in the region and defining the classic glacial and interglacial phases for Europe and North America. Subsequently, this data was supplemented by observations on a variety of materials such as pollen contained in the sediment profiles, which could be used to infer a complex pattern of Quaternary climatic changes. These climatic shifts resulted in the development of a series of named glacial/interglacial phases as well as less pronounced interphase variations—termed stadial and interstadial series—within a glacial or interglacial phase. Associated with the waxing and waning of the continental ice sheets in the Northern Hemisphere were worldwide changes in sea levels that left a series of terrace deposits at the ocean-land interfaces.[7]

Other data used to infer Quaternary climate history include studies of varves, fossil pollen that reflects changes in dominant plant communities, and loess, windblown fine grain sediments that reflect widespread regional and continental aridity. These and other data have been synthesized to provide the classic terrestrial chronological framework for the Quaternary.

Over the past thirty years, an added component has been oxygen isotope data obtained from cores of ocean sediments and ice cores of glaciers. These data have made a profound impact on the study of Quaternary climate and thus on the nature of Quaternary geochronological reconstructions. Oxygen isotopic variations provide a record of global warm-cold transitions that have been correlated with glacial-interglacial and stadial-interstadial stages. These variations are interpreted as primarily reflecting the amount of water locked up in the polar ice caps and in glaciers.[8]

CHRONOLOGY BUILDING

Chronology building in archaeology involves a wide-ranging set of approaches and methods reflecting the highly diverse nature of the archaeological record. The multiplicity of approaches also reflects institutional and organizational aspects of professional archaeological studies since, unlike geology or paleontology, archaeological scholarship has not developed within a single disciplinary tradition with a common set of understandings about how to approach data and consider evidence.

An important factor that contributes to the diversity in emphasis and approach to the archaeological record is whether the material culture being examined is that of a society whose activities have been documented by an extensive written record providing narrative data or whether the archaeological record is that of a society lacking any textual corpus. In the first case, the archaeological data to be examined would be those of historic human cultures and in the second case, the archaeological record is of prehistoric human cultures. It should be noted that writing systems and the textual corpus derived from their use arose within the earliest civilizations or state political systems in Western Eurasia and Egypt only within the last 5,000 years. Because of this, the cultural histories of only a small fraction of human societies are reflected in textual data provided by writing systems. For most of the time of human existence and for most human societies, the only basis on which to reconstruct past cultural activity is the material objects recovered by archaeological excavation and survey along with an analysis of their physical and environmental contexts.

A second important factor conditioning an approach to the archaeological record in general (and chronology building specifically) is whether an archaeologist considers a study being undertaken to be a scientific or humanistic enterprise. There has been a general tendency for archaeologists working with the material culture of historic societies (e.g., classical Greco-Roman archaeology) to view their efforts within a humanistic and art history tradition. In contrast, prehistorians include many who view themselves as operating within a scientific framework. This contrast in orientation reflects a fundamental difference—almost at the level of a world view; the scientific perspective posits that human behavior is best viewed as one element within a complex, evolving natural environment, while the humanistic understanding views humans as possessing some special and unique capability and status that sets them apart, in some manner, from the natural world.

Reflecting the historic/prehistoric distinctions, a related factor contributing to the diversity of approaches is the existence of different institutional traditions concerning the placement of archaeology within university curriculums. In the United States, archaeologists who deal with prehistoric cultures are to be found principally within departments of anthropology. In England and Europe and in institutions of higher education modeled on them, separate departments of archaeology and prehistory are the norm. Such contrasting institutional arrangements have influenced attitudes toward the processes used in approaching the archaeological record. For example, anthropologically-oriented archaeological studies would typically have a greater awareness of the structural variations in hunter-gatherer cultures, focus attention on environmental and ecological factors to explain changes in cultural adaptive strategies, and would be much more comfortable in using ethnographic analogies in their interpretation of the archaeological record.[9]

Formal archaeological investigations dealing with historic societies have their origin during the sixteenth-century European Renaissance. They were initiated at the same time that the early modern European historic consciousness segmented Western history into its traditional taxonomy of *ancient*, *medieval*, and *modern*. The modern period was defined as that during which the Renaissance intellectuals were then currently living. The medieval or middle period was the interval of time that separated the modern from the world of the ancients, which to the Renaissance writers included the classic Greek and Roman civilization along with those cultures identified within the corpus of Judaeo-Christian literature.

Chronologies of the classical historic societies of the circum-Mediterranean region are derived primarily from analyses of the Greek and Latin textual corpus supplemented by materials excavated at various classical sites. Modern knowledge of the chronological systems employed within the Greek city states, the Roman Republic, and later the Roman Empire was transmitted by various Byzantine and Western medieval chronicles, commentaries, and compendiums, and edited and summarized in terms of the interests of European Renaissance scholars beginning in the sixteenth century.

Sixteenth-century excavations carried out first in Italy, at Roman sites such as Pompeii, and then in Greece, provided an ever increasing amount of textual data and various categories of artifacts—from ceramics to statuary. Early excavations were typically concerned with the recovery of whole ceramics and statuary that were viewed as having significant artistic merit and that could be exhibited in the developing national museums of Europe. Discoveries of caches of ancient papyri, the "paper" of the ancient Mediterranean world, allowed scholars to examine the dating notations contained on a broad spectrum of written communications in the ancient classical world.[10]

In the late eighteenth and early nineteenth century, French and English military incursions into various parts of the Near East opened this area to European scholars. Up until this time, essentially the only source of primary chronological data for this region was based on statements contained in the Hebrew Biblical text and the narratives of various classical authors: for example, the 4 B.C. Greek historian Herodotus and Hellenistic period writers such as Manetho, a Greek-speaking Egyptian writing in 2 B.C.

In 1789, a stela containing a three-part inscription dating to the Hellenistic period was recovered in a wall of a military fort being rebuilt by French forces near the Rosetta mouth of the Nile. The stela that became known as the Rosetta Stone, contained a Greek text and two forms of ancient Egyptian writing (hieratic and hieroglyphic). Although the text itself is of little historical significance, the insight into the nature of the ancient Egyptian writing afforded by having the same text in Greek set into motion a process by which the corpus of ancient Egyptian texts on monuments and in tombs could be now deciphered. From these sources, texts that listed the sequence of Egyptian rulers, their family groupings (dynasties), and their reign years could now be directly read from the monuments and other ancient Egyptian texts and compared with the information contained in the classical texts.

The nineteenth-century recognition of geologists and paleontologists that earth history and the fossil record that went with it—including hominid (human-like) fossils—had a greatly expanded temporal dimension provided a major stimulant for the undertaking of European archaeological investigations. Archaeological field studies examining cultural developments in "deep time" became closely associated with the understandings of geologists and others of the complex nature of the geological and paleoenvironmental record.

Stratigraphic analysis of archaeological sites employed many of the same techniques that had been developed by geologists over the preceding century. Chronology building for archaeologists, particularly those concerned with Pleistocene sites, often closely followed geological stratigraphic analysis of sediments in which the cultural materials were embedded.

A nineteenth-century development that also contributed to the undertaking of archaeological investigations in nonhistoric contexts was initiated in northern Europe by Scandinavian scholars. Their motivation reflected the emergence of a desire to develop an "ancient history" for their region—one that had not come under the hegemony of the Roman Empire and thus lacked cultural connections with the rest of the Western classical world and the text-based chronologies developed within it. Since the initial historic documentation of Scandinavian societies occurred with the arrival of Christian missionaries in the early European medieval period, the only basis on which their pre-Christian cultural history could be constructed was through analyses of the prehistoric material culture.

Fortunately, in a number of regions in Denmark and Sweden, extensive collections of mortuary materials from *barrows* or tomb mounds had been collected and deposited in various museums. Although not collected in any controlled manner, through a fortunate set of circumstances, the contextual integrity of many of the collected artifact items were maintained intact. It permitted the first generation of Scandinavian archaeologists in the mid-nineteenth century to examine systemically the physical properties of the materials comprising the collection and, more importantly, relationships between and among various classes of artifacts. This approach laid the foundation for what later became known as *seriation*—the development of a sequential time series for a given category of object based on changes in design elements of a collection of these objects. Using an early form of seriation, the first general model of prehistory emerged in a Stone Age, Bronze Age, and Iron Age taxonomy. Initially employed only for descriptive purposes in museum contexts, subsequent field work demonstrated that a temporal series was reflected in these categories in this region.[11]

Stratigraphic and seriation approaches provided the foundation on which temporal frameworks for archaeological materials were mounted in the late nineteenth and early twentieth century. In prehistoric studies, they initially constituted the only means by which temporal relationships could be established. While only relative placement is possible with such approaches, both stratigraphy and seriation remain as important elements of contemporary archaeological studies even though physical science-based dating methods can now provide direct chronometric data.

STRATIGRAPHY

The recognition that many parts of the earth's crust were made up of an ordered sequence of layers of sediment or strata and that different attributes characterized different sedimentary sections was the foundation on which a modern understanding of the geological column was mounted. Although many of the basic principles of stratigraphic analysis were set out as early as the Renaissance, they were only extensively employed in geology beginning in the early decades of the nineteenth century. At first, these techniques were employed principally for practical purposes such as the identification of economically important geological features such as coal seams and iron ore deposits. Only later, with the realization of the reality of "deep time" in the geologic record, were they employed to explicate the entire geologic column. Tentative use of stratigraphic data in archaeology occurred in the 1880s and 1890s to supplement arguments about the association of humans and extinct fauna, but such approaches were not generally employed in wider contexts until the early twentieth century.[12]

The underlying basis of stratigraphic analysis involve the application of relatively straightforward, even common sense, principles. Superposition posits that, in an undisturbed context, the oldest stratum is at the bottom of a sequence, with progressively younger deposits at progressively higher levels. The principle of initial horizontality holds that strata have been deposited in a horizontal plane and that any nonhorizontal strata must have been the result of subsequent movement. A third principal, lateral termination, assumes that strata will extend until terminated at the edge of the deposit or until progressively thinned to zero.

Stratigraphic concepts were combined with a more general uniformitarian view that geological processes now being observed are sufficient to account for the observed sedimentary record. These basic concepts and others derived from them—in combination with analyses of the sediments' various plant and animal fossils, and mineralogical and geochemical/geophysical characteristics—have become powerful tools in the analysis of archaeological sediments. The more recent development of geoarchaeology as a subspeciality within geology reflects a new focus in the interpretation of archaeological sediments.

The greatest successes in applying stratigraphic principles in archaeology are observable in regions where sites are characterized by extensive and deep deposits reflecting long periods of occupation. Such contexts are often encountered in the study of Upper Paleolithic archaeology during the late Pleistocene period in western Europe where cave and rock shelters contain lengthy stratigraphic records. In the New World, stratigraphic analyses were particularly important in the examination of North American late Pleistocene and early Holocene Paleoindian sites. Analyses of the association of artifacts and extinct fauna within well-studied geological contexts became a notable characteristic of Paleoindian archaeological research by the 1930s.

In sites where there are extensive deposits with multiple, distinct sedimentary layers, stratigraphic analysis can be undertaken by excavations that follow natural stratigraphy. Such analysis documents the visible horizontal and vertical relationships in the sequence of natural sediments deposited at a site and reconstructs the processes that were responsible for the creation of the site's observed stratigraphic record. Figure 2-2 illustrates, however, that the process of interpreting stratigraphic sequences can be complex. This figure is taken from a discussion by Sir Mortimer Wheeler that contrasts an (a) "undifferentiated section," (b) a section "unintelligently differentiated," and (c) a section "intelligently differentiated."[13]

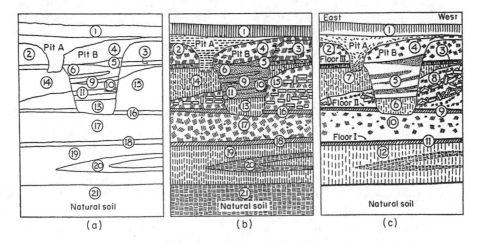

FIGURE 2-2   ILLUSTRATION OF INTERPRETATIONS OF A STRATIGRAPHIC PROFILE
Source: From M. Wheeler, *Archaeology from the Earth* (Oxford: Clarendon Press, 1954).

In a number of regions where archaeological deposits are found primarily in thin soils, where occupations were of short duration, or where the depositional processes deposited soil of homogeneous character, stratigraphic excavation can be undertaken in arbitrary levels using variable units depending on the individual circumstances of the site location. Arbitrary stratigraphy is used to provide horizontal controls for artifacts and materials recovered from buried sediments that can document past subsistence activities and paleoenvironmental data.

SERIATION

Seriation or serialization analyses are based on the observation that different formal or stylistic elements (e.g., a standardized design) observed on a given artifact type (e.g., ceramic) will increase and decrease in frequency within a given geographic region or cultural context over time. A fundamental assumption of all seriation approaches is that formal similarity denotes temporal similarity: Artifact types that share the most stylistic elements will lie close together in time. The underlying assumptions of evolutionary biologists in their study of the phylogenetic history of species are very similar to those postulated by archaeologists, if one substitutes "species" for "artifact type" and "morphological characteristic" for "stylistic element." The study of the historical relationships of languages also makes use of the principle that lexical and structural similarity denote chronological proximity.[14]

This simple principal was used impressionistically by the Greek historian Herodotus in attempting to place in chronological order Egyptian monuments that he observed during his travels. Unfortunately, he was not aware that Egyptian builders had recently copied earlier architectural styles and thus his chronological reconstructions were invalid. For example, he placed the period of the construction of the great pyramids at Giza, now known to date to some 2400 to 2200 B.C., at only a few hundred years prior to his own time.

The classic use of seriation is exemplified in the approach taken by the late nineteenth- and early twentieth-century British archaeologist, Sir William Matthews Flinders Petrie, in ordering the temporal relationship of ceramics recovered from over 4000 predynastic burials in Egypt. Using changes primarily in the form of the handles on ceramic vessels, he conceptualized a series of relative "Sequence Dates" for these vessels and thus, by association, for the burials from which they were derived. Seriation and stratigraphic observations were the basis on which the prehistoric chronologies in New World archaeology were initially developed during the first three decades of the twentieth century. This is particularly exemplified in the work of A. V. Kidder at the Pecos Pueblo in New Mexico: Kidder studied variations in ceramic design, noting the chronological significance of a particular design element becoming less detailed or intricate over time.

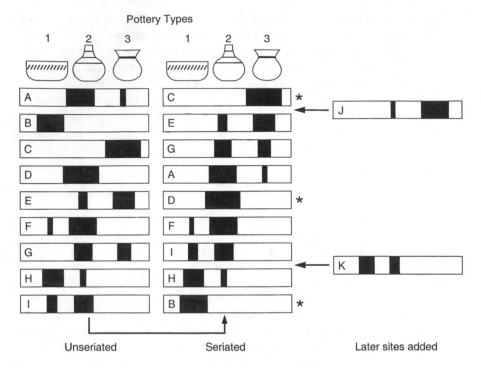

FIGURE 2-3   ILLUSTRATION OF SERIATION PROCESS

Source: Taken from Figure 7.7 in B. M. Fagan, *In the Beginning: An Introduction to Archaeology*, 10th ed. (New Jersey: Prentice Hall, 2001).

In archaeology, using formal changes in stylistic elements to temporally order these elements assumes the existence of archaeological *types*. These types are abstract or ideal categories into which single items are grouped on the basis of one or more defined, shared trait. An archaeological type can stand in the place of or as a proxy for clustered individual items of a class of artifact. Obviously, all such types reflect the criteria used to create them and thus, strictly speaking, there are no archaeological types-as-such but only types-as-defined: for example, functional, decorative, morphological, descriptive, or chronological. Ideally, chronological types are constructed of elements that are assumed or known to change over time.

Two types of seriation can be distinguished. Following the terminology of John Rowe, *evolutionary* seriation orders artifact types on the basis of some assumed developmental principal, such as technologies proceeding from simple to complex or artistic designs proceeding from abstract to realistic. In contrast, *similarity* seriation makes its temporal ordering exclusively on the basis of physical resemblance between defined types with no assumption about the validity or reality of any assumed developmental schema. R. Lee Lyman has further divided similarity seriation into frequency seriation, occurrence seriation, and phyletic seriation.

Figure 2-3 illustrates the use of seriation principles to order three pottery types (labeled 1, 2, 3) collected from nine sites (labeled A through I). The different percentages of each of the three types at each site have been represented by variations in the width of the black segment of the bar that represents each site. In the left hand column is the unseriated listing. In the right hand column is the seriated rearrangement of the bars to yield the characteristic "battleship" curve representing the variation in frequency over time for each type at each site. On the basis of the seriation, the relative order of the sites could be determined. However, it was not possible to determine if site C or B was the earliest. With such seriation representations, it was also possible to add additional sites as in the case of J and K.[15]

CHRONOMETRIC DATING METHODS

Within the last fifty years, chronology building in archaeological studies involving the reconstruction of prehistoric culture histories has been transformed with the introduction of a wide range of physical science–based dating methods. In essentially all cases, the methods were originally developed by non-archaeologists (e.g., chemists, physicists, biologists), and their successful application in archaeology depends on a knowledge and understanding of the physical and chemical principles on which the techniques themselves are based. Table 2-1 lists the dating methods that have been employed in archaeological contexts and the bases on which they operate. We will discuss the techniques that are most often employed in the development of archaeological chronologies.[16]

TABLE 2-1   MAJOR OPERATIONAL QUARTERNARY
DATING METHODS USED IN ARCHAEOLOGY

A. FIXED-RATE PROCESSES [TIME PLACEMENT]

1. Radiometric-decay: radiocarbon, potassium-argon/argon-argon
2. Radiometric-equilibrium: uranium series
3. Radiometric-radiation damage accumulation: thermoluminescence, fission-track
4. Geological: varve (regionally specific)

A. PATTERN-RECOGNITION PROCESSES [TIME/RELATIVE PLACEMENT]

1. biological: dendrochronology (regionally specific)
2. geophysical: archaeomagnetic (regionally specific)

A. VARIABLE-RATE PROCESSES [TIME/RELATIVE PLACEMENT]

1. Chemical: obsidian hydration (regionally specific)
2. fluorine/uranium/nitrogen, amino acid racemization (regionally specific)

Source: Based on R. E. Taylor and M. J. Aitken, eds., *Chronometric Dating in Archaeology* (New York: Plenum, 1997).

RADIOCARBON

Since its introduction more than five decades ago, the radiocarbon (^{14}C) method has become the principal chronometric method used in archaeological studies for late Pleistocene and Holocene sites and materials. Over the last three decades, the vast majority of chronological age estimates for prehistoric sites and artifacts younger than about 40,000 years are based, directly or indirectly, on ^{14}C values.[17]

Radiocarbon dating is one of a number of nuclear decay or radiometric methods of dating that takes advantage of radioactivity to provide a nuclear-based "clock." Radiocarbon takes it name from the contraction of "radioactive carbon." The method was conceived by an American chemist, Willard F. Libby, and developed at the University of Chicago immediately following World War II by Libby, James R. Arnold, and Ernest C. Anderson. Libby received the 1960 Nobel Prize in Chemistry for the development of the method.[18]

The natural production of ^{14}C is a secondary effect of cosmic-ray interactions with atmospheric gas molecules. Cosmic rays are very high energy radiation received by the earth from external sources—mostly from far beyond our solar system. One of the effects of such bombardment is the creation of neutrons, which, after losing energy in collisions and reaching appropriate energies, react with ^{14}N to form ^{14}C. Following production, ^{14}C is rapidly oxidized to form ^{14}CO$_2$. In this form, ^{14}C is distributed throughout the earth's atmosphere by stratospheric winds, becoming generally well mixed by the time ^{14}C-tagged CO$_2$ molecules reach the planetary surface. Most ^{14}C is absorbed in the oceans while a small percentage (1 to 2 percent) becomes part of the terrestrial biosphere, primarily by terrestrial plants fixing ^{14}C into their cellular structures by means of photosynthesis. Other terrestrial organisms such as animals obtain it secondarily by ingestion of plant materials.

Metabolic processes maintain the ^{14}C content of living organisms in approximate equilibrium with atmospheric ^{14}C. While ^{14}C decays in living tissue, it is continually replaced through the ingestion of plant or animal tissue. However, once metabolic processes cease—as at the death of an animal or plant—the amount of ^{14}C will begin to decrease by one form of radioactivity—beta decay—at a rate measured by the ^{14}C half-life. The term half-life is used to refer to the characteristic rate at which a given radioactive isotope decays. In the case of ^{14}C, it takes approximately 5,700 years for the ^{14}C concentration in a sample to be reduced by one-half of the original activity or concentration through beta decay. The radiocarbon age of a sample is based on measurement of its residual ^{14}C content and a knowledge of the half-life. For example, a sample that contains 50 percent of the concentration of ^{14}C in the contemporary or modern standard would be about 5,700 ^{14}C years old.

Depending on particular laboratory configurations and experimental conditions, the maximum age that can be routinely inferred from the measurement of the residual content of ^{14}C in most samples ranges from about 40,000 to 75,000 years. For recent archaeological and historic samples, the minimum age than can be resolved on a routine basis by ^{14}C data is about 300 years. Required sample sizes have been reduced from 1 to 10 grams of carbon to several milligrams as the result of the development of accelerator mass spectrometry (AMS).[19]

The ^{14}C method currently enjoys the status of the final arbiter in disputes concerning the age of historic or archaeological artifacts or related materials. The most recent major application of ^{14}C as a means of providing authentication for objects of disputed age and/or historicity that has drawn international interest was the analysis of the Shroud of Turin, which since the 1350s has been the object of religious veneration as the linen burial cloth of Jesus of Nazareth. If such an attribution was correct, fibers from the linen object would have to date to the first century B.C. The ^{14}C values obtained from the Shroud demonstrated that the plants from which the linen was woven were growing in the fourteenth century A.D., not the first century A.D.[20]

Similarly, the ^{14}C method was used for authentication purposes on human bone materials recovered in the mid-nineteenth century from a mine shaft near Angel's Camp in Calaveras County, California. The Calaveras Skull was from the beginning widely suspected to be a "plant" in the mine shaft. However, during the late nineteenth and early twentieth century, several highly reputable anthropologists advanced the view that the skull was actually of Pliocene age—making it, in their view, the oldest anatomically modern *Homo sapiens* known. While most anthropologists had long dismissed the Calaveras Skull as a fraud—the New World equivalent of the Piltdown hoax in Europe— no final, definitive evidence as to its actual age was obtained until a ^{14}C age estimate determined that human bone fragments associated with it were, at most, 2,000 years old.[21]

POTASSIUM-ARGON/ARGON-ARGON DATING

The potassium/argon ([40]K/[40]Ar) method, together with its more recently developed analytical variant, the argon/argon ([39]Ar/[40]Ar) method, historically provided the geochronological framework for the study of sites documenting early hominid biological and cultural evolution. These techniques can be applied to the dating of sedimentary units—under optimal conditions, as young as 30,000 (±10,000) years—if appropriate igneous (volcanic) deposits are present. These techniques have provided core chronological data for the Pleistocene archaeological and paleoanthropological record older than that which can be documented by the ^{14}C method in regions where appropriate sediments are present, such as in East Africa (e.g., Olduvai Gorge), and Java.[22]

Potassium, a widely distributed element in crustal sediments and the eighth most abundant element in terrestrial rocks, has three naturally-occurring isotopes: two stable ([39]K and [41]K) and one radioactive ([40]K). [40]K decays to [40]Ar and [40]Ca by beta emission and electron capture with a half-life of about 1,250 million years. After nitrogen and oxygen, argon is the third most abundant gas in the atmosphere. Since ^{40}Ar exists as a gas, when sufficient heat is applied, it will be removed or *outgased* from minerals and rocks. This process occurs primarily in igneous sediments, namely, rock types associated with volcanism and igneous rock–derived components of sedimentary and metamorphic rocks. If a set of assumptions hold, by measuring the ^{40}Ar/^{40}K ratio, one can calculate the time elapsed since the last heating episode experienced by a given rock sample or a specific mineral separate.

Argon/argon dating is based on the same general model and assumptions as the K/Ar method. The principal difference is the manner in which the potassium is measured. In this approach, potassium and argon can be measured virtually simultaneously since the sample is irradiated with high-energy neutrons. This converts ^{39}K in the sample to ^{39}Ar, an isotope that does not occur in nature and the ^{39}Ar concentration becomes a proxy measurement for the potassium concentration. The advantages of the Ar/Ar method over the K/Ar technique are that ages are based entirely on measurement of Ar isotopic ratios in a single sample, smaller samples can be dated, precision and accuracy are improved because problems of sample heterogeneity are eliminated, and ratios, not amounts, are measured. Finally, rock samples or mineral separates can be heated to progressively higher temperatures and the Ar released in each step can be measured. Also, highly selective sampling of single mineral grains are possible using laser techniques. The use of these procedures permits quantitative measurements of the contamination of samples to be evaluated.

DENDROCHRONOLOGY

Dendrochronology (tree-ring dating) was the first effective time-placement method used in North American archaeology. The technique was developed in the mid-1920s by Andrew E. Douglass, a University of Arizona astronomer, who was interested in establishing a proxy for sunspot and ancient climatic cycles in the sequence of tree-rings widths recorded in ancient wood collected from various prehistoric sites in the southwestern United States.[23]

Dendrochronology is based on a phenomenon known at least since the time of the Hellenistic Greeks—namely, that some species of trees exhibit recognizable annual growth rings. Based on observations of Douglass and others, it was recognized that, in some species of trees in some regions, the width of each annual ring varies as a function of variations in one or more environmental parameters (e.g., annual variations in temperature or amount or timing of rainfall). These trees are known as *sensitive* trees (i.e., the width of the annual ring was sensitive to variation in a given environmental parameter). This is in contrast to *complacent* trees that show no significant variation in tree-ring thickness from year to year in response to environmental changes—other than the thinning of the rings in response to the increasing diameter of the tree.

It was observed that, in some environments, different trees of the same sensitive-type species in the same environment/geographic region will exhibit a similar ring pattern. By comparing tree-ring patterns in different trees in the same environment, cross dating between trees is possible. A regional master tree-ring series for a particular species of tree in a specific geographical/environmental range could then be assembled by cross dating a series of trees from the same environment that exhibit increasing age. Once a regional master tree-ring series has been developed, the dating of an unknown-age tree can be accomplished by comparing its ring pattern with the master tree-ring series.

Like all techniques, the utility of dendrochronology depends on several assumptions being fulfilled in the samples. First, it is assumed that any multiple or missing tree-rings can be identified in samples examined. Multiple rings involve the production of two or more rings over a twelve-month period; missing rings involve the absence of one or more rings over at least a twelve-month period. Finally, it is assumed that a master tree-ring series accurately represents the actual age of the trees exhibiting a given tree-ring pattern in the defined geographic region and that all trees of the species of the master tree-ring series and unknown-age trees exhibit the same tree-ring pattern once any multiple or missing rings are identified and filtered out.

ARCHAEOMAGNETIC DATING

Archaeomagnetic dating derives from the study of geomagnetism, the branch of geophysics that examines the origin, characteristics, and short- and long-term changes in the magnetic field of the earth. Paleomagnetism refers to the history of earth's magnetic field over geologic time; archaeomagnetism deals with the same phenomena associated with human contexts within the geologically recent past.[24]

The temporal mechanism used in archaeomagnetic dating reflects a knowledge of changes over time in the direction and field strength (intensity) of the earth's magnetic (geomagnetic) field. The geomagnetic field at any one time at any point on the earth's surface can be characterized by vector values describing its two components: declination (the angle between geographic north and the horizontal components of the field), and inclination (the angle or vertical dip of the field vector with respect to the horizontal). Archaeometric dating is possible because these values—along with the strength or intensity of the field—change over time at any one place on the earth's surface. The temporal changes in the magnetic field (with time scales of decades to millennia) are referred to as geomagnetic secular variation.

The process of deriving age estimates based on archaeomagnetic data begins with the construction of secular variation curves for different geographic regions. This involves obtaining measurements of the declination and inclination angles on certain classes of materials of known age. The materials amenable to archaeomagnetic dating are objects that have been subjected to heating above a characteristic temperature and that are composed of fine-grain sediments (e.g., clays, soils, bricks) containing a few percent of various types of iron oxides. In these materials, each grain acts as a very small, single magnet. In unfired materials, grains are randomly oriented and thus the net magnetic effect is small. However, heating these materials above what is called a characteristic *blocking temperature* causes thermal agitation of crystal lattice structures allowing these grains to magnetically reorient in the same direction as the geomagnetic field at that place and time. On cooling below the blocking temperature, the orientation and intensity of the field is frozen and the sample exhibits thermoremanent magnetism (TRM).

The measurement of TRM in a series of known-age materials allows the construction of a geomagnetic secular variation curve for a given geographical region. Thus, archaeomagnetic dating involves the inference of the age of a sample—defined as the time since the last heating event—by comparing the TRM orientation values of the sample with a master regional secular variation curve.[25]

OBSIDIAN HYDRATION

Obsidian is a naturally occurring volcanic glass that was extensively used by prehistoric populations in all areas of the world where geological conditions produced Quaternary volcanism and where the obsidian was exposed on the surface and able to be quarried. Because obsidian could be worked into a wide variety of artifact types (e.g., projectile points, scrapers) with very sharp cutting edges, it was the preferred lithic type used by those making tools in hunter and gatherer societies. Groups traveled long distances to secure this valuable resource and it was widely traded far beyond the areas where it was exposed on the surface and mined.[26]

The obsidian hydration technique derives from the observation first extensively studied by Irving Friedman of the U.S. Geological Survey in the early 1960s that a newly exposed surface of obsidian—such as that created by chipping during artifact manufacture—will hydrate. Hydration is the process by which a material absorbs "water" from the environment and creates a new material with a higher density. The process forms a hydration front or rim parallel to the surface. (The actual physical mechanism involved in hydration rim formation is not precisely known, so "water" is used in a very general sense). Hydration formation in obsidian is a near-surface process measured in microns (1 micron = 10^{-3} millimeter). The hydration rim can be observed in thin section in an optical microscope since the hydrated obsidian band or rim contrasts with the unhydrated obsidian mass. The difference in density can be highlighted by viewing the thin section in polarized light.

Typically, the depth of penetration of the hydration rim will increase as a function of the time that has elapsed since a new surface was exposed. Since the hydration process involves primarily chemical reactions between the "water" and the obsidian, the hydration rate (i.e., the rate at which the hydration rim increases in depth), is primarily a function of the environmental temperature that is experienced by the obsidian—sometimes referred to as the *effective hydration temperature* (EHT)—and the chemical characteristics of the obsidian. If the actual hydration rate of obsidian of a given chemical composition in a particular region/site can be established to an appropriate level of accuracy and precision and the hydration rim on a particular sample can be measured to an appropriate level of accuracy and precision, then the time that has elapsed since the surface of that sample was exposed can, in theory, be determined.

Extensive studies over the last three decades have identified the important parameters of the method. First, hydration in obsidian is treated as a first-order diffusion process. There are other mass-transport mechanisms in solids, but it is generally accepted that the hydration process in obsidian (i.e., the transport of "water" into the obsidian mass) is governed by diffusion mechanisms. Secondly, it appears that the principal factors influencing the rate of diffusion in obsidian are the effective hydration temperature (EHT) and the specific chemical characteristics of the obsidian; no other factor, such as environmental humidity, plays a significant role.

Several studies have suggested that, under some circumstances, the amount of "water" contained within the unhydrated obsidian as well as the degree of available environmental "water" can influence the hydration process. With regard to the variation in chemical characteristics of obsidian, the measurement of various minor and trace elements have been used to distinguish different types of obsidian from different sources/subsources. For a given obsidian source/subsource type, it has been generally assumed that the hydration rate can be determined either by calibration or by experimentally induced hydration.

Calibration involves independently dating (e.g., by association with ^{14}C-dated samples) a time series of obsidian artifacts from a given environmental zone and establishing the hydration rate by inference. Induced hydration involves exposing a given type of obsidian to elevated temperatures in a controlled experiment, measuring the artificially-produced hydration rims, and assuming that the rims so produced in the laboratory are analogous to those formed naturally at a much slower rate.

REFLECTIONS

Since one of the fundamental purposes of archaeological research is the study of the evolution of human cultures, and since evolution denotes *change over time*, chronology is a fundamental archaeological parameter. Archaeology shares with geology, paleontology, and other sciences concerned with temporal relationships the need to view its data within as accurate and precise a temporal context as possible. For archaeology, such a requirement needs to be met if any meaningful understanding of evolutionary processes is to be inferred from the examination of the physical residue of past human behavior.

Sophisticated higher level generalizations and approaches that seek to understand the dynamics of cultural evolution by examining the complex interplay of ideological, environmental, ecological, functional, and/or adaptive factors must, in the end, depend on having an accurate chronology for the events that the theories and models are attempting to explain.

NOTES

1. Colin Renfrew and Paul Bahn, *Archaeology Theories, Methods, and Practice* (New York: Thames and Hudson, 1991), pp. 102–148.
2. Martin J. Aitken, *Science-Based Dating in Archaeology* (New York: Longman, 1990).
3. Stephen Jay Gould, *Time's Arrow, Times's Cycle: Myth and Metaphor in the Discovery of Geological Time* (Cambridge: Harvard University Press, 1987).
4. J. Barr, "Why the World Was Created in 4004 B.C.: Archbishop Ussher and Biblical Chronology," *Bulletin of the John Rylands University Library of Manchester* 67 (1985): 575–608.
5. Donald K. Grayson, *The Establishment of Human Antiquity* (New York: Academic Press, 1983).
6. Martin J. Aitken and Stephen Stokes, "Climatostratigraphy" in R. E. Taylor and Martin J. Aitken, eds., *Chronometric Dating in Archaeology* (New York: Plenum, 1997), pp. 1–30.
7. J. A. Imbrie and K. P. Imbrie, *Ice Ages* (Cambridge: Harvard University Press, 1986).
8. W. L. Prell, J. Imbrie, D. G. Martinson, J. J. Morleyh, N. G. Pisias, N. J. Shackleton, and H. E. Streeter, "Graphic Correlations of Oxygen Isotope Stratigraphy and Application to the Late Quaternary," *Paleoceanography* 1 (1986): 137–162.
9. R. E. Taylor, "Archaeometry and the 'Two Cultures Effect' in American Anthropology," in Prudence Rice and Donald Price, eds., *The Past and Future of Anthropological Archaeometry* (Carbondale: Southern Illinois University, in press).
10. J. T. Hooker, *Reading the Past: Ancient Writing from Cuneiform to the Alphabet* (Berkeley: University of California Press, 1990).
11. Bo Graslund, *The Birth of Prehistoric Chronology: Dating Methods and Dating Systems in Nineteenth Century Scandinavian Archaeology* (Cambridge: Cambridge University Press, 1987).
12. M. J. O'Brien and R. L. Lyman. *Seriation, Stratigraphy, and Index Fossils: The Backbone of Archaeological Dating* (New York: Kluwer Academic/Plenum, 2000).
13. Sir Mortimer Wheeler, *Archaeology from the Earth* (Oxford: Clarendon Press, 1954).
14. O'Brien and Lyman. *Seriation, Stratigraphy, and Index Fossils.*
15. Brian M. Fagan, *In the Beginning: An Introduction to Archaeology*, 10th ed. (New Jersey: Prentice Hall, 2001), Figure 7.7.
16. R. E. Taylor and Martin J. Aitken, eds. *Chronometric Dating in Archaeology* (New York: Plenum, 1997).

17. R. E. Taylor, *Radiocarbon Dating: An Archaeological Perspective* (New York: Academic Press, 1987),

18. R. E. Taylor, "Fifty Years of Radiocarbon Dating," *American Scientist* 88 (2000): 60–67.

19. R. E. Taylor, "Radiocarbon Dating: The Continuing Revolution," *Evolutionary Anthropology* 4 (1996): 169–181.

20. Paul Damon, et al., "Radiocarbon Dating the Shroud of Turin," *Nature* 337 (1989): 611–615.

21. R. E. Taylor, Louis A. Payen, and Peter J. Slota, Jr. "The Age of the Calaveras Skull: Dating the 'Piltdown Man' of the New World," *American Antiquity* 57 (1992): 269–275.

22. Robert C. Walter, "Potassium-Argon/Argon-Argon Dating Methods" in R. E. Taylor and Martin J. Aitken, eds. *Chronometric Dating in Archaeology* (New York: Plenum, 1997), pp. 97–126.

23. Jeffrey S. Dean, "Dendrochronology" in R. E. Taylor and Martin J. Aitken, eds. *Chronometric Dating in Archaeology* (New York: Plenum, 1997), pp. 31–64.

24. Jeffrey L. Eighmy and Robert S. Sternberg, eds., *Archaeomagnetic Dating* (Tucson: The University of Arizona Press, 1990).

25. Robert S. Sternberg, "Archaeomagnetic Dating," in R. E. Taylor and Martin J. Aitken, eds., *Chronometric Dating in Archaeology* (New York: Plenum, 1997), pp. 323–356.

26. Irving Friedman, Fred W. Trembour, and Richard E. Hughes, "Obsidian Hydration Dating," in R. E. Taylor and Martin J. Aitken, eds., *Chronometric Dating in Archaeology* (New York: Plenum, 1997), pp. 297–322.

SUGGESTED READINGS

Baillie, M. G. L. *Tree Ring Dating and Archaeology.* Chicago: University of Chicago Press, 1982. Provides an overview and summary of the development and application of dendrochronology in archaeology.

Ehrich, R. W. ed. *Chronologies in Old World Archaeology*, 3rd ed. Chicago: University of Chicago Press, 1993. A series of chapters written by area specialists summarizing the archaeological chronologies and cultural histories of various regions of the Eastern Hemisphere.

Geyh, M. A. and H. Schleicher. *Absolute Age Determination: Physical and Chemical Dating Methods and Their Application.* New York: Springer-Verlag, 1990. This presents a concise summary of the major time placement and relative placement chronometric techniques.

Nash, Steven E. *It's About Time: A History of Archaeological Dating in North America.* Salt Lake City: The University of Utah Press, 2000. An historical review of the development of strategies and approaches to dating in prehistoric North American archaeology.

Taylor, R. Ervin. and Clement W. Meighan, eds. *Chronologies in New World Archaeology.* New York: Seminar Press, 1978. A series of chapters written by area specialists summarizing the archaeological chronologies and cultural histories of the regions of North, Meso-, and South America.

THE CONSERVATION
OF ARCHAEOLOGICAL MATERIALS

CATHERINE SEASE

When most people go to a museum or see an exhibit, they look at the artifacts on display. When I go to a museum, I start by looking at the artifacts, but my attention invariably wanders. I find myself looking at how the artifacts are displayed or assessing how well a broken pot has been restored. While others are reading exhibit labels, I read the humidity monitoring equipment. I can't help it. I am an archaeological conservator and it is an occupational hazard.

As a conservator, I am concerned with the overall preservation of the collections under my care. This means that I am involved in all aspects of collections care and handling. How artifacts are stored is of as much concern to me as what materials will be in the same exhibit case with them or whether they will travel by truck or airplane to an institution borrowing them for study or exhibit. I frequently use a medical analogy to describe what I do: I am a doctor for artifacts. Just like a physician, I am concerned with the total well-being of my patients. Unlike human patients, however, mine cannot speak for themselves. They need someone to speak for them, someone to look out for their needs, and look at situations solely from their point of view. That is the role of the conservator.

Conservators are uniquely qualified to do this. In graduate school we spend several years learning about artifacts: the materials of which they are made, how and under what conditions they deteriorate, how to prevent deterioration from occurring, and how to treat specific problems. We are trained to look at situations involving collections holistically, taking into consideration all factors involved in their preservation. This is not to say that others are not concerned with the well-being of collections, but they come from a different perspective and the specific needs of an artifact are not necessarily their first consideration. The conservator has no other agenda than what is best for the collections. This is an awesome responsibility, and it is a crucial job. If we do not preserve our archaeological collections, their full research potential will not be realized and our knowledge of history will suffer as a result. Unfortunately, research based on material culture is all too frequently hindered by artifacts too deteriorated to be of any use.

Conservators do not work in a vacuum. It is imperative that we work closely with archaeologists, both in the field and in the museum. Teamwork is essential for the well-being of the artifacts; conservators are not experts in archaeology nor are archaeologists experts in conservation. Rather, the expertise of both is complementary and should be used together to address the central challenge of preserving collections. It stands to reason, however, that if conservators have an understanding of basic archaeological procedures and archaeologists of conservation techniques, we will be able to communicate better and thus form a stronger team.

PRESERVATION VERSUS RESTORATION

Conservation consists of two main activities: preservation and restoration. While both are important, one can frequently take on more importance than the other, depending on the nature of the collection involved, its specific needs, and how it is to be used. Preservation involves stabilizing the condition of artifacts; its goal is to prevent further deterioration or damage from taking place. This usually involves controlling the environment around the artifacts, as well as how they are handled and used. There are times, however, when stabilization requires active treatment. If the surface of a pot, for example, is powdery and flaking, consolidation may be necessary to prevent the loss not only of the surface, but of any decoration that might be on it.

In contrast, restoration involves purposely changing the material and structure of an artifact. Its purpose is to return an artifact as closely as possible to its original or previous appearance to make it more understandable. Restoration is usually done for exhibit or educational purposes, to increase the interpretive value of the artifact. Thus, sherds pieced together give the museum visitor a better idea of what that vessel looked like than does a mere pile of sherds. Restoration can also be done to stabilize an artifact, for example, when missing portions render an artifact too fragile for handling and study. A collection of potsherds from a site in the Middle East containing water soluble salts illustrates this distinction between preservation and restoration. These salts can do considerable damage to the sherds if they are not removed or the relative humidity in the room where the sherds are kept is not strictly controlled. Either removing the salts or keeping the sherds in a climate-controlled storeroom is a preservation activity. Piecing the sherds back together to form a vessel, however, is restoration. Both fall within the purview of conservation.

THE PHILOSOPHY OF CONSERVATION

While the conservation of archaeological material is governed by the same principles and procedures as for other types of collections, its approach differs somewhat due to the nature of archaeological collections. Artifacts are the tangible, and frequently the only, remains of past societies. They reflect the ideas, beliefs, and activities of that society and, as such, are valuable sources of information about human behavior and can be regarded as primary documents of history. Even the most insignificant artifact is capable of relinquishing some information about its history—who made it or how it was used. More important artifacts can give us information about larger issues, such as technological methods and trade. Together, all artifacts from a site form an assemblage that provides us with a picture of a group of people who lived in the past.

Most archaeological materials have been collected through modern excavation techniques, with photographic and written records documenting their retrieval and associations. This documentation provides context for artifacts. Without it, our information about the artifacts would be diminished and they would lose much of their research potential, for context is what gives artifacts their meaning. Recently, a zooarchaeologist analyzing animal bones from an early Iron Age tomb on Cyprus found a dozen horse bones. Initially, these bones were thought to be intrusive, having nothing to do with the burial itself. However, an examination of the excavation records and artifacts produced horse blinkers indicating that the horse bones were, in fact, interred as part of the burial of a royal personage. In this instance, knowing the correct context of the bones demonstrated that they were a unique find among the eight hundred tombs excavated at the site. Thus, artifacts from a site, along with their documentation, form a valuable systematic research collection in which the material as a whole takes on a significance far beyond the importance of a single artifact within that collection. The potential research and informational value of the collection becomes of overriding importance.

Preservation, or stabilization, rather than restoration should be the primary and ethical aim of archaeological conservation. Any treatment should be kept to a minimum and, whenever possible, noninvasive procedures should be used. Everything done to an artifact must be carefully weighed and justified, for all conservation treatment alters an artifact in some way. If undertaken without forethought, an ill-advised treatment can mislead interpretation. I am reminded of an excavation publication many years ago that reported two distinct types of pottery from the site. The body of one was dense and strong while that of the other was porous and crumbly. Great significance was placed on the difference. Some time later, it was discovered that the conservation treatment the pottery had received in the field was actually responsible for the difference. The porous sherds differed from the others only in that they had had a calcareous temper that was dissolved away when the sherds were cleaned with acid, leaving the fabric porous and friable.

Deciding on a treatment or course of action, then, is not as easy or as straightforward as it might at first seem. Compromises must almost always be made, but they must be made taking all aspects of the artifact into consideration, including possible uses. As one noted conservator stated, "What is gained in stability may be offset by some undesirable change in aesthetic quality, the veiling of a characteristic feature or the accentuation of something that is undesirable."[1] Artifacts can also be unwittingly diminished by the removal of seemingly inconsequential material. The consequences of this loss may not be obvious to us today, but could well turn out to be significant to future scientists. For example, pottery has always been washed with relative impunity. It is only with the development of certain analytical techniques over the past few years that we are now aware that not only do food residues exist in vessels, but they can be identified if they are not washed away.

Respect for the integrity of an artifact also means not imposing one's own cultural values on it by making assumptions about how it should look. Unfortunately, this was frequently done in the past, when the treatment of artifacts was subject to fashion. In the 1920s and 1930s, for example, it was the vogue for archaeological bronzes to be green. If bronzes were not green because of corrosion, great pains were taken to paint them to simulate corrosion and to make them look more "antique."

The conservator must bear in mind that the preservation of an artifact is not necessarily restricted solely to its appearance or to the material of which it was originally made. Any technological information embodied in an artifact is part of the total information that can be obtained from its study and must be preserved. It is not uncommon to excavate artifacts that were repaired in antiquity. These repairs may seem crude and unsightly to us today, but they are part of the history of the use of the artifacts and should not be removed. Repair materials and techniques may indicate that the artifact was an heirloom, repaired many years after it was made. I always find it fascinating that some artifacts were of sufficient value to someone in antiquity that they bothered to repair them while others were thrown away and replaced.

ACTIVE CONSERVATION

In caring for collections, conservators, like physicians, practice both active and passive techniques in caring for collections. Active treatment is the equivalent of setting a broken bone. When a pot has lost its structural stability through burial in the ground, it is necessary to strengthen or consolidate it in order first to get it out of the ground and then to enable us to handle, study, and possibly exhibit it. Whenever we must actively treat artifacts, our work is guided by the concept of minimum intervention. This means that any treatment undertaken should never be more extensive than absolutely necessary. Although it may sound peculiar, the best treatment is always the least, leaving the artifact as close as possible to its original condition.

It follows, then, that when treatment is necessary, the adhesives, consolidants, and other conservation materials applied to an artifact should be used to the least possible extent so as to alter the artifact as little as possible. Thus, only the smallest quantities needed to ensure the stabilization of the artifact should be used. While the practice of minimal intervention is important in all conservation work, it takes on special importance when treating artifacts that may be used for dating or elemental analysis. We must always bear in mind that any treatment of an artifact, including merely cleaning it, can falsify or invalidate any future analytical techniques. Therefore, if a sherd, for example, is to be used for thermoluminescence dating, it is best to leave part or all of it untreated. Just as the archaeologist frequently leaves part of a site unexcavated for future researchers armed with better, more effective field techniques, it is wise for the conservator to leave, if not whole artifacts, at least fragments of them untreated for future studies.

In keeping with this approach, we strive to use only conservation materials that are reversible. This means that any treatment materials applied to an artifact, such as adhesives or consolidants, should be removable at a later date with no damage to the artifact. Reversibility, a principle that has long guided all conservation work, grew out of the recognition that conservation knowledge is constantly changing. As technology improves, we may find we need to undo tomorrow what we did yesterday. We have come to recognize, however, that some treatments by their very nature are not reversible. For example, if we were to try to remove the consolidant from the pot mentioned earlier, we would not be able to get it all out. No matter how carefully we try to remove it, traces of consolidant will remain. In addition, the pot would suffer considerable damage from our efforts to try to remove the consolidant.

So reversibility, although no longer regarded as a principle, remains a goal of conservation treatment and guides our work. It is of particular importance in excavation work, for here the field conservator is frequently forced to carry out procedures under less than ideal conditions. When the artifact gets to a lab, what was done in the field must be undone first before it can be properly treated. If irreversible materials are used in the field, this job becomes much more difficult, if not impossible.

DOCUMENTATION

Documentation is an integral part of any active conservation treatment that takes place. Careful records must document everything that is done to an artifact, including justifications for action taken. Written reports and photographs, augmented with drawings when appropriate, should fully and accurately describe the condition of the artifact both before and after treatment, the materials and methods involved in the treatment, and any technological information revealed during the course of treatment. Notation must also be made of any tests performed on the artifact and their results, even if inconclusive. Any material removed from an artifact, including dirt, should also be noted. While this may seem unnecessary, the fact that something was present could be of significance later; dirt and other substances removed from artifacts can sometimes provide valuable clues in determining how an artifact was used or what activities took place at the site.

Treatment records are just as important to the artifacts as the excavation documentation. Together with the artifacts themselves, they form an integral part of the archaeological collection. They must remain with the collection and be made accessible to archaeologists and conservators alike. Information in the reports could aid future archaeological research, while treatment information will certainly facilitate any future conservation work.

RESTORATION

While restoration is generally not an important aspect of archaeological conservation, there are times when it is appropriate. It is usually done for exhibit purposes, to increase the interpretive value of an artifact by restoring its missing parts. These restorations can serve to strengthen and, thus, stabilize the artifact as well.

The approach to restoration must be in keeping with the principles that govern other forms of treatment already mentioned. Restoration must be done as clearly and honestly as possible with a clear distinction being made between what is original and what is restoration. Repairs and restorations should not be hidden nor should the artifact be made to appear to be in better condition than it actually is. This is not to say, however, that restorations need be obtrusive or inharmonious. Quite the contrary. When done skillfully and sensitively, they are readily seen without being a dominant element. We usually strive to make a restoration blend in with the original parts of the artifact when viewed from a distance of ten feet or so. On closer inspection, however, they must be readily apparent.

When restoring artifacts, we must be careful not to impose our own aesthetics, cultural values, or interpretations on them, as in the case of painting bronzes green. Assumptions should not be made about how an artifact looked. Missing elements must not be added unless unequivocal evidence exists of what the shape should be and where it should be placed. Neither should we guess at decoration. If half of a painted design is missing on a bowl, there is no way we can know the artist's intent and accurately reconstruct the picture. In this instance, the only thing we can do is restore the shape of the missing area, but either leave the restoration uncolored or paint it a solid color that blends in with the original parts of the bowl. Even when the decorative scheme is repetitive or symmetrical, we must have clear evidence to support its restoration. Certainly, when the scheme is asymmetrical, it cannot be restored.

The same holds true for an artifact that is part of a group; we cannot assume that it was exactly like the others in shape, surface texture, or decoration. We can only restore that for which we have definite evidence.

Two silver lyres from Ur (an early city in Mesopotamia) illustrate how inappropriate restorations can lead archaeologists into drawing wrong conclusions about artifacts. These lyres are the only two with boat-shaped soundboxes and, from the early 1930s until a few years ago, archaeologists were convinced that they were unique. It turns out, however, that they were incorrectly restored. The British Museum lyre was actually parts of two soundboxes mistakenly put together to form one, while the lyre at the University of Pennsylvania's University Museum was restored to look like the British one. Because the two making up the British lyre were found squashed together in a burial, it was assumed that there was only one instrument. As no one had ever seen anything like it before, they didn't know what the lyre had looked like and, therefore, had guessed at the restoration. Given the circumstances of burial and the rudimentary state of conservation at the time, the erroneous restoration was not altogether unreasonable. It wasn't until recently, some sixty years later, that conservators at both institutions, using careful examination and modern analytical techniques, discovered the mistaken restorations. The problem with such restorations, of course, is that erroneous information is perpetuated in the literature and becomes very hard to correct.

PREVENTIVE CONSERVATION

Over the past decade, we have become much more conservative in the treatment of artifacts. We have come to rely more heavily on passive, or preventive, treatment. Preventive conservation is based on the premise that deterioration can be reduced greatly by controlling its causes. Thus, if we prevent damage from occurring by removing the causes of deterioration, we will not need to treat artifacts using invasive techniques. Again, the medical analogy is a good one. By taking care of yourself, eating right, and having regular check-ups, you are less likely to develop conditions that require intrusive procedures, such as taking medications or having surgery. Similarly, through proper handling, collection maintenance, and controlling the environment in which collections are stored, studied, and exhibited, we can achieve the stabilization of large assemblages of archaeological material. Preventive conservation, then, puts the emphasis of preservation on the collection as a whole rather than on any single artifact within the collection. Preventive conservation, by its very nature, enables us to care better for large numbers of artifacts at the same time, frequently an important consideration when caring for many archaeological assemblages. Active treatment is labor intensive and, given the lack of conservators in museums, only small numbers of artifacts can be treated actively or invasively. By concentrating on providing the appropriate overall conditions for artifacts, however, whole storerooms of artifacts can be treated at the same time. Thus, preventive treatment is much more time and cost effective, particularly where large collections are involved.

So in practicing preventive conservation, we are concerned with removing as many of the causes of deterioration as possible. Probably the greatest amount of damage to artifacts comes from improper or careless handling. Ironically, this is the most unnecessary damage that can occur. Thus, conservators have developed procedures and guidelines for all activities involving artifacts: proper ways of picking up and transporting them, putting numbers on them, and mounting them in exhibit cases, to name a few. While many of these procedures might seem fairly fundamental and obvious, it is astounding how frequently people who should know better take unnecessary risks when handling artifacts.

The majority of archaeological materials, especially sherds, do not have much exhibit value and will spend most of their existence in storage. As this storage is usually permanent, we spend considerable time and effort overseeing the preparation of artifacts for storage. We make sure that artifacts are appropriately padded and supported so that they will not suffer physical damage while in storage. Decisions must be made about which materials can be packed together in groups and which artifacts should be individually housed. How do you store large assemblages of lithics (artifacts made of stone), for example? Ideally, each should be individually housed, but this is hardly practical. If you store them in groups in boxes, how do you prevent them from rubbing against and abrading each other, possibly ruining their surfaces for future studies of wear? How can hundreds of bags of sherds be stored to take up as little space as possible? If packed efficiently into boxes, how do you prevent them from being crushed under their own weight? These are some of the questions we deal with on a daily basis.

Conservators are also involved with exhibit work, for exhibits can be regarded as a form of storage. When artifacts are used for exhibit, it is the role of the conservator to make sure that the security and well-being of the artifact is not sacrificed for aesthetic effect. Mounting hardware must be designed that is compatible with the artifact yet provides adequate support. While we do not generally make mounts, we must advise the mountmaker, communicating the needs of the artifacts. For example, insufficient support means poor distribution of the artifact's weight, which can lead to warping and breakage, while hard abrasive mount hardware can permanently disfigure the surface of an artifact.

Controlling the environment in which artifacts are housed is an important part of preventive treatment, but it is also the most difficult to achieve. We are concerned with the levels of relative humidity, light, and pollution, all of which can be extremely damaging to artifacts.

Relative humidity can adversely affect all types of material. High levels of relative humidity can cause metals to corrode, while low levels allow artifacts made of organic materials to dry out. Fluctuating levels of relative humidity can be particularly damaging to artifacts containing water soluble salts. These salts go in and out of solution in response to changes in the relative humidity. As the salts take up a larger volume in the solid state than in solution, the constant cycling in and out of solution causes the salts to exert mechanical pressure against the surface of the artifact, literally pushing it off.

Light, on the other hand, generally damages only organic materials. As light damage is restricted to those areas that it touches, initially it is superficial in nature, taking the form of fading or bleaching. If allowed to continue, however, it will eventually result in serious structural damage to the artifact.

The idea of pollution affecting artifacts may seem a bit far fetched, but, in fact, it is a grave reality. The pollution generally comes from the very materials meant to protect artifacts, the packing materials used to house them. Thus, we are adamant in insisting that only inert, stable materials are used for packing and housing artifacts. Materials known to emit harmful vapors are avoided. These include the woods and paints used to make shelving and drawers as well as the plastic bags, cardboard boxes, tissue paper, and foams that come in contact with the artifacts, and also the materials used in making and furnishing exhibit cases. Any harmful vapors emitted by these materials can be especially damaging as they are held in a small enclosed space with the artifacts and cannot dissipate. I recently had to treat some Roman bowls, spoons, and vases made out of silver that were badly corroded by sulphur emitted by the rubber gaskets in the case in which they were displayed. They suffered from a virulent form of sulphur attack that has left their surfaces permanently pitted and defaced. Had inert gasketing been used, this damage would have been avoided.

I think one can see that preventive conservation by its very nature is a long-term commitment, the key to which is careful and constant vigilance. Artifacts as well as environmental conditions must be monitored consistently and regularly to enable remedial action to be taken as soon as possible when the need arises.

INVESTIGATIVE WORK

While archaeological conservators spend much of their time caring for collections, we also do detective work that can play a significant role in the study of artifacts. If active and passive treatment are the meat and potatoes of what we do, then investigational work is the gravy, at least for me. Investigative work does not entitle us to interpret artifacts; this is the domain of the archaeologist. However, we can bring an important perspective to this process and should participate in it. We can also assist the archaeologist with important research questions, such as those concerning technology, provenience, and authenticity. Again, our training makes us uniquely qualified to do this.

Examination is one of the skills we learn early on in our training. It is just as important an aspect of archaeological conservation as stabilization and restoration. Examination can be regarded as a form of investigative work that over time enables us to develop a familiarity with and understanding of materials and the technology involved in the fabrication of artifacts. Examination is the primary means by which archaeological conservators systematically extract information from artifacts that helps answer questions about technology, provenience, and authenticity.

Work I did a few years ago illustrates this point nicely. The collections of the Field Museum in Chicago include a famous copper alloy rein-ring from the Mesopotamian site of Kish. When first excavated in 1928, the animal atop the ring was identified as a Mesopotamian fallow deer. A famous paleontologist, however, later interpreted the figure as a likeness of an extinct fossil giraffe called *Sivatherium*. His theory, based on two small structures on the forehead of the animal and the lack of antlers, was widely accepted by scholars up to the present day. Acceptance meant that this animal lived at the same time as the people of ancient Mesopotamia (ca. 2700 B.C.), considerably more recently than previously thought. A few years ago, a zooarchaeologist studying the rein-ring strongly doubted the *Sivatherium* theory. He brought the ring to me, along with a box of copper alloy fragments from the site, and asked if I could make any sense out of all the pieces. It did not take long to recognize antlers in two knobbly pieces. By carefully examining the head of the animal, it was not difficult to find where they had broken off the animal's head. Once re-adhered, it became obvious that the animal was indeed the more likely Mesopotamian fallow deer, and a peculiar anomaly was laid to rest.

Our training in materials science has taught us about the structure of materials and how they deteriorate. Over time, we gain considerable experience in looking at a variety of materials and artifacts from different time periods and locations. This experience, along with our knowledge of materials science, helps us to recognize and identify the materials of which artifacts are made. Our training in chemistry and analytical techniques enables us to carry out simple tests to verify our identifications. A recent nondestructive study of ivory artifacts from Bronze Age Greece used the researcher's familiarity and knowledge of morphological characteristics of different kinds of ivory, along with careful examination of artifacts, to identify much of the material as being hippopotamus ivory. Previously, most Aegean Bronze Age ivory artifacts were thought to have been made only from elephant ivory. This important work has led to a reappraisal of Aegean ivories, which has provided a better understanding of Bronze Age ivory-working as well as the larger issue of trade.[2]

On many sites, burial conditions are not conducive to the preservation of organic materials, such as seeds, leaves, leather, or wood. Evidence of these materials is preserved more often than you might think, however, if you know what to look for and where to search for it. If a piece of wood, for example, is buried next to a metal artifact, part or all of it may be preserved by or in the corrosion products of that artifact. The corrosion products either preserve the wood by acting as a biocide, preventing it from deteriorating, or by replacing the wood as it disintegrates, forming an exact replica called a pseudomorph. I once cleaned an Anglo-Saxon iron sword that was heavily corroded. As I examined and cleaned the blade, I uncovered preserved bits of wood from the scabbard and pseudomorphs of the fleece that once lined the scabbard. Always on the lookout for such evidence when cleaning metal artifacts, I was able to recognize this evidence, document it carefully, and preserve it. Had the sword been cleaned by an inexperienced person, especially with chemicals, this information would certainly have been lost without anyone ever knowing it had been there.

Identifying freshly excavated materials in the field can be a much more difficult task than working in a laboratory. I am reminded of a field season on Crete several years ago where the excavators sent up a bag of sherds labeled "fineware." They were sent directly to me, bypassing the sherd-cleaning women, as they were unusual for the trench in which they were found. In cleaning them, I quickly realized that they were not pottery. Closer examination, along with having seen the material before, enabled me to identify the pieces as fragments of imported ostrich eggshell.

Our training has also made us knowledgeable about ancient fabrication techniques. I don't know a single archaeological conservator who is not fascinated by how artifacts are made. I personally get extraordinary pleasure out of cleaning a freshly excavated artifact. To be the first person in thousands of years to carefully examine it, to reveal fingerprints of the potter in the clay or the metalsmith's file marks in the bronze, is tremendously exciting. With our specialized training, we are in the unique position of being able to reveal such information about artifacts that might otherwise be missed.

CONCLUSION

I think one can see that the discipline of conservation is an integral part of archaeology. Through its various procedures and functions, it can make major contributions to the study of archaeological material and our understanding of the past. Our preservation activities help to prolong the life of archaeological collections and ensure that they will be around for future generations of researchers, undoubtedly equipped with better, more sophisticated means of extracting information from artifacts. Without our investigative work, much information would never be recovered from artifacts, and worse, would be lost without anyone ever knowing that it had been there.

NOTES

1. Harold J. Plenderleith, "Preservation and Conservation: Introductory Statement," in S. Timmons, ed., *Preservation and Conservation: Principles and Practices* (Washington: Preservation Press, 1976), p. xx.
2. Olga H. Krzyszkowska, "Ivory in the Aegean Bronze Age: Elephant Tusk or Hippopotamus Ivory?" *The Annual of the British School of Archaeology at Athens* 83 (1988): 209–234.

SUGGESTED READINGS

Bleed, Peter, and Robert Nickel. "Optimal Management of Archaeological Collections." *Curator* 32 (1989): 26–33. A brief discussion of some of the issues involved in the care of archaeological materials.

Freed, Stanley A. "Research Pitfalls as a Result of the Restoration of Museum Specimens." In A. Cantwell, J. B. Griffin, and N. A. Rothschild, eds. *The Research Potential of Anthropological Museum Collections.* New York: New York Academy of Sciences, 1981, pp. 229–245. A profusely illustrated discussion of how restorations can be misleading.

Oddy, Andrew. "Introduction." In Andrew Oddy, ed. *The Art of the Conservator.* London: British Museum Press/Washington: Smithsonian Institution Press, 1992, pp. 7–27. A good general discussion about the issues and ethics involved in conservation work.

Sease, Catherine. *A Conservation Manual for the Field Archaeologist,* 3rd ed. Los Angeles: UCLA Institute of Archeology, 1994. A manual designed to aid the archaeologist in retrieving artifacts safely from the ground.

Ward, Philip. *The Nature of Conservation—A Race against Time.* Marina del Rey, CA: The Getty Conservation Institute, 1986). A brief, general discussion of what conservation entails, including the differences between preservation and restoration, the various roles of the conservator, and conservation training.

Webster, Laurie, "Altered States: Documenting Changes in Anthropology Research Collections." *Curator* 33 (1990): 130–160. A good discussion about how conservation and collection care procedures can affect the research potential of artifacts.

LITHIC ANALYSIS:
CHIPPED STONE TOOLS
AND WASTE FLAKES IN ARCHAEOLOGY

ROBERT L. KELLY

The air was thick with the sweet smell of sage that hot Nevada afternoon in 1973, my first day of archaeological survey. We had huffed and puffed our way to the top of a windy ridge overlooking Big Smoky Valley. Our crew leader, Robert Bettinger, always ahead of the rest of us, paused at the crest of the hill. I caught up with him first. Looking down at the ground, he asked me if I saw "it." Following his gaze, I saw dozens of small flecks, brilliant red against the parched earth. I bent down to pick one up and was surprised to find they were stone. I had thought they were flower petals! Nearby was a broken knife of the same material, its surface covered with neat symmetrical fractures as if someone had carved it from clay. In my hand I held the stone, hot from the noon sun, and ran my thumb over its undulating surface. I thought that I had never seen anything so beautiful. At that moment my future was charted for me.

LITHIC ANALYSIS

Lithic analysis is the study of chipped stone tools and the waste flakes from their manufacture and maintenance. Stone tools and waste flakes form the largest class of archaeological data. They record the earliest instances of tool making by our ancestors (just over two million years ago) and are the bulk of the archaeological remains left behind by hunting and gathering peoples. They even continued to be an integral part of prehistoric technology after the introduction of metals. Flaked stones were used for the manufacture of projectile points (arrowheads and spear points) scrapers, engraving tools, knives, choppers, drills, and shredders; these tools were used to work leather, wood, bone, antler, and sinew to make clothing, bags, baskets, bows, amulets—to make all the necessities of life. Understandably, then, archaeologists have devoted a considerable amount of time to the study of stone tools.

IS IT A TOOL?

Students frequently ask me to look at stones found in their fields that they think are spear points or scrapers or something else (I also get lots of petrified brains and hearts). Usually the students are right, but sometimes what they show me is just an unusually shaped rock. How does an archaeologist know what's a tool and what's just a broken rock?

Most of the time the answer is easy because the probability that a stone could naturally fracture into, for example, a projectile point is extremely small. But prehistoric people often fashioned tools expediently by quickly striking a few flakes off a handy cobble. How can we tell if such cobbles are tools? This issue is especially important to archaeologists who try to determine when humans first arrived in the Americas.

All archaeologists agree that people were in the Americas by 11,200 years ago—they were the ones who fashioned Clovis spear points (see Figure 4-1 on page 50). But some argue that people were here earlier—fifty thousand or more years ago—based on the excavation of crudely fractured cobbles at a few localities, such as the Pedra Furada site in Brazil. The "tools" at this site's earliest levels are simple quartzite cobbles from which a few flakes were removed; they look like crude chopping or cutting tools. While living peoples made frequent use of such tools, we also find fractured stones that look like tools along a river's rapids where they were pounded against one another; at the base of cliffs where they shattered upon impact; in *alluvial fans*, the geologic deposits that form vast and deep skirts on mountain ranges where stones broke under pressure or in mudslides; or in glacial deposits where stones broke beneath the crushing force of a thick sheet of ice.

Pedra Furada is a cliffside rock shelter, far above which is a geologic deposit containing quartzite nodules; these nodules have been breaking off, tumbling down the cliff, shattering and rolling into the rock shelter for millenia. How do we know if the casually fractured stones in Pedra Furada's early deposits were made by humans or by natural forces?

First, we can sometimes rule out natural processes by the kind of rock that was used to make tools. Through visual inspection or chemical analysis it is often possible to trace a rock to the geologic strata from which it came. If the tools occur in large numbers in a site located higher in elevation than the geologic strata, then there is a good chance that people brought them there (or, as archaeologist Dennis Stanford once said, there must have been one heck of a windstorm). Or if fractured stones are found in geologic deposits that were deposited with little force (e.g., pond sediments or a peat bog), Mother Nature cannot be blamed. But if the stone comes originally from a geologic strata "upslope" from where it is found (as at Pedra Furada), someplace from which the stone could have rolled down and into the site, or if the stone is found in a deposit that was (at least in times past) deposited violently, then it is less likely that the tools were created by people.

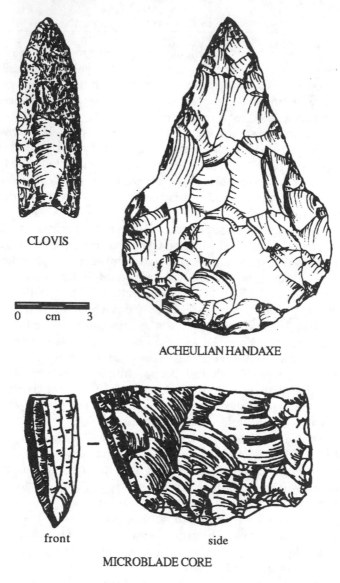

CLOVIS

0   cm   3

ACHEULIAN HANDAXE

front   side

MICROBLADE CORE

FIGURE 4-1   THREE STONE TOOLS: A CLOVIS SPEAR POINT,
AN ACHEULIAN HAND AX, AND A MICROBLADE CORE

Second, if we knew how stones tend to break in nature, uninfluenced by
people, then we might be able to say whether casually flaked cobbles in a site
could or could not be products of nature. What do stones look like if they fracture naturally as they roll down rivers, bounce along in a mudflow, topple off
cliffs, or are crushed by glacial ice? Archaeologists can simulate these situations

by churning cobbles, water, and mud into cement mixers or by dropping rocks off a cliff. The results could provide "signatures" of the frequency of different kinds of broken rock in natural deposits, showing, for example, the percentage of the stones in a mudflow that have only one flake removed, the percentage that have two, or the percentage that have two flakes removed from the same edge.

Although more detailed studies need to be conducted, current experiments suggest that natural processes only rarely produce stones that look like those called stone tools at Pedra Furada. It seems that if Mother Nature breaks hundreds of thousands of rocks blindfolded, she will produce only one or two that look like casual tools. This means that if the archaeologist looks at enough broken rocks, he or she will certainly find a few that look like tools but that are probably not tools. If I only find three dozen rocks in a site, including artifacts and unmodified stones, and ten of these each have three or four flake scars, then there is a good chance that they were produced by humans. But at a site like Pedra Furada, where researchers recovered tens of thousands of broken rocks, only a few of which were thought to be tools, there is an infinitesimally small chance that these few pieces really are tools.[1]

HOW WERE STONE TOOLS MADE AND HOW DO ARCHAEOLOGISTS KNOW?

The first stage in making a stone tool is selecting the right kind of stone. The kind of stones that prehistoric peoples preferred to use were primarily flint, chert, jasper, and obsidian. The reason is that when stones of these materials are struck they break with a *concoidal* or glassy fracture that creates sharp edges and that gives the flintknapper control over flake removal. Quartz, quartzite, and fine-grained basalts were also used. Other kinds of rock can be flaked, but they can be awfully frustrating. Prehistoric peoples often visited the same locales to obtain stone, even transporting it long distances. Prehistoric quarries demonstrate this fact. At Spanish Diggings in Wyoming, for example, acres and acres of hillsides are covered with a dense carpet of quartzite flakes and discarded tools and are pitted with deep holes where people excavated into solid rock, using only fire to loosen pieces and stout poles to wedge them out. Prehistoric peoples knew that stone on the surface had "dried out" (yes, rock can dry out) and would not flake as well as the buried "wet" rock.

Now our flintknapper has a piece of stone; how does he or she make it into a tool? There are many ways to flake stone, and they are differentiated primarily in terms of the degree of control the flintknapper wishes to exercise over the size and shape of flakes removed. One could simply throw a hunk of stone against another and select suitable flakes from the resulting shatter. Most prehistoric peoples, however, preferred methods with a bit more control, such as *direct percussion*. Here one holds a stone, the *core*, and strikes it with the *hammer*. There are two kinds of hammers: *hard hammers*, normally fist-sized, slightly oblong cobbles (hammerstones), and *soft hammers*, antlers or hardwood batons, which permit a bit more control over the shape of flakes. With practice, you can learn how to strike a stone with just the right amount of force and at just the right angle to detach the kind of flake you want. Still greater control can be achieved by using *indirect percussion*, in which an antler punch is used in conjunction with a hard hammer to direct the force of the blow to a very small area on a core's edge.

An unmodified flake was probably suitable for many prehistoric tasks, but often a tool had to be shaped. After removing a flake from a core, the flintknapper could continue to remove flakes from all margins and both sides of that flake. This results in a tool that is flaked on both sides and is therefore called a *biface* or a *bifacial* tool. The technique used for the final flaking of implements—to sharpen the edges of a knife or to put notches in an arrowhead—is *pressure flaking*. Here the tine of an antler or a pointed hard stone is used. Instead of striking the margin of the stone, the flintknapper removes flakes by pressing on the edge of the tool until a flake pops off the opposite side of the tool. To assist in this process, a tool's edge is first ground with a flat cobble to roughen it up and provide the pressure flaker with a purchase on its edge. Bifacial tools can be of many different sizes, from large Acheulean hand axes (manufactured throughout much of the Old World some 1.7 to .5 million years ago) to projectile points smaller than a U.S. dime.[2]

Sometimes prehistoric people found themselves with only small cobbles as the source of flakes for tools. In this case, they normally used the *bipolar* technique. Here the flintknapper holds a small cobble on an anvil or, if it is especially small, wraps grass around it to provide a "handle," and then unceremoniously strikes it with a hammer stone. The result is often a shatter of flakes, most of which could not be further modified but which were useful for expedient tasks.

Finally, there are *prismatic blades* and *microblades* (see Figure 4-1 on page 50). These are rectangular razor-bladelike tools that vary in size but are generally at least twice as long as they are wide. Large blades were removed from conical or cylindrical cores, while microblades were often removed from small, wedge-shaped cores. Blades could be handheld and used for a variety of fine cutting or skilled carving tasks. They could also be set into slots carved into appropriately shaped bone, wood, or antler to form razor-edged spear points or long sickles. Blades were produced through indirect and direct percussion as well as pressure flaking. Sometimes the flintknapper used a *chest crutch*, a meter-long T-shaped pole, pointed at one end. The pointed end was placed on the edge of a cylindrical core, which was held in a wooden vice or between the flintknapper's feet. The flintknapper then bent over, placing his or her chest on the top of the T-shaped pole, and with a quick motion downward drove off a flake. In my experience, this method works best if you weigh about two hundred pounds—otherwise you end up with nothing more than flint dust and bruised ribs.

It takes no time at all to learn the simplest of these methods of making stone tools, and a considerable amount of time to learn others. It helps if you have the skills of a sculptor because you have to be able to "see" the arrowhead in the lump of stone before you. Archaeologist Bruce Bradley, certainly one of the world's finest living flintknappers, says that it takes about two years of practice to make an acceptable Clovis spear point (which entails the removal of one or more blades from the surface of a biface). If you wish to practice making stone tools, I would recommend apprenticing yourself to a flintknapper. Also, be sure to hold the stone you are working on in a thick leather pad to prevent flakes from being driven through your palm (you'll know an extremely hard-core flintknapper by the number of band-aids on his or her hands), wear protective goggles to protect your eyes from flying slivers, and work in an open environment—eighteenth-century gunflint makers in England frequently died of silicosis, contracted from breathing flint dust for years on end.

Practicing making stone tools is the first step in learning how to recognize evidence of different stone tool manufacturing methods from archaeological data. Different manufacturing methods leave behind different kinds of traces besides the tools themselves. Blade production, for example, leaves behind a very distinctive core, one with narrow flake scars running along its long axis. Learning how to recognize different methods of stone tool production also requires learning how to recognize the different sorts of flakes each technique produces. Flintknapping is a messy activity; for every shaped tool a knapper produces he or she may leave hundreds of waste flakes behind. Sometimes these waste flakes are a clue as to what technique was being used. The kinds of tools found in a site are certainly indicative of the reduction methods used, but the same tool can be made through different techniques. And although some tools were brought to a site fully manufactured, others were made on the spot and discarded, and still others might have been partially completed and then transported from the site. Understanding what stone tools have to tell us about prehistoric lives means understanding how tools are used across a landscape, not just at one location. And this means reconstructing stone tool technology not just from the tools themselves, but from the waste flakes left behind. This is not easy, for a given technique may produce more than one kind of flake. But experimental archaeology suggests that the different ways of manufacturing tools leave discernible patterns in their waste flakes.

Before going further we need to define a few terms (see Figure 4-2 on page 54). A flake has two sides: Its *dorsal* side is the side that was outside the core and its *ventral* side is the side that was inside the core. The dorsal side is normally covered with flake scars, evidence of previous flake removals from the core. The dorsal side of the first flakes removed from a core, however, are covered with *cortex* or *patina*, the weathered surface of the core. At the flake's "top," the point where the hammer stone or pressure flaker made contact with the core, is the *striking platform*; on the ventral surface of the flake just below the striking platform is a slight bulge, the *bulb of percussion*. The "bottom" of

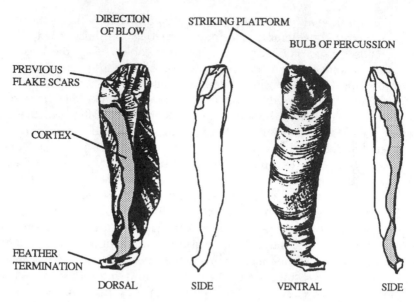

DIRECTION OF BLOW

STRIKING PLATFORM

BULB OF PERCUSSION

PREVIOUS FLAKE SCARS

CORTEX

FEATHER TERMINATION

DORSAL   SIDE   VENTRAL   SIDE

FIGURE 4-2   THE BASIC ATTRIBUTES OF STONE FLAKES
Source: Modified from Crabtree, 1972.

the flake has a *feather termination* if it comes to a thin, featherlike end, or a *step* or *hinge fracture* if the flake broke off the core abruptly. Archaeologists record all sorts of observations on flakes—length, width, thickness, platform width, platform depth, weight, platform angle, the number and directions of flake scars on the dorsal surface, the amount of cortex on the dorsal side, the kind of termination, the type of platform, and a range of other arcane measures.

Experimental replicative flintknapping suggests that these variables can be used to detect prehistoric flintknapping methods. To see how, consider the following scenario. Imagine a family of hunter-gatherers who spend some time one summer in a rock shelter. They have brought a number of spear points fashioned from a distinctive red chert. While at the shelter, these points are used in hunting, but also for cutting meat; some break and are reflaked and used to scrape hides. Needing to prepare willow branches to make baskets, a woman brings some small quartzite cobbles from a nearby stream and makes some flakes through percussion knapping; some of the cobbles are small and so she reduces them bipolarly. She uses the flakes for a day, then discards them. Meanwhile, some of the men decide that they do not have enough spear points for the next place they plan to inhabit, which is good hunting territory, and so they make a special trip to a quarry they know is two days' journey away. Once there, they make some large bifaces of a brown chert—not wanting to bring back stone that contains flaws—and return home, where they work on them further. Some of these bifaces are heated in the family hearth, for these foragers know that chert often flakes better if it is baked for a while.[3] After a month, the family leaves. The wind blows dust into the rock shelter, covering the flakes and tools left behind; time passes, and the site is left for the archaeologist to excavate.

Sorting the waste flakes and artifacts into three raw material categories, the archaeologist notices several patterns. In the red chert pile there are broken bits of bifacial spear points, some recycled into scrapers. The flakes in this pile are all very small and have no cortex on their dorsal surface but, for their size, they do have many dorsal scars. Their platforms are small and are covered with many facets, suggesting they were removed late in a tool's "life." In the quartzite pile are many flakes with cortex on their dorsal surface, indicating that they entered the site as complete river cobbles. Looking more closely, we see primarily two kinds of flakes: some with wide or deep platforms with only one or two facets, and some with platforms completely crushed that also lack prominent bulbs of percussion—some of these are crushed at the end opposite the platform. Many of the flakes in both piles terminate in hinge or step fractures. The first pile represents simple percussion knapping while the second indicates bipolar reduction. There are regular cores and bipolar cores present, but no bifacial tools of quartzite. Finally, the pile of brown chert contains medium to large flakes with prominent bulbs of percussion, and platforms with only a few facets. There is no cortex on the dorsal surfaces, which are instead covered by a few previous flake scars. The flakes are generally thin, with unpronounced bulbs of percussion suggesting they were struck with a soft hammer. These flakes point to an early stage in the manufacture of bifaces.

An additional line of evidence the archaeologist could use at this site is *refitting*.[4] If our archaeologist excavated most of the site, he or she could try to fit the flakes, cores, and tool fragments together, reconstructing the knapping sequence in reverse order. This is not easy; it takes hours and hours and is like trying to put together a 3-D jigsaw puzzle with half the pieces missing and no picture on the box. Some people are very good at it while others like me don't have the patience. But it can be an extremely valuable addition to or confirmation of an analysis of waste flakes. Putting the quartzite flakes together, the archaeologist would see that some flakes refit back to cores and some to bipolar cores, forming entire river cobbles; he or she could probably see that some of the heated and unheated pieces of chert fit back together again (sometimes heat-treating completely changes a rock's color and texture), and that many flakes of the red chert fit back together, forming the outside of a biface, but the biface itself is missing. A biface fragment recycled into a scraper may fit back to the rest of the discarded biface. Refitting can also trace the movement of items across a site—showing where different activities occurred—or it can even indicate whether a site was used more than once, whether natural factors affected the distribution of material in a site, or if there has been much vertical movement of artifacts in a buried site (caused by burrowing rodents, for example).

Returning to our analysis, we could interpret the patterns in the waste flakes and tools as indicating that the red chert entered the rock shelter as completed bifaces that were then resharpened and occasionally recycled into scrapers. The quartzite flakes came from a source so close that no preliminary reduction was done at the quarrying location. Only expedient flake tools were produced from them, and small cobbles were reduced bipolarly. The brown chert was brought into the site after being initially reduced into large bifaces at the quarry; these were further worked into bifacial implements, perhaps spear points, but were generally not used as tools at the site—they were taken with the occupants to be used elsewhere.

In reality, analysis of tools and waste flakes is far more complex than the earlier example suggests. It is often difficult to sort raw materials, and post-deposition factors such as trampling can break flakes in ways that have nothing to do with flintknapping. The relationship between flake characteristics and knapping techniques is still not clear. Some archaeologists suggest that we look only at simple characteristics, such as the degree of flake completeness, or size grade distributions of flakes. Others advocate more complex approaches, preferring to measure many variables and crunch these through high-powered statistical routines to search for patterns. Personally, I am of the "less-is-more" school, but the jury is still out. Finally, stone tool analysis is inevitably complicated by the fact that tools, cores, and flakes could be changed into something completely different at any stage in their use-lives. While we often look upon stone tools romantically as artistic endeavors, I suspect they were just rocks to prehistoric peoples. A flintknapper could set out to make a biface, but if the stone broke along the way, as often happens, it might be turned into something else; bifaces can also be smashed bipolarly to produce small expedient flake tools, or points can break and be turned into scrapers. The past is never as neat and tidy as we would like it to be.

WHAT WERE STONE TOOLS USED FOR?

For many years archaeologists interpreted the function of stone tools based on a tool's shape: Projectile points were used for hunting, scrapers for scraping, drills for drilling. But we now know that the shape of a tool does not always tell us its use. And shape tells us nothing about what simple unmodified flakes were used for (probably the most common tool prehistorically). And even if we correctly identify a scraper as a scraper, this does not tell us on what material it was used (hide, wood, bone, antler?).

It makes sense that using stone tools on different materials will produce different kinds of wear on the tool. The Russian archaeologist Sergei Semenov initiated the microscopic study of use-wear in the 1950s. His method has since been refined by a number of archaeologists.[5] This research entails experiments. Archaeologists make stone tools or flakes, record their unused edges under a microscope fitted with a camera, then use the tools to cut open animals (road kills, or zoo animals that died of natural causes), and cut or scrape hides, wood, antler, bone, etc. Using a tool on any of these materials leaves three major sorts of traces on its edge: microscopic edge chipping, striations, and polish. Chipping is the most obvious, and the harder the material involved the larger the chipping. Striations indicate the motion involved: Striations perpendicular to the tool edge point to a scraping motion while striations more parallel to the edge indicate a cutting or sawing motion. As the tool is used friction sends silica from both the tool and the material being worked into solution and builds up polishes that vary in luster, brightness, roughness, and pitting depending on the kind of material being worked. This polish can be seen beneath a microscope at x 200 to x 400, although some analysts advocate the use of lower powers—less than x 100. Experimental research demonstrates that polish of different degrees of luster, brightness, etc., can be attributed to some very specific materials: green bone, old bone, wood, hides, meat, etc.

Use-wear studies of stone tools have altered some of our ideas about prehistory by betraying archaeologists' assumptions about stone tools. For example, George Odell argues that the bow and arrow came into use in the midwestern United States some 2,000 years before the long-accepted date of A.D. 1000 based on the presence of projectile use-wear on small triangular flakes—artifacts not typically labeled as projectile points. He also notes that many artifacts in the eastern United States traditionally labeled as projectile points bear no use-wear of having been employed as projectiles.[6]

Use-wear has been a tremendous boon for archaeology but it is not without its limitations and difficulties. It is difficult to see some types of polish on certain types of stone; the method works best on cherts and flints (which have plenty of silica to form polishes). Also, since tools could be used for a variety of purposes, the analyst may only see the most recent use, or may not be able to decide what kind of polish is present. It also takes some time for a tool to build up a polish. In fact, Douglas Bamforth argues that it takes about 30 minutes or 1,500 strokes of continuous use for a tool to build up a polish that is distinctive of the particular kind of material being worked.[7] Many prehistoric tools were probably used for very quick tasks and use-wear on their edges tells us they were used, but nothing more. Although early claims of extreme accuracy in identifying the worked material have now been tempered, use-wear analysis remains an important part of the archaeologist's tool chest.

WHAT DO STONE TOOLS TELL US ABOUT PREHISTORIC LIVES?

Stone tool production is a complex sequence of stone quarrying, manufacture, use, repair, recycling, scavenging, and discard. Many analysts focus on reconstructing the particular sequence at a specific site. Others, however, are more interested in what stone tool production has to say about prehistoric economy and society.[8]

For example, several archaeologists argue that nomadic hunter-gatherers made greater use of bifacial implements than did sedentary peoples because the shape of bifacial implements allows them to be resharpened and the potential source of more flake tools than a simple core of similar weight. Thus, bifaces maximize the number of tools carried while minimizing the amount of stone carried—an obvious advantage for nomadic peoples.[9] But not all prehistoric nomadic hunter-gatherers used bifaces: Where stone tool raw material is widely available, they used simple expedient flake tools. We have not as yet found any simple correlations between technology and other social, economic, or political variables.

The type of tool made is affected by four factors: material type, size, regional distribution, and function. Material type and size will constrain the types of tools that can be produced: If only small, grainy material is present, even an experienced flintknapper will not be able to produce blades or large bifaces. If raw material is rare, then some aspect of tool manufacture and use must respond to the fact that the tool supply will be difficult to replenish. The task at hand also directs a tool's final form—you don't make a scraper if what you need to do is kill a mastodon.

But it is not always easy to define which of these variables are at work. Microblades, for example, may be an alternative to bifaces as a way to make efficient use of raw material, but they may also be a way to make efficient use of very small nodules (like bipolar knapping, but with much greater control). Then again, they may be a way to manufacture long, straight edges, as are needed, for example, to make a grass-harvesting sickle (a single blade, thirty centimeters to fifty centimeters long, would break far too easily for the effort it would take to manufacture one; microblades can be set into a slot in a wooden handle and if one of the blades breaks only the blade must be replaced, not the entire tool).

As yet there is no coherent body of theory that accounts for how stone tool production and use respond to changes in economic, social, or political behavior. In the Great Basin, for example, projectile points became smaller in size about 1,500 years ago. Earlier points were resharpened and recycled more frequently than later points. The later points probably came in with the introduction of the bow and arrow, but this does not account for why earlier points were larger and frequently resharpened. What might the change in technology have to say about changes in the role of hunting in Great Basin societies—a change from long-distance hunting to hunting that occurred only in the immediate vicinity of camp? a reduction in the amount of meat in the diet? a shift in the division of labor, the time men devote to hunting? Going back further in time, what does it mean that our early human ancestors' stone tools, especially Acheulean hand axes (see Figure 4-1 on page 50), were manufactured in a remarkably redundant fashion across entire continents for tens of thousands of generations (whereas later in time we see a diversity of stone tool manufacturing methods that are responsive to differences in raw material type, distribution, and tool function)? Perhaps this pattern is a clue to a fundamental qualitative difference in the reasoning abilities between ourselves and the maker of hand axes, *Homo erectus*.

WHAT DOES THE FUTURE HOLD?

One might think that since stone tools have been the focus of so much archaeological research, there would be little more that could be said about them, but this is not true. In fact, there is an enormous amount of work to be done. Use-wear analysis, while moving far in recent years, still needs further experimental work, and more accurate, more easily replicable methods of analysis (I must admit that when I look at photographs of different kinds of polish they all look like the same blurry, mottled surface to me). We need far more replicative experiments to determine how to differentiate the various reduction techniques based on waste flakes. Few people today make even moderate use of stone tools, which were replaced long ago with traders' goods, or tools manufactured from iron (car springs are a preferred raw material, in my experience). Nonetheless, ethnographic research with living peoples may still help point to the relationships between technology and behavior to help us develop ways to make inferences about prehistoric behavior from stone tool remains. Researchers interested in understanding the use of stone tools by our early human ancestors face an especially difficult barrier because these earliest of all stone tool users were neither biologically nor behaviorally similar to modern humans. In this area, one innovative approach implemented by paleoanthropologists Nicholas Toth and Kathy Schick has been to observe chimpanzees as they learn to make and use simple flake tools.[10]

Others are working on better ways to date stone tools. For many years archaeologists have been unable to date the many stone tools that are found on the surface of sites in arid parts of the world, where organic artifacts that could be dated through more conventional radiocarbon methods have long since disintegrated. Accelerator radiocarbon dating of organic residues trapped in a stone's patina and cation-ratio dating of the patina itself are now being developed.[11] Others are using a variety of methods to extract and identify blood residue from the cracks in tools, even tools that are thousands of years old.[12] In sum, the field of lithic analysis still holds some distant horizons and uncharted territories. Stone tool studies will continue to play an important role in archaeology for many years to come. Sometimes, in fact, I feel as though I am back on that windy ridge in Nevada, looking for the first time at a scatter of red chert flakes.

NOTES

1. See N. Guidon and B. Arnaud, "The Chronology of the New World: Two Faces of One Reality," *World Archaeology* 23 (1991): 167–178; and D. Meltzer, J. M. Adovasio, and T. D. Dillehay, "On a Pleistocene Human Occupation at Pedra Furada, Brazil," *Antiquity* 68 (1994): 695–715.
2. Small points are popularly known as "bird points" but there is no reason to think they were used for hunting birds. In fact, birds were more usually hunted with bunts, and if an arrow was well placed (and especially if it was dipped in poison beforehand) a small arrowhead could still be used to kill game the size of bison or giraffes.
3. Heating siliceous rocks at 300°C to 400°C recrystallizes stone and improves its fracture qualities.
4. J. L. Hofman and J. G. Enloe, eds., *Piecing Together the Past: Application of Refitting Studies in Archaeology*, British Archaeological Reports, no. 578 (Oxford, England: Archaeological and Historical Associates limited, 1992).
5. L. Keeley, *Experimental Determination of Stone Tool Uses* (Chicago: University of Chicago Press, 1980); G. H. Odell and F. Odell-Vereecken, "Verifying the Reliability of Lithic Use-Wear Assessments by 'Blind Tests': The Low-Power Approach," *Journal of Field Archaeology* 7 (1980): 87–120.
6. G. H. Odell, "Addressing Prehistoric Hunting Practices through Use-Wear Analysis," *American Anthropologist* 90 (1988): 335–356.
7. D. G. Bamforth, "Investigating Microwear Polishes with Blind Tests: The Institute Results in Context," *Journal of Archaeological Science* 15 (1988): 11–23; D. B. Bamforth, G. R. Burns, and C. Woodman, "Ambiguous Use Traces and Blind Test Results: New Data," *Journal of Archaeological Science* 17 (1990): 413–430.
8. M. Nelson, "The Study of Technological Organization," in M. Schiffer, ed., *Archaeological Method and Theory*, vol. 3 (Tucson: University of Arizona Press, 1991), pp. 57–100.
9. R. L. Kelly, "The Three Sides of a Biface," *American Antiquity* 53 (1988): 717–734.
10. K. D. Schick and N. Toth, *Making Silent Stones Speak* (New York: Simon & Schuster, 1993).
11. R. I. Dorn, D. B. Bamforth, T. A. Cahil, J. C. Dohrenwend, B. D. Turrin, D. J. Donahue, A. J. T. Jull, A. Long, M. E. Macko, E. B. Weil, D. S. Whitley, and T. H. Zabel, "Cation-Ratio and Accelerator-Radiocarbon Dating of Rock Varnish on Mohave Artifacts and Landforms," *Science* 231 (1986): 830–833.
12. B. Kooyman, M. E. Newman, and H. Ceri, "Verifying the Reliability of Blood Residue Analysis on Archaeological Tools," *Journal of Archaeological Science* 3 (1992): 265–270. Note that recent experimental research suggests that blood may not be preserved even after only a few months in the ground. See J. Eisele, "Survival and Detection of Blood Residues on Stone Tools," *Technical Report*, no. 94-1 (Reno: University of Nevada–Reno, Department of Anthropology).

SUGGESTED READINGS

Bordes, Francois. *The Old Stone Age*. New York: McGraw Hill, 1968. A description of stone tools in the European lower and middle Paleolithic by the founder of the European school of flintknapping.

Crabtree, Don. *An Introduction to Flintworking.* Occasional Papers of the Idaho State Museum, no. 28. Pocatello: Idaho State University Museum, 1972. An introduction to the basics of flintknapping by the founder of the American school of flintknapping.

Hayden, Brian. *Paleolithic Reflections: Lithic Technology and Ethnographic Excavation among the Australian Aborigines.* Canberra: Australian Institute of Aboriginal Studies, 1979. Ethnographic research in Australia that includes the manufacture and use of stone tools.

Toth, Nicholas, Desmond Clark, and Giancarlo Ligabue. "The Last Stone Ax Makers." *Scientific American* (July 1992): 88–93. A description of stone ax making among the Langda, a people of highland New Guinea.

Whittaker, John. *Flintknapping: Making and Understanding Stone Tools.* Austin: University of Texas Press, 1994. A thorough review of flintknapping for the beginner.

Learning about the Past through Archaeological Ceramics: An Example from Vijayanagara, India

Carla M. Sinopoli

In 1983 I came to the archaeological site of Vijayanagara in southern India to work as a ceramic analyst. Intensive archaeological research at this imperial capital (fourteenth–sixteenth century A.D.) had been underway since 1979, and previous work at the site spans more than a century.[1] The ceramic vessels used by Vijayanagara's inhabitants, however, remained completely undocumented. The site of Vijayanagara, like many historic sites in India, contains massive and impressive architectural remains that extend over an area of more than twenty square kilometers (see Figure 5-1). Architecture includes fortification walls and gates of elegant stone masonry, monumental temples, royal palaces and administrative buildings, wells, watch towers, and hundreds of sculptures of Hindu gods and royal scenes. It is little wonder that the many thousands of undecorated earthenware ceramic fragments, or sherds, visible on the ground surface and found in excavations, received little attention from earlier archaeologists working at the site.

Ceramics are among the most common category of artifacts recovered by archaeologists. Ceramic vessels are most often used for the preparation, storage, or serving of food; they may also serve a variety of other functions, including industrial uses, use in mortuary contexts, or use in the trade and transport of commodities. Because of their widespread use, frequent breakage, and durability in the archaeological record, ceramics are extremely important in archaeological analysis and interpretation. Chronological sequences can be constructed through the study of stylistic or technological changes in their form or decoration. Ceramics can also provide evidence of patterns of trade and local and supralocal interaction by identifying sources of raw material and the places where the finished products were distributed. The organization of craft production can be studied through analysis of production sites such as kilns or workshops, as well as from the documentation of technological

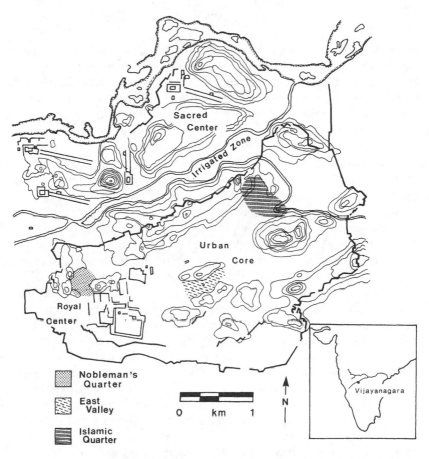

FIGURE 5-1   VIJAYANAGARA CITY PLAN

traces on the vessel fragments themselves. Further, the spatial distribution of ceramics within sites and across regions provides important evidence concerning the nature of ancient social structures, status relations, and activity distributions.

The study of ceramics is relevant not only in prehistoric contexts but also in the study of historic periods. In cities such as Vijayanagara only a very small portion of the population was literate or lived in the impressive monumental structures that dominate the landscape. The vast majority of the city's residents lived in small huts of impermanent materials and left no written accounts of their lives. They are thus completely unknown to us, except for the scattered remains that they left behind. The most common of these remains are earthenware ceramics.

THE FIRST STEP: CERAMIC CLASSIFICATION

In many regions of the world an archaeologist commencing a study of ceramics builds on the work of earlier generations of scholars, developing research strategies and research questions in the context of an established body of knowledge. The questions asked by a later generation of archaeologists may vary significantly from those of their predecessors as a result of changing theoretical perspectives or research goals, as well as the increased sophistication and availability of new analytical tools and techniques, such as computer-assisted analysis or chemical sourcing techniques. Nonetheless, scholars working in an area with an established tradition of ceramic analysis have an established language for talking about the materials they study—in the form of a ceramic classification.[2]

The classification of archaeological remains is the first step in any analysis. In order to be able to describe ceramics and examine how they vary over time and space, archaeologists must first document basic characteristics, including raw materials and production technology as well as vessel shape, size, color, and decoration. Classification is a tool that allows us to group individual ceramic fragments—whether sherds or whole vessels—into coherent and meaningful groups whose members share some essential characteristics. The characteristics that are chosen in constructing classifications will vary depending on the nature of the ceramics and the questions that the researcher is seeking to answer. For example, a scholar interested in ceramic use and the distribution of activities at a site might attempt to classify vessels into functional categories such as cooking, serving, or storage vessels. A scholar interested in documenting long distance trade might develop a classification based on the specific raw materials used in ceramic production, as well as regional stylistic variations in decoration or vessel shape. And a scholar interested in constructing or documenting chronological sequences would base a classification on those traits or attributes that appear to have changed over time. The classifications that archaeologists produce and use in analyses are contemporary creations; we cannot know how the ancient people we study grouped their ceramic vessels. However, by basing our classifications on patterned and verifiable variations in archaeological materials, we can encode categories that we believe were in some way significant to the past makers and users of ceramic vessels.

There is a potentially infinite number of variables, or measurable traits, that can be used in the development of a ceramic classification, and there are many different ways that classifications can be derived—from sorting ceramics into piles of similar sherds to detailed metric, chemical, and statistical analyses. Most classifications used by archaeologists have been developed inductively, through trial and error and direct observations and measurement of physical similarities in vessels from a particular site or region. Variables commonly used in the creation of ceramic classifications include color, decoration, and evidence for ceramic manufacturing techniques, as well as characteristics of vessel size and shape.

As the first scholar to study South Asian ceramics of the late historic period, my initial priority was to develop a ceramic classification. My ultimate research aim was to use ceramic data to examine patterns of ceramic use and their relation to social identity across this large, complex, and culturally diverse historic Indian city. That is, I was interested in seeing if different segments of Vijayanagara's population could be identified on the basis of differences in the kinds of ceramic vessels they used. Such differences, I reasoned, could be expected in a hierarchical, caste-based society such as Vijayanagara, where distinct social groups were characterized by status differences as well as by their dietary practices. Because most ceramics at Vijayanagara were used in food preparation or consumption, I hypothesized that the dietary differences known to distinguish caste groups should be evident in the ceramics used in those activities. Studying the distribution of ceramic forms across the city should make it possible to learn about the distribution of the diverse social groups that comprised the city. The analysis of ceramic distributions could also reveal something about the organization of ceramic production and distribution at the capital. As a caste-based society, Vijayanagara was characterized by a well-developed system of craft specialization. Ceramics were produced by members of the potter's caste (*Kumbhar*) in workshops. But how were these workshops organized? Were they large, centralized workshops controlled by the imperial government, or were they small neighborhood workshops of local producers serving local communities within Vijayanagara? In the absence of the workshops themselves, the ceramic forms and technology might provide some answers to these questions.

In order to examine these kinds of questions, I needed to develop a ceramic classification that would be sensitive to relatively fine degrees of variation in the Vijayanagara ceramics. It would not, for example, be sufficient to merely distinguish between cooking and serving vessels or between bowls and jars. Instead, a classification was needed that would be sensitive to small-scale variations among vessels used for similar activities by different social groups. Because most of the Vijayanagara vessels were black or dark brown in color and undecorated, those variables could not provide a basis for sorting the vessels into meaningful categories. Instead, I chose to divide the vessels based on details of vessel shape, size, and rim form. To develop this kind of detailed classification I took a quantitative approach, recording information on more than seventeen thousand individual rim fragments.[3]

The ceramics that I studied came from two sources: (1) excavated materials from ten elite residential compounds excavated by the Government of Karnataka (the Indian state where Vijayanagara is located) Department of Archaeology and Museums, and (2) surface artifacts from two areas—the city's main Islamic Quarter and the East Valley, an area including both elite and nonelite residential areas and a market. By using ceramics from several locations I hoped to develop a classification that would encompass the full range of variation in the Vijayanagara ceramics.

Because there were relatively few complete vessels preserved at Vijayanagara, most of my analyses focused on identifiable vessel fragments, or *diagnostic* sherds—rims, bases, handles, or decorated body sherds. The vast majority of these were rims, and I recorded a broad range of *quantitative* and *qualitative* information on each rim sherd (see Figure 5-2). The quantitative, or metric, information I recorded included measurements of vessel diameters at rim, neck, and the widest point of the vessel; thicknesses and heights at several defined points; and measurement of angles or vessel orientation. I also estimated the percentage of inclusions visible in the vessel's cross section—inclusions are any materials larger in size than clay particles that may occur naturally in clays or may be added to clay by potters to make them easier to work and to give the fired vessel desired characteristics (deliberately added inclusions are known as *temper*). Common inclusions in ceramic pastes include sand, ash, ground-up potsherds (grog), shell, and organic materials such as straw or chaff. The qualitative, or categorical, information that I recorded included information on the color of the surface and interior body of the vessel; surface treatment (i.e., whether the vessel surface was painted, smoothed, highly polished, etc.); decoration and design motifs; and some general information on vessel and rim shape (i.e., whether the vessel was a bowl or jar, whether the outer edge of a jar rim was straight or rounded or had a bulge or flange). For each sherd I also recorded information on where in the site it came from—its archaeological context.

This approach to ceramic recording, though labor intensive, is comparatively low-tech. All information was recorded in the field using relatively simple equipment: a chart of concentric circles ranging from two to forty centimeters in diameter to measure diameters, a vernier calipers to record thicknesses and heights, a modified protractor to record angles, and a geological chart and ten-power magnifying hand lens for estimating types and densities of inclusions. Values were recorded on large data recording sheets and were later transferred to a computer data base. (This work was done before the common availability of small, portable, battery-powered computers—today one could simply record all of the information directly onto a computer.) Because this was the first project to document historic South Indian ceramics, I also devoted quite a lot of time to drawing rim *profiles*, or sections, so that they would be available for use by future scholars working in the region. For the purposes of this study I did not conduct any chemical or mineralogical analyses, which would have required more sophisticated technology than was available in rural India. (Archaeological materials from India legally belong to the Indian national or state governments. Foreign archaeologists are obliged to study materials in the confines of the country and cannot take them back to their home country for analysis.)

STRAIGHT RIM RESTRICTED VESSELS

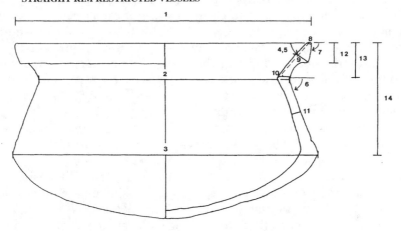

FLANGE RIM RESTRICTED VESSELS

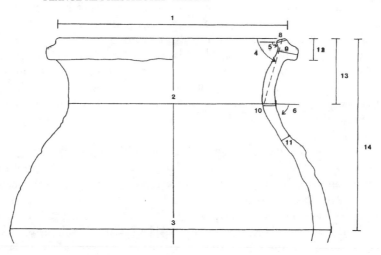

1. Rim Diameter
2. Neck Diameter
3. Maximum Diameter
4. Rim Angle
5. Lip Angle
6. Body Angle
7. Rim Top Angle (Straight Rim Only)

8. Lip Thickness
9. Rim Thickness
10. Neck Thickness
11. Body Thickness
12. Rim Height
13. Neck Height
14. Maximum Body Height

FIGURE 5-2   QUANTITATIVE VARIABLES RECORDED ON VIJAYANAGARA VESSELS

The next step in the construction of the classification was to use the recorded information to group the vessels into classes or categories. The recording techniques used and the measurements taken on individual sherds were at the level of the individual variable or feature—for example, rim diameter, neck thickness, or rim height. However, the goal of the classification was to go beyond the variable level to look at broader vessel characteristics such as vessel shape or size. Such *dimensions of variation* cannot necessarily be measured by a single variable; shape, for example, is a product of complex geometric relations between diameters, heights, and angles. Assessing these dimensions is made even more complex by the partial nature of the sample; given the small number of complete vessels, I had to reconstruct vessel shape and size from rim fragments alone. In attempting to define significant dimensions of ceramic variation I took a statistical approach, focusing on the range and distribution of individual variables and their interrelations.

Statistics is a set of methods for dealing with data in one of two ways: *Descriptive statistics* allows us to summarize our data in standardized form (concepts such as mean, standard deviation, and median are very important here); *inferential statistics* allows us to use principles of probability to infer something about entire populations from subsets or samples of those populations.[4] Archaeologists almost always work with samples. The ceramics I examined were only a small sample of all of the Vijayanagara ceramics, yet I wanted to be able to say something about Vijayanagara ceramics in general. Inferential statistics, based on probability theory, allows us to do this in much the same way that political pollsters attempt to infer general public opinion from interviewing a sample of voters.

The precise statistical methods used in the analysis of Vijayanagara ceramics do not concern us here. Essentially, I focused on the distributions of individual variables and groups of related variables to subdivide the vessels into overall vessel form categories. I defined nine general shape classes (referred to as *vessel use classes*; see Figure 5-3). These included three categories of unrestricted (i.e., neckless) vessels or bowls: (1) small saucers (used as lamps); (2) round-bottomed shallow bowls; and (3) other bowls (a miscellaneous category); and six categories of restricted (i.e., with neck constrictions) vessels or jars: (1) small serving vessels (perhaps drinking cups, ritual vessels, or individual serving vessels); (2) medium broad-necked food preparation vessels; (3) large broad-necked food preparation vessels; (4) small vertical-necked serving or transport vessels; (5) medium vertical-necked serving, transport, or storage vessels; and (6) large vertical-necked transport or storage vessels. Other less common ceramic forms included incense burners, gaming pieces, water pipes, ceramic braziers, and architectural fittings such as roof tiles and well linings.

I used three separate lines of reasoning to interpret vessel use or function: (1) analogies with modern vessels still produced in the area; (2) traces

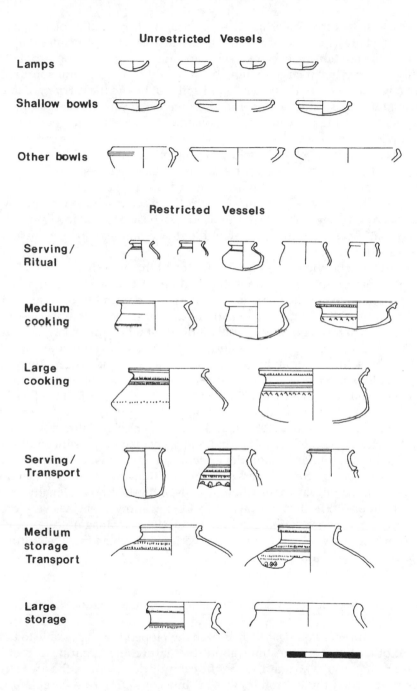

FIGURE 5-3   VIJAYANAGARA VESSEL USE CLASSES

of vessel use (*use wear*) such as burning around the base of a cooking pot or abrasion where a lid was used; and (3) general geometric principles that play a role in the relations between vessel shape and function.[5] For example, it is highly unlikely that a large shallow bowl would be used to transport water from a well, as most of the water would spill out before the carrier got home; nor would we use such a vessel to store water because the large opening would lead to a high rate of evaporation and the water would get dirty very quickly. Similarly, we would not expect people to dine out of a tall narrow-necked jar because they could neither reach nor see their meal; and a cooking pot should have an opening wide enough so that we can stir and serve the food within it. This does not mean that humans always use the most efficiently shaped pot for a particular task; at times we reach for whatever vessel is nearest, whether it is the best for our purpose or not. However, we do expect that there are some general and logical relations between vessel use and vessel form.

I further subdivided vessels within each of the nine shape categories on the basis of more subtle variations that could reflect the activities of different ceramic producers or the demands of different communities of ceramic consumers. Ultimately, I defined a total of more than seventy ceramic classes on the basis of rim form, base form, orientation, or other distinguishing features.

This approach to ceramic classification is far more cumbersome than the traditional technique of laying sherds out on a table and sorting them into piles that look more or less alike. It does, however, provide several benefits. First, it is explicit. Rather than relying on an intuitive sense of which pots look most alike (a difficult challenge in a ceramic inventory where different forms grade continuously into one another), I examined clearly defined traits measured in clearly defined ways. Second, the Vijayanagara classification is potentially replicable. It is not dependent on my personal expertise or experiences; rather, other scholars could record the same information and analyze it in the same way (or in different ways, if they so chose). Finally, unlike most traditional classifications, which tend to group vessels into very broad categories and ignore variation within them, the Vijayanagara ceramic classification explicitly examines fine-scale variations, which may be culturally or behaviorally meaningful.

CERAMIC USE AND ACTIVITY DISTRIBUTION IN THE NOBLEMEN'S QUARTER

When the ceramic classification had been developed it was possible to begin asking other kinds of questions about the nature and organization of the imperial city of Vijayanagara, using the ceramic data. One of the areas from which I recorded these ceramics was an area consisting of several large architectural compounds that had been excavated by the Government of Karnataka Department of Archaeology and Museums, who graciously allowed me to study their ceramics. They designated this area "The Noblemen's Quarter" (NMQ) because the major structures that comprised it were interpreted as elite residences (see Figure 5-4). Twelve walled architectural compounds had been excavated between 1982 and 1986, when I was conducting my initial research at the site. Each compound consisted of a large central structure with between two and four stepped tiers and several chambers, surrounded by subsidiary structures on carved stone platforms or basements, poorly constructed rubble wall structures, and, in some compounds, by wells and toilet facilities.

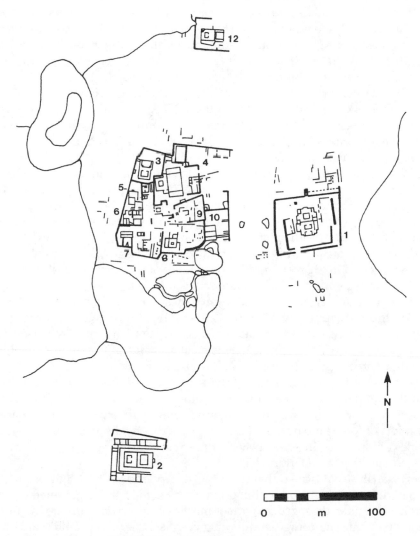

FIGURE 5-4   THE NOBLEMEN'S QUARTER

The NMQ compounds provided me with an unusual opportunity to examine the organization of space in a well-defined elite residential area of the site. Fortunately for archaeology (though not for the original occupants of the compound), the NMQ structures had burned down, presumably in the sacking that followed the city's abandonment after a major military defeat in A.D. 1565. The inhabitants of Vijayanagara fled precipitously on learning of the defeat and did not bother to straighten out their houses or pack and move their utilitarian ceramics. It is also highly unlikely that the people who looted these compounds paid much attention to low-value items such as earthenware pots. Therefore, many of the shattered ceramic vessels found beneath layers of burnt debris in the NMQ areas could be assumed to be located in the area where they were last used. By examining the distribution of functional or vessel use classes from floor areas in the burned structures of the NMQ, I could potentially contribute to the understandings of the activities that occurred within these complex architectural compounds. I could also compare overall distributions in each of the compounds to examine differences in the activities that occurred within them. And finally, I could compare NMQ ceramics to ceramics collected from other areas of the site in order to examine variations between elite and nonelite areas, as well as other sources of variation in ceramic use, such as religious or caste identification.

I recorded information on approximately eight thousand diagnostic sherds from eighty-seven different excavations or provenience units in the NMQ. Ceramics are common throughout the NMQ area. In general, low ceramic densities occur within the central structures and higher densities are found in open areas and in subsidiary structures within compounds. Although the residents of these compounds no doubt also used metal vessels (very few of which are found in excavations), the abundance of ceramics suggests that they were the most common kind of container used by Vijayanagara's inhabitants.

I used a number of analytical approaches to examine ceramic distributions in the NMQ provenience units. These ranged from simply plotting the relative frequencies of individual vessel classes to using more sophisticated computer-assisted techniques, such as cluster analysis. The analyses helped to classify areas using distinct ceramic signatures, which reflected the predominant activities in which vessels were used or deposited. Areas identified include dump areas (with a wide range of vessel use classes, roughly in proportion to their overall frequencies in the ceramic inventory), kitchen areas (with lots of food preparation and storage vessels, and few serving vessels), shrines (with lamps, incense burners, and small offering vessels), and serving and storage areas (see Figure 5-5).

The analyses indicated that the NMQ compounds varied significantly in the activities that occurred within them. Some compounds contained ceramics that were indeed congruent with domestic compounds, with the full range of food preparation, storage, and serving vessels. Other compounds contained a much more restricted range of ceramic forms, focused especially on serving

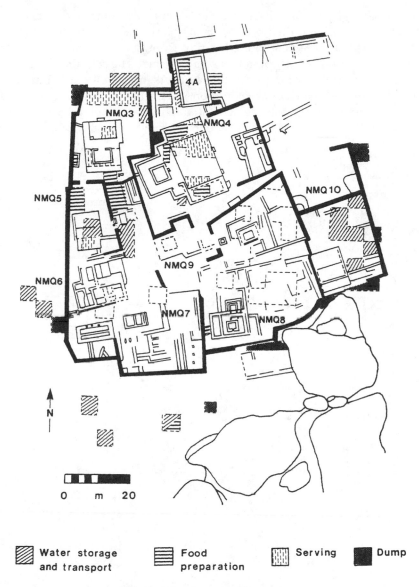

FIGURE 5-5   ACTIVITY DISTRIBUTION
IN NOBLEMEN'S QUARTER COMPOUNDS NMQ3—NMQ10

and water-storage vessels. The latter may have served largely as public or administrative areas and may not have been residential areas at all. The small rubble wall structures that surrounded the walled compounds appear to have been residences of lower status people, who may have served the inhabitants of the palace compounds. These structures typically contained many food preparation vessels, and their occupants may have been involved in preparing meals for their elite neighbors. Judging from their ceramic contents, at least two of the compounds contained small shrines. The ceramics from these areas included many oil lamps, incense burners, and well-made miniature jars (see Figure 5-6). Shrines are common in Hindu households, with each family maintaining a small shrine dedicated to the family god. In compound NMQ12 the shrine was located in the central room of the structure.

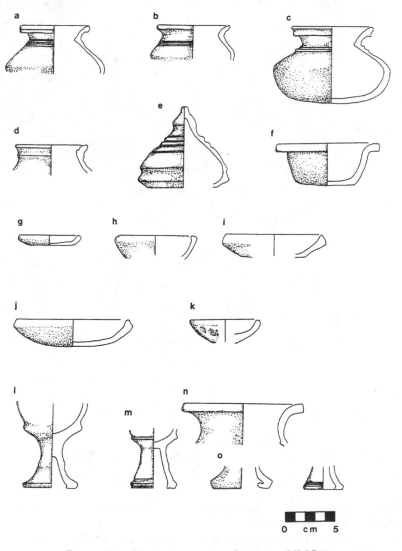

FIGURE 5-6   VESSELS FROM THE SHRINE IN NMQ12

SPATIAL AND SOCIAL VARIATION IN CERAMIC USE

In the next stage of my research I wanted to broaden my scope—to use ceramics to consider the social and spatial organization of Vijayanagara at a larger scale. Were there differences in how ceramics were used by different castes or religious groups? Could high- and low-status areas be distinguished on the basis of the ceramics their inhabitants used? Could residential areas be distinguished from marketplaces, workshops, or temple zones? Did inhabitants of different neighborhoods at Vijayanagara acquire their ceramic vessels from different ceramic-producing workshops, and could these be identified?

In order to look at these broader issues concerning Vijayanagara's organization, I compared the NMQ ceramics to collections from two other areas of the site. These were the city's main Islamic Quarter, occupied by Muslim mercenaries who served in the Vijayanagara army, and an area known as the East Valley, which contained high- and low-status occupation areas.[6] The inner wall of the city's core bisects the East Valley, and an inscription near the gate in the wall refers to it as the "Monday Gate," alluding to the occurrence of a weekly market. These three areas housed very different segments of Vijayanagara's population: the Hindu elites of the Noblemen's Quarter, the soldiers and other Muslim inhabitants of the Islamic Quarter, and the inhabitants of the commercial zone of the East Valley, in addition to its diverse Hindu, Jain, elite, and nonelite residential zones.

The ceramics that I examined from the East Valley and Islamic Quarter were not recovered in excavations but came from the surface of the site. Surface collection units were systematically placed across each of the areas, using a combination of judgment and random sampling techniques. In the Islamic Quarter, where ceramic densities were relatively low, I collected ceramics from seven ten-meter square units. Some ceramics from the Islamic Quarter came from Government of Karnataka excavations at the quarter's main mosque and from a nearby well. The total samples collected from the Islamic Quarter were 1,661 sherds, of which 584 were measurable diagnostics. In the East Valley, where it was literally impossible to walk without stepping on fragments of pottery, collection units were much smaller—circular units four meters in diameter. A total of 294 units were collected from across the Valley. Unit location was determined through random sampling to assure even and representative coverage of the valley. Because of the large number of ceramics that the collection produced, analysis focused on roughly half of the units; approximately 7,000 rim sherds and more than 33,600 body sherds were documented from 143 collection units.

Analysis of overall patterns of ceramic distributions of the three areas focused on multiple levels of ceramic variation. These included vessel ware (defined by color and surface treatment), the nine functional or vessel use classes described previously, and the finer variants within each of those functional classes. Significant differences in ceramic use were identified at all levels of ceramic variation. Differences were especially pronounced between the city's Islamic Quarter and the two non-Muslim areas of the site.[7] Inhabitants of the Islamic Quarter used more red ware vessels than were used in either the Noblemen's Quarter or the East Valley. It is uncertain whether the preference for red wares is a function of different cultural conceptions concerning appropriate colors of ceramic vessels or of differences in the production practices of workshops serving these different areas of the city.

Variation also existed between the Islamic Quarter and the other areas in frequencies of different functional classes of vessels. In particular, the inhabitants of the Islamic Quarter used significantly more bowls than did people in predominantly Hindu neighborhoods. The three bowl forms (lamps, shallow bowls, and other bowls) comprised nearly 23 percent of the ceramics from the Islamic Quarter, and only 10.9 percent of vessels from the East Valley and 12.3 percent of vessels from the Noblemen's Quarter. Thus, bowls were roughly twice as common in the Islamic Quarter as in other areas—a statistically significant difference. Cultural differences in food consumption practices appear to account for these differences. Elaborate rules exist in Hinduism concerning food consumption. In particular, cooked foods are believed to be particularly potent vehicles for absorbing and conveying ritual impurities, and earthenware ceramics are believed to be especially vulnerable to absorbing impure substances. Thus high-caste and low-caste Hindus cannot eat foods from the same dishes, and Brahmins, the highest ritual caste, are required to discard earthenware dining vessels after a single use. As a consequence of these beliefs, Hindus typically do not eat from ceramic vessels; instead, food is served on banana leaves or on metal plates, which are believed to be less vulnerable to ritual impurities and more easily cleansed.

Other differences were also observed in the frequency of vessel use classes among the three areas. The Noblemen's Quarter contained higher than expected frequencies of large food preparation vessels and water-storage and transport vessels than the other areas, suggesting a greater emphasis on the preparation of large quantities of food and the serving and storage of higher quantities of liquid than occurred in the East Valley. This pattern makes sense, given that the NMQ was a high-status area, in which public gatherings and private receptions would have been important. The ceramics of the East Valley appeared to be more typical domestic assemblages, with high frequencies of small and medium cooking, storage, and serving vessels. The area near the Monday Gate in the East Valley yielded a great diversity of ceramic forms, supporting the interpretation that a market in which ceramics were sold may have existed there.

The frequencies of the finer formal variants defined for the Vijayanagara ceramics also differed among these three areas. These differences were more in frequency than in kind; that is, certain variants were more common in one area than in another, but all variants were found across the site. The significance of this kind of variation is difficult to interpret at present. It may be the result of social or temporal variation in ceramic use and distribution, or it may be the result of relatively open distribution networks, in which individual households could obtain vessels from any of a large number of ceramic workshops.

The analysis of the spatial distribution of Vijayanagara ceramics provided evidence for pronounced variations in ceramic use and distribution within the Noblemen's Quarter and among the three quite distinct areas of the site. The study of these materials adds considerably to our knowledge of the imperial capital of Vijayanagara, both to refine interpretations based on architectural remains and to provide information on areas such as the East Valley, where there are few monumental structures and elite constructions.

The Organization of Ceramic Production at Vijayanagara

No ceramic manufacturing workshops have yet been identified at Vijayanagara, either in the city core or in the suburban outskirts of the imperial capital. There is thus no direct evidence concerning the organization of ceramic production in the city. However, the sherds themselves can provide some clues to the scale and technology of production. Ceramics can be produced using a variety of hand-building or wheel-throwing techniques. Each manufacturing technique leaves distinct traces on vessels—for example, the interior striations of wheel throwing, or the identifiable joints that appear when individual rolls of prepared clay are rolled and linked together to form handmade coiled jars or bowls. The Vijayanagara ceramics were produced using a combination of the wheel-throwing and the paddle-and-anvil technique. In the paddle-and-anvil technique vessels are thinned and shaped by banging a wooden paddle against a stone anvil held on the interior of a vessel. This allows potters to produce very thin-walled vessels with characteristic surfaces, and also permits the construction of round-bottomed vessels, preferred by Vijayanagara's consumers. Some Vijayanagara vessel forms were produced entirely by hand, through coiling or a technique known as slab building, in which large flat slabs of clay were joined together to form large storage and other irregularly-shaped vessels, such as three-sided ovens or braziers.

As noted earlier, the ceramics at Vijayanagara exhibit a wide range of variability. Vessels conform to some broadly accepted ideas concerning what cooking, storage, or other functional categories of pots should look like, but within each of these categories there is a high degree of variation in shape and rim form. In other words, the Vijayanagara vessels were not highly standardized.[8] Archaeologists expect that ceramics produced in large-scale or centralized workshops should be standardized as a result of increased regularity and efficiency of production in workshops that produced many vessels over short time periods. Because Vijayanagara had a population of more than two hundred thousand inhabitants there was clearly a need for a very large number of ceramic cooking, storage, and serving vessels. The lack of standardization in ceramic forms suggests that these vessels were produced in many small workshops rather than in a small number of large workshops. These workshops may have distributed their products to distinct neighborhoods of Vijayanagara, accounting at least in part for some of the variation in ceramic distributions among different areas of the site.

CHRONOLOGY

One of the most important uses of ceramic analysis in archaeology is in the construction of cultural chronologies. Like other items of material culture, the ceramic vessels used by a community tend to change over time. These changes can result from a variety of causes: stylistic innovations by creative artisans, the emergence of new technologies, imitations of exotic or status items, or fashion trends. Temporal changes in ceramic forms or decoration allow archaeologists to place ceramics in a chronological sequence. Ceramics from well-defined stratigraphic excavations can be studied to develop temporal frameworks. Archaeologists can also use materials' nonstratified contexts to develop ceramic chronologies using a technique known as seriation. Seriation is a relative dating technique that is based on the assumption that new styles appear slowly, become increasingly popular, and then gradually decline in popularity as new fashions appear and replace them. By comparing relative frequencies of different ceramic wares from individual sites or excavation units, using this basic assumption about material culture change, it is often possible to place individual assemblages in a relative chronological order.

As noted previously, it is possible that chronological differences may play a role in differences in ceramic frequencies across Vijayanagara. One of the goals of my research at the site was to understand patterns of chronological change in Vijayanagara ceramics. So far, however, I have not been successful at this. The city of Vijayanagara was occupied for slightly more than two hundred years, a relatively short time from the perspective of archaeological analysis. Although the ceramics exhibit a tremendous amount of variability, at present it is not possible to attribute any of that variation to change over time. Attempts at seriation and the analysis of ceramics from dated structures and stratigraphic excavations have not provided evidence for any clear patterns of change over time. It may well be that the Vijayanagara ceramics did not change much over the two hundred years that the site was occupied, and indeed, some vessel forms made by Vijayanagara potters continue to be manufactured by local potters in the area today. Perhaps as more archaeologists begin to study the ceramics of earlier and later periods in South India we will be able to identify general patterns of temporal change in ceramic forms and styles.

DISCUSSION

The city of Vijayanagara is a large and complex archaeological site, yielding a wide range of archaeological remains. The ceramics of Vijayanagara provide archaeologists with a unique perspective on this ancient city. The ceramics were produced by specialists and distributed in markets to all of the inhabitants of Vijayanagara. Unlike other kinds of archaeological remains at the site, such as architecture or metal goods, ceramics were used by both high- and low-status people from a range of religious and economic groups. A careful study of ceramics from across the site can provide information on aspects of Vijayanagara's social, economic, and sacred life that could not be learned from either written records or elite archaeological remains.

This chapter has examined a study of archaeological ceramics at a single site to illustrate the contributions that ceramic analysis can make to the study of the human past. The questions I asked and the approaches I took in analyzing Vijayanagara ceramics were oriented toward my specific research interests and the kinds of data available to me. The issues addressed in this chapter in no way encompass the full range of questions about the past that archaeologists can address through the study of ceramics. The broad range of uses to which ceramics are put and their excellent preservation in archaeological contexts means that archaeological ceramics are often the most numerous class of artifacts found in archaeological sites (at least from those time periods and societies that produced ceramics). Further, the technology of ceramic production and decoration allows for a great deal of variability in the finished products. Vessel shape, size, color, raw material composition, and a wide range of other variables can vary widely as a result of the conscious decisions made by individual potters as they formed and fired their vessels. These decisions are culturally informed; that is, potters (and consumers of pottery) within any society tend to share basic cultural values about what pots should look like, how they should be made, and how they should be decorated. Within the parameters defined by these broadly shared values, ceramics will vary as a result of individual and group preferences, skill, technologies used in their manufacture, and available raw materials.

The study of archaeological ceramics thus provides an important way to look at cultural norms (the shared values of communities) as well as internal variation within or between societies on the basis of deviations from those norms. Interaction between different societies can also be approached through ceramic analysis, through documenting the movement of ceramics over space and time. Studies of ceramic exchange can be approached through documenting the presence of exotic styles of ceramics in sites (such as the presence of Egyptian-style ceramics in sites on Cyprus) or through chemical and microscopic studies of ceramic raw materials, many of which are derived from a small number of source areas. Chemical studies can also allow the analysis of the contents of ceramic vessels; archaeologists have been able to identify residues of milk, meat, oils, beer, and wine in ceramics from a range of archaeological contexts. The extremely wide range of questions that can be asked about the human past through the study of archaeological ceramics makes their careful study an essential part of any archaeological analysis.

NOTES

1. John M. Fritz, George A. Michell, and M. S. Nagaraja Rao, *Where Kings and Gods Meet: The Royal Center of Vijayanagara* (Tucson: University of Arizona Press, 1984).
2. Robert Whallon and James A. Brown, eds., *Essays on Archaeological Typology* (Evanston, IL: Center for American Archaeology Press, 1982).
3. Carla M. Sinopoli, *Pots and Palaces: The Earthenware Ceramics of the Noblemen's Quarter of Vijayanagara* (New Delhi: Manohar Press, 1993).
4. David H. Thomas, *Refiguring Anthropology: First Principles of Probability and Statistics* (Prospect Heights, IL: Waveland Press, 1986).
5. James M. Skibo, *Pottery Function: A Use-Alteration Perspective* (New York: Plenum Press, 1992).
6. Carla M. Sinopoli, *Material Patterning and Social Organization: A Study of Ceramics from Vijayanagara South India* (Ann Arbor: University Microfilms, 1986).
7. Carla M. Sinopoli, "The Archaeological Ceramics of the Islamic Quarter of Vijayanagara," in D. V. Devaraj and C. S. Patil, eds., *Vijayanagara Progress of Research* (Mysore: Department of Archaeology and Museums, in press).
8. Carla M. Sinopoli, "The Organization of Craft Production at Vijayanagara, India," *American Anthropologist* 90 (1988): 580–597.

SUGGESTED READINGS

Rice, Prudence M. *Pottery Analysis: A Sourcebook.* Chicago: University of Chicago Press, 1987. A comprehensive overview of ceramic analysis in archaeology.

Rye, Owen. *Pottery Technology: Principles and Reconstruction.* Washington, D.C.: Taraxacum Press, 1981. An important source on ceramic production and firing techniques and how they can be identified through archaeological analysis.

Saraswati, Baidyanath. *Pottery Making Cultures and Indian Civilization.* New Delhi: Abhinav Publications, 1970. A useful overview of the production and use of ceramics in South Asia.

Sinopoli, Carla M. *Approaches to Archaeological Ceramics.* New York: Plenum Press, 1989. A general introduction to ceramic analysis, illustrated with case studies.

The Analysis
of Archaeological Plant Remains

Naomi F. Miller

An otherwise sophisticated prehistorian once remarked to me, "I can see why you'd collect plant remains if your interest is in the origins of agriculture, but once you're dealing with literate, urban civilizations, why bother?" Why indeed? Agriculture was the economic base of the early civilizations. The specialization of labor and consequent social differentiation we associate with "civilization" would not have been possible without surplus-generating production. Even for literate societies, textual evidence provides only a narrow window into agriculture and the effects of land clearance, fuel gathering, irrigation, and other land-use practices. Because plants play such an important role in food, fuel, and items of trade, they reflect many dimensions of society—including cuisine, the organization of labor, and social differentiation—in all times and places. It is for these reasons that I am interested in plant remains.

Paleoethnobotany concerns itself with the relationship between people and plants in the archaeological record—including aspects of ecology, economy, society, and ideology.[1] To understand that relationship, it is necessary sometimes to go beyond studying plant remains from archaeological sites (*archaeobotany*). We may also need to consider the evidence of history, ethnohistory, folklore, and botany.

Types of Plant Remains

The three most important categories of plant remains from archaeological contexts are macroremains (e.g., seeds and charcoal), pollen, and phytoliths (microscopic silica bodies found in some plant tissue). Other less common sources of information are plant impressions in clay, artistic representations of plants, lipid analysis (which identifies fat sources, animal or vegetable), and artifacts made from plants.

To recover plant remains, we have to separate them from the sediment matrix of the archaeological site. Flotation and screening for macroremains mechanically separate the plant materials from the dirt, stones, and artifacts. No special laboratory facilities are required. For pollen analysis, we mechanically remove and chemically dissolve everything that is not pollen—the organic materials, silicates, and carbonates that comprise the sediment matrix. Similarly, phytolith analysis uses mechanical and chemical means to concentrate the items of interest. Since hydrofluoric acid dissolves sand (i.e., silicates), phytoliths (which are made of silica) in a sediment sample analyzed for pollen will be destroyed, so separate analyses are required. In contrast to macroremain analysis, pollen and phytolith analyses require special laboratory facilities.[2]

MACROREMAINS

Macroremains are relatively large items that generally comprise the bulk of plant remains recovered from archaeological sites. They include seeds and seed-like plant structures, fruits, wood, leaves, tubers, and so on. But remember that most of the plant parts brought to a site by people will not remain on the site. After all, plant matter used as fuel is burned, people eat the food plants, animals eat the fodder. Artifacts like wooden tools, baskets, and mats represent a small and easily lost portion of the total plant material people use over the years and are usually encountered less frequently than ancient trash.

The preservation environment determines which plant parts left after people abandon a site will actually persist in the soil. For organic materials to be preserved, biological, chemical, and mechanical degradation must stop. In temperate, open-air conditions like those prevalent on the east coast of North America, we expect to find charred remains only.[3] Plant remains may also be preserved in dry caves, deserts, pyramids, or in waterlogged deposits.[4]

Typically, macroremains are recovered manually, as seen during excavation and screening, or they are recovered through flotation. Only fairly large botanical items will be recovered through screening, as archaeologists commonly use quarter-inch or centimeter mesh in the field. Chunks of wood charcoal and large seeds like olive pits or nuts are readily removed. However, individual seeds and other charred bits are usually fairly meaningless without their archaeological context. Therefore, the unit of paleoethnobotanical analysis is ordinarily not the individual seed or piece of charcoal, but rather a sampling of the material available within a particular volume of sediment from a clearly defined location on the site. As long as the remains do not explode upon contact with water, flotation is the most efficient way to concentrate small seeds and plant parts scattered in the soil matrix.[5]

As a rule, one ought to be able to develop a flotation system and sampling design for any project and budget, no matter how small. The simplest flotation systems consist basically of a bucket, a sieve, and some water. Dirt may be poured into the bucket and stirred, and floating material is then poured off onto a cloth or sieve. Alternatively, the soil sample may be poured into a large sieve that is swirled in a barrel of water; floating material is scooped up with a small strainer and emptied onto a cloth to dry. More elaborate flotation systems take advantage of running water piped into a modified barrel. The soil sample is poured into the screen-lined barrel and sinks; an upward flow of water helps lift the plant remains, which are caught in a cloth or screen after they float over the lip of the barrel.

After the flotation sample has dried, analysis begins. The assemblage of macroremains is identified and quantified. Archaeobotanists use morphological criteria (size, shape, and surface features of seeds, and ring patterns of wood). Some seeds and plant parts are only identifiable at the very gross level of plant family (e.g., grass), and others may be identified even to variety (e.g., six-row barley). Unfortunately, many specific and varietal distinctions are based on flower morphology, and flowers are almost never preserved. Therefore, one must frequently be satisfied with identifications just to the genus level. Many botanists and archaeobotanists are working on refining the taxonomy of early domesticates (e.g., goosefoot in North America, wheat in the Old World, and plant tissues).[6]

How one chooses to measure and assess the different types and quantities of plant remains reflects the assumptions and inferences one makes about deposition, preservation, and recovery processes. For example, American Indians ate both hickory and acorns, but hard, dense hickory shell is much more readily preserved than acorn shell. Burned remains of hickory are better able to survive flotation, as well. Because a simple comparison of nutshell weight would severely underestimate the quantity of acorn, experimentally derived estimates of nutmeat based on the weight of modern burnt nutshell permit more accurate estimates of the importance of hickory and acorn in the ancient diet.[7] Cultural interpretations are based not only on the relative quantities of plant remains, but also on their spatial distribution and archaeological contexts. For example, four hundred wheat grains from a storage context (i.e., food remains) cannot be interpreted the same way as four hundred wheat grains distributed unevenly over forty hearth or trash deposits (i.e., remnants of dung fuel or crop-processing debris).

POLLEN

Pollen is the male germ cell of seed-bearing plants. It may be dispersed by wind, insects, other animals, water, and so on. Under anaerobic, undisturbed conditions, such as those found on lake bottoms, the pollen exoskeleton persists indefinitely, which allows the palynologist to identify the plants that produced the pollen. As is true of macroremains, however, some pollen types are more distinctive than others. For example, members of the daisy family are generally not distinguishable from one another—all have spiny pollen, and the only distinction is between high spine and low spine pollen. But many members of the pine family, with two air sacs, can be distinguished from other conifers.[8]

The identification of pollen types allows one to reconstruct ancient vegetation and, by inference, climate. Changes in the relative amounts of different pollen types provide evidence of vegetation and climate history in a region. However, plants contribute widely differing quantities of pollen to the pollen record. Palynologists therefore study the modern "pollen rain" in order to see which plants may be over- or underrepresented. Most pollen analyses are done on lake and bog sediments and focus on reconstructing local and regional vegetation patterns.

Archaeological pollen cores, or profiles, are usually not directly comparable to lake cores; the air currents and other "natural" means of pollen transport and deposition associated with lakes are not relevant to settlements, where people have erected roofed structures or brought in wild or cultivated crops. In temperate conditions, like those prevailing in eastern North America, mechanical abrasion, exposure to oxygen in disturbed soils, and earthworms (which eat high-protein pollen) reduce pollen preservability, so most archaeological sediments are unsuited to pollen preservation.

Despite these drawbacks, the special conditions provided by archaeological context have some advantages for palynological studies. For example, James Hill and Richard Hevly were able to recognize three types of rooms in a prehistoric pueblo in Arizona. Habitation areas where food was prepared and eaten had low but consistent quantities of the pollen of maize and other crops; food storage areas had high densities of maize and squash pollen; and ceremonial areas had pollen from plants that, based on the ethnohistoric record, would have been ritually important.[9]

PHYTOLITHS

Phytoliths are formed when plants absorb soluble silica from the water they take in through their roots. A silica body forms, which may take on the shape of the cell in which it is deposited. Because the silica is differentially deposited in plant cells, frequently in distinctive shapes, different plant types are recognizable. In addition, phytoliths are virtually indestructible under many conditions, the exception being soils where the pH is above 8.5. Stem tissue of some plants, especially grasses, is particularly rich in phytoliths. This is of great interest to archaeologists because the grasses include the economically important cereals that are difficult to identify by pollen analysis alone. As a relatively new technique applied to archaeological problems, advances in the principles of phytolith interpretation are made with each new analysis. Taxonomic studies are particularly important because phytolith analysis is such a new field.[10]

SAMPLING SEDIMENTS FOR PLANT REMAINS

From the previous discussion it should be clear that the three types of archaeobotanical analysis discussed are complementary, not mutually exclusive. Soils that preserve macroremains may be poor in pollen or phytoliths. Similarly, soils rich in pollen or phytoliths may lack macroremains. For example, Deborah Pearsall found early evidence for maize cultivation in Ecuador through phytolith analysis, despite the poor preservation of charcoal and other organic remains in tropical soils.[11] In addition, different plant structures and plant products may document the variety of ways people use plants—for example, cherry wood might come from furniture and cherry pits from food use; a room full of wheat grains may provide evidence for food storage, while a high density of wheat phytoliths from straw may show a fodder storage area.

The cultural meaning of archaeological plant remains is not self-evident. Interpretation of a particular archaeobotanical assemblage must take a variety of factors into account—how the material was deposited, preserved, recovered, and analyzed. Some of these factors can be accounted for, but not controlled, by the archaeobotanist (e.g., how and when the botanical material arrived on the site, and how it came to be preserved). Recovery procedures, including sampling design and recovery techniques (flotation, screening) should be under the control of the archaeobotanist, although in practice it is the archaeologist in the field who makes many of the recovery decisions. The archaeobotanist has most control over analysis—choosing which samples to identify, how to quantify the remains, and how to relate the plant assemblage to the people that produced it.

All sampling for plant remains aims at representativeness. Because of differences in the nature of deposition and preservation, specific sampling strategies for macroremains, pollen, and phytoliths will vary. A good sampling design will satisfy several requirements. First, it will provide an overview of deposits with or without plant remains. Second, it will yield representative samples of those plant remains. Because macroremains are frequently visible as flecks of charcoal or concentrations of seeds, archaeologists who would otherwise not sample for botanical remains will frequently take samples of opportunistically discovered caches. Although this type of "grab" sampling is better than no sampling at all, I prefer to analyze material from sites where there has been a systematic attempt at recovering all types of remains, immediately visible or not. Pollen and phytoliths, invisible to the unaided eye, must be sampled for on faith.

To find out which deposits yield plant remains, one takes soil from a variety of archaeological contexts. Many "sterile" samples so obtained will serve as control samples for the ones rich in plant remains. Achieving a representative assemblage should be an automatic result of such a sampling strategy. Depending on the archaeological (i.e., cultural) context and the preservation environment, however, some deposits are particularly likely to yield plant remains—whether macroremains, pollen, or phytoliths—and special attention should therefore be paid to them.

ISSUES ADDRESSED BY PALEOETHNOBOTANISTS

Although archaeologists have been saving plant remains from archaeological sites since the mid-nineteenth century, the systematic sampling of archaeological sediments is a relatively recent development. The research topic that inspired modern archaeobotanical studies was agricultural origins in the Near East. Beginning in the late 1940s and early 1950s, Robert Braidwood of the University of Chicago recognized the significance of plant remains, and he arranged for Hans Helbaek, a Danish botanist, to study macroremains from the early village site of Jarmo, in Iraq.[12] Around the same time, Americanists were investigating the beginnings of agriculture in the midwestern United States. Since the 1960s, archaeobotanical studies have increasingly become a standard component of archaeological projects around the world, and archaeobotanists continue to address many new topics.[13]

AGRICULTURAL ECONOMIES OF COMPLEX SOCIETIES

In both the Old World and the New, complex societies depended on agriculture for their survival and expansion. For example, evidence from plant remains has helped document the economic and political influence of the Inka in Peru. Prior to Inka expansion, there appears to have been more maize, a prized food, in the homes of local elites. The Inka promoted some social leveling at the expense of local elites, however, for even commoner households in later, imperial times had high frequencies of maize.[14]

As previously mentioned, archaeobotanical data is not always valued for the historical periods of the Near East, where textual evidence for plant use consists of lists of rations, sowing and yield rates, untranslatable plant names, and similar esoterica. Yet even here, texts refer to the activities of the temple or palace, and many archaeological sites have few or no relevant texts. Thus, trash deposits and human waste deposits may be the only way to document which crops were grown, how animals were foddered and, by inference, environmental and social constraints on production (see the following discussion).[15]

FORMATION OF THE ARCHAEOBOTANICAL RECORD AND ITS INTERPRETATION

Much current research in archaeobotany either focuses on or acknowledges how important it is to understand how plant remains arrive on a site and how they are preserved; that is, how cultural practices and natural conditions "filter" the materials that are recovered. Some studies compare modern vegetation with archaeobotanical assemblages; others use ethnographic models to interpret the remains.[16] Archaeobotanists, more than most archaeologists, recognize that the minute items they concern themselves with do not speak for themselves, and that one's analytical tools must correct for these potential distortions.[17]

To give just one example of the importance of context and preservation for accurate interpretation, we can consider a seeming inconsistency in the composition of the archaeobotanical assemblage at the third millennium B.C. city of Malyan, Iran. In the present day, where both wheat and barley can be grown, wheat tends to be preferred for food because the grain is easier to process. At ancient Malyan, however, most of the charred grain is barley; the ratio of charred barley to charred wheat is about thirteen to one. In contrast, mineralized grains from a human waste deposit had a barley to wheat ratio of about one to two. This discrepancy was explained by applying an ethnographic model of plant use, which suggests that many seeds from ancient sites in the Near East were inclusions in dung that was burned as fuel. That is, the charred grains from trash had passed through animals, and those in the human waste deposit had passed through people![18]

ENVIRONMENT, ECONOMY, AND LAND USE

No matter what the time period or geographical area, plant remains can provide important primary data about the natural environment and land use practices. My own research focuses on long-term human impact on the environment. In central Turkey, at the site of Gordion (and presumed home of King Midas at around 700 B.C.), shifts in the proportions of wood charcoal between about 2000 B.C. and A.D. 1000 suggested that nearby juniper woodland was reduced, oak became more prominent in the landscape, and overall dominant forest woods (juniper, oak, and pine) were replaced with secondary types. Coincident with the decline in woodland, seed evidence suggested pasture quality lessened as well; high-quality fodder legumes declined in the assemblage, and there was a small increase in spiny and alkaloid-rich plants avoided by animals.

Like all archaeologists, archaeobotanists study the variation in time and space in many aspects of ancient life. For example, in tracing the influence of the environment on foddering practices and crop choice, I have examined several fourth and third millennium B.C. sites along the Euphrates river in southeastern Turkey and northwestern Syria. Rainfall increases as you go north, and the natural vegetation changes from steppe to open oak woodland. Shifts in the proportions of charred seeds of wild and cultivated plants that originated in dung fuel—direct evidence of fodder choice—follow geography. On the steppe, where rainfall agriculture is riskier, sheep and goats would be put out to graze, but as you go north, it becomes more economical to grow fodder, and cereals make a correspondingly greater contribution to the animal diet. Archaeobotanically, this is reflected in a decline in the wild seed to cereal ratio from south to north. In this example, change through time is not pronounced.[19]

The spread and exchange of crop plants began almost as soon as people began farming in both the Old and New Worlds. Globally, however, the pace of change quickened with the European invasion of the Americas, which resulted in major change to the existing Native American land use systems.[20] The most obvious effect was two-way exchange of crops. For example, Old World plants like peach and watermelon were rapidly accepted by the Native Americans.[21] The Europeans brought many of their own crops (grains, fruits, nuts, ornamentals, etc.) to grow. The settlers also began to grow Indian cultigens, like maize, beans, and squash, and they introduced these crops to the Old World. The goal of crop studies is not to develop a laundry list of historically documented introductions. Rather, tracing the spread of introduced plants helps one trace the spread of European influence and enables one to see that the foreigners kept many of their old food and farming habits, but also learned how to grow and use the new crops.

Of course, useful crops were not the only plants that were exchanged. Weedy "camp followers" like crabgrass radically changed the vegetation, not only around the new settlements, but in the interior as well, for plants do not recognize the same cultural boundaries that people do.[22] Thus, even the weeds help document the effects of European expansion.

TRADE

Exchange of crop plants represents one type of trade but, if a group successfully adopts a new crop, the initial trading relationship can cease. In some cases, however, an important exotic plant could not be grown easily, or at all. For example, Mediterranean plants like the olive do fine in California, but not on the east coast of North America. Nonetheless, olive pits were found in a dry crawl-space below an orangery at the home of the prominent family of Charles Calvert, colonial governor of Maryland.[23] If the pits were deposited when the space was actively used for growing warmth-loving plants, we might suspect olive was grown as a high-status plant, for it requires special growing conditions. This hypothesis would be tremendously strengthened by the discovery of olive pollen, or even wood, as evidence of the tree itself growing. Rodent-gnawed olive pits found in a trash deposit post-dating the crawl-space could be the remains of an imported (but still relatively high-status) food. Thus, depending on the archaeological context and the total archaeobotanical assemblage, occurrence of an exotic plant may show important facets of historic economy.

SPATIAL ORGANIZATION—ESPECIALLY
OF URBAN AREAS, FARMSTEADS, AND GARDENS

A city is more than just a collection of buildings. Open space, tended or not, is part of the urban scene, and even the most desolate tract will soon sprout hardy weeds. As Wilhelmina Jashemski has shown for Pompeii, urban areas may have gardens, both private and commercial.[24] Plant remains found on an ancient garden or field surface may reveal fertilizing practices or what was growing on the plot itself. For example, charred remains mixed with small eroded pot sherds indicated that household debris was worked into the soil as fertilizer at Herod the Great's palace in Jericho. Maize and squash pollen has been found in ancient fields in northern Arizona, but it was absent from adjacent areas, clear evidence that the field once supported those crops.[25]

CONCLUSION

All peoples have some direct relationship with the botanical world, and the material evidence they leave behind can be recovered and interpreted. Paleoethnobotany is one of the most important tools we have for developing a picture of ancient life and landscape.

NOTES

1. Richard I. Ford, "Paleoethnobotany in American Anthropology," *Advances in Archaeological Method and Theory* 2 (1979): 285–336.
2. For discussion and instructions on different recovery techniques, see Deborah M. Pearsall, *Paleoethnobotany: A Handbook of Procedures* (San Diego: Academic Press, 1988).
3. Paul E. Minnis, "Seeds in Archaeological Sites: Sources and Some Interpretive Problems," *American Antiquity* 46 (1981): 143–152.
4. Gayle Fritz, "Identification of Cultigen Amaranth and Chenopod from Rock Shelter Sites in Northwest Arkansas," *American Antiquity* 49 (1984): 558–572; Sheila Pozorski, "Changing Subsistence Priorities and Early Settlement Patterns on the North Coast of Peru," *Journal of Ethnobiology* 3 (1983): 15–38; Christian de Vartavan, "Contaminated Plant-Foods from the Tomb of Tutankhamun: A New Interpretive System," *Journal of Archaeological Science* 17 (1990): 473–494; G. H. Willcox, "Exotic Plants from Roman Waterlogged Sites in London," *Journal of Archaeological Science* 4 (1977): 269–282.
5. See Pearsall, *Paleoethnobotany*, pp. 15–105 for an extensive discussion of flotation systems.
6. Bruce Smith, "The Independent Domestication of Indigenous Seed Bearing Plants in Eastern North America," in William Keegan, ed., *Emergent Horticultural Economies of the Eastern Woodlands* (Carbondale: Southern Illinois University Press, 1987), pp. 3–47; Mordechai E. Kislev, "Botanical Evidence for Ancient Naked Wheats in the

Near East," in W. van Zeist and W. A. Casparie, eds., *Plants and Ancient Man* (Rotterdam: A. A. Balkema, 1984), pp. 141–152; Jon Hather, *An Archaeobotanical Guide to Root and Tuber Identification, Volume 1: Europe and Southwest Asia* (Oxford: Oxbow Monograph 28, 1993).

7. Neal B. Lopinot, "Archaeobotanical Formation Processes and Late Middle Archaic Human-Plant Interrelationships in the Midcontinental U.S.A.," Ph.D. diss., Department of Anthropology, Southern Illinois University (Ann Arbor: University Microfilms, 1984).

8. For overviews, see G. W. Dimbleby, *The Palynology of Archaeological Sites* (New York: Academic Press, 1985); Richard G. Holloway and Vaughn M. Bryant, "New Directions of Palynology in Ethnobiology," *Journal of Ethnobiology* 6 (1986): 47–65; Suzanne K. Fish, "Archaeological Palynology of Gardens and Fields," in Naomi F. Miller and Kathryn L. Gleason, eds., *The Archaeology of Garden and Field* (Philadelphia: University of Pennsylvania Press, 1994), pp. 44–69.

9. James N. Hill and Richard H. Hevly, "Pollen at Broken K Pueblo: Some New Interpretations," *American Antiquity* 33 (1968): 200–210.

10. For overviews, see Deborah M. Pearsall, "Phytolith Analysis: Applications of a New Paleoethnobotanical Technique in Archeology," *American Anthropologist* 84 (1982): 862–878; Dolores R. Piperno, *Phytolith Analysis: An Archaeological and Geological Perspective* (San Diego: Academic Press, 1988).

11. Deborah M. Pearsall, "Phytolith Analysis of Archeological Soils: Evidence for Maize Cultivation in Formative Ecuador," *Science* 199 (1978): 177–178; Deborah M. Pearsall and Dolores R. Piperno, "Antiquity of Maize Cultivation in Ecuador: Summary and Reevaluation of the Evidence," *American Antiquity* 55 (1990): 324–337.

12. Hans Helbaek, "The Paleoethnobotany of the Near East and Europe," in Robert J. Braidwood and Bruce Howe, eds., *Prehistoric Investigations in Iraqi Kurdistan* (Chicago: University of Chicago Press, 1960), pp. 99–118.

13. For overview, see Ford,"Paleoethnobotany in American Anthropology," in David R. Harris and Gordon C. Hillman, eds., *Foraging and Farming: The Evolution of Plant Exploitation* (London: Unwin Hyman, 1989).

14. Christine A. Hastorf, "The Effect of the Inka State on Sausa Agricultural Production and Crop Consumption," *American Antiquity* 55 (1990): 262–290.

15. Naomi F. Miller, "The Near East," in W. van Zeist, K.-E. Behre, and K. Wasylikowa, eds., *Progress in Old World Palaeoethnobotany* (Rotterdam: A. A. Balkema, 1991), pp. 133–160.

16. See Minnis, "Seeds in Archaeological Sites"; Naomi F. Miller, "The Use of Dung as Fuel: An Ethnographic Example and an Archaeological Application," *Paléorient* 10 (1984): 71–79; Gordon C. Hillman, "Reconstructing Crop Husbandry Practices from Charred Remains of Plants," in R. Mercer, ed., *Farming Practice in British Prehistory* (Edinburgh: The University Press, 1981), pp. 123–162.

17. See papers in Christine A. Hastorf and Virginia S. Popper, *Current Paleoethnobotany* (Chicago: University of Chicago Press, 1988).

18. Naomi F. Miller, "The Interpretation of Some Carbonized Cereal Remains as Remnants of Dung Cake Fuel," *Bulletin on Sumerian Agriculture* 1 (1984), pp. 45–47.

19. Naomi F. Miller, "Environmental Constraints and Cultural Choices along the Euphrates between the Fourth and Second Millennia B.C.," paper presented at the annual meeting of the Society for American Archaeology, Anaheim, 1994.

20. William Cronon, *Changes in the Land: Indians, Colonists, and the Ecology of New England* (New York: Hill and Wang, 1983); Alfred Crosby, *Ecological Imperialism: The Biology of European Expansion, 900–1900* (Cambridge: Cambridge University Press, 1987).
21. Leonard W. Blake, "Early Acceptance of Watermelon by the Indians of the United States," *Journal of Ethnobiology* 1 (1981): 193–199.
22. Crosby, *Ecological Imperialism*.
23. Naomi F. Miller, "What Mean These Seeds: A Comparative Approach to Archaeological Seed Analysis," *Historical Archaeology* 23 (1989): 50–58.
24. Wilhelmina F. Jashemski, *The Gardens of Pompeii* (New Rochelle, NY: Caratzas Brothers, 1979).
25. Naomi F. Miller and Kathryn L. Gleason, "Fertilizer in the Identification and Analysis of Cultivated Soil," in N. F. Miller and K. L. Gleason, eds., *The Archaeology of Garden and Field* (Philadelphia: University of Pennsylvania Press, 1994), pp. 24–43; Suzanne K. Fish, "Archaeological Palynology of Gardens and Fields," in N. F. Miller and K. L. Gleason, eds., *The Archaeology of Garden and Field* (Philadelphia: University of Pennsylvania Press, 1994), pp. 44–69.

SUGGESTED READINGS

Hastorf, Christine A., and Virginia S. Popper. *Current Paleoethnobotany: Analytical Methods and Cultural Interpretations of Archaeological Plant Remains*. Chicago: University of Chicago Press, 1988. The papers in this collection—directed toward students of archaeobotany—discuss the many ways archaeobotanists extract cultural meaning from the bits of charred seeds and wood recovered from archaeological sites.

Miller, Naomi F. "The Near East." In W. van Zeist, K-E. Behre, and K. Wasylikowa, eds. *Progress in Old World Paleoethnobotany*. Rotterdam: A.A. Balkema, 1991, pp. 133–160. An overview of archaeobotanical discoveries in the Near East.

Pearsall, Deborah M. *Paleoethnobotany: A Handbook of Procedures*. San Diego: Academic Press, 1988. An essential resource for all archaeologists, filled with practical information about archaeobotanical sampling and recovery procedures in the field. For the professional as well as the student, it details how to set up an archaeobotanical laboratory and begin the analysis of plant remains. The analysis of macroremains, pollen, and phytoliths are all covered.

Watson, Patty Jo, and C. Wesley Cowan, eds. *The Origins of Agriculture: An International Perspective*. Washington D.C.: Smithsonian Institution Press, 1992. Chapters directed toward college students and other interested people focus on the archaeobotanical evidence for cultivation in east Asia, the Near East, Africa, Europe, eastern North America, the southwestern United States, Mesoamerica and Central America, and South America.

The Study of Human Subsistence Behavior Using Faunal Evidence from Archaeological Sites

Richard W. Redding

> Any country that produces more than 265 kinds of cheese cannot be governed.
> —*Charles de Gaulle*

Charles de Gaulle's culinary-based description of the diversity of France and its consequence should serve as a warning to the reader about my attempt to describe the intellectual diversity among researchers who study human subsistence utilizing animal remains and other evidence of animal use left by past inhabitants of archaeological sites. Indeed, this activity is so diverse that arguments have ensued over what the field should be called! Most researchers refer to themselves as archaeozoologists, but others use paleontologist, zooarchaeologist, ethnozoologist or paleoethnozoologist. I estimate that there are over 500 individuals worldwide who study archaeological faunal evidence and, while I doubt that over 265 approaches to the study of archaeological faunal evidence can be identified within this group, substantial differences obtain among individual researchers in goals, methods, and techniques. Any attempt to describe the field is probably doomed to failure and will certainly create acrimony. Hence, I will provide in this paper a personal view of the field, discussing its goals and methods while recognizing its diversity.

Before continuing, I would like to emphasize the potential of animal remains and other evidence of animal use from archaeological sites to answer a kaleidoscopic range of fascinating questions about the past. How did our earliest ancestors of the Paleolithic periods live and how did they obtain meat— were they scavengers, hunters, or some combination of the two? How did humans survive in the frigid wastes of the north during glacial periods, and how were they able to cross into the Americas before the end of the last glaciation? When and why were animals first domesticated for food and other products? How and why were animals first used for transport and warfare?

Additionally, more general questions may be addressed with faunal remains and other evidence of animal use. How do people make decisions about which animals to consume and when to consume them? What is the relationship between decisions made about animal use and socioeconomic organization? What is the relationship between changing animal use and culture change?

I will begin with a brief summary of the scope of the study of faunal evidence from archaeological sites. This will be followed by a personal view of the history of research in the field. This is undertaken to introduce and explain the broad range of goals and allow readers to recognize and understand fundamental schisms that shape the literature. Finally, I will discuss how I think research in the field should be done and illustrate the approach with a discussion of two questions regarding animal use from archaeological sites.

THE SCOPE OF FAUNAL STUDIES

As already noted, the study of faunal evidence from archaeological sites is different things to different people. Some researchers would argue that it is simply the study of animal bones and shells recovered from excavations. However, I think this definition is vague and limiting. A better definition includes a statement of the goal(s), as in the following definition: The study of faunal evidence is a subdiscipline of archaeology whose focus is the evidence of human use and manipulation of animals. Researchers seek to identify patterns of relationships in the faunal data from archaeological contexts and to explain these patterns. Indeed, researchers have often used bone and shell fragments from sites in their studies, but arguments about animal use have been made based on analyses of skin and other tissue fragments, feces, artistic representations of animals and animal use, and archaeological features related to animal use. Individuals working with areas and in time periods with written records have used these to examine animal use in the past and, in fact, the use of early texts in Mesopotamia, Egypt, and Europe has yielded considerable insight.[1]

A BRIEF HISTORY OF THE STUDY OF FAUNAL EVIDENCE FROM ARCHAEOLOGICAL SITES

Why is it important to discuss the history of the study of archaeological faunal evidence? The short answer is that the development of a field and the way in which its practitioners are trained conditions the goals and methods of the field. If multiple goals evolve this may lead to schisms in the field. If methodological differences arise this also may result in schisms. Schisms in a field may yield obvious disagreements in the literature that may be difficult for the reader in the field to comprehend. However, understanding the schisms and their origins is critical to evaluating the literature. Because authors frequently do not clearly explain their goals and methods it is often difficult to tease out their biases. People who study archaeological faunal evidence are not immune to these problems. Recently I was called by the editor of a journal. He had sent out an article on faunal remains from a site in Turkey for review by three researchers and received one glowing, one critical, and one outright hostile review. He asked me to look over the paper and give him my opinion as to whether he should publish the article. He sent me copies of the three reviews along with a copy of the article. It was clear that the writers of the hostile and the critical reviews were on one side of a major schism in the field, and the authors of the article and the glowing review were on the other side. The criticisms were not based on the article but on strong disagreements on goals and methodology.

The following brief discussion of the development of the study of archaeological faunal evidence will lead to a discussion of important divisions within the field. Before I begin, however, I wish to make two facts very clear. First, as I describe the various approaches to the study of faunal evidence I do not wish to give the reader the impression that I am denigrating any approach or any individual who uses that approach. In general, the individuals who study faunal evidence from archaeological sites are all doing excellent work and making solid contributions. We differ over goals and methods, not intellect or personality. Second, not all of the individuals working in the field fit into the niches that I describe.

The growth of the field, from the earliest studies to the present, has been characterized by a strong relationship with paleontology. Indeed, the roots of the field of archaeological faunal studies are in paleontology. The first break with the paleontological orientation in archaeological faunal studies occurred in the early 1900s when some researchers began to focus on questions related to the origin of animal domestication. By the 1950s some researchers, particularly in Europe, were being trained as anatomists or in veterinary anatomy. These individuals were primarily interested in research on the origins and evolution of domestic animals but their methodology was still borrowed from paleontology. Those whose approach to archaeological faunal evidence is based on paleontology or veterinary medicine usually refer to themselves as archaeozoologists or zooarchaeologists. These are the "traditionalists" in the field.

It was in the late 1950s and early 1960s that individuals interested in archaeological faunal evidence begin to show increased diversification in research goals and methods. This diversification was most evident among North American researchers. In the late 1950s some researchers began to develop goals beyond those of paleontology. They recognized that archaeological faunal evidence may provide insight on human behavior. Most of these individuals were trained in North America and had been exposed to method and theory either in anthropology or in ecology and evolutionary biology. Not surprisingly, they began applying method and theory from those fields. The

questions that this group has focused on, in addition to the traditional paleontological questions, include the following:

1. What were human subsistence behaviors and how did they change over
   time?
2. How were past economies organized and how did they change over time?
3. What do the faunal data tell us about human evolution?

Further, their basic approach to the faunal data was quite different. The
more traditional approach was to examine the faunal data for patterns of relationships and anomalies and then to explain the observed patterns and
anomalies by reference to the data or information from other sources. This
frequently led to explanations that were accepted without testing and evaluation. As researchers began to use faunal data to ask questions about human
behavior they also began to use a new approach. This involved the construction of models and/or expectations based on ideas about how humans may
have used animals, and then the comparison of expectations to the faunal
data. The goal of this approach is a reciprocal relation among theory, explanation, and evaluation. These individuals prefer to call what they do ethno-
zoology or paleoethnozoology, thus emphasizing their ties to anthropology.
The individuals in this branch of the field will be referred to subsequently as
the "radicals."

A very important group of researchers began to appear in the late 1970s.
It was composed primarily of researchers who had been radicals or who had
at least found the radical approach attractive. These individuals had great
hopes for using archaeological faunal data to examine human behavior but
they became skeptical of the assumption that faunal remains are evidence of
human subsistence behavior. They were heavily influenced by developments
in paleontology. Paleontologists had for a considerable period of time recognized that patterning in the paleontological record might be due to pre- and
post-depositional biasing forces, hence paleontological samples were not a
direct reflection of the living community. Articles on studies of how fossil
samples had been biased by formational processes began appearing in the
1950s. This study of the formational processes in the paleontological record is
referred to as taphonomy. A seminal article in paleontological taphonomy was
published in 1969 by M. R. Voorhies, "Taphonomy and Population Dynamics
of an Early Pliocene Vertebrate Fauna, Knox County, Nebraska."[2] This article
influenced many of those who were working with archaeological faunal data
and by 1975 articles on taphonomic processes at archaeological sites were appearing. This group of researchers has become so important that taphonomic studies of archaeological faunas have come to dominate the methodological
literature. In general, individuals in this group refer to their work as ar-
chaeozoology, although a few see themselves as ethnozoologists. I will refer
to this group of researchers as the "taphonomists."[3]

Most taphonomists would like to be able to examine changes in human subsistence behavior and cultural change using faunal data but feel they must first determine what patterns of relationships in the data reflect human behavior. The group includes individuals who think that fauna cannot be used to examine human behavior, "depressed taphonomists," and those who think that they can compensate for the taphonomic processes, "taphonomic optimists." This latter group of researchers study carcass handling by modern humans and non-human carnivores and the biasing effect of natural processes in an attempt to understand how faunal remains accumulate in an archaeological context.

In the early 1980s a number of researchers appeared who were trained and see themselves primarily as archaeologists. Like other archaeologists, they specialize in the study of some archaeological data set like ceramics, lithics, or in their case, fauna. They are archaeologists who use data on human subsistence behavior to address archaeological problems. Individuals in this group tend to be radicals but prefer to call themselves anthropological archaeologists.

As a final note to this section, I need to mention a different approach to animal use at archaeological sites that developed among classical and biblical archaeologists, Egyptologists, and historians. A number of researchers in these fields have used ancient texts, carvings, and paintings to document and explore animal use by humans.[4] The questions they sought to answer have been as follows:

1. What species and breeds were used and what were they called?
2. What were they used for?
3. How were they used?

Although their research has focused on quite different questions than the traditionalists or the radicals, I have found it extremely useful.

SCHISMS

I believe two major schisms plague the study of archaeological faunal evidence at present. The first schism is based on perceptions of what goals are valid for the field. The second is based on a disagreement over what is represented by patterns of variation in archaeological faunal remains.

On one side of the first schism are researchers whose goals are, at most, those of the paleontological approach previously noted. Included in this group are almost all European and Asian and many North American archaeozoologists. The papers they produce tend to focus on the bones and how to identify them, on seasonal and environmental reconstruction, and on what was eaten and how it was obtained. They argue that the data do not support the deeper analyses of the radicals; they are frequently suspicious of theoretically based models, and they have embraced the taphonomists (particularly the depressed taphonomists) because they feel taphonomy supports this position.

On the other side of the first schism are individuals whose goals, in addition to those listed earlier, are to explain the evolution of human subsistence behavior. Included in this group are, primarily, some North American and British archaeologists specializing in faunal evidence and ethnozoologists.[5] This group includes the radicals and many of the taphonomic optimists. They tend to produce theoretically based models that relate faunal remains to human behavior and cultural change.

The second major schism exists primarily among North American researchers. On one side are the depressed taphonomists, who consider faunal data to be heavily biased by taphonomic factors. They feel, at least at present, that little can be done with faunal remains other than to tease out the taphonomic factors. The papers they produce may explain how to identify and quantify faunal remains, seasonality, and environmental reconstruction, but frequently focus as well on understanding the taphonomic factors that have altered the faunal assemblage. This group publishes studies on recent assemblages, how they are biased, or how to identify the activities of biasing agents. Examples include studies on the following:

1. Modern hunters, their butchering patterns, and what body parts they return to the site
2. The disposal of bones by modern hunter-gatherer groups and how the assemblages are modified by forces after site abandonment
3. Deposits of bones from the dens of scavengers and carnivores
4. Relative survivability of different bones

On the other side of the second schism are researchers, mostly archaeologists who specialize in faunal studies, who feel that patterns of variability found in faunal assemblages are most likely the result of human subsistence behavior. The articles published by this group tend to focus on the development of models and expectations based on human behavior and the comparison of models and expectations to faunal data.

Who is right? Probably both groups. The depressed taphonomists primarily work with sites that were occupied by hunters and gatherers, while the radicals and archaeologists specializing in faunal evidence primarily work with sites occupied by food producers. Faunal assemblages derived from sites occupied by food producers are qualitatively different from sites occupied by hunter-gatherers. At sites that were inhabited by food producers the faunal samples are much larger and result from more intensive deposition. For example, five hundred identifiable bone fragments from a hunter-gatherer site might have been deposited over hundreds if not thousand of years, while five hundred identifiable fragments at a site occupied by food producers may represent one week's garbage. At a site in Iran, Tepe

Sharafabad, we encountered a large garbage pit ten meters long, four meters across, and about four meters deep. The pit dated to about 3400 B.C. We excavated a 1.5-meter-wide trench through the garbage pit that provided us with about a 15 percent sample of its contents. The bone fragments in the sample were very well preserved and showed little evidence of mechanical battering or carnivore gnawing. This along with the stratigraphy suggests that the pit was rapidly filled and little disturbed. The excavation yielded 1,177 limb and skull fragments from sheep, goats, pigs, and cattle. Based on the stratigraphy, the four meter deep deposit represents human subsistence behavior over only 2.5 years![6] Clearly, biasing of the samples by taphonomic processes is much more likely at hunter-gatherer sites than at those occupied by food producers.

I was working on an Old Kingdom village site, dating to about 2200 B.C., in the Nile Delta of Egypt when the site was visited by a taphonomist. After examining some of the bone fragments from the site and finding evidence of carnivore and rodent chewing, he asked how I knew any of the bones I was examining were the result of human activity. I replied that the problem I had was not in determining which elements were the result of human activity but which ones were not. This, I think, captures the essence of the difference between the two groups.

HOW I STUDY ARCHAEOLOGICAL FAUNAL EVIDENCE

I am one of the radicals who think of themselves as anthropological archaeologists who study the evolution of human subsistence behavior. Like all researchers in the field, my perspective shapes what I see as interesting problems to work on and how I approach those problems. My perspective has been shaped by my educational background, which is strongly based in evolutionary ecology and evolutionary theory. I believe the study of the evolution of human subsistence behavior is critical to understanding the evolution of human behavior. In my view, the study of archaeological faunal evidence addresses one component of human subsistence behavior.

For many the research process starts with the identification of animal remains from archaeological contexts. However, I would argue that if faunal remains and evidence are going to provide real insight into human behavior, they will do so only if we use fauna to test ideas about human subsistence behavior. To accomplish this, we must begin with models of human subsistence behavior that suggest what we might find at sites and where we might look for patterns of relationships. Because we are in the early stages of the development of theory in the study of archaeological faunal evidence, the models that are being used are relatively simple. Particularly important are models that make minimal assumptions about human subsistence behavior. Such models form a baseline against which we can compare the archaeological faunal data. I will illustrate this approach with two examples.

SCAVENGER OR SCHLEPPER?

Dexter Perkins and Patricia Daly published a study in *Scientific American* in 1968 on the fauna from the site of Suberde in southwestern Turkey.[7] Suberde is an early Neolithic site dating to about 7000 B.C. Based on an examination of the animal bone fragments recovered, Perkins and Daly concluded that the ancient residents of Suberde obtained meat by hunting, primarily sheep, goats, pigs, deer, and cattle. They noted in their analysis a disparity between the kinds of body parts found for large bovids (cattle) and medium bovids (sheep and goats).[8] The limb bones of animals can be divided into two types. The first are limb bones like the scapula, humerus, radius, ulna, femur, and tibia that are enclosed in large masses of muscle. These may be referred to as meat-bearing limb bones or proximal limb bones.[9] The second type are the sinewy bones of the hand and foot, the metapodials, podials, and phalanges. These may be referred to as non-meat-bearing limb bones or distal limb bones.[10] In the sample of cattle at Suberde, meat-bearing limb bones were scarce when compared to the meat-bearing bones for sheep and goats.

> The foot bones of sheep and goats [non-meat-bearing] comprised about 55 percent of the combined total; the leg [meat-bearing] bones made up the remaining 45 percent. With the oxen 83 percent of the bones were foot bones and only 17 percent were leg bones.[11]

Perkins and Daly suggest that this difference between cattle and sheep/goats is because cattle were treated differently by the ancient inhabitants of Suberde than were sheep and goats. Perkins and Daly maintain that cattle were probably butchered away from the base camp. The hide was stripped off the carcass and the feet, which contain the non-meat-bearing limb bones, were left attached to it. The meat that was stripped from the bones and most of the meat-bearing limb bones were discarded at the butchering site. The meat was placed into the hide and the combined package was dragged (schlepped) back to the base camp using the feet as handles. They noted that sheep and goats are smaller and, though killed away from the site, the entire carcass could be easily carried back. The proposed disparity between large and small bovids in body part distribution resulting from differences in butchering and transport Perkins and Daly named the "schlepp effect."

The schlepp effect became a standard explanation in the literature for a disparity between large and medium-small bovids in percentage of meat-bearing versus non-meat-bearing limbs in the sample. Its use by Richard Klein in the analysis of the fauna from Cave 1 of the Klasies River Mouth Sites, a series of Middle Stone Age sites in South Africa, has resulted in considerable controversy.[12] In particular, Lewis Binford has attacked the use of the schlepp effect and the associated assumption that the occupants of the site were hunters.[13] Binford, using the same data, argues that the occupants of Cave 1 scavenged the remains of larger bovids and may have hunted the small and medium bovids.[14] To quote the respective authors:

> The basic observation to be explained is a striking contrast between smaller bovids and larger bovids in the degree to which skeletal part abundance departs from anatomical expectations. It tends to be significantly more uneven or discrepant in the larger bovids, and the contrast is more than locally interesting, since it also tends to characterize most other archaeological occupation sites where smaller and larger ungulates occur....as I show below, for Klasies, and most comparable sites, pre-excavation differential transport and/or differential destruction are far more likely explanations.[15]
>
> In short, the bias present among the bones from the large animals is the very pattern that attracted me to the study of the material—a pattern of high head-and-lower-limb-bone frequencies, the pattern that all actualistic evidence suggested should be characteristic of a scavenged assemblage.[16]

This controversy has involved one book, a number of articles, book reviews and several authors. The fauna from Cave 1 at the Klasies River Mouth and its interpretation now has larger implications because of attempts to expand the use of Binford's and Klein's explanations to other sites in other areas and indeed to establish strategies of human subsistence behavior during the Pleistocene.

Critical to both authors' analyses is the assumption that the percentage of non-meat-bearing fragments in the sample of limb fragments found among the small and medium-small categories of bovids is "normal" and it is the anomalous percentage of the medium-large and large categories of bovids that requires explanation. This assumption needs to be carefully examined. This can be done with a simple, baseline model I have developed to examine body part representation in sites.

The goal of constructing a baseline model for body part representation in this case is to establish an expected percentage of non-meat-bearing fragments in the sample of limb fragments, given the assumption that complete carcasses are returned to the site. This is the simplest case and involves the simplest assumption. I start by noting that larger limb bones tend to break into proximal and distal fragments, and indeed these are the general categories we use in classifying fragments of large limb bones from archaeological contexts. Given this assumption and a skeleton of a bovid (all bovids should have the same number of limb bones), one can count bones and using expected fragmentation, establish expected counts for meat-bearing and non-meat-bearing fragments. The expected counts for Cave 1 for an entire skeleton are fifty-two for non-meat-bearing limb fragments and twenty-two for meat-bearing fragments. Thus, if complete skeletons of bovids are being returned to the site then non-meat-bearing bones should form 70 percent of the sample of limb bones.

Using the counts provided by Klein and calculating percentages of non-meat-bearing fragments in the total sample of limb fragments, the following percentages are observed:

Large bovids, 79.1 percent
Medium-large bovids, 68.6 percent
Medium-small bovids, 44.4 percent
Small bovids, 35.4 percent

The percentages for the large and medium-large bovids are close to what one would expect if whole animals were being returned to the site. Clearly the percentages for the small and medium-small bovids are not as expected if whole animals were being returned to the site. The observed percentages for small and medium-small bovids indicate that non-meat-bearing fragments are relatively underrepresented in the sample. Remember that Klein and Binford both *assumed* that for the larger categories of bovids, non-meat-bearing fragments were over-represented in the sample. What appears to be true from my analysis is that non-meat-bearing fragments in large bovids are occurring in about the percentage expected if whole animals are being returned to the site and are relatively underrepresented in the small and medium-small bovids.

Is there a reasonable explanation of the relative underrepresentation of non-meat-bearing fragments in the samples for small and small-medium bovids? The site was excavated using one-half inch screens to recover the small fragments of bone and other small artifacts. The majority of the non-meat-bearing bones are carpals and tarsals, the small bones of the feet. Not surprisingly, in the larger bovids the carpals and tarsals are much larger than in the smaller bovids. Could we be seeing the effect of poor recovery of the carpals and tarsals from the smaller bovid categories? If carpals and tarsals are being recovered in the percentage they occur in the carcass then 59 percent of the limb bones recovered should be carpals or tarsals. Interestingly, the observed percentages for Cave 1 are as follows:

Large bovids, 43.5 percent
Medium-large bovids, 22.3 percent
Medium-small bovids, 4.7 percent
Small bovids, 2.6 percent

These data show that carpals and tarsals are underrepresented in the samples for all sizes of bovids, but the underrepresentation for the medium-small and small bovids is dramatic. Clearly for these size categories of bovids, carpals and tarsals are missing from the samples in substantial numbers. This is a pattern congruent with the loss of carpals and tarsals through the screen. A further test of this explanation for the underrepresentation of the carpals and tarsals of the medium-small and small bovids is possible by looking at the expected percentage of the other non-meat-bearing bones, the metapodials. These bones (the longer bones of the feet) are about the size of the meat-bearing limb bones. Fragments of metapodials should not have been lost through the screens at the same rate as the much smaller carpals and tarsals and, hence, should occur in about the expected percentage. The expected percentage of metapodial fragments in the sample of limb fragments is 10 percent. The observed percentages are as follows:

Large bovids, 14 percent

Medium-large bovids, 10 percent

Medium-small bovids, 7.5 percent

Small bovids, 3.8 percent

These data indicate metapodials are not extremely underrepresented, except in the small bovids. Hence, the most reasonable explanation for the underrepresentation of non-meat-bearing fragments in the samples for medium-small and small bovids is that the carpals and tarsal were lost during excavation, probably through the screen.

Klein and Binford both maintain that the pattern to explain in the fauna from Cave 1 of the Klasies River Mouth is the over-representation of non-meat-bearing fragments in large bovids. This analysis indicates that non-meat-bearing fragments are not over-represented in large bovids and that the important pattern to explain is the underrepresentation of non-meat-bearing fragments in medium-small bovids! A simple explanation for the observed underrepresentation is the loss of small and medium bovid carpals and tarsals in the excavation process. This example illustrates the danger of attempting to explain patterns of relationships in the archaeological record without first constructing baseline models.

The study of animal evidence from sites associated with early humans has potential for solving some of the issues involving early human subsistence behavior. In fact it is probably only through the study of faunal remains that we will be able to determine whether the early humans obtained meat by hunting, scavenging, or a combination of the two. Interesting and exciting work is being done on the faunal remains from many early sites—how faunal remains accumulate in archaeological contexts and how faunal remains may be biased over time by physical factors.

MANAGEMENT STRATEGIES AND TACTICS
FOR DOMESTIC ANIMALS IN THE ANCIENT MIDDLE EAST

I have put considerable effort into developing a baseline model to examine tactics of domestic animal use at archaeological sites in the Middle East and North Africa.[17] The model is based on two data sets. The first is recent reproductive, production, survivorship, feeding, and physiological data published for unimproved breeds of domestic animals kept in the Middle East and North Africa. Most of this information has been obtained from the animal management literature. The second is ethnographic data on domestic animal use by agricultural and pastoral groups in the Middle East and North Africa. I have synthesized these data to yield expectations for four variables that reflect animal management practices, estimates of which can be recovered from archaeological samples. These four variables are as follows:

1. Species ratios (e.g., the ratio of sheep to goats, or sheep/goats to cattle). A direct estimate of species ratios for sites has been obtained from the relative abundance of fragments of each taxa.
2. Survivorship for each domestic taxa. An estimate of survivorship for each taxa at a site can be derived from bone fusion data and tooth eruption data.[18] The data is usually presented in the form of a curve with the x-axis representing increasing age (usually in months) and the y-axis representing increasing percentage of animals surviving. A point on the curve is an estimate of the percentage of animals born that survive to that age.
3. Sex ratio for each domestic taxa. A direct estimate of sex ratio for each taxa at a site can be derived from a number of sources.[19]
4. Body part distribution for each domestic taxa. An estimate of the relative abundance of body parts for each taxa at a site can be derived from counts of fragments.

The model is based on three important assumptions. The first is that the site is primarily a producing/consuming site (the majority of animals produced at the site are consumed locally). A second is that the goal of the management system is herd security. The third is that the sample is a complete representation of the activities at the site. The model yields predictions about four variables that provide evidence of animal management practices.

The model uses species ratios for cattle, sheep, goats, and pigs as an indicator of subsistence tactics and management practices. The species ratios only provide the initial expectations for the other three variables (survivorship, sex ratios, and body part distribution). If the other three variables do not conform with expectations set by the species ratios, then we must examine the possibility that the assumptions have been violated (e.g., the animals at the site are not being obtained locally and/or the local herders are engaged in some form of specialized production).

As previously noted, species ratios are the first variable examined because they provide the best first estimate of the management tactics. Certainly the exact value for any species ratio may be affected by local environmental conditions but in general the numbers and ranges I describe should obtain if flocks and herds are being maintained locally with a goal of herd security. The ratio of sheep/goats to cattle is an estimator of the degree of involvement of the occupants in intensive agriculture. When cattle are consumed in about the same numbers or in greater numbers than sheep and goats at a site (a ratio of 1:1 or less), the area around the site was intensively farmed. A ratio of 2:1 or 5:1 reflects a mixed herding and farming strategy. If the ratio is higher, the site was probably a locus of sheep/goat pastoralism. The ratio of sheep to goat should vary inversely to the ratio of sheep/goat to cattle. That is, as cattle increase in the sample so should the number of goats in the flocks. If the site was a center of sheep/goat pastoralism the ratio of sheep to goats should be about 8:1.[20]

Expected survivorship curves can be modeled using reproduction and mortality data from recent flocks or herds of unimproved breeds of any of the domesticates. A computer algorithm modeling growth in a population based on these data can be used to model off take. Using these data in a series of management goals for maximizing the flock/herd, the survivorship curve for each domestic taxa can be estimated. These goals include flock/herd security, meat production, milk production and, for sheep/goats, wool/hair production.[21] By comparing these expected survivorship curves to those derived from archaeological samples, we perform a test of the underlying subsistence goals.

The sex ratio for each taxa can provide insight into the tactics used in herding the animals and can be used to test the conclusion derived from the species ratios. A ratio of males to females in sheep/goats consumed that is biased toward males reflects herd management for milk, meat, or herd security.[22] This is the ratio one should see given the assumptions of our baseline model. A ratio that is strongly biased toward males could result from importation of young males onto the site from other producing areas. A ratio of about 1:1 is due to management for wool production. Establishing expectations for cattle sex ratios is complicated by the castration and use of males for plowing. In general, a heavily male-biased ratio is expected when males are brought into the site from other areas. A slightly male-biased ratio results from herding for security, meat, or milk. An unbiased ratio may reflect the use of cattle for milk, meat, and plowing.

The percentage of non-meat-bearing limb fragments in the sample of limb fragments may be used to test whether animals are being obtained locally or being imported. The expected percentage of non-meat-bearing fragments in the limb fragment sample for sheep/goats and cattle in the Middle East is 66 percent; for pigs it is 73 percent. If the animals at a site are all obtained locally, the ratios of non-meat- to meat-bearing specimens should approximate the expected values. Ratios that approach these values indicate that entire animals are being butchered on the site. A bias toward meat-bearing elements is indicative of offsite butchering or butchering that occurred in some other area of the site; hence parts of animals are probably being imported to the site or into the area of the site excavated. A ratio biased toward non-meat-bearing elements would suggest on site/local butchering with the export of meat-bearing parts.

I do not have space to provide a complete example of how such modeling of management practice for domestic animals has been used with archaeological fauna, but the following is a summary of how it has been used with faunal data from two Old Kingdom sites in Egypt.[23] One is a village site in the Nile Delta that dates to about 2200 B.C., Kom el-Hisn. The other site is the workers' area next to the pyramids complex at Giza.

The analysis of the fauna from the village site, Kom el-Hisn, indicated the following:

1. The site was a center of cattle rearing but the residents rarely had access to the cattle meat. Based on survivorship data, the residents ate cattle that were either very young or old. The prime, eighteen- to twenty-four-month-old males apparently were not consumed at the site.
2. Sheep and goats were herded around the site. The goats were consumed locally but the sheep were rarely available. The prime young male sheep of twelve to twenty-four months were apparently removed from the site.
3. Domestic pig bone fragments are more common in the samples than cattle or sheep/goat fragments. Pigs were the most commonly consumed animal at the site and the survivorship data suggest that the pigs were managed to maximize meat offtake from the herd.

The conclusion reached was that Kom el-Hisn was a production center for cattle and sheep controlled by a central authority. The young males harvested from the Kom el-Hisn herds and flocks were taken to other sites for consumption by individuals working for that central authority. This yields a number of predictions of how the faunal remains from a site provisioned by the central authority should be structured:

1. Cattle should dominate.
2. Sheep should be the second most common mammal. The ratio of sheep to goats should be about 6.6:1.
3. In the samples of cattle and sheep the survivorship curves should be dominated by individuals between sixteen and twenty-four months.
4. In the samples of cattle and sheep bones, males should dominate.

Fortunately, recent excavations in a workers' village next to the pyramids at Giza have yielded faunal samples that are the result of provisioning by a central authority. In these samples the ratio of cattle to sheep/goat bone fragments is 3.1:1. At most other Egyptian Pharaonic sites for which we have faunal data, the ratio is less than 1:1 (0.6:1 to 0.9:1). Sheep/goats are the second most common mammal in the samples and the ratio of sheep to goats is 3.3:1. The survivorship data for cattle indicate that 88 percent of the animals represented in the samples are less than twenty-four months of age. The sex ratio for the cattle material is four males for every female, an unusually biased ratio for sites in Egypt. The survivorship data for the sheep/goat samples indicate that over half of the animals represented are less than fifteen months old. The sex ratio for sheep/goats is four males for every female.

Comparing the baseline model to the Kom el-Hisn data yielded discrepancies that were used to construct an explanation for the observed pattern of relationships. In turn, this explanation yielded predictions that may be tested in future work at Kom el-Hisn. Additionally, the explanation had implications for the fauna from sites provisioned by a central authority. These implications provide insight into the socioeconomic system of Old Kingdom Egypt.

The importance of this approach is that it has focused research and yielded considerable insight into the use of fauna to answer questions about economic decision making. It has even helped us focus our basic research on methods. A colleague at a meeting once told me that he had tried applying the model but because we are, at present, unable to construct separate survivorship curves for sheep and goats he thought the model was useless. My reply was that at least now we know one place to focus our research—developing techniques to develop separate survivorship curves for sheep and goats—that will yield substantial return.

SUMMARY

As should be clear, I believe that archaeological faunal remains have tremendous potential for exploring temporal and geographic variation in human subsistence behavior. Understanding the evolution of human subsistence behavior is critical to explaining the origin and evolution of culture. However, the potential of faunal evidence from archaeological sites can be realized only if we approach the data with some theoretical framework within which we can study faunal remains. This theoretical framework will guide the collection of faunal data; it can be used to direct future archaeological research and indicate where and how to look for patterns, and it can suggest productive lines of research on methodology. At this stage in the development of the discipline an important part of this framework is the development of simple, baseline models that help us examine faunal data. Specifically, models that predict what we will find in faunal data using the simplest assumptions will provide us with insight into what causes deviations from the expected. The application of these types of models to archaeological data has led and will lead researchers to more complex models reflecting a deeper understanding of human subsistence decision making.

This is not a widely held position. Many individuals who study archaeological faunal evidence are skeptical of the use of theory and models in explaining patterns in archaeological faunal data. Others think it can not be done because too many factors have acted on the samples and the patterns resulting from human behavior have been partially erased. My argument is that we should seek patterns in the faunal data and attempt to explain them. As an initial research position we should assume that patterns in the data for sites, at least those based on food production rather than hunting and gathering, are more likely to be explained by spatial and temporal variation in human subsistence behavior. If this position is incorrect, over time we will find that serious discrepancies exist between the explanatory constructs and the data. Even if the empirically identified patterns prove to be the result of biasing processes, by using this approach we should gain insight into biasing agencies and learn where and how they affect faunal samples.

Only by trying to explain faunal data in terms of a theoretical framework will researchers studying archaeological faunal evidence make progress in understanding variation and patterning in the archaeological faunal data. Only by creating a framework and challenging ourselves and the data will the study of archaeological faunal evidence make a substantial contribution to the study of human evolution.

NOTES

1. Studies of faunal use based on texts and faunal remains have tremendous potential. I recommend the following references for people wishing to explore this potential: J. N. Postgate, *Early Mesopotamia: Society and Economy at the Dawn of History* (London: Routledge, 1992); Ignace J. Gelb, "Growth of a Cattle Herd in Ten Years," *Journal of Cuneiform Studies* 21 (1965): 64–69; Melinda A. Zeder, "Of Kings and Shepherds: Specialized Animal Economy in Ur III Mesopotamia," in Gil Stein and Mitchell S. Rothman, eds., *Chiefdoms and Early States in the Near East* (Madison: Prehistory Press, Monographs in World Archaeology, vol. 18, 1994), pp. 175–191.
2. M. R. Voorhies, *Taphonomy and Population Dynamics of an Early Pliocene Vertebrate Fauna, Knox County, Nebraska*, University of Wyoming, Contributions to Geology Special Paper, no. 1, 1969.
3. Two recent books provide an excellent summary of the state of taphonomic studies in archaeology: Jean Hudson, *From Bones to Behavior: Ethnoarchaeological and Experimental Contributions to the Interpretation of Faunal Remains*, Center for Archaeological Investigation, Southern Illinois University at Carbondale, Occasional Paper no. 21, 1993; R. Lee Lyman, *Vertebrate Taphonomy* (Cambridge: Cambridge University Press, Cambridge Manuals in Archaeology, 1994).
4. One of the most recent and complete of these is William J. Darby, Paul Ghalioungui, and Louis Grivetti, *Food: The Gift of Osiris* (New York: Academic Press, 1977). A number of early works using this approach exist. I recommend E. Douglas Van Buren, "The Fauna of Ancient Mesopotamia as Represented in Art," *Analecta Orientalia* 18 (1939). Another interesting general work using this approach is Alan Houghton Brodrick, ed., *Animals in Archaeology* (New York: Praeger Publishers, 1972).
5. I do not mean to insult my colleagues in other areas of the world by omission.
6. The excavation, stratigraphy, and archaeology of the garbage pit at Tepe Sharafabad have been described and discussed in two articles: Henry T. Wright, Naomi Miller, and Richard W. Redding, "Time and Process in an Uruk Rural Center," in C.N.R.S., ed., *L'archaeologie de L'Iraq perspectives et limites de L'interpretation anthropologique*

des documents, C.N.R.S. Colloques Internationaux, no. 580, 1980, pp. 263–280; Henry T. Wright, Richard W. Redding, and Susan Pollack, "Monitoring Interannual Variability: An Example from the Period of Early State Development in Southwestern Iran," in Paul Halstead and John O'Shea, eds., *Bad Year Economics* (Cambridge: Cambridge University Press, 1989), pp. 6–113.

7. Dexter Perkins, Jr. and Patricia Daly, "A Hunter's Village in Neolithic Turkey," *Scientific American* 219 (1968): 96–104.

8. Bovids is the common name for members of the family Bovidae. The bovids include most of the domestic herbivores, sheep, goats, and all the cattle, as well as gazelles, antelopes, and buffalo. This includes over fifty-five species of herbivores that live in Africa.

9. *Proximal* is an anatomical term meaning closer to the center of the body.

10. *Distal* is an anatomical term meaning away from the center of the body.

11. Perkins and Daly, "A Hunter's Village in Neolithic Turkey," p. 104.

12. Richard G. Klein, "The Mammalian Fauna of the Klasies River Mouth Sites, Southern Cape Province, South Africa," *South African Archaeological Bulletin* 31 (1976): 75–98; Richard G. Klein, "Why Does Skeletal Part Representation Differ between Smaller and Larger Bovids at Klasies River Mouth and Other Archaeological Sites?" *Journal of Archaeological Science* 6 (1989): 363–381; Lewis R. Binford, *Bones: Ancient Men and Modern Myths* (New York: Academic Press, 1981); Lewis R. Binford, *Faunal Remains from Klasies River Mouth* (New York: Academic Press, 1984); Lewis R. Binford, "Response to Turner," *Journal of Archaeological Science* 16 (1989): 13–16; Alan Turner, "Sample Selection, Schlepp Effects, and Scavenging: The Implications of Partial Recovery for Interpretations of the Terrestrial Mammal Assemblage from Klasies River Mouth," *Journal of Archaeological Science* 16 (1989): 1–11.

13. Binford, *Bones: Ancient Men and Modern Myths*, pp. 184–185.

14. The sample of bovids in the Klasies River Mouth fauna includes at least fifteen species. At present it is impossible to identify even complete limb ends to species. Indeed, it is usually teeth and skull elements that are used to identify the species present. Hence, for the purpose of analysis the bones have been sorted into size categories: small, small-medium, large-medium, large, and very large.

15. Klein, "Why Does Skeletal Part Representation Differ between Smaller and Larger Bovids at Klasies River Mouth and Other Archaeological Sites?" p. 364.

16. Binford, *Faunal Remains from Klasies River Mouth*, p. 86.

17. Richard W. Redding, *Decision Making in Subsistence Herding of Sheep and Goats in the Middle East* (Ph.D. diss., University of Michigan, 1981); Richard W. Redding, "Theoretical Determinants of a Herder's Decisions: Modeling Variation in the Sheep/Goat Ratio," in Juliet Clutton-Brock and Caroline Grigson, eds., *Animals and Archaeology: Early Herders and Their Flocks*, British Archaeological Reports, International Series 202, 1984, pp. 223–241; Richard W. Redding, "The Role of Faunal Remains in the Explanation of the Development of Complex Societies in Southwest Iran: Potential, Problems, and the Future," *Paleorient* 11, no. 3 (1985): 121–124.

18. The most frequently used type of survivorship data is bone fusion. Limb bones are composed of at least three parts: a shaft and two ends that form the articulations. Limb bones grow by adding material to the ends of the shaft, in effect pushing the two ends apart. When growth ceases the ends fuse onto the shaft, forming a single element. The ends of limb bones fuse at different ages. For example, in

sheep and goats, the proximal humerus (upper arm bone) fuses at about thirty-six to forty-two months and the distal humerus fuses at about ten months. If 80 percent of the distal humerus fragments are fused, then at least 80 percent of the animals in the flock at the site must have lived to at least ten months. If 20 percent of the proximal humerus fragments are fused, then at least 20 percent of the animals at the site must have lived to at least thirty-six to forty-two months. Using fusion data for all the limb elements one can construct a curve as described in the article that estimates survivorship for each taxa at a site. Baby and adult teeth erupt at different ages and by examining a mandible or maxilla one can assign an approximate age of death for the animal. Using a sample of aged mandibles and maxillae for a species one can also construct a curve that estimates survivorship for each taxa.

19. Two types of data on sex ratios are available. First, there are morphological differences between the sexes in the pubis and the first two vertebrae, the atlas and axis. Second, metric differences between the sexes in some limb bone ends obtain. Note that I have not included horn cores.

20. For an explanation of the derivation of these expected ratios and subsequent expectations for survivorship curves, sex ratios, and body part ratios, see Redding, "Theoretical Determinants of a Herder's Decisions: Modeling Variation in the Sheep/Goat Ratio," pp. 223–241; Richard W. Redding, "The Role of the Pig in the Subsistence System of Ancient Egypt: A Parable on the Potential of Faunal Data," in Pam J. Crabtree and Kathleen Ryan, eds., *Animal Use and Culture Change*, MASCA, The University Museum of Archaeology and Anthropology, University of Pennsylvania, Research Papers in Science and Archaeology, supplement to vol. 8, 1991, pp. 20–30; and Richard W. Redding, "Egyptian Old Kingdom Patterns of Animal Use and the Value of Faunal Data in Modeling Socioeconomic Systems," *Paléorient* 18, no. 2 (1992): 99–107.

21. At present it is very difficult to separate the limb bones of sheep and goats. The survivorship curves we construct use limb fragments that are, in general, only identified as sheep/goat. Hence, the curves reflect some combination of survivorship in sheep and goats.

22. As with survivorship data, the sex ratio data is for sheep and goats.

23. Redding, "Egyptian Old Kingdom Patterns of Animal Use and the Value of Faunal Data in Modeling Socioeconomic Systems," pp. 99–107.

SUGGESTED READINGS

Brain, C. K. *The Hunters or the Hunted: An Introduction to African Cave Taphonomy*. Chicago: University of Chicago Press, 1981. This is one of the early books in taphonomy and is constantly cited. Chapters 1 through 8 are interesting and readable.

Clutton-Brock, Juliet. *Domesticated Animals for Early Times*. Austin: University of Texas Press, 1981. Although I did not discuss the origin of animal domestication in the main text, this is an important problem being addressed with archaeological faunal data. This is a readable volume that focuses on the problem of animal domestication. Its author was trained as a zoologist and this permeates the text. This book does not adequately address the issue of why humans domesticated animals.

Davis, Simon J. M. *The Archaeology of Animals*. New Haven: Yale University Press, 1987. This is the best of the easily available "how to" manuals for the study of archaeological faunal remains. The caveat is that it was written by an individual with a "traditional" approach.

Gebauer, Anne B., and T. Douglas Price. *Transitions to Agriculture in Prehistory*. Madison, WI: Prehistory Press, Monographs in World Archaeology 4, 1992. I have included this book, even though it does not specifically focus on animal bones, because it presents strong discussions on the problem of why humans domesticated plants and animals. The first two articles examine some of the explanations offered for the origin of domestication. The other articles explore the evidence for domestication in various regions of the world.

Lyman, R. Lee. *Vertebrate Taphonomy*. Cambridge, UK: Cambridge University Press, Cambridge Manuals in Archaeology, 1994. This is the most recent and complete of the books dealing with taphonomy. It is written by a "depressed" taphonomist and is slow reading. If you really want to get into taphonomy this is the book. If you want an overview of the taphonomic approach as it has developed, see the Hudson book in footnote 3. Unfortunately, the Hudson volume is not readily available in most college libraries.

Zeder, Melinda A. *Feeding Cities: Specialized Animal Economy in the Ancient Near East*. Washington, D.C.: Smithsonian Institution Press, 1991. This is one of the best books that presents an analysis from a "radical" perspective. It is extremely innovative and has been the subject of some controversial reviews. It elaborates on the model of domestic animal use presented earlier.

BARE BONES ANTHROPOLOGY:
THE BIOARCHAEOLOGY
OF HUMAN REMAINS

CLARK SPENCER LARSEN

I have always been intrigued with the behavior and quality of life of prehistoric peoples—their activities, the difficulty of their lifestyles, what they ate, how they lived, and what their health was like. In my freshman year in college at Kansas State University, I came to realize that archaeology and physical anthropology had a great deal to offer in addressing these topics. During that year, I had the good fortune of taking a class in human osteology—the study of bones and teeth—with then-visiting professor of anthropology William M. Bass. In his course I learned about skeletal and dental identification, age estimation, sex identification, and prehistoric disease. That summer, Dr. Bass secured a place for me on an archaeological project excavating human skeletons near Mobridge, South Dakota, under the direction of Smithsonian physical anthropologists Douglas H. Ubelaker and T. Dale Stewart. We spent long hours after work piecing together skeletons and discussing various topics dealing with the biology and behavior of past humans. By the time I returned for classes in the fall, I was hooked.

Since then, I've studied—in college, in graduate school, and now as a professional physical anthropologist—hundreds of skeletons from all over the world. In this chapter I share with you the kinds of exciting knowledge to be learned from analysis of ancient human remains, most of which has been made possible by new technology and imaginative hypotheses. Everything that I talk about here revolves around one simple question: What can we learn about past peoples through the study of their remains?

BIOARCHAEOLOGY DEFINED

The specialty within anthropology that is concerned with this question has been given various names over the years, including osteology, osteoarchaeology, human zooarchaeology, archaeological skeletal biology, biological archaeology, human skeletal analysis, and so forth. All of these terms adequately describe the content of the field. However, I have settled on *bioarchaeology*, a name that captures the interdisciplinary tone of this field and its emphasis on biological (or physical) anthropology in the archaeological setting.[1] Put more simply, I define bioarchaeology as the study of the human biological component of the archaeological record.

The human biological component of the past includes anything representing once-living tissues or remains found in archaeological sites. These types of remains have been found in locations worldwide, such as the ancient mummies in Egypt, the bog people in Denmark and England, and the remarkably well-preserved corpses in Greenland, Peru, and Chile, some of which are thousands of years old.[2] Certain of these remains are well known. The recent discovery and follow-up study of the "Ice Man," a well-preserved 5,300-year-old body found frozen in ice in the Austrian Alps, has received more attention in *Newsweek*, *Time*, *The Today Show*, and other popular media than have the elections of some political leaders abroad!

However, the preservation of whole or partial bodies—mummies—requires very special circumstances, such as the extremely dry conditions in the American Southwest or the practice of intentional mummification as in dynastic Egypt and prehistoric Chile.[3] Far and away, the most commonly found human remains in archaeological settings are bones and teeth, with no trace of accompanying soft tissues (for example, muscle, hair, skin). The much greater preservation of bones and teeth is made possible by the fact that they are comprised of mostly mineral matter. Teeth, for example, have a very tough outer covering—called enamel—that is highly mineralized. Consequently, teeth are especially resistant to natural processes of decay following burial. Overall, teeth and bones are better represented in the archaeological record than are soft tissues of the body. Therefore, I'll limit the scope of this chapter to what bioarchaeology reveals about past peoples based on their skeletal remains.

THE STUDY OF BONES AND TEETH IN ANTHROPOLOGY: FROM TYPOLOGY TO PROCESS

Analysis of human skeletal remains has a long tradition in anthropology, going back centuries to the time when early anatomists, paleontologists, and natural historians were attempting to comprehend the position of living representatives of *Homo sapiens* in a greater natural order. Bones and teeth were used to determine evolutionary and biological relationships among different geographic groups of people, between living humans and potential fossil ancestors, and among humans and other living species in the order Primates.[4] For much of the past couple of centuries, this field emphasized measurement of skulls and other bones (for example, the femur or thigh bone) for identifying racial characteristics of human groups. These typologically oriented studies resulted in generating literally hundreds of different measurements.

In the early 1900s, the founding fathers of physical anthropology in the United States, Ales Hrdlicka of the Smithsonian Institution and Earnest A. Hooton of Harvard University, developed a kind of typological analysis that was highly influential in determining the direction that the field would take in the following decades. Hooton, for example, constructed a classification scheme for the American Southwest, whereby he argued that individual crania could be typed and racial history could be inferred.[5] Other physical anthropologists began to develop cranial typologies for classifying populations within broad geographical areas.

Typological approaches to skeletal analysis have some major drawbacks, which cast doubt on their validity and meaning. Most importantly, none of the typological studies sought to address the biological significance of variation among and between human populations—the singular purpose was to identify boundaries. In recent years, however, physical anthropologists have been emphasizing the role of environmental and developmental processes that underlie the variability we see in human skeletal remains, such as in the shapes of skulls and other bones. Bones in the living person are very plastic and respond to mechanical stimuli over the course of an individual's lifetime. We know, for example, that food consistency (hard vs. soft) has a strong impact on the masticatory (chewing) muscles, which in turn influence the way skull form develops as the person grows and matures.[6] Similarly, physical activity has a dynamic influence in determining the shape of cross-sections of the femur bone.[7] New technological advances developed in the past ten years or so now make it possible to reconstruct and interpret in amazing detail the physical activities and adaptations of humans in diverse environmental settings. I'll discuss some of these advances later.

My point here is that there has been a fundamental shift in emphasis in the study of skeletal remains of past populations from typology to *process*, which means trying to explain the variation that is observed in skeletal remains throughout the world. The challenge is to understand past peoples as members of living and functioning populations—as though they were alive today. I emphasize here that bones and teeth in the living person are tissues that are remarkably sensitive to the environment. As such, human remains from archaeological sites offer us a retrospective biological picture of the past that is not available from other lines of evidence. With this perspective, we have the basis for understanding earlier peoples as members of real populations rather than as meaningless typological groups.

CURRENT APPROACHES TO THE STUDY OF HUMAN SKELETAL REMAINS

Like all scientists, bioarchaeologists formulate their research agendas by asking specific questions. Consistent with this approach, I pose four key questions and discuss the kinds of information that are used to address them in analyzing archaeological skeletal remains.

⌐WHAT DID PEOPLE EAT?⌐DIETARY PATTERNS IN PAST HUMAN POPULATIONS

This is an important question in anthropology because the diet (the foods that are eaten) and nutrition (the way that these foods are used by the body) of a population play an integral role in its adaptive success. We've all heard the expression, "You are what you eat." To the bioarchaeologist, the metaphor is literally true because a large number of foods leave a diagnostic chemical signature in the bones of what the person ate during his or her lifetime.[8] By looking at a group or population of skeletons from one archaeological site or prehistoric culture, we are able to document characteristics of the diet in general as well as how it varied by age, sex, or social group. Moreover, in comparing different samples of skeletons from different time periods within a region, we are able to look at how diets are altered in response to a change in circumstances, such as the adoption of a new food, technological change, population increase, or environmental disruption.

Until now, most of what we knew about the diet of past populations came from plant and animal remains excavated from prehistoric sites. Unfortunately, this kind of information rarely tells how much was eaten or in what proportions, because of the highly variable preservation of food remains. Without this information, we cannot draw inferences about the nutritional quality of the diet.

Much more precise information about diet is available from newly developed quantitative approaches based on the measurement of ratios of stable isotopes of carbon (^{12}C, ^{13}C) and nitrogen (^{14}N, ^{15}N) in bones. The isotope values are physically determined by taking a small bone sample of perhaps a few grams or so from a skeleton, converting the bone sample into a gas, and measuring the isotope values with an isotope ratio mass spectrometer.[9] This approach is based on the premise that carbon and nitrogen stable isotope ratios directly reflect the foods that the consumer ate.[10] Briefly, the isotopic ratio (denoted by the Greek letter delta, δ) values are related to the role of terrestrial (land-based) plant or marine food sources in diet. Terrestrial plants follow one of three photosynthetic pathways, either C_3 (Calvin), C_4 (Hatch-Slack), or Crassulacean Acid Metabolism (CAM). Typically, C_3 plants have very negative $\delta^{13}C$ ratios, C_4 plants have less negative ratios, and CAM plants lie somewhere between C_3 and C_4 ratios. Nitrogen isotope ratios ($\delta^{15}N$) are useful for distinguishing consumption of marine vs. terrestrial foods. These distinctions are passed along to the consumers, eventually leaving a dietary signature in the bone tissues of the humans.

Corn (or maize) was the only C_4 plant of dietary importance in North America (most other plants were C_3) at the time Europeans first arrived in the New World.[11] For some time, archaeologists have wanted to know when corn achieved its dietary importance in native New World societies. This new technique helps answer this question. Based on the measurement of stable isotope ratios of carbon from human bone samples taken from archaeological sites all over the eastern United States dating from the period of 500 B.C. to A.D.

1500, we have learned that the rate of increased dependence on corn varied from region to region. In general, heavy reliance on this plant did not occur until late in prehistory, certainly after A.D. 800 to 900.[12]

Why is it important to know that corn was so heavily used by Native Americans, or by any other population for that matter? For understanding prehistoric health, the answer is simple. Corn is a notoriously poor source of nutrition—it lacks a couple of essential amino acids (amino acids that the human body doesn't produce by itself), it is deficient in niacin, and it has phytate, a chemical substance that actually prohibits iron from being absorbed by the body tissues. These factors alone indicate that if there is an over-reliance on corn—which we see in many third world nations today—then growth potential is compromised and there is a risk of iron deficiency.[13] Moreover, maize is a carbohydrate with a high sugar component. Anyone who eats sugar knows the outcome of its consumption—tooth decay! It comes as no surprise, then, that mounting bioarchaeological evidence shows a decline in quality of life among many late prehistoric societies of the eastern United States and elsewhere.[14]

From a sociopolitical perspective, corn played an important role in both the emergence of complex societies and in the increase in population size of Native Americans during late prehistoric times. Therefore, in one sense, corn agriculture contributed to the "success" of Native Americans before contact with Europeans, if we measure success by population increase and greater social complexity. However, the cost of this apparent success was a reduction in quality of life for many thousands of individuals.

Isotopic analysis of bones in bioarchaeological studies has also increased our understanding of status and gender differences within prehistoric societies. For example, at the ancient Maya center of Copán, Honduras, high-status individuals buried in elaborate tombs have a much greater range of carbon isotope values than commoners—in fact, more than two times greater.[15] This suggests that higher-status individuals had a more varied diet and better nutrition than lower-status individuals. Moreover, in this society, females had a higher prevalence of dental caries (tooth decay), probably due to their higher consumption of carbohydrate-rich corn. This gender distinction has also been documented in many other late prehistoric sites in North America where the populations were dependent on corn.[16]

WHAT WERE ACTIVITY PATTERNS AND WORKLOADS LIKE?
RECONSTRUCTING LIFESTYLES IN THE PAST

A defining characteristic of humans is their lifestyle, which to a bioarchaeologist includes their physical behaviors and other attributes that contribute to movement and habitual activities. Hunter-gatherers, or populations dependent on wild plants and animals for sustenance, are often said to be highly mobile—they seem to be always on the move in search of food, never settling down in one place. Agriculturalists, on the other hand, are often perceived as sedentary. They seem to stay in one place year-round tending their crops and livestock. These characterizations of hunter-gatherer and agricultural lifeways point to the important link between mobility and the business of acquiring food and other essential resources in human populations.[17]

In addition to being highly mobile, it is often assumed that hunter-gatherers lead difficult and physically demanding lives. The archaeologist Robert J. Braidwood went so far as to say, in his popular textbook in the late 1960s, that hunter-gatherers live "a savage's existence, and a very tough one...following animals just to kill them to eat, or moving from one berry patch to another (and) living just like an animal."[18]

In order to address the general discussion of hunter-gatherer lifestyles, an international conference called "Man the Hunter"was held in 1966. Following the conference—and especially the provocative findings of Richard B. Lee's observations of the !Kung of northern Botswana[19]—a consensus developed among anthropologists that, contrary to the popular perception of hunter-gatherer lifeways as "nasty, brutish, and short," hunter-gatherers actually had it pretty good—they were not subject to much work, and, overall, life for them was leisurely and plentiful.[20]

Physical anthropologists have been looking at levels of difficulty of work in different lifeways for quite some time. Osteoarthritis is an important indicator of level and pattern of activity in humans. Osteoarthritis is a disorder that results from cumulative physical wear and tear on the joints, especially those joints involved in movement from one place to another (for example, the hip and leg joints).[21] In addition, nonweight-bearing joints that are involved in other types of motion—such as the elbow, wrist, and shoulder—are subject to different kinds of physical demands, such as in the lower back.

What does osteoarthritis look like in the skeleton? Bioarchaeologists typically observe tiny projections or spicules of bones that protrude from the margins of the bones that make up joints (Figure 8-1). Nonarthritic joints lack these projections. In more severe cases, the cartilage that normally lines the ends of the bones wears away if the stress on the joint is severe enough. This results in direct rubbing of bone on bone within an articular joint and produces polishing (eburnation) of joint surfaces (Figure 8-1). In prehistoric skeletons, common sites of polishing are the ends of the femur and tibia, especially in the knee joint, and the ends of the radius (one of two bones of the lower arm) and humerus in the elbow joint.

The observation of these degenerative changes in archaeological skeletons gives important insight into past activity loads and patterns. For example, physical anthropologists have been able to reconstruct in some detail the different kinds of activities that people undertook in the past based on the pattern of osteoarthritis within individual skeletons, that is, from the joints most commonly affected. Comparison of the elbow joints of Eskimos and ancient

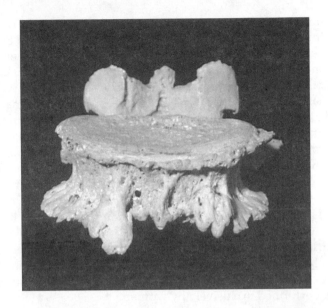

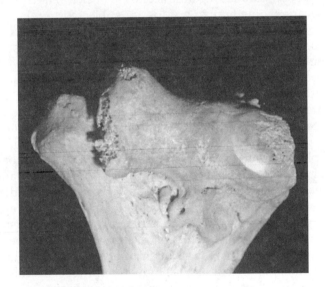

FIGURE 8-1

Top: Osteoarthritis of Lumbar Vertebra. Note the projections of bone on the margin of the joint surfaces. Bottom: Elbow Joint Showing Polishing (Eburnation) on Part of Surface. The bone shown is the end of the humerus, or upper arm bone.

Source: Photographs by Barry Stark; reproduced with permission of Academic Press, Inc., from Clark Spencer Larsen, "Bioarchaeological Interpretations of Subsistence Economy and Behavior from Human Skeletal Remains," in Michael B. Schiffer, ed., *Advances in Archaeological Method and Theory*, vol. 10.

Peruvian Indians indicates very different patterns of osteoarthritis involvement.[22] Eskimos have more osteoarthritis of the elbow joint than Peruvian Indians. How is this difference between populations linked with their activities? Through ethnographic field studies, anthropologists know that Eskimos make heavy use of the atlatl (spear thrower) in hunting animals such as seals. Thrusting of the atlatl places severe demands on the elbow, which ultimately results in osteoarthritis in older adults. Because most individuals are right handed, there is a higher frequency of degenerative changes in the right elbow than in the left elbow in Eskimos. Peruvian Indians did not use the atlatl and, therefore, experienced relatively less mechanical demand in the elbow. The differences between Eskimos and Peruvian Indians in elbow osteoarthritis is related directly to how they used the elbow joint.

Physical anthropologists have found that, in contrast to Eskimos, some prehistoric native groups in the American Southwest have equal distribution of osteoarthritis involving both elbow joints, especially in women.[23] This pattern likely relates to the use of grinding stones, an activity that involves both arms for processing corn kernels into flour. In recent Southwestern societies this work is performed exclusively by women.

All human populations, regardless of time or place, have osteoarthritis. However, because some human groups are subjected to relatively greater amounts of physical labor than other groups, we should expect to see more osteoarthritis in them. In general, mobile hunter-gatherer groups tend to have relatively higher levels of osteoarthritis than sedentary groups.[24] In order to examine the effects of major adaptive shifts on human populations, I have looked at patterns of osteoarthritis in a large number of skeletons from prehistoric hunter-gatherers dating from about A.D. 500 to 1150 from the Georgia Atlantic coast and compared them with later corn agriculturalists from the same region dating from about A.D. 1150 to 1450. The hunter-gatherers collected wild plants, hunted animals (for example, deer), and did a great deal of fishing. Their descendants in later prehistoric times ate the same kinds of foods, but maize was introduced about A.D. 1100 or so and rapidly became a central part of diet. Based on my reading of bioarchaeological reports on osteoarthritis in hunter-gatherers and agriculturalists from prehistoric sites—showing that hunter-gatherers have a tendency for higher levels of osteoarthritis—I thought that the earlier hunter-gatherers would have more osteoarthritis than the agriculturalists living on the Georgia coast. Comparison of the two groups of skeletons from the region confirmed my hypothesis.[25] This finding suggests that there was a decline in workload with the increased focus on corn in this region.

Since the early 1980s I have been collaborating with archaeologists and physical anthropologists on the study of skeletons from Spanish missions located in coastal Georgia and in northern Florida.[26] These missions were established by the Spanish Crown in cooperation with the Roman Catholic Church during the late 1500s and throughout the 1600s in order to introduce

Christianity to native populations and also to stake a claim to this region of southeastern North America. The Spanish relied on Indians as a labor source for raising crops, building projects, and labor transport. By all accounts, these labor demands were excessive, and they took a heavy physical toll on Indian groups in the region.[27] What should we expect to see in osteoarthritis prevalence in these mission Indians, the descendants of the prehistoric populations from the region? In looking at their skeletons, my colleagues and I have found that osteoarthritis increased dramatically in mission Indians.[28] For example, if we look at one joint—the adult male lumbar (lower back) vertebra—the frequency of individuals affected by osteoarthritis jumped from 16 percent in late prehistoric agriculturalists to 53 percent in mission Indians. As predicted, the increase in osteoarthritis indicates that the workload of mission native groups was indeed much higher. In this case, historic writings for the time period are verified by human skeletal analysis.

Although the osteoarthritis findings allow the bioarchaeologist to characterize patterns and levels of workload in extinct human societies, the accurate interpretation of the disorder is clouded by the fact that genetic predisposition, body weight, age, and other predisposing factors influence its presence. Therefore, like any scientific investigation, it is important that we go to other lines of evidence that might confirm findings based on the study of osteoarthritis in archaeological skeletons. So we turned to the analysis of bone structure in relation to physical activity.

In the late 1800s the German anatomist and orthopaedic surgeon Julius Wolff recognized the great sensitivity of bone to physical or mechanical stimuli.[29] He argued that in the living human skeleton, bone is placed where it is needed in response to physical demands. A century of follow-up experimental and other evidence has accrued that strongly supports what has become known as Wolff's Law of Bone Remodelling (abbreviated as Wolff's Law).

We now know that over the period of one's lifetime the long tubular bones of the skeleton (for example, femur) are constantly subjected to mechanical stimuli, especially bending and twisting forces resulting from all sorts of physical activity, such as walking, running, lifting, climbing, or even standing. In archaeological remains, we can actually measure the bone's response to the stresses that the person experienced while he or she was alive. We do this by measuring the "strength" of the bone's cross section anywhere along the diaphysis (the long shaft of the bone), just as an engineer would measure the strength of an I-beam or other materials that are used to construct a building.[30] This is based on a simple engineering principle: For any given location along a beam (or long bone diaphysis), the further the material is away from the center of a cross section, the greater its overall strength or resistance to mechanical forces (especially bending and twisting) at that location.[31] Bending a ruler illustrates this principle. If you hold each end of a ruler—one end with your left hand and one end with your right hand—and apply pressure with your thumbs to the middle of the ruler's flat surface in the direction away from your body, it bends easily. However, if you rotate the ruler 90° and try to bend the ruler by applying pressure along the narrow edge, there is little or no give. The small amount of give is due to the fact that there is simply more material in the cross section that is distributed away from a central axis, thus giving the ruler more strength or resistance to bending in this direction.

A long bone is a special kind of beam in that it is hollow. Therefore, we have to be able to measure the cross section of just the bone matter excluding the hollow space. There are a couple of ways of doing this. One way is to physically cut the bone with a saw at the region where the strength is to be measured, but this results in destroying some of the bone in order to get the measurement. A more desirable alternative has been made possible in recent years by the availability of noninvasive technology, such as computed axial tomography (CAT scans), whereby accurate images of bone cross sections are produced without cutting.

When we have a cross section image, it is then projected onto a screen, and the bone cross section is traced with an electronic stylus interfaced directly with a computer. This stylus records key points along the bone perimeter and automatically calculates cross-sectional geometric properties (values that represent measures of bone strength). This approach is especially valuable because it allows for the recording and storing of thousands of strength values and the study of many skeletons at one time.

The elegance of the structural approach is that we can directly measure the strength of bones—high values of strength indicate that the person's bones adapted to high physical demands during his or her lifetime, and conversely, low values of strength indicate reduced exposure to physical demands. In a decade-long collaboration between Christopher Ruff and me, we have determined section properties for prehistoric and mission period femora and humeri from Georgia and Florida. This comparison was ideal for testing our hypotheses about work load and activity because of the availability of the osteoarthritis data base for these same populations. The cross-sectional analysis showed a reduction in bone strength in comparing the prehistoric agriculturalists with prehistoric hunter-gatherers, which is consistent with our earlier conclusions about decline in workload.[32] The comparison of the mission femora and humeri revealed that the Indians had generally stronger bones than the prehistoric Indians, thus representing a reversal of the trend that we saw in the prehistoric populations. Our hypothesis of increasing workloads in mission Indians was also confirmed.

HOW HEALTHY WERE EARLIER PEOPLES?
HEALTH STATUS AND ILLNESS IN THE PAST

Human skeletons from archaeological sites offer an enormous opportunity to examine the history of human health, especially before the time of written records. The drawback of skeletal evidence of disease is that relatively few specific diseases leave a diagnostic signature on the skeleton. Moreover, some diseases result in either rapid death or rapid recovery, thus leaving no time for a skeletal impression to be made. On the other hand, there are a number of chronic infectious diseases—diseases that the individual lives with for a lengthy period of time (months or years)—for which there is a distinctive pattern of skeletal involvement. The study of disease in the past, called *paleopathology*, is very important to bioarchaeology because it has fostered a greater under-standing of the problems that human populations experienced in the past, es-pecially in regard to factors such as diet, environment, population size, and other circumstances that might affect disease susceptibility and transmission.

Paleopathological investigations have contributed a great deal of infor-mation for dispelling misunderstandings about disease and quality of life in prehistoric societies. For example, the myth persists that before Columbus ar-rived in the New World, Native Americans lived in an essentially disease-free environment.[33] Sociologist Russell Thornton stated that "there are over-whelming indications that the peoples of North America and the entire West-ern Hemisphere were remarkably free of serious diseases before the Europeans and Africans arrived."[34] Based on my own studies and in reviewing numer-ous reports of human skeletons from prehistoric archaeological sites in North America and South America, I have come to the conclusion that prehistoric Native Americans were far from disease-free. Tuberculosis, an infectious dis-ease caused by the bacillus *Mycobacterium tuberculosis*, was long thought to have been transported to the Americas from Europe. However, tubercular bone lesions—expressed in the form of pitting and loss of bone tissue, espe-cially in the lower vertebrae (spine)—have been documented in many pre-historic remains in North and South America (Figure 8-2 on page 122).[35] New evidence supporting the presence of TB in prehistoric societies has for the first time been observed in DNA extracted from lung and lymph tissue from a one-thousand-year-old Peruvian mummy.[36]

In addition to TB, a group of infections called treponematosis—which in-cludes both venereal (sexually-transmitted) and nonvenereal forms of syphilis—has also been observed in numerous prehistoric skeletons through-out the Americas. Among other skeletal changes, this disease results in ab-normal expansion of long bone diaphyses, such as in the tibia. The form of syphilis in prehistoric skeletons is probably nonvenereal.

Most infectious conditions observed in human skeletons are not identifi-able as to the specific diseases that caused them. The study of nonspecific in-fections lends important insight into general characteristics of human health prior to European contact. The most common of these infections are called periostitis or periosteal reactions because they involve the periosteum, the outer covering of bone. In this regard, the periosteum becomes swollen, and the surface is roughened (Figure 8-3 on page 123). There is now abundant ev-idence from the study of skeletons from numerous archaeological sites for the presence of these infections well before European contact. In some prehistoric

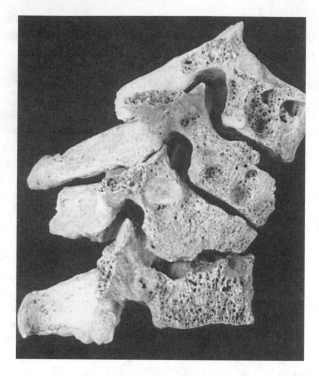

FIGURE 8-2

Large pits on sides of vertebrae, which are probably
due to advanced tuberculosis in an Indian from prehistoric Georgia

Source: Photograph by Mark C. Griffin.

sites, well over half of adults have periostitis (or a more severe form of the infection called osteomyelitis).[37]

Interestingly, bioarchaeologists are finding that populations with relatively high frequencies of infections—specific and nonspecific—tend to be
late prehistoric, especially in eastern North America.[38] I believe that this is
likely related to the fact that population size was highest during this time
and that population tended to be concentrated in some regions in sedentary,
densely crowded communities. Population crowding provides the conditions that are conducive to the spread of infectious disease because of closer
contact between people and rapid transmission of pathogens (agents such
as bacteria that cause disease). Additionally, crowding oftentimes results in
reduced sanitary conditions, thus creating an additional health hazard. Recall from my previous discussion that the increased reliance on corn resulted in a decline in nutrition in late prehistoric societies in the eastern United
States. Infection and poor nutrition have a synergistic relationship. That is,

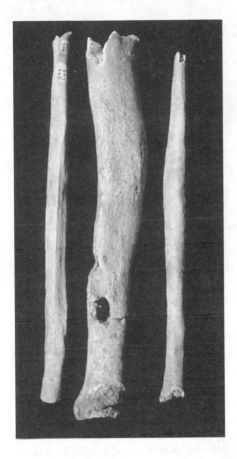

FIGURE 8-3
Periostitis or osteomyelitis from prehistoric
Georgia Indian.
Source: Photograph by Mark C. Griffin.

an infection interferes with nutrition and undernutrition lowers resistance to infection. Therefore, the general decline that we see in health was likely caused by poor nutrition, by infections, and by the synergy of nutrition and infection.

Teeth from archaeological sites offer a unique perspective on the human condition. Unlike bone tissue, once formed, teeth do not change their shape or structure except from excessive wear or cavities. Teeth are also highly sensitive to physiological problems that might arise during the years that they are developing. The crowns of secondary, or permanent, teeth (the teeth that replace the primary, or milk, teeth) begin to form a little after birth (the first molar) and are completely formed by about age twelve (the third molar). During this period, disease, poor nutrition, or a combination of both may result in disruption of the enamel formation, resulting in defects called hypoplasias. The most common type of defect is a linear groove around the tooth crown that reflects the completeness of the tooth at the time of the disruption (Figure 8-4 on page 124).[39]

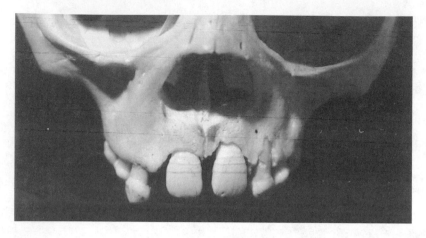

FIGURE 8-4

Hypoplasias on incisors (two middle teeth) of child. Note the series of horizontal lines across these teeth.

Source: Photograph by Barry Stark.

Hypoplasias have been found in numerous archaeological teeth worldwide.[40] These stress markers provide bioarchaeologists with an important source of information on quality of life in past human groups. Alan Goodman and his colleagues have examined the frequency of hypoplasias in populations undergoing the transition to intensive corn agriculture in the prehistoric Midwest at the Dickson Mounds site, Illinois. Given what I have said elsewhere in this chapter about declining health in corn agriculturalists in prehistoric North America, I think you can probably guess what they found in their research on dental defects. In comparison of incipient agriculturalists with full-blown corn agriculturalists they found an increase in the frequency of people affected by hypoplasia from 45 percent to 80 percent, thus demonstrating an elevation in physiological stress levels.[41]

HOW CAN INTERACTIONS BETWEEN POPULATIONS BE OBSERVED? MEASURING CONFLICT IN PAST SOCIETIES

Violence is a form of interaction that has been studied by anthropologists from a variety of approaches, but it is not always easy to find in the archaeological record. Bioarchaeologists have recently made a contribution by methodical study of the skeletal remains of the victims of conflict. We are learning that human remains offer an important perspective on the biological costs of conflict that is not available from other data sources.

George Milner has recently completed a study of a series of several hundred skeletons from the late prehistoric (ca. A.D. 1300) Norris Farms cemetery located in west-central Illinois.[42] He presents incontrovertible evidence that a significant portion of deaths in this population were due to violence. Some 16 percent of the skeletons show evidence of malevolent trauma, including scalping, mutilation, decapitation, massive skull fractures, and arrow wounds. Most injuries were lethal, but at least five adults—all women—have well-healed scalping marks on their skulls, indicating that they survived an attack or attacks. Archaeological evidence indicates that the attacks likely occurred over the span of several decades. Thus, the deaths were accretional rather than catastrophic, which is a feature of chronic intergroup warfare that anthropologists have documented in small-scale societies in the twentieth century (for example, among the Yanomami).[43]

Although warfare in the Norris Farms population could be due to several factors, Milner points to the fact that population conflicts may have surfaced because of competition with other groups in the region for food resources. Analysis of food remains from the Norris Farms village indicates that there was an abnormally low diversity of animal and plant resources available to the local population. Other evidence from the study of these skeletons shows that the population was highly stressed. For example, presence of tuberculosis, enamel hypoplasias, and lesions in the eye sockets and flat bones of the skull (called cribra orbitalia and porotic hyperostosis, respectively, representing bouts with iron deficiency anemia) indicate generally poor health.

Milner's reading of the bioarchaeological literature shows that the Norris Farms site is not an isolated occurrence of warfare in the past, but rather represents a pattern of widespread conflict, especially during later prehistory in eastern North America. He argues that escalation of conflict occurred during a time of population growth, sedentism, and probable increase in competition for productive land for raising crops.[44]

FUTURE GROWTH OF BIOARCHAEOLOGY

From early in the nineteenth century, human skeletal analysis has been recognized by anthropologists and allied disciplines as important for understanding variation and evolution of earlier societies. In recent years, the appreciation for human remains in archaeological settings for informing us of past lifeways and the human condition generally has resulted in a tremendous growth in the field.

The study of human remains in some areas of the world has become increasingly controversial as many native groups express religious and political concerns and indicate their desire for "repatriation" of skeletal remains to affiliated tribes. However, largely as an outgrowth of discussions leading to the development of the Native American Graves Protection and Repatriation Act in 1990,[45] a new spirit of compromise between anthropologists advocating permanent preservation of existing collections and members of many Native American groups has emerged. I am optimistic that this emerging dialogue between anthropologists and native groups, coupled with the advances made in recent years in bioarchaeology, will result in continued growth in the field for many years to come.

NOTES

1. Clark Spencer Larsen, "Bioarchaeological Interpretations of Subsistence Economy and Behavior from Human Skeletal Remains," in Michael B. Schiffer, ed., *Advances in Archaeological Method and Theory*, vol. 10 (San Diego: Academic Press, 1987), pp. 339–445.
2. Aidan Cockburn and Eve Cockburn, eds., *Mummies, Disease, and Ancient Cultures* (Cambridge, England: Cambridge University Press, 1980); Don Brothwell, *The Bog Man and the Archaeology of People* (Cambridge, MA: Harvard University Press, 1987); Jens Peder Hart Hansen, Jorgen Meldgaard, and Jorgen Nordqvist, eds., *The Greenland Mummies* (Washington, D.C.: Smithsonian Institution Press, 1991).
3. Ibid.
4. George J. Armelagos, David S. Carlson, and Dennis P. Van Gerven, "The Theoretical Foundations and Development of Skeletal Biology," in Frank Spencer, ed., *A History of American Physical Anthropology: 1930–1980* (New York: Academic Press, 1982), pp. 305–328.
5. Earnest A. Hooton, *The Indians of Pecos Pueblo: A Study of Their Skeletal Remains* (New Haven, CT: Yale University Press, 1930).
6. David S. Carlson and Dennis P. Van Gerven, "Masticatory Function and Post-Pleistocene Evolution in Nubia," *American Journal of Physical Anthropology* 46 (1977): 495–506.
7. Christopher B. Ruff, "Biomechanical Analyses of Archaeological Human Skeletal Samples," in Shelley R. Saunders and M. Anne Katzenberg, eds., *The Skeletal Biology of Past Peoples: Advances in Research Methods* (New York: Wiley-Liss, 1992), pp. 37–58.
8. George J. Armelagos, "You Are What You Eat," in Kristin D. Sobolik, ed., *Paleonutrition: The Diet and Health of Prehistoric Americans* (Carbondale, IL: Center for Archaeological Investigations, Southern Illinois University, Occasional Paper, no. 22, 1994), pp. 235–244.
9. Stanley H. Ambrose, "Isotopic Analysis of Paleodiets: Methodological and Interpretive Considerations," in Mary K. Sandford, ed., *Investigations of Ancient Human Tissue: Chemical Analyses in Anthropology* (Langhorne, PA: Gordon and Breach, 1993), pp. 59–130.
10. Ibid.
11. Henry P. Schwarcz and Margaret J. Schoeninger, "Stable Isotope Analyses in Human Nutritional Ecology," *Yearbook of Physical Anthropology* 34 (1991): 283–321.
12. Bruce D. Smith, "Origins of Agriculture in Eastern North America," *Science* 246 (1989): 1566–1571.
13. Larsen, "Bioarchaeological Interpretations of Subsistence Economy and Behavior from Human Skeletal Remains," pp. 357–362.

14. Mark Nathan Cohen and George J. Armelagos, eds., *Paleopathology at the Origins of Agriculture* (Orlando, FL: Academic Press, 1984).
15. David M. Reed, "Ancient Maya Diet at Copán, Honduras, as Determined through the Analysis of Stable Carbon and Nitrogen Isotopes," in Kristin D. Sobolik, ed., *Paleonutrition: The Diet and Health of Prehistoric Americans* (Carbondale, IL: Center for Archaeological Investigations, Southern Illinois University, Occasional Paper, no. 22, 1994), pp. 210–221.
16. Larsen, "Bioarchaeological Interpretations of Subsistence Economy and Behavior from Human Skeletal Remains," p. 377.
17. Robert L. Kelly, "Mobility/Sedentism: Concepts, Archaeological Measures, and Effects," *Annual Review of Anthropology* 21 (1992): 43–66.
18. Robert J. Braidwood, *Prehistoric Men*, 7th ed. (Glenview, IL: Scott, Foresman, 1967), p. 113.
19. Richard B. Lee and Irven DeVore, eds., *Man the Hunter* (Chicago: Aldine, 1968).
20. Marshall Sahlins, *Stone Age Economics* (Chicago: Aldine, 1972).
21. Larsen, "Bioarchaeological Interpretations of Subsistence Economy and Behavior from Human Skeletal Remains," pp. 388–394.
22. Donald J. Ortner, "Description and Classification of Degenerative Bone Changes in the Distal Joint Surfaces of the Humerus," *American Journal of Physical Anthropology* 28 (1968): 139–156.
23. Robert J. Miller, "Lateral Epicondylitis in a Prehistoric Central Arizona Indian Population from Nuvakwewtaqa (Chavez Pass)," in Charles F. Merbs and Robert J. Miller, eds., *Health and Disease in the Prehistoric Southwest* (Tempe: Arizona State University Anthropological Research Papers, no. 34, 1985), pp. 391–400.
24. Larsen, "Bioarchaeological Interpretations of Subsistence Economy and Behavior from Human Skeletal Remains," pp. 388–394.
25. Clark Spencer Larsen, Margaret J. Schoeninger, Christopher B. Ruff, and Dale L. Hutchinson, "Population Decline and Extinction in La Florida," in John W. Verano and Douglas H. Ubelaker, eds., *Disease and Demography in the Americas* (Washington, D.C.: Smithsonian Institution Press, 1992), pp. 25–39.
26. Ibid.
27. Ibid.
28. Ibid.
29. Julius Wolff, *The Law of Bone Remodelling*, trans. P. Maquet and R. Furlong (Berlin: Springer-Verlag, 1986).
30. Ruff, "Biomechanical Analyses of Archaeological Human Skeletal Samples."
31. Ibid.
32. Larsen, Schoeninger, Ruff, and Hutchinson, "Population Decline and Extinction in La Florida."
33. Clark Spencer Larsen, "In the Wake of Columbus: Native Population Biology in the Postcontact Americas," *Yearbook of Physical Anthropology* 37 (1994): 109–154.
34. Russell Thornton, *American Indian Holocaust and Survival: A Population History since 1492* (Norman: University of Oklahoma Press, 1987), p. 39.
35. Jane E. Buikstra, ed., *Prehistoric Tuberculosis in the Americas* (Evanston, IL: Northwestern University Archaeological Program, Scientific Papers, no. 5, 1981).
36. Wilmar Salo, Arthur C. Aufderheide, Jane Buikstra, and Todd A. Holcomb, "Identification of *Mycobacterium tuberculosis* DNA in a Pre-Columbian Peruvian Mummy," *Proceedings of the National Academy of Sciences* 91 (1994): 2091–2094.

128   CHAPTER 8

37. Larsen, "Bioarchaeological Interpretations of Subsistence Economy and Behavior from Human Skeletal Remains," pp. 380–382.
38. Ibid.; Cohen and Armelagos, eds., *Paleopathology at the Origins of Agriculture.*
39. Alan H. Goodman and Luigi L. Capasso, eds., *Recent Contributions to the Study of Enamel Developmental Defects* (Chieti, Italy: Journal of Paleopathology, Monographic Publications, no. 2, 1992).
40. Ibid.
41. Alan H. Goodman, John W. Lallo, George J. Armelagos, and Jerome C. Rose, "Health Changes at Dickson Mounds, Illinois (A.D. 950–1300)," in Mark Nathan Cohen and George J. Armelagos, eds., *Paleopathology at the Origins of Agriculture* (Orlando, FL: Academic Press, 1984), pp. 271–305.
42. George R. Milner, "Warfare in Late Prehistoric West-Central Illinois," *American Antiquity* 56 (1991): 581–603.
43. Ibid.
44. Ibid.
45. Douglas H. Ubelaker and Lauryn Guttenplan Grant, "Human Skeletal Remains: Preservation or Reburial," *Yearbook of Physical Anthropology* 32 (1989): 249–287; Julie A. Pace, ed., *Symposium: The Native American Graves Protection and Repatriation Act of 1990 and State Repatriation-Related Legislation* (Tempe: Arizona State Law Journal, 24, 1992).

SUGGESTED READINGS

Chamberlain, Andrew. *Human Remains.* Berkeley: University of California Press, 1994. An introduction to osteological analysis.
Cybulski, Jerome S. *A Greenville Burial Ground: Human Remains and Mortuary Elements in British Columbia Prehistory.* Ottawa: Archaeological Survey of Canada, Mercury Series Paper, no. 146, 1992. This is a fairly detailed description of human remains presented in a biocultural perspective. Definitions of scientific jargon are provided throughout.
Glob, P.V. *The Bog People: Iron-Age Man Preserved.* New York: Ballantine Books, 1971. A popular account of bog mummies in Denmark and northern Europe.
Larsen, Clark Spencer. "Bioarchaeological Interpretations of Subsistence Economy and Behavior from Human Skeletal Remains." In Michael B. Schiffer, ed., *Advances in Archaeological Method and Theory*, vol. 10 (San Diego: Academic Press, 1987). A comprehensive coverage of many of the issues discussed in this chapter.
Larsen, Clark Spencer. "Telltale Bones." *Archaeology* (March/April, 1992): 43–46. A popular article on Spanish mission period bioarchaeology in Georgia and Florida.

Dental Deductions:
Why and How
Anthropologists Study Teeth

John R. Lukacs

The news crew gave blank stares of disbelief, then replied, "Dental anthropology!" "I had no idea!" "You're kidding, is it really a field of study?" The local hospital had just donated their radiographic and CT scan services to assist us in the analysis of Iron Age jaws and teeth from the Sultanate of Oman. The hospital public relations office notified the press about the unusual nature of the afternoon's patients, and representatives of two TV stations and the local newspaper were there to cover a unique story.[1] My German colleague, Paul Yule, an archaeologist specializing in South Asian and Arabian Gulf cultures, had sent me several boxes containing the teeth and jaws of people he had excavated from 2,500-year-old burials at Samad Oasis (Figure 9-1 on page 130). He had requested a thorough anthropological analysis of these fragmentary but ancient specimens. At this point you might rightfully interrupt to ask several pointed questions: (1) "Why would Professor Yule, or anyone else for that matter, request an 'anthropological analysis' of a collection of ancient teeth and jaws?" (2) "What does an anthropological analysis of human teeth and jaws include?" (3) "How is such a study conducted?" (4) "What kinds of information and insights can be gained from the study of ancient teeth?" These are the kinds of questions that will be answered in the following pages. This introduction to the design, conduct, and results of research in the field of dental anthropology will use examples from my fieldwork in India and Pakistan to illustrate the research process in this unique but exciting subfield of biological anthropology.

The discipline of *dental anthropology* can be defined as the study of teeth and jaws of living or prehistoric people and their ancestors for insights concerning human behavior, health and nutritional status, or genetic relationship of populations to one another. Any process or mechanism that influences the structure or function of teeth, jaws, or face is within the domain of dental anthropology.[2] The wide range of ways in which culture and

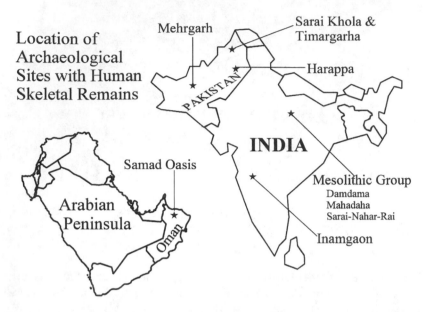

FIGURE 9-1   LOCATION MAP OF ARCHAEOLOGICAL SITES WITH DENTAL REMAINS

environment interact with the human dentition makes dental anthropology a diverse discipline; one that embraces subjects as different as genetic influences on the formation of dental tissues of modern humans, to the varied nondietary ways in which Neandertals may have used their teeth. This area of study differs in several important ways from dentistry, orthodontics, and other clinical approaches to the dentition. Anthropologists are concerned primarily with the interaction of biological and cultural systems in a natural setting. Dentists and their clinical colleagues seek to preserve the health or eliminate diseases of the teeth and jaws of their patients. Dentists treat individuals and family members who are often from ethnically diverse backgrounds. For anthropologists, the primary unit of study is a sample derived from a natural biological or breeding population, and ideally all anthropological studies of the dentition are conducted within the analytic framework of evolutionary biology. Anthropologists see variation in the morphology (form and structure), size, and patterns of disease of modern human teeth as the outcome of a long evolutionary history in which the interaction of biology, culture, and environment has produced different dental variations in every human population.

The importance of teeth in anthropological studies derives from attributes of the teeth themselves and from the indelible marks that bio-cultural interactions leave on the teeth during and after they form. First, since teeth and jaws are among the hardest parts of the body, they preserve better and more abundantly than other body parts in archaeological sites and in fossil deposits. Initially this may seem strange, given the high rates of dental decay documented for many agricultural and industrial societies; however, during life the oral cavity contains food debris as well as chemical and bacterial conditions that may lead to their rapid destruction in the absence of good hygiene. Once buried, and free from the bacterio-chemical environment of the living oral cavity, teeth and jaws may be preserved in excellent condition for thousands or millions of years. Second, many aspects of dental anatomy, including size of the teeth, their morphological details, and the timing of their development, for example, are known to be under genetic control. This feature of the dentition leads to the corollary that populations that display many similarities in tooth structure and size are more closely related to one another than those whose dental structure is quite different. Third, since our two sets of teeth develop slowly over a long period of time, and are not easily modified after they form, our teeth provide an indelible and retrospective indicator of physiological status during development—from prenatal times to about twenty years of age.

The Iron Age Omani specimens revealed an interesting finding. Most adults in this series had experienced some loss of their permanent teeth before death. This is not necessarily an unusual situation in archaeologically derived skeletal collections, depending on the age structure of the sample and on the diet and the environment in which the group lived. However, in the Omani series, molar teeth were lost quite early in life—adolescents and young adults commonly suffered loss of one or more molar teeth. A review of the archaeological record shows that date palms were a common feature of the Samad Oasis. These trees provided shade for humans and crops, and also provided an abundant source of sweet foods for youth of the Iron Age. Frequent consumption of dates, perhaps coupled with somewhat less frequent episodes of dental hygiene, resulted in high rates of dental caries (popularly called cavities), dental infections, and early loss of teeth.[3] The radiographic analysis of the Samad jaws, so intriguing to the press and public, showed that no root fragments were imbedded in them. This finding implies that crude dental extractions were not practiced by these ancient Omanis, and that loss of teeth early in life was exclusively due to dietary factors—consumption of dates. This finding is of interest to archaeologists because it permits them to gain a more complete picture of behavioral patterns in the Samad Oasis 2,500 years ago. Yet it is only one aspect of our multifaceted analysis of the Samad dentition. In association with the analysis of dental diseases, the size and morphology of the teeth have also been documented so that interrelationships between tooth size, morphology, and dental disease can be investigated. This review will begin by introducing several key concepts in dental anthropology. These concepts are prerequisite to considering three examples in which the careful study of teeth has enhanced our knowledge of biocultural interaction among prehistoric humans in Asia.

BASIC CONCEPTS IN DENTAL ANTHROPOLOGY

Teeth are composed of four biological tissues: enamel, dentine, pulp, and cementum. Enamel is the white outermost covering of the portion of the tooth
that projects into the oral cavity (Figure 9-2). It is the most durable tissue in
the body and is derived from the embryonic tissue ectoderm. Due to its embryonic origin, enamel is the only dental tissue that lacks recuperative power;
it cannot respond to stress or regenerate if damaged. Dentine is the tissue that
comprises the bulk of a tooth's substance. Dentine formed at the time a tooth
is initially developing is referred to as primary dentine. It is yellowish in color,
softer than enamel, and derived from mesodermal tissue embryonically. In
response to decay or heavy chewing stresses, cells lining the internal surface
of the dentine layer will respond by initiating additional dentine production.
This recuperative dentine is called secondary or reparative dentine, and can
be visually differentiated from primary dentine. The third dental tissue, cementum, is also of mesodermal origin and covers the roots of the tooth. Teeth
are held in their sockets (or alveoli) by the periodontal ligament, a band-like
tissue that is anchored in cementum on one end and attaches to the alveolar
bone on the other. The dental pulp is composed of loose connective tissue that
fills the internal chamber of the tooth—the pulp chamber. Blood vessels and
nerves enter the pulp chamber through a small opening at the apex of the
root. Major anatomical parts of the tooth are the crown, neck (cervix), and
root (Figure 9-2). The crown may be more specifically designated as the

Basic Anatomical Structures of Teeth

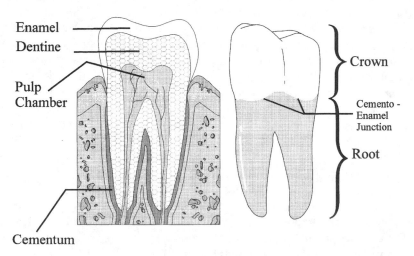

FIGURE 9-2   BASIC ANATOMICAL STRUCTURES OF TEETH:
CROSS-SECTION AND SURFACE FEATURES

anatomical crown, or the portion of the tooth above the cemento-enamel junction, or the surgical crown, that portion of the tooth projecting into the oral cavity or visible above the gum. The dental cervix is the line of contact between the enamel and cement, known as the cemento-enamel junction.

Humans, like most mammals, have two sets of teeth. The first set of teeth is generally called the "baby" or "milk" dentition, though anthropologists commonly refer to them as the "primary" or "deciduous" dentition. You may think of deciduous teeth, which are lost and replaced by their permanent successors, as similar to deciduous trees that lose their leaves each fall but are replaced by new ones each spring. Modern humans have twenty deciduous teeth, which are normally replaced by thirty-two permanent teeth. Differences in morphology and size of crown and roots make it easy, after training and some practice, to identify isolated teeth as either deciduous or permanent. Another mammalian feature of the human dentition is the morphological difference between tooth types, a characteristic known as heterodonty. The permanent dentition consists of four tooth classes: spatulate incisors, conical and single cusped canines, premolars with two or more cusps, and the rectangular, complexly structured molar teeth. Different structures are associated with different functions; the nipping and cutting of incisor teeth is distinct from the crushing and grinding function of the molars. A heterodont dentition permits mammals to masticate, or thoroughly chew food, thus beginning the digestive breakdown of food in the oral cavity. This is essential for animals such as mammals that have a high and constant body temperature in association with an energetic activity pattern. The single, holding-grasping function of the reptilian mouth is associated with a homodont dentition (teeth with the same shape), low and variable body temperature, and a less active lifestyle. This contrast between mammalian and reptilian dental structure shows that tooth shape and function are closely interrelated, and dental function is tightly linked to the behavioral activity pattern of an organism. Having established the basic fundamentals of dental anthropology, a series of examples will be considered with the intention of revealing both the methods and techniques used, as well as the significance of the results and conclusions derived from this research.

GETTING THE FACTS: FIELDWORK PLACES
DENTAL DATA IN CULTURAL CONTEXT

The three examples of research in dental anthropology to be discussed later involve the analysis of (1) dental disease and subsistence, (2) dental morphology and biological relationships, and (3) tooth size, technology, and biological relationships. Each of these topics represents an area of dental anthropology research to which I have personally contributed. My research involves the field excavation (Harappa) and laboratory preparation of human skeletal and dental remains (Ganges Plains sites, Inamgaon, Mehrgarh) for analysis. Such work is very time consuming and requires repeated visits of several months duration each year to remote field locations in Baluchistan and Punjab Provinces, Pakistan, and to laboratory and field sites in the cities of Pune and Allahabad, India.[4] The results reported here are based upon skeletal remains from archaeological sites excavated within the past twenty years, and represent new insights into the prehistoric peoples and cultures of the Indian subcontinent.

Late stone age cultures of the middle Gangetic Plains north of Allahabad consist of microlithic tools and grinding stones, but lack pottery, and date approximately from 8000 to 5000 B.C. (see Figure 9-1 on page 130 for site locations). A similar pattern of "mesolithic" culture, including a nomadic hunting and gathering lifestyle and dependence on wild plant and animal species, was discovered from archaeological excavations at *Damdama* (DDM), *Mahadaha* (MDH), and *Sarai-Nahar-Rai* (SNR).[5] Archaeological sites in the greater Indus Valley of Pakistan include *Neolithic Mehrgarh* (MR 3), a preceramic, early agricultural site with a mixed economic subsistence pattern found in Baluchistan Province ca. 6000 B.C.; *Chalcolithic Mehrgarh* (MR 2), where agriculture, animal husbandry, and wheel-made pottery was common at approximately 4500 B.C.; and *Bronze Age Harappa* (HAR) to the northeast, in Punjab Province, a significantly more urban and intensively agricultural site of the Indus Valley (or Harappan) Civilization (ca. 2500 B.C.).[6] In western India, the early agricultural village site that has yielded abundant human skeletal remains, mostly of infants, is known as *Inamgaon* (INM).[7] Associated with a chalcolithic culture known as Jorwe, most human remains from Inamgaon derive from levels dating between 1100 and 700 B.C. Two post-Harappan, early iron-using cultures of northwestern Pakistan that have provided dental remains for analysis, include *Sarai Khola* (SKH) and *Timargarha* (TMG).[8]

DENTAL DISEASE AND SUBSISTENCE TRANSITIONS

The study of dental disease in prehistoric human skeletons is usually undertaken for different reasons by different anthropologists. The absence of archaeological indications of diet may lead one investigator to analyze the pattern of dental disease in a skeletal series to gain insight into the kinds of food people consumed. In another case, dental disease patterns may be investigated to determine if sex or status subgroups within an ancient society consumed the same or different kinds of food, and how this relates to their general health status. While people may rely on one key staple or resource, differences in food preparation methods between societies may produce distinctive patterns of dental disease of interest to the anthropologist. In the example given later, dental diseases in several skeletal series from one region are compared to reveal how changing patterns of subsistence have a direct impact upon changing patterns of dental health.

One of the most profound and significant changes in human subsistence systems (how people get their food) is the shift from hunting and gathering for food to reliance upon the products of agriculture and of domesticated animals. This transition in subsistence behavior, and its corollaries such as increased population density and increased sedentary habits, has directly affected human health, the robustness of our skeletal system, the degree of sexual dimorphism, and the type and frequency of dental diseases that afflict us.[9] The investigation of a relationship between dental disease and subsistence pattern requires the adoption of a research design consisting of a specific methodology that is consistently applied to several skeletal collections whose archaeological context provides a clear indication of subsistence pattern.

Generally, the anthropologist will observe and record the presence or absence of several pathological dental lesions in all skeletons from a site that contains a large collection of teeth and jaws. A typical list of dental disease lesions to be studied might include abscesses, antemortem loss of teeth, caries, calculus, enamel hypoplasia, exposure of the pulp chamber, hypercementosis, and resorption of alveolar bone. A dental abscess, for example, is a well-defined pocket of pus associated with an infected tooth. Bone resorption within the jaw accompanies a chronic infection and produces a bony space within the jaw. Antemortem tooth loss refers to loss of teeth prior to death, a condition recognized by the partial or complete obliteration of tooth sockets through the process of bone resorption and remodeling. An affliction commonly observed in agricultural peoples is dental caries, or a demineralization and cavitation of tooth surface. Oral bacteria produce acidic byproducts that cause the breakdown of dental tissues. Enamel hypoplasia is a deficiency in enamel thickness due to reduced activity of enamel forming cells at the time of enamel formation. Defects appear as linear grooves, pits, or depressed areas, especially evident on the anterior surfaces of incisor and canine teeth. The results of a pathological analysis of the dentition are often portrayed in two ways: individual count frequency and tooth count frequency. The first method presents the number of individuals afflicted with a dental disease divided by the total number of individuals for which a dental condition could be observed. Since human skeletons derived from archaeological contexts are often incompletely preserved or damaged, the sample size for computing the individual frequency of dental conditions will vary. The second, or tooth count method, presents results as the number of teeth affected by a dental condition divided by the total number of teeth in which the condition could be observed.

Dental pathology profiles based upon individual count frequencies for three archaeological sites in the greater Indus Valley—Neolithic Mehrgarh (MR 3), Chalcolithic Mehrgarh (MR 2), and Bronze Age Harappa (HAR)—are presented in Figure 9-3 on page 136. The progressive increase in most dental diseases with time and increasing cultural complexity is clearly evident. The gradual deterioration of dental health through time in the greater Indus

DENTAL DISEASE AT HARAPPA: A COMPARATIVE VIEW

(individual count)

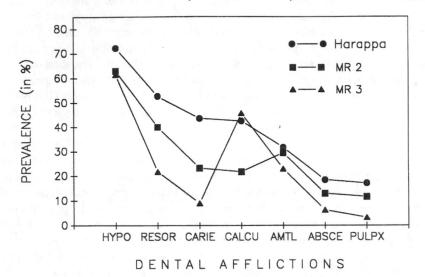

FIGURE 9-3   DENTAL PATHOLOGY PROFILES
OF ARCHAEOLOGICAL SITES IN THE GREATER INDUS VALLEY

Valley appears to coincide with an increasing dependence upon agriculture as a means of subsistence. The greater reliance upon agriculture and more sophisticated food processing equipment results in foods that are more refined, finer in texture, and stickier—features that increase the potential for causing dental caries. Similar relationships between diet and dental disease have been demonstrated elsewhere, especially among Native North Americans, whose dental health declined even more dramatically with the adoption of maize (corn) as a dietary staple.

Caries is the dental condition most responsive to changes in diet, and serves as an accurate barometer for the shift from a coarse and varied diet like that of hunters and gatherers, to one that is less diverse, soft, and sticky—typical of many agriculturalists. The use of an alternative reporting method, based on tooth count frequencies, confirms the findings reported earlier on the basis of individual count frequencies. The tooth count frequency for dental caries in prehistoric human skeletal series from the Indian subcontinent shows that mesolithic hunting and foraging peoples have very low dental caries rates (between 0.0 percent and 1.2 percent) compared with Iron Age peoples (between 4.4 percent and 7.7 percent), who are generally more reliant upon agriculture. Second, within the greater Indus Valley, tooth count caries rates increase dramatically through time, in association with developing material culture and increased reliance upon agricultural products. This trend is visible in the progressively higher caries rates from Neolithic Mehrgarh (MR 3; 1.8 percent) to Chalcolithic Mehrgarh (MR 2; 6.9 percent) to Harappa (HAR; 12.1 percent).[10]

In conclusion, a clear relationship has been shown between major cultural variables of diet and subsistence, and their impact on dental health. Generally, the subsistence shift from hunting and foraging to agriculture, and the attendant dietary change from coarse, unrefined food to soft, finely textured, and highly processed foods results in a dramatic increase in dental disease. This escalation of poor dental health is evident in both the number of individuals afflicted and the percentage of teeth affected by specific dental diseases.

DENTAL MORPHOLOGY AND BIOLOGICAL RELATIONSHIPS

The question of biological relationships between people is an important one. Some people worship their ancestors, others seek genealogical links to colonists (Mayflower descendants), or to important people in world history. Anthropologists investigate the biological relationships of prehistoric and living peoples of the world for a variety of reasons. One goal is to better understand the early history of human populations and how they dispersed and colonized the earth. A biological history of humanity is the ultimate objective of this research.[11] This research approach is well illustrated by the attention anthropologists have devoted to people whose biology and culture appear inconsistent with their modern surroundings. The Ainu of Japan, pygmies of the Andaman and Philippine Islands, the Gypsies of eastern Europe, and the Lapps of northern Europe are some typical examples. Unfortunately, tracing the biological history of human populations through time is difficult. Complications arise in part because the genetic traits upon which the assessment of biological relationship are typically based, such as blood types and variation in DNA structure, are not always reliably determined for prehistoric skeletons. Another complicating factor is that human skeletons are not available from all time periods or from all regions of the world, so availability of data is patchy. Relying on *genetic features of the dentition*, anthropologists are able to trace human and prehuman history over millions of years into the distant past when we shared a common ancestor with the great apes of Africa. In the absence of DNA and genetic features of blood, teeth are ideal for reconstructing biological relationships between human populations because they preserve well after burial, display many genetically controlled variations of the crown and root, are easily observable in living and prehistoric specimens, and vary in anatomy from one region of the world to another.

The early farming village of Inamgaon in western India is unique in many ways. In addition to several unusual clay coffin burials of adults, abundant child and infant burials were discovered at this site. Infants and children are very rarely found in prehistoric cemeteries because their bones are incompletely developed, thin, and much more fragile than adult bones. However, at Inamgaon 85 percent of the skeletons are immature. In this unique case infants and children were buried in twin urns placed mouth-to-mouth beneath the house floor, thus protecting the bones from destruction by soil compaction and chemical deterioration. The abundance of children's teeth preserved at the site provided an opportunity to investigate the question of the biological identity or affinity of the people of Inamgaon. Since Asian and European people differ in a number of their genetically determined dental features, a question arose regarding which dental pattern the people of Inamgaon were most like. The dental traits generally included in a study of morphological variation may include twenty-five or more variations in shape and form of crown and root. Typical observations might note the number of cusps on a molar tooth, distinctive shape of incisor teeth (shovel shape), the pattern of grooves on a molar crown, or the presence or absence of several specific extra cusps on molar teeth. The vocabulary of dental morphology is complex, and standards have been established so anthropologists studying dental morphology can be assured that they evaluate and compare similar attributes.[12] Typically observed morphological traits, including those that distinguish Asian and European dental patterns, are listed in Table 9-1 and illustrated in Figure 9-4. A graphic presentation of primary differences in deciduous dental trait frequencies that distinguish Asian and European dental complexes is provided in Figure 9-5. The Asian dental complex is characterized by high frequencies

TABLE 9-1   DEFINITION OF DENTAL MORPHOLOGICAL TRAITS

Shovel Shape (Incisors): Elevated margins or ridges along the lingual surface of the upper incisor teeth give this surface of the tooth a shovel-like appearance. Variation is categorized as absent, slight, moderate, or marked.

Carabelli's Trait (Upper Molars): A variation in enamel surface on the anterior lingual aspect upper molar teeth. Expression is graded as absent, pit, groove, or cusp.

Cusp Number (Premolar and Molar): A simple count of the number of cusps (elevated or projecting points) on the tooth crown. Normally molars display either three, four, or five cusps; less frequently six or seven may be present.

Cusp-6 or Entoconulid (Lower Molars): A specific extra cusp that occasionally appears on the posterior margin of lower molar teeth. It may be recorded as present or absent, or scored along a size continuum.

Cusp-7 or Metaconulid (Lower Molars): A specific extra cusp that may be expressed between the two major cusps on the lingual surface of the tooth. Variation is scored in the same way as cusp-6.

Protostylid (Lower Molars): A trait occurring on the anterior cheek surface of lower molar teeth that displays a pattern of variation similar to Carabelli's trait. Variation evaluated as pit, groove, or cusp.

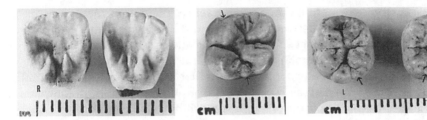

FIGURE 9-4   DENTAL MORPHOLOGICAL TRAITS OF THE DECIDUOUS DENTITION
Left: INM-163. Lingual surface of maxillary central incisor teeth. Note the double median lingual ridges and trace shovel. **Middle:** INM-163. Upper left first molar. Note the well developed metaconule (C-5) and the Carabelli's trait (top). **Right:** INM-177. Occlusal view, lower first molar teeth. Note the Y groove pattern and the moderately developed entoconuclid (C-6).

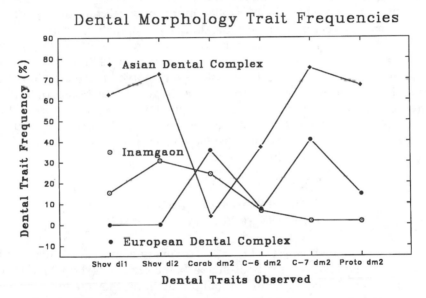

FIGURE 9-5   DECIDUOUS DENTAL TRAIT FREQUENCIES FOR ASIANS,
EUROPEANS, AND PREHISTORIC SKELETONS FROM CHALCOLITHIC INAMGAON

of incisor shoveling, extra molar cusps six and seven, and the protostylid, but Carabelli's trait is infrequent. By contrast, the European dental complex is distinguished by low frequencies of incisor shoveling and molar cusp six, moderate frequencies of Carabelli's trait and molar cusp seven, and low incidence of the protostylid. These patterns of deciduous dental variation, and similar frequency differences that are found in the permanent teeth of adults, were initially described by the Japanese anthropologist Kazuro Hanihara. The pattern of dental trait frequencies found in primary teeth at prehistoric Inamgaon displays values intermediate between the Asian and European dental complexes. In the frequency of molar cusp six, Inamgaon and Europeans are essentially similar; and in two traits, molar cusp seven and the protostylid, the Inamgaon dentition displays values lower than either Asian or European dental patterns. The overall impression one gains from this trait-by-trait comparison is that the prehistoric people of Inamgaon exhibit a dental trait pattern that is in some features intermediate between the Asian and European dental complexes, but that certain traits are clearly closer to the European pattern. This greater degree of affinity in dental variation between prehistoric Inamgaon and Europeans is generally consistent with archaeological and recent historical evidence suggesting the importance of population movement into the Indian subcontinent from the northwest. By contrast, the Himalayas form a less easily penetrated geographical barrier between India and east Asia, precluding major biological influences from central and eastern Asia.

In summation, genetically controlled morphological traits of the human dentition provide very different insights about past populations than the study of dental diseases. The study of morphological variations of the deciduous and permanent teeth yields clues about the biological relationships among prehistoric peoples and between past and living peoples. In conjunction with archaeological and linguistic evidence, clues of genetic relationship derived from the teeth assist anthropologists in tracing the biological history of humanity. Documenting the northeast Asian origins of Native Americans and the northwest African origins of Canary Islanders on the basis of dental traits are examples of the success of this research approach.[13]

TOOTH SIZE AND TECHNOLOGY: "WHAT BIG TEETH YOU HAD, GRANDMA!"[14]

The most conspicuous aspect of biological diversity in human populations is skin color. While differences in body shape, hair color and texture, blood proteins, and DNA also characterize human populations, they are not nearly as strikingly obvious. Variations in tooth morphology (see earlier section) and tooth size (this section) are more subtle and are concealed from the eyes of most people (with the exception of dentists and dental anthropologists). While discrimination has primarily been based upon differences in skin color, cases of differential treatment based on body size (fat people) and stature (short people) also occur. By contrast, no cases of differential treatment of people with large or small teeth are known to exist, despite the considerable variation that exists in size and morphology of our teeth. The purpose of this section is to show how anthropologists study tooth size, to describe patterns of tooth size variation through space and time, and to explain how and why this variation exists.

Unlike morphological traits of the teeth that are either present or absent, tooth size varies along a continuous scale, like stature or body weight. While sophisticated methods of analyzing dental dimensions are continuously being developed and tested, such as moiré contourography and digital photography, they are often expensive and laborious, and may require technical equipment.[15] The most widely used technique of dental measurement is the simple measurement of two dimensions of the tooth crown: length (mesio-distal dimension) and breadth (bucco-lingual dimension) (see Figure 9-6 on page 142). Many other aspects of tooth size are occasionally measured by researchers for specific purposes. These include crown height, root length, cusp volume, and intercuspal distance, for example. However, common problems associated with normal tooth use or structure prevent easy determination of dental dimensions. For example, loss of enamel and dentine through wear reduces crown height, roots are often concealed in the bony tissue of the jaws, and the lack of systematic standards for dental measurement results in variations between researchers. On a worldwide basis our current knowledge of tooth size variation is largely based upon the mesio-distal and bucco-lingual dimensions of unworn, or very slightly worn teeth. Variation in dental dimensions has been described for many living and prehistoric people of the world, though some continents, like Europe, are much better documented than others, like Africa and South America. Many published studies of dental dimensions, however, are of little value to anthropologists. These clinical studies, often conducted by orthodontists for the purpose of understanding dental crowding and malocclusion, are based on groups comprising people from a variety of different ethnic backgrounds. Such groups do not represent valid biological populations, nor do they represent populations that shared a specific culture or adapted to a particular environment over long periods of time.

Two different perspectives have been employed in attempting to understanding human variation in dental dimensions: (1) the techno-cultural approach, and (2) the genetic affinity approach. The techno-cultural approach, championed by anthropologist C. Loring Brace, envisions an inverse relationship between tooth size and culture. The basis for this perspective is that populations with small teeth generally tend to exhibit technologically developed or complex material culture. Agriculturalists with complex food-processing equipment and pottery have smaller teeth than hunter-gatherers and foragers whose cultures and food processing technologies are much more basic, and associated with much larger teeth. This approach is based upon the overall size of the dentition and stresses the role that teeth play in food processing. Variation in tooth size among peoples reflects differences in the extent to which material culture has replaced the functions of teeth in food-processing activities. The techno-cultural approach focuses on crown area as a biologically meaningful measure of tooth size. Crown area is easily computed by multiplying crown length by crown breadth. Individual

MEASUREMENT OF DENTAL CROWN DIAMETERS

MD   Mesiodistal
BL   Buccolingual
●   Mesial surface of tooth

INCISOR	LOWER MOLAR	UPPER MOLAR

OCCLUSAL   OCCLUSAL   OCCLUSAL

LINGUAL   LINGUAL   LINGUAL

MESIAL   MESIAL   MESIAL

DENTAL CROWN INDICES

CROWN AREA   = MD x BL   measures occlusal surface area

CROWN INDEX = $\dfrac{MD}{BL}$ x 100   measures crown shape

CROWN MODULE = $\dfrac{MD + BL}{2}$ measures crown perimeter

MD = 12.2   MD = 10.3

BL = 10.5   BL = 9.4

128 I mm²	CROWN AREA	96.82 mm²
116.19	CROWN INDEX	109.57
11.35 mm²	CROWN MODULE	9.85 mm

● mesial surface of tooth

**FIGURE 9-6   MEASUREMENT OF DENTAL CROWN
DIMENSIONS AND COMPUTATION OF CROWN INDICES**

values for each tooth can then be summed for all upper and lower teeth, resulting in a quantity known as total crown area that is expressed in millimeters squared. Australian aboriginals display very large teeth with a total crown area of 1,500 mm^2, while some European and Chinese populations exhibit crown areas of between 900 and 1,000 mm^2 and have the smallest teeth yet recorded.

The progress of tooth size reduction through time can be readily seen in South Asia, where over a period of about 7,000 years human tooth size decreased by about 125 mm^2. Adherents to the techno-cultural perspective on tooth size envision this progressive decrease in dental dimensions as being causally linked to changes in diet and improvements in material culture. The presence of a loose but obvious correlation between increasing cultural complexity and decrease in tooth size is graphically displayed for South Asia in Figure 9-7. Techno-cultural complexity increases from left to right across the horizontal axis, while the vertical axis indicates total tooth crown area in mm^2. Note that sites included in this graph embrace a broad range of cultural adaptations, from late stone age cultures on the left to iron-using cultures on the right. In association with the increase in cultural complexity,

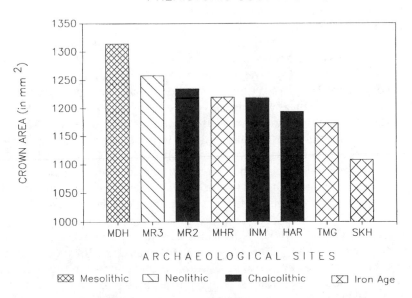

FIGURE 9-7   BI-VARIATE PLOT OF TOOTH SIZE AND MATERIAL CULTURE

tooth size reduces. The evolutionary mechanisms that bring about the observed reduction in dental crown dimensions are a matter of continuing controversy, and little consensus exists over competing models that favor one or another of the primary forces of evolution.[16]

The dental dimensions and biological affinity approach to variation in dental dimensions, espoused by Ed Harris, emphasizes similarities and differences in the patterning of dental dimensions between populations. In this approach, multivariate statistical methods are used to elucidate a small number of genetic factors that influence the pattern of dental dimensions in a population.[17] Populations with similar factors and patterns are interpreted to be more closely related to one another than populations that display different factors and patterns. Principal components analysis (PCA) is a multivariate method that is used to reduce the sixty-four length and breadth measurements on thirty-two teeth to three or four major components that account for the pattern of variation in dental dimensions in a population. A comparison of these components and other factors derived from PCA are interpreted to reflect genetic controls that contribute to patterns of tooth size variation between tooth classes (incisor, canine, premolar and molar) and dimensions (length and breadth). Principal components analysis was recently used in a study of permanent tooth size in an eighteenth century slave population of South Carolina.[18] As comparative samples, dental dimensions of permanent teeth from Inamgaon and Neolithic Mehrgarh were included in the analysis with interesting results. When components of permanent tooth size are plotted graphically, the group most similar to Inamgaon is a sample of American whites, an observation that reaffirms the results of dental morphology reported earlier on the basis of deciduous teeth. This plot of tooth size components also reveals a close relationship between the prehistoric dental sample from Neolithic Mehrgarh and the Inamgaon sample, a relationship initially discovered during my comparative analysis of dental morphological traits among prehistoric South Asians.[19] The high level of correspondence between results obtained from the independent analysis of dental morphology and tooth size variation is encouraging, especially since different data sets and distinct statistical methods point to identical results. More recently, Hemphill has applied multivariate statistical methods to the dimensions of permanent teeth of living castes and tribes of India. His findings reveal that patterns of tooth size in South Asia are indirectly influenced by the impact of social organization and linguistic factors on mating systems.[20]

In summary, each approach to variation in human tooth size emphasizes a different aspect of dental dimensions: The tooth size and technology school stresses the functional importance of total tooth size, while the dental dimensions and biological affinity school regards patterns of dental variation—from incisors, to canines, to premolars, to molars—as indicative of underlying genetic determinants of size variation and consequently indicative of genetic relationships between human populations.

DENTAL ANTHROPOLOGY: SUMMARY AND PROSPECTS

This brief review of the field known as dental anthropology provides a limited introduction to the kinds of questions, methods, and results often derived from an analysis of the dentition of living and prehistoric human populations. The topics selected for discussion in this review included diet, subsistence and dental health, dental morphology as a measure of biological affinity, and tooth size variation in relation to masticatory function and population relationships. These are topics in which I have had personal research experience, and though they appear to be wide-ranging, these subjects represent a limited array of the potential fields of enquiry within dental anthropology. Other exciting topics in the discipline of dental anthropology include: the rates of dental maturation and age assessment, dental indicators of tooth wear and tool use, enamel defects as a measure of health and nutritional deficiency, dental wear and dietary differences between the sexes. The sources cited in the notes below and in the Suggested Readings list will direct you to more detailed discussion of many of these specific topics. If this introduction to dental anthropology inspires some students to read and study further in the area of biological anthropology generally, or dental anthropology in particular, it will have accomplished its main objective.

NOTES

1. Thanks are due to Dan Steinberg, Public Relations; and thanks are due to the Department of Radiology, Sacred Heart Hospital, Eugene, Oregon, for collaborative assistance in research and for taking the initiative in organizing news coverage for this phase of our research. The analysis of the human remains from Oman was conducted by University of Oregon graduate student Greg Nelson, under my supervision.
2. For additional information about the discipline of dental anthropology and examples of the range of research topics embraced by it, see G. Richard Scott, "Dental Anthropology," *Encyclopedia of Human Biology* 2 (1991): 789–804; G. Richard Scott and Christy G. Turner, II, "Dental Anthropology," *Annual Reviews in Anthropology* 17 (1988): 99–126.
3. For further information refer to Greg C. Nelson and John R. Lukacs, "Early Antemortem Tooth Loss Due to Caries in a Late Iron Age Sample from the Sultanate of Oman," *American Journal of Physical Anthropology,* suppl. 18 (1994): 152. For additional details on the dental health of prehistoric people of the Arabian Gulf states, consult Judith Littleton and Bruno Frohlich, "An Analysis of Dental Pathology and Diet on Historic Bahrain," *Paleorient* 15 (1989): 59–75; Judith Littleton and Bruno Frohlich, "Fish-Eaters and Farmers: Dental Pathology in the Arabian Gulf," *American Journal of Physical Anthropology* 92 (1993): 427–447.
4. My research at Mehrgarh was possible through the courtesy of Jean-Francois and Catherine Jarrige; at Harappa by invitation of the late George F. Dales, Jr.; at Inamgaon through the courtesy of Hasmukh D. Sankalia, Shantaram B. Deo, Madhukar

K. Dhavalikar, and Virenda N. Misra, successive Directors of Deccan College Post-Graduate and Research Institute, Pune; at Allahabad through the co-operation of the late Govardhan R. Sharma, U. N. Roy, and Sibesh C. Bhattacharya, Department of Ancient History, Culture, and Archaeology, Allahabad University. Funding for this work has been provided by the Alexander von Humboldt Foundation, American Institute of Indian Studies, American Philosophical Society, Council for International Exchange of Scholars, Fulbright-Hayes Program, National Geographic Society, National Science Foundation, and Smithsonian Institution. The research results reported here would not have been accomplished without the continuing financial support of these agencies.

5. Archaeological reports include G. R. Sharma, V. D. Misra, D. Mandel, B. B. Misra, and J. N. Pal, *Beginnings of Agriculture* (Allahabad: Abinash Prakashan, 1980); J. N. Pal, "Some New Light on the Mesolithic Burial Practices of the Ganga Valley: Evidence from Mahadaha, Pratapgarh, Uttar Pradesh," *Man and Environment* 9 (1985): 28–37; J. N. Pal, "Mesolithic Double Burials from Recent Excavations at Damdama," *Man and Environment* 12 (1988): 115–122; and J. N. Pal, "Mesolithic Human Burials from the Gangetic Plain, North India," *Man and Environment* 17 (1992): 35–44. The biological features of human skeletons from these sites are discussed in monographs by Kenneth A. R. Kennedy, Nancy C. Lovell, and Christopher B. Burrow, "Mesolithic Human Remains from the Gangetic Plain: Sarai Nahar Rai," *Occasional Papers and Theses, South Asia Program*, vol. 10 (Ithaca: Cornell University, 1986), pp. 1–89; Kenneth A. R. Kennedy et al., "Mesolithic Human Remains from the Gangetic Plain: Mahadaha," *Occasional Papers and Theses, South Asia Program* (Ithaca: Cornell University, 1992); and in a review article by John R. Lukacs and J. N. Pal, "Mesolithic Subsistence in North India: Inferences from Dental Pathology and Odontometry," *Current Anthropology* 34 (1993): 745–765.

6. The best general synthesis of Indian archaeology is by Bridgit and Raymond Allchin, *The Rise of Civilization in India and Pakistan* (Cambridge: Cambridge University Press, 1982). Excavations at Mehrgarh are summarized by Jean-Francois Jarrige and Richard Meadow, "Antecedents of Civilization in the Indus Valley," *Scientific American* 243 (1980): 122–133; Monique Lechevallier and G. Quivron, "The Neolithic in Baluchistan: New Evidences from Mehrgarh," in H. Hartel, ed., *South Asian Archaeology, 1979* (Berlin: Dietrich Reimer Verlag, 1981), pp. 71–92. Burial practices have been described for neolithic Mehrgarh by Pascal Sellier, "The Contribution of Paleoanthropology to the Interpretation of a Functional Funerary Structure: The Graves from Neolithic Mehrgarh Period IB," in Catherine Jarrige, ed., *South Asian Archaeology, 1989* (Madison: Prehistory Press, 1992), pp. 253–266; and for chalcolithic Mehrgarh by A. Samzun and Pascal Sellier, "First Anthropological and Cultural Evidences of the Funerary Practices of the Chalcolithic Population of Mehrgarh, Pakistan," in Janine Schotsmans and M. Taddei, eds., *South Asian Archaeology 1983* (Naples: Instituto Universitario Orientale, 1985), pp. 91–119. The dental anthropology of human remains from these sites is discussed in greater detail by John R. Lukacs, D. H. Retief, and Jean-Francois Jarrige, "Dental Disease in Prehistoric Baluchistan," National Geographic Research 1 (1985): 184–197; John R. Lukacs "Dental Morphology and Odontometrics of Early Agriculturalists from Neolithic Mehrgarh, Pakistan," in Donald E. Russell, Jean-Pierre Santoro, and Denise Sigogneau-Russell, eds., *Teeth Revisited: Memoires du Museum*, serie (C) 53 (Paris: Musee d'Histoire Naturelle, 1988), pp. 287–305; and John R. Lukacs and

Lori Minderman, "Dental Pathology and Agricultural Intensification from Ne-olithic to Chalcolithic Periods at Mehrgarh [Baluchistan, Pakistan]," in Catherine Jarrige, ed., *South Asian Archaeology 1989* (Madison: Prehistory Press, 1992), pp. 167–179. For recent archaeological results at Harappa, see Richard H. Meadow, "Harappa Excavations 1986–1990: A Multidisciplinary Approach to Third Millen-nium Urbanism," *Monographs in World Archaeology*, no. 3 (Madison: Prehistory Press, 1991); for an analysis of Harappan dental pathology, see John R. Lukacs, "Dental Paleopathology and Agricultural Intensification in South Asia: New Evi-dence from Bronze Age Harappa," *American Journal of Physical Anthropology* 87 (1992): 133—150; John R. Lukacs, "The Osteological Paradox and the Indus Civi-lization: Problems Inferring Health from Human Skeletons at Harappa," in Jonathan Mark Kenoyer, ed., *From Sumer to Meluhha: Contributions to the Archaeol-ogy of South and West Asia, in Memory of George F. Dales, Jr., Wisconsin Archaeological Reports*, vol. 3 (Madison: University of Wisconsin, Dept. of Anthropology, 1994), pp. 143–156.

7. The final excavation report for Inamgaon was published by M. K. Dhavalikar, H. D. Sankalia, and Z. D. Ansari, *Excavations at Inamgaon*, vol. 1 (Pune: Deccan College Post-Graduate and Research Institute, 1988); an overview of significant cultural findings at Inamgaon is presented in condensed form by M. K. Dhavalikar, *The First Farmers of the Deccan* (Pune: Ravish Publishers, 1988). A catalog and invento-ry of human remains from the site is available in John R. Lukacs and Subhash R. Walimbe, *Excavations at Inamgaon, Vol. II: The Physical Anthropology of Human Skele-tal Remains, Part I: An Osteobiographic Analysis* (Pune: Deccan College Post-Gradu-ate and Research Institute, 1986); numerous short reports on dental anthropology and paleodemography have been published in John R. Lukacs, Moreshwar R. Joshi, and Parmanand G. Makhija, "Deciduous Tooth Crown Dimensions in Living and Prehistoric Populations of Western India," *American Journal of Physical Anthropolo-gy* 61 (1983): 383–397; John R. Lukacs and Subhash R. Walimbe, "Paleodemogra-phy at Inamgaon: An Early Farming Village in Western India," in John R. Lukacs, ed., *The People of South Asia* (New York: Plenum Press, 1984), pp. 105–132; and John R. Lukacs and Subhash R. Walimbe, "Deciduous Dental Morphology and the Bi-ological Affinities of a Late Chalcolithic Skeletal Series from Western India," *Amer-ican Journal of Physical Anthropology* 65 (1984): 23–30.

8. The archaeology of these early iron-using sites of the northwest can be found in reports by Ahmed Hassan Dani, "Gandhara Grave Complex in West Pakistan," *Asian Perspectives* 11 (1966): 99–110; A. H. Dani, "Timargarha and the Gandhara Grave Culture," *Ancient Pakistan* 3 (1967): 1–407; A. H. Dani, "Northwest Frontier Burial Sites in Their Wider Archaeological Setting," in H. H. E. Loofs-Wissowa, ed., *The Diffusion of Material Culture, Asian and Pacific Archaeology*, series 9 (Manoa: University of Hawaii, 1980), pp. 121–137; M. A. Halim, "Preliminary Report on the Excavations of Sarai Khola," *Pakistan Archaeology* 5 (1968): 28–40; M. A. Halim, "Excavations at Sarai Khola, Part I," *Pakistan Archaeology* 7 (1970–1971): 23–89; and M. A. Halim, "Excavations at Sarai Khola, Part II," *Pakistan Archaeology* 8 (1972): 3–112. The physical anthropology of human skeletons from SKH and TMG was described by Wolfram Bernhard, "Human Skeletal Remains from the Ceme-tery of Timargarha," *Ancient Pakistan* 3 (1967): 291–407; W. Bernhard, "Human Skeletal Remains from the Prehistoric Cemetery of Sarai Khola," *Pakistan Archae-ology* 6 (1967): 100–116; W. Bernhard, "Ethnic and Morphological Affinities of the

Iron Age Cemetery of Sarai Khola near Taxila [Pakistan]," *Journal of Mediterranean Archaeology and Anthropology* 1 (1981): 180–210. The dental anthropology of these series was reported by John R. Lukacs, "Dental Paleopathology: Methods for Reconstructing Dietary Patterns in Prehistory," in M. Yasar Iscan and Kenneth A. R. Kennedy, eds., *Reconstruction of Life from the Skeleton* (New York: Alan R. Liss, 1989), pp. 261–286; John R. Lukacs, "Dental Anthropology and the Origins of Two Iron Age Populations from Northern Pakistan," *Homo* 34 (1983): 1–15.

9. Questions regarding changes in human health and longevity associated with the transition from hunting and gathering to agriculture have been addressed in a general overview by Mark N. Cohen, *Health and the Rise of Civilization* (New Haven: Yale University Press, 1989); for specific regions of the world by the contributors to Mark N. Cohen and George J. Armelagos, eds., *Paleopathology at the Origins of Agriculture* (Orlando: Academic Press, 1984).

10. For further discussion of the caries correction factor and its impact on reconstructing the dental health of prehistoric human skeletal series, see John R. Lukacs, "The 'Caries Correction Factor': A New Method of Calibrating Dental Caries Rates to Compensate for Antemortem Loss of Teeth," *International J. Osteoarchaeology* 5 (1995): 151–156; John R. Lukacs, "Dental Caries Rates Differentially Impact Women with the Rise of Agriculture in South Asia," *Current Anthropology* 37 (1996): 147–153.

11. A recent holistic approach to the prehistory of global colonization that integrates archaeological and anthropological evidence is by Clive Gamble, *Timewalkers: the Prehistory of Global Colonization* (Cambridge: Harvard University Press, 1993).

12. The most widely used method of analyzing dental morphology is based upon a set of standardized dental models prepared by the Department of Anthropology, Arizona State University, under the direction of Christy Turner; for details, see Christy G. Turner, II, Christian R. Nichol, and G. Richard Scott, "Scoring Procedures for Key Morphological Traits of the Permanent Dentition," in Marc A. Kelley and Clark S. Larsen, ed., *Advances in Dental Anthropology* (New York: Wiley-Liss, 1991), pp. 13–31.

13. For a concise discussion of the dental evidence for an Asian origin of native Americans, see Christy G. Turner, II, "The Dental Search for Native American Origins," in R. Kirk and E. Szathmary, ed., *Out of Asia: Peopling of the Americas and the Pacific* (Canberra: The Journal of Pacific History, 1985). pp. 31–78; Christy G. Turner, II, "Teeth and Prehistory in Asia," *Scientific American* 260 (1989): 88–96. Evidence from dental morphology suggests a North African origin for prehistoric inhabitants of the Canary Islands: see José Bermudez de Castro, "The Carabelli Trait in Human Prehistoric Populations of the Canary Islands," *Human Biology* 61 (1989): 117–131; José Bermudez de Castro and S. Lopez de Ipiña, "Analisis de la variabilidad dental an las poblaciones prehistoricas de Canarias." *Cuadernos de Sección, Antropología y Etnografía* 4 (1987): 133–168; and Joel D. Irish, "Dental Morphometric Affinity of Canary Islanders with North African Maghreb Populations," *American Journal of Physical Anthropology*, suppl. 16 (1993): 114.

14. The subtitle of this section is derived from the clever title of an article that discusses tooth size variation and evolutionary mechanisms of dental reduction in greater detail: see C. Loring Brace, S. L. Smith, and Kevin D. Hunt, "What Big Teeth You Had, Grandma! Human Tooth Size, Past and Present," in M. A. Kelley and C. S. Larsen, ed., *Advances in Dental Anthropology* (New York: Wiley-Liss, 1991), pp. 33–57.

15. For a review of moiré contourography and other hi-tech methods of assessing dental morphology and tooth size, see John T. Mayhall, "Techniques for the Study of Dental Morphology," in Shelley R. Saunders and M. Anne Katzenberg, eds., *Skeletal Biology of Past Peoples: Research Methods* (New York: Wiley-Liss, 1992).

16. The controversy over evolutionary mechanisms responsible for the reduction of human tooth size through time is well represented in Brace, Smith, and Hunt, "What Big Teeth You Had, Grandma!" and James M. Calcagno and Kathleen R. Gibson, "Selective Compromise: Evolutionary Trends and Mechanisms in Hominid Tooth Size," in M. A. Kelley and C. S. Larsen, eds., *Advances in Dental Anthropology* (New York: Wiley-Liss, 1991), pp. 59–76.

17. A recent review of human odontometrics includes introductions to several widely-used multivariate methods as applied to the analysis of human dental crown dimensions: see Julius A. Kieser, *Human Adult Odontometrics,* Cambridge Studies in Biological Anthropology, no. 4 (Cambridge: Cambridge University Press, 1990); Milford H. Wolpoff, "Metric Trends in Hominid Dental Evolution," *Case Western Reserve University, Studies in Anthropology* 2 (1971): 1–244. For a discussion of metric trends in human dental evolution, see David W. Frayer, *The Evolution of the Dentition in Upper Paleolithic and Mesolithic Europe* (Lawrence: University of Kansas, Publications in Anthropology, no. 10, 1978).

18. This discussion is based upon the analysis conducted by Edward F. Harris and Ted A. Rathbun, "Small Tooth Sizes in a Nineteenth Century South Carolina Plantation Slave Series," *American Journal of Physical Anthropology* 78 (1989): 411–420.

19. The first comparative study of dental morphology to document a close relationship between Neolithic Mehrgarh and Inamgaon was by John R. Lukacs, "Dental Morphology and Odontometrics of Early Agriculturalists from Neolithic Mehrgarh, Pakistan," in D. E. Russell, J. P. Santoro, and D. Sigogneau-Russell, eds., *Teeth Revisited: Memoires du Museum,* serie (C) 53 (Paris: Musee d'Histoire Naturelle, 1988), pp. 287–305. This study was based upon a univariate analysis of trait frequencies, and has subsequently been reaffirmed by multivariate methods of comparison in John R. Lukacs and Brian E. Hemphill, "Dental Anthropology of Prehistoric Baluchistan and the Peopling of South Asia," in M. A. Kelley and C. S. Larsen, eds., *Advances in Dental Anthropology* (New York: Wiley-Liss, 1991). pp. 77–119.

20. The statistical analysis of dental dimensions among south Indian castes and tribes has been presented in Brian E. Hemphill, *Tooth Size Apportionment among Contemporary Indians: An Analysis of Caste, Language, and Geography* (Ph.D. diss., Eugene, University of Oregon, 1991); Brian E. Hemphill, John R. Lukacs, and V. Rami Reddy, "Tooth Size Apportionment in Modern India: Factors of Caste, Language, and Geography," in John R. Lukacs, ed., *Culture, Ecology, and Dental Anthropology* (Delhi: Kamla-Raj Enterprises, 1992), pp. 231–253; and Brian E. Hemphill and John R. Lukacs, "Odontometry and Biological Affinities in South Asia: Analysis of Three Ethnic Groups from Northwest India," *Human Biology* 65 (1993): 279–325.

SUGGESTED READINGS

Cruwys, E., and Robert A. Foley. *Teeth and Anthropology.* British Archaeological Reports, International Series, S 291, 1986. Provides a good example of the interdisciplinary nature of research in dental anthropology.

Kelley, M. A., and C. S. Larsen. *Advances in Dental Anthropology*. New York: Wiley-Liss, 1991. Contains articles devoted to a wide range of dental topics (attrition, occlusion, pathology, morphology, and cultural modification), as well as several that focus on the teeth of people from specific geographical regions.

Kieser, Julius A. *Human Adult Odontometrics*. Cambridge: Cambridge University Press, Cambridge Studies in Biological Anthropology, no. 4, 1990. Reviews the methods and objectives employed in the analysis of tooth size in human populations.

Hillson, Simon. *Teeth*. Cambridge: Cambridge University Press, Cambridge Manuals in Archaeology, 1986. A good introduction to dental anthropology that includes microscopic structures and a summary of dental evolution. This book also includes drawings that help in identifying teeth of animals often found in archaeological sites.

Scott, G. Richard. "Dental Anthropology." *Encyclopedia of Human Biology* 2 (1991): 789—804. A brief introduction to the field that includes examples of cultural modification of teeth and use of teeth as tools in manufacturing and manipulating objects.

Turner, Christy G., II. "Southwest Indian Teeth." *National Geographic Research & Exploration* 9 (1993): 32–53. A well-illustrated summary of what can be learned about Native Americans from their teeth.

WERE OUR ANCESTORS
HUNTERS OR SCAVENGERS?[1]

JOHN D. SPETH

Modern humans frequently eat meat, and often in prodigious amounts. For many of us it is probably hard to imagine a week passing without at least some beef, lamb, pork, or chicken on our plate. The fact that we eat animal flesh, therefore, doesn't seem like anything noteworthy or unusual, and might seem almost trivial were it not for the fact that our closest living relatives, the primates, for the most part do not. These denizens of the forest subsist largely on fruits, leaves, shoots, pith, resin, and other vegetal foods. Hence, understanding the origin of what at first seems like a pretty mundane behavior in humans is actually a very intriguing issue, one that has fascinated scholars of human evolution ever since the time of Darwin. If we are descended from a primate ancestor, and primates are largely vegetarians, then hunting, especially of large and dangerous prey, must somehow have played a pivotal role in transforming a small-brained quadrupedal ape into a brainy, tool-making, bipedal human. Working largely without the benefit of either a fossil record or an archaeological record, Darwin well over a century ago theorized about the central role of hunting in human origins; and with only minor modifications, Darwin's "hunting hypothesis" has pretty much guided anthropological thinking ever since. Over the years, archaeology and paleoanthropology have provided the "hard" evidence for the evolution of "man the hunter," essentially filling out the details of a process that, at least in broad outline, we thought we already pretty well knew and understood.

To our great surprise, however, the past decade has witnessed developments that seriously challenge some of the basic premises of the "hunting hypothesis." In fact, "man the hunter" is beginning to look more and more like "man the scavenger." In this brief paper, we will look at the "hunting hypothesis" more closely, and then explore the fascinating controversy that now rages as to whether our early hominid ancestors, more than two million years ago, had already become highly skilled big-game hunters, or instead were

mere scavengers of partly consumed animal carcasses that had been abandoned on the landscape by lions, hyenas, and other big carnivores, the true
"hunters" of the animal kingdom.

THE "HUNTING HYPOTHESIS"

It is now widely accepted that humans are descended from a primate ancestor, and that we share a common ancestor with the chimpanzee, a great ape
found in the tropical forests and woodlands of sub-Saharan Africa.[2] Moreover, a wealth of genetic, paleontological, geological, and other evidence supports a growing consensus that the human and ape line diverged quite recently
by geological standards, perhaps only five or six million years ago.[3] Our understanding of the "when," "where," and "how" of hominid origins and evolution is improving rapidly, as new hominid fossils are discovered and
previous finds are reanalyzed and more securely dated, and as ever more detailed paleoenvironmental, archaeological, and other kinds of studies reveal
the context in which these early hominids lived, died, and became incorporated into the fossil record.

Anthropologists and biologists are also approaching this fascinating issue
from the other end of the time scale. Some are studying the diet, behavior, and
ecology of free-ranging chimpanzees and other higher primates,[4] while others
are focusing on the adaptations and subsistence practices of contemporary
hunter-gatherers or foragers, people who, like our ancestors in the distant past,
continue to this day to make their living without the benefits of agriculture.[5]
These behavioral and comparative studies of living humans and primates help
pinpoint important similarities and differences between ourselves and our
closest living nonhuman relatives, and in the process shed light on the very
processes that may have given rise to the human line in the first place.

One of the most striking contrasts between modern hunter-gatherers and
most living primates, a difference that was clearly recognized by Darwin over
a century ago, is that humans are very effective predators, even of large and
dangerous prey.[6] Modern hunter-gatherers, armed only with spears, bow and
arrows, or harpoons, are fully capable of killing prey much larger than themselves. And while humans are basically omnivores, not carnivores, they are
clearly capable of eating (and often do eat) large amounts of meat. Nowhere is
this more strikingly apparent than among traditional Eskimos. Before the far
reaches of the arctic were invaded by Western missionaries and traders, who
brought with them a vast array of new foods, technologies, and diseases, these
northern hunters subsisted almost entirely on a diet of meat and fat obtained by
killing large and often very dangerous sea mammals, such as seals, walruses,
and even whales, as well as caribou, polar bears, arctic foxes, and many other
terrestrial mammals and birds.[7] In fact, traditional Eskimo diet contained almost no carbohydrates, other than small amounts found in liver, as well as

berries and other plant foods collected during the short arctic summer. In striking contrast, most primates are largely or entirely vegetarian, deriving the bulk of their diet from fruits, leaves, shoots, nuts, resin, and other plant parts.[8] There is clearly no analogue to the Eskimos among the higher primates.

Darwin, in fact, believed this contrast was so fundamental that he used it as the basis for a theory of human origins that, somewhat modified, still remains very persuasive today. In its modern form, Darwin's "hunting hypothesis," as it is often called, holds that during the Miocene—a geological period lasting from roughly twenty-five to six million years ago—global climatic conditions steadily deteriorated, becoming cooler, drier, and more markedly seasonal. The dense tropical rainforests of Eurasia and sub-Saharan Africa, which once covered vast areas, began to shrink and were gradually replaced by woodlands and broad expanses of open savanna grasslands. Many species of great ape, adapted to the forests, were unable to cope with these dramatic habitat changes and became extinct, but some populations of one of these species, thought by most to have been the common ancestor of both chimpanzees and humans, successfully adapted to the changing conditions by turning to the one obvious new resource that the expanding grasslands offered—huge herds of grazing antelopes and other herbivores. But to kill these animals, many of which certainly weighed considerably more than the hunters themselves, and to be able to cut through their thick tough hides, these puny "proto-hominids," known as Australopithecines, needed effective, sharp-edged cutting and piercing tools. Moreover, in order to venture out into the grasslands in pursuit of game, these intrepid hunters had to have tools with which they could defend themselves against attacks by dangerous predators such as lions and hyenas that were also preying on the herbivores. With time these venturesome pioneers of the grasslands became heavily dependent on tools, perhaps first made of wood or bone, then of flaked stone, to stake out their claim in this emerging new world.

Gradually, a positive feedback relationship emerged, in which increasing reliance on tools by the hominids favored a bipedal or two-legged stance in order to free their hands, as well as greater intelligence (and hence larger brain size) as they came to rely more and more on tools and other forms of learned or culturally mediated behavior. These changes were also accompanied by a gradual reduction in the size of their initially very large and intimidating canines as the function of these teeth for both defense and gaining access to tough vegetable foods was supplanted by tools.

More recent variants of this basic "hunting hypothesis" attribute other characteristically human traits to hunting as well. For example, some anthropologists have suggested that the bonanza of meat provided by a single large animal carcass favored the emergence of food-sharing, not just between mother and offspring or among siblings, as is common in nonhuman primates, but among a much broader network of less closely related kin, and perhaps even among nonkin.[9] A single hunter certainly could not consume an entire large carcass alone before the meat spoiled, and the costs to the hunter of trying to "defend" the carcass in the face of demands for meat from other members of the group probably far outweighed the benefits of "sharing" it with them.

A few anthropologists have taken the "hunting hypothesis" to the extreme, arguing that the skills and knowledge needed to find and kill large, dangerous game selected for new and more effective means of communication, a process that culminated in the emergence of true language. According to these scholars, the same factors might also have favored increased levels of cooperation among larger numbers of hunters, enhancing the importance of group integration and kinship beyond the biological family and ultimately giving rise to new and more complex forms of social organization.[10]

These few examples are sufficient to show the favored place that big-game hunting has occupied in our theories of human origins and evolution. While other theories have come and gone, none has captured the scholarly or public imagination as completely or as tenaciously as the "hunting hypothesis."

However, despite its elegance and compelling simplicity, various lines of evidence are now beginning to raise serious doubts about the validity of the "hunting hypothesis." And while no equally comprehensive and compelling new theory has emerged to replace it, our views about the role of big-game hunting in the evolutionary history of the human line have begun to change, in some respects dramatically. The new evidence and insights are coming from many different sources, including detailed ethnographic studies of the world's last remaining groups of hunters and gatherers; long-term field studies of chimpanzees and other primates; archaeology; and taphonomy, a relatively new field that studies the processes (e.g., natural decay, trampling, transport by flowing water, transport and destruction by carnivores) that affect an assemblage of bones from the time an animal dies until its bones have become incorporated into the fossil record. We will now briefly look at the more important of these new insights, and especially at the growing controversy surrounding the role that hunting and scavenging played in hominid origins and evolution.

MODERN HUNTER-GATHERERS

Hunters and gatherers (or foragers) are peoples who live entirely or largely without agriculture or animal husbandry. Prior to the end of the Pleistocene or "Ice Age," humans everywhere subsisted exclusively by hunting, fishing, and gathering, and even after the origins of agriculture, many foraging populations persisted, some right up to the present. Even as recently as the period of European colonial expansion in the fifteenth and sixteenth centuries, there were still hundreds of hunting and gathering groups scattered throughout the Old and New World (e.g., San or Bushmen, Australian Aborigines, Eskimos, Pygmies, etc.).[11]

All of these historically or ethnographically known foragers did a great deal of hunting and they also attributed considerable social importance to it, although the actual contribution of animal foods in kilograms or calories to their diet varied from group to group.[12] Despite this variability, there is a fairly strong positive correlation between latitude and proportion of meat (or fish) in the diet. Not unexpectedly, in the arctic and subarctic plant foods contribute only minimally to the diet, while hunting of both land and sea mammals, as well as fishing, constitute the bulk of the foods consumed. In the temperate latitudes, diets are more varied, but hunting and fishing remain very important. As one continues toward the equator, the contribution of plant foods to the larder of many forager groups, particularly those living far from the sea, steadily increases, reaching as much as 60 to 80 percent by weight of the total food intake among many of the groups that live in the tropics.[13]

This observation—that outside of the temperate and northern latitudes plant foods form a substantial and at times the dominant component of the foragers' diet—is not new. It was already recognized over a century ago by Frederick Engels,[14] but for some reason was brushed aside by the vast majority of anthropologists until the 1960s, when intensive fieldwork among the Kalahari Bushmen (San) in southern Africa and similar work among Australian Aborigines made it impossible for the anthropological establishment to continue to focus primarily on hunting while largely ignoring the role of plant foods (and the women who collect them) in the subsistence activities of many of the world's hunters and gatherers. In fact, the change in perspective was so dramatic that some anthropologists now insist that we refer to foraging populations as "gatherer-hunters" rather than "hunter-gatherers."[15]

This change in perspective has led anthropologists to question some of the basic assumptions of the classic "hunting hypothesis." If plant foods constitute a major part of the diet among many tropical latitude foragers today, perhaps this was also true of early hominid diet in the distant past, since our earliest ancestors, the Australopithecines, evolved in the African tropics. This observation, of course, in no way implies that hunting played no role in the origins or evolution of early hominids. But it does suggest that the "hunting hypothesis" may be overly simplistic in downplaying or ignoring the role of plant foods (and of course nonsubsistence factors) in this process.

This new look at hunter-gatherers has also underscored the serious gender bias built into the "hunting hypothesis." So long as big-game hunting held center stage in our theories of hominid origins, the role of females in the early stages of our evolution was ignored.[16] The origins of tools and weapons, food sharing, the division of labor, the reckoning of kin and other social ties, even language and human intelligence, could all be conveniently attributed, one way or another, to the forces set in motion by males hunting large, dangerous prey. In such views females played virtually no role, beyond that of procreation, in our evolution. However, if plant foods were as important to early hominids as they are to contemporary foragers, then females must have been far more important actors in the events of the past than most theories based on the "hunting hypothesis" would lead us to believe.

Unfortunately, we presently have no way of directly determining the contribution of plant foods to the diet of our Pleistocene forebears. Archaeology is almost totally silent in this matter, since plant foods rarely preserve for such long periods of time. In contrast, animal remains, especially the bones of very large animals like buffalo and elephants, are far more likely to survive in the fossil record, and obviously a great deal easier to find, no doubt contributing to the appeal of the "hunting hypothesis." Studies of striations and other forms of wear on the chewing surfaces of the teeth of ancient human fossils have provided more direct clues to the nature of Australopithecine diet, particularly with respect to the hardness and abrasiveness of the foods being eaten, but they tell us little or nothing about the actual caloric contribution of vegetal foods. Moreover, such wear studies may have much more to say about the last few meals an individual ate before entering the fossil record than about his or her average lifetime diet.

More promising are exciting new biochemical techniques that use the abundance of trace elements, such as strontium, in fossil bone as measures of the proportion of plant foods in the diet.[17] The logic underlying this approach is relatively straightforward. Strontium, which occurs naturally in the soil, accumulates in plants. An animal that consumes plant foods will incorporate strontium into its bones. Carnivores, in contrast, get their strontium indirectly by consuming herbivores. As a consequence, carnivores have much lower levels of strontium in their bones than either browsers or grazers. In archaeological materials, one measures the amount of strontium in the bones of the fossil human whose diet is unknown, and then compares the results with the strontium levels in the bones of known carnivores and herbivores (e.g., hyena and gazelle), ideally prehistoric ones from the same site as the human remains. This is done to control for differences that occur from area to area in the amount of strontium that is naturally available in the soil. The degree to which the strontium content of the fossil human specimen approaches or matches the level in either the known meat-eater (low strontium) or the vegetarian (high strontium) provides a reasonably good measure of the overall makeup of the ancient human's diet. Many other biochemical techniques are now being explored, including a wide range of trace elements in addition to strontium, as well as numerous isotopes, particularly of carbon and nitrogen.[18] There are still many difficulties in applying these biochemical techniques to ancient fossils, not the least of which is the fact that part of a precious fossil specimen must be destroyed to determine its trace element or isotopic composition, as well as the complex chemical changes, known as diagenesis, that invariably accompany the very process of fossilization. Nevertheless, these "high tech" approaches may one day provide us with relatively accurate quantitative measures of the amount of plant food consumed by early hominids, and perhaps even tell us something about the variety.

CHIMPANZEE HUNTING

Another approach to the study of human evolution is to look at the diet and behavior of chimpanzees, our closest living primate relative. Patterns of behavior shared by both chimpanzees and modern foragers should provide us with invaluable clues about the behavior of "proto-hominids." Until the early 1960s, however, when Jane Goodall began her pioneering work in the Gombe National Park—a strip of rugged, forested terrain along the eastern shore of Lake Tanganyika in Tanzania—very little was actually known about free-ranging chimpanzees. Over the three decades since her studies began, our understanding of chimpanzees, and other primates, under natural conditions has improved tremendously, and not surprisingly, our views about the origins and evolutionary significance of human carnivory have been altered in the process.[19]

In Darwin's time, and in fact right up into the 1960s, chimpanzees were thought to be strictly vegetarians, actually frugivores, animals whose diet includes large quantities of fruits. As field studies proceeded, however, it became clear that chimpanzees also ate insects, especially termites, which they collected from nests using simple "fishing" tools made from grass stems. But perhaps the most dramatic change in our views of chimpanzee diet came when researchers first began to observe these supposedly peaceful vegetarians killing and eating mammals, especially the young of several species of monkeys and small antelopes. Chimpanzees were turning out to be omnivores, not strict vegetarians.[20]

Until the chimpanzees became habituated to the presence of their human observers, however, researchers had great difficulty following them in the forest closely enough to get reliable information on the frequency of meat-eating or the conditions that triggered such behavior. Thus, in the early stages of the Gombe research, the chimpanzees were provisioned with bananas at a central feeding station so that they could be observed more easily. Unfortunately, the concentrated food resource provided by the bananas also attracted baboons, a situation that often led to intense competition and conflict between the two primate species. Many of the cases of killing and meat-eating seen in the early stages of the Gombe research occurred when chimpanzees suddenly attacked immature baboons at the provisioning site. Many researchers therefore tended to attribute chimpanzee predation to the artificially competitive environment created by food provisioning.

Over the years, however, more and more incidents of killing and meat-eating were observed, and they continued to be reported long after provisioning had ceased. Moreover, cases of killing and meat-eating began to be reported from other chimpanzee study sites as well, both in Central and West Africa. As field studies progressed, it became evident that chimpanzee predation was neither just an occasional event, nor an artifact of provisioning, but occurred repeatedly and with design. It is now clear that chimpanzees actually hunt deliberately, often cooperatively, and share meat with other group members, particularly females in estrus. In fact, recent work in the Ivory Coast has shown that West African chimpanzees hunt on average almost once every three days, far more frequently than do their cousins in Gombe.[21] They also hunt in larger groups, focus more on adult prey, share the kill more actively and more widely, and in at least one case consumed an estimated 1.4 kg (3.1 pounds) of meat and bone per individual. And while chimpanzees do not use tools to kill their prey, the Ivory Coast chimpanzees occasionally use sticks to extract marrow from the limb bones.

These ongoing studies of chimpanzees in the wild clearly demonstrate that our closest living relatives hunt and share meat, behaviors that until quite recently anthropologists had jealously reserved solely for humans. In fact, it now seems very likely that the common ancestor of both chimpanzees and humans already hunted, making it improbable that proto-hominids were the first primates to "discover" carnivory, a discovery that supposedly then transformed them from apes into hominids. But the insights from chimpanzee studies have in no way made the "hunting hypothesis" obsolete. Instead, many anthropologists now feel that the explanation for hominid origins lies not in the discovery of hunting per se, but in the quantity of meat that early hominids were able to procure; in other words, in their success at locating, pursuing, and killing large game.

HUNTING AND SCAVENGING IN THE PAST

Since the pioneering work of the Leakeys in the 1950s and 1960s at Olduvai Gorge, Tanzania, our understanding of the archaeological record of early hominids has improved dramatically. They painstakingly excavated, mapped, and analyzed many well-preserved archaeological sites or localities buried within deposits that accumulated along the shores of what was once a shallow lake.[22] The Leakeys' careful excavations began to provide tantalizing "snapshots" of the behavior of these ancient hominids, revealing places where they had foraged and camped almost two million years ago. Some of the Olduvai sites produced thousands of sharp-edged stone flakes and heavy-duty chopping or pounding tools together with the broken bones and teeth of many different species of animal, ranging from tiny rodents, birds, and turtles to huge and dangerous buffalo, hippopotamus, and distant relatives of the modern African elephant. The repeated association of tools and bones seemed incontrovertible proof that early hominids were avid and highly successful hunters, and thus became one of the principal cornerstones of the "hunting hypothesis."

While archaeology was uncovering the "hard" evidence of past human activities, another field—taphonomy—was beginning to explore other issues that would ultimately force archaeologists to reexamine many of their basic assumptions. Taphonomy is the study of the processes that can alter and distort an assemblage of bones from the time an animal dies until its bones become incorporated into the fossil record.[23] Before we can draw reliable conclusions about the behavior of ancient humans from the fossilized animal bones we recover in an archaeological site, we have to examine the bones taphonomically to be sure that they are what we think they are—the food remains of early hominids. Taphonomic studies began to make it clear that the mere juxtaposition of stone tools and animal bones did not demonstrate their functional association. Flowing water could have brought the two together in a channel deposit, or hyenas and humans could each have taken advantage of the same shade tree but at slightly different times, producing a fortuitous association of bones and tools. Because of these very basic taphonomic questions, archaeologists found themselves almost having to start from scratch, demonstrating through painstaking analyses what they had previously merely assumed.[24] While very tedious, this process of reevaluation, which is still going on today, has proven to be extremely fruitful.[25]

For example, we now know that some, but by no means all, of the early sites where stone tools and animal bones occur together do in fact represent places where hominids butchered animal carcasses. The best evidence is provided by unambiguous cutmarks on many of the bones produced by sharp-edged flakes, and by use-wear studies of some of the stone tools themselves, which reveal distinct polishes on their edges shown by experimental work to be the product of meat-cutting.[26] Other, somewhat less direct and hence more controversial evidence includes the fact that bones of many different species occur together in a single place, a pattern clearly distinct from that found at hyena or lion kills.[27] And while hyenas accumulate the remains of many different species in their dens, the array of skeletal elements one typically finds in hyena dens differs from what the Leakeys found in many of the Olduvai sites.[28]

But the taphonomic studies of these sites have raised a different issue, one that has far-reaching implications for the "hunting hypothesis." Many of the bones at these sites have gnaw marks, punctures, and other clear evidence of carnivore damage. Moreover, even in sites where it can be shown convincingly that flowing water and differential decay played no significant role in altering the composition of the bone assemblages, nevertheless the less dense parts of limb elements, those with lots of porous, "spongy" tissue such as the proximal ends (the ends closest to the body) of femurs, tibias, and humeri, are almost always conspicuously underrepresented. Detailed studies of the feeding behavior of many different carnivores suggest that these bones have most likely been destroyed or carried off by hyenas.

These observations have raised an even more fundamental question, one that had not been seriously considered until quite recently. Did humans kill the animals and hyenas scavenge the remains that littered the campsite once its human occupants had left? This scenario of course would be entirely compatible with the traditional "man the hunter" view. Or did lions or hyenas kill the animals and humans merely scavenge the carcasses for edible scraps of meat and marrow after the carnivores had finished feeding or were driven off by the humans? After rather protracted and often very heated exchanges, most scholars are now convinced that the latter is more likely.[29]

This discovery marks a radical turning point in our understanding of our distant past. Archaeologists have often been criticized for relying too heavily on analogies with living primates and hunter-gatherers in arriving at their reconstructions of the past. The fear is that we are simply "creating" a past that is nothing more than a mirror image of the present. But in the hunting/scavenging debate we have discovered a pattern in the past that has no modern analogue. No living primate or human group obtains its meat primarily by scavenging.

If we accept the view that early hominids were basically scavengers, not hunters, what role did scavenging play in hominid origins and evolution? The answer to this question remains far from resolved, but certain facets of the problem are becoming clear. One facet concerns the kinds of scavenging opportunities that would have been available to early hominids as they began to exploit the expanding woodlands and open grasslands of sub-Saharan Africa. Ongoing studies of hyenas scavenging in the wild offer some very interesting insights.[30]

Field studies of hyenas have shown them to be very capable hunters as well as scavengers, and in a matter of minutes they can consume the entire carcass, bones and all, of a small antelope such as a gazelle. Hyenas typically first eat the soft underbelly and the organs within the body cavity. They next tackle the meaty haunches and the upper forelimb.[31] If they continue to consume the carcass, the facial area and brain is often next, followed by the tissues along the back and finally the feet. Not unexpectedly, however, the larger the carcass, the more of it the hyenas are likely to leave behind, other things being equal (such as the level of competition among the feeding hyenas, or between the hyenas and other predators, at the carcass). Thus, hyenas may consume most of the carcass of medium-sized animals such as wildebeest and zebras (live weights between about 100 kg and 350 kg), but leave behind the vertebrae, braincase, and lower limbs partly or largely intact. From these elements, early hominids would have been able to scavenge scraps of edible muscle tissue, marrow, and of course the brain, which is particularly rich in fat. Sharp flakes would have made it possible for them to open the hide around the limb bones in order to get at the marrow within the shaft; a stone or limb bone could have been used as a hammer to break open the shaft or to open the skull to get at the brain. Because they lacked appropriate boiling technology, however, the calorie-rich grease in the spongy tissue of the limb bones and vertebrae would have been largely inaccessible to early hominids.

Hyenas often abandon the largest carcasses, those weighing in excess of about 350 kg (e.g., buffalo, rhinoceros, giraffe, and elephant), more or less intact. These would of course have provided early hominids with a bonanza of meat, but kills or natural deaths of these megafauna are not very frequent events and therefore would not have provided a very reliable food base.

These observations suggest that early hominid scavengers would have been most likely to encounter the partial remains of medium-sized animals from which they could have gleaned scraps of meat and marrow, particularly from the lower limbs, and perhaps the brain. If they transported the edible parts back to a central place to process them in comparative safety (and perhaps to share with other members of the group), these marginal skeletal elements are the ones that we would expect to find in greatest abundance in early hominid archaeological sites such as at Olduvai. Initial study of the animal bones from several of the major Olduvai localities, in fact, found that these elements far outnumbered bones from more meaty parts of carcasses, seemingly clinching the scavenging argument.

But the debate didn't stop there. Were early hominids passive or active scavengers, that is, did they have to wait until hyenas and other predators had finished feeding on a carcass or were they instead capable of driving them away soon after the kill?[32] If they were active scavengers, they would have been able to transport back to their home base many more of the less marginal, meaty parts such as the upper forelimbs and haunches.

The difficulty in resolving whether early hominids were active or passive scavengers is largely methodological at this point. Limb bones are rarely found intact in ancient archaeological sites. In part this is due to geological and other processes, such as soil compaction, weathering, and the penetration of roots and insects, that over the millennia gradually weaken the bones and break them into tiny pieces. Early hominids undoubtedly contributed to the breakage as well, by smashing open shafts to get at the marrow. Unfortunately, faunal analysts can usually only identify the ends or joints (epiphyses) of the limbs to genus or species; shaft fragments are virtually impossible to identify. Understandably, therefore, the bones that faunal analysts most often focus on are the epiphyses, not the fragmentary shafts. But the spongy tissue in the epiphyses of many of the meatiest limb bones is also very rich in grease and is therefore relished by carnivores. This means that even if early hominids had transported lots of meaty limbs back to their camp, hyenas would almost certainly have carried off the joints as soon as the camp had been abandoned. The result is that, to the faunal analyst, the archaeological bone assemblage from the site would appear to be devoid of meaty limbs. One would then very likely conclude on the basis of the identified bones that hominids did not have access to carcasses until hyenas or other carnivores had already largely stripped them of the most desirable parts; in other words, that they must have been passive scavengers.

To get around this thorny problem, archaeologists are now beginning the monumentally tedious task of identifying the thousands, sometimes tens of thousands, of tiny shaft fragments, not by genus or species, but by approximate body-size class (i.e., small, medium, or large mammal). The initial results have been very intriguing but controversial. They suggest that, on some early hominid sites at least, upper limbs originally may have been quite well represented but only shaft fragments now remain.[33] This perhaps indicates that early hominids were active scavengers capable of driving predators away from carcasses before the meatiest portions had been totally devoured. On the basis of these shaft-fragment studies, some archaeologists have even suggested that early hominids may have hunted some of the larger animals, a position that if correct brings us full circle to where we began when taphonomic insights first began to seriously challenge the "hunting hypothesis."

Scavenging studies have revealed another interesting facet of hyena behavior. During the rainy season, many herbivores move away from permanent water sources into the open grasslands where they rely on temporary pools of water. In these open habitats, hyenas are extremely aggressive scavengers (and hunters), and often leave little remaining of a carcass that could then be scavenged profitably by hominids. Groups of hyenas may even drive a pride of lions away from a carcass before they have finished feeding. In contrast, during the dry season, when many of the herbivores stay much closer to permanent water sources, hyenas often leave lion kills untouched or only partly devoured. The reason for this seasonal difference in hyena feeding behavior appears to be related to their fear of lions, which are much more likely to ambush them in the dense thickets and woodlands near water courses than out in the open. This suggests that the opportunities for hominid scavenging are likely to have been greater during the dry season than during the rainy season, and close to water sources, assuming of course that early hominids were less intimidated in vegetated areas by lions than modern hyenas seem to be. In addition, the dry season is also the time when very young and very old or sickly animals are most likely to die of hunger, disease, or other natural causes, providing additional potentially scavengable carcasses.

The idea of hominids scavenging where hyenas feared to go may not be as far-fetched as it might at first seem. Hyenas and lions do much of their hunting at night. On the other hand, early hominids, like ourselves, may not have been very adept at foraging in the dark and may instead have been most active during the heat of the day, taking advantage of a time when the big carnivores are much less active.

Thus, answers to these critical and interesting questions—whether early hominids were hunters or scavengers and, if the latter as many now believe, whether they were active or passive scavengers; also whether they procured meat year-round or focused primarily on scraps of tissue gleaned from carcasses during the dry season—hinge ultimately on the ability of archaeologists to find ways to determine, among other things, whether meaty upper limbs were actually present in large numbers on early hominid sites, and on their success in establishing the seasonality of these ancient occupations.

A great deal of the research by archaeologists today is devoted to finding answers to just these questions. We have already noted that archaeologists are beginning to look seriously at the fragmentary limb shafts to determine just how well represented meaty limb bones really were on these ancient sites, and in a few years this issue may be largely resolved. Many other kinds of research are also underway. For example, archaeologists are trying to find ways to tell from the nature and placement of cutmarks on the surfaces of animal bones, traces that are left by sharp stone flakes used in butchering, whether there had been a lot of meat on the bones, or merely small scraps of edible tissue, at the time the cutmarks were made.

Similarly, studies of cutmarks and bone breakage patterns may help archaeologists determine whether the hominids were butchering carcasses when they were still fresh and supple, a sign of early access to the carcasses, or stiff and dry, a sign of passive scavenging.[34] When a carcass is still fresh, limb joints can be dismembered fairly easily by bending them a little, slicing through exposed ligaments and muscles, bending them further, then cutting some more, and so forth until the joints are separated. This method obviously doesn't work very well, particularly in a large carcass, once rigor mortis has set in, since the joint becomes very stiff and hard to bend. In such cases, butchering is more effectively done using a heavy chopping tool rather than a sharp but delicate cutting flake, leaving very different kinds of marks on the bones.

Methods are also being developed to determine the season of death of the animals whose remains are found in early hominid sites. One approach involves making thin sections of teeth from the lower jaw or mandible of an animal, in order to study growth layers in the dental cementum.[35] The cementum is a hard substance that develops around the roots of the teeth and serves as a kind of shock absorber when the animal chews. It forms in distinct layers or bands, with a new one added each year, and under a microscope the bands look very much like tree rings. Thin, dark bands represent seasons of little or no growth (dry season); thick, light rings represent seasons of accelerated growth (rainy season). By examining the nature and thickness of the outermost layer, the last layer to be formed, one can estimate the approximate time of year when the animal died or was killed. The total number of cementum rings also tells the archaeologist how old the animal was when it died, indicating whether early hominids exploited an animal in its prime, or one that was old and perhaps sickly. However, since the cementum method is destructive, archaeologists obviously first must demonstrate its effectiveness and reliability in modern animals before they begin cutting up the precious fossils themselves.

Slowly but surely we are gaining a better understanding of how our distant ancestors some two million years ago made their living in the expanding grasslands of sub-Saharan Africa. Obviously at stake in this entire debate is much more than just the issue of whether early hominids were scavengers rather than hunters, but whether they actually possessed the necessary cognitive and organizational sophistication to plan, coordinate, and carry out successful hunts of large and dangerous prey. The issues are controversial, and the debate sometimes quite heated, but it is always exciting. And in the process we are gradually piecing together a picture of where we came from, tracing the complex chain of events that gradually transformed a small-brained quadrupedal ape into the unique creature that we are today. And we are unique. After all, what other animal finds pleasure and satisfaction probing its own origins?

NOTES

1. Portions of this chapter are reprinted by permission of the publisher from John D. Speth, "Carnivory," in R. Dulbecco, ed., *Encyclopedia of Human Biology*, vol. 2 (Copyright © 1991 by Academic Press, Inc.).
2. Roger Lewin, *Human Evolution*, 2nd ed. (Boston: Blackwell Scientific Publications, 1989).
3. Richard G. Klein, *The Human Career: Human Biological and Cultural Origins* (Chicago: University of Chicago Press, 1989).
4. Jane Goodall, *The Chimpanzees of Gombe* (Cambridge, MA: Belknap Press of Harvard University Press, 1986).
5. Kim Hill, "Hunter-Gatherers of the New World," *American Scientist* 77 (1989): 437–443.
6. Charles Darwin, *The Descent of Man and Selection in Relation to Sex* (London: Murray, 1871).
7. Asen Balikci, *The Netsilik Eskimo* (Garden City, NY: Natural History Press, 1970).
8. Katharine Milton, "Primate Diets and Gut Morphology: Implications for Hominid Evolution," in Marvin Harris and Eric B. Ross, eds., *Food and Evolution: Toward a Theory of Human Food Habits* (Philadelphia: Temple University Press, 1987), pp. 93–115.
9. Glynn Isaac, "The Food-Sharing Behavior of Protohuman Hominids," *Scientific American* 238 (1978): 90–108.
10. Sherwood L. Washburn and C. S. Lancaster, "The Evolution of Hunting," in Richard B. Lee and Irven DeVore, eds., *Man the Hunter* (Chicago: Aldine, 1968), pp. 293–303.
11. Richard B. Lee and Irven DeVore, eds., *Man the Hunter* (Chicago: Aldine, 1968).
12. Brian Hayden, "Subsistence and Ecological Adaptations of Modern Hunter/Gatherers," in Robert S. O. Harding and Geza Teleki, eds., *Omnivorous Primates: Gathering and Hunting in Human Evolution* (New York: Columbia University Press, 1981), pp. 344–421; the importance of hunted foods and fish among many of the world's foraging populations is also clearly demonstrated by Carol R. Ember, "Myths about Hunter-Gatherers," *Ethnology* 17 (1978): 439–448.
13. Richard B. Lee, "What Hunters Do for a Living, or, How to Make Out on Scarce Resources," in Richard B. Lee and Irven DeVore, eds., *Man the Hunter* (Chicago: Aldine, 1968), pp. 30–48.
14. Frederick Engels, *The Origin of the Family, Private Property, and the State* (New York: Pathfinder Press, 1972).
15. Barbara Bender and Brian Morris, "Twenty Years of History, Evolution, and Social Change in Gatherer-Hunter Studies," in Tim Ingold, David Riches, and James Woodburn, eds., *Hunters and Gatherers, Volume 1: History, Evolution, and Social*

Change (Oxford: Berg, 1988), pp. 4–14. Unfortunately, merely reversing the order of the term from "hunter-gatherer" to "gatherer-hunter" adds little to our understanding of the reasons for the tremendous variability among foragers in the composition of their diet.

16. Adrienne L. Zihlman, "Women as Shapers of the Human Adaptation," in Frances Dahlberg, ed., *Woman the Gatherer* (New Haven, CT: Yale University Press, 1981), pp. 75–120.

17. T. Douglas Price, Margaret J. Schoeninger, and George J. Armelagos, "Bone Chemistry and Past Behavior: An Overview," *Journal of Human Evolution* 14 (1985): 419–447.

18. Margaret J. Schoeninger and Katherine Moore, "Bone Stable Isotope Studies in Archaeology," *Journal of World Prehistory* 6 (1992): 247–296.

19. A. Whiten and E. M. Widdowson, eds., *Foraging Strategies and Natural Diet of Monkeys, Apes, and Humans* (Oxford: Clarendon Press, 1992).

20. Geza Teleki, "The Omnivorous Chimpanzee," *Scientific American* 228 (1973): 32–42.

21. Christophe Boesch and Hedwige Boesch, "Hunting Behavior of Wild Chimpanzees in the Taï National Park," *American Journal of Physical Anthropology* 78 (1989): 547–573.

22. Mary D. Leakey, "A Summary and Discussion of the Archaeological Evidence from Bed I and Bed II, Olduvai Gorge, Tanzania," in Glynn Llewellyn Isaac and E. McCown, eds., *Human Origins: Louis Leakey and the East African Evidence* (Menlo Park, CA: W. A. Benjamin, 1976), pp. 431–459.

23. Anna K. Behrensmeyer and Andrew P. Hill, *Fossils in the Making: Vertebrate Taphonomy and Paleoecology* (Chicago: University of Chicago Press, 1980); C. K. Brain, *The Hunters or the Hunted? An Introduction to African Cave Taphonomy* (Chicago: University of Chicago Press, 1981).

24. Lewis R. Binford, *Bones: Ancient Men and Modern Myths* (New York: Academic Press, 1981).

25. Henry T. Bunn, "A Taphonomic Perspective on the Archaeology of Human Origins," *Annual Review of Anthropology* 20 (1991): 433–467.

26. Lawrence H. Keeley and Nicholas Toth, "Microwear Polishes on Early Stone Tools from Koobi Fora, Kenya," *Nature* 293 (1981): 464–465.

27. Robert J. Blumenschine, "Man the Scavenger," *Archaeology* 42 (1989): 26–32.

28. Henry T. Bunn, "Patterns of Skeletal Representation and Hominid Subsistence Activities at Olduvai Gorge, Tanzania, and Koobi Fora, Kenya," *Journal of Human Evolution* 15 (1986): 673–690.

29. One unambiguous way to determine whether humans or predators got to a carcass first would be to observe patterns of superposition of cutmarks and gnawing damage on the ancient animal bones. If the cutmarks consistently underlay the gnaw marks, one could conclude that the predators scavenged the bones after they had been discarded by hominids. On the other hand, if the gnaw marks were always underneath, the hominids most likely scavenged remnants of dead carcasses. This interesting approach to the problem was tried by Pat Shipman, "Scavenging or Hunting in Early Hominids: Theoretical Framework and Tests," *American Anthropologist* 88 (1986): 27–43, using the fossil animal remains from several early sites in Olduvai Gorge, Tanzania. Unfortunately, the marks left by stone tools and predator teeth, while often occurring on the same bone, seldom were directly superimposed on each other, yielding ambiguous results.

30. Robert J. Blumenschine, "Characteristics of an Early Hominid Scavenging Niche," *Current Anthropology* 28 (1987): 383–407.
31. Robert J. Blumenschine, "Carcass Consumption Sequences and the Archaeological Distinction of Scavenging and Hunting," *Journal of Human Evolution* 15 (1986): 639–659.
32. Henry T. Bunn and Ellen M. Kroll, "Systematic Butchery by Plio/Pleistocene Hominids at Olduvai Gorge, Tanzania," *Current Anthropology* 27 (1986): 431–452.
33. Henry T. Bunn and Ellen M. Kroll, "Fact and Fiction about the *Zinjanthropus* Floor: Data, Arguments, and Interpretations," *Current Anthropology* 29 (1988): 135–149.
34. Lewis R. Binford, *Faunal Remains from Klasies River Mouth* (Orlando, FL: Academic Press, 1984).
35. Daniel E. Lieberman, T. W. Deacon, and Richard H. Meadow, "Computer Image Enhancement and Analysis of Cementum Increments as Applied to Teeth of *Gazella gazella*," *Journal of Archaeological Science* 17 (1990): 519–533.

SUGGESTED READINGS

Binford, Lewis R., M. G. L. Mills, and N. M. Stone. "Hyena Scavenging Behavior and Its Implications for the Interpretation of Faunal Assemblages from FLK 22 (the Zinj Floor) at Olduvai Gorge." *Journal of Anthropological Archaeology* 7 (1988): 99–135. This study discusses habits of hyenas when bones with different amounts of edible tissue are laid out for them experimentally.

Bunn, Henry T., L. E. Bartram, and Ellen M. Kroll. "Variability in Bone Assemblage Formation from Hadza Hunting, Scavenging, and Carcass Processing." *Journal of Anthropological Archaeology* 7 (1988): 412–457. An ethno-archaeological study of living foragers in Tanzania who still obtain a lot of their food from hunting. Looks at how the animals are killed and butchered and which parts are transported back to camp.

Gordon, Kathleen D. "Evolutionary Perspectives on Human Diet." In Francis E. Johnston, ed. *Nutritional Anthropology*. New York: Alan R. Liss, 1987, pp. 3–39. A broad overview of the literature on early hominid diet.

O'Connell, James F., Kristen Hawkes, and Nicholas Blurton Jones. "Hadza Scavenging: Implications for Plio/Pleistocene Hominid Subsistence." *Current Anthropology* 29 (1988): 356–363. An ethno-archaeological study of scavenging by contemporary foragers in Tanzania. Documents how often they scavenge and the caloric returns.

Speth, John D. "Early Hominid Hunting and Scavenging: The Role of Meat as an Energy Source." *Journal of Human Evolution* 18 (1989): 329–343. A look at the problems posed by early hominid diets high in protein during times of the year when other nutrients are scarce.

Speth, John D. "Protein Selection and Avoidance Strategies of Contemporary and Ancestral Foragers: Unresolved Issues." In A. Whiten and E. M. Widdowson, eds. *Foraging Strategies and Natural Diet of Monkeys, Apes, and Humans*. Oxford: Clarendon Press, 1992, pp. 105–110. This article also deals with high protein diets, but looks specifically at the impact of excess protein on pregnancy outcome.

WHEN AND HOW DID HUMANS POPULATE THE NEW WORLD?

WILLIAM J. PARRY

For almost five hundred years, European and American scholars have wondered about the origins of the native people (or "Indians") of the Americas. They had somehow reached the New World before Columbus, but when? How long had they been there? Where did they come from? Or had they always been there?

Philosophers, clergy, and scientists debated this topic for centuries. Lacking any direct evidence, they were forced to rely on speculation and guesswork. The famous American writer Washington Irving, in a satirical piece published in 1809,[1] summarized many of the most popular theories: that the Native Americans were descendants of Israelites, Vikings, Chinese, Egyptians, Celts, Phoenicians, Romans, Africans, or people from the mythical lost continent of Atlantis; that they came by land or by water via Greenland, Siberia, or Antarctica; or even that they had come from the moon!

As Washington Irving sadly noted,

> It is an evil much to be lamented, that none of the worthy writers…could ever commence his work, without immediately declaring hostilities against every writer who had treated on the same subject…. If…these learned men can weave whole systems out of nothing, what would be their productions were they furnished with substantial materials![2]

In subsequent years, our knowledge of this topic has grown, even if the tone of the debate has not improved much. The development of archaeology in the United States during the nineteenth century was largely in response to this controversy, as early archaeologists attempted to discover when and how and from where did the ancestors of the Native Americans first colonize the Americas.[3]

AGREEMENTS AND DISAGREEMENTS

[handwritten margin note: Dennis Stanford Solutrean]

Almost all modern anthropologists would agree that the ancestors of the Native Americans came from eastern Asia, and that they first crossed from Siberia into Alaska during the last Ice Age, at least twelve thousand years ago. Once in Alaska, they moved south, eventually spreading throughout North and South America. The best evidence for this migration is not archaeological but biological. Studies of DNA, blood groups, tooth shapes, and other genetic traits clearly show that all modern Native Americans are biologically related to each other, and to the native peoples of eastern Asia.[4]

[handwritten margin note: 3) by land or by sea]

There are basically two major areas of controversy. First, how many migrations were there? Are all Native Americans descended from one single band of immigrants, or did several different groups migrate into the Americas at different times? Second, how long ago did the *first* migrants enter the New World?

From archaeological research, we know that humans had settled in what is now the United States sometime before 11,600 years ago. There are a number of discovered sites that yield traces of these "Paleoindians" (early Indians); when dated by radiocarbon dating,[5] they all turn out to be about 11,500 to 10,500 years old.[6] Because some of the first evidence of these Paleoindians was found near the town of Clovis, in New Mexico, they are often referred to as the "Clovis people." Their handiwork is relatively easy to recognize, because they made a very distinctive style of spearpoint. These "Clovis fluted points" are finely flaked and symmetrical, with a characteristic groove or "flute" running up each face.

The Clovis people lived near the end of the Pleistocene epoch (the "Ice Age"), at a time when the climate was distinctly colder than today. Most of what is now Canada was then covered with glaciers, thick sheets of ice. In order to reach the interior of North America, the earliest immigrants would have had to thread their way between (or around) these massive barriers of ice and snow. During the peak glaciation, about seventeen thousand to thirteen thousand years ago, it was probably impossible to cross Canada.[7] So the first immigrants might not have been able to reach the United States until sometime after thirteen thousand years ago, in which case the Clovis people were probably the first immigrants.

However, it is physically possible for people to have crossed at an earlier date, sometime before seventeen thousand years ago. In that case, the Clovis people would *not* have been the first Americans. Rather, they might have been the descendants of pre-Clovis immigrants, or the descendants of a separate group of later migrants. This is the crux of the controversy: Is there any evidence of pre-Clovis people in the Americas, or were the Clovis people the first immigrants?

WHY IS THIS AN INTERESTING QUESTION?

Archaeologists, like everyone else, are motivated by many complex feelings. Almost all of us went into archaeology because we enjoy doing fieldwork, and more importantly, we want to satisfy our intellectual curiosity. We want to know what *really* happened in the distant past, and it's thrilling to be able to answer a question that no one else has been able to answer before. But many arguments begin from less altruistic motives, as Washington Irving pointed out. Sometimes we compete with each other, seeking older or more spectacular finds, or attacking someone else's theories (and defending our own), not to discover the truth, but to make ourselves look superior to our colleagues.

This has been a particular problem in seeking the First Americans. We could call this the "Guinness Book of Records" syndrome: Every archaeologist wants to find the *oldest* site in the Americas, just for the sake of the recognition that would come from making a record-setting discovery. But why should anyone else care? What difference would it make if the oldest site turns out to be twelve thousand years old, fourteen thousand years old, twenty thousand years old, or one hundred thousand years old?

In fact, it makes a big difference, because the answer that you give to the question "How old is the oldest site in the Americas?" determines how you will answer a whole series of other questions about how humans behave in general. The first peopling of the Americas provides us with a unique case study of how people behave in certain situations. We begin with two large continents, teeming with animal life but devoid of humans. When the first humans arrived in this New World, what did they do? How did they react to this new situation? What impact did they have on the environment? The answers to all of these questions depend on first determining exactly *when* they first entered the Americas.

Let me mention just two examples. First, we know that the Clovis people, who were living in North America shortly after twelve thousand years ago, hunted a variety of large animals, including mammoth and mastodon (extinct varieties of elephant), wild horse, camel, caribou, and an extinct variety of bison. Except for the caribou, all of these animals became extinct between eleven thousand and ten thousand years ago.[8]

If the Clovis people were the first humans in the New World, then they might be responsible for these mass extinctions. As soon as they arrived in Americas, they started hunting animals that had never before seen humans (and maybe didn't know how to defend themselves). Within a thousand years, all of these animals were gone. Some archaeologists have concluded that the Clovis people killed off nearly all of the large animals (or "megafauna") in the Americas.[9]

On the other hand, if the Clovis people were *not* the first settlers in the Americas, then the animals must have coexisted with humans for thousands of years. In that case, it is unlikely that human hunting can be blamed for the extermination of the animals, and we must seek a different explanation. It has been suggested that environmental change might be the cause: The climate was rapidly warming around ten thousand years ago, and perhaps the animals couldn't adjust.[10]

A second question focuses on human population growth and expansion. The earliest Clovis sites that we know of, in the northern Plains of the United States, have radiocarbon dates no earlier than 11,600 years old.[11] A Clovis site in Nova Scotia, on the east coast of Canada, dates to about 10,600 years ago.[12] The site of Fell's Cave, at the very southernmost tip of South America, yielded a radiocarbon date of 10,700 years old.[13] If the Clovis people were the first inhabitants of the Americas, then they must have spread incredibly rapidly, even explosively, since they had reached the farthest shores of North and South America within one thousand years of their first entry into the continental United States, migrating through diverse environments to reach those points. On the other hand, if the Clovis people were *not* the first inhabitants of the Americas, then their population might have increased and spread much more slowly, and it may have taken tens of thousands of years to populate the two continents. We know that it is possible for human populations to increase and expand very rapidly, under certain special conditions,[14] but we won't know if that was the case for the first Americans, unless we can determine *when* they first entered the New World.

If the Clovis people were the first, arriving no more than twelve thousand years ago, then they had a profound impact on the Americas. It would appear that their populations grew explosively, expanded rapidly, and had a massive impact on the natural environment, culminating in the destruction of most of the large animal species that inhabited the New World. On the other hand, if some pre-Clovis people were the first inhabitants, arriving more than seventeen thousand years ago, then their populations and their impact on the environment would seem to have been much less.

WHAT IS THE EVIDENCE?

In order to discover whether the Clovis or the pre-Clovis people were the first inhabitants of the Americas, we must carefully weigh the evidence on both sides. If we want to know what really happened, it is not enough to support one side or the other just because we wish the theory to be true, or we are friends with the people who support the theory, or because a majority of our colleagues believe it and we want to be on the winning side. You do not discover truth in science just by taking a vote.

Unfortunately, much of what has been written on the first peopling of the Americas borders on pseudo-science. Some scholars who claim to have discovered very early sites have been slow to publish their actual data and evidence.

Rather than let the rest of us decide for ourselves whether or not they have proved their claims, they just say, "Trust us. Take our word for it." When you ask them to show you proof that their claims or interpretations are correct, some of them respond with personal attacks, saying that anyone who doubts them is narrow-minded and dogmatic, or jealous and elitist.[15] This may be a good way to gain sympathy, but it's a bad way to discover scientific facts.

One of the difficulties I had in writing this summary is that so few of the claims for pre-Clovis occupations are backed up by published data. As of this writing (June 1993), not a single one of the sites that I will be discussing has been described in print in enough detail that I can really be sure that their claims are valid. I had to rely on the incomplete information found in brief preliminary reports, popular articles, and in one case the first volume of a planned multi-volume series (the other volumes not yet published).

In theory, it should be easy to prove that the Clovis people were not the first inhabitants of the Americas. All you would need is a single site that had indisputable evidence of human occupation before twelve thousand years ago; that would be sufficient to prove that there were pre-Clovis people in the Americas. On the other hand, it would be very difficult to prove that there *weren't* any pre-Clovis people, even if this were the truth. Just because you haven't been able to find any pre-Clovis sites, even after a long search, doesn't mean that one might not be discovered somewhere tomorrow. After all, there are still many places where we haven't looked, so it's almost impossible to prove that there are *no* pre-Clovis sites anywhere. We might think that pre-Clovis sites are unlikely, but we really can't prove it.

However, many people do claim to have discovered pre-Clovis sites, and thereby proven that the Clovis people were not the first to arrive in the New World. What sorts of evidence would be needed to demonstrate a pre-Clovis occupation? There are three basic points that need to be established, before a site can be accepted as valid evidence for pre-Clovis inhabitants.

The first point that must be demonstrated is that humans did in fact occupy the site—that the traces found there were left by people, not by wild animals or natural forces. The best evidence would be actual human skeletal remains. However, no human skeletons more than eleven thousand years old have yet been discovered in the Americas.[16] If human bones are not present, then there must be some other clear evidence: artifacts (tools and implements) and features (hearths, pits, and other constructions) of unquestionable human manufacture.

The second point that must be established is the age of the site. If a site is to provide evidence for pre-Clovis occupation, not only must it be shown that humans lived there; they must also have lived there more than twelve thousand years ago. Radiocarbon dating is the most commonly used technique (see note 5), but there are also many other ways of establishing the age of a site.[17] Ideally, it would be most convincing if several independent techniques all point to the same date.

③/   Third, and most important, the archaeologist must demonstrate a valid *association*. This is the key to almost all archaeological inferences. In other words, are the dated materials really related to the evidences of human occupation? Were all of the materials deposited together at the same time, or have materials of different age been mixed together? Perhaps genuine tools, of relatively recent date, have been accidentally inserted into natural features of much greater age.

It can be very difficult to determine whether or not the items found in an archaeological site are really associated. A lot depends on the archaeologist's experience, ability to distinguish subtle changes in the soil that might mark some disturbance or discontinuity in the deposits, and the amount of care taken in excavating and precisely recording the locations and relationships of all finds.

Much of the debate surrounding pre-Clovis sites focuses on the question of association. It can be difficult to tell from a written report whether or not the archaeologist has correctly observed and interpreted the relationships among the finds. It is doubly difficult when, as is the case with almost all of the claimed pre-Clovis sites, the archaeologist doesn't bother to tell you exactly what was observed in the field, and why he or she concluded that certain materials were associated.

To illustrate the arguments that surround most pre-Clovis sites, I focus on several specific examples. Each of these has been claimed, at one time or another, to represent the definitive proof of pre-Clovis settlement in the Americas. But each of these is also deficient in at least one of the key points: Either the evidence for human presence, early dates, or the association of the two has been disputed.

THE CALICO SITE: HUMAN PRESENCE?

The Calico site, located in the Mohave Desert of California, is perhaps one of the most famous of the claimed pre-Clovis sites. It owes much of its notoriety to the involvement of Louis Leakey, the famed investigator of Olduvai Gorge in Africa. Late in his life, Leakey turned his attention to the Americas, determined to find traces of Early Man here, just as he had in Africa. The endorsement of such a famous scholar put Calico on the map.[18]

Excavations at Calico began in 1964 and still continue, at least on a small scale, thirty years later. There is no dispute about the great age of this site. Originally believed to be more than seventy thousand years old, it has now been shown to be about two hundred thousand years old.[19]

The Calico site is located in an ancient alluvial fan—a mass of mud and gravel that slid down the side of a mountain. This gravel includes many chunks of flint. Not surprisingly, many of these rocks are broken, since they must have clashed against each other when they flowed down the slope. However, the excavators claim that there are some humanly produced stone tools mixed in with this mass of naturally broken rocks. After decades of excavation that have uncovered millions of broken rocks, they have identified about three thousand that they believe were *possibly* flaked by humans. From those three thousand they selected three hundred that they consider to have *probably* been of human manufacture. Of those three hundred there are about thirty that are considered to be crude but unmistakable tools made by humans.[20]

Except for the crude stone "tools," there is no other evidence for a human presence at the site: There are no human skeletons, no animal bones, and no convincing features. Thus, the entire claim for pre-Clovis occupation at Calico hinges on whether or not the broken rocks were fractured by humans (as opposed to natural forces). Several investigators have measured a sample of the specimens, and compared these measurements to naturally broken rocks and to genuine tools from other sites. Based on their measurements, one group of archaeologists has claimed that all of the specimens are natural,[21] while another group claims that their measurements prove that some specimens are humanly worked.[22]

The biggest problem with the Calico site is the way the evidence was collected. In principle, one of the worst sins that scientists can commit is to bias their data by selectively discarding any observations that don't fit their preconceived theories, in order to alter the final results. This is considered to be a form of scientific cheating only slightly short of outright fraud.[23]

In essence, this is what was done at Calico, by selecting a small number of "good" specimens and ignoring the vast majority that clearly were not tools. Even Louis Leakey's wife Mary, a noted archaeologist in her own right, was critical:

> However meticulous the excavation, he was still arguing in a completely unscientific way.... To me, it was the treatment of the finds that was most shocking....[The excavator] sorted through each heap [of stones] and selected certain pieces as possibly pleasing to Louis. Later, whenever Louis happened to be in California next, he would take certain pieces from the selection kept for him and pronounce them to be artifacts.[24]

My own opinion, and I think the consensus of most other archaeologists, is that all of the stones from Calico are naturally fractured and that none of them were worked by humans. There are some good criteria for distinguishing stone tools from natural rocks if you have an unbiased sample to study.[25] But it's impossible to tell if a single rock is a tool or not, when that rock has been singled out from an otherwise random assortment just because it is the one in a million that happens to look like a tool.

There are a number of other claimed pre-Clovis sites that have been the center of similar controversies. They are clearly very ancient, and in some cases have fossil animal bones as well as broken rocks, but none have human skeletal remains or definite cultural features. In each case, the only evidence for a human presence is broken rocks (or broken animal bones) that are in-terpreted as crude tools manufactured by humans. A few of the best-known examples are the Texas Street site in California, the recently reported Pende-jo Cave site in New Mexico, Richmond Hill in Belize (Central America), Piki-machay Cave in Peru, and Pedra Furada in Brazil.[26]

The most spectacular example is Monte Verde in Chile. This site has multiple occupations, of which the two earliest are claimed to be pre-Clovis, dating about thirteen thousand and thirty-three thousand years ago. Most, if not all of the stone "tools" that are associated with these early layers ap-pear to be naturally fractured rocks. The excavators concede this point, but still claim that they were *used* as tools by humans, even if not deliberately manufactured.[27]

Because of its setting in a wet location, Monte Verde is exceptional in hav-ing pieces of preserved wood and other organic materials. In one area, a num-ber of logs were found, lying in roughly rectangular arrangements, that the excavators interpret as the remains of wooden houses. Many archaeologists find this evidence very impressive, although a few skeptics have suggested that the logs are just natural dead trees, and don't provide convincing evi-dence of a human presence.[28] Until a detailed final report—with clear illus-trations—is published, it is difficult to evaluate the claims made for this site, so it is best to suspend judgment for the time being.

THE LEWISVILLE SITE: DATING?

When the Lewisville site was excavated in Texas in 1956 it appeared that it would finally prove the presence of pre-Clovis populations in North Ameri-ca. The presence of humans was unquestionable: There were simple but def-inite stone tools (choppers and scrapers), features (hearths), and bones from extinct animals (some burned, in the hearths). Several radiocarbon dates from the hearths were all greater than thirty-seven thousand years old.[29]

The only objection to Lewisville was that one of the stone tools was a Clo-vis point. By definition, it could not be a pre-Clovis site, and it was thought impossible that a Clovis site could be thirty-seven thousand years old. There-fore, the Clovis point could not be associated with the dates. Some archaeol-ogists suggested that the Clovis point was accidentally (or even fraudulently) introduced into the site from somewhere else. Others suggested that none of the stone tools was really associated with the dates, but that materials of dif-ferent ages were mixed, and that the "hearths" were natural formations.

Curiously, no archaeologists ever questioned the accuracy of the dates—only their association. After the excavation, the site was flooded by a reservoir, and could not be reexamined. This situation changed in 1980, when a drought lowered the water level and exposed the site once again. Reexcavation yield-ed more hearths and stone tools. Additional samples were taken from the hearths for new radiocarbon dates. When these samples were closely examined in the laboratory, however, it was discovered that they were *not* wood charcoal. Rather, they were lignite (soft coal)—the fossilized remains of plants that had died many tens of thousands of years ago.

Evidently, the native people who occupied the Lewisville site dug coal out of the ground and used it for fuel in their hearths. The radiocarbon dates tell us when the plants died, but do not tell us that they were burned in the hearths many thousands of years later (see note 5). Lewisville is apparently a Clovis site, probably dating to about eleven thousand years ago. It is an authentic site, but the dating was wrong.[30]

MEADOWCROFT ROCKSHELTER: DATING AND ASSOCIATION?

Many archaeologists believe that the Meadowcroft site, located in western Pennsylvania, provides the most convincing evidence for pre-Clovis occupation in the Americas. This site is protected by an overhanging cliff (or "rockshelter"), which makes it an attractive place for humans to camp. Eleven distinct layers of debris were distinguished by the excavators, representing almost continuous occupation over the past several thousand years. The deepest layer in the site, Stratum 1, produced several radiocarbon dates ranging from twenty thousand to thirty-one thousand years ago. It is believed that these samples represent naturally occurring charcoal (perhaps from forest fires), and are not the result of human activities.

The oldest evidence for human occupation is found in Stratum 2a, which has radiocarbon dates ranging from 8,000 to 19,600 years ago. All of the dates from the bottom third of this layer are from before 12,800 years ago, which points to a pre-Clovis occupation. This same layer also had a number of unquestionable stone tools, including a spearpoint (shaped like a Clovis point but lacking the distinctive "flutes") and a number of chipped knives and scrapers, as well as animal bones and even two small fragments of human bone.[31] The evidence of a human presence at the site is unquestionable. The only real weakness in the evidence from Meadowcroft is that the radiocarbon dates are not independently supported by any other evidence that the site is very ancient. In particular, all of the plant and animal remains are of forest-dwelling species that still live in the vicinity of the site today, such as acorns and flying squirrels. This is surprising, because thirteen thousand to seventeen thousand years ago the climate would have been very different: It was much colder then, and forests probably would have been restricted to small, protected locations. Yet no extinct or arctic animals were found at Meadowcroft.

This has led at least a few archaeologists to question the dating of the site. Some have argued that the charcoal samples might have been contaminated by coal, which occurs naturally around the site. In this case, the radiocarbon dates would be wrong, just like the case of Lewisville. However, the excavators of the site have argued emphatically that this is not a problem at Meadowcroft.[32]

The other objection that has been raised does not question the accuracy of the dates, but rather their association with the human occupation.[33] Since it is conceded that at least some of the early dates represent naturally occurring deposits (even if not coal), it is possible that all of the dated charcoal samples represent natural events such as forest fires. Perhaps Stratum 2a contains material of different ages that have been mixed together. It is a typical problem in caves or rockshelters that the deposits become mixed and churned by animal burrows, falling rocks, and so on. However, the dates from Meadowcroft are so consistent—the deeper within the level, the earlier the date—that it does not appear that mixing has been a very serious problem.

In my opinion, the best way to settle this question would be to radiocarbon-date the two fragments of human bone. Unlike the charcoal, there can be no doubt that the bones are associated with human presence. If either of these two bone fragments turned out to be more than twelve thousand years old, then that would conclusively prove the presence of pre-Clovis people in the New World. Unfortunately, this has not yet been done, so the association of the early dates and the human remains has not been absolutely proved. The question of associations at this site must remain moot for the time being, since a detailed, final descriptive report has not yet been published.

CONCLUSION

In order to discover when and how the first people came to the Americas, it is not enough just to list the claims that have been made on either side of the controversy. We should always ask, "What is the evidence?" How can we decide which claims are true? A scientist does not rely on other people's opinions, or on second-hand accounts (like this chapter) that claim to report what other people have said. Rather, we should go back to the original publications, and see if the facts really support the claims that have been made. As one of the proponents of the pre-Clovis theory has very correctly pointed out,

> It is clear that in the current controversy about the circumstances of the initial settlement of the Americas, a reader must follow the basic principle of good scholarship. Never rely on secondary sources for basic information. Always go to the original sources, read them carefully and thoroughly...and judge the matter for yourself.[34]

NOTES

1. Washington Irving, "Showing the Great Difficulty Philosophers Have Had in Peopling America," in *Diedrich Knickerbocker's History of New York* (New York, 1838), pp. 244–249.
2. Ibid., pp. 247–248.

3. Edwin N. Wilmsen, "An Outline of Early Man Studies in the United States," *American Antiquity* 31 (1965): 172–192; David J. Meltzer, "The Antiquity of Man and the Development of American Archaeology," in Michael B. Schiffer, ed., *Advances in Archaeological Method and Theory* 6 (1983): 1–51.

4. Joseph H. Greenberg, Christy G. Turner II, and Stephen L. Zegura, "The Settlement of the Americas: A Comparison of the Linguistic, Dental, and Genetic Evidence," *Current Anthropology* 27 (1986): 477–497.

5. Radiocarbon dating is based on the fact that all living tissues contain minute amounts of naturally occurring radioactive isotopes. These radioactive isotopes decay at a constant rate, so by measuring how much radioactivity remains in a sample of organic material (such as wood charcoal, bone, etc.), we can estimate how many years have elapsed since the organism died. There are several limitations. First, the date is an estimate, and may be off by several hundred (or even thousand) years. Second, it cannot date things that are more than about forty thousand years old (it can tell us that they are *more* than forty thousand years old, but not how much more). Third, it only tells you the date that an organism died. It doesn't tell you when that organism was used by humans. That is, if you date a piece of wood charcoal, it tells you when the tree died, *not* when the wood was actually burned in the fireplace. And it can't be used at all to date things that were never alive, like stone tools. For more details, see a textbook such as: Colin Renfrew and Paul Bahn, *Archaeology: Theories, Methods, and Practice* (New York: Thames and Hudson, 1991), pp. 121–129.

6. Robson Bonnichsen and Karen L. Turnmire, eds., *Clovis: Origins and Adaptations* (Corvallis: Center for the Study of the First Americans, Oregon State University, 1991).

7. Knut R. Fladmark, "Times and Places: Environmental Correlates of Mid-to-Late Wisconsinan Human Population Expansion in North America," in Richard Shutler Jr., ed., *Early Man in the New World* (Beverly Hills, CA: Sage, 1983), pp. 13–41.

8. David J. Meltzer and Jim I. Mead, "Dating Late Pleistocene Extinctions," in Jim I. Mead and David J. Meltzer, eds., *Environments and Extinctions: Man in Late Glacial North America* (Orono: Center for the Study of Early Man, University of Maine, 1985), pp. 145–173. The "wild horses" that now roam the Great Plains were introduced by the Spaniards in the 1500s, and are not descended from the native wild horses of the Ice Age.

9. Paul S. Martin, "Prehistoric Overkill: The Global Model" in Paul S. Martin and Richard G. Klein, eds., *Quaternary Extinctions: A Prehistoric Revolution* (Tucson: University of Arizona, 1984), pp. 354–403; Larry D. Agenbroad, "Clovis People: The Human Factor in the Pleistocene Megafauna Extinction Equation," in Ronald C. Carlisle, ed., *Americans before Columbus: Ice-Age Origins* (Pittsburgh, PA.: University of Pittsburgh, Department of Anthropology, Ethnology Monographs 12, 1988), pp. 63–74.

10. Ernest L. Lundelius, Jr., "What Happened to the Mammoth? The Climatic Model," in Ronald C. Carlisle, ed., *Americans before Columbus: Ice-Age Origins* (Pittsburgh, PA: University of Pittsburgh, Department of Anthropology, Ethnology Monographs 12, 1988), pp. 75–82.

11. George C. Frison, *Prehistoric Hunters of the High Plains*, 2nd ed. (San Diego, CA: Academic Press, 1991), p. 25.

12. George F. MacDonald, *Debert: A Paleo-Indian Site in Central Nova Scotia* (Buffalo, NY: Persimmon Press, 1985), p. 53.

13. Junius B. Bird, *Travels and Archaeology in South Chile* (Iowa City: University of Iowa Press, 1988).

14. Harry L. Shapiro, *The Pitcairn Islanders* (New York: Simon & Schuster, 1962), pp. 208–210.

15. John R. Cole, "Anthropology beyond the Fringe," *Skeptical Inquirer* 2 (Spring/Summer 1978): 62–71; John R. Cole, "Cult Archaeology and Unscientific Method and Theory," in Michael B. Schiffer, ed., *Advances in Archaeological Method and Theory* 3 (1980): 1–34.

16. R. E. Taylor et al., "Major Revisions in the Pleistocene Age Assignments for North American Human Skeletons by C-14 Accelerator Mass Spectrometry: None Older Than 11,000 C-14 Years B.P.," *American Antiquity* 50 (1985): 136–140.

17. Colin Renfrew and Paul Bahn, *Archaeology: Theories, Methods, and Practice* (New York: Thames and Hudson, 1991), pp. 101–148.

18. Louis S. B. Leakey et al., *Pleistocene Man at Calico* (Redlands, CA: San Bernardino County Museum, 1972).

19. J. L. Bischoff et al., "Uranium-Series and Soil-Geomorphic Dating of the Calico Archaeological Site, California," *Geology* 9 (1981): 576–582.

20. Ruth D. Simpson, Leland W. Patterson, and Clay A. Singer, "Lithic Technology of the Calico Mountains Site, Southern California," in Alan Lyle Bryan, ed., *New Evidence for the Pleistocene Peopling of the Americas* (Orono: Center for the Study of Early Man, University of Maine, 1986), pp. 89–105; Herbert L. Minshall, *The Broken Stones: The Case for Early Man in California* (Van Nuys, CA: Copley Books, 1976), pp. 30–40.

21. James G. Duvall and William T. Venner, "A Statistical Analysis of the Lithics from the Calico Site (SBCM 1500A), California," *Journal of Field Archaeology* 6 (1979): 455–462.

22. Leland W. Patterson, Louis V. Hoffman, Rose Marie Higginbotham, and Ruth D. Simpson, "Analysis of Lithic Flakes at the Calico Site, California," *Journal of Field Archaeology* 14 (1987): 91–106.

23. Alexander Kohn, *False Prophets: Fraud and Error in Science and Medicine* (Oxford: Basil Blackwell, 1986), pp. 3–4.

24. Mary Leakey, *Disclosing the Past: An Autobiography* (Garden City, NY: Doubleday, 1984), p. 143.

25. Martin F. Hemingway and Dick Stapert, "Early Artifacts from Pakistan? Some Questions for the Excavators," *Current Anthropology* 30 (1989): 317–318.

26. David J. Meltzer, "Pleistocene Peopling of the Americas," *Evolutionary Anthropology* 1 (1993): 157–169.

27. Tom D. Dillehay, "The Cultural Relationships of Monte Verde: A Late Pleistocene Settlement Site in the Sub-Antarctic Forest of South-Central Chile," in Alan Lyle Bryan, ed., *New Evidence for the Pleistocene Peopling of the Americas* (Orono: Center for the Study of Early Man, University of Maine, 1986), pp. 319–337.

28. Thomas F. Lynch, "Glacial-Age Man in South America? A Critical Review," *American Antiquity* 55 (1990): 12–36.

29. Dennis Stanford, "Pre-Clovis Occupation South of the Ice Sheets," in Richard Shutler Jr., ed., *Early Man in the New World* (Beverly Hills, CA: Sage, 1983), pp. 65–72.

30. Ibid., p. 70.

31. J. M. Adovasio et al., "Paleoenvironmental Reconstruction at Meadowcroft Rockshelter, Washington County, Pennsylvania," in Jim I. Mead and David J. Meltzer,

eds., *Environments and Extinctions: Man in Late Glacial North America* (Orono: Center for the Study of Early Man, University of Maine, 1985), pp. 73–110; R. C. Carlisle and J. M. Adovasio, eds., *Meadowcroft: Collected Papers on the Archaeology of Meadowcroft Rockshelter and the Cross Creek Drainage* (Pittsburgh, PA: Department of Anthropology, University of Pittsburgh, 1982).

32. J. M. Adovasio, J. Donahue, and R. Stuckenrath, "The Meadowcroft Rockshelter Radiocarbon Chronology 1975–1990," *American Antiquity* 55 (1990): 348–354.

33. Dena F. Dincauze, "The Meadowcroft Papers," *Quarterly Review of Archaeology* 2 (1981): 3–4.

34. Ruth Gruhn and Alan L. Bryan, "A Review of Lynch's Descriptions of South American Pleistocene Sites," *American Antiquity* 56 (1991): 342–348.

SUGGESTED READINGS

Canby, Thomas Y. "The Search for the First Americans." *National Geographic* 156 (September 1979): 330–363. Somewhat out-of-date, but beautifully illustrated.

Fagan, Brian M. *The Great Journey: The Peopling of Ancient America.* New York: Thames and Hudson, 1987. A general overview.

Fladmark, Knut R. et al. "The First Americans." A series of fourteen articles in *Natural History* (November 1986–February 1988). An excellent selection that covers all aspects of the controversy.

Meltzer, David J. "Pleistocene Peopling of the Americas." *Evolutionary Anthropology* 1 (1993): 157–169. Excellent but technical summary.

Wolkomir, Richard. "New Finds Could Rewrite the Start of American History." *Smithsonian* (March 1991): 130–144.

WERE EARLY AGRICULTURALISTS LESS HEALTHY THAN FOOD-COLLECTORS?

MARK NATHAN COHEN

The study of the Neolithic Revolution—why prehistoric people switched from hunting and gathering to agriculture and how that switch affected human lives and human health—has generated a good deal of controversy in recent years. The controversy may now be moving toward a new synthesis, but opinion remains divided.

Until recently, consideration of the early history of human health was largely implicit in discussions that focused explicitly on technology and on human economic choices. Prior to the mid-1960s, the study of the origins of agriculture focused on when, where, and how the principle of plant and animal domestication was discovered and on when and how that understanding diffused to other regions. Research focused on identifying the original "hearths" of invention; and controversy revolved around the number of places in which agriculture had been invented "independently" (that is, without diffusion of crops or the concept of planting seeds from other regions).[1]

Archaeologists and botanists did not ask, however, why domestication and agriculture, once invented, were adopted as a way of life by human populations. That is because, in the earlier view, the answer seemed obvious: Agriculture was simply assumed to provide a better and more reliable diet than hunting and gathering and to promote better health; to permit larger numbers of people to gather permanently in one place; to provide increased leisure time; and to underwrite construction of the great architectural landmarks that distinguish incipient civilization.[2]

In the mid-1960s three things dramatically altered our perception of the origin of agriculture. First, agricultural economist Ester Boserup offered a new model of economic growth in human history. Second, anthropologist Richard Lee presented a description of life among contemporary hunter gatherers that seemed to fit well into Boserup's model. Third, anthropologists such as Morton

Fried and Marvin Harris reexamined our understanding of the basis of civilized wealth and monumental construction

Boserup,[3] studying the evolution of agricultural systems, suggested that growing population—rather than technological invention—had been the primary stimulus to economic growth in human history. She argued that simple technology such as shifting or impermanent cultivation was actually the relatively efficient technology of small and dispersed human populations; and that technological "progress," such as the adoption of continuous cultivation of permanent fields, the use of the plow, and irrigation, was actually technological accommodation to high density population, often with declining rather than increasing returns for labor. In short, she suggested that simpler technology often represented the most efficient use of labor, while advanced technology represented the efficient use of space. Boserup allowed us to think of the simple technology of small groups as a small-scale, low-density adaptation rather than as "primitive."

Lee[4] provided a description of a group of contemporary hunter-gatherers, the !Kung San of the Kalahari Desert in southern Africa, a group with very simple technology. The San, by his description, did not farm but actually enjoyed considerable leisure time, worked relatively little and enjoyed relatively good nutritional returns. Lee pointed out that they understood the principle of planting crops but could not be bothered to do so (in apparent accord with Boserup's model). He suggested that in return for labor averaging about 20 hours per week for adults, San enjoyed diets of about 2,100 calories (technically, kilocalories) per person per day combined with a healthy intake of protein, vitamins, and minerals. Further study of the San by Truswell and Hansen[5] and by Howell[6] suggested, moreover, that they enjoyed relatively good health and nutritional status and had a life expectancy at birth of about thirty years (roughly the average length of life, balancing the deaths of infants and children with the deaths of older adults, some of whom died in their sixties and seventies). This figure, although low by twentieth-century European and American standards was reasonably good compared to many eighteenth and nineteenth-century European populations; and it compared favorably with many Third World populations such as India until well into the twentieth century.[7] Apparently, such food collectors were not necessarily the least healthy nor the shortest lived of human groups.

Anthropologists Fried[8] and Harris,[9] meanwhile, argued that the great monuments of civilization should not be considered primarily as evidence of technological sophistication and affluence but rather as evidence of the coercive power of political elites who could control very large amounts of human labor. The economic surplus necessary to underwrite the building of a pyramid resulted not from a simple ability to produce more food (since even !Kung San could apparently do this if they wanted to) but from political organization, which forced people to get more and to concentrate their surplus production. The social engineering to build a pyramid was at least as important as the mechanical engineering. It was the emergence of this coercive power, they argued, rather than any technological advance, that marked the origins of civilization.

In response to the work of Boserup, Lee, Harris, and Fried, a number of archaeologists began to ask why hunting and gathering societies (now considered relatively "affluent,"[10]) ever adopted agriculture at all, since agriculture seemed to offer no obvious advantages. Many concluded that some sort of stress such as changing climate or changing sea level would have been necessary to force populations to give up a successful hunting and gathering lifestyle; and several archaeologists[11] concluded, following Boserup, that an imbalance between population and resources (caused either by resource decline or growing human population) was the stimulus to economic change. Some new theories also argued that political incentives and coercion, artificially increasing the demand for production, might have been the stimulus for agriculture.[12]

Most of these theories, however, suggested that human populations, like all animal populations, were normally self-regulating and did not normally outgrow the "carrying capacity" of their resources (the capacity of their resources to regenerate themselves).[13] Therefore, they suggested, the imbalance that necessitated the adoption of agriculture had to be a local and temporary phenomenon distorting an otherwise well-regulated equilibrium. However, recent work in the emerging field of biology called "sociobiology" has questioned whether such "self-regulation" has ever existed in the biological world and has, in my opinion, effectively eliminated this issue from discussion.[14]

In 1977, I proposed that human populations might commonly, if slowly, outgrow their resources (or at least their preferred resources, since human groups always seem to have some less desirable resources in reserve). According to this theory,[15] population growth would slowly force groups to modify their behavior and to make more and more economic and dietary compromises in much the same manner that slow inflation gradually forces people in the modern world to change their buying habits. I suggested that the adoption of agriculture was only one in a long sequence of such adjustments to population growth. This sequence also included the later intensification of agriculture, as Boserup had suggested, as well as the earlier adoption of aquatic hunting and fishing, the adoption of tools for hunting small game, and the adoption of grindstones for processing wild seeds and nuts. (The last three developments marked the Mesolithic or "broad spectrum revolution" that preceded the origins of agriculture in most regions of the world.)[16] Each of the steps leading to the adoption and later intensification of agriculture represented diminishing economic returns, I argued.

In short, I argued that slowly growing human population had forced gradual expansion of a relatively elastic resource base with ever diminishing returns for labor. An alternate theory proposed by Brian Hayden[17] also suggested that population and food technology grew in an interactive manner and had tracked one another very closely in human history; but Hayden argued that technological development was the main stimulus to growth and that the new technologies added increasing efficiency and greater certainty to the food quest.

Meanwhile, the conclusions of Boserup and Lee were being challenged from several perspectives. Some anthropologists and agricultural historians argued that empirical measurements of efficiency and the observed sequence of agricultural development in different parts of the world often did not follow Boserup's predictions.[18] Other workers with the !Kung San and their neighbors called into question both their "affluence" and their authenticity as representatives of an ancient lifeway. Wilmsen,[19] for example, suggested that San dietary intake fell well below Lee's estimates, at least seasonally. Further study suggested that the San actually were relatively inefficient foragers.[20] And it was suggested that they devoted a lot of their time to leisure because of extreme seasonal heat and dryness. It was also suggested that hot, dry seasons placed severe limits on the numbers of children that a family could rear and thereby contributed to the apparent leisure of parents in less stressful and more productive seasons.[21] Schrire[22] and others argued also that the !Kung San were not pristine remnants of an ancient way of life but creations of twentieth century political conditions in South Africa and therefore their lives had little if any meaning for studying the human past.

In an effort to sort out the meaning of the !Kung San data, I undertook a review of published data on the health and nutrition of other contemporary hunter-gatherers. I studied more than forty additional hunting and gathering societies from all of the world's continents for which at least some comparable data were available.[23] For the purposes of this review, I argued that groups like the !Kung San, even if they were not pristine remnants of ancient life, might nevertheless act as twentieth-century experiments in hunting and gathering lifestyle through which we could evaluate certain aspects of the health and nutrition of hunter-gatherer groups. For example, whether or not contemporary hunter-gatherers were "pristine," we could use them to evaluate the potential for obtaining a balanced diet by foraging in various environments; the amount of labor involved in obtaining and processing various foods; and the impact of group size and nomadism on the transmission of infectious disease.

The comparative data[24] suggested that modern hunter-gatherers are indeed commonly well nourished in qualitative terms (vitamins, minerals, protein) although calories may be in short supply at least on a seasonal basis. Anemia was very infrequent in such groups. Diseases like kwashiorkor or marasmus (protein and protein-calorie deficiency), pellagra (niacin deficiency) or beri beri (thiamine deficiency), which plague modern poor populations world-wide, essentially do not occur among hunter-gatherers (until they are forced to adopt modern diets.) In short, although they are occasionally hungry, modern hunter-gatherers are conspicuously well nourished by modern Third-World standards. Moreover, the !Kung San, living in a desert, far from being the most affluent, seem to be relatively impoverished in comparison to other hunter-gatherers. Groups such as the East African Hadza, living in game-rich areas, seem to be far more affluent and also better models for prehistoric hunter-gatherers who chose similarly rich environments in which to live.[25]

The data also suggested that small group size and the mobility that characterizes hunters seems commonly to act to protect them against parasites of various types. This relative freedom from parasites contributes to the good nutritional health of hunter-gatherers since parasitic infestation typically robs the body of nutrients in a variety of ways.[26]

In particular, intestinal parasites spread by human feces are rare among hunter-gatherers populations who tend to move on before feces accumulates and who therefore suffer relatively little diarrhea. Perhaps most important, hunter-gatherers seem to suffer relatively little of the diarrhea of infancy and early childhood that contributes so heavily to the death of children in the modern Third World.[27]

The comparative data also suggested that contemporary hunter-gatherers are at least as successful as most historic populations in rearing children to adulthood. On the average, such groups seem to lose about 20 percent of their children as infants and about 40 percent of children overall before they reach adulthood. These figures are comparable to what was true for most of Europe in the eighteenth and nineteenth centuries and significantly better than European and American cities at the beginning of the twentieth century. Adult life expectancy is not as great in most hunter-gatherer groups as Howell suggests for the !Kung. But overall life expectancy at birth averages twenty-five years or so in these groups, a figure that is still moderate by historic standards.[28]

Two relatively new lines of inquiry contributed further to the debate in the 1980s. First, optimal foraging research[29] stimulated once again by a movement in biology and involving the precise measurement of time, work, and returns for labor has resulted in the careful reevaluation of the different foraging and hunting techniques with results that are of interest to the present discussion. Several such studies suggest that, as long as large game animals are to be found with reasonable ease, big game hunting is a far more efficient activity (measured in caloric returns per hour of work) than other foraging strategies. One study suggests that hunters in rich environments can *average* 7,500–15,000 calories per hour of work.[30] Other studies suggest that once a large animal has been encountered, it can be harvested and converted to food at the rate of 15,000 to 45,000 calories per hour of work. In contrast, many of the more recent resources associated with the mesolithic or broad spectrum revolution such as small game, shellfish, and small seeds can be harvested at rates of only about one thousand calories per hour even after they are located, even with the best and most "modern" stone or iron age equipment.[31]

These caloric studies strongly support the argument that economic changes leading up to the adoption of agriculture were motivated by necessity, not progress. The implication is that prehistoric foragers are likely to have focused more heavily on big game when they were available and to have turned increasingly to secondary resources such as shellfish, small seeds, and small game not because of technological advances but only because choicer resources, particularly large game animals, became scarce. The data also suggest that nutritional health is likely to have declined over this time span rather than improved. A further implication is that modern hunter-gatherers who often rely heavily on the low-return resources may not be as well nourished as their (and our) prehistoric forebears. Most simple agricultural systems average about three thousand to five thousand calories per hour of labor suggesting that they are less efficient than big game hunting but more efficient than "broad spectrum" foraging. This may explain why agriculture began only after the broad spectrum revolution in most parts of the world.

The second major new line of evidence that emerged during the 1970s and 1980s was the development of paleopathological techniques for the direct assessment of prehistoric health from the study of archaeological skeletons, mummies, and feces. Research techniques that had previously focused on the analysis of pathological individuals or the history of specific diseases began instead to provide quantitative, statistically based descriptions of whole populations that could, with caution, be used to compare the health of human groups from different periods of prehistory.[32]

Paleopathology can assess the presence and frequency of some specific, chronic diseases such as syphilis and tuberculosis in the skeleton. (When mummies are found their preserved soft tissues permit diagnosis of a far wider range of illnesses.) Paleopathology can also assess some specific nutrient deficiencies such as iron deficiency anemia. But it can also be used to assess a number of chronic but nonspecific indicators of nutrition, health, growth, and the disruption of growth, which permit the comparison of general health between populations.

In 1982, paleopathologist George Armelagos and I organized a conference of paleopathologists for the express purpose of evaluating the significance of the adoption of agriculture for human health.[33] We asked paleopathologists working in twenty-two regions of the world to use standard paleopathological indicators to assess health trends of populations prior to, at, and after the adoption of agriculture. Although each region of the world is subject to unique historical patterns we hoped that common trends shared by various regions would tell us something about the overall health of hunter-gatherers and farmers.

I had hoped that the data would display clear declines in health *prior* to the adoption of agriculture in support of my population-pressure model of agricultural origins. In this respect the data were disappointing. Fragmentary archaeological samples most often did not permit us to recognize more than one population that had existed prior to the adoption of agriculture in any region. The few comparisons that could be made were limited by small sample size and imperfect preservation. However, throughout the Old World where preagricultural samples are available (India, the Middle East, Mediterranean Europe, Northern Europe) the data suggest that people did get smaller *before* the adoption of agriculture. In at least one region (the Mediterranean) the trend in stature is combined with other signs of declining nutrition. Since decline in stature itself is often used as an index of declining nutrition in other historical contexts, this may be an indicator of declining nutrition among prehistoric groups. I consider this the best explanation of the trend. However, various authorities suggest that declining stature is, instead, an indication either of changing climate or of changing human activities.[34] In any case, few data from this period suggest that preagricultural human beings are making "progress" in health or nutrition. One population from Peru, however, counter to my expectations, does display an increase in stature and in other indications of health and nutrition prior to the adoption of agriculture.[35]

The comparison of prehistoric farmers with their hunting and gathering forebears provided much more interesting results. In most regions of the world, early farmers, living in larger and more sedentary communities than their ancestors, also displayed higher rates of infection in the skeleton (or preserved tissues or feces.) In particular, periostitis, the non-specific infection of bone surfaces usually attributed to staphylococcus or streptococcus infection, is almost invariably more common after the adoption of sedentary farming. A comparison of mummies from Peru suggested that intestinal infection also increased after the adoption of farming.[36] The same conclusion was suggested by comparison of human feces from different periods of prehistory in the American southwest.[37] Treponemal infection (yaws) also seems to be more common after the adoption of farming (its venereal form, syphilis, seems to be a much more recent affliction, rarely if ever being diagnosed with certainty in human groups of any region before the age of Columbus). Tuberculosis is almost entirely confined to relatively recent populations living in large urban aggregates, which do not occur in the absence of agriculture.[38]

Farmers also almost invariably displayed more frequent anemia than earlier hunter-gatherers in the same region. There is some controversy about the source of the anemia. One possibility is that it reflects iron deficiency resulting from farmers' dependency on cereal crops such as maize (corn), which are poor in iron and actually tend to inhibit iron absorption.[39] A more likely possibility is that it reflects the secondary loss of iron to parasites such as hookworm, malaria, or tuberculosis, all of which become more frequent when large sedentary aggregates of people are formed.[40]

Other signs of malnutrition such as retarded growth among children or premature osteoporosis (loss of bone) among adults also seem to be more common after the adoption of agriculture. Farmers also displayed higher rates of imperfections in the enamel of teeth (enamel hypoplasia and Wilson's bands) thought to be a permanent record of severe episodes of poor health in childhood.[41] This suggests, contrary to popular expectation, that prehistoric hunter-gatherers may have been *better* buffered against stressful episodes than their descendants.

The data, unfortunately, cannot be used to assess changing life expectancy. A cemetery may not be an accurate reflection of the community from which it is derived.[42] Immigrants and emigrants skew the age distribution in a cemetery, the former adding older individuals to the cemetery who were not born locally, and the latter subtracting older local individuals. Moreover, if a population is growing rapidly, each cohort (annual crop) of babies is larger than the last and the cemetery will have a disproportionately large number of young people—producing an apparent increase in infant and child mortality even if the actual risk of dying as an infant or child has not changed. A population that is declining and producing fewer babies each year will show the opposite effect. The available data, therefore, cannot be used to show a decline in life expectancy associated with the origins of agriculture as I anticipated; but neither do they provide evidence of the improvement in life expectancy archaeologists once took for granted as a concomitant of human progress.

Overall, these data seem to me to be a fairly substantial body of evidence in support of the hypothesis that the adoption of agriculture resulted in a decline in human health. This conclusion has been challenged, however, by individuals who question the value of skeletal samples.[43] These authors point out that skeletons in a cemetery may not be a true reflection of a once-living population. (As simply one example, skeletal lesions or scars of disease take time to form, so the number of lesions in a skeletal population *might* reflect not the number who were ever sick but the number who survived the illness long enough for the lesions to form. By this argument, a high frequency of pathology in a cemetery *might* perversely be an indication of relatively good health!)

Paleopathologist Alan Goodman has responded to this argument[44] by pointing out, among other things, that enamel hypoplasia do occur in living populations in proportion to deprivation and poverty, suggesting that they are a reliable and direct indicator of health stress. My own response[45] is to point out that several different lines of evidence can often combine to bolster conclusions when no single line of reasoning is sufficient. (It is this cross-checking of one kind of evidence against another that is the real hallmark of science.) For example, archaeological skeletons regularly display an increase in frequencies of infection with the adoption of large sedentary communities associated with farming. This might, as the critics suggest, be a misleading artifact of skeletal samples. But the increase in infection with large groups and sedentism is in accordance with standard modern epidemiological expectations based on knowledge of the life cycles of parasites. Moreover, the same increase is displayed over and over again when contemporary hunter-gatherers are settled in large communities. It seems reasonable to conclude, then, that the increase in infection with the adoption of farming is historic fact and not a mere artifact of skeletal sampling.

Similarly, anemia becomes more visible in skeletal populations after the adoption of farming. But we also know that anemia is infrequent in contemporary hunter-gatherers and that rates of parasitism (the most probable explanation of anemia for most populations) increase with farming. Again it seems reasonable to conclude that the increase in anemia is a matter of historic fact. Similarly, dental defects indicating disrupted growth in children become more common in skeletal populations after farming. But observations on living groups suggest that weaning diarrhea—which is thought to be a major cause of such dental defects—also increases with sedentism suggesting that the prehistoric trend is real and not the product of a sampling error. Similarly, tuberculosis, which occurs only in relatively recent, dense, sedentary populations in the archaeological sequence is also primarily a disease of cities in the modern world, suggesting that we are not being misled about its prehistoric distribution.

In short, data from a variety of sources seem to be converging on a new way of viewing the origins of agriculture and other episodes in human history. Taken together, evidence from paleopathology, from ethnographic studies of contemporary hunter-gatherers, epidemiology or knowledge of disease mechanics, and optimal foraging research all suggest that human health declined with the adoption of agriculture—and these data also suggest more generally that much human "progress" has been a matter of diminishing returns for all but privileged groups and classes.

One final point needs to be made. One of the problems with our initial ideas about agriculture is that some of the basic assumptions—such as that agriculture represents "progress" (or indeed that human history as a whole has been about "progress")—were never tested. All ideas, no matter how plausible or how much in accord with prevailing beliefs, should be tested in many different ways.

The idea of "progress" is itself nothing more than an hypothesis that was created by scientists and scholars like ourselves who were working from similar data (although generally from *less* data and never from more data than are now available). If it is to be believed, the hypothesis of progress must be supported by empirical evidence from contemporary populations or skeletons, like any other competing hypothesis. At present it is not supported and I believe it has less actual empirical evidence in support than the alternative hypothesis offered here. I think it is time to change our thinking and our assumptions about what happened in history.

NOTES

1. Jack R. Harlan, "Agricultural Origins: Centers and Non-Centers," *Science* 174 (1971): 168–174.
2. V. Gordon Childe, *Man Makes Himself* (New York: Mentor, 1950).
3. Ester Boserup, *The Conditions of Agricultural Growth* (Chicago: Aldine, 1965).
4. Richard Lee, "What Hunters Do for a Living, or, How to Make Out on Scarce Resources," in Richard B. Lee and Irven DeVore, eds., *Man the Hunter* (Chicago: Aldine, 1968), pp. 30–43; Richard Lee, "!Kung Bushman Subsistence—an Input/Output Analysis," in A. P. Vayda, ed., *Ecological Studies in Cultural Anthropology* (New York: Natural History Press, 1969), pp. 47–79.
5. A. S. Truswell and J. D. L. Hansen, "Medical Research among the !Kung," in Richard Lee and Irven DeVore, eds., *Kalahari Hunter-Gatherers* (Cambridge, MA: Harvard University Press, 1976), pp. 166–195.
6. Nancy Howell, *Demography of the Dobe !Kung* (New York: Academic Press, 1979).
7. Mark N. Cohen, *Health and the Rise of Civilization* (New Haven, CT: Yale University Press, 1989).
8. Morton H. Fried, *The Evolution of Political Society* (New York: Random House, 1967).
9. Marvin Harris, "The Economy Has No Surplus?" *American Anthropologist* 61 (1959): 189–199.
10. Marshall Sahlins, *Stone Age Economics* (Chicago: Aldine, 1968).
11. Lewis R. Binford, "Post-Pleistocene Adaptations," in Lewis R. Binford and Sally Binford, eds., *New Perspectives in Archaeology* (Chicago: Aldine, 1968), pp. 313–341; Kent V. Flannery, "Origins and Ecological Effects of Early Farming in Iran and the Near East," in P. J. Ucko and J. W. Dimbleby, eds., *The Domestication and Exploitation of Plants and Animals* (London: Duckworth, 1969), pp. 73–100; J. T. Meyers, "The Origins of Agriculture: An Evaluation of Hypotheses," in Stuart Struever, ed., *Prehistoric Agriculture* (Garden City, NJ: Natural History Press, 1971), pp. 101–121.
12. T. D. Price and J. A. Brown, eds., *Prehistoric Hunter-Gatherers: The Emergence of Cultural Complexity* (Chicago: Aldine, 1985).
13. V. C. Wynne-Edwards, *Animal Dispersion in Relation to Social Behavior* (Edinburgh: Oliver and Boyd, 1962).
14. Edward O. Wilson, *Sociobiology* (Cambridge, MA: Harvard University Press, 1975).
15. Mark N. Cohen, *The Food Crisis in Prehistory* (New Haven, CT: Yale University Press, 1977).
16. Kent V. Flannery, "The Origins of Agriculture," *Annual Review of Anthropology* 2 (1973): 271–310.
17. Brian Hayden, "Research and Development in the Stone Age," *Current Anthropology* 22 (1981): 519–548.
18. Brian Spooner, ed., *Population Growth: Anthropological Implications* (Cambridge, MA: MIT Press, 1972).
19. Edwin Wilmsen, "Seasonal Effects of Dietary Intake on the Kalahari San," *Federation Proceedings* 37 (1978): 65–72.
20. Kristen Hawkes and James F. O'Connell, "Optimal Foraging Models and the Case of the !Kung," *American Anthropologist* 87 (1985): 401–405.
21. Nicholas Blurton-Jones and P. M. Sibley, "Testing Adaptiveness of Culturally Determined Behavior: Do Bushman Women Maximize Their Reproductive Success?"

in *Human Behavior and Adaptation,* Society for the Study of Human Biology, Symposium 18 (London: Taylor and Francis, 1978), pp. 133–157.

22. Carmel Schrire, "An Inquiry into the Evolutionary Status and Apparent Identity of San Hunter Gatherers," *Human Ecology* 8 (1980): 9–32.

23. Mark N. Cohen, *Health and the Rise of Civilization* (New Haven, CT: Yale University Press, 1989).

24. Ibid., pp. 184–192.

25. James Woodburn, "An Introduction to Hadza Ecology," in Richard B. Lee and Irven DeVore, eds., *Man the Hunter* (Chicago: Aldine, 1968), pp. 49–55; James F. O'Connell, Kristen Hawes, and Nicholas Blurton-Jones, "Hadza Scavenging: Implications for Plio/Pleistocene Hominid Subsistence," *Current Anthropology* 29 (1988): 256–263.

26. Cohen, *Health and the Rise of Civilization,* pp. 63–64.

27. Ibid.

28. Ibid., pp. 100–102, 195–204.

29. Bruce Winterhalder and Eric A. Smith, eds., *Hunter-Gatherer Foraging Strategies* (Chicago: University of Chicago Press, 1981).

30. Stuart Marks, *Large Mammals and a Brave People* (Seattle: University of Washington Press, 1976).

31. Rhys Jones, "Hunters in the Australian Coastal Savanna," in David Harris, ed., *Human Ecology in Savanna Environments* (New York: Academic Press, 1981); P. Rowly-Conwy, "The Laziness of the Short Distance Hunter," *Journal of Anthropological Archaeology* 38 (1984): 300–324; Roderick Blackburn, "In the Land of Milk and Honey," in Eleanor Leacock and Richard B. Lee, eds., *Politics and History in Band Society* (Cambridge: Cambridge University Press, 1982), pp. 283–306.

32. Jane Buikstra and Della Cook, "Paleopathology: An American Account," *Annual Review of Anthropology* 9 (1980): 433–470.

33. Mark N. Cohen and George J. Armelagos, eds., *Paleopathology at the Origins of Agriculture* (New York: Academic Press, 1984).

34. David Frayer, "Body Size, Weapon Use, and Natural Selection in the European Upper Paleolithic and Mesolithic," *American Anthropologist* 83 (1981): 57–73.

35. Robert Benfer, "The Challenges and Rewards of Sedentism: The Preceramic Village of Paloma, Peru," in Mark N. Cohen and George J. Armelagos, eds., *Paleopathology at the Origins of Agriculture* (New York: Academic Press, 1984), pp. 531–555.

36. Marvin J. Allison, "Paleopathology in Peruvian and Chilean Populations," in Mark N. Cohen and George J. Armelagos, eds., *Paleopathology at the Origins of Agriculture* (New York: Academic Press, 1984), pp. 515–530.

37. Carl Reinhard, "Cultural Ecology of Prehistoric Parasites on the Colorado Plateau as Evidenced by Coprology,"*American Journal of Physical Anthropology* 77 (1988): 355–366.

38. Cohen and Armelagos, *Paleopathology at the Origins of Agriculture.*

39. Mahmoud El Najjar, "Maize, Malarias, and the Anemias in the Pre-Columbian New World," *Yearbook of Physical Anthropology* 28 (1977): 329–337.

40. Patty Stuart Macadam and Susan Kent, eds., *Diet Demography and Disease* (Hawthorne, NY: Aldine de Gruyter, 1992).

41. Jerome Rose, Alan Goodman, and Keith Condon, "Diet and Dentition: Developmental Disturbances," in R. I. Gilbert and J. Mielke, eds., *The Analysis of Prehistoric Diets* (New York: Academic Press, 1985), pp. 281–306.

42. Lisa Sattenspiel and Henry Harpending, "Stable Populations and Skeletal Age," *American Antiquity* 48 (1983): 489–498.
43. James W. Wood, George R. Milner, Henry C. Harpending, and Kenneth Weiss, "The Osteological Paradox: Problems of Inferring Prehistoric Health from Skeletal Samples," *Current Anthropology* 33 (1992): 343–358.
44. Alan Goodman, "On the Interpretation of Health from Skeletal Remains," *Current Anthropology* 34 (1993): 281–288.
45. Mark N. Cohen, "Comment," *Current Anthropology* 33 (1992): 358–359.

SUGGESTED READINGS

Cohen, Mark N. *The Food Crisis in Prehistory.* New Haven, CT: Yale University Press, 1977. The first comprehensive statement about the impact of population growth on prehistoric populations.

____. *Health and the Rise of Civilization.* New Haven, CT: Yale University Press, 1989. A readable summary of theory and evidence concerning the impact of civilization on human health.

Lee, Richard B., and Irven DeVore, eds. *Man the Hunter.* Chicago: Aldine, 1968. The modern classic description of hunting and gathering.

____. *Kalahari Hunter Gatherers.* Cambridge, MA: Harvard University Press, 1976. The most concentrated discussion of the life and health of the !Kung San.

Marks, Stuart. *Large Mammals and a Brave People.* Seattle: University of Washington Press, 1976. A description of a modern African hunting economy.

MAYA HIEROGLYPHS:
HISTORY OR PROPAGANDA?

JOYCE MARCUS

The Maya—an American Indian group that numbers four million people and speaks some twenty-eight related languages—occupy parts of Mexico, Guatemala, Belize, El Salvador, and Honduras. In ancient times they were one of the most highly advanced peoples of the Americas. At the peak of their political power, between A.D. 300 and 800, they occupied large cities and proclaimed the exploits of their rulers in a complex system of hieroglyphic writing.

Maya writing is found on thousands of carved stone monuments, painted pottery vessels, and objects of jade, bone, and shell. The earliest examples appeared on stone by A.D. 300, while the most recent appeared in "books" of painted deerskin around A.D. 1500.

Maya hieroglyphs have been studied by a wide variety of scholars for more than a hundred years. These studies reveal that the field has passed through many stages, during which researchers have repeatedly changed their opinions on the content of the ancient texts. Often, in fact, later scholars have returned to positions taken by earlier scholars. Such returns are sometimes called pendulum swings, and they are typical of science as a whole. Frequently one generation takes a position on a question; their immediate successors counter that by taking the opposite position; and the next generation returns to the original position.[1]

In this chapter we use the study of Maya hieroglyphs as an example of how science undergoes such pendulum swings. In particular, we ask the question: "What is the subject of Maya inscriptions? Is it astronomy and myth? Is it history? Or is it political propaganda?"

FROM 1830 TO 1920: MAYA WRITING IS HISTORY

In 1839 an American lawyer named John L. Stephens decided to explore the Maya ruins of Mexico, Guatemala, and Honduras. He took with him Frederick Catherwood, an accomplished artist who was to draw all the sights they would see. Both Stephens and Catherwood were already world travelers, with Stephens's earlier trips having resulted in two best-selling books—*Incidents of Travel in Egypt, Arabia Petraea, and the Holy Land* and *Incidents of Travel in Greece, Turkey, Russia, and Poland.*

Those Old World adventures predisposed Stephens to develop a comparative perspective, one that took note of the similarities and differences among Old and New World civilizations.[2] In particular, Stephens compared Maya stone sculpture and hieroglyphic writing to those of Egypt, suggesting that both civilizations had depicted kings and recorded history.

Stephens's views were shared by a later Maya scholar, Herbert J. Spinden, who in 1913 agreed that the subject of Maya texts was history:

> In addition to what is now known we may expect to find in the Maya inscriptions some hieroglyphs that give the names of individuals, cities, and political divisions and others that represent feasts, sacrifices, tributes, and common objects of trade as well as signs referring to birth, death, establishment, conquest, destruction and other such fundamentals of individual and social existence.[3]

FROM 1920 TO 1960: MAYA WRITING IS ASTRONOMY, MYTH, AND THE PHILOSOPHY OF TIME

New and influential Maya scholars such as Sylvanus G. Morley and J. Eric S. Thompson emerged during the 1920s and 1930s. Unlike Stephens and Spinden, Morley and Thompson believed that Maya texts contained astronomy, myth, cosmology, and philosophy.[4] The human figures seen on many stone monuments were thought to be priests and astronomers rather than kings. The fact that some figures wore long robes or loose dresses only reinforced the notion that they were priests, perhaps the leaders of an ancient theocracy or "government headed by gods." In 1950 Thompson forcefully disputed the views of earlier scholars when he wrote, "It has been held by some that Maya dates recorded on stelae [free-standing stone monuments] may refer to historical events or even recount the deeds of individuals; to me such a possibility is well-nigh inconceivable."[5]

Why did Thompson and others of his generation come to this conclusion? It had to do with the portion of Maya texts that could be translated at that time. Maya inscriptions often include dates, given in an ancient calendric system that the Indians of Mexico had invented hundreds of years earlier. By the 1940s different correlations linking the Maya dates to our calendar had been worked out, and both Morley and Thompson were proficient at such correlations. They had also determined that some Maya monuments give data on various planetary cycles, including those of Venus and the moon. Despite the fact that he himself had catalogued 862 of the noncalendric hieroglyphs, Thompson could not translate most of them.[6] Deprived of what we now know to be the main subject matter of the inscriptions, Morley and Thompson concentrated on the calendric and astronomical portions of the texts. Small wonder they saw the hieroglyphic inscriptions as "impersonal," and considered the Maya "obsessed with time." This view was only reinforced when it was discovered that the Maya were making calculations that involved millions of years and were recording events that took place thousands of years ago in our calendar.[7]

Thus, despite the fact that scholars of the period from 1920 to 1960 could read more of the inscriptions than could Stephens and Spinden, the limited portions of the text that could be read led them away from history. That situation lasted until 1958–1960, when two major breakthroughs took place.

FROM 1960 TO 1990: A RETURN TO HISTORY

In the late 1950s two scholars, working independently, returned to the "historical" position advocated by Stephens and Spinden. One scholar was Heinrich Berlin, a German emigré to Mexico; the other was Tatiana Proskouriakoff, a Russian emigrée to the United States.

Berlin's breakthrough came while he was studying hieroglyphs on the stone coffin of a ruler buried in the Temple of the Inscriptions at Palenque, a Maya city in the jungles of southeastern Mexico. Here, for the first time, Berlin identified the personal names of Maya rulers and their relatives.[8] He also noted that the last hieroglyph in each name phrase at Palenque usually had the same compound structure. He called it the Palenque Emblem Glyph (see the upper left of Figure 13-1 for one of the Palenque emblem glyphs, and see the lower right of Figure 13-5 on page 201 for a variant).

Berlin then turned to texts at other Maya sites, where he found that rulers' name phrases ended with a similar hieroglyphic compound, but with a different central element; he suggested that the final glyphic compounds referred to different cities (see Figure 13-1). Berlin concluded that these different emblem glyphs functioned as rulers' titles, dynastic names, or place names.[9] Subsequent work has shown that these glyphs are compounds of a ruler's title plus the name of a place—for example, "Lord of Palenque"—and therefore do provide geographic references.

Proskouriakoff's breakthrough was the demonstration that Maya texts, just as Stephens and Spinden had suspected, recorded important events in the lives of rulers. She reasoned that the calendric phrases were the dates of rulers' births, accessions to the throne, and deaths. Initially, Proskouriakoff concentrated on Piedras Negras, a Maya city in northwest Guatemala, which she chose because its monuments were numerous and had been conveniently erected at five-year intervals.[10]

Proskouriakoff began by dividing the dated monuments into seven consecutive series. She noted that each series began with the same pictorial motif:

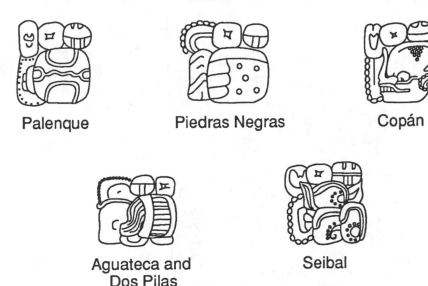

Palenque **Piedras Negras** **Copán**

Aguateca and Dos Pilas **Seibal**

FIGURE 13-1 EMBLEM GLYPHS OF FIVE MAYA CITIES
Source: Redrawn from Marcus, 1976, Figures 1.7, 4.11.

a human being seated cross-legged on a throne set in a niche or doorway, with a ladder leading up to it. Proskouriakoff called this scene the Ascension Motif (see Figure 13-2 on page 196). In the accompanying texts she noted one hieroglyph that was consistently associated with a date falling in the five-year period before the erection of the monument; she called this the Inaugural Date, and suggested that it marked the day the ruler ascended to the throne. Proskouriakoff also noted that each of the seven series began with a still earlier date that fell some twelve to thirty-one years before the Inaugural Date; she suggested that this might refer to the ruler's date of birth (see Figure 13-3 on page 197).

Proskouriakoff went on to identify the hieroglyphs associated with Maya women, rituals of sacrificial bloodletting, and the capture of one Maya lord by another in battle.[11] Thanks to her, we now know that the robed figures considered to be priests by Morley and Thompson were in fact royal women.

While some admirers have described Proskouriakoff's breakthrough as a single stroke of brilliant intuition (like the lightbulb going on over a cartoon character's head), she herself considered it to be the result of logic and deduction. She said that she had relied on earlier work—including that of Spinden and Morley, who had already noted that the Piedras Negras monuments bearing the Ascension Motif were separated by time intervals "no greater than a human lifetime."[12] Thus Spinden's and Morley's earlier work allowed Proskouriakoff to start her study with a testable hypothesis—that each monument displaying the Ascension Motif marked the beginning of a new ruler's reign.

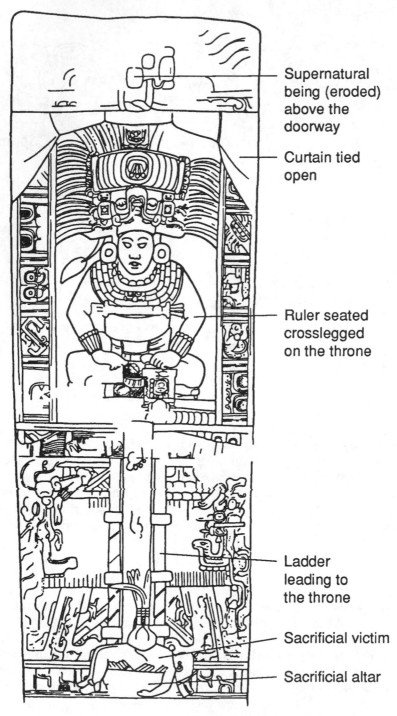

Supernatural being (eroded) above the doorway

Curtain tied open

Ruler seated crosslegged on the throne

Ladder leading to the throne

Sacrificial victim

Sacrificial altar

FIGURE 13-2   MONUMENT AT PIEDRAS NEGRAS, GUATEMALA, DISPLAYING THE ASCENSION MOTIF

Source: Redrawn from Marcus, 1992, Figure 10.14.

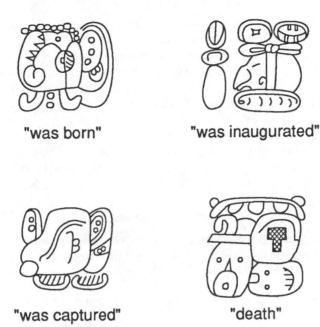

"was born"   "was inaugurated"

"was captured"   "death"

FIGURE 13-3   HIEROGLYPHS REFERRING
TO MAJOR EVENTS IN THE LIFE OF A MAYA RULER
Source: Redrawn from Marcus, 1976, Figure 1.2.

We need to remember that most breakthroughs in research are not gained in an instant through luck or intuition. Most are the hard-won products of combining past work with new questions and fresh approaches. New research may follow past work or contradict it, but it will always be affected by it in some way.

THE ALTAR Q STORY

To see how our interpretations of Maya writing have changed over the past 150 years, let us follow one carved stone monument through the whole process. That monument is Altar Q at Copán, an ancient Maya city that once had ten thousand inhabitants.

Copán lies at 1,968 feet above sea level in a fertile, green valley in western Honduras. Supported by cornfields stretching along the floodplain of the Copán River, the city of Copán was built of blocks of greenish volcanic tuff quarried from cliffs flanking the valley.

Altar Q, a striking monument carved from a block of such tuff four feet seven inches square, sits today beneath a protective roof in front of Copán's Temple 16. The altar's layout reveals a very careful plan that paid particular attention to symmetry. It is four-sided, and its flat top bears thirty-six units, or blocks, of hieroglyphs. Around its sides are sixteen human figures—four to a side—each seated on a hieroglyphic compound (a glyph block containing several glyphs). The faces of all sixteen individuals are directed toward the west side of the altar, which is the principal side. On that side, the two main protagonists face each other (see Figure 13-4).

Between the faces of these two protagonists are two glyphs in the Maya calendar—6 Caban 10 Mol—that correspond to July 2, A.D. 763 in our calendar. That date is repeated several times at Copán, and so are the tenth, twentieth, thirtieth, and fortieth anniversaries of the same date. From the frequency of its use, we are given a clue: This was a very important date in the history of Copán.

TIMELINE OF ALTAR Q

1. In 1840 John L. Stephens found Altar Q. Given his comparative perspective on ancient civilizations, he concluded that "beyond doubt [its texts] record some event in the history" of the Maya.[13] Stephens was the first to conclude that the two figures facing each other on the west side of the altar were the protagonists and suggested that the other fourteen were following those leaders. He perceptively suggested that the hieroglyphic compound on which each figure sat might refer to that individual's name and political office, and he pointed out that one of the two protagonists was holding a scepter.

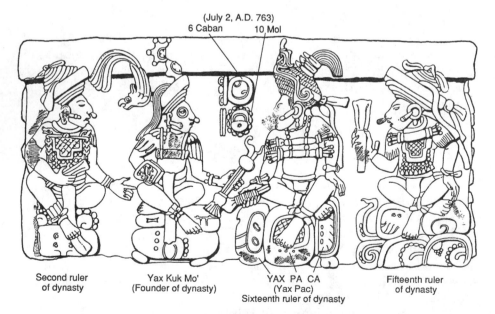

FIGURE 13-4   THE WEST SIDE OF ALTAR Q, COPÁN, HONDURAS
Source: Redrawn from Marcus, 1976, Figure 4.48.

2. In the 1930s an astronomer named John Teeple studied Altar Q.[14] Because Mayanists at that time believed that the hieroglyphic texts dealt with astronomy and cosmology, he concluded that the sixteen figures were ancient Maya astronomers attending an astronomical congress. Suspecting that these Copán astronomers had produced the most up-to-date computation of the length of the tropical year, Teeple compared Altar Q to "a group photograph of the Copán Academy of Sciences taken just after their sessions." This position was supported by J. Eric S. Thompson and most other Mayanists of the 1920–1960 era.[15]

3. Following the breakthroughs of Berlin and Proskouriakoff, the individuals on Altar Q suddenly became historical figures again. By 1974 Mayanists such as Tatiana Proskouriakoff, David H. Kelley, and I suggested that one of the two main protagonists was a Copán ruler whose hieroglyphic name was Yax "Sun at Horizon."[16] We also agreed that this ruler was inaugurated on July 2, A.D. 763, and that the protagonist on the left was handing him the scepter of office (see Figure 13-4).

The discovery (or rediscovery) that Maya inscriptions dealt with real historic figures greatly speeded up the process of analysis. Soon linguists like Floyd Lounsbury were at work on the actual pronunciation of the glyphs, combining their efforts with those of archaeologists (David Kelley and Peter Mathews) and an art historian (Linda Schele).[17] The decipherment of Stela 3 from the site of Piedras Negras, Guatemala, provides an example of such multidisciplinary approaches. As a student of Proskouriakoff, I used her approach to translate the entire inscription glyph by glyph.[18] Victoria Bricker, a linguistic anthropologist, then showed how each glyph might have been pronounced by the ancient Maya.[19]

By the 1980s most scholars working on the Maya were in agreement that Altar Q recorded a sequence of sixteen consecutive Copán rulers, all but one seated on his hieroglyphic name. Most also believed that one of the protagonists on the west side of the altar was the sixteenth ruler in the sequence, whose name could finally be pronounced *yax* + *pa* + *ca*, or Yax Pac ("First Dawn").[20] Lord Yax Pac was shown facing to his right, where he looked upon the glyphs that gave the date of his inauguration. Handing him the scepter of office was the other protagonist, a ruler named Yax Kuk Mo' or "Blue-green Quetzal Macaw." His headdress supplies the hieroglyphs of his name, and he sits on the hieroglyphic compound meaning *ahau*, "hereditary lord."

THE 1990S: MAYA WRITING IS A COMBINATION OF PROPAGANDA, MYTH, AND HISTORY

The 1990s is a period of real irony, because the breakthroughs of 1958–1960—which returned us to an historical perspective on Maya hieroglyphs—now threaten the notion that Maya writing is history. So many Maya texts have now been translated that we can no longer defend the notion that the Maya were only recording true events in the lives of their rulers. They were also employing heavy doses of political propaganda.

Altar Q is a prime example of such a combination of history and propaganda. Because the two protagonists, Yax Pac and Yax Kuk Mo', are shown facing each other, we might assume that they were contemporaries. We might also assume that we are witnessing an historic event during which Yax Kuk Mo' passed the scepter of office to his successor, Yax Pac.

In fact, Yax Kuk Mo' was *not* Yax Pac's immediate predecessor in office; he was the *first* in the sequence of sixteen rulers, ostensibly the "founder of the dynasty." Based on other monuments at Copán, it appears that Yax Kuk Mo' actually ruled ca. A.D. 430, some 333 years before Yax Pac's inauguration.[21] Thus the west side of Altar Q cannot record an actual historic event, since Yax Kuk Mo' would have been long dead by the time Yax Pac received his scepter of office. Having discovered this fact, our curiosity is aroused. Let us see what else we can discover about these rulers of Copán.

We turn first to the text on the upper surface of Altar Q, expecting it to feature Yax Pac, the ruler who commissioned it. Instead, the hieroglyphic text features the deeds of Yax Kuk Mo', who is proclaimed the founder of the dynasty. We learn that the monument was carved in A.D. 775 (twelve years after Yax Pac's inauguration), and that the two featured accomplishments of Yax Kuk Mo' took place in A.D. 426, some 350 years before Altar Q was carved. Why, we wonder, would Yax Pac devote so much space on his own altar to the accomplishments of a long-dead predecessor?

We turn now to a stone bench in Temple 11, another building at Copán. This bench was carved in A.D. 773—two years before Altar Q—and also commissioned by Yax Pac. On the bench we see twenty seated figures, divided into two groups of ten, one of whom is Yax Pac himself. Who are these figures, and how do they relate to the sixteen on Altar Q? Since Yax Pac always refers to himself as the sixteenth ruler in his dynasty, who are the additional four people on the Temple 11 bench?

Finally, we turn to Stela 8 at Copán.[22] This is a free-standing stone monument carved in A.D. 783, on the twentieth anniversary of Yax Pac's inauguration to the throne (see Figure 13-5 on page 202 and Figure 13-6 on page 203). In its text, Yax Pac discloses for the first time that his mother was a royal woman from the ancient Maya city of Palenque, 265 miles northwest of Copán. Nowhere on this monument, nor on any commissioned by Yax Pac, is the name of his father given. Now our curiosity is heightened even more. Who was Yax Pac's father? If he were one of the sixteen members of the dynasty founded by Yax Kuk Mo', would he not be mentioned by Yax Pac? And why are there no monuments recording Yax Pac's father's marriage to the royal woman from Palenque?

Let us now summarize the evidence we have. In A.D. 763 a ruler named Yax Pac ascends to the throne of Copán. In A.D. 775 he dedicates Temple 16 at

Copán, and he has Altar Q set in front of it. On the upper surface of the altar he orders the carving of a long inscription concerning the accomplishments of Yax Kuk Mo', a ruler preceding him by more than 333 years. On one side of the altar he orders a scene in which Yax Kuk Mo' hands him the scepter of office, and on the other sides he shows other members of the dynasty founded by Yax Kuk Mo'. At no point on any monument does he establish his biological relationship to any of the other rulers on the altar. Finally, on the twentieth anniversary of his inauguration he commissions a stela, on which he reveals that his mother was a royal woman from a city 265 miles away.

In my opinion, we are dealing with political propaganda. Yax Pac had Altar Q carved not to record an historic event, but to legitimize his right to a throne to which he had ascended twelve years earlier.[23] He achieved this by showing himself receiving the scepter of office from a long-dead heroic king whose exploits were recorded on top of the altar. He claimed royal bloodlines through his mother, but never mentioned his father nor proved his descent from the heroic king. This is the kind of propaganda one might expect when there was a break in Copán's dynastic succession. Perhaps the previous ruler had died without heirs; or perhaps Yax Pac—emphasizing his mother's royal credentials—had managed to wrest the throne from the legitimate heir.

OTHER EXAMPLES OF PROPAGANDA

The Altar Q story is only one case of Maya history manipulated for political purposes. Three carved stone monuments from the Pasión River drainage of western Guatemala provide an equally interesting story, one that combines war, astronomy, propaganda, and history.

The story begins at the Maya sites of Dos Pilas and Aguateca, two cities so closely allied that they used the same emblem glyph (see Figure 13-1 on page 195). In the eighth century A.D. two monuments alleging the same series of events were erected at both cities. The stela at Dos Pilas displays superior carving, has a longer hieroglyphic text, and is twenty-two feet high. The stela at Aguateca was carved more hurriedly, has a shorter text, and is 9½ feet high.[24]

Both monuments mention three events from an eight-day period in A.D. 735. The first event, on November 29, has been interpreted as a battle with Seibal, another city in the Pasión River drainage. The second event, on November 30, has been translated as the "decapitation" of the defeated lord of Seibal. The third event, on December 6, has been interpreted as "the adorning of the prisoner."

On both monuments, the defeated lord of Seibal (whose name was "Jaguar-paw Jaguar") is shown beneath the feet of the Dos Pilas ruler. The lord of Seibal has ropes tied around his arms, is bent over in a posture of submission, and is carved at much smaller scale than his standing captor (see Figure 13-7 on page 204). Given their translation of the November 30 event as

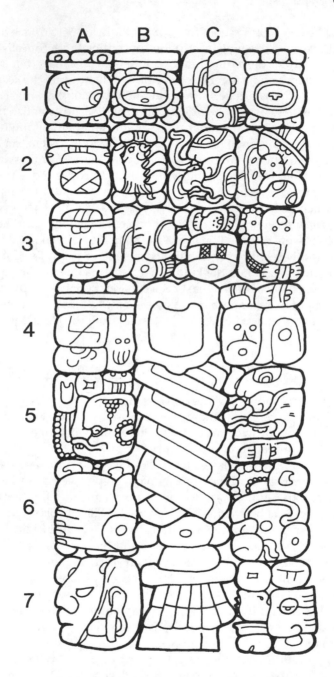

FIGURE 13-5   HIEROGLYPHIC TEXT ON STELA 8 AT COPÁN

Read across line 1 (A1–D1), then across lines 2 and 3. Then read down from A4–A7 and D4–D7.

Source: Redrawn by J. Klausmeyer from Schele and Freidel, 1990, p. 331.

	A	B	C	D
1	6 Caban July 2, A.D. 763 (his accession to the throne)	10 Mol	Forward count to	a day 9 lk
2	and a month 15 Zip (5 days after his 20th anniversary)	His autosacrifice was performed by	ruler's title	Yax Pac
3	sky title	royal title	2 units of 20 years	celebration event
4	(he is the) 16th ruler in the sequence			a royal title
5	lord of Copán,			title
6	offspring of a female,			in the royal line of
7	the royal woman			Palenque.

FIGURE 13-6   TRANSLATION OF THE STELA 8 TEXT,
GIVING YAX PAC'S CLAIM THAT HIS MOTHER WAS FROM PALENQUE

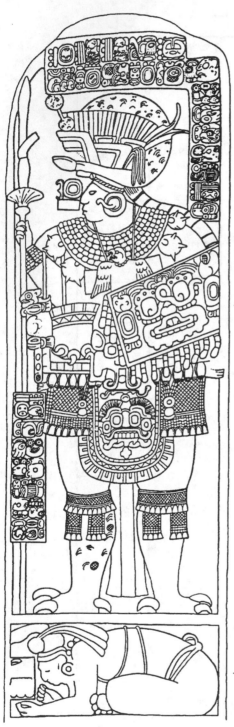

Hieroglyphic text reporting battle with Seibal and awarding of "captor" title to the ruler of Dos Pilas

← Dos Pilas ruler holding spear and shield

FIGURE 13-7   STONE MONUMENT FROM AGUATECA

The monument shows the ruler of Dos Pilas standing above the cramped body of his prisoner, the ruler of Seibal.

Source: Redrawn by Kay Clahassey from Graham, 1967, Figure 5.

← Seibal ruler tied up with rope

a "decapitation," some Mayanists—following the 1960–1990 framework, which views all Maya texts as "history"—have concluded that the Seibal ruler was defeated and killed by his Dos Pilas rival. In celebration of this military victory, the Dos Pilas ruler erected a twenty-two-foot stela at Dos Pilas and a smaller version at the allied city of Aguateca.[25]

Let us turn next to the city of Seibal. Among its monuments are carved stone steps that record the date October 30, A.D. 747, an event that took place twelve years after the alleged battle. To our surprise, we read about the same Seibal ruler we saw tied up on the stelae at Dos Pilas and Aguateca as the loser in an important ritual ballgame. Such ballgames have been interpreted as mechanisms of "conflict resolution," deadly serious contests designed to eliminate the need for war by resolving disputes between neighboring cities. Some scholars now think that the Seibal ruler was sacrificed following that ballgame, rather than twelve years earlier. But if we find yet another monument showing the Seibal ruler alive and well five years after the ballgame, will we be forced to revise our thinking again?

What is going on here? Was the Seibal ruler really captured? Was he decapitated or not? How could he participate in a ballgame twelve years after he was killed by the lord of Dos Pilas? Were any of the hieroglyphic claims true, or was it all propaganda?

One answer is that we are seeing two different versions of history, each publicly displayed by one of two rival cities. Dos Pilas claims that its ruler defeated (and may have sacrificed) the lord of Seibal in A.D. 735. Seibal claims that its ruler not only survived the battle, but played in a ballgame in A.D. 747. Each city has its own political agenda. This situation is analogous to the daily press releases put out by both the Iraqi government and the U.S. Pentagon during the early stages of the 1991 Persian Gulf War. Both sides agreed there was a war going on; that part was history. Each side claimed it was winning; that part was propaganda.

In my opinion, there probably was a battle between Dos Pilas and Seibal, and that was history. The Seibal lord was, however, probably not decapitated or sacrificed; that was propaganda fomented by the Dos Pilas ruler. If we had only the Dos Pilas version of the events, we might have believed their story; but once we read Seibal's version, we could see the conflict between the two versions.

In the case of the Maya, we may even have reason to question the specific dates of some battles. Thanks to the work of Floyd Lounsbury, David Kelley, and Mary Miller,[26] we know that the ancient Maya followed the behavior of the planet Venus and used it as an important augury, or predictor of success, in warfare. November 29, A.D 735—the alleged date of the battle between Seibal and Dos Pilas—coincided with the appearance of Venus as the Evening Star. October 30, A.D. 747—the alleged date of the Seibal ruler's participation in a ritual ballgame—coincides with what astronomers call the inferior conjunction of Venus.

The ancient Maya wanted us to believe that such battles were all timed to important astronomical events, and many probably were. Because some battles were reported seventy or more years after the fact, however, there was always the opportunity to assign auspicious dates to them retroactively. The latter possibility is hard to rule out for the following reason: We have other Maya texts that link both historical and mythical events to astronomical cycles thousands of years in the past, indeed so far in the past that they may not have happened at all.[27]

THE PROSPECTS FOR FUTURE STUDY

I argued in a recent book that Maya hieroglyphic texts were not really history, but a *combination* of history, myth, and propaganda.[28] Maya writing was controlled by the ruling elite, and while it was based on real persons and events, it was biased and distorted in ways that suited the current needs of those rulers.

Maya studies are now divided into two opposing theoretical camps: those who think that the Maya were writing unmanipulated history, and those who believe that the inscriptions included large doses of royal propaganda. The first group are humanists who believe that the texts can be used to write a straightforward history of the Maya. The second group, to which I belong, are social scientists who believe that the texts provide material for an analysis of Maya rulers' political goals, strategies, and agendas. What we hope to gain from the texts is an understanding of what Maya rulers wanted their subjects, their fellow nobles, their allies, and their enemies to believe. We do not believe they were trying to write impartial history.

One reason we believe this is that it was true of every other early writing system of the ancient world. The neighbors of the Maya—the Aztec, Mixtec, and Zapotec Indians of ancient Mexico—also used heavy doses of propaganda, mixing mythological and legendary events with historic ones in order to present their rulers in the best light.[29]

So, too, did the elites of Old World civilizations. The ancient Egyptians, like the Maya, portrayed their rulers as giants standing on the crumpled bodies of their enemies.[30] Were their military victories all "true history"? No. Egyptologist John Wilson has shown that five different pharaohs, spanning a period of 1,600 years, claimed to have executed the same Libyan noble prisoner in the presence of his wife and two sons. The hieroglyphic names of those Libyans, including the names of the wife and two sons, are duplicated exactly.[31] Nothing could be clearer than that later Egyptian pharaohs simply repeated the identical conquest claims of earlier rulers, much as Copán's Yax Pac used the surface of Altar Q to recite the accomplishments of the much earlier ruler Yax Kuk Mo'.

Over the next decade, many scholars will understandably devote themselves to translating more of the undeciphered Maya glyphs, to correcting past mistakes in translations, and to improving our understanding of how glyphs were pronounced. A major new frontier for Maya studies, however, will be the use of these ancient texts to understand broad anthropological issues. We need to know how rulers bolstered their position with strategic political and marital alliances; how their territories expanded and contracted; how major and minor lords interacted; and how subjugated towns battled for independence from the larger cities that controlled them.

We will not be able to achieve those anthropological goals as long as we continue to treat every Maya ruler's text as gospel, failing to recognize it as the biased, self-serving claim that it was. It is ironic that at the dawn of Maya studies 150 years ago, John L. Stephens pointed us in the right direction when he compared Maya writing to that of Mesopotamia and Egypt. Ask scholars in those two regions whether the texts they study are history or propaganda, and they will unhesitatingly answer, "both."

NOTES

1. Joyce Marcus, "Lowland Maya Archaeology at the Crossroads," *American Antiquity* 48 (1983): 454–488.
2. John Lloyd Stephens, *Incidents of Travel in Central America, Chiapas, and Yucatan* (New York: Harper and Brothers, 1841).
3. Herbert J. Spinden, *A Study of Maya Art*, Memoir VI of the Peabody Museum of American Archaeology and Ethnology (Cambridge, MA: Peabody Museum, Harvard University, 1913), pp. 94–95.
4. Sylvanus G. Morley, *The Ancient Maya* (Stanford, CA: Stanford University Press, 1946); J. Eric S. Thompson, "Maya Chronology: Glyph G of the Lunar Series," *American Anthropologist* 31 (1929): 223–231; J. Eric S. Thompson, *Maya Hieroglyphic Writing* (Washington, D.C.: Carnegie Institution of Washington, Publication 589, 1950).
5. Thompson, *Maya Hieroglyphic Writing*, p. 155.
6. J. Eric S. Thompson, *A Catalog of Maya Hieroglyphs* (Norman: University of Oklahoma Press, 1962).
7. Sylvanus G. Morley, *An Introduction to the Study of Maya Hieroglyphs* (Washington, D.C.: Bureau of American Ethnology, Bulletin 57, 1915), pp. 114–129; Thompson, *Maya Hieroglyphic Writing*, pp. 314–316.
8. Heinrich Berlin, "Glifos nominales en el sarcófago de Palenque: un ensayo," *Humanidades*, vol. 2, no. 10 (Guatemala City: University of San Carlos, 1959), pp. 1–8.
9. Heinrich Berlin, "El glifo 'emblema' en las inscripciones mayas," *Journal de la Société des Américanistes de Paris* 47 (1958): 111–119.
10. Tatiana Proskouriakoff, "Historical Implications of a Pattern of Dates at Piedras Negras, Guatemala," *American Antiquity* 25 (1960): 454–475.
11. Tatiana Proskouriakoff, "Portraits of Women in Maya Art," in S. K. Lothrop, ed., *Essays in Pre-Columbian Art and Archaeology* (Cambridge: Harvard University Press, 1961), pp. 81–99; Tatiana Proskouriakoff, "Historical Data in the Inscriptions of Yaxchilan, Part I," *Estudios de Cultura Maya* 3 (1963): 149–167; Tatiana Proskouriakoff, "Historical Data in the Inscriptions of Yaxchilan, Part II," *Estudios de Cultura Maya* 4 (1964): 177–201.
12. Herbert J. Spinden, "Portraiture in Central American Art," in F. W. Hodge, ed., *Holmes Anniversary Volume* (Washington: J. W. Bryan Press, 1916), p. 446; Morley, *The Ancient Maya*, Plate 66.
13. Stephens, *Incidents of Travel in Central America, Chiapas, and Yucatan*, p. 140.

14. John E. Teeple, *Maya Astronomy* (Washington, D.C.: Carnegie Institution of Washington, Publication 403, Contributions to American Archaeology, vol. 1, no. 2, 1930).

15. Thompson, *Maya Hieroglyphic Writing*, pp. 205, 317.

16. Proskouriakoff, "Historical Implications of a Pattern of Dates at Piedras Negras, Guatemala," p. 468; David H. Kelley, "Glyphic Evidence for a Dynastic Sequence at Quiriguá," *American Antiquity* 27 (1962): 332–333; Joyce Marcus, *An Epigraphic Approach to the Territorial Organization of the Lowland Classic Maya* (Ph.D. diss., Harvard University, 1974), pp. 173–180; Joyce Marcus, *Emblem and State in the Classic Maya Lowlands: An Epigraphic Approach to Territorial Organization* (Washington, D.C.: Dumbarton Oaks, 1976), pp. 139–143.

17. Daniel G. Brinton, "The Ancient Phonetic Alphabet of Yucatan," *American Bibliopolist* 2 (1870): 143–148; Benjamin L. Whorf, "The Phonetic Value of Certain Characters in Maya Writing," *Papers of the Peabody Museum of American Archaeology and Ethnology* 13 (Cambridge: Harvard University, 1933); Yuri V. Knorozov, *The Writing of the Maya Indians*, trans. Sophie Coe, Peabody Museum of Archaeology and Ethnology, Russian Translation Series, vol. 4 (Cambridge: Harvard University, 1967); David H. Kelley, "Kakupacal and the Itzas," *Estudios de Cultura Maya* 7 (1968): 255–268; Floyd G. Lounsbury, "Pacal," p. ii, and Peter Mathews and Linda Schele, "Lords of Palenque—The Glyphic Evidence," pp. 63–76, in Merle G. Robertson, ed., *Primera Mesa Redonda de Palenque, Part I* (Pebble Beach, CA: Robert Louis Stevenson School, 1974).

18. Joyce Marcus, "The Origins of Mesoamerican Writing," *Annual Review of Anthropology* 5 (1976): 62–63.

19. Victoria R. Bricker, *A Grammar of Mayan Hieroglyphs* (New Orleans: Middle American Research Institute, Tulane University, Publication 56, 1986), pp. 192–198.

20. Floyd G. Lounsbury, "The Names of a King: Hieroglyphic Variants as a Key to Decipherment," in William F. Hanks and Don S. Rice, eds., *Word and Image in Maya Culture* (Salt Lake City: University of Utah Press, 1989), pp. 73–91; Linda Schele and David Freidel, *A Forest of Kings* (New York: William Morrow, 1990).

21. Linda Schele, "The Founders of Lineages at Copán and Other Maya Sites," *Copán Note 8* (Tegucigalpa, Honduras: IHAH); William L. Fash, *Scribes, Warriors, and Kings: The City of Copán and the Ancient Maya* (London: Thames and Hudson, 1991), pp. 79–83.

22. Sylvanus G. Morley, *The Inscriptions at Copan* (Washington, D.C.: Carnegie Institution of Washington, Publication 219, 1920), Plate 32; Marcus, *Emblem and State in the Classic Maya Lowlands: An Epigraphic Approach to Territorial Organization*, p. 145; Schele and Freidel, *A Forest of Kings*, pp. 330–331.

23. Joyce Marcus, *Mesoamerican Writing Systems: Propaganda, Myth, and History in Four Ancient Civilizations* (Princeton, NJ: Princeton University Press, 1992), pp. 256–257.

24. Ian Graham, *Archaeological Explorations in El Peten, Guatemala* (New Orleans: Middle American Research Institute, Tulane University, Publication 33, 1967), p. 14.

25. Ibid., pp. 9–19; Stephen D. Houston, *Hieroglyphs and History at Dos Pilas* (Austin: University of Texas Press, 1993).

26. F. G. Lounsbury, "Astronomical Knowledge and Its Uses at Bonampak, Mexico," in Anthony F. Aveni, ed., *Archaeoastronomy in the New World* (Cambridge: Cambridge University Press, 1982), pp. 143–168; David H. Kelley, "Maya Astronomical Tables and Inscriptions," in Anthony F. Aveni, ed., *Native American Astronomy* (Austin: University of Texas Press, 1977), pp. 57–74; Mary E. Miller, *The Murals of Bonampak* (Princeton, NJ: Princeton University Press, 1986).

27. Floyd G. Lounsbury, "Maya Numeration, Computation, and Calendrical Astronomy," in C. C. Gillispie, ed., *Dictionary of Scientific Biography*, vol. 15, Supplement 1 (New York: Scribner's and Sons, 1978), pp. 759–818; Floyd G. Lounsbury, "A Rationale for the Initial Date of the Temple of the Cross at Palenque," in Merle G. Robertson, ed., *The Art, Iconography, and Dynastic History of Palenque, Part III: Proceedings of the Segunda Mesa Redonda de Palenque* (Pebble Beach, CA: Robert Louis Stevenson School, 1976), pp. 211–224; Floyd G. Lounsbury, "Some Problems in the Interpretation of the Mythological Portion of the Hieroglyphic Text of the Temple of the Cross at Palenque," in Merle G. Robertson, ed., *Third Palenque Round Table 1978, Part 2* (Austin: University of Texas Press, 1980), pp. 99–115; Schele and Freidel, *A Forest of Kings*, pp. 244–254; Thompson, *Maya Hieroglyphic Writing*, pp. 314–317.

28. Marcus, *Mesoamerican Writing Systems: Propaganda, Myth, and History in Four Ancient Civilizations.*

29. Ibid., pp. 143–152.

30. Bruce Trigger, "The Narmer Palette in Crosscultural Perspective," in M. Gorg and E. Pusch, eds., *Festschrift Elmar Edel 1979* (Bamberg: Kurt Urlaub, 1979), pp. 409–416.

31. John A. Wilson, "The Royal Myth in Ancient Egypt," *Proceedings of the American Philosophical Society* 100 (1956): 439–442; Jean Leclant, "La 'famille libyenne' au Temple Haut du Pepi Ier.," *Le Livre du Centenaire 1880–1980* (Cairo: Institut Français d'Archéologie Orientale, 1980), pp. 49–54.

SUGGESTED READINGS

Fash, William L. *Scribes, Warriors, and Kings: The City of Copán and the Ancient Maya*. New York: Thames and Hudson, 1991. A comprehensive overview of recent excavations and newly discovered texts from Copán, the city of Altar Q.

Henderson, John S. *The World of the Ancient Maya*. Ithaca, NY: Cornell University Press, 1981. A well-balanced synthesis of major topics in Maya archaeology.

Marcus, Joyce. *Mesoamerican Writing Systems: Propaganda, Myth, and History in Four Ancient Civilizations*. Princeton, NJ: Princeton University Press, 1992. This book develops a typology of four different types of propaganda and then applies it to the Maya, Zapotec, Mixtec, and Aztec writing systems.

Sabloff, Jeremy A., and John S. Henderson. *Ancient Maya Civilization in the Eighth Century A.D*. Washington, D.C.: Dumbarton Oaks, 1993. A recent synthesis of Maya civilization during its heyday, from A.D. 700 to 800.

Sabloff, Jeremy A. *The New Archaeology and the Ancient Maya*. New York: Scientific American Library Series, 1990. Discusses the necessity of formulating questions before conducting research and the importance of establishing a good fit between evidence and interpretations.

Sharer, Robert J. *The Ancient Maya*, 5th ed. Stanford: Stanford University Press, 1994. An up-to-date and highly informative overview of Maya archaeology.

Stephens, John L. *Incidents of Travel in Central America, Chiapas, and Yucatan*. Reprint, New York: Dover Paperbacks, 1969. This adventure story is set in the mid-nineteenth century, with Stephens and Catherwood leading us on a trip to discover Maya ruins covered by jungle.

GENDER AND ARCHAEOLOGY

CHERYL CLAASSEN

As I entered college in 1971, the Women's movement was generating much activity on campus and in the field of anthropology, my major. As I read my archaeology books I began collecting ways to identify women in the archaeological record. The sexing of skeletons was one obvious way in which archaeologists were able to identify women. Vitamin C storage is higher in women's vertebrae and this difference had been used in a European study to sex poorly preserved skeletons. The types of grave goods could also suggest the sex of those buried. Further, ethnography suggested that the size of the house pattern indicated if a community was matrilocal (the new couple lived with the family of the wife). And archaeologists argued that spatial clustering of design elements on women's or men's tools could differentiate matrilineal from patrilineal societies (inheritance was transmitted through either the mother or the father). My advisor in graduate school told me that comparing the chemistry of children's teeth with those of adult women and men in a burial population could tell us which parent married in and which parent was resident in the region from birth.[1]

I presented all these possibilities for identifying women in the classes I taught as a graduate student in the late 1970s. During this time I contemplated the difference in learning atmospheres I encountered during my schooling. At the University of Arkansas during the early 1970s most of the graduate student assistantships went to women, the state archaeologist was a woman, several of the affiliated field archaeologists were women, the crews often had as many or more women than men, and many of the graduate students were women. At Harvard in the mid-1970s through the early 1980s—my graduate school years—there was one woman archaeologist on the faculty and about five women graduate students. It was only later that I learned that it is typical to find more women in state universities than in private ones. Ironically, my undergraduate mentor was a man and my graduate mentor a woman.

As I considered the relationship of gender to the current field of archaeology, I worked on a research project that explored the relationship of gender to archaeological study. In the mid-1980s I was working on a particularly pesky problem in the prehistory of the eastern United States. About two thousand to seven thousand years ago there was a phenomenon known as the Shell Mound Archaic, in which freshwater shells were often mounded on the landscape along the Green River in Kentucky and the Ohio, Tennessee, Savannah, and St. John rivers. These mounds are striking not only for their size and the high density of artifacts but also for their use as cemeteries. Why were these mounds begun and why had shell mounding ceased? The traditional explanation was that this mounding behavior began because shells were available during that time but not before seven thousand years ago nor after two thousand years ago.

But I had my doubts about this explanation. Freshwater shellfish occur today in hundreds of rivers, streams, and lakes and they have been intensively commercially exploited since 1891, first for the shell button industry and now for the Japanese cultured pearl industry. If the shell mounds were simply food debris and the timing of the shell mounds was simply because of the presence of shellfish in the rivers, why had these mounds not appeared along hundreds of rivers in the eastern United States? I found a few other explanations in the literature of the 1950s and 1960s—humans had harvested all the shellfish, or people migrated out of the Green and Tennessee river valleys. Again the question arose as to why these people had not moved to other rivers and resumed shellfish harvesting there.

In 1985 I had one of those cherished moments in science when a totally new awareness of my research problem came to me—the environmental explanation, the overharvesting explanation, and the migration explanation all implied the same social consequences. Assuming, as do most archaeologists, based on ethnographic examples, that women and children did the shellfishing, these three explanations meant that the end of shellfishing impacted the schedules and workload of women and children. What if shellfishing and shell mounding stopped not because of environmental reasons but because of social reasons? What if women and children *decided* not to harvest shellfish anymore?

This simple change in thinking from women and children being passive to women and children being agents of change in the course of prehistoric events freed my imagination. New hypotheses based on stereotypical concepts of gendered activities flowed easily. Why would women stop shellfishing? Could domesticated plants now be taking women's time, providing an equivalent source of nutrition? If men were the shellfishers, why would men stop shellfishing? Maybe shellfish flesh was used as fish bait and they changed from baited fishing techniques to unbaited techniques, such as nets. There were other hypotheses as well. In each hypothesis it was not the gender of the actor that needed further research but rather the implied activity—what was the evidence for the presence of domesticated plants 3,500 years ago, when most of the mounding activity ceased along the Tennessee or Green or Savannah rivers? What was the evidence for fishing technology 4,500 years ago and 3,000 years ago? Thinking about gender was key in this process for it forced me to conceptualize real people—their decisions, their workloads, their communities, their activities. I imagined that not all women were shell-fishers, that some simply did not like the food and spent their time in other activities while other women and children excelled at it, earning the respect of their neighbors and kin.

In tackling the research problem I have just described, as well as in any other research endeavor, imagination is a key element for the scientist. The point of the various academic degrees in anthropology is to bring the student to a common understanding of the culture history, the key pieces of research, the contemporary ideas. While this academic training has many merits, it also has the unwanted side effect of standardizing the hypotheses, theories, and references we use to solve research problems. Sexism has a similar impact: It standardizes the way we view women and men, now and in the past. While sexism has an immediate, often painful impact on men and women in our modern societies, there is a subtler influence on scientists: Sexism limits our imaginations. Once the imagination is freed, new hypotheses and theories will emerge to shake loose entrenched ideas and tabled problems.

Thinking of women and children as agents of cultural change—in fact, thinking of men as agents of cultural change—was out of fashion among most archaeologists from about 1970 until the mid-1980s. During those years most archaeologists thought that the dominant factor in culture history was the ecosystem—that the changes and challenges brought by the physical environment could and did explain everything that we saw in the archaeological record. But beginning in the 1980s a noticeable number of archaeologists began positing that people could and did cause change—in their own kin groups and in their communities. Gender, class, and ethnic struggles have assumed a new level of respect from archaeologists.[2]

For some archaeologists the task at hand has been to make women in the past visible, or to devise methods whereby gender can be deduced from objects.[3] But many feminist archaeologists want the enterprise to result in more than the reclamation of past women. Feminist archaeologists have the goal of exploring past social relationships, specifically those between social groups that differ in age, gender, status, occupation, class, or ethnicity. Increasingly, feminist archaeologists are concerned with our modern relationship to our voluntary audience and to the descendants of our subjects. Feminist archaeologists are striving to be more inclusive of past and present peoples, particularly in how they write about the past.[4]

The impact of feminism and gender studies on the discipline has been startling but mirrors that on every other academic field. Feminist positivists—those who believe that there is a knowable past if one correctly employs the scientific method—have exposed biases that not only inhibited the scientist's imagination but resulted in the obstruction of the work of science, even to the point of having obscured basic research simply because the data were collected by a woman. Feminist poststructuralists—those who view humans primarily as symbol makers and users—have questioned the Western privileging of words over signs and the automatic acceptance of the male/female opposition. Postprocessual feminist archaeologists—those placing social interactions, particularly involving gender, as central to understanding cultural changes in the past—have done serious damage to the tenets of ecological determinism and even to postprocessual analyses generated by men who have ignored gender issues.[5] Feminist research has shown that every form of social organization archaeologists have typically used—class, tribe, state, sex, egalitarian, craft specialist, etc.—needs to be redefined incorporating gender and the conclusions drawn from their application reexamined. And the endeavor is growing.[6]

While some people would say that gender is a new topic in archaeology, in fact, gender has always been present. Book and article titles talk about man the hunter, the evolution of man, man the inventor, and archaeologists occasionally mention woman the childkeeper, woman the cook, woman the plant gatherer. What is new in archaeology is an explicit examination of gender, the use of gender to test theories, to develop hypotheses, to set up research problems. The pivotal paper in the history of both gendered and feminist archaeology, "Archaeology and the Study of Gender," was written by Margaret Conkey and Janet Spector in 1984. Since that time, numerous symposia on gender have been organized at regional and national archaeology conferences (some of which were published), courses have been offered on gender and archaeology, and several conferences exclusively addressing gender have been held.[7] Not since the early 1970s has there been such a flurry of intellectual activity in archaeology as now surrounds the topic of gender.

ENGENDERING THE PROFESSION

What are the gendered research questions being tackled by scholars in archaeology? The area of inquiry attracting the most attention so far is that of the structure of the discipline of archaeology itself. Surveys of archaeologists have found that women more often have nontenure track jobs when affiliated with universities, that a larger percentage of women archaeologists teach at state universities (versus private universities or government entities) than men archaeologists, that women working in contracting companies and in cultural resource management are paid less than are men at the same rank, even after holding the position longer and having more education.[8] Surveys have found that in proportion to their membership in professional organizations, women submit papers for publication less frequently than do men, their writings are cited less often, their books are reviewed less often, and they act as reviewers less often than do men.[9] Women feel less confident about their field skills or may actually learn less than men in field schools, they are given fewer chances to teach as graduate students, and they are more likely to drop out of the field after graduation.[10]

I have already pointed out that sexism hurts the scientific process by limiting the imagination of scientists (as does racism, heterosexism, ethnocentrism, and the professionalization process). Sexism has other, more obvious impacts on the practice of archaeology. Because of the nature of elementary and secondary education, girls are usually less prepared and less comfortable with mathematics and hard sciences. When these girls become archaeologists, they continue to stay away from statistical tests and useful techniques such as archaeometry (physics of dating techniques), chemical studies for sourcing raw materials and studying diet and environmental change, and simulation modeling. Our cultural equation of boys associated with weapons, military items, rocks, and dirt and girls associated with tidying, sewing, and cooking have translated into adult research domains: Men numerically dominate the study of military archaeology, nautical archaeology, lithic tool replication, metallurgy, and geomorphology, while women numerically dominate the study of buttons, foods (particularly floral analysis), weaving, and are more often found in archaeological laboratories.

Biographies are beginning to appear about specific women archaeologists, and several individuals have begun researching women's roles in specific archaeological organizations, specific long-term field schools, historical eras, states, countries, and university programs. Women have participated in the work of archaeology in a much broader range of ways than have men.[11] Lacking education or career time, women have resorted to volunteering on digs, recording and collecting at sites on weekends and vacations, buying sites, establishing and running archaeological and historical societies and preserves, working in museums, performing analyses at home, funding expeditions, donating collections, and editing archaeological newsletters and journals. Women also assisted professional men (not their husbands) by leading them to sites, hosting conferences in their homes, editing men's papers, and housing them while in school. Virtually all of these women were white but black women excavated several sites in the South during the Works Progress Administration program.[12]

Writings about theoretical issues are very popular in the effort to engender archaeology. Women, in particular, believe they have something to say about gender and many women archaeologists have appropriate theoretical backgrounds via their own participation in the Women's movement to contribute to this discourse. The large number of theoretical papers addressing gender contradicts the impression from our professional journals that women are not engaged in theoretical discussions. It suggests instead that there is a social network surrounding journals that few women can penetrate, that the theoretical issues discussed in professional journals are of minor interest to women archaeologists when compared to their interest in gender, or a combination of both these factors. One of the striking aspects of the body of literature addressing gender in archaeology since 1989 is the large number of new authors.

ENGENDERING THE PAST

Theoretical discussions about gender in the past have focused on topics such as mothering, the number of genders, origins of division of labor, expedient stone tools versus formal stone tools, gender negotiations as a cause of social change, landscape, architecture, pottery, style change, colonization, class and state formation, household archaeology, activity areas, methodology, etc. The usefulness of burial data has attracted much attention.[13]

Gender is often defined as a cultural category and sex as a biological category. It is customary in Western society of the twentieth century to view gender as determined by biological sex. Most people, anthropologists included, go so far as to assume that at other times in the history of Western society, gender has always followed from sex, or from soft tissue. Mary Ellen Morbeck, for instance, states that "Gender traditionally has been defined as classification by sex."[14] In fact, the tradition referred to by Morbeck, the determination of gender from genitalia, has a short history in Western thinking. In the Middle Ages, sex was not limited to two categories, but gender was. During the Renaissance, "there was no privileged discourse that could even claim to establish a definitive method by which one distinguished male from female," for the heats of the body could alter genitalia.[15] Until the eighteenth century, and present in the culture of the writer of the Book of Deuteronomy some three thousand years earlier, gender was determined by dress and consequently chosen by the individual. Gender display was used to determine the sex of the one viewed.[16]

Gender was and is attributed among many Native American groups on the basis of both dress and behavioral display.[17] Visions the child recounts and the activities and objects the child is drawn to instruct the relatives as to which gender the child has assumed. In iconographic and glyphic studies of the Maya, dress is the basis for assigning gender because primary sexual characteristics are usually omitted from the depiction. Apparently the Maya viewer was to determine gender from dress.[18]

These examples suggest that prior to the ascendency of biological and medical discourse, many of the world's cultures may have used dress and behavior—rather than biology—as the means by which gender was deduced. Twentieth-century archaeologists, products of a worldview that privileges biological discourse, derive gender in the distant past through the sexing of recovered skeletal material. The trouble with that route is that the two sexes are thought to be synonymous with two genders.

   Not all feminists or anthropologists agree that sex is simply biological, distinct from cultural influence or cultural definition, however. In the burial setting, sex is certainly culturally created. Consider the following example: Sex is assigned to a complete adult skeleton using either an implicit or explicit set of observations. Examples of female traits are more gracile bones, U-shaped mandibles, broader pelves, wide sciatic notch, etc. After examining the skeleton, the archaeologist tallies the traits within the male range of variation and the traits within the female range of variation; whichever percentage of traits is greater is used to determine a sex for the skeleton. That a body should be and must be assigned a sex is cultural baggage carried by the investigator. That statistics are used for deciding a sex is cultural baggage. Sexing a skeleton is a cultural act built on observations of the distribution of sexual characteristics in Western skeletons. Even within Western skeletal populations, systematic error favoring the label "male" has been uncovered.[19] Furthermore, contemporary sexing criteria are particularly suspect when applied to other hominid species. For instance, the australopithecines were quite small and their heads may not have required an enlarged birth canal for passage. In the next several million years, while the female pelves were widening, the male pelves may have been narrowing. For chimps and gorillas, more accurate sexing of skeletons is achieved with dental traits and crania than with pelves.[20]

   These errors of culture aside, archaeologists, following the Western convention, assume that gender follows from sex. Such an equation of sex with gender is probably wrong and denies past individuals the choice of gender they may well have had. Additionally, it homogenizes people into two genders, the same two as are found today in U.S. society. There might be some research questions for which we would need to know sex rather than gender (such as how often did sex and gender not equate in a particular culture) but they have not been the subject of study by archaeologists to date. Instead, the unanimous concern so far has been with gender. Skeletal data lead us astray unless we want to make the simplistic and ethnocentric assumption that sex has always equaled gender.

   Artifacts are one possible way to address gender and circumvent the problem of sex. Burials often contain artifacts. Objects in graves, however, are not simple reflections of who the person was in life. Objects in and on the grave as well as the grave itself can convey information about the deceased, the kin group, the mourners, and the community. Artwork, particularly iconography, may be the most direct expression of gender available to archaeologists. For this reason, the icon-rich highland Mexico and Maya worlds have been fruitful arenas for archaeologists investigating gender relations.[21]

   Just which sex or gender made a particular fishhook or invented pottery or established a fishing camp probably cannot be known. But our inability to assign gender to artifacts need not keep us from asking questions about gender in the past. When in the past did sex became gendered?[22] What has been the relative social status of the genders "man" and "woman" in different past societies? Several archaeologists expect different social functions for gender in different societies and further expect gendering to function differently within the same society at different points in its history. What is the social function of gender? Contrary to a concept of a changing function for gender is one that the function of gender has always been to mark sexuality.[23] A very interesting question that follows from either perspective is: "When, and under what conditions, are gender distinctions emphasized and when are they relaxed or nonexistent?"[24]

Several studies have posited reasons for why an ancient society had more or less concern with gender. Margaret Conkey posited that public gatherings would call forth more concern and attention to gender than would small group household interaction because spouses would be drawn from the larger groups. As the number of public occasions increased in the Upper Paleolithic as population and group size grew, there was a greater social concern with gender and the public and material display of gender.[25] Ian Hodder found that as domestication intensified in central and eastern Europe and the Near East four thousand to six thousand years ago, the elaboration of domestic symbolism—female figurines, in houses and ovens; miniature sets of women, houses, ovens, and pots; pottery decoration; and architecture—increased.[26] When the Catholic leadership sought to separate itself from the laity in the tenth through the twelfth centuries, it equated sexuality, flesh, menstrual blood, and women with sin, thus emphasizing differences not only between celibate priests and their congregations but also between women and men.[27] These examples should make it clear that there can be no universal relationship between gender and either the material expression of gender concerns or the form the concern will take. In fact, one can argue that as concern with gender increases in a society, the material expression of gender could either increase or decrease.

NORTH AMERICAN PAST

To make the discussion of gender more tangible, I will briefly summarize thinking about the North American past generated by gendered research.[28] To organize information, archaeologists have divided the past of every river valley and state into subperiods. The earliest subperiods (Paleoindian and Archaic) are recognizable by the shapes of projectile points, which were presumably men's tools and are found most often in special activity sites rather than in base camps; the later two subperiods in the eastern United States (Woodland and Mississippian) are distinguished by ceramics, which were presumably women's tools and are found most often in villages. The two halves of prehistory are incomparable in either site type or gender focus.[29]

The most focused research into the archaeological record of pre-European North America on gender has been in the southeastern United States during the late Archaic period, three thousand to five thousand years ago. Several phenomena in particular have drawn attention over the past decade: the cessation of shell mounding, the beginnings of plant cultivation, and the rate of adoption of pottery.[30] A closer look at the recent gendered discussion of plant domestication and cultivation will serve to show how an idea creates a discourse in science and how a gendered perspective stimulates thinking.

Throughout the history of American archaeology, it has been assumed that native women were the plant gatherers in prehistory because they were during historic times. When writing about domestication, however, most authors gave no role to women. For example, Bruce Smith of the Smithsonian first published his Floodplain Weed theory in 1987, advancing the idea that there were at least seven domesticated or cultivated indigenous crops prior to the arrival of the tropical domesticates, maize and beans.[31] These early domesticated local crops had adapted from their floodplain habitats to the disturbed soils of human camps. Smith made no mention of gender in his discussions. When a gender was specified, as it was in a 1986 article by Guy Prentice, at that time a graduate anthropology student at the University of Florida, the agents of the change to cultivation were men. Prentice argued that shamans were the individuals who probably introduced the Mexican domesticated gourd into the cultures of the southeastern United States. His thinking was innovative in that he was stressing the significant role that individuals could play in culture change but it was predictable that he would think all shamans were men.[32]

Patty Jo Watson of Washington University and her graduate student Mary Kennedy prepared a paper in 1988 that critiqued the ideas of Prentice, Smith, and other paleoethnobotanists.[33] They pointed out that the women and men involved in the domesticating and cultivating of these plants were seldom mentioned. Ethnographic and ethnohistorical information frequently mentioned women and children planting, reaping, collecting, and processing plants and seeds, yet Smith and other writers degendered the process. Men's hunting is characterized in articles by archaeologists as active work, but women's gathering is seen as passive work. However, in the one example of gender attribution to the introduction of domesticated plants and of the active manipulation of plants and engineering of culture change—that proposed by Prentice—it was assumed that men were the actors.

Smith argued that the continual disturbance of the soil in camps and the constant introduction of seeds to camp soils made it easy for these plants to adapt to human camps. Watson and Kennedy argue that "actual women" disturbed the soil in camp, chose from which plants to harvest and store seeds, processed the seeds into flour, and planted the seeds in the spring. Therefore women were the ones causing the genetic changes in the target plants and women were the ones causing the habitat changes. "[W]e are leery of explanations that remove women from the one realm that is traditionally granted them, as soon as innovation or invention enters the picture."[34] They extend this point to the development of Maiz de Ocho (eight-rowed corn) in the northeastern United States, which was farmed from A.D. 800 to historic times. They reason that Maiz de Ocho was developed from tropical Chapalote maize, which was ill-suited to the environment of the Northeast; women must have consciously developed Maiz de Ocho, conducting breeding experiments, observing the progeny, selecting seed stock that was hardier—in short, consciously manipulating the gene pool of Chapalote maize.

In 1992 Bruce Smith had an opportunity to respond to the criticism of Watson and Kennedy in a restatement of the Floodplain Weed theory of plant domestication in eastern North America. He credits their "interesting and thought provoking potential expansion of the [Floodplain Weed] theory" with providing a valuable correction. "They point out that deliberate planting was down-played...rather than highlighted as a major transition point in human history."[35] That same year Patty Jo Watson published another paper on domestication of plants in the eastern United States in which she reiterated her objection to ideas that denied or trivialized the role that women undoubtedly had in domesticating some native weeds.[36]

In an article published in 1993, "Reconciling the Gender-Credit Critique and the Floodplain Weed Theory of Plant Domestication," Smith elected to address Watson and Kennedy's critique on a point-by-point basis. He detailed four major areas in which the two perspectives disagree: (1) the Mexican origin of gourds; (2) the presence of any truly gender-neutral approaches in archaeology; (3) human intention in plant domestication; and (4) the initial economic importance of the earliest domesticated plants. As he proceeds he examines a number of specific statements and implications of statements by Watson and Kennedy, finding several errors in their presentation of the data. But at the end of the article, Bruce Smith concludes that the two perspectives are compatible rather than competitive. He again acknowledges their writing in helping to clarify and develop his thoughts on the Floodplain Weed theory, particularly in the area of human intention in the domestication process. Of even greater importance, he writes, are the research questions for the period of 2250 to 250 B.C. in the eastern United States that are born as a result of Watson and Kennedy's gendered examination of the development of domesticates and agriculture—questions like, "What social mechanisms might have constrained an expanded...early role for these crop plants?"[37]

CONCLUSION

What feminism has brought to archaeology is a renewed focus on the people in the past, people who negotiated gender, ethnic, power, and spiritual relations. It has moved us away somewhat from a twenty-year focus on the environment and the natural sciences. This explicitly feminist archaeology has gained great momentum in the past decade. Far from being faddish or marginalized in the community of archaeologists who do not call themselves "feminist," these writings are influencing their work as well. What we are finding is that a gendered perspective is offering new vigor to research as it has in many other academic fields. Without a doubt, gender impacts the archaeological record as well as archaeologists; gender must be an issue for all of us who study the past and work in this profession.

NOTES

1. I. Kiszely, "On the Possibilities and Methods of the Chemical Determination of Sex from Bones," *OSSA* 1 (1974): 51–62; Melvin Ember, "An Archaeological Indicator of Matrilocal versus Patrilocal Residence," *American Antiquity* 38 (1973): 177–182; William T. Divale, "Living Floor Area and Marital Residence," *Behavior Science Research* 12 (1977): 109–116; William Longacre, "Archeology as Anthropology: A Case Study," *Science* 144 (1964): 1454–1455; James Deetz, *The Dynamics of Stylistic Change in Arikara Ceramics*, Illinois Studies in Anthropology, no. 4 (Urbana: University of Illinois Press, 1965); Jon Ericson, personal communication, 1981.
2. Elizabeth Brumfiel, "Distinguished Lecture in Archeology: Breaking and Entering the Ecosystem—Gender, Class, and Faction Steal the Show," *American Anthropologist* 94 (1992): 551–567.
3. Marcel Kornfeld and Julie Francis, "A Preliminary Historical Outline of Northwestern High Plains Gender Systems," in Dale Walde and Noreen Willows, eds., *The Archaeology of Gender* (Calgary: The Archaeological Association of the University of Calgary, 1991), pp. 444–451; Margaret Ehrenberg, *Women in Prehistory* (Norman: University of Oklahoma Press, 1989); Janet Spector, "Male/Female Task Differentiation among the Hidatza: Toward the Development of an Archaeological Approach to the Study of Gender," in Patricia Albers and Betrice Medicine, eds., *The Hidden Half: Studies of Native Plains Women* (Washington, D.C.: University Press of America, 1983), pp. 77–100.
4. Janet Spector, *What this Awl Means: Feminist Archaeology at a Wahpeton Dakota Village* (St. Paul: Minnesota Historical Society Press, 1994).
5. A number of feminists trained in the sciences have seriously questioned the ability of scientists to be objective, particularly Sandra Harding, *The Science Question in Feminism* (London: Milton Keynes, Open University Press, 1986). See also B. Imber and N. Tuana, "Feminist Perspectives on Science," *Hypatia* 3 (1988): 139–155; Sue Rosser, *Female Friendly Science* (New York: Teacher's College Press, 1990); and Alison Wylie, K. Okruhlik, S. Morton, and L. Thielan-Wilson, "Feminist Critiques of Science: The Epistemological and Methodological Literature," *Women's Studies International Forum* 12 (1988): 379–388. For a discussion of the feminist antiscience perspective in archaeology, see Ericka Engelstad, "Images of Power and Contradiction: Feminist Theory and Post-Processual Archaeology," *Antiquity* 65 (1991): 502–514. Engelstad points out that postprocessual archaeologists, including feminist postprocessualists, criticize "positivist, functionalist, adaptational models of the past that emphasize a scientific, objective, hypothesis-testing approach." Several women archaeologists believe that doing science better will not eliminate the androcentric bias in the profession or in our interpretations.

6. The third Gender and Archaeology Conference in Australia was held in February 1995. The third Archaeology and Gender Conference at Appalachian State University in North Carolina was held in September 1994 with a theme of gender in ancient America. A huge conference was held in Exeter College, England, in July 1994, focusing on gender and material culture. A gender symposium was held at the first meeting of the European Archaeological Association in September 1994.

7. Margaret Conkey and Janet Spector, "Archaeology and the Study of Gender," in Michael Schiffer, ed., *Advances in Archaeological Method and Theory* (New York: Academic Press, 1984), pp. 1–38; Joan Gero and Margaret Conkey, eds., *Engendering Archaeology: Women and Prehistory* (Oxford: Basil Blackwells, 1991); Virginia Miller, ed., *The Role of Gender in Pre-Columbian Art and Architecture* (Lanham: University Press of America, 1988); Walde and Willows, *The Archaeology of Gender*; Cheryl Claassen, ed., *Exploring Gender through Archaeology* (Madison: Prehistory Press, 1992); Cheryl Claassen, ed., *Women in Archaeology* (Philadelphia: University of Pennsylvania Press, 1994).

8. See articles in Walde and Willows, *Archaeology and Gender*; and Claassen, *Women in Archaeology*.

9. Katharine Victor and Mary Beaudry, "Women's Participation in American Prehistoric and Historic Archaeology: A Comparative Look at the Journals *American Antiquity* and *Historical Archaeology*," in Claassen, *Exploring Gender through Archaeology*, pp. 11–21.

10. Tracey Sweely, "Male Hunting Camp or Female Processing Station?" in Claassen, *Women in Archaeology*, pp. 173–201.

11. Claassen, *Women in Archaeology*; Ute Gacs, Aisha Khan, Jerrie McIntyre, and Ruth Weinberg, eds., *Women Anthropologists: Selected Biographies* (Urbana: University of Illinois Press, 1989); Jonathon Reyman, ed., *Rediscovering Our Past: Essays on the History of American Archaeology* (Aldershot, England: Avebury/Ashgate Publishing, 1992).

12. Cheryl Claassen, "Black and White Women at Irene Mound," *Southeastern Archaeology* 12 (1993): 137–147.

13. Charlotte Damm, "From Burials to Gender Roles: Problems and Potentials in Post-Processual Archaeology," in Walde and Willows, *The Archaeology of Gender*, pp. 130–136; Wendy Eisner, "The Consequences of Gender Bias in Mortuary Analysis: A Case Study," in Walde and Willows, *The Archaeology of Gender*, pp. 352–357; Mary Ellen Morbeck, "Bones, Gender, and Life History," in Walde and Willows, *The Archaeology of Gender*, pp. 39–45; Mary Whelan, "Gender and Archaeology: Mortuary Studies and the Search for the Origins of Gender Differentiation," in Walde and Willows, *The Archaeology of Gender*, pp. 358–367.

14. Morbeck, "Bones, Gender, and Life History," p. 39.

15. Ann Rosalind Jones and Peter Stallybrass, "Fetishizing Gender: Constructing the Hermaphrodite in Renaissance Europe," in Julia Epstein and Kristina Straub, eds., *Body Guards: The Cultural Politics of Gender Ambiguity* (New York: Routledge, 1991), pp. 80–111.

16. Druann Pagliassotti, "The Discursive Construction of Sex and Gender in Europe from Early Christianity to the Twentieth Century," paper read at the Forty-Third Annual Meeting of the International Communication Association, Washington, D.C., 1993, p. 10.

17. Harriet Whitehead, "The Bow and the Burdenstrap: A New Look at Institutionalized Homosexuality in Native North America," in S. B. Ortner and H. Whitehead, eds., *Sexual Meanings: The Cultural Construction of Gender* (New York: Cambridge University Press, 1981), pp. 80–115.

18. Rosemary Joyce, "Images of Gender and Labor Organization in Classic Maya Society," in Claassen, *Exploring Gender through Archaeology*, pp. 63–70.

19. P. Bennike, *Paleopathology of Danish Skeletons: A Comparative Study of Demography, Disease, and Injury* (Copenhagen: Akademisk Forlag, 1985).

20. Lori Hager, "The Evidence for Sex Differences in the Hominid Fossil Record," in Walde and Willows, *The Archaeology of Gender*, p. 46.

21. Elizabeth Graham, "Women and Gender in Maya Prehistory," in Walde and Willows, *The Archaeology of Gender*, pp. 470–478; Rosemary Joyce, "Women's Work: Images of Production and Reproduction in Pre-Hispanic Southern Central America (with comments)," *Current Anthropology* 34 (1993): 255–274; Tatiana Proskouriakoff, "Portraits of Women in Maya Art," in Samuel Lothrop, ed., *Essays in Pre-Columbian Art and Archaeology* (Cambridge: Harvard University Press 1961), pp. 81–99; Sharisse McCafferty and Geoffrey McCafferty, "Powerful Women and the Myth of Male Dominance in Aztec Society," *Archaeological Review from Cambridge* 7 (1988): 45–59; Sharisse McCafferty and Geoffrey McCafferty, "Engendering Tomb 7 at Monte Albán (with comments)," *Current Anthropology* 35 (1994): 143–166; Miller, *The Role of Gender in Pre-Columbian Art and Architecture*; María J. Rodríguez V., "La Condición Femenina en Tlaxcala Según las Fuentes," *Mesoamérica* 17 (1989): 1–23.

22. Mary Whelan, "Gender and Archaeology: Mortuary Studies and the Search for the Origins of Gender Differentiation," in Walde and Willows, *The Archaeology of Gender*, pp. 358–365.

23. Cheryl Claassen, "Questioning Gender: An Introduction," in Claassen, *Exploring Gender through Archaeology*, pp. 1–10.

24. Margaret Conkey and Joan Gero, "Tensions, Pluralities, and Engendering Archaeology: An Introduction to Women and Prehistory," in Gero and Conkey, *Engendering Archaeology*, pp. 3–30.

25. Margaret Conkey, "Contexts of Action, Contexts for Power: Material Culture and Gender in the Magdalenian," in Gero and Conkey, *Engendering Archaeology*, pp. 57–92.

26. Ian Hodder, "Gender Representation and Social Reality," in Walde and Willows, *The Archaeology of Gender*, p. 11.

27. J. LeGoff, *The Medieval Imagination* (Chicago: University of Chicago Press, 1985).

28. Donna Seifert, ed., "Gender in Historical Archaeology," *Historical Archaeology* 25, special issue (1991); Cheryl Claassen, "Gender, Shellfishing, and the Shell Mound Archaic," in Gero and Conkey, *Engendering Archaeology*, pp. 276–300; Sandra Hollimon, "Health Consequences of Sexual Division of Labor among Prehistoric Native Americans: The Chumash of California and the Arikara of the North Plains," in Claassen, *Exploring Gender through Archaeology*, pp. 81–88; Tom Jackson, "Pounding Acorn: Women's Production as Social and Economic Focus," in Gero and Conkey, *Engendering Archaeology*, pp. 301–328; Marcel Kornfeld, ed., *Approaches to Gender Processes on the Great Plains* (Plains Anthropological Society, memoir 26, 1991); Madonna Moss, "Shellfish, Gender, and Status on the Northwest Coast: Reconciling Archeological, Ethnographic, and Ethnohistorical Records of the Tlingit," *American Anthropologist* 95 (1993): 631–652; Guy Prentice, "Origins of Plant Domestication

in the Eastern United States: Promoting the Individual in Archaeological Theory," *Southeastern Archaeology* 5 (1986): 103–109; Ken Sassaman, "Gender and Technology at the Archaic-Woodland Transition," in Claassen, *Exploring Gender through Archaeology*, pp. 63–70; Ken Sassaman, *Early Pottery in the Southeast: Tradition and Innovation in Cooking Technology* (Tuscaloosa: University of Alabama Press, 1993); Patty Jo Watson and Mary Kennedy, "The Development of Horticulture in the Eastern Woodlands of North America: Women's Role," in Gero and Conkey, *Engendering Archaeology*, pp. 255–275.

29. Sassaman, "Gender and Technology at the Archaic-Woodland Transition," pp. 63–70.
30. Claassen, "Gender, Shellfishing, and the Shell Mound Archaic," pp. 276–300; Prentice, "Origins of Plant Domestication in the Eastern United States: Promoting the Individual in Archaeological Theory," pp. 103–109; Bruce Smith, "Reconciling the Gender-Credit Critique and the Floodplain Weed Theory of Plant Domestication," in James B. Stoltman, ed., *Archaeology of Eastern North America Papers in Honor of Stephen Williams*, Archaeological Report no. 25 (Jackson: Mississippi Department of Archives and History, 1993), pp. 111–125; Watson and Kennedy, "The Development of Horticulture in the Eastern Woodlands of North America," pp. 255–275; Sassaman, *Early Pottery in the Southeast.*
31. Bruce D. Smith, "The Independent Domestication of Indigenous Seed-Bearing Plants in Eastern North America," in William Keegan, ed., *Emergent Horticultural Economies of the Eastern Woodlands*, Occasional Paper no. 7 (Carbondale: Southern Illinois University at Carbondale Center for Archaeological Investigations, 1987), pp. 3–48.
32. Prentice, "Origins of Plant Domestication in the Eastern United States," pp. 103–109.
33. Watson and Kennedy, "The Development of Horticulture in the Eastern Woodlands of North America."
34. Ibid., p. 264.
35. Bruce Smith, *Rivers of Change* (Washington, D.C.: Smithsonian Institution, 1992), p. 31.
36. Patty Jo Watson, "Origins of Food Production in Western Asia and Eastern North America," in Linda Shane and Edward Cushing, eds., *Quaternary Landscapes* (Minneapolis: University of Minnesota Press, 1992), pp. 1–37.
37. Smith, "Reconciling the Gender-Credit Critique and the Floodplain Weed Theory of Plant Domestication," p. 123.

SUGGESTED READINGS

Bacus, Elisabeth, Alex Barker, Jeffrey Bonevich, Sandra Dunavan, Benjamin Fitzhugh, Debra Gold, Nurit Goldman-Finn, William Griffin, and Karen Mudar, eds. *A Gendered Past: A Critical Bibliography of Gender in Archaeology.* Technical Report 25. Ann Arbor: University of Michigan Museum of Anthropology, 1993. Collection contains annotations of 197 published articles and books as well as evaluations of their arguments.

Claassen, Cheryl, ed. *Women in Archaeology.* Philadelphia: University of Pennsylvania Press, 1994. Extended biographies are found here on Dorothy Poponoe, Madeline

Kneberg Lewis, and Marian White. Forty-four other women are discussed. Surveys cover archaeologists in Arizona, Mesoamericanists, contract archaeologists, and the journal *Historical Archaeology*.

Gero, Joan, and Margaret Conkey, eds. *Engendering Archaeology: Women and Prehistory.* Oxford: Basil Blackwells, 1991. A collection of papers that addresses gender in past societies on several continents. Specific categories of material remains are addressed, such as housing, pottery, shellfishing, spindel whorls, art, and bedrock mortars.

Miller, Virginia, ed. *The Role of Gender in Pre-Columbian Art and Architecture.* Lanham: University Press of America, 1988. A collection of papers on art and architecture in the New World prior to the arrival of Columbus.

Seifert, Donna, ed. "Gender in Historical Archaeology." *Historical Archaeology* 25, special issue (1991). All articles address women in the past. They cover the logging and dairy industries, Dakota women, Spanish women, and women in the fur trade, in New York City, Washington, D.C., and the Chesapeake region.

Walde, Dale, and Noreen Willows, eds. *The Archaeology of Gender.* Calgary: The Archaeological Association of the University of Calgary, 1991. Sixty-nine short papers covering a plethora of topics and geography. Topics include hominids, women in the prehistoric past, women in history, and women in the profession.

PREHISTORIC SOCIAL EVOLUTION

KENT V. FLANNERY

Human beings today are unique in the animal kingdom because they have undergone two fundamentally different types of evolution. As the result of natural selection operating on their genes, they have descended biologically from apelike ancestors who are now extinct. As the result of social evolution, which has nothing to do with genes, they now live in societies more complex than anything their Stone Age ancestors could have imagined.

We know more about biological evolution than we do about social evolution. By studying living species intensively, zoologists and geneticists have constructed theories about the ways that earlier animals gave rise to later ones. By excavating the fossils of earlier animals, paleontologists have tested these theories and constructed their own. Because biological evolution is better understood, it has inevitably been used as an analogy for social evolution. Ethnologists have studied living peoples intensively, and constructed theories about the ways that earlier societies gave rise to later ones. Archaeologists, by excavating the remains of earlier societies, have tested those theories and constructed their own.

Unfortunately, as we shall see, biological evolution is an imperfect analogy for social evolution. In this paper we look at the contexts in which the analogy is useful, as well as contexts in which it can mislead.

CULTURAL VERSUS SOCIAL EVOLUTION

In this chapter I distinguish between *social evolution* and *cultural evolution*. By "culture" I mean that set of shared beliefs, values, cosmologies, ideologies, customs, and traditions that distinguishes one group of people from other groups, giving it its ethnic identity. *Cultural evolution* would thus be analogous to what biologists call *divergent evolution*—the rise of two or more new forms from a common ancestor. For example, the ancient Mixtec and Zapotec Indian cultures of southern Mexico are believed to have diverged from a common prehistoric ancestral culture, referred to as Proto-Otomanguean.[1] While they shared many cosmological principles as a result of their common ancestry, the ancient Mixtec and Zapotec spoke different languages, worshiped different deities, had different styles of art and architecture, used different kinship terms, and displayed many different customs.

I use the term *social evolution*, on the other hand, to refer to the reorganization of society at a different level of complexity—as, for example, when a small society based on egalitarian relationships becomes a larger society based on hierarchical relationships. Such a change can take place within a human group without thoroughly transforming its culture or ethnic identity. For example, during the early part of this century the Kachin people of highland Burma sometimes reorganized their normally egalitarian, or *gumlao*, society as a hierarchical, or *gumsa*, society, while still retaining their identity as Kachin.[2] Thus, while acknowledging that culture and society are linked, we will use the term *social evolution* for organizational changes that do not produce a whole new ethnic group.

ANALOGIES BETWEEN BIOLOGICAL AND SOCIAL EVOLUTION

Biologists believe that evolution is a continuous process. Many paleontologists, however, argue that there have been periods of (1) *rapid change*, which produced significant new forms, and (2) *slower change*, which produced what appear to be long periods of stability.[3] The archaeological record also seems to show long periods of stability, separated by moments of rapid social change. In both fields of study, it is the periods of stability about which we know the most. We also suspect that in both fields the moments of rapid change hold many of the keys to understanding evolution.

In both fields, scholars have defined *stages of evolution*, mutually agreed-upon units that allow researchers to discuss common problems. Among the higher vertebrates, for example, zoologists recognize the living classes *bony fishes, amphibians, reptiles, birds*, and *mammals*. Paleontologists have provided data to suggest that amphibians evolved from bony fish, reptiles evolved from amphibians, and both birds and mammals evolved from reptiles.[4] They also point out that the fossil record has evidence for many more species of higher vertebrates than those that have survived to be studied by zoologists. The fossil record contains extinct animals that appear to be intermediate between two of the living classes, providing clues to the process of change. An example would be the cynodonts, a group of mammal-like reptiles who lived 250–150 million years ago. While the cynodonts' individual limb bones were still reptilian, their teeth already had the characteristic division into incisors, canines, and molars seen in mammals.[5]

Are there also classes of living human societies that might represent stages of social evolution? Many anthropologists believe so. Scholars such as Julian Steward,[6] Elman Service,[7] Marshall Sahlins,[8] Morton Fried,[9] and Robert Carneiro[10] have all made contributions to the definition of such classes. During the years 1955–1995 there was considerable debate over the number, nature, and appropriate names for these classes. The following list gives my current preferences.

Hunting-and-gathering bands constitute the simplest societies known for our species. While few remain today, our world still contained many bands as recently as the nineteenth century. Such societies subsisted entirely on wild plants and animals, often living a nomadic or semi-nomadic existence. The modal size of most bands was twenty-five to thirty-five persons, although larger groups occupied more permanent encampments when wild resources permitted.

Hunting-and-gathering bands had no hereditary differences in rank or authority, and their leadership was ephemeral, based on differences in age, experience, skill, and charisma. Divisions of labor were largely along the lines of age and gender, and most hunting-gathering bands had an egalitarian ethic that downplayed any differences in prestige that arose. This class of society is important as a kind of baseline for future evolution: Fifteen thousand years ago virtually all of our ancestors lived in such bands. The Eskimo, the Australian aborigines, the Bushmen of Africa's Kalahari Desert, and the Alacaluf of Patagonia are well-studied examples.

The whole world would still be living as hunters and gatherers were it not for the adoption of agriculture and animal domestication. Our best estimates are that cereal agriculture began in the Near East by 7000 B.C. and spread quickly to the Nile Valley and the Indus River. In the New World, cereal agriculture began in Mexico and Peru between 5000 and 3000 B.C., then spread gradually north and south. With agriculture came larger and more sedentary settlements, and our first examples of what are now called *autonomous village societies*.

There is great worldwide variation in autonomous village societies. Communities may be large or small, their houses circular, rectangular, or oval. At the start of this century they included people as diverse as the Pueblo Indians of the American Southwest, the villagers of highland New Guinea, and many native peoples of the Amazon Basin. While they may live in larger communities than most hunter-gatherers, such societies still display no hereditary differences in rank, nor do large villages have authority over smaller villages nearby. One mechanism integrating large numbers of families is the belief that they all descended from a common ancestor.

While everyone is equal at birth in such villages, significant differences in prestige can be acquired during one's lifetime. Most autonomous village societies provide individuals of talent and ambition with ways to rise within a ritual system, creating what Raymond Kelly has called a "hierarchy of virtue."[11] Often each group maintains a ceremonial structure such as a Men's

House, which one can enter only after he has proven that he deserves to be initiated. While men's ritual may thus be *exclusionary* (dividing the village into initiates and noninitiates), women's ritual often remains *nonexclusionary*, carried out by every woman in the context of her household.

In some Pueblo societies, those who have risen in the ritual hierarchy through years of community service may be called "Made People," while the uninitiated are called "Dry Food People."[12] A similar hierarchy of achievement in highland New Guinea has produced terms like "Prominent Men," "Ordinary Men," and "Rubbish Men."[13] Highest among the Prominent Men are "Big Men"—self-selected, ambitious individuals who sponsor feasts, brag, threaten, engage in long-distance trade, accumulate valuables, and lead raids against other villages. Significantly, however, these Big Men cannot bequeath their achieved prestige to their offspring. When they die, they and their valuables may even be burned. This is done to rid their community of the powerful magic to which their fellow villagers attribute their success.

It appears that under certain conditions a third class of society, called *rank society*, can evolve from such village cultures. In rank societies the egalitarian ethic has been overcome, replaced by an ideology in which individuals are unequal at birth. Large groups of families are still integrated by the belief that they share a common ancestor, but community leaders now tend to come exclusively from the descendants of prestigious ancestors, individuals who possessed magic even greater than that of Big Men. The more closely related one is to such ancestors, the higher his or her rank; the more distantly related, the lower the rank. There is thus a continuum of inherited status from the highest to the lowest individuals, and whom one marries can greatly affect the rank of one's future children.

Our world had many such societies during the nineteenth century, but Robert Carneiro points out that they could be divided into two categories.[14] Some rank societies, like the Northwest Coast Indians of Canada and the United States, had hereditary differences in rank, but each village was independent of every other. In other rank societies, such as the Natchez of the southeastern United States or the Cauca and Chibcha of Colombia, small villages had lost their autonomy and were under the command of paramount leaders at large villages. Large rank societies with loss of village autonomy are usually called *chiefdoms*.

Once large villages begin to break down the autonomy of the small villages around them, ambitious chiefs can bring very large territories and thousands of people under their control. Because of the superior size and manpower of chiefdoms, they can usually overwhelm the autonomous village societies in their region. This is often done by raiding—a simple version of warfare—and may result in the conversion of defeated villagers into slaves. Warfare among chiefdoms can be particularly nasty, involving terror tactics such as torture, mutilation, ritual cannibalism, human sacrifice, and the taking of trophy heads.[15]

Chiefs and their close relatives are generally allowed to distinguish themselves from lesser individuals through the use of sumptuary goods—prestigious valuables such as gold, silver, jade, imported shells, exotic feathers and animal hides, stools on which they alone can sit, litters in which they alone are carried by servants. In Mexico and Peru, where the earliest chiefdoms were flamboyant in their use of sumptuary goods, we can identify societies of this type in archaeological sites of the first millennium B.C. In Egypt they were surely present by 3500 B.C. In Mesopotamia, where the earliest chiefdoms were noticeably less flamboyant, it is correspondingly harder to identify them in the archaeological record. By the fifth millennium B.C., however, Mesopotamia shows us (1) residences appropriate for chiefly individuals; (2) prominent villages whose temples probably served a network of smaller, subject communities; and (3) the kinds of defensive works usually associated with chiefdom-level warfare.

Under the right conditions still another kind of society, called an *archaic state*, can arise in the context of competing chiefdoms. Archaic states differed from most modern states, which are run by presidents, prime ministers, and other elected officials. Most archaic states were *kingdoms*. These societies were divided into at least two social strata who did not intermarry. At the top was a stratum of hereditary nobles from whom the ruler would likely come, either by inheriting his or her title from the previous ruler, or as the result of having been chosen by other nobles, or both. At the bottom was a stratum of citizens not of noble birth and therefore not eligible to rule. This stratum of "commoners" had many routes for advancement through achievement; they could become wealthy merchants or craftsmen, rise through military service, or be appointed to bureaucratic positions by the ruler. On the other hand, through misfortune they could become landless serfs who worked the fields of more fortunate families. Through misdeeds, or by being taken captive in war, they could even become slaves.

The first archaic states arose on the alluvial plains of southern Iraq and southwestern Iran around 3000 B.C. They were large societies with populations in the tens or hundreds of thousands, depending on where archaeologists choose to draw the boundaries around them. The capital of each state was a city, sometimes defended with a wall, often with large public buildings in prominent places. In the hinterland beyond the city were smaller communities of at least three sizes: towns, large villages, and small villages.[16] At both towns and large villages there seem to have been administrators who interacted on a regular basis with the city. By 2000 B.C., early written texts reveal a society with complex divisions of labor: ruler, priest, scribe, mason, carpenter, soldier, smith, servant, and many others.[17]

The valleys of the Nile and Indus Rivers had major states by this time as well. Archaic states did not arise as early in the New World, but by the first century A.D. they were present in several parts of Mexico. These early states had large palaces in which their rulers lived; standardized two-room temples in which a state religion was conducted; ballcourts in which an official state game was played; densely packed cities, some with defensive works; hiero-glyphic writing; and a hierarchy of towns, large villages, and small villages analogous to that of Mesopotamia.[18] While less is known about the origins of the state in the Andes, all along the river valleys of the northern Peruvian coast one can still see immense pyramids left behind by precocious early states. A recent survey of Peru's Casma Valley by David Wilson suggests that a state-like hierarchy of city, town, large village, and small village was present there by at least the first century B.C.[19]

Eventually, by expansion and conquest, some archaic states grew large enough to incorporate within their boundaries people speaking different lan-guages and belonging to different cultures or ethnic groups. We refer to these multicultural conquest states as *empires*. Of all the classes of society we have examined, empires were the largest and the least stable. Most broke down within two hundred years or less, perhaps telling us something about the upper size limits of human social organization.[20]

HOW ARCHAEOLOGISTS STUDY SOCIAL EVOLUTION

Zoologists study living animals in their entirety: the skeleton, the soft tissues, and the behavior. Their analyses include the ways that behavior is reflected in both the soft tissues and the skeleton. Paleontologists usually find only skeletons, but they can use the analyses of zoologists to reconstruct the soft tis-sues and behavior of extinct creatures.

For an example of how this can be done, let us examine the evolution of mammals from reptiles. Zoologists tell us that modern mammals require approximately ten times more food and oxygen than do reptiles of compa-rable size. According to paleontologist Robert R. Caroll, their higher rate of metabolism "allows mammals to be active more continuously and to main-tain a high, constant body temperature that is independent of the environ-ment. Such a radical difference in metabolic rate affects nearly all the systems of the body and is responsible, directly or indirectly, for nearly all the dif-ferences we observe between reptiles (be they modern or Paleozoic) and mammals."[21]

In general terms, it was the early mammals' high rate of activity—including their ability to be active at night because of their high body temperature—that gave them an evolutionary advantage over the more sluggish reptiles, who depend on the sun to raise their temperature.

How are such differences in behavior reflected in the skeletons? Let us look again at the cynodonts, the extinct mammal-like reptiles we mentioned earlier. We see that their feeding apparatus was adapted for longer chewing, reducing their food to smaller particles and ultimately deriving from it the increased calories required for a higher level of activity. Most lizards seize their food with uniformly dagger-like teeth, gulping it down whole or in large chunks. The cynodonts had canines for seizing food, but also molar-like cheek teeth for grinding it into smaller particles. Clues to their prolonged chewing can also be found in their secondary palate and their larger adductor (jaw) muscles, both mammal-like traits. Their hip and shoulder girdles also show that their limbs, rather than being splayed to the side like those of lizards, were drawn in below the torso in the manner of mammals. This would have allowed them to run faster, another trait associated with the higher metabolism. Thus a paleontologist, although he might only have the skeleton of a cynodont, would know that its behavior had been mammal-like because of the relationships between skeleton, soft tissue, and behavior.

Here is one area where zoology and paleontology do provide an analogy for ethnology and archaeology. Ethnologists study living societies in their entirety: cosmology, ideology, social and political organization, religion, economics, settlement, and subsistence. Archaeologists recover only the imperishable physical remains of ancient societies. They can, however, use the analyses of ethnologists to reconstruct some of the missing "soft parts" and the behavior of past societies. In so doing, they rely on the fact that there are relationships between a society's behavior and its residences, shrines, temples, artifacts, activity areas, storage facilities, burials, settlement and subsistence patterns, at least some of which will be preserved.

As an example of how this can be done, let us examine three of the major transitions from one class of society to another, and consider what an archaeologist might look for.

FROM HUNTING AND GATHERING TO AUTONOMOUS VILLAGE SOCIETY

In some parts of the world, such as the Near East and the coast of Peru, sedentary life in villages seems to have preceded agriculture. In other regions, such as highland Mexico, agriculture seems to have preceded village life.[22] Whether the economic basis for sedentary life was a reliable source of wild food or a newly domesticated species, many of the same principles applied: Societies [People] began to live together in larger and more permanent groupings than before, and sought to establish long-term rights to an economically important patch of resources.

In a world without written deeds, one of the ways to establish one's long-term right to land is by showing that one's ancestors have lived and died there since time immemorial. Cemeteries—which were relatively rare among ancient hunting-gathering bands—became common among autonomous village societies. In Upper Egypt and Nubia, small cemeteries were present near resource-rich embayments of the Nile as early as 10,000 B.C., long before agriculture had taken hold. In Mexico, cemeteries were common among the village farmers of 1500–1000 B.C. Such permanent resting places for one's ancestors helped to establish a group's territorial priority.

Members of hunting-gathering bands live and work mostly with their blood relatives and in-laws. This becomes difficult in large villages, where the population may be far greater than anyone's kinsmen. Autonomous village societies integrate larger groups of people by several means. First, they create larger groups of "blood relatives" by asserting that many seemingly unrelated persons were all descended from the same mythological ancestor. Second, they create a series of community-wide fraternal orders, or *sodalities*, to which deserving individuals from several descent groups can be initiated. These fraternal orders may maintain their own ritual features or buildings, such as a kiva in a New Mexico pueblo or a Men's House in a New Guinea village.

Like hunting and gathering bands, autonomous village societies are "egalitarian" in the sense that everyone is equal at birth. However, unlike most hunting-gathering bands, autonomous village societies allow significant differences in prestige to develop during the course of one's lifetime. Individuals of greater intelligence, charisma, talent, or social skills rise rapidly by initiation through a series of increasingly exclusive fraternal orders until they have become village leaders, while other people are left behind. Such differences in prestige are tolerated because they are seen as being based on community service. We still describe such societies as egalitarian, however, because parents cannot pass on such acquired prestige to their children.

Archaeologists excavating autonomous village societies, like paleontologists working with fossils, attempt to reconstruct their behavior from physical remains. Usually such societies have relatively permanent architecture—thatched huts whose post holes survive, pit houses whose subterranean parts survive, mud brick houses whose wall stubs survive. Sometimes such societies leave behind small shrines, temples, or Men's Houses (it should be noted that in societies that reckon descent through the female line, there are sometimes Women's Houses). Since prestige is acquired, not inherited, it is unlikely that the houses of village leaders will be readily distinguishable from anyone else's. However, families claiming descent from the same mythical ancestor may share symbols (whether on pottery, figurines, carved bone, shell, or some other material) referring to that ancestor; they may also be buried in the same manner in the same cemetery.

In some autonomous village societies, like those of the Solomon Islands fifty years ago, ambitious leaders might work hard to increase their prestige further.[23] They might organize labor for the building of Men's Houses, attract a coterie of followers, accumulate trade goods, and lead raids against enemy villages. Archaeologists should take care not to interpret the remains of these activities as evidence for rank society. Big Men in autonomous village societies might accumulate (or even be buried with) masses of shell ornaments, and they might be responsible for impressive public buildings. What they could not do was extend their power to neighboring villages, or bequeath to their offspring the prestige they had achieved during a lifetime of self-aggrandizement.

FROM AUTONOMOUS VILLAGE SOCIETY TO CHIEFLY SOCIETY

For many areas of the ancient world, autonomous village societies persisted well into this century. For other regions—including Mexico, Guatemala, Peru, Egypt, Mesopotamia, and Southeast Asia—rank societies evolved from autonomous village societies not long after the latter first appeared.

Key to the appearance of rank society is an ideological change: The belief that all humans are equal at birth is replaced by a system in which everyone is ranked from top to bottom, depending on how closely he or she is related to the society's highest-ranked individual.

Ethnologists working in Southeast Asia have made major contributions to our view of the way such an ideological shift might be accomplished.[24] They have shown us that inherited differences in rank will not be accepted by lower-ranking members of society unless they are seen as having a supernatural basis—that is, unless society's most important families are seen as having descended from very powerful ancestral spirits or deities. Only then is it considered appropriate for society to be directed permanently by hereditary leaders drawn from the highest-ranking lineages. These leaders are seen as having supernaturally-sanctioned authority, although most also work hard to keep their followers satisfied.

Chiefdoms arise when the leaders of larger communities are able to break down the independence of the smaller communities around them—something the Big Men in autonomous village societies are unable to do. One way this can be accomplished is through *hypogamy*, the practice of sending a high-ranked woman from a large village to marry the lower-ranked headman of a small village. The headman of the smaller village thereby has his prestige raised, and his children are guaranteed higher rank; on the other hand, his village also comes under the control of his chiefly father-in-law.

Archaeologists have detected such processes at work in Mexico between 1200 and 500 B.C. One can see large villages building up networks of smaller villages that contributed construction materials for public buildings, shared in the fruits of long-distance trade, and imitated the pottery styles of their local chiefly center. And at those smaller villages, some of the richest burials are those of women—likely hypogamous brides from a larger village.

Entitled by their elite status to accumulate sumptuary goods, highly-ranked men and women in such societies were often buried with prestige goods. Gold and silver were favored in early Egypt and Peru; jade was favored in Mexico and Southeast Asia. The question for the archaeologist has always been: Was the buried individual entitled to these goods through inherited high status, or through a lifetime of achievement? The answer may be complicated, since achievement continues to be important in chiefdoms; not everyone born to an elite family actually becomes a chief.

Archaeologists often take it as a sign of inherited status when impressive sumptuary goods are buried with infants or children—individuals too young to have acquired their high status through a lifetime of community service. Infants buried with alabaster statues at 5300 B.C. in Mesopotamia are frequently-cited examples (assuming that they are burials, rather than examples of infant sacrifice).

In many chiefdoms, the competition for positions of authority is intense. There may be a whole group of brothers, sisters, and cousins of almost equally high rank, resulting in competition that can lead to political assassination or even warfare. In addition, the ambitious subchiefs who command the smaller settlements below the paramount chief's village are a constant threat to the latter's authority. Warfare in chiefdoms may be so intense that some villages have palisades, ditches, moats, or defensive walls, or may be relocated to defensible hilltops.

In Mesopotamia, settlements of the fifth and sixth millennium B.C. sometimes have watchtowers, defensive ditches, and heaps of sling missiles for repelling attackers; in spite of this, some villages were overrun and their leaders' residences burned.[25] On the coast of Peru, at least one public building of the second millennium B.C. displays carvings of enemies who appear to have been hacked to pieces.[26] And some chiefly centers in the lowland Maya region of Mexico and Guatemala, dating to A.D. 1–400, had ditches, parapets, and palisades encircling them.[27]

Many ancient chiefdoms seem to have a hierarchical settlement pattern in which a paramount chief's large village is surrounded by smaller villages, administered by his subchiefs. In turn, these smaller villages may be surrounded by even smaller subject hamlets. It may therefore be necessary for archaeologists to survey relatively large regions in order to determine whether or not they are dealing with a rank society in which the autonomy of smaller settlements has been lost.

FROM CHIEFDOM TO ARCHAIC STATE

In many parts of the ancient world, the chiefdom was the most complex class of society ever to appear. When European explorers first reached North America, they found impressive chiefdoms operating in what are now the states of Georgia, Alabama, and Mississippi; others were found to the south in Panama, Hispaniola, Colombia, and Venezuela. On the Pacific Islands of Tonga, Tahiti, and Hawaii there were elaborate chiefdoms as well.

In places like Egypt, Mesopotamia, and southwest Iran, on the other hand, archaic states had already formed by 3000 B.C. In both Mexico and Peru, such states had emerged by the end of the first millennium B.C.

How do states evolve from chiefdoms? That question is hard to answer in the case of the world's first states, since no social scientists were present to record the process. We can get insights, however, by looking at more recently formed states in Hawaii and southern Africa. These more recent cases suggest that individual chiefdoms do not simply turn into states. States arise in the context of a group of competing chiefdoms, when one of the latter succeeds in taking over its neighbors and turning them into the provinces of a larger political unit.

In the late 1770s, each of the larger islands of the Hawaiian archipelago—Hawai'i, Maui, O'ahu, and Kaua'i—was the scene of a native chiefdom. Rival chiefs from O'ahu and Maui competed for control of the smaller islands of Lana'i and Moloka'i. By 1782, the paramount chief of Maui had seized those two smaller islands and administered a significant defeat to his rival, the chief of Hawai'i. We have a record of what happened next, because British sailors had begun visiting the islands by 1778.

When the defeated chief of Hawai'i died, his title was usurped by his ambitious nephew Kamehameha, who mustered enough support to assassinate the real heir and seize control. By trading with European ships who docked at his port, he acquired cannons and muskets, and hired two British officers as military advisors. Between 1792 and 1810, Kamehameha succeeded in conquering all the other Hawaiian Islands, turning them into subject provinces of a single state of which he was now the king.[28]

The origins of South Africa's Zulu state were equally grounded in chiefly competition. That story also begins in the 1770s, among a group of Bantu-speaking pastoralists and shifting cultivators who were organized into competing chiefdoms. Each chief ruled a large group of people divided into local units, each of which was usually commanded by one of his brothers.

After 1775, a chief named Shaka hit upon the strategy of organizing regiments of warriors, each made up of young men who were about the same age. So successful were these regiments that in the space of ten years, "by his personal character and military strategy," Shaka was able to reduce many rival chiefdoms to provinces of a single Zulu state of which he was now king. This archaic state covered eighty thousand square miles and had at least one hundred thousand subjects. From this point on, Shaka's relatives became a kind of "royal family" from which future rulers would come.[29]

This brings us to the difference in social inequality between chiefdoms and states. We have seen that rank societies have a continuum of status from highest to lowest. Archaic states, on the other hand, had actual *stratification*—the separation of citizens into at least two classes, the rulers and the ruled, which remained apart by not intermarrying. Often this stratification was supported by a political ideology in which nobles were seen as having a completely different genealogical origin from commoners. The Mixtec Indians of Mexico, for example, believed that their nobles had descended from a divine couple who had emerged from a sacred tree; commoners, on the other hand, were seen as descending from "stone people" who had crawled out of a crack in the earth's surface.[30] This difference in genealogical origin gave nobles the right to live in palaces, wear gold and jade, deform their skulls as a sign of beauty, and receive tribute. The Mixtec believed that although commoners died, nobles only "fainted"; while commoner women gave milk to their nursing infants, noble women's breasts provided "honey." The parts of a noble's body were described using a different set of words from those used for commoners, almost as if the latter were a separate species.

Again, data from eighteenth-century Hawai'i provide insight into the evolution of stratification from ranking. In the traditional chiefly system, every Hawaiian occupied a position in the continuum from highly ranked to lowly. At the bottom of the social system were people whom no highly-ranked person wanted to marry, since the children of such a marriage would have no chance of rising in the hierarchy. With the rise of the state, these lowest-ranking families were simply "divorced" from the continuum, which severed their ties to the ancestors and converted them into a permanent underclass.[31]

There are many archaeological clues to the existence of an archaic state. The rulers of states were kings and queens who lived in palaces, and the ground plans of those palaces can be recovered archaeologically. In some archaic states, such as those of highland Mexico, the palace was an elegant residence with an interior patio, built by commoners under the direction of architects. In other states, like the Minoan civilization of ancient Crete or the Chimu civilization of Peru, the ruler's residence might be only one small part of a larger complex of storage rooms, artisans' quarters, audience halls, and royal burial areas.

The rulers of archaic states were often given spectacular burials, usually in tombs. One of the most famous was the tomb of Tutankhamun in Egypt's Valley of the Kings. In addition to his gilded coffin, Tutankhamun's tomb was so filled with royal furniture, chariots, and elegant offerings that it took archaeologists a decade to excavate it.[32] Another famous burial was that of Queen Shub-ad of Ur in ancient Mesopotamia. Female attendants, male soldiers, musicians with their harps and lyres, even teams of oxen hitched to wagons had been sacrificed on the ramp leading to her tomb.[33] In a chamber deep inside a pyramid at Palenque, Mexico, the Maya ruler Pacal—adorned with a jade mosaic mask—lay inside a stone sarcophagus whose hieroglyphic inscriptions described his royal ancestors.[34]

Archaeologists excavating the burials of stratified societies, however, must be careful to distinguish between the perquisites of *status* and *office*. In an archaic state numbering one hundred thousand persons, as many as ten thousand to fifteen thousand might belong to the stratum of nobles. At any point in time, however, only one noble would occupy the office of king. While every noble's status as a member of the hereditary elite entitled him or her to a fine burial, only an individual holding the office of king or queen received a spectacular burial of the kind described earlier. Sometimes archaeologists, finding a tomb intermediate in elegance between that of a king and a commoner, believe that they have found evidence for an ancient "middle class." More often than not, it is either the tomb of a minor noble or of a wealthy commoner such as an artisan or merchant. Most archaic states did not have a middle class in the sense of a third *social* stratum. What they did have were individuals intermediate in wealth between the royal family and the average commoner. Such individuals were middle class only in the *economic* sense.

Archaic states often had an official religion, conducted in formal temples by full-time priests. As in the case of the palace, the ground plans of these temples are recognizable. In Mexico they might be two-room buildings on pyramidal mounds, their doorways flanked by columns. In ancient Mesopotamia, temples often had a long central chamber and podium flanked by smaller rooms; their outer walls could be decorated by intricate brickwork or mosaics of colored cones. In ancient Peru, many early temples had a ground plan in the form of a block U.

Still another characteristic of many archaic states, first pointed out in the Near East by Henry Wright and Gregory Johnson, is a settlement hierarchy of at least four levels.[35] At the top of the hierarchy is a city; below the city are a number of towns; below each town are a number of large villages; below these are even more small villages. Only the upper three levels—city, town, and large village—had administrative functions. Since states were large political units, often covering thousands of square miles, a great deal of archaeological survey is necessary to recover this settlement hierarchy.

Wright and Johnson found that artifacts related to administration occurred from top to bottom of the hierarchy. Cylindrical seals—used by Mesopotamian administrators to seal up bales, bundles, or jars for shipment by pressing the seal into wet clay—occurred most often in the debris of cities and towns. On the other hand, broken blobs of clay with seal impressions were often found in the debris of towns and villages to which the shipments had been sent. There were also public buildings that occurred only at the upper levels of the settlement hierarchy.

In Mexico, the Zapotec state also showed a hierarchy of four (or more) levels of settlement during its early stage of development. Palaces were found at the upper two levels of the hierarchy (cities and towns); temples, on the other hand, were found at the upper three levels.[36] In the lowland Maya region, where the use of hieroglyphic place names was well developed, Joyce Marcus has discovered that many carved inscriptions reflected the administrative hierarchy: Second-level centers mentioned the local capital, while third-level centers mentioned the second-level centers.[37]

While archaic states were powerful political entities, with a high degree of occupational specialization and an elaborate military apparatus, they seem to have been less stable than the smaller-scale societies discussed earlier. Marcus has suggested that many Mesoamerican states had an early burst of growth (perhaps analogous to Shaka's takeover of the Zulus' neighbors), after which they began to lose many of their outer provinces and shrink in size.[38] Nicholas Postgate has demonstrated a similar pattern for Mesopotamia.[39] There the Uruk state of 3500–3000 B.C. may have been not only the earliest, but also the largest in terms of territorial extent. This archaic

Uruk state, however, broke down during the Early Dynastic period into a series of smaller (but densely populated) polities. Later, Mesopotamia was re-
unified under the ruler Sargon of Akkad at 2350 B.C. With the collapse of
Sargon's dynasty, Mesopotamia again fragmented into a series of smaller polities. This cyclic "rise and fall" seems to have been typical of archaic states in
the Andes as well; there the collapse of the early Moche state was followed by
the Wari state and later by the Chimu.[40]

Perhaps we should not be surprised that it proved hard to maintain huge
states and empires for long periods of time. After all, humans' biological evolution only prepared them for life in hunting-and-gathering bands; everything larger is the result of social evolution.

WHERE THE ANALOGY BREAKS DOWN

We have now looked briefly at hunting-gathering bands, autonomous village
societies, rank societies, and archaic states. We have seen that, just as the study
of living animals provides a level of detail that paleontology cannot, so the
study of living societies provides a level of detail that archaeology cannot. We
will not let this discourage us, however, since paleontology and archaeology
provide long-term perspectives on evolutionary change that the study of living animals and societies cannot.

Now, however, we must bring up a problem with the analogy we have
been using: The bony fishes-amphibian-reptile-mammal evolutionary sequence is not really analogous to what happens in social evolution.

One of the major differences between biological and social evolution can
be seen by comparing Figures 15-1 and 15-2. Figure 15-1 shows the way many
paleontologists believe that the classes of higher vertebrates evolved. At some
point in time, conditions being right, the first reptiles branched off from amphibians. All reptiles, living and extinct, are the descendants of those first reptiles. At a later time, conditions being right, the first mammals branched off
from reptiles. All mammals, living and extinct, are the descendants of those
first mammals.

That is not at all how various classes of societies evolved. For example, we
believe that in ancient Egypt, rank societies evolved from autonomous village societies some time between 4000 and 3000 B.C. In Mexico, on the other
hand, rank societies evolved some time between 1200 and 800 B.C., in ways unrelated to the earlier events in Egypt. In no sense are all rank societies, living
or extinct, the descendants of the first rank society to appear; nor are all archaic
states the descendants of the first state to appear. In addition, some early states
collapsed in such a way that their citizens went back to living in rank societies.
There are many mammals that have become extinct, but none that returned
to being reptiles.

Are there better analogies for our classes of societies? Perhaps there are.
A better analogy is provided by certain types of organs—such as eyes—that

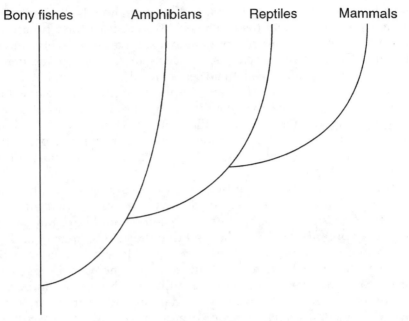

FIGURE 15-1

The biological evolution of bony fishes, amphibians, reptiles, and mammals. This diagram does not provide a suitable analogy for social evolution.

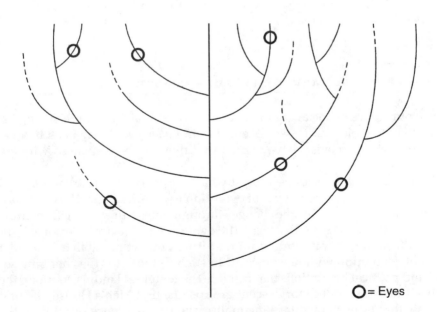

FIGURE 15-2

The evolution of eyes, which has happened repeatedly in very different branches of the animal kingdom. This diagram provides a better analogy for social evolution.

have evolved independently in many classes of animals. Biologist Ernst Mayr has pointed out that the eye has evolved at least forty times, independently, in very different groups of animals.[41] Eyes have evolved in flatworms, in molluscs like the octopus, in insects, in vertebrates, and in many other creatures great and small. In no sense are all eyes descended from the first eye that ever evolved. They are simply structures that have evolved over and over again, whenever conditions were right, because they work efficiently. Rank societies show a similar pattern. They have evolved independently many times, when conditions were right, in many parts of the world, perhaps because they represent one of the five or six most effective ways of organizing human beings.

What we see in social evolution is not the kind of process that gave rise to amphibians, reptiles, and birds. Instead, we see that out of the hundreds of possible ways that human societies could be organized, certain types of organization work so well that they show up over and over again throughout the world. Anthropologist Marvin Harris has called this "the principle of limited possibilities."[42] No one would suggest that hunting-gathering bands, autonomous villages, chiefdoms, and archaic states represent the only ways that human societies can be organized. However, those particular types of organization have repeatedly survived to be studied, while others have broken down and disappeared. Almost certainly, the long stable periods we see in the archaeological record were periods when one of the former types of society was in existence. Thus archaeologists need to study the ethnographic descriptions of such kinds of societies.

ARE EVOLUTIONARY STAGES EVEN NECESSARY?

Since our stages of social organization are more analogous to recurring organs than to biological classes like *reptile* and *mammal*, do we need them at all? Some archaeologists have argued that they can be dispensed with entirely. I disagree.

In a recent article, archaeologist Charles Spencer argues that we need to engage in two different types of evolutionary studies.[43] One, basically *historic* in nature, documents the changes through time within a specific culture. Joyce Marcus and I recently traced the evolution of Mexico's Zapotec Indian civilization this way, and found that it was in fact possible to present a kind of "evolution without stages."[44] In such a study it is the changing social and political institutions that provide the temporal landmarks along the way—the first evidence for descent groups, the first Men's House, the first burials that reflect hereditary inequality, the first evidence of raiding, the first recognizable royal palace.

Spencer's second type of evolutionary study is *comparative* in nature. It seeks not to trace the history of one specific culture, but to compare the evolution of unrelated cultures in different regions of the world. Such a comparative study needs terms like "autonomous village," "chiefdom," and "archaic state," for the same reasons that paleontology needs terms like "reptile," "bird," and "mammal." In spite of the fact that such labels do not necessarily describe every "fossil" society in the archaeological record, they provide us with shorthand references to some very common types.

ARE SOCIETIES "TRANSFORMED" OR "SELECTED FOR"?

Some archaeologists, desiring the analogy between biological and social evolution to be even stronger than it is, maintain that societies are subject to a process analogous to natural selection.[45] They contrast their approach with that of the majority of evolutionary archaeologists, whom they have labeled "transformationists."

The emergence of the Hawaiian and Zulu states, to which we have already referred, provides us with a chance to compare these two views of evolution. Selectionists (with some justification) could argue that Kamehameha's acquisition of European cannons and Shaka's development of military regiments gave those leaders a "selective advantage" over their rivals. Transformationists, on the other hand, would argue that neither leader did what an animal with a selective advantage does—that is, produce so many more offspring than his rivals that he eventually displaces them. (Shaka, in fact, left no offspring at all.) They would maintain that in both cases an archaic state was created by "transforming" several formerly independent chiefdoms into a single larger unit. This is not even vaguely similar to the way that new classes of animals arise in biological evolution.

I would argue, therefore, that neither the "transformationist" nor the "selectionist" position is more than an imperfect analogy for biological evolution. These alternatives are simply two ways of looking at the same phenomenon—moments of change in social institutions, set in motion by real human actors, succeeding only when conditions are right, and proceeding rapidly by the standards of prehistory.

What fascinates both ethnologists and archaeologists is how similar the results of social evolutionary changes look, at different times and different places, all over the world. Because the prehistoric record, like the paleontological record, contains a huge sample of evolutionary change, archaeologists have a particularly strong obligation to study it. At the same time, one of the most compelling aspects of the study of social evolution is that it gives archaeologists and ethnologists the chance to work together on a common problem.

NOTES

1. Kent V. Flannery and Joyce Marcus, eds., *The Cloud People: Divergent Evolution of the Zapotec and Mixtec Civilizations* (New York: Academic Press, 1983).
2. Edmund R. Leach, *Political Systems of Highland Burma: A Study of Kachin Social Structure* (London: G. Bell and Sons, 1954).
3. Niles Eldredge and Stephen J. Gould, "Punctuated Equilibria: An Alternative to Phyletic Gradualism," in T. J. M. Schopf, ed., *Models in Paleobiology* (San Francisco: Freeman, Cooper and Co., 1972), pp. 82–115.
4. Robert R. Caroll, *Vertebrate Paleontology and Evolution* (New York: W.H. Freeman and Co., 1988).
5. Thomas S. Kemp, *Mammal-Like Reptiles and the Origin of Mammals* (New York: Academic Press, 1982).
6. Julian H. Steward, *Theory of Culture Change* (Urbana: University of Illinois Press, 1955).
7. Elman R. Service, *Primitive Social Organization: An Evolutionary Perspective* (New York: Random House, 1962).
8. Marshall D. Sahlins, "Poor Man, Rich Man, Big-Man, Chief: Political Types in Melanesia and Polynesia," *Comparative Studies in Society and History* 5 (1963): 285–303.
9. Morton A. Fried, *The Evolution of Political Society* (New York: Random House, 1967).
10. Robert L. Carneiro, "The Chiefdom: Precursor of the State," in Grant D. Jones and Robert R. Kautz, eds., *The Transition to Statehood in the New World* (Cambridge: Cambridge University Press, 1981), pp. 37–79.
11. Raymond C. Kelly, *Constructing Inequality: The Fabrication of a Hierarchy of Virtue among the Etoro* (Ann Arbor: University of Michigan Press, 1993).
12. Alfonso Ortiz, *The Tewa World: Time, Space, Being and Becoming in a Pueblo Society* (Chicago: University of Chicago Press, 1969).
13. Paula Brown, *The Chimbu: A Study of Change in the New Guinea Highlands* (Cambridge, MA: Schenkman Publishing Co., 1972).
14. Robert L. Carneiro, "The Nature of the Chiefdom as Revealed by Evidence from the Cauca Valley of Colombia," in A. Terry Rambo and Kathleen Gillogly, eds., *Profiles in Cultural Evolution* (Ann Arbor: Museum of Anthropology, University of Michigan Anthropological Paper 85, 1991), pp. 167–190.
15. Elsa M. Redmond, *Tribal and Chiefly Warfare in South America* (Ann Arbor: Museum of Anthropology, University of Michigan Memoir 28, 1994).
16. Henry T. Wright and Gregory A. Johnson, "Population, Exchange, and Early State Formation in Southwestern Iran," *American Anthropologist* 77 (1975): 267–289.
17. Nicholas Postgate, *Early Mesopotamia: Society and Economy at the Dawn of History* (London: Routledge, 1992).
18. Joyce Marcus and Kent V. Flannery, *Zapotec Civilization: How Urban Society Evolved in Mexico's Oaxaca Valley* (London: Thames and Hudson, 1996).
19. David J. Wilson, "Prehispanic Settlement Patterns in the Casma Valley, North Coast of Peru," Report to the National Geographic Society, 1995.
20. Joyce Marcus, "Dynamic Cycles of Mesoamerican States," *National Geographic Research and Exploration* 8 (1992): 392–411.
21. Caroll, *Vertebrate Paleontology and Evolution*, p. 379.

22. Kent V. Flannery, "The Origins of the Village as a Settlement Type in Mesoamerica and the Near East: A Comparative Study," in Peter J. Ucko, Ruth Tringham, and G. W. Dimbleby, eds., *Man, Settlement and Urbanism* (London: Duckworth, 1972), pp. 23–53.

23. Douglas L. Oliver, *A Solomon Island Society: Kinship and Leadership among the Siuai of Bougainville* (Boston: Beacon Press, 1955).

24. Jonathan Friedman, *System, Structure, and Contradiction: The Evolution of "Asiatic" Social Formations* (Copenhagen: National Museum of Denmark, 1979).

25. A. J. Tobler, *Excavations at Tepe Gawra*, vol. 2 (Philadelphia: University of Pennsylvania Press, 1950).

26. Julio C. Tello, *Arqueología del Valle de Casma: Culturas Chavín, Santa o Huaylas, Yunga y Sub-Chimu* (Lima: Universidad Nacional Mayor de San Marcos, 1956).

27. David L. Webster, *Defensive Earthworks at Becán, Campeche, Mexico: Implications for Maya Warfare* (New Orleans: Tulane University, Middle American Research Institute, Publication 41, 1976).

28. Elman R. Service, *Origins of the State and Civilization* (New York: W.W. Norton, 1975), pp. 154–158.

29. Max Gluckman, "The Kingdom of the Zulu of South Africa," in Meyer Fortes and E. E. Evans-Pritchard, eds., *African Political Systems* (London: Oxford University Press, 1940), pp. 25–55.

30. Joyce Marcus, *Mesoamerican Writing Systems: Propaganda, Myth, and History in Four Ancient Civilizations* (Princeton, NJ: Princeton University Press, 1992), pp. 274–277.

31. Patrick V. Kirch, *The Evolution of the Polynesian Chiefdoms* (Cambridge: Cambridge University Press, 1984), pp. 243–263.

32. Howard Carter and A. C. Mace, *The Discovery of the Tomb of Tutankhamen* (New York: Dover Publications, 1977).

33. Sir Leonard Woolley, *Excavations at Ur* (New York: Thomas Y. Crowell, 1955), pp. 52–90.

34. Alberto Ruz L., "Exploraciones arqueológicas en Palenque: 1953–1956," *Anales del Instituto Nacional de Arqueología e Historia* 10 (1958): 69–299.

35. Wright and Johnson, "Population, Exchange, and Early State Formation in Southwestern Iran."

36. Marcus and Flannery, *Zapotec Civilization*.

37. Joyce Marcus, *Emblem and State in the Classic Maya Lowlands: An Epigraphic Approach to Territorial Organization* (Washington, D.C.: Dumbarton Oaks, 1976).

38. Marcus, "Dynamic Cycles of Mesoamerican States."

39. Postgate, *Early Mesopotamia*, p. 45 and Figure 2.11.

40. Michael E. Moseley, *The Incas and their Ancestors: The Archaeology of Peru* (London: Thames and Hudson, 1992).

41. Ernst Mayr, a professor emeritus at Harvard University, made these remarks during an interview with a newspaper reporter in November, 1994.

42. Marvin Harris, *The Rise of Anthropological Theory* (New York: Thomas Y. Crowell, 1968), pp. 624–627.

43. Charles S. Spencer, "On the Tempo and Mode of State Formation: Neoevolutionism Reconsidered," *Journal of Anthropological Archaeology* 9 (1990): 1–30.

44. Marcus and Flannery, *Zapotec Civilization*, Chapter 16.

45. Some ethnologists share this belief. See, for example, Robert L. Carneiro, "The Role of Natural Selection in the Evolution of Culture," *Cultural Dynamics* 5 (1992): 113–140.

SUGGESTED READINGS

Fried, Morton H. *The Evolution of Political Society*. New York: Random House, 1967. A worldwide look at hunters and gatherers, autonomous villages, rank societies, and archaic states that serves as a guide to archaeological reconstruction.

Service, Elman R. *Origins of the State and Civilization*. New York: W.W. Norton, 1975. A noted ethnologist's reconstruction of the processes involved in the rise of archaic states, in both ancient and recent times.

Kirch, Patrick V. *The Evolution of the Polynesian Chiefdoms*. New York: Cambridge University Press, 1984. A detailed analysis of social evolution in the Pacific Islands, from their first colonization to Kamehameha's pan-Hawaiian state.

Marcus, Joyce, and Kent V. Flannery. *Zapotec Civilization: How Urban Society Evolved in Mexico's Oaxaca Valley*. New York: Thames and Hudson, 1996. A detailed analysis of social evolution in southern Mexico, from hunters and gatherers to the archaic state.

ETHICS IN ARCHAEOLOGY

MARK J. LYNOTT

My first field experience in archaeology was in the summer of 1971. Like most students at the time, my only opportunity to participate in archaeology was as part of a university field school in archaeological methods. I was a student at Western Michigan University, and the Anthropology Department was involved in a project to conduct salvage excavations at a site in Michigan's Upper Peninsula. The site was a mound and village complex on a point of land along the southern shore of Lake Superior. The opportunity for a summer of adventure in the beautiful north woods was more than enough to attract my attention. I did not realize at the time that, in addition to being introduced to archaeological methods, many aspects of that first summer of fieldwork would also introduce me to ethical issues that I and the archaeological profession would face in the years to come.

My summer of 1971 was spent at the Sand Point site near Baraga, Michigan. The site is comprised of a series of mounds and habitation areas on a point of land along the south shore of Lake Superior. In 1968, a significant part of the site along the lakeshore was privately owned, and the owner planned to greatly modify the landscape and build a resort with cabins and a marina. The presence of archaeological remains at that location became known when human bones were exposed by a bulldozer pushing soil from a sand knoll into swampy areas to level the site. Two years later, Western Michigan began archaeological investigations at the site. Most of the 1970 work focused on excavation of a large mound. My own participation in the project began a year later, and included work on smaller mounds and habitation areas. In addition to learning archaeological field methods, I was also informally exposed to three issues that continue to be relevant to archaeology today.

As a student just getting started in archaeology, I had little knowledge about the laws that govern the management and protection of archaeological sites in the United States. Our project of excavating mounds and village areas of the Sand Point site before they were destroyed by lakeshore developments seemed intuitively the "right" thing to do. It only made sense that someone should study archaeological sites before they were destroyed. Issues of stewardship and conservation of the archaeological record, which we see as a foundation of contemporary archaeology, were less widely discussed and not formally taught at that time. Although salvage archaeology associated with road, pipeline, and reservoir construction was practiced throughout the United States,[1] there was very little literature that addressed the philosophical basis for preserving and protecting archaeological sites. It was not until the appearance of Public Archaeology[2] by Charles R. McGimsey III in 1972 and "A Conservation Model for American Archaeology"[3] by William D. Lipe in 1974 that archaeologists began to refine this paradigm.

During the summer of 1971, my fellow students and I excavated several small mounds at the Sand Point site. The mounds contained human burials and were built from beach sand and soil from the nearby village sites. I recall being thoroughly intrigued by the carefully organized bundles of bones we encountered, and fascinated by our instructor's explanation of different mortuary practices. At the time, I gave no thought to the possibility that our excavations might offend some Native Americans. My own family heritage was unknown to me beyond my great grandparents, so I didn't anticipate that other people would object to the excavation of graves that were a thousand or more years old. I simply viewed the excavation of these mounds before they were to be bulldozed as logical and important to understanding the past. In subsequent years, I would be exposed to the strong and diverse views that exist about archaeological excavation of human remains.

Our instructor in the summer of 1971 was Winston D. Moore, who has studied at Washington State University and worked with Richard Daugherty at the Ozette site near Neah Bay, Washington. The Ozette site is a late prehistoric Makah village that was covered by a mudslide and excavated as a cooperative effort between Washington State University and the Makah tribe. Our instructor's experience at Ozette must have been positive, because in the summer of 1971 he arranged to have two local Ojibwa people join the archaeological field crew. Although he never instructed us on the ethical value of this action, it is plain to me in retrospect that he anticipated and respected their interest and desire to be involved in the archaeological study of their past. Thirty years later, this is still an important issue for archaeologists, and it is being incorporated into formal archaeological training.

Upon completion of my undergraduate training, I entered graduate school in 1973. In retrospect, I see now that my undergraduate years in archaeology were associated with a period when most archeological research was the private domain of university and museum archaeologists. My graduate studies and subsequent career have been associated with the development of cultural resource management. During the past thirty years, I have had the good fortune to participate in the tremendous growth of the archaeological profession.

During this time we have seen increasing opportunities for archaeological employment and tremendous public support for archaeological research. Along with these benefits there are also responsibilities and the need for archaeological ethics.

ARCHAEOLOGICAL ETHICS: ORIGINS

As a student in the 1970s, my formal training in archaeological ethics was unfortunately limited. This was typical for most students at that time, and the tradition continues to some extent today. The reluctance to discuss ethics in archaeological courses is probably due in part to the history of archaeology.

Most historians of archaeology point to the nineteenth century as the start of systematic archaeological investigation. At that time, there were no "professional" archaeologists. People who conducted archaeological investigations were either independently wealthy or had other employment to support themselves and their families. The development of museums in cities in the eastern United States in the last half of the nineteenth century generated a demand for artifacts associated with the earthen and stone monuments of North and Central America. This demand provided a number of self-taught individuals with employment to excavate mounds and earthworks in eastern North America, pueblo ruins in the southwest, and ruins and temples in Meso-America. As reports of these expeditions were published, eastern preservationists became concerned about the loss of important sites to looting and vandalism. This eventually resulted in the passage of federal legislation that protected archaeological sites on federal lands. The Smithsonian Institution and the Archaeological Institute of America were instrumental in passage of the Antiquities Act of 1906, and this likely represents the origins of archaeological ethics in the United States.

Throughout the first half of the twentieth century, archaeology was conducted by a small number of professionals in universities and museums. The number of archaeologists in these early years was small enough that the Annual Meeting of the Society for American Archaeology was often held at a university in cities like Ann Arbor, Michigan, Norman, Oklahoma, and Lincoln, Nebraska. The first Annual Meeting of the Society for American Archaeology was held in 1935 in Andover, Massachusetts with approximately 75 people in attendance.[4]

Due to the small size of the archaeological profession, the number of research projects and resulting reports were quite few. Even with the growth of the archaeological profession following World War II, the number of archaeologists was still sufficiently small so that all the archaeologists working in a region like the Plains knew each other fairly well. With archaeologists focused mainly on research and teaching, the need for formal statements about ethics was limited.

In a review of the history of archaeological ethics, Charles R. McGimsey III[5] notes that the major federal funding through the River Basin Surveys in the late 1940s and 1950s awakened a desire among the archaeological profession to better define the basic qualifications of an archaeologist. Consequently in 1960, Jesse Jennings, President of the Society for American Archaeology, established a Committee on Ethics and Standards. A year later that Committee published a report titled "Four Statements for Archaeology."[6] The four statements represent the first published ethics policy for the Society for American Archaeology and reflect the concerns of that time. The statements warn of censure or expulsion from the Society for disregard of proper archaeological field methods, buying and selling of artifacts, and willful destruction, distortion or concealment of archaeological data. The fourth statement recommends that archaeologists have formal training consisting of a B.A. or B.S. degree followed by two years of graduate study in archaeology and anthropology, with two years of summer field school experience under the supervision of a trained archaeologist. A Ph.D. in anthropology was highly recommended, but not required.

In 1971 when I participated in my first summer of archaeological fieldwork, this ethics policy was not part of the formal archaeological curriculum. During the 1960s and 1970s, students in archaeology were deeply concerned about changes in the paradigm of archaeology. The writings of Lewis R. Binford and his students promoted an interest in processual theory. Processualist views promoted problem-oriented research and the search for laws and theory through research designs and hypothesis testing. The change from a culture-historical orientation to a processualist orientation dominated archaeological discussion and debate even as the foundations of contemporary cultural resource management programs were being developed.

CULTURAL RESOURCE MANAGEMENT

When I was an idealistic student, it seemed only logical that archaeologists should conduct research at sites before they are destroyed by construction or other activities. The archaeological heritage that was salvaged by the TVA and River Basin Survey programs, although it did not live up to the standards of processual or "New" archaeology, still served as a reminder of what could be lost without archaeological salvage. Fortunately, through the efforts of archaeologists and other preservationists, the U.S. Congress passed the National Historic Preservation Act of 1966, the National Environmental Policy Act of 1969, and the Archeological and Historic Preservation Act of 1974. These three laws form the core of what has become known as Cultural Resource Management in the United States.

As a graduate student at Southern Methodist University, I had the opportunity to participate in a wide variety of contract archaeology projects throughout northern Texas. At that time, most of the archaeological research associated with Cultural Resource Management was being done by universities. Major projects like New Melones in California, Orme and Santa Rosa Wash in Arizona, and Cache River in Arkansas offered opportunities for enthusiastic young archaeologists to apply processualist approaches on an increasingly large scale. Private sector involvement at this time was just beginning, and public funding for archaeology was on the rise. At the same time, some of the same individuals who had worked to pass the laws that formed the basis for the new Cultural Resource Management movement were able to see the need for an expanded code of ethics for archaeology.

SOCIETY OF PROFESSIONAL ARCHEOLOGISTS

Throughout the first half of the 1970s, members of the Society for American Archaeology discussed the need for certification of archaeologists. After several conferences and meetings, a Society for American Archaeology committee met in Fayetteville, Arkansas in January 1976 and decided to develop certification procedures, a code of ethics, and standards of research performance for a new organization, totally independent of SAA and other existing archaeological societies. In May 1976, the Society of Professional Archeologists (SOPA) was incorporated in Illinois and began the process of establishing a registry of professional archaeologists.

Unlike the earlier ethics code developed by the SAA, the new SOPA code was more comprehensive and more specific. The Code of Ethics addressed the responsibility of archaeologists to the public, colleagues, employees, students, and clients. The Standards of Research Performance addressed the responsibility of archaeologists to be properly prepared and trained for any research they undertake, to implement the research in a systematic and scientific manner, to report the results of the research in a reasonable period of time, and to insure that the artifacts and records resulting from the research are curated in an appropriate institution. The Society of Professional Archeologists also implemented a Grievance Procedure that allowed individuals to charge SOPA-certified archaeologists with violations of the Code of Ethics and Standards of Research Performance. After investigation by the Grievance Coordinator and a hearing in front of the Standards Board, an archaeologist who had violated the Ethics Code and Standards of Research Performance could be admonished, suspended, or expelled from SOPA. The creation of a mechanism to enforce the Code of Ethics and Standards of Research Performance represented a bold precedent for American archaeology.

Between 1976 and 1998, the Society of Professional Archeologists was the only organization in the United States that certified individuals as professional archaeologists. Although there was widespread support for the creation of SOPA, many archaeologists objected to the certification process and never joined the organization. The inability to convince substantial numbers of archaeologists to be certified and accept the Code of Ethics and Standards of Research Performance reduced the effectiveness of the organization. Although expensive, the Grievance Process proved effective and SOPA gradually built a body of case law about ethical behavior.

During this same period, archaeology experienced major growth in employment resulting from the passage of cultural resource management legislation. The number of archaeologists boomed from hundreds to thousands, and raised questions about minimum professional qualifications and standards of performance. During this period, SOPA was the only organization to regularly and explicitly address the ethical issues facing the archaeological profession. However, the relatively small number of dedicated SOPA members were unable to have the full impact they desired on the ethics of the archaeological profession.

1980s AND BEYOND

While the field of cultural resource management continued to grow, the threat to archaeological resources also grew. Illegal trade in antiquities threatened sites around the world, and archaeologists worked with legislators to pass laws to protect archaeological sites from looting by antiquities hunters. Despite serious efforts by many nations to protect their archaeological heritage, the antiquities trade continued to flourish. Archaeological organizations like the Archaeological Institute of America and the Society for Historical Archaeology developed policies to discourage archaeologists from working with looters and antiquities traders to avoid any appearance of approval of their activities.

At the same time, archaeologists were confronted by an increasing expression of interest among Native Americans in the archaeological record and the treatment of the archaeological record. This interest eventually grew into political activism that resulted in the passage of state and federal legislation relating to the repatriation of human remains and associated artifacts. While some archaeologists opposed these developments as anti-science, others argued that these laws offered an opportunity to build upon a history of cooperation between archaeologists and some Native American groups. However archaeologists felt about the Native American Graves Protection and Repatriation Act (NAGPRA), it fueled further discussion about archaeological ethics.

In 1990, the editors of the *American Journal of Archaeology* (published by the Archaeological Institute of America) and *Latin American Antiquity* and *American Antiquity* (published by the Society for American Archaeology) issued policies that prohibited publication of papers that were based on looted data. In May 1991, Alison Wylie made a presentation to the SAA Executive Board about the ethical issues associated with publishing papers that utilized data from looted sites. The SAA Executive Board recognized that the Society's ethics policy was outdated and the editorial policies of their journals were not fully compatible with Society bylaws. The Executive Board asked Alison Wylie and me to cochair a task force on ethics in archaeology.

With funding from the National Science Foundation and the National Park Service, we were able to organize a three-day workshop (November 5–7, 1993) at the CRM Policy Institute, University of Nevada-Reno. At that workshop, a diverse range of participants drafted six principles of archaeological ethics and agreed upon a process for presenting them to the SAA membership. The six principles developed at the Reno Workshop addressed stewardship, accountability, commercialization, public education and outreach, intellectual property, and records preservation.

The six draft principles were presented to the SAA membership at the fifty-ninth Annual Meeting of the Society in a Special Forum in Anaheim, California. The Special Forum included an introduction, six position papers about the draft principles, and commentaries from five discussants. The proceedings from the Forum were compiled and edited and published by the SAA as a Special Report.[7] The Special Forum and subsequent Special Report were intended to encourage discussion and inform archaeologists about the draft principles. Verbal and written comments were further solicited by the presentation of papers at regional conferences and at discussion sessions at the sixtieth Annual Meeting of the SAA in Minneapolis in 1995.

After reviewing the comments that were received, the Ethics in Archaeology Task Force made editorial and other minor changes and developed an additional principle that addressed the responsibility of archaeologists to publish reports of their research. The principles were then submitted to the SAA Executive Board for review and approval in September 1995. At the next meeting, the Executive Board discussed the draft principles expressing concerns about aspects of two of the draft principles and recommending that an eighth principle addressing training and resources be developed by the Task Force. The Task Force made the recommended changes and resubmitted them to the SAA Executive Board, which adopted them in 1996.

PRINCIPLES OF ARCHAEOLOGICAL ETHICS

The Principles of Archaeological Ethics are statements of ethical goals or ideals. They are intended to guide archaeologists through the increasing complexity of conducting their professional lives in the modern world. The Principles of Archaeological Ethics represent what Alison Wylie[8] has called "ceilings" of ethical behavior, rather than "floors" that might identify minimum acceptable levels of conduct. The Ethics in Archaeology Task Force, in developing the Principles, never intended that they be enforceable. The Principles were intended to stimulate discussion, encourage teaching about ethics, and serve as ethical guidelines.

PRINCIPLE 1: STEWARDSHIP

The archaeological record—that is, in situ archaeological material and sites, archaeological collections, records, and reports—is irreplaceable. It is the responsibility of all archaeologists to work for the long-term conservation and protection of the archaeological record by practicing and promoting good stewardship of the archaeological record. Stewards are both caretakers of and advocates for the archaeological record. In the interests of stewardship, archaeologists should use and advocate use of the archaeological record for the benefit of all people; as they investigate and interpret the record, they should use the specialized knowledge they gain to promote public understanding and support for its long-term preservation.

PRINCIPLE 2: ACCOUNTABILITY

Responsible archaeological research, including all levels of professional activity, requires an acknowledgement of public accountability and a commitment to make every reasonable effort, in good faith, to consult actively with affected group(s), with the goal of establishing a working relationship that can be beneficial to all parties involved.

PRINCIPLE 3: COMMERCIALIZATION

The Society for American Archaeology has long recognized that the buying and selling of objects out of archaeological context is contributing to the destruction of the archaeological record on the American continents and around the world. The commercialization of archaeological objects— their use as commodities to be exploited for personal enjoyment or profit— results in the destruction of archaeological sites and of contextual information that is essential to understanding the archaeological record. Archaeologists should therefore carefully weigh the benefits to scholarship of a project against the costs of potentially enhancing the commercial value of archaeological objects. Wherever possible, they should discourage, and should themselves avoid, activities that enhance the commercial value of archaeological objects, especially objects that are not curated in public institutions, or readily available for scientific study, public interpretation, and display.

PRINCIPLE 4: PUBLIC EDUCATION AND OUTREACH

Archaeologists should reach out to, and participate in, cooperative efforts with others interested in the archaeological record with the aim of improving the preservation, protection, and interpretation of the record. In particular, archaeologists should undertake to (1) enlist public support for the stewardship of the archaeological record; (2) explain and promote the use of archaeological methods and techniques in understanding human behavior and culture and (3) communicate archaeological interpretations of the past. Many publics exist for archaeology, including students and teachers; Native Americans and other ethnic, religious, and cultural groups who find in the archaeological record important aspects of their cultural heritage; lawmakers and government officials; reporters, journalists, and others involved in the media; and the general public. Archaeologists who are unable to undertake public education and outreach directly should encourage and support the efforts of others in these activities.

PRINCIPLE 5: INTELLECTUAL PROPERTY

Intellectual property, as contained in the knowledge and documents created through the study of archaeological resources, is part of the archaeological record. As such it should be treated in accord with the principles of stewardship rather than as a matter of personal possession. If there is a compelling reason, and no legal restrictions or strong countervailing interests, a researcher may have primary access to original materials and documents for a limited and reasonable time, after which these materials and documents must be made available to others.

PRINCIPLE 6: PUBLIC REPORTING AND PUBLICATION

Within a reasonable time, the knowledge archaeologists gain from investigation of the archaeological record must be presented in accessible form (through publication or other means) to as wide a range of interested publics as possible. The documents and materials on which publication and other forms of public reporting are based should be deposited in a suitable place for permanent safekeeping. An interest in preserving and protecting in situ archaeological sites must be taken into account when publishing and distributing information about their nature and location.

PRINCIPLE 7: RECORDS AND PRESERVATION

Archaeologists should work actively for the preservation of, and long-term access to, archaeological collections, records, and reports. To this end, they should encourage colleagues, students, and others to make responsible use of collections, records, and reports in their research as one means of preserving the in situ archaeological record and of increasing the care and attention given to that portion of the archaeological record that has been removed and incorporated into archaeological collections, records, and reports.

PRINCIPLE 8: TRAINING AND RESOURCES

Given the destructive nature of most archaeological investigations, archaeologists must ensure that they have adequate training, experience, facilities, and other support necessary to conduct any program of research they initiate in a manner consistent with the foregoing principles and contemporary standards of professional practice.

STEWARDSHIP

The concept of stewardship is at the center of the Principles of Archaeological Ethics. It has become widespread in archaeology with the development of cultural resource management. The term became a catchword for archaeological site protection following the publication of a booklet titled "These are the Stewards of the Past."[9] Stewardship responsibilities for archaeologists were further defined by William Lipe in one of the most important archaeological papers in the past three decades. In that 1974 paper, "A Conservation Model for American Archaeology," Lipe offered many excellent and logical reasons why archaeologists should work to protect and preserve the archaeological record for future study.[10] A generation of archaeologists embraced this model and worked to weave it into the fabric of current cultural resource management practices.

Recently, Lipe has refined his thinking on stewardship and reminds archaeologists that understanding the past through the study of the archaeological record is the ultimate goal of archaeology. Since the value of many archaeological sites is tied to their information potential, well-designed and implemented archaeological research is important to the advancement of the discipline and benefits the public. "Long-term, frugal consumption of the archaeological record by well-justified research—both problem-oriented, and mitigation driven—must be an accepted and integrated part of the preservation program."[11]

Although much of my own archaeological training emphasized that professionally trained archaeologists have the most legitimate interest in the archaeological record, the interest of the general public and specific interest groups in the use and management of archaeological sites and objects is clearly increasing. Coincident with the development of the draft Principles of Archaeological Ethics, Christopher Chippindale[12] published an eloquent dialogue on the importance of holding archaeological resources in "common" for everyone. Since the vast majority of archaeological research and archaeological site management is now funded by the public, this seems to be a practical as well as principled approach. Archaeologists have long recognized that one of the primary factors that distinguish professional archaeologists from looters is that our training, specialized knowledge, and skills permit us to serve a wide range of public interests.

ACCOUNTABILITY AND PUBLIC EDUCATION AND OUTREACH

The principles of accountability and public education and outreach reflect the growing awareness among archaeologists that our obligations extend beyond the archaeological community. When I first became involved in archaeology, many archaeologists viewed talking with the media or giving a lecture at a rotary luncheon as something to be avoided. This is clearly changing. Not only do the principles encourage archaeologists to share their specialized knowledge about the past with the diverse public, but archaeologists recognize that most of their work is sponsored by public funding. At a time when there is increasing competition for public funds at all levels, it is clearly in our best interest to share our knowledge and discoveries with the public. The Society for American Archaeology has established a nationwide network of Public Education Coordinators who work with local archaeologists to arrange and schedule public lectures, assist teachers and administrators in adding archaeology to school curricula, and organize and schedule statewide archaeology week activities.

There is also growing awareness among archaeologists that our research and professional activities affect many individuals and groups beyond the archaeological profession. Archaeologists have always been aware of their responsibilities to landowners on whose property they wish to work, but now there is increasing awareness of responsibility to the people whose past we study. Many native people around the world are interested in what archaeology can tell them about their heritage, and some are uncomfortable with the methods of archaeology. In the United States, the Native American Graves Protection and Repatriation Act recognizes that Native Americans should have a voice in the treatment of human remains and associated funerary objects recovered from archaeological sites. Similar legislation in Canada and other nations is encouraging archaeologists and First Nations to communicate and collaborate on the study of the past.

COMMERCIALIZATION

The loss of archaeological sites and damage to the archaeological record from looters is a major problem throughout the world. A search of almost any American flea market will reveal a dealer selling arrow heads and other artifacts. While many of these may, in fact, be recent replicas, they demonstrate the market for even common and broken objects from the past. The finest archaeological objects usually sell through international auctions. The demand for antiquities is worldwide and is big business. Competition among museums to display the best and finest artifacts also fuels this market. The demand for antiquities is encouraging illegal and unscientific excavation of archaeological sites all over the world.

One of the oldest, and still most important, ethical problems for archaeologists is deciding how to deal with collections owned by amateur archaeologists and art collectors. Archaeology in general, and professional archaeologists in particular, have benefited greatly from information provided by amateur archaeologists. Most professional archaeologists are comfortable working with amateur archaeologists and landowners who collect surface artifacts, record their provenience, and report site locations to professional archaeologists. What becomes more difficult is deciding how to treat individuals who dig for artifacts without proper training.

Ten years ago, *Archaeology* magazine published a special report on the extent of looting in Arkansas.[13] The report emphasized the extent and intensity of the problem. Since it is largely rural and one of the poorest states, many people in Arkansas see digging for artifacts as a way to increase their income. Individuals have been digging prehistoric graves to collect pots and other artifacts for sale for more than a hundred years, and Mississippian and Caddoan pottery from Arkansas is found in private collections and museums around the world. Unfortunately, when an archaeologist examines artifacts from a private collection and provides an opinion about their age, function, or authenticity, that opinion may be used to legitimize the artifacts. A professional archaeologist's opinion might also result in an increase in the sale price of artifacts. This is even more likely when an archaeologist incorporates data from looted contexts into their research and publications. By increasing the commercial value of looted collections, archaeologists unintentionally provide fuel for further looting of archaeological sites. Art and antiquities collectors are very much aware of the literature of archaeology, and opinions, writing, and activities of professional archaeologists have an impact on collecting activities and interests.

INTELLECTUAL PROPERTY AND PUBLIC REPORTING AND PUBLICATION

As a student, one of the first informal lessons I received in ethics was a discussion by a professor about the importance of writing reports that describe our excavations. The professor never really said why reporting was important, but it was clear that failure to do so would tarnish our reputations. With most archaeological research today is supported by public funding, the obligation to prepare reports is still widely accepted. The need to publish our research results, particularly books and papers that synthesized work from cultural resource management projects, is particularly important. Most cultural resource management reports are produced in very small numbers, and they are only accessible to specialists and close colleagues. This "gray literature," as it is known, contains a tremendous amount of information that is inaccessible to many professionals and most of the public. For most people working in cultural resource management, it is difficult to find the time needed to synthesize projects and prepare papers and books for publication. However, it is widely understood that this is necessary if we are ever going to fully justify the continuing expenditure of public funds on archaeology.

My student training also included informal lessons about intellectual property. As noted in Principle 5, the knowledge and documents that are created as part of archaeological research are just as much a part of the archaeological record as are artifacts and objects. When I first started in archaeology, many archaeologists viewed their records and notes as personal property. Although they accepted that the artifacts from a project belonged in a museum, they kept the written notes and records in their personal possession. The importance of properly curating records and notes with artifact collections is also addressed in Principle 7. More than one older research collection has been reduced in value through the loss of records and notes that describe the provenience of artifacts or the circumstance of their discovery.

It is logical that project archaeologists should have primary access to the original records and documents for a limited and reasonable period of time. However, when a project report is complete, collections and records should be made available to others. Our stewardship responsibilities require that we share our knowledge, notes, and records with colleagues, to maximize the information potential of the archaeological record.

RECORDS AND PRESERVATION

From some of our earliest years in school, we are taught that scientific research includes systematic, objective, and precise experiments or observations that can be replicated under the same circumstances. In archaeology, the process of excavating a site removes artifacts from their original context. This process is destructive in that it leaves little or nothing for future researchers to study, except the artifacts, photographs, notes, and records of the excavation. Once excavated, a site cannot be reconstructed and excavations cannot be replicated. Consequently, we must preserve the artifacts and records from our research so that other archaeologists can decide if they concur with our interpretations of the archaeological record.

The stewardship principle recognizes that the artifacts, records, notes, and photographs from archaeological research are an important part of the archaeological record. Preserving these materials in a museum or curatorial repository is as much a part of a successful archaeological project as developing a research design. We must recognize that the products of our research are valuable resources that permit us to restudy the archaeological record, even after the site(s) from which the data came has been destroyed. The federal government recognizes that artifacts and records from archaeological research are important resources and worthy of preservation, and the Secretary of the Interior has issued detailed guidelines for the preservation of these materials.

The growth of cultural resource management has produced a crisis in the management of archaeological collections. Although some new facilities are being constructed, and some existing facilities are being expanded, there is not enough museum or repository space to properly house all the existing collections. As archaeological research continues, it is essential that we work to help develop new facilities. The preservation of these collections is important to the continued study of the archaeological record, and it is each archaeologist's ethical obligation to insure that artifacts and other products of research are properly curated.

TRAINING AND RESOURCES

The growth of cultural resource management has made archaeology a significant business in the United States. Thousands of people are employed in archaeology every year. Increasing competition for contracts and grants have led some archaeologists to undertake projects for which they were not fully qualified. Since archaeology is a destructive process, it is important that practitioners be properly trained for the research they undertake. Principle 8 was developed to remind archaeologists that we must have the appropriate training, experience, preparation, and facilities before undertaking an archaeological project.

REGISTER OF PROFESSIONAL ARCHAEOLOGISTS

While the Principles of Archaeological Ethics were being developed, the Society for American Archaeology, Society of Professional Archeologists, Archaeological Institute of America, and the Society for Historical Archaeology were discussing the creation of a Register of Professional Archaeologists. The Register was formally established in 1998, from the Society of Professional Archeologists under the joint sponsorship of the other three organizations. The Register of Professional Archaeologists (RPA) adopted most of the procedures developed by SOPA, including the Code of Ethics, the Standards of Research Performance, and the Grievance Procedure.

The grievance procedure and certification process are at the heart of the RPA. Through the certification process, individuals submit their credentials to demonstrate that they have met the minimum education and experience levels necessary to be registered as Professional Archaeologists. Individuals listed on the Register also agree to accept the Code of Ethics and Standards of Research Performance. By doing this, individuals agree to participate in the grievance process if there is a credible challenge to their conduct or research performance. The grievance process establishes a system where any concerned individual can ask that the actions of anyone listed on the Register be reviewed by a panel of professional archaeologists.

The grievance process represents a mechanism, with more than twenty years of success under SOPA, by which archaeologists can investigate the conduct and performance of colleagues. This self-policing program provides a venue where legitimate complaints are reviewed, and if necessary, sanctions recommended against individuals who perform substandard work.

Since the establishment of the RPA in 1998, the number of archaeologists who have applied for and received certification as professional archaeologists has more than doubled. While only a small fraction of the individuals currently working at archaeology have been certified by the RPA, the substantial increase in applications for certification is encouraging. This implies that more and more archaeologists recognize and accept that there is a need for a formal ethics code for archaeologists.

ETHICS AND THE FUTURE

After nearly thirty years of participating in archaeology, it is obvious to me that change in our profession, just like society in general, is occurring at an increasing rate. The Principles of Archaeological Ethics that have been adopted by the Society for American Archaeology are intended to serve as guidelines to help archaeologists make informed and wise professional choices in a rapidly changing world. The principles represent ideals, and they are intended to encourage discussion and formal training about archaeological ethics.

Until recently, ethics were not commonly part of formal training in archaeology. This is changing as archaeologists become more informed about their ethical responsibilities and the conflicts that confront us throughout the profession. Continued discussion about the Principles is essential, because we cannot possibly anticipate all the future ethical issues that will face us individually and collectively in the coming years. Consequently, the Principles must be reviewed regularly, and possibly updated or revised as needed. Formal discussion and training about ethics is important to this process, and is the best way to introduce future professional archaeologists to the difficult choices they may face.

As archaeology matures as a profession, there is an increasing need for ethical guidelines. The recent, rapid growth in the archaeological profession has clearly created an environment where the Principles of Archaeological Ethics (developed by the Society for American Archaeology), and the Register of Professional Archaeologists both serve an important function. The combination of ethical ideals, professional certification, and standards of minimally acceptable conduct from these two ethical codes offer guidelines to operate in most of the practical real-world situations being encountered by contemporary archaeologists.

NOTES

1. Robert Silverberg, *Men Against Time* (New York: MacMillan, 1967).
2. Charles R. McGimsey III, *Public Archaeology* (New York: Seminar Press, 1972).
3. William D. Lipe, "A Conservation Model for American Archaeology," *Kiva* 39 (1974): 213–245.
4. Carl E. Guthe, "Report, Society for American Archaeology," *American Antiquity* 1 (1936): 310.
5. Charles R. McGimsey III, "Standards, Ethics, and Archaeology: A Brief History," in M. J. Lynott and A. Wylie, eds., *Ethics in American Archaeology: Challenges for the 1990s* (Washington: Society for American Archaeology Special Report, 1995).
6. J. L. Champe, D. S. Byers, C. Evans, A. K. Guthe, H. W. Hamilton, E. B. Jelks, C. W. Meighan, S. Olafson, G. I. Quimby, W. Smith, and F. Wendorf, "Four Statements for Archaeology," *American Antiquity* 27 (1961): 137–138.
7. Mark J. Lynott and Alison Wylie, eds., *Ethics in American Archaeology: Challenges for the 1990s* (Washington: Society for American Archaeology Special Report, 1995).
8. Alison Wylie, "Ethical Dilemmas in Archaeological Practice: Looting, Repatriation, Stewardship, and the (Trans)formation of Disciplinary Identity," in M. J. Lynott and A. Wylie, eds., *Ethics in American Archaeology* (Washington: Society for American Archaeology, 2000).
9. Charles R. McGimsey III, Hester A. Davis, and Carl Chapman, "These Are the Stewards of the Past" (Columbia: University of Missouri, Extension Division, 1970).
10. See note #3.
11. Ibid.
12. Christopher Chippindale, "The Concept of the 'Commons,'" *Antiquity* 68 (1994): 191–192.
13. Spencer P. M. Harrington, "The Looting of Arkansas," *Archaeology* 44 (1991): 22–31.

SUGGESTED READINGS

Green, Ernestene L., ed. *Ethics and Values in Archaeology.* New York: Free Press, 1984.
Lynott, Mark J. "Ethical Principles and Archaeological Practice: Development of an Ethics Policy." *American Antiquity* 62, no. 4 (1987): 589–599.
Lynott, Mark J. and Alison Wylie, eds. *Ethics in American Archaeology.* Washington: Society for American Archaeology, 2000.
Messenger, Phyllis Mauch, ed. *The Ethics of Collecting Cultural Property: Whose Culture? Whose Property?* Albuquerque: University of New Mexico Press, 1989.
Vitelli, Karen D., ed. *Archaeological Ethics.* Walnut Creek, CA: Altamira Press, 1996.

CLOTH PRODUCTION AND GENDER RELATIONS IN THE INKA EMPIRE

CATHY LYNNE COSTIN

Since the 1960s, archaeologists have worked at developing methodologies to identify and analyze variability within and between ancient societies. Prior to that time, most "traditional" archaeologists—and, more generally, anthropologists—approached the cultures they studied as though they were homogeneous units of mind and behavior, making the implicit assumption that everyone within a society thought the same and acted in the same sorts of ways. The "new" approach to archaeology explicitly acknowledged many forms and causes of cultural heterogeneity: geographic and environmental differences, occupational differences and specialization, class and wealth differences. Although some argue that the potential for incorporating these ideas has yet to be fully achieved,[1] most archaeologists today recognize that individuals of different occupation, class, or place of residency engage in different activities, pursue different strategies for survival and success, and are likely to be affected differently by the actions of others within and outside their societies.

Recently, some archaeologists have begun to include another dimension of social variability in their research. This dimension is gender, the distinction between feminine and masculine.[2] In all human societies women and men do different things and are thought about in different ways. Because of this, it is probable that they will contribute to, as well as experience, cultural change in different ways. To gloss over or ignore this fundamental difference is to miss an important dynamic of social process.

But how can we identify and analyze how gender helped structure ancient societies? After all, the people we study are dead! We cannot directly observe people making tools, stirring food, growing crops, selling wares at the market, or deciding to declare war or sue for peace in order to document and analyze gendered differences in behavior. Even more invisible—so the argument goes—is what people *thought* about gender: the relative values placed on the products of men's and women's labor, their activities, and their very lives. It is important that we do not assume that gender-based behavior, personality, status, and treatment have been universal across space and time or that they conform to twentieth-century Western ideals. Rather, we must develop methods to identify and explain the similarities and differences in the ways men and women acted, participated, and were treated in ancient societies.[3] In the remainder of this chapter I will present the wealth of data we can use to study gender differences in ancient societies, just as we can analyze other key dimensions of variability such as occupation, settlement, and class. I will do so with examples from my own research on the immediately pre-Inka and Inka societies of the Yanamarca Valley in the Central Highlands of Peru.

DATA APPROPRIATE FOR THE STUDY OF GENDER IN ANCIENT SOCIETIES

There are many categories of data that can be used to study gender differences in past societies. We can broadly divide these into ethnohistorical and archaeological data. Ethnohistory is a term used by both anthropologists and historians to refer to the reconstruction of native cultures from written sources. There are many types of sources available to the ethnohistorian. First are indigenous documents. These come from ancient civilizations that developed their own writing systems. The earliest of these documents include Maya hieroglyphic texts; Mesoamerican pictorial books (called codices); Mesopotamian cuneiform texts; Mycenaean clay tablets; and Egyptian hieroglyphic texts. These sources are particularly informative because they present the insiders' view. The audience for whom these documents were written was that small segment of society that was literate, namely the elites. Hence, the topics covered were those that would be of most interest to them, such as elite genealogies, military and political histories, taxation and other economic matters, and state religious ritual and belief.

The second category of ethnohistoric sources are transcribed native oral traditions. Like native written documents, they were probably composed and/or maintained by the elite. These texts include myths, legends, poetry, literature, genealogical histories, legal codes, and other bodies of information traditionally retained by memory but eventually written down.

A third category of ethnohistoric sources consists of firsthand accounts and descriptions by outsiders such as traders, explorers, missionaries, and conquerors.

A fourth category of ethnohistorical data consists of colonial administrative documents, including censuses, official questionnaires, tribute lists, court transcripts, and legal codes. Many of these documents exist because colonial administrators often relied upon indigenous forms of labor organization, tax collection, and administration to achieve their ends, and the native systems incorporated into the colonial structure were recorded in an attempt to regularize and standardize them. Indigenous peoples also sought to take advantage of new legal systems to preserve and advance their own interests, and their testimony to courts and judicial advocates about title to land, rights of access to resources, marriage patterns, inheritance rules, and other practices is preserved in archives around the world.

None of these ethnohistoric sources is without problems and/or biases. For most, the topics and domains covered are narrow, usually focusing primarily on things of interest to the ruling class. The information in both native and colonial documents was often collected from and recorded by men—usually upper-class men—and therefore most ethnohistoric sources represent the viewpoint and practices of only a small segment of society.

One of the main problems with colonial sources is that they rarely represent the native point of view. Few of these works are consciously objective "ethnographic" investigations of native culture. Outsiders sometimes failed to comprehend what they were witnessing and often were contemptuous of the practices they observed. For both native and colonial texts, we have problems of translation. These problems include our own ability to decipher and translate ancient texts as well as errors in translation made by those who compiled oral histories and recorded native languages and practices many centuries ago. The third problem is one of imprecision in chronological and spatial focus. Oral histories—which are often passed down *with modification* for hundreds of years—may combine attitudes and practices that pertain to different eras. Similarly, colonial chronicles and administrative documents may indiscriminately record the practices of different regions and/or subgroups without noting where or from whom the information was obtained. We need to evaluate the veracity, reliability, and usefulness of each source, taking into account when it was written, where it was written, for whom it was written, why it was written, and the background of the writer.

Despite their shortcomings, the documentary sources are particularly valuable as sources of certain kinds of information, especially for those intangibles of culture that often leave no material record. These include rules, ideas, abstract beliefs, marriage patterns and practices, systems of access to resources, and historical information. Many aspects of gender—including the division of labor and gender ideology—are among the topics that can be accessed with ethnohistoric data.

I have found that ethnohistorical materials are particularly useful when used in conjunction with archaeological data. The advantage of archaeological data is that, if collected and analyzed appropriately, these data do not suffer from the same types of problems discussed for the documentary materials. First, archaeological materials are more broadly representative of the society as a whole. We should be able to recover the garbage of rich and poor, men and women, children and adults, farmers and priests, villagers and city-dwellers. Also, since most human activities leave some sort of material record, the archaeological data may reflect a wider variety of activities than do the ethnohistoric data: from the mundane, humdrum acts necessary for daily survival to the great pageantry and spectacle of ritual and nobility.

Second, the archaeological data themselves are more objective. The processes of deposit formation—loss, discard, and abandonment—are rarely consciously manipulated to present an image or bias an opinion; neither is there self-reflective commentary in patterns of deposit. That is, people rarely worry about the image they create when they throw out their trash (because they don't expect anyone to really look at it, let alone scientifically analyze it to recreate their lifestyle).

The archaeological record is not without its drawbacks and limitations, however. Not all things people use preserve equally well over the centuries. Organic materials are much less likely to be preserved than nonorganic materials. This can lead to an incorrect interpretation of a culture. For example, if we recover all the stone tools but none of the wooden ones, we may incorrectly reconstruct the range of activities people pursued. Similarly, some organic materials preserve better than others, so that animal bones (which represent the flesh component of the diet) may be well represented, while botanical remains (which represent the vegetal component of the diet) may not be recovered. Such a pattern of recovery may cause us to overestimate dependence on meat and underestimate the importance of plant foods in the diet. Similarly, there may be some parts of culture that are invisible in the archaeological record because they do not have a direct, material component. Language and beliefs are two often cited examples, but other items include marriage and kinship patterns, property systems, and historical data. Also, there are parts of the archaeological record that are not immediately identifiable and interpretable, often because they have no modern counterpart to which we can compare them, or because the record is incomplete or ambiguous. "What *is* this?" is probably among the most frequently asked questions in the field and in the lab. Problems of objectivity and reliability figure in the analysis, and it is incumbent on us to use rigorous and appropriate methodologies for drawing our conclusions about the past.

Despite these problems, archaeological data *can* be used to study gender. In fact, there are five general categories of archaeological data pertinent to the study of sex/gender. The first is skeletal data. While most sex differences are expressed in soft tissues (which are rarely recovered), it is also possible to use the shape and size of some bones to identify the sex of an adult with reasonable accuracy. Examination of bone can yield information about age at death; number of pregnancies (obviously, females only); trauma; stress; diet and malnutrition; and some infectious and degenerative diseases. These analyses provide straightforward information on the physical well-being, activities, differential care, prestige, and status of men and women.

The second category of archaeological data that may reflect gender differences consists of grave goods—the objects with which individuals were buried. Archaeologists assume that these reflect some of the basic activities the individual participated in in life (or at least those activities ideologically or symbolically associated with his/her social category); and his or her status and prestige.

The third category of data consists of two-dimensional or three-dimensional figurative representations, which may record information about gender differences in activities and status. As with most archaeological materials, some artistic traditions are easier to interpret than others. For example, the division of labor is fairly easy to identify from images painted on the walls of ancient Egyptian tombs,[4] while the nature and meaning of Paleolithic female "Venus" figures remains enigmatic.[5]

The fourth category of data consists of various artifacts themselves. We must first try to determine which particular artifacts and/or activities were regularly associated with which gender. We can then compare this with the variable distribution of these artifacts and activities throughout time and location. This will enable us to identify changes in the location of particular activities, the relative intensities of activities in different periods or different communities, changes in people's work loads, and changes in activity scheduling. All of these things may in turn affect economic and social relationships.

The fifth category of archaeological data consists of analysis of activity patterns in their spatial and architectural contexts. The identification of certain activities and artifacts with certain individuals permits discussion of where those activities took place. We can consider the degree to which certain activities are domestic or public, unrestricted or secluded, universal or limited. We can then further discuss the impact any restrictions may have on people's lives and on other activities they may pursue.

In sum, we students of the past are lucky in that archaeology and ethnohistory generally have complementary strengths, errors, and omissions. They can thus be combined quite effectively for the study of the past. The two types of data often cover different domains and aspects of society. Second, the archaeological and ethnohistorical records were generally formed independently of one another, and so should not contain the same errors, biases, and omissions. Of the roughly nine different categories of data, I used seven in my study of Wanka and Inka gender.

RESEARCH BACKGROUND

The archaeological data discussed in this chapter were collected by the Upper Mantaro Archaeological Research Project (UMARP). UMARP was established in 1977 to study culture changes in the Yanamarca Valley of highland Peru (see Figure 17-1 on page 266). We were particularly interested in the development of small scale chiefdoms among the indigenous Wanka ethnic group between A.D. 1300 and 1470, and the effects of the Inka conquest, which occurred in about A.D. 1470, on the local population. The project members were an international team, each of whom contributed their expertise in an area of data collection and/or materials analysis (pottery, lithics, animal bone, botanical remains, architecture, etc.).

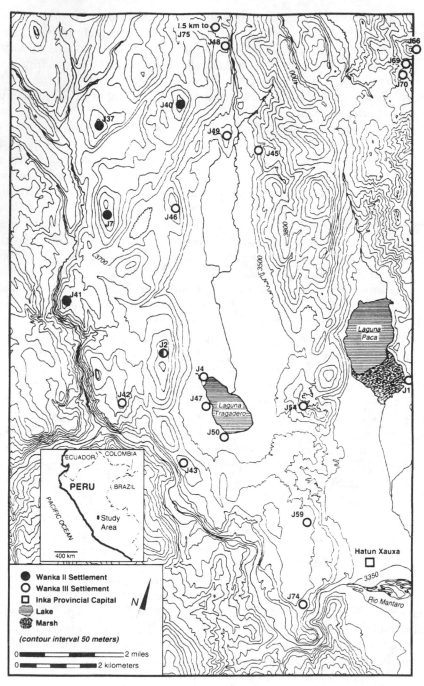

FIGURE 17-1   MAP OF THE UPPER MANTARO
ARCHAEOLOGICAL RESEARCH PROJECT RESEARCH AREA

To achieve our goal of reconstructing and explaining change in Wanka society, we collected archaeological data from sites that pertained to the immediately pre-Inka period (which we call Wanka II), and the period during which the Wanka population was under Inka domination (which we dubbed Wanka III). Surface collections were made at over thirty sites, and intensive excavations were conducted at seven of those sites. In our excavations, we focused our efforts on houses and their adjoining "private" patio space. We excavated in thirty-one households. Although this is an extremely small fraction of the tens of thousands of households that populated the region, because we used scientific sampling procedures we believe that the sample is probably representative of the Wanka population as a whole.

We recovered, catalogued, and analyzed hundreds of thousands of artifacts and ecofacts. In all, approximately 300,000 pottery sherds, 50,000 stone artifacts, 80,000 animal bones, many kilos of botanical materials, 106 human burials, and hundreds of pieces of metal and shell comprise the dataset from which we drew our conclusions about Wanka and Inka society in the Yanamarca. In addition, we analyzed the architecture and settlement patterns of the communities from which we collected our data. All the materials were processed and catalogued in Peru. Computer analyses of the data were conducted at UCLA.

When we developed our research design, we were careful to include methods of data collection and analysis that would allow us to discuss differences in the Wanka population in terms of socioeconomic class, occupation, and community type. However, to be honest, we did not include gender as an analytic category in our original research and therefore did not explicitly collect data to address gender-related issues. It was not until a decade later that I realized we should have included gender as an analytic category! It is a credit to the potency of our research design—which generated data to address a wide variety of questions, including some not anticipated when the research began—that I was able to expand our analytic categories and pursue this "gender-informed" research.

Let me digress for a minute, to discuss the non-gendered conclusions we drew from our analyses.[6] As mentioned earlier, the Wanka were the native inhabitants of the Yanamarca Valley. At about A.D. 1300, they developed a chiefdom level society, probably as the indirect result of intensified warfare among communities. We infer a high level of conflict among the Wanka from the locations and configurations of their settlements. Most people lived in walled/fortified communities located on knolls high above the valley floor, where they could easily defend themselves. This conclusion is supported by ethnohistoric documents that report a high degree of warfare among the Wanka prior to the Inka conquest.[7] There was some socio-economic stratification in the Wanka II period. We differentiate between elite and commoner households on the basis of house size, location, and the quantities and types of artifacts recovered in those households. According to the documentary sources, the Wanka lords (called sinchi) initially achieved their positions of power and authority as successful leaders in battle.[8] We can also identify a settlement hierarchy. There were people living in both large towns and smaller villages. The ethnohistoric documents tell us nothing about the division of labor and occupational specialization during the Wanka II period. However, our archaeological work did identify some occupational differences among the pre-Inka population. Based on the distribution of tools used for agriculture, pottery making, stone working, and weaving, we determined that most people were farmers. However, there were some households that specialized part-time in pottery production, stone tool production, and perhaps textile production.

As recorded in the colonial-era chronicles, the Wanka were conquered by the Inka during the reign of the Inka Emperor Pachakuti (in about A.D. 1470) as a part of that leader's explosive military expansion through the Andes. After the Inka conquest, the area was transformed physically and organizationally. We learn from documentary sources that the region was incorporated as a province within the Empire. The state sent a governor and many bureaucrats from the imperial capital of Cuzco to establish Inka rule. These rulers built a new administrative center (the archaeological site of Hatun Xauxa) and set up a provincial government. Some local Wanka rulers were given low-level positions in the Inka provincial bureaucracy. There was a change in the nature and structure of socioeconomic class differences. The Inka conquerors (bureaucrats and military personnel) formed the uppermost level in Yanamarca society. Although the Wanka elite were able to maintain their wealth and power differentiation from the commoners, the local lords lost much of their independence, in that they obtained their power and wealth as vassals of the Inka state. This dependence on the conquerors is reflected materially in the fact that the Wanka elites became great imitators of all things Inka.[9] They used large quantities of imitation Inka pottery and built Inka-style additions to their homes.[10] Interestingly, the archaeological data indicate that while overall status differences continued, the commoners were in some ways better off under the Inkas. For example, the higher quantities of maize and animal bones found in Inka period houses compared with that found in pre-Inka houses suggests commoners had better diets after the conquest. Similarly, higher frequencies of certain types of pottery and other artifacts indicate increased access to some types of material goods with Inka domination. Finally, comparative analyses of skeletal remains indicate commoners experienced slightly better health and longer lifespans after the Inka conquest.[11]

In our study of settlement patterns, we identified changes in community location and structure. Most fundamentally, people moved out of the large, walled Wanka II hill towns into smaller villages closer to agricultural lands near the valley bottom. This move likely increased agricultural productivity—since people didn't have to spend an hour or more commuting each day. The breakup of the fortified towns also enhanced the Inka's ability to control the local population, since the Wanka could not retreat behind their walls to plot and carry out a rebellion. Finally, the shift from the dense, crowded towns may have contributed to the generally better health experienced by the Wanka after the Inka conquest.

The ethnohistoric sources provide some information about the craft artisans who worked for the Inka government, but provide little information regarding those artisans who produced utilitarian goods for local consumption. However, the archaeological data provide a wealth of information about craft producers. From these data, we recognize changes in the occupational structure of Wanka society after the Inka conquest. Most basically, the economy became more specialized as people in some villages focused intensively on agriculture while in other villages most households focused more intensively on craft production, such as pottery making or stone-tool making.

WANKA GENDER RELATIONS: CLOTH

The foregoing discussion demonstrates that we can reconstruct quite a bit about social and economic differences within a given cultural group, and we can document how cultural change—in this case, change brought about by the Inka conquest—affects different social groups in different ways. Can we also explore how the Inka conquest affected women and men differently? Yes!

In my own research, I have combined ethnohistorical and archaeological data to study gender relations as reflected in one small slice of ancient life: cloth production. By engendering my discussion of textile production, I have been able to explore the division of labor, the nature of the economic and political process, and social relations.

The first step I took in my work was to identify each sex/gender with certain activities, symbols, and/or places. Unfortunately, the burial data from the UMARP excavations were of minimal use in identifying sex/gender differences in the Wanka and Inka populations. There were few strong associations between artifacts of known function or symbolism and a particular sex. Also, there was little in the way of artistic data that could be used in the study, as neither the Wanka nor the Inka had strong figurative artistic traditions.

However, the ethnohistoric documents are rich in their discussion of sex/gender patterns and differences and therefore offer a starting point from which to conduct the analysis. The pre-colonial Andean peoples were nonliterate; therefore, there are no native/indigenous written sources from which to draw information pertaining to a time prior to the Spanish conquest. However, we do have a variety of early Spanish documents from which we can draw information. The Inka had a rich oral tradition, which was recorded soon after the Spanish conquest of Peru. Second, we have a large body of legal documents, including censuses, official questionnaires (*visitas*), and court documents. Finally, we have a relatively large corpus of diaries, letters, and other written works of the Spanish conquerors, later European administrators, and literate natives.

The ethnohistoric documents provide information on the general division of labor along both age and gender lines. Ideally, children and adults of both genders had specific tasks they were expected to perform. Young girls were expected to carry water, collect herbs and flowers (for cooking and dyeing), help with the cooking, and watch their younger siblings; young boys were expected to trap birds and other small animals, carry wood, and herd. Adult men and women both worked in the agricultural fields, but at somewhat different tasks: Men plowed and helped with the harvest, while women planted, weeded, and harvested. Men also built houses and other structures and served in the army. Women were responsible for cooking food, brewing beer, and watching small children. Females of all ages performed various tasks associated with cloth production, such as spinning thread and weaving (see Figure 17-2).

It was the study of cloth production that led me to the study of gender in Wanka and Inka society. As the person on the project responsible for the analysis of all ceramic artifacts, it fell to me to say something interesting about several thousand round, perforated objects recovered consistently in our excavations (see Figure 17-3). I quickly identified these as spindle whorls, which are weights used in the spinning process to keep the thread tight and even (see Figure 17-2). Having identified these objects with a specific activity, I began my investigations of that activity (spinning), its final product (cloth), and the people who made that product.

The ethnohistoric documents make clear the extreme importance and value of cloth and cloth production in Wanka and Inka societies. Cloth—in the highlands woven primarily of llama and alpaca wool—was obviously necessary for survival. Cloth had a role in many important ceremonies and rituals, including puberty rites, marriage, and burial. Cloth was also the primary form of wealth in most Andean societies, which had no money as we know it.

Because the pre-Columbian Andean peoples had no true money or coinage, the activities of the government were financed in kind (goods such as food items, pottery, and especially cloth). Revenues were raised by imposing tribute levies on subordinate populations. For example, when the Inka conquered a new territory they imposed a cloth tax on the local population. Each village was required to produce a certain amount of cloth to be turned over to state tax collectors on a regular basis. The cloth requisitioned by the state was used to clothe men serving in the army and to "pay" or reward bureaucrats and other personnel working for civilian and military institutions. State tax collectors told local leaders how much cloth to produce, and these leaders then divided the work among the villagers under their control. Not surprisingly, the cloth tax burden fell on the "traditional" spinners and weavers, that is, on girls and women. Thus, in addition to spinning and weaving to make clothing and blankets for their own families—as they had done before the Inka conquest—women under the Inka additionally spun thread and wove cloth that was turned over to state tax collectors.[12]

FIGURE 17-2   SIXTEENTH-CENTURY DRAWINGS
ILLUSTRATING ANDEAN WOMEN (A) SPINNING AND (B) WEAVING

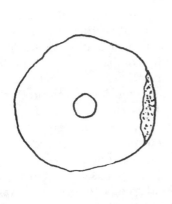

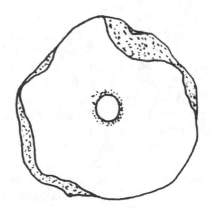

FIGURE 17-3   SPINDLE WHORLS

The ethnohistoric documents tell us that most cloth was manufactured in a domestic setting and that women were the primary producers of thread and cloth.[13] Given the strength of the association between weaving and women in Inka (and likely pre-Inka) society, I would argue that the study of cloth production provides an ideal way to study women in particular and gender relations more generally in Inka society. I make the leap from technology and production to social relations for the following reason. Cloth was a good that was produced in part for exchange. People who exchange goods must have some sort of an economic and social relationship. Asking questions about the nature of production ultimately gives us information about the nature of those economic and social relationships. Given this argument, our next questions become: How can we see cloth production archaeologically? What can the study of cloth production tell us about the effects of the Inka conquest on women's labor and gender relations?

In the Andes, the tools and materials associated with cloth production that were recovered by archaeologists include spindles and whorls used in thread production, pieces of the simple backstrap looms favored by Andean women, and needles used in finishing and embellishing woven cloth. On the coast of Peru where the dry climate leads to unusually good preservation of organic materials, my colleagues often recover a wide variety of tools associated with weaving, including entire "weaver's baskets" replete with unspun wool, half-finished thread, wooden spindles, and other accoutrements. Unfortunately, the cool, damp conditions of the highlands where I conducted my investigations do not promote such preservation. Thus, I have virtually no cloth, raw wool, spun yarn, or tools made out of perishable materials available for analysis.

The primary archaeological data I used consisted of several thousand ceramic spindle whorls, several dozen bone and metal needles, and a few ambiguous bone tools that may have served as thread bobbins, shuttles, or battens. I combined an analysis of the distribution of these artifacts (and their association with other activities) with ethnohistoric descriptions of cloth specifically and Inka society more generally to understand how cloth production changed over time, its contexts of production and distribution, and how this all affected women (and their relations with men). I used the relative numbers of tools recovered in different households to determine whether and how the amount of cloth production varied by site, class, and time period.

First, I reconstructed pre-Inka cloth production as a baseline against which to test changes after the Inka conquest. We found spindle whorls in all Wanka II households, which I interpret to mean that all households—and, therefore, I presume all females—spun and made cloth. Whorls were not, however, *evenly* distributed. Some households had significantly more whorls than others, suggesting some households—and therefore some females—worked more at cloth production than did others. The intensity of production varied in two ways. First, the density of whorls increased with elevation. This indicates that women living closer to the high elevation *puna* grasslands—where the Andean villagers kept their flocks of wool-bearing llamas and alpacas—spun more thread and possibly made more cloth than did villagers living further from good pastures. I propose a straightforward ecological/environmental explanation for this pattern: People exploited most intensively those resources located closest to where they lived.

Second, elite households yielded twice the density of whorls as did commoner households. This pattern supports a conclusion that elite women made more cloth than did commoner women. This is an interesting observation that requires further discussion, as it is at odds with our twentieth-century Western perception that wealthy women enjoy great leisure. I turned to the ethnohistoric record for an explanation of this pattern. The colonial-era documents describing pre-Inka and Inka society indicate that elites generally did not work at hard labor in the agricultural fields, but this does not mean that they did nothing all day. Rather than being idle, I argue that elite women spent their time weaving, a conclusion that is indirectly supported by statements in the documents describing the wives, daughters, and other female relatives of leaders as weaving intensively.[14] Considering what we know about the importance of cloth as a measure of wealth in Andean societies, we see that women and girls created wealth for their families by using their time and labor to turn raw fiber into valuable cloth.

The cloth created by women was an important part of the Andean political process as well as an economic asset. We learn from the documentary sources that powerful families gave away large quantities of cloth as a way of creating alliances, enlarging their power bases, and rewarding loyal followers.[15] Cloth distribution took place as a part of large feasts sponsored and hosted by elite families.[16] Archaeological materials help us identify the locations of these feasts. The distribution of bowls used to serve special foods and drinks indicates that these feasts took place within elite houses, rather than in some other nondomestic, public place. Since Wanka houses were built in such a way that no one could be secluded in an inaccessible part of the house, all members of the household sponsoring the feast must have been present at and likely participated in the activities. Thus, elite women—as the creators of textile wealth—directly contributed to and participated in the political strategies of their families.

Using the Wanka II data and conclusions as a baseline in the analysis, I then asked: What happened after the Inka conquest? Several interesting patterns emerged from the data. First, the number of spindle whorls recovered in Wanka III households is twice that recovered in Wanka II households. From this I conclude that the overall amount of spinning doubled after the Inka conquest. I believe this reflects the Inka cloth tax described in the colonial documents. There is no indication—archaeological or ethnohistoric—that women were freed from any other tasks to make more time for spinning and weaving. Thus, it would appear that the production of thread and cloth to meet state demands was accomplished in addition to all the other work for which women were responsible. By combining evidence from documentary sources and archaeological data, we might conclude that women worked harder and longer under Inka domination.

A second pattern that emerged is that, after the conquest, elite women were no longer making more cloth than commoner women: We recover roughly the same number of whorls in Wanka III commoner and elite households. The significance of this change will become clear in the subsequent discussion.

The changes in cloth production were accompanied by changes in distribution. Cloth retained its important economic and political functions, but the location of distribution and the identities of those who participated in its distribution changed. Cloth distribution no longer took place within a household context (where women would invariably have been involved). Rather, cloth was removed from the local villages and taken to regional Inka storage facilities and to the capital of the Empire itself, from where it was redistributed. In fact, the colonial-era documents make clear that all fine cloth "belonged" to the emperor (no matter who made it). Technically, people could obtain it only as a gift from the state.

As in pre-Inka times, large amounts of cloth were given away during official feasts and festivities, but the sponsorship and nature of these events changed after the Inka conquest. The number of large bowls and other artifacts associated with feasting fell dramatically in Wanka III household contexts, indicating that local Wanka lords no longer hosted large feasts and large cloth give-aways within their homes. Rather, the Inka governors and state bureaucrats assumed this role, which was carried out in large public plazas at Inka administrative centers.

Under Inka domination, cloth distribution became an increasingly masculine activity on both the giving and receiving ends. It is clear from the ethnohistoric sources that all Inka bureaucrats—including the tax collectors and administrators who distributed cloth—were male. My colleague Christine Hastorf has presented important evidence that women did not attend the state-sponsored feasts—the events where cloth was distributed—as frequently as did men. Hastorf's analysis of bones from Inka-period graves indicates women ate less maize (corn) than did men.[17] The chemical composition of women's bones closely reflects the types and proportions of foods recovered in domestic settings, indicating women mostly ate at home. In contrast, men consumed more maize than was served up at home. Hastorf concludes that men were "eating out" more than women. In the Andes, maize was often consumed as *chicha* beer, which was a key component of elaborate state-sponsored feasts. In sum, the skeletal and botanical data provide circumstantial evidence that men were partying (feasting) more than women. If women were attending fewer feasts, they may not have been the direct recipients of cloth as frequently as men. Likely, women would have received state-distributed cloth from their male relatives (husbands, brothers, fathers, sons) who did attend the feasts. This established a new set of dependencies, whereby women could not directly obtain necessary and/or valuable goods for themselves, but had to rely on others (men) for them.

Women were not directly distributing or receiving cloth, and they may not have been the ultimate consumers of this fine cloth either. Very few of the textiles that women made have survived: The organic materials from which they were made decomposed long ago. However, virtually all that have survived the past five hundred years are *men's* shirts.[18] Based on the increase in textile production activities and the lack of evidence that women were weaving for themselves, we might conclude that under Inka domination women increased their labor but presumably did not benefit from it directly. Under Inka domination, Wanka women produced more but consumed less of what they produced.

Let us return now to the specific labor taxes imposed on the conquered population. Ethnohistoric documents indicate that women wove cloth and brewed beer. The archaeological evidence indicates that they did much of this work *within* their own houses. Women, however, were not the only ones who worked harder under Inka domination. The men were also taxed. Most commonly, men worked in state agricultural and construction projects *outside* their homes. Although both women and men were taxed, there was a structural difference in the nature of men's and women's taxes: Women worked in a domestic setting, while men worked in a more public context. It was the latter type of work that was rewarded with preferred foods such as meat, maize, and chicha during and after state service. Thus, while everyone "paid taxes" by producing goods and providing services for the state, men received greater rewards for that labor.

As the nature of cloth production and distribution changed, women became further removed from direct participation in the political process. The fine cloth that elite women wove went not toward their own families' political activities, but to the state, which generally excluded women from the larger political and bureaucratic functions. Irene Silverblatt and others have argued that the pre-Inka Andean ideology viewed men and women as complementary—each working for the benefit of the other within the domestic unit and within the society.[19] But under Inka domination we see an increasing flow of highly desirable goods (such as cloth and preferred foods) from women to men, without a complementary increase in the flow of valuable "masculine" products to women. Women also lost control over the products of their labor, as these items were increasingly distributed outside the home by men unrelated to the female producers. At the same time, women may have become more dependent on men for the acquisition of necessary and valued items, such as cloth.

To follow through on this line of thought, I ask one last question: How might this change in the distribution of goods have changed household and social structure and gender relations in general? The increasingly lopsided apportionment of privileges and dependencies surely must have disrupted the formerly balanced, complementary gender relations of the Andes. We can speculate that there might have been an increase in tension between men and women as women produced more beer and cloth but participated less in the public activities in which these goods were distributed. Might the Inka conquest have begun to set men and women in opposition to each other instead of seeing themselves as working together? Returning to the original hypothesis that men and women experience culture change differently, men and women would probably have different degrees of acceptance of or resistance to Inka domination in part because they experienced their tax burdens differently. A differential, gender-based reaction to Inka rule may have spawned more gender-conscious policies of governance and administration, which might then change traditional Andean society even further.

CONCLUSIONS

I hope that the foregoing discussion has demonstrated the strength of combining archaeological and ethnohistorical inquiry in our studies of the past. Frankly, my discussion could not be as vivid, my conclusions not as detailed, if I did not have both types of data from which to draw. My students often ask me what conclusions I might have reached had I not had the ethnohistorical materials to complement my archaeological data. My archaeological data on the Wanka (and Inka) are probably insufficient to engender activities—including cloth production—in the first place and certainly not to the degree they are made gender specific in the ethnohistorical literature. I could have studied cloth production using only archaeological data, but could not have derived the conclusions about the gendered division of labor, gender relations, and women's power (or lack thereof).

At the same time, the documentary sources alone are also insufficient to generate these conclusions. The ethnohistorical record provides virtually no information on patterns of variability in cloth production. For example, in discussions of the location of cloth production, there is no distinction made between elite and commoner, high- and low-altitude villages. Similarly, there is little in the documents on how the cloth tax was implemented, the actual burden it created, or the effects of changes in cloth distribution on local populations. There is little in the documents on the seemingly "incidental" information—such as diet and the locations of feasts—which ends up being crucial for piecing together the story of gendered socioeconomic relationships and political process. Archaeological and ethnohistorical data are frequently—indeed usually—used independently of one another. In many cases, it is because we have available to us only one or the other, but not both. As this work shows, however, when both can be employed, the old proverb holds true: The whole is clearly greater than the sum of the parts.

NOTES

1. See, for example, Elizabeth Brumfiel, "Distinguished Lecture in Archaeology: Breaking and Entering the Ecosystem—Gender, Class, and Faction Steal the Show," *American Anthropologist* 94 (1992): 551–567.

2. Although the two terms are often used interchangeably, *sex* and *gender* are two different phenomena. *Sex* refers to the genetically determined, physiological differences between males and females that relate directly to their respective roles in biological reproduction. *Gender* refers to the socially defined, *learned* behaviors that are considered appropriate for individuals of a particular sex. Sex is universal in the sense that no matter where you go, all females have the same genitalia and potentially the same roles in biological reproduction (they gestate and lactate), while males have a distinctive set of genitalia and their own role in biological reproduction (they impregnate). In contrast, while all human societies have gender systems, the specific personalities and behaviors that are considered appropriately masculine or feminine vary from one group to the next. For example, in some societies making pottery is considered "women's work," while in others it is "men's work." Similarly, in some societies it is considered feminine to be passionate and headstrong and masculine to be calm and rational, while in others the near opposite holds true.

3. A few of the pioneering studies are published in Cheryl Claassen, ed., *Exploring Gender through Archaeology* (Madison, WI: Prehistory Press, 1992); Joan Gero and Margaret Conkey, eds., *Engendering Archaeology: Women and Prehistory* (Oxford: Basil Blackwell, 1991); and Dale Walde and Noreen Willows, eds., *The Archaeology of Gender: Proceedings of the 22nd Annual Chacmool Conference* (Calgary: Archaeological Association of the University of Calgary, 1991).

4. Elizabeth J. W. Barber, *Prehistoric Textiles: The Development of Cloth in the Neolithic and Bronze Ages* (Princeton, NJ: Princeton University Press, 1991), p. 286.

5. Sarah M. Nelson, "Diversity of the Upper Paleolithic 'Venus' Figurines and Archeological Mythology," in Sarah M. Nelson and Alice B. Kehoe, eds., *Powers of Observation: Alternative Views in Archeology* (Washington, D.C.: American Anthropological Association, 1990), pp. 11–22.

6. Many of the major conclusions of the UMARP work have been published in Cathy Costin, *From Chiefdom to Empire State: Ceramic Economy among the Prehispanic Wanka of Highland Peru* (Ph.D. diss., University of California, Los Angeles; Ann Arbor: University Microfilms, 1986); Terence D'Altroy, *Provincial Power in the Inka Empire* (Washington, D.C.: Smithsonian Institution Press, 1992); Timothy Earle, Terence D'Altroy, Christine Hastorf, Catherine LeBlanc, Cathy Costin, Glenn Russell, and Elsie Sandefur, *Archaeological Field Research in the Upper Mantaro Peru, 1982–1983: Investigations of Inka Expansion and Exchange* (Los Angeles: Institute of Archaeology, University of California, Los Angeles, 1987); Christine Hastorf, *Agriculture and the Onset of Political Inequality before the Inka* (Cambridge: Cambridge University Press, 1993); Catherine LeBlanc, *Late Prehispanic Huanca Settlement Patterns in the Yanamarca Valley, Peru* (Ph.D. diss., University of California, Los Angeles; Ann Arbor: University Microfilms, 1981); and Glenn Russell, *The Impact of Inka Policy on the Domestic Economy of the Wanka, Peru: Stone Tool Production and Use* (Ph.D. diss., University of California, Los Angeles; Ann Arbor: University Microfilms, 1987).

7. LeBlanc, *Late Prehispanic Huanca Settlement Patterns in the Yanamarca Valley, Peru*, pp. 349–352.

8. Ibid., pp. 339–371.

9. Cathy L. Costin and Timothy Earle, "Status Distinction and Legitimation of Power as Reflected in Changing Patterns of Consumption in Late Prehispanic Peru," *American Antiquity* 54 (1989): 691–714.

10. Prior to the Inka conquest, the Wanka built exclusively round houses. Inka architecture, in contrast, is characterized by rectangular buildings with trapezoidal niches, windows, and doorways. In the Wanka III period, these Inka architectural canons were selectively used by the Wanka, but only in elite houses.

11. Bruce Owen and Marilyn Norconk, "Analysis of the Human Burials, 1977–1983 Field Seasons: Demographic Profiles and Burial Practices," Appendix 1 in Earle et al., *Archaeological Field Research in the Upper Mantaro Peru, 1982–1983*, pp. 107–123; Marilyn Norconk "Analysis of the UMARP Burials, 1983 Field Season: Paleopathology Report," Appendix 2 in Earle et al., *Archaeological Field Research in the Upper Mantaro Peru, 1982–1983*, pp. 124–133.

12. According to the documentary sources, the state supplied the fiber while women theoretically supplied only their labor. My research suggests women probably supplied their own tools. The fiber likely came from state-controlled cotton fields and camelid herds.

13. There is some discussion as to how exclusively "feminine" cloth production was. Some argue that all women produced domestically while some men were specialists; others argue that men and women made different things and/or used different types of looms. Two points are relatively clear. First, spinning and weaving were such labor intensive activities, and demand for cloth was so high, that it is likely that all "idle" hands were recruited to help with these never-ending tasks. Second, despite the fact that the reality was that at least some boys and/or adult men spun thread and wove cloth, these activities were viewed as archetypal feminine roles.

14. Juan Polo de Ondegardo, "Informe…al licenciado Brivesca de Muñatones 1561," *Revista Histórica* 13 (1940): 141.

15. John V. Murra, "Cloth and Its Functions in the Inca State," *American Anthropologist* 64 (1962): 710–728.

16. We learn from ethnographic literature that feasting is a strategic *political* activity in ranked societies. During these "social" events, status differences are marked and reinforced, political alliances are forged, the allocation of resources is negotiated, and decisions about marriages, warfare, and other events are made.

17. Christine Hastorf, "Gender, Space, and Food in Prehistory," in Joan Gero and Margaret Conkey, eds., *Engendering Archaeology: Women and Prehistory* (Oxford: Basil Blackwell, 1991), pp. 148–152.

18. John Rowe, "Standardization in Inca Tapestry Tunics," in Ann Rowe, ed., *The Junius Bird Pre-Columbian Textile Conference* (Washington, D.C.: Dumbarton Oaks, 1979), pp. 239–264.

19. Irene Silverblatt, *Moon, Sun, and Witches: Gender Ideologies and Class in Inca and Colonial Peru* (Princeton, NJ: Princeton University Press, 1987).

SUGGESTED READINGS

Barber, Elizabeth J. W. *Women's Work: The First 20,000 Years*. New York: Norton, 1994. Good discussion of women and weaving in the Old World.

Costin, Cathy. "Textiles, Women, and Political Economy in Late Prehispanic Peru." *Research in Economic Anthropology* 14 (1993): 3–28. This article discusses the research presented in this chapter in greater detail.

Ehrenberg, Margaret. *Women in Prehistory*. Norman, OK: University of Oklahoma Press, 1989. This text provides a good introduction to the study of women in prehistory. The substantive discussion focuses primarily on the Old World.

Gero, Joan, and Margaret Conkey, eds. *Engendering Archaeology: Women and Prehistory*. Oxford: Basil Blackwell, 1991. This collection of essays offers a balanced overview of archaeological approaches to gender.

Patterson, Thomas. *The Inca Empire: The Formation and Disintegration of a Pre-Capitalist State*. New York: Berg, 1991. This discussion of the Inka focuses on social, economic, and political relationships within the empire.

Silverblatt, Irene. *Moon, Sun, and Witches: Gender Ideologies and Class in Inca and Colonial Peru*. Princeton, NJ: Princeton University Press, 1987. The best general discussion of gender in the Inka empire, based entirely on documentary sources.

INVESTIGATING CRAFT SPECIALIZATION DURING THE LONGSHAN PERIOD OF CHINA[1]

ANNE P. UNDERHILL

I will never forget the first time I saw some of the famous thin-walled, black polished pottery from the Longshan Period (ca. 2600–1900 B.C.) in Shandong province of northern China. The time was 1987. I was exhausted from weeks of traveling alone, by bicycle and on unbelievably crowded trains and buses, to study pottery vessels from the Longshan Period. I had only seen this pottery in photographs, and I was spellbound as I gazed at the incredible eggshell-thin vessels on display. The elegant, tall-stemmed cups had walls that were literally as thin as eggshells, approximately one millimeter in thickness. These vessels represent the climax of ceramic technology in ancient China and, as far as I am aware, no prehistoric vessels of this kind have been found in any other area of the world (Figure 18-1). I stayed transfixed in front of those museum display cases, lost in thought, as families with small children moved past me.

What were these tall stemmed cups used for? Surely they were too fragile to be used for daily eating and drinking. Besides, most of these vessels were found in burials, so they probably were used in rituals. Judging by the relatively large quantities of goods in burials, probably only the wealthy and powerful people had the privilege of using the cups. How I wished I could jump in a time machine and observe people from the Longshan Period using these cups at funeral ceremonies. Who were the potters who made the eggshell-thin vessels? As many archaeologists have suggested, they must have been craft specialists, since clearly they had unusual skills. What kind of craft specialization existed? My mind drifted off, imagining potters in workshops carefully thinning vessel walls by scraping, as an overseer inspected their work.

Then I remembered the less elaborate vessels from Longshan sites in the Huang or Yellow River valley that I had examined in museums and storerooms at archaeological work stations (see Figure 18-2 on page 282 for the

**FIGURE 18-1 EGGSHELL-THIN CUP
FROM THE LONGSHAN PERIOD**

Source: Reproduced from Zhong guo Taoci (1985), p. 20, Figure 20, by permission of Science Press, Beijing.

location of this area). There is great variety in the shapes of vessels that people must have used on a daily basis for food preparation, cooking, storage, and serving. (See Figure 18-3 on page 283 for a pitcher that may have been placed over a fire and used to prepare soups or heat liquids.) More questions arose. What kind of organization of labor existed for the production of these vessels? Was it different for the eggshell pottery? Did most communities have a few craft specialists who made vessels for every family? Was there more than one kind of craft specialization during the Longshan Period? Were there important changes in the way pottery vessels were made and used during this period?

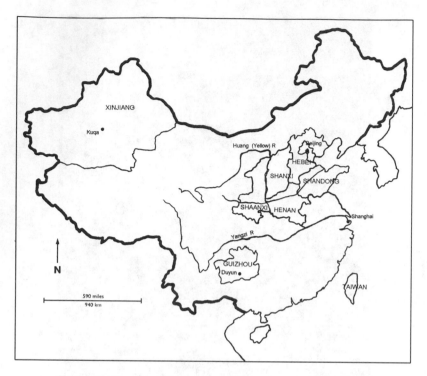

FIGURE 18-2   GEOGRAPHIC AREAS MENTIONED IN THE TEXT

Archaeologists in several areas of the world have suggested that change in craft specialization played a role in the development of complex societies. Since that initial trip to study pottery collections, I have continued to investigate craft specialization during the late prehistoric Longshan Period. After discussing some of the approaches archaeologists in China have used for investigating the Longshan Period, I will describe my own attempts to investigate change in craft specialization.

RESEARCH IN CHINA ON THE LONGSHAN PERIOD

The Longshan Period is extremely important in Chinese archaeology because it provides information on the precursors of civilization in China. For over fifty years, archaeologists have excavated late prehistoric and early historic sites in the Huang River valley in order to learn how early Chinese civilization developed. One significant characteristic of archaeology in China is that practitioners regard the field as part of history.[2] Archaeologists work to trace the history of their long, continuous civilization, one with which they feel a direct and personal connection. In contrast, most archaeologists in North

FIGURE 18-3   TRIPOD PITCHER FROM THE LONGSHAN PERIOD
Source: Reproduced from Zhong guo Taoci (1985), p. 21, Figure 21, by permission of Science Press, Beijing.

America regard archaeology as a subfield of anthropology. Most archaeologists working in North America are not Native Americans and have no ancestral ties to the prehistoric cultures they study. These American archaeologists seek to identify similarities and differences among prehistoric cultures in various areas, rather than to trace the origins of their own culture.

In China, one priority in archaeological research is to trace the origins of key features of early Chinese civilization. These features include large settlements with surrounding walls of rammed earth, bronze metallurgy, writing, and clear social differentiation represented in mortuary ritual. These features characterize the earliest undisputed dynasty in China, the Shang (ca. 1700–1100 B.C.) as well as the Western Zhou (ca. 1100 B.C.–770 B.C.), which followed the Shang Dynasty. A dynasty is a succession of kings from the same line of descent. Archaeologists also use the terms *Shang* and *Zhou* to refer to time periods.

Legends and written records suggest that an even earlier dynasty, the Xia, existed in the Huang River valley sometime before ca. 1700 B.C. Therefore, another priority in research is identifying archaeological remains from the Xia Dynasty. Archaeologists have faced difficulties in this task, however, because no writing from the period has been found. Most archaeologists think that remains of what is called the Erlitou Culture in central and western Henan as well as southwestern Shanxi province, represent the Xia, judging from expected location, dating, and the degree of social complexity represented by the remains. However, there is great debate over which specific periods of Erlitou Culture remains belong to the Xia Dynasty.[3]

An important goal in archaeological research is to identify the sequence of cultures over time in each major area along the Huang River valley, especially to identify the sequence of cultures that led to the development of each early dynasty. Archaeologists identify different types, or *leixing*, of Longshan Culture in different areas, such as western Henan and eastern Shandong provinces, on the basis of variation in pottery styles and other factors. Archaeologists believe that remains from Longshan Period sites in western Henan and southern Shanxi provinces belong to one type of Longshan Culture and represent the predecessors of people who lived during the Xia Dynasty. Similarly, remains from northern Henan and southern Hebei provinces are ancestral to the Shang Dynasty.[4] Another important goal of research on the Longshan Period is to document the first appearance of bronze metallurgy, walled towns, and other key characteristics of early Chinese civilization.[5]

There are many debates about the Longshan Period. A central debate concerns the level of social complexity represented by the large, walled sites such as Wangchenggang in western Henan province. Some archaeologists believe that this site actually represents the earliest remains of the Xia Dynasty rather than a pre-state society.[6] Some researchers even argue that the Longshan Period as a whole represents the first development of states, urbanization, and civilization in China. It is likely that complex societies developed in a parallel fashion in more than one region of the Huang River valley, not just western Henan. Sites with surrounding walls, traces of metallurgy, and rich burials that appear to symbolize social stratification have been found from Shanxi province in the west to Shandong province in the east.[7] In addition, recent discoveries in other areas of China are forcing archaeologists to evaluate their views about where civilization first evolved. Archaeologists have discovered late prehistoric sites with remains indicating cultural complexity in other areas—most notably, the lower and middle Yangzi River valley (see Figure 18-2 on page 282). This area has large sites with surrounding earthen walls and extremely rich burials.[8] For example, burials from the Liangzhu Culture (ca. 3300–2200 B.C.) are known for their large quantities of elaborate jade objects.[9] These sites challenge the long established notion that the Huang River valley is the single center for the origins of Chinese civilization. Complex societies developed in more than one area, and probably several were contemporary with one another. One should consider that each area contributed to the development of Chinese civilization.[10]

Some current research in China is also devoted to determining the processes by which civilization evolved. Archaeologists in China, as in other countries, have investigated topics such as warfare, the rise of urbanization, and social stratification as indicated by burials.[11]

One of my goals has been to tell English-speaking archaeologists about the exciting research being done on the Longshan Period, because it is difficult for foreigners to get access to archaeological reports published in Chinese. I have also offered my own interpretations about the processes by which complex societies developed in China. Trained in North American anthropological archaeology, I have approached the development of civilization in China partially from a comparative perspective. I have sought to understand whether processes of change were similar to or different from those in other areas of the world where early complex societies emerged.

The concept of *chiefdom* is useful for describing general characteristics of Longshan sociopolitical organization.[12] The Longshan Period appears to have features similar to pre-state societies known as chiefdoms in other areas of the world.[13] These features include regional settlement hierarchies (interrelated groups of settlements with political centers that may have had important economic or religious functions, and smaller settlements such as villages), social stratification as indicated by differences in burials and houses, craft specialization (such as pottery vessels and jade items), and competition between elites to increase their political power. I have examined these features in an effort to examine how and why cultural change occurred during the Longshan Period.[14] Researchers have particularly remarked that the elaborate pottery vessels from the Longshan Period indicate the existence of craft specialization.[15] I have investigated the relationship between change in craft specialization and the development of complex societies.

CURRENT MODELS OF CRAFT SPECIALIZATION

Many archaeologists assume that the organization of labor to produce craft goods changes as social and political systems become more complex. For example, they expect change from part-time to full-time craft specialization as chiefdoms evolve into states.[16] Also, researchers expect that societies with social ranking such as chiefdoms would have two different kinds of craft goods, utilitarian and prestige goods. The former represent goods used on a daily basis and those that are accessible to all households. Prestige goods are those made from costly, rare, or difficult to obtain materials and often represent considerable labor input. Only households with sufficient resources would have the means to acquire these objects. To ensure a steady supply of these luxury goods, high status households might support the craftspeople who made them (providing materials, food, etc.).[17] Archaeologists call this kind of sponsored production "attached specialization." Elites could set up workshops for craftspeople in the vicinity of their residences in order to oversee production more effectively. In contrast, archaeologists call production of utilitarian items by specialists free of elite control "independent specialization."

There has been much debate about how craft specialization changes as complex societies develop. Were there more significant changes in attached specialization or in independent specialization? Some archaeologists argue that more changes occurred in attached specialization. As elites competed with others to increase their wealth and political power, they sought to acquire greater quantities and varieties of prestige goods. Thus, elites attempted to increase their control of production, distribution, and use of these goods. Other archaeologists argue that there were also important changes in independent specialization, such as making greater quantities of goods more efficiently and exchanging them over longer distances. These changes integrated communities over greater distances and were accompanied by greater occupational specialization in general.[18]

Archaeologists who work in different areas of the world have developed criteria to identify organization of pottery production at sites. Researchers use information on traditional pottery production obtained from ethnography, ethnohistory, and archaeology to describe the variation in organization of labor that could have existed in prehistory. Archaeologists have also collected their own information on traditional pottery production. These studies are called "ethnoarchaeological," because archaeologists study the material culture of contemporary peoples in order to improve methods for interpreting remains on ancient sites.[19]

Some archaeologists have described the different kinds of organization of labor to produce pottery as "modes of production." By this they mean models or descriptions of the organization of labor, including information about craftspeople and where they work.[20] Who were these craftspeople—what was their sex, age, and kin group? Did they work in their own houses or in workshops? What kinds of techniques did they use—hand building techniques, wheels, or molds? What was the division of labor to make vessels? Archaeologists have identified several modes of production, from simple to complex, and most of these involve specialization.

Two of these modes are useful as starting points for investigating the organization of labor to make pottery vessels during the Longshan Period. One is called "household industry" and refers to specialization on a relatively small scale. A few households in a village specialize in pottery production and exchange their vessels for goods from other households. "Individual workshop industry" may have existed during the Longshan Period, too. This term refers to specialized production in spaces exclusively for pottery and involves production of greater quantities of vessels as well as exchange of vessels over longer distances.[21]

In order to identify organization of ceramic production in prehistory, archaeologists have relied upon two criteria. One is the degree of standardization of vessels. For example, archaeologists expect pots in a system of individual workshop industry to exhibit a greater degree of standardization than those produced in a system of household industry. There should be a relatively small number of producers within a given area, and each one should strive to make vessels efficiently. Researchers assess degree of vessel standardization by measuring the major dimensions of pots, such as height and maximum diameter. It is also worthwhile to assess the variety of decorative techniques and the like used to make individual shapes of vessels.[22] The second kind of evidence archaeologists use to assess organization of pottery production is remains of production areas in sites. Some scholars believe that it should be possible to recognize individual workshop industry by the presence of a small quantity of structures exclusively devoted to pottery production. Similarly, more production areas in or near residences should indicate household industry.[23]

STUDYING POTTERY FROM THE LONGSHAN PERIOD

When I initially chose to work on craft specialization, I considered the materials realistically available for study in China and designed methods of data collection that involved examination of excavated vessels described in published reports. Pottery vessels constitute the most abundant category of remains from late Neolithic sites, and they are well described in archaeological reports. Also, I had good reason to expect that I would be allowed to examine many vessels in museum displays and in storage areas.

When I went to China to do my initial research, I planned to investigate the organization of pottery production during the Longshan Period by assessing degree of vessel standardization, varieties of vessels, and direct evidence for production at sites, such as tools and kilns. My first step was to choose sites with clear dating of periods and published reports with detailed descriptions of pottery. During my six-month stay in China in 1987, I learned about the Longshan Period from archaeologists at Beijing University and also visited several museums and archaeological research stations in Henan and Shandong provinces where vessels from my sites of interest were stored. I examined as many as possible from each site.

Sometimes finding and examining particular pottery collections was difficult. After a long, crowded train trip I might find that a particular town did not have the vessels in question after all. I learned to accept the fact that occasionally I would make a fool of myself as I became more acquainted with each area. One day my hosts thoughtfully took me to visit the location of an archaeological site. I stood in front of the stone marker to get a closer look at the Chinese characters, noticing that my hosts kept their distance. I soon realized that I was sinking up to my knees in a pile of compost, containing night soil, for the fields. My hosts kindly kept from laughing too hard as they led me to a local family's water pump to wash off.

Being able to see particular vessels mentioned in site reports helped me understand the kinds of information these reports provide. I examined primarily whole, reconstructed vessels from Longshan sites. In China, one of the main purposes of describing pottery vessels is for identifying different time periods and tracing the historical development of a culture. Archaeologists reconstruct as many vessels from sites as possible in order to obtain information for establishing a relative chronology based on morphological and stylistic features. Therefore, these kinds of data are emphasized in Neolithic site reports. Some of the information I needed for my study could only be obtained by my own observations. When my hosts gave me permission, I measured as many vessels of each different shape as possible to assess degree of standardization. I brought the necessary equipment with me. I also recorded diversity of shape classes and decorative techniques per period at these sites.

As is often the case, doing fieldwork causes one to learn unexpected things. I saw a greater variety of utilitarian and possible prestige vessels from Longshan sites than I had anticipated. For example, there were several kinds of thin-walled vessels in addition to the famous eggshell vessels. When I returned to North America to analyze my data, I realized that I should think in broader terms about the ways in which pottery production and use can change as change in sociopolitical organization occurs. Focusing exclusively on change in mode of production is too limiting. The development of complex societies can be accompanied by more than one kind of ceramic change, involving utilitarian or prestige vessels. Important changes in ceramics may not be accompanied by a change in organization of labor. For instance, new shapes of pottery vessels can emerge to accommodate new cooking techniques or new foods in the diet.[24]

I formulated a more comprehensive model outlining the kinds of ceramic changes that can occur in a context of increasing cultural complexity. The model allows for consideration of more than one kind of possible prestige vessel during the Longshan Period. I saw several varieties of labor intensive vessels (thin-walled, highly polished, elaborately shaped, and very large vessels) in Henan and Shandong provinces. Archaeological reports indicate that these vessels were made in other areas along the Huang River valley, too. The very large vessels were a complete surprise. I researched the use of large containers for feasting by elites in traditional societies (ethnographic and archaeological) as one means to display status. I also examined cross-cultural data on conspicuous consumption with containers. In addition, I looked at data on the use of bronze and pottery vessels by elites during the Shang Dynasty in China. Then I incorporated these uses of containers in my model, outlining different possible trajectories of ceramic change during the Longshan Period. Finally, I considered the processes that could result in similarities in labor intensive techniques in different areas, such as exchange of vessels between elites and emulation (deliberate copying of techniques used in neighboring regions).[25]

I concluded that attached specialists made labor intensive vessels for high status people in several areas throughout the Longshan Period. Some techniques, such as making thin-walled vessels, were probably copied in neighboring regions as elites sought to outdo others in displays of status. Although I do not have data on large quantities of labor intensive vessels, I do not think there is any evidence that these vessels became more standardized in shape or decoration over time. Thus, I do not see any evidence for a change in mode of production for prestige vessels, such as a change from household industry to individual workshop industry. I think that elites tried to make greater varieties of prestige vessels over time, but that this kind of change was not accompanied by a change in mode of production.

Most of the vessels that I was permitted to measure in China were probably utilitarian vessels, such as jars and small bowls. I do not see any evidence for increase over time in degree of dimensional standardization for these vessels, either. The limited data on decorative varieties per shape class do not indicate increasing standardization in production. I infer that there was no change in organization of production for utilitarian vessels either. Thus, contrary to expectations for areas in which complex societies developed, I do not see any evidence for change in organization of pottery production. Since there are many varieties of vessels on sites, and excavators have not discovered any large workshops for pottery production, I suggest that many communities during the Longshan Period had potters, and that household industry (independent specialization) characterized most areas rather than individual workshop industry. Prestige vessels probably were made under a system of small-scale attached specialization (household industry near elite residences). I conclude that, in China, significant change in the organization of pottery production did not occur until after states were well established.

My study was the first systematic investigation of specialization of pottery production during the Chinese Neolithic Period. My results should be regarded as hypotheses rather than firm conclusions, since the samples of vessels available for study were small. I hope to test these hypotheses in future work by obtaining a larger sample of vessels and by examining other kinds of evidence. More information on the contexts in which labor intensive vessels occur at sites must be obtained in order to strengthen the hypothesis that they were used by elites. In addition, more direct evidence for pottery production at sites is needed, such as tools, spatial areas for shaping pots, and kilns. Also, it is necessary to compare these kinds of remains at sites within a given settlement hierarchy. At least some large, walled sites should yield evidence for attached specialization of labor intensive vessels. Many smaller sites where ordinary people lived should yield evidence for small scale specialization of production of utilitarian vessels. Whether or not people agree with my conclusions, I hope that I demonstrated the value of using the approach that I did. I also concluded during the course of my study that I could more effectively assess organization of ceramic production in the future by collecting my own ethnoarchaeological data in China.

CERAMIC ETHNOARCHAEOLOGICAL RESEARCH

Archaeological studies have been hampered by the limited methods available for investigating the organization of ceramic production. More ethnoarchaeological studies are needed to test the validity of criteria such as degree of vessel standardization.[26] It is not clear, for example, what the difference in degree of standardization of vessels should be for household industry versus individual workshop industry. When I began to plan my own ethnoarchaeological study, I wondered if there were other material indicators of variation in organization of ceramic production that had not been considered by scholars. After much inquiry, I learned that there were several areas in China with potters using traditional techniques, especially in the western provinces. Traditional pottery production is declining at a rapid rate throughout the world as economic change occurs, and it is imperative not to lose this opportunity to conduct ethnoarchaeological studies.[27]

I worked to find areas in China where pottery is produced with traditional techniques and where vessels are used on a regular basis by local people. I also looked for areas with an organization of production equivalent to household industry, since this was likely an important kind of organization of labor during the Longshan Period. Of course, I also needed to find local researchers who would permit my study and were willing to assist me. I learned that many potters using traditional techniques are located in areas occupied by minority ethnic groups in western provinces. Chinese researchers have done important studies in some areas for over thirty years, but their main goal has been to document the history of a particular technological tradition, rather than organization of production.[28]

In 1992, I had the opportunity to conduct a pilot study in two very different areas—Xinjiang province in northwest China and Guizhou province in the southwest (see Figure 18-2 on page 282). The purpose was to visit a number of communities where pottery production takes place, to begin to collect data, and to determine which communities were more feasible for an in-depth project.

Xinjiang is an arid province with mountains and deserts interspersed with small farming villages. Uighur (Uygur) potters, Muslims who speak a Turkic language, make large water jars and flower pots by using earthen molds. There are several large dome-shaped mounds of packed earth in the courtyards of potting families. Potters spread clay on top of these molds to form the two halves of each vessel. In Guizhou province, potters from the Buyi ethnic group as well as Han (the majority ethnic group in China) potters live in small villages surrounded by terraced rice fields and lush, green mountains. They make a variety of vessels, such as large storage jars and the small containers used to serve popular condiments of hot chili peppers that are eaten with every meal. (I was gradually able to increase my intake!) Potters in Guizhou use kick (fast) wheels of wood or dried clay to make the majority of vessels and, in some communities, wooden hand wheels to make small bowls.

In each area, the majority of potters are male, but they rely on the help of family members in more than one step of production. Thus, I think it is appropriate to describe this kind of system as family specialization. It is not surprising to find potters in these provinces also using some techniques that were developed after the late Neolithic Period, such as adding glaze to vessels. Pottery production has been an important activity in China since the Neolithic Period, and it would be difficult to find a community using purely Neolithic techniques. I do not claim that these communities directly represent pottery production as it was during the Longshan Period, but it is likely that they do represent a partially analogous situation.

I decided to continue my research in Guizhou province because there are more potting communities in which a greater variety of vessels are made. Also, the people speak Mandarin Chinese, the language I had been studying (although the dialect is very different from that of other areas such as Beijing). In Xinjiang I could not talk with potters directly, since I had not studied Uygur. I relied on the assistance of a skilled interpreter who translated from Uygur to Chinese, and vice versa. Another important factor in my decision was that potters in Guizhou use the fast wheel to make most vessels, a major technique used during the Longshan Period. I continued my study in Guizhou during the summers of 1993 and 1994, comparing specialization of pottery production in two different communities. The village I studied in 1994 is "closed" to foreigners, but thanks to the local Public Security Bureau I obtained permission to work there. I am now in the process of completing my analyses. At this point I can outline the methods I used during those three years as well as my preliminary results.[29]

One of my goals was to interview potters to learn details about the organization of labor in production. I tried to take into account recent criticisms about archaeological studies of organization of production, particularly the need for scholars to investigate organization of production more thoroughly. Archaeologists must investigate variation in factors such as intensity or time spent in production, output, and scale.[30] For example, the term *household industry* could include much variation along these lines. I asked potters questions about the time they spend in production (versus other activities such as farming), the varieties and quantities of pots they make, and distribution areas for their vessels.

I found that there is much more variation in organization of production among these family specialists than I expected. Some potters could be called "part-time" specialists because they are also farmers, while others are "full-time" producers. However, these terms are not very meaningful because there is considerable variation within each category of producers with respect to time spent making pottery vessels throughout the year, and the kinds of vessels made. Two factors that affect time spent in production are the availability of family members to help and the weather. (The drier seasons, summer and fall, are the most suitable.)

I studied vessels and workshops to see if any of this variation in organization of production would be recognizable from remains left in archaeological deposits. I noted varieties of vessels made by each potter and measured a large quantity of vessels to assess the degree of vessel standardization. I observed potters making vessels and the specific methods they used to standardize their products. Also, I measured and described the spatial areas where each step of the production process took place, including preparing clay, shaping, decorating, and firing.

One of my preliminary conclusions is that both part-time and full-time potters make highly standardized pots. It would not be possible to distinguish the difference in intensity or time spent in production by differences in degree of vessel standardization. Potters achieve remarkable standardization in shape by using their hands and simple bamboo tools. Potters have the incentive to make standardized vessels because consumers prefer to buy vessels of this kind.[31] People told me they judge a potter's skill at the village street markets on the basis of his ability to make vessels that look similar in size.

I have also concluded that archaeologists can learn a great deal about variation in organization of pottery production if they can identify locations in sites where different steps in production took place.[32] Unfortunately, archaeologists often face difficulties in doing this because tools made of perishable materials are not preserved. I suggest that characteristics of work spaces can help reveal information, such as the intensity or time a potter spends in production. In Guizhou, there is much variation in the spatial areas potters use in each step of the production process: preparing clay, shaping, decorating, drying vessels, and firing. A potter may use one or more whole rooms of a house, partial rooms, or a separate structure—a workshop. Potters who spend the most time in making vessels often choose to use relatively large workshops suitable for most steps in production.

It was a tremendous experience to observe pottery production, distribution, and use firsthand. I am extremely grateful to the local workers who provided so much assistance in studying these communities. I am also indebted to the patience and kindness of the potters and their families. I soon realized that ethnoarchaeologists have to accept the fact that local people, understandably, find our activities bizarre. Imagine if a person from another country came to your town for the summer and engaged in activities such as measuring containers in your kitchen. However, I do know that my interest and respect for the tremendous skills of the potters was appreciated. I hope that my report can help document a vibrant way of life in these villages.

Conclusions

The goal of my research on the Longshan Period of the Huang River valley has been to explain how specialization of pottery production changes in relation to the development of social complexity. This chapter illustrates the process I have gone through in conducting my research to date: learning about the kinds of research being done by archaeologists in China on the Longshan Period, considering theoretical arguments for change in craft specialization as complex societies develop, studying vessels from Longshan sites in China, evaluating the results of my research, and conducting an ethnoarchaeological study in order to evaluate methods for investigating specialization of ceramic production.

My concluding hypotheses about change in specialization of pottery production in a context of increasing cultural complexity should be tested at other late Neolithic sites in China. My limited data do not indicate that there was a change in organization of labor to make pottery vessels during the Longshan Period. There is no evidence for increasing standardization of utilitarian or prestige vessels, contrary to expectations of archaeologists working in other areas. However, I suspect that elites in many regions sponsored production of a variety of labor intensive vessels for use in displays of status. More studies of change in pottery production and use should be undertaken in different regions of the Huang River valley as well as other areas, such as the Yangzi River valley, where complex societies developed. The unit of analysis should be individual settlement hierarchies, so that information on the kinds of vessels elites and other people used can be compared. It is likely that labor intensive vessels such as the eggshell-thin cups were made at centers of settlement under a system of attached specialization. Most communities, however, probably had independent specialists making many kinds of vessels for daily use. More direct evidence for pottery production at sites is needed. Change in the production and use of different kinds of pottery vessels during the Longshan Period must be studied in conjunction with change in other components of culture as more data become available. For example, did increasing warfare or the development of bronze metallurgy cause change in pottery production and use? Did increasing political centralization have an impact on the production of prestige vessels, but not utilitarian vessels?

On the basis of my ethnoarchaeological research in Guizhou province, I think that variation in organization of ceramic production within individual communities would have been common during the late prehistoric period. It is likely that there was variation in the time potters spent in production as well as the scale of production within a region, depending on the particular kinds of pottery vessels involved. Family specialization, an enduring organization of ceramic production in more than one region of China, is useful as a plausible general model for organization of labor during the Longshan Period, for the production of both utilitarian and prestige vessels—while recognizing that there may be variation in factors such as intensity or scale of production. Finally, my on-going statistical analyses of vessels from Guizhou suggest that difference in degree of vessel standardization may not always be a reliable indicator of differences in organization of ceramic production. One must consider factors such as consumer demand for standardization of particular kinds of vessels. I suggest that during the Longshan Period there was more incentive on the part of potters to standardize utilitarian vessels than prestige vessels, since efficiency in production was a major concern. However, identifying variation in spatial areas used in different steps of production may help archaeologists more profitably examine variation in organization of labor and, ultimately, help them investigate change in specialization of pottery production in relation to the development of complex societies.

NOTES

1. I am grateful for the financial support from the Social Sciences and Humanities Research Council of Canada for my research in China on Longshan pottery vessels in 1987. My pilot project on ceramic ethnoarchaeology in Xinjiang and Guizhou provinces during 1992 was supported by the Committee on Scholarly Communication with China (Archaeology Subcommittee). My ceramic ethnoarchaeological project in Guizhou during 1993 and 1994 was funded by the National Science Foundation, Division of International Programs, Program for Research at Foreign Centers of Excellence, Grant No. INT-9303334. I also thank the Wenner-Gren Foundation for Anthropological Research for a supplemental research grant for my ethnoarchaeological research in 1993. Finally, I thank Erika Evasdottir of Harvard University for preparing Figure 18-2.
2. John Olsen, "The Practice of Archaeology in China Today," *Antiquity* 61 (1987): 282–290; Lothar von Faulkenhausen, "On the Historiographical Orientation of Chinese Archaeology," *Antiquity* 67 (1993): 839–849.
3. K. C. Chang, "Sandai Archaeology and the Formation of States in Ancient China," in David Keightley, ed., *Origins of Chinese Civilization* (Berkeley: University of California, 1983), pp. 495–521; K. C. Chang, *The Archaeology of Ancient China*, 4th ed. (Cambridge: Harvard University, 1986).
4. Richard Pearson and Anne Underhill, "The Chinese Neolithic: Recent Trends in Research," *American Anthropologist* 89, no. 4 (1987): 807–822.
5. Anne P. Underhill, "Variation in Settlements during the Longshan Period of Northern China," *Asian Perspectives* 33, no. 2 (1994): 197–228.
6. Henan Province Cultural Research Institute and The Archaeology Department, Museum of Chinese History, *Dengfeng Wangchenggang Yu Yangcheng [The Wangchenggang Site at Dengfeng and the Site of Yangcheng]* (Beijing: Cultural Relics).
7. Underhill, "Variation in Settlements"; Anne P. Underhill, "Craft Production and Social Evolution during the Longshan Period of Northern China," in Bernard Wailes, ed., *Craft Specialization and Social Evolution: In Memory of V. Gordon Childe* (Philadelphia: University of Pennsylvania, 1996).
8. Underhill, "Variation in Settlements."

9. Sun Zhixin, "The Liangzhu Culture: Its Discovery and Its Jades," *Early China* 18 (1993): 1–40.

10. Yan Wenming, "Zhongguo Shiqian Wenhua de Tongyixing Yu Duoyangxing [Unity and Diversity in Chinese Neolithic Culture]," *Wenwu* 3 (1987): 38–50.

11. Yan Wenming, "Jiangou de Tougai Bei he Botoupi Fengsu [Skull Cap Cups from Jiangou and the Custom of Scalping]," *Kaogu Yu Wenwu* 2 (1982): 38–41; Cao Guiling, "Huaiyang Pingliangtai Yizhi Shehui Xingzhi Tanxi [An Analysis of the Nature of Society at the Pingliangtai Site at Huaiyang]," *Zhongyuan Wenwu* 2 (1990): 89–92; He Zhangfeng, "Youguan Wo Guo Zaoqi Chengshi Tansuo Zhong De Jige Wenti [A Few Issues Concerning the Investigation of Early Cities in Our Country]," *Kaogu Yu Wenwu* 4 (1989): 91–96; Richard Pearson, "Chinese Neolithic Burial Patterns: Problems of Method and Interpretation," *Early China* 13 (1988): 1–45.

12. Underhill, "Variation in Settlements"; Anne P. Underhill, "Regional Growth of Cultural Complexity during the Longshan Period of Northern China," in C. Melvin Aikens and Song Nai Rhee, eds., *Pacific Northeast Asia in Prehistory: Hunter-Fisher-Gatherers, Farmers, and Socio-Political Elites* (Pullman: Washington State University, 1992), pp. 173–178.

13. Timothy Earle, ed., *Chiefdoms: Power, Economy, and Ideology* (New York: Cambridge University, 1991).

14. Underhill, "Variation in Settlements"; Underhill, "Craft Production and Social Evolution"; Anne P. Underhill, "Pottery Production in Chiefdoms: the Longshan Period in Northern China," *World Archaeology* 23, no. 1 (1991): 12–27; Anne P. Underhill, "Changing Patterns of Pottery Production during the Longshan Period of Northern China, ca. 2500–2000 B.C." (Ph.D. diss., University of British Columbia, 1990); Anne P. Underhill, "Warfare during the Neolithic Period: A Review of the Evidence," in Diana Tkaczuk and Brian Vivian, eds., *Cultures in Conflict: Current Archaeological Perspectives* (Calgary: University of Alberta, 1989), pp. 229–237.

15. Song Zhaolin, Li Jiafang, Du Yaoxi, *Zhongguo Yuanshi Shihui Shi [A History of Chinese Primitive Society]* (Beijing: Cultural Relics, 1983); David Keightley, "Archaeology and Mentality: The Making of China," *Representations* 18 (1987): 91–128.

16. Kent Flannery, "The Cultural Evolution of Civilizations," *Annual Review of Ecology and Systematics* 3 (1972): 399–426.

17. Peter Peregrine, "Some Political Aspects of Craft Specialization," *World Archaeology* 23, no. 1: 1–11.

18. Elizabeth Brumfiel and Timothy Earle, "Specialization, Exchange, and Complex Societies: An Introduction," in Elizabeth Brumfiel and Timothy Earle, eds., *Specialization, Exchange, and Complex Societies* (New York: Cambridge University), pp. 1–9; Prudence Rice, *Pottery Analysis: A Sourcebook* (Chicago: University of Chicago, 1987); Prudence Rice, "Evolution of Specialized Pottery Production: A Trial Model," *Current Anthropology* 22, no. 3 (1981): 219–240.

19. Rice, *Pottery Analysis*; Dean Arnold, *Ceramic Theory and Cultural Process* (New York: Cambridge University, 1985); William Longacre, ed., *Ceramic Ethnoarchaeology* (Tucson: University of Arizona, 1991); Philip Arnold, *Domestic Ceramic Production and Spatial Organization* (New York: Cambridge University, 1991).

20. Rice, *Pottery Analysis*, pp. 170, 182–191.

21. Ibid; Underhill, "Variation in Settlements"; Flannery, "The Cultural Evolution of Civilizations"; Underhill, "Pottery Production in Chiefdoms."

22. Rice, *Pottery Analysis.*
23. Ibid.
24. Prudence Rice, "Change and Conservatism in Pottery-Producing Systems," in S. E. van der Leeuw and A. C. Pritchard, eds., *The Many Dimensions of Pottery: Ceramics in Archaeology and Anthropology* (Amsterdam: Institute for Pre- and Proto-History, University of Amsterdam, 1984).
25. Underhill, "Changing Patterns of Pottery Production"; Underhill, "Craft Production and Social Evolution"; Underhill, "Regional Growth of Cultural Complexity"; Underhill, "Pottery Production in Chiefdoms"; Anne P. Underhill, *Craft Specialization and the Development of Complex Societies in China: A Study of Pottery Production and Use during the Longshan Period.* (Book manuscript in preparation.)
26. Rice, *Pottery Analysis.*
27. William Longacre, "Ceramic Ethnoarchaeology: An Introduction," in William Longacre, ed., *Ceramic Ethnoarchaeology* (Tucson: University of Arizona, 1991), pp. 1–10.
28. Li Yangsong, "Cong Wazu Zhitao Tantao Gudai Taoqi Zhizuoshangde Jige Wenti [Some Problems of Ancient Pottery Making as Seen from an Inquiry of Pottery Manufacture among the Wa Nationality]," *Kaogu* 5 (1959): 220–254.
29. Anne P. Underhill, "Ceramic Ethnoarchaeology in China: A Pilot Project on Variation in Organization of Production," in Charles Kolb and Philip Arnold, ed., *Ceramic Ecology: Material Culture Past and Present* (Madison, WI: Prehistory Press, in press); Anne P. Underhill, "Ceramic Ethnoarchaeology in China: Implications for Investigating Craft Specialization in Prehistory," paper presented at symposium Ceramic Ecology 1994: Current Research on Ceramics, American Anthropological Association Meeting, Atlanta, GA, November 30–December 4, 1994; Anne P. Underhill, "Ceramic Ethnoarchaeology in China: Evaluation of Archaeological Criteria for Identifying Variation in Specialization of Ceramic Production." (Manuscript in preparation.)
30. Cathy Costin, "Craft Specialization: Issues in Defining, Documenting, and Explaining the Organization of Production," in Michael Schiffer, ed., *Advances in Archaeological Method and Theory*, vol. 3 (New York: Academic, 1980), pp. 1–56.
31. See Dean Arnold and A. Nieves, "Factors Affecting Ceramic Standardization," in George Bey and Christopher Pool, eds., *Ceramic Production and Distribution* (Boulder: Westview, 1992).
32. See P. Arnold, *Domestic Ceramic Production.*

SUGGESTED READINGS

Barnes, Gina. *China, Korea, and Japan: The Rise of Civilization in East Asia.* New York: Thames and Hudson, 1993. An introduction to the prehistoric and early historic periods of East Asia.

Chang, K. C. *The Archaeology of Ancient China*, 4th ed. Cambridge: Harvard University, 1986. The most complete account of archaeology in China available in English.

Murowchick, Robert, ed. *Cradles of Civilization. China.* Norman: University of Oklahoma Press, 1994. A well illustrated volume with a collection of essays on the Neolithic and historic periods of China.

Rice, Prudence. *Pottery Analysis. A Sourcebook.* Chicago: University of Chicago Press, 1987. An excellent reference book for pottery analysis in archaeology.

Underhill, Anne P. "A Guide to Understanding Ceramic Change." In Erica Weeder, ed. *The Rise of a Great Tradition: Japanese Archaeological Ceramics from the Jomon through the Heian Periods (10,500 B.C.–A.D. 1185).* New York: Agency for Cultural Affairs, Government of Japan, and the Japan Society, 1990, pp. 10–14. Explains how archaeologists study change over time in ceramics and the social significance of this change.

READING THE LAND:
THE ARCHAEOLOGY
OF SETTLEMENT AND LAND USE

CAROLE L. CRUMLEY

Where are you from? This familiar question opens conversation with strangers the world over. The answer is full of information: Preferences, attitudes, abilities, politics, and social standing are only some of the things one can learn from a simple question about origins.

In the four million years since ancestors of our species found food, water, and shelter in subtropical Africa, genus *Homo* has made more and more of the planet home. The places people make their homes vary greatly: Our ancestors found shelter in caves and overhangs, or made shelters with brush, or hides and mammoth tusks, heaped-up earth, adobe, or sun-dried brick. Contemporary shelters—a steel-and-glass skyscraper, an isolated cabin, or a tiny room overlooking a narrow street—all look just fine to the tired returning traveller, as long as they are "home," a place that is familiar and, relatively speaking, predictable and safe.

Home is bigger than the physical space in which we eat, sleep, and relax. Our surroundings—full of landmarks, familiar sounds and smells, and memories of people and events—are extensions of the structures we occupy. We have hometowns and home states or provinces, and even inveterate world travelers generally have what they consider a home country, although it may not be the same as the country on the passport. And, of course, we all share a home planet, the third from the star we call Sun.

There were not always so many human beings on the planet and, as a species, we have not always lived as close as we do today to people we don't know. Millions of people live in the largest cities, with densities of thousands per square mile. Extreme environments such as polar or desert regions attract fewer residents than our species' home tropics or the temperate latitudes, although contemporary desert cities such as Cairo and

Phoenix call even such general statements into question. In short, human beings, thanks to broad adaptive abilities, can and do live in every conceivable environment.

The physical limitations on where people can live are, however, the same as they have always been: We must be supplied with food and water, and we have to be sheltered from the extremes of weather.

HOME IS WHERE THE RESOURCES ARE

Although miles of water pipelines and several means of long-distance transport now allow people to live very far from sources of water, food, and fuel, this is a very recent development. For most of human history, the work of finding (or tending) and preparing food for the group of people to which one belonged took up most of the working day.

Today supermarkets offer a wide variety of prepared foods, and most of their cost is payment for the work of production, preparation, and transport to the store from wherever the food was grown or raised. Most of us live far from the Kansas or Argentine feedlots where the beef cattle were raised for our hamburgers and the Idaho fields where potatoes were harvested for our french fries. We can get vegetables and fruit year-round from Florida, California, the Caribbean, and South America.

The desire to prepare and eat food in safe and social circumstances is still a hallmark of our species, but now a far greater percentage of the population is free to pursue activities unrelated to food production. While a few people were always excused from daily food-getting tasks (specialists in religion or certain crafts, the very young or old), now only a few, relatively speaking, produce food for all the rest of us.

GLOBAL HOUSEKEEPING

All this has had a profound and not unproblematic effect on where we live. As the human niche (that is, the kinds of environment humans could call home) expanded with new solutions to resource problems, the very success of the species has caused increased human impacts on fragile landscapes. Today, with the combined effects of greater numbers, long-distance transport, and gigantic land-modification machinery, the human mark on our home planet can be seen easily from space. What the satellites show us are polluted oceans and lakes, eroded croplands, sediment-choked rivers, and, in the ozone layer that protects us from deadly ultraviolet rays, a growing hole.

Issues of population control aside, there remains the fact that humans are disproportionately distributed upon the planet in a pattern characterized by huge urban areas and sparsely populated rural areas. Because they are so far from the sources of supply, this pattern puts urban populations at risk. As recently as the beginning of the twentieth century, 99.9 percent of the world's population lived close enough to food and water to obtain it themselves. Today many urban residents would have no idea where to get water if taps were dry, or food if the store shelves were bare.

How did this new landscape develop? How old are cities? What is the history of pollution? Could knowledge of past land use and the distribution of settlements give us ideas about how to solve contemporary social and environmental problems?

OBSERVING THE LANDSCAPE

When my family took trips, my job was always to navigate. My dad showed me how to use maps, read signs, find north, and keep my eyes open for landmarks. Soon (if I was confident of our route) I was looking at other things, too: buildings, fields, and other evidence of human activity. The abandoned farmhouse and its tumbledown outbuildings and fences right next to the diner where we stopped for lunch told me that the road hadn't always been a busy highway. Bricked-up doors and windows in a city warehouse and a barely-readable sign told me the structure had once been a grain mill serving an agricultural countryside. These were clues to a vanished landscape, in which the land was put to different uses.

We often travelled between the black earth and ancient lakebeds of southeastern Michigan and the rolling, red clay hills of northeast Tennessee. I loved the game of waking from a nap and trying to guess where we were from analyzing the landscape: the architecture and materials of buildings, the topography, the vegetation, the *feel* of the place.

Soon enough, I discovered that archaeology allowed me views into the landscapes of distant times and places, even when all above-ground clues had been swept away. One sunny afternoon in third grade, my teacher asked me to read from our social science book. The subject was ancient Egyptian burial customs, and the text explained that much of what was known about Egyptian life had come from the tombs of the dead, the very existence of which had been forgotten for thousands of years.

This evidence was even more challenging than "seeing" old landscapes still above ground. In places where peoples of the past had discarded smashed pottery, broken and used-up tools, or other household garbage, there were landmarks from the past. I realized that by studying how and where people used the land and made their homes, one could imagine the sights, sounds, and smells of the past and understand changes that distinguished them from those of the present.

CHRONICLES OF VANISHED LANDSCAPES

Modern archaeologists are not the first to notice landmarks of the past. The most easily recognized, and therefore the earliest recorded evidence of past human activity, were the big building projects. The great monuments of the old world (that is, the eastern hemisphere), such as the Egyptian pyramids, were already thousands of years old when Greek traveler-scholars wrote of them in the centuries just before the birth of Christ. Even the sites of big disasters, like the Italian towns of Pompeii and Herculaneum that were buried by the eruption of the volcano Vesuvius in A.D. 79, were known in the Middle Ages.

Renaissance (ca. A.D. 1350–1650) naturalists and antiquarians made painstaking records of monuments, such as Stonehenge and Avebury in England and Carnac in France, on their home soil. Their colonial counterparts, when the duties of conquest allowed, recorded the sites and monuments that figured in more distant landscapes.

Most easily recognized were burial monuments (mounds, pyramids) and large religious or domestic structures (temples, palaces). Built to impress, they continued to do so as elements of much later landscapes. Considered romantic and mysterious, ruined structures appeared as elements of an idealized landscape in Renaissance paintings.[1] Also easy to spot were the extensive heaps of debris: the great ruined cities of the past such as Assur (near modern Baghdad), Teotihuacan (near modern Mexico City), and Great Zimbabwe (near Mas Vingo [colonial Fort Victoria], Zimbabwe).

While some naturalists and antiquarians concentrated on sites that were still a visible element in the contemporary landscape, others searched for much less visible dwellings, tools, and other debris left by peoples of more modest means. By the end of the eighteenth century, empirical methods of study had become standard in the physical and natural sciences (geology, botany, anatomy); these methods were applied to bones and stone tools found at considerable depth in caves and quarries and in the company of extinct plants and animals. In particular, advances in geology permitted sites to be placed in the context of their surrounding strata and dated to thousands of years earlier than the events in the Bible.

These sites, mostly invisible on the surface of the ground, were the homes, game butchering spots, and workshops of humans who lived thousands of years before the Pharaohs built the pyramids; considerably greater effort was required to imagine them or their surroundings. The clergy was especially disinclined to recognize a human antiquity that predated biblical events, and new theories of technological and biological evolution differed dramatically from the catastrophic version of human history found in the Bible. Religious authorities found themselves in heated defense of an interpretation of the Bible that placed the world's creation only six thousand years ago; according to Bishop Ussher of Armagh (in Northern Ireland), who had added up all the generations in Genesis and calculated backward, the world began in exactly 4004 B.C.

By the mid-nineteenth century, the ecclesiastical crisis had been resolved in favor of a less literal interpretation, in part through the offices of scientists who were also religious. Thus unpretentious sites, yielding evidence of everyday human activity, were instrumental in revising our understanding of all human history; the geological, biological, and archaeological data they contained gave Charles Darwin and others solid historical evidence for anatomical change and species extinction.

Thus, two "strands" of archaeology came into being. One studied humanity's great works, the other pieced together the lives and surroundings of ordinary people. The findings of both were sometimes commandeered in support of ethnic, nationalist, and colonial causes.[2] These two traditions began the history of the discipline and shaped subsequent study of human settlement and land use. Today, a fresh perspective on the ways settlement and land use can be studied suggests some provocative questions for the future.

SYSTEMATIC STUDIES OF SETTLEMENT AND LAND USE

Airborne, one becomes quickly enamored with landscapes and their various elements. After the Wright brothers and others succeeded in making the long-held human dream of flight come true, the First World War made flight routine and gave many British and American archaeologists a new perspective. They saw the larger setting of the burial mounds at Cranbourne Chase, the limits of ancient fields, and other features of prehistoric and historic Britain; they spotted roads, overgrown with vegetation, which connected Maya centers in Yucatan.[3]

Archaeologists began to place sites in the larger spatial context of society, exploring in turn the diverse elements that comprised vanished landscapes. In Egypt, they searched for the quarries where stone for the pyramids was procured; realizing the mechanical and human effort that went into pyramid construction, they looked for access roads, workshops, workers' towns and cemeteries. In Chaco Canyon (NW New Mexico), they spotted ancient paths that connect abandoned pueblos.

Searching the land for archaeological sites, called surveying in North America and fieldwalking in the British Isles, joined excavation as standard practice. One of the first systematic regional surveys by American archaeologists was conducted as part of a large project designed to understand the origins of complex society in the Viru Valley, Peru.[4] The analysis of *settlement patterns*, the study of all simultaneously occupied sites, enabled the first visualizations of those ancient landscapes.

In the 1950s both British and American archaeologists began to reconstruct vanished environments to better understand past economies. They reasoned that the systematic collection of economic data (in the form of evidence for domestic and trading activity) was predicated upon the reconstruction of the physical environment (climate, plant and animal life, and other natural resources), which then permitted the interpretation of daily and seasonal activities, the division of labor, and patterns of trade. J. G. D. Clark's study of the prehistoric environment surrounding the British Mesolithic site of Starr Carr was influential on both sides of the Atlantic.[5] In the Americas, Richard MacNeish assembled an impressive multi-disciplinary team including botanists, geologists, and other environmental experts in the Tehuacan Valley of Mexico.[6] By the end of the 1960s, environmental studies were an indispensable element in every archaeological report.[7]

ARCHAEOLOGY AND THE INFORMATION AGE

Although settlement pattern studies had been a part of archaeology for over a decade, the expanded potential for the study of trade, politics, and social organization caught the imagination of a new generation of computer literate and statistically oriented archaeologists.[8] The respected quantitative archaeologist Albert C. Spaulding set the new agenda when he argued that the three dimensions of archaeology were space, time, and form, and that the spatial dimension could use a lot more attention.[9]

This reorientation changed the scale and focus of archaeological investigations. Chronological and typological studies did not disappear—they remained necessary but were not sufficient in the study of past human settlement. The patterning of artifacts within a site (as well as between sites) was analyzed to detect variation among individuals and groups. The various activity areas (for example, where food was prepared or a tool was made) were then related to social distinctions among inhabitants of the site (e.g., kinship status, occupation, gender).[10] Long-distance trade was reconstructed by finding the sources of excavated materials (e.g., obsidian, galena).[11]

Greater interest in individual behavior and in social relations moved Euro-American archaeology away from technological and typological studies to sociopolitical analysis. While settlement pattern archaeology had primarily charted the relation among dwellings and other buildings as they pertained to community life, now the term *settlement system* began to be used.[12] It emphasized regional connections among settlements and reflected the impact of systems theory on archaeology. For example, mining of a resource like gold or tin might take place in the mountains, but the material might only be made into ingots at the extraction site; from there it would be transported by caravan to an urban workshop, where expert metalsmiths would fashion exquisite jewelry from the gold and mix the tin with copper from elsewhere to make bronze. On the return trip, the caravans would be laden with the artifacts of city life, destined for the elites who controlled the mines: spices from distant lands, wine, pottery, and other artisan-made goods. Thus did archaeologists turn to the study of reciprocal economic, social, and political relations among contemporaneous sites.

Taking their cue from geographers (many of whom had served as map-makers and meteorologists and in other technical capacities during World War II), archaeologists enthusiastically embraced computer-based statistical and spatial modeling to predict where sites of varying function would be located. Sampling problems—both statistical and in archaeological surveys—began to dominate discussions of method. While the use of computers vastly increased the speed and even the very possibility of some calculations, computer modeling measured the always-flawed sampling universe of known archaeological sites against an ideal landscape in which all actors acted "rationally," that is, to maximize efficiency in resource procurement. These and other optimizing assumptions underlay what was to be known as the *new archaeology*. The problem is, of course, that people act in ways that are not always economically optimal. Kinship and political obligations between and within societies, trade routes rendered inhospitable by pirates or terrain, and many other reasons keep people from choosing the most economically sensible site for their homes and other activities.

THE NEW ARCHAEOLOGY AND SPATIAL MODELING

By the late 1960s, general availability of computers allowed large amounts of environmental and archaeological data to be statistically combined, offering a new approach to the study of settlement and land use. Researchers designed computer models of settlement systems based on hypotheses (for example, if agricultural yield diminishes, there is more warfare). Collectively termed locational analysis, these approaches to settlement concentrated on habitation sites and their relationship to one another and to economic resources.

Many archaeologists hoped that these methods offered the possibility of predicting the location of sites; however, they had been designed for rather different purposes than finding archaeological sites. For example, central place models were employed in the analysis of mercantile activities such as the siting of fast-food restaurants or the deployment of trucks carrying bananas. These activities had characteristics archaeological sites would never have: The data were complete (one knew how many patrons, trucks, or bananas were required for the system to work properly), those elements' simultaneous existence in the world (contemporaneity) was assured, and the model dealt with only retail distribution, which more often than not obeyed certain rules of cost/benefit analysis. On the other hand, one could never be sure that all the archaeological sites of a period had been found, or that it could be said with certainty that the ones found had all been in existence at the same time.

Finally, and most problematically, past human behavior (except in narrowly defined circumstances) did not follow twentieth century Western economic principles.[13] Even in the contemporary data the geographers collected, people still had preferences and personal and social histories that took them out to dinner or shopping in another part of town or even to another city. The consumption of fast food and bananas varied from one neighborhood to another. By the late 1960s geographers had abandoned central place models except in specialized circumstances that combined the economic data with reliable social indicators.

Some locational techniques have had greater longevity. Gravity models (sometimes called distance-decay) predict that progressively less of a resource (for example, good clay for making pottery) will be found the further away one is from its origin. Theissen polygons (created by drawing a straight lines between sites in a region and bifurcating them at their midpoints) approximate the area of influence around a particular site in relation to the position of its neighbors.

These and other geometric techniques, while of use to archaeologists in posing research questions, still failed to account for the more interesting social, political, and historical reasons people do not make unanimous choices about anything. These very issues, dear to the heart of anthropologists, were termed "noise" by modelers who employed the assumptions of rationalist economic theory. Yet even sociocultural anthropologists constructed "ideal types" to aid their analysis of cultures; the urge to contrast real and ideal human behavior seemed irresistible for a time throughout the social sciences.

THEORETICAL QUANDARIES AND SOME SOLUTIONS

This was the situation when I began a career in anthropology and archaeology. With undergraduate and graduate training in both the humanities (classics) and in the social and natural sciences (anthropology, geology), I felt theoretically homeless. I was intrigued by the idea that ancient texts could illuminate individual lives (although usually those of elites) and great historical movements, but, to my sorrow, classical archaeology seemed more an adjunct to art history than a window to life in the past. The new archaeology treated the lives of everyday people, but seemed too mechanistic in its search for laws governing human behavior. I began my own search for the work of archaeologists and others who offered a critique of the status quo, and for an alternative.

The first work I found was *A Study in Archaeology*, the dissertation of Walter W. Taylor.[14] Critical of the overly scientific approach to the interpretation of archaeological evidence, he advocated a contextual approach, by which he meant not just the physical environment but social and historical circumstances as well. Unfortunately, the work was admired and taught more for its spirited criticism of prominent archaeologists than for its persuasive argument for the integration of history and the humanities into archaeological interpretation.

Taylor, an American prisoner of war in Europe during WWII, may have been influenced by an important historical tradition in France, referred to as the *Annales* school. Shortly after finding Taylor's book, I discovered the Annales historian Marc Bloch, who was a member of the French Resistance and, unlike Taylor, did not survive the war.[15] In the 1920s the Annales founder, Lucien Febvre, had launched an unrelenting attack on the "old school" of history, in which narrow particularism and mind-numbing chronology held sway and the context of events was left unexamined.[16] Instead, Febvre and his colleagues proposed an interdisciplinary history distinguished by its emphasis on pattern recognition at three temporal scales: the event, groups of conditions and events (*conjoncture*), and long-term (*longue durée*) history. By the 1940s, when Taylor was imprisoned, the Annales was the reigning paradigm in France.

It seemed to me that archaeology could use similar housecleaning. Enter Lewis Binford, whom many would credit with starting the revolution against the old "chronologies and typologies" school of American archaeology; this "new broom" would come to be known as the "new archaeology." Binford has always argued that "archaeology is anthropology or it is nothing."[17] Since the 1960s, he has exhorted American archaeologists to look for patterns of individual and collective behavior in the analysis of artifacts and the patterning of debris within sites. He employs ethnographic research to better understand the formation of the archaeological record, a tactic termed *ethnoarchaeology*.

My search led me next to the work of David Clarke, who had begun to refine and broaden locational analysis in Britain. He defined *spatial archaeology* as "the study of the flow and integration of activities within and between structures, sites, and resource spaces." Spatial archaeology "deals with human activities at every scale, the traces and artifacts left by them, the physical infrastructure that accommodated them, the environments that they impinged upon, and the interaction between all these aspects. Spatial archaeology deals with a set of elements and relationships."[18] Archaeologists on both sides of the Atlantic realized that by examining patterns of archaeological remains at different spatial scales (e.g., deriving regional economic and social conditions by studying gravestone art), long-term change could be more readily inferred than by examining archaeological patterns at a single (usually site-specific) scale.[19]

During the past two decades, I have drawn on Taylor, Bloch, Binford, Clarke, and others to redefine the concept of *landscape*, using it to integrate diverse temporal and spatial studies. Landscape is the "spatial manifestation of the relations between humans and the environment" and, as such is itself an artifact.[20] As archaeologists' units of spatial analysis became more inclusive (artifact to site to landscape), changes in landscapes could be studied over both the short- and long-term. Today, a theoretical and methodological framework for the interdisciplinary study of landscape is in place, with implications well beyond any single field of study.

CONTEMPORARY LANDSCAPE AND REGIONAL STUDIES

Today the many strands that enable us to understand the domestic relationship humans have with the earth have begun to come together. Archaeologists study elements (artifacts, features, sites) and spaces as they form the landscape, charting the ways regions have changed over time. Of course, excavations and the search for locales of activity (survey or fieldwalking) are still fundamental to archaeology everywhere, but now the goal is to understand landscapes and entire regions in the past rather than a single site, and to read the history of human activity all the way up to the global scale.

Multiple-investigator projects, often organized by archaeologists based both in cultural resource management (CRM) and in research institutions, seek to do this by assembling teams of scholars who can cooperate to maximize the scope, complexity, rapidity, and quality with which such projects can be completed. Such an approach is traditional for archaeologists, who regularly employ both natural and physical sciences (biology, geology, physics, chemistry) and the humanities (history, classics, philosophy, linguistics). Despite what sometimes appear to be rather parochial interests, archaeologists routinely consult science and humanities colleagues or have training themselves in these disciplines. Most important, archaeology offers the temporal and spatial breadth required for long-term ecological analysis.

A suite of specialized studies are undertaken, and preliminary findings are shared among the researchers. A beginning assumption is that humans can modify the environment and vice versa. Although the physical environment of a region (topography, soils, water, climate, plants, and animals) may have changed as humans utilized various resources, other events and conditions (volcanic activity, a cold period) could also have played a role. Researchers also expect that human responses to changing environmental conditions, whether they had caused those changes or not, can yield valuable insight into contemporary human ecology. These integrated, regional histories of human-environment relationships are termed historical ecology.[21] The word ecology is from the Greek *oikos* (household); it is related to *oikonomos* (the setting from which households draw provisions), which gives us the word economy.

Ecofacts, the natural scientific evidence of human activity, can yield as much information as artifacts. For example, a paleoethnobotanist (someone trained to identify the plant remains humans used in the past) might examine burned seeds from all levels of an archaeological site, finding that a native plant species becomes more common as time goes on *and* that it underwent marked genetic change. A biological anthropologist, looking at human skeletal material from the same site, reports that the people who lived there began eating almost solely grain, with marked negative effect on their nutrition, and that many of the site's later inhabitants died violently. A geologist notes that erosion becomes a problem in the entire region during the period that corresponds to the latter part of the site's occupation. A climatologist, using information collected locally, regionally, and globally, finds evidence for a dry period in the entire region.

Archaeologists, surveying and excavating sites throughout the region, report that settlements were small and widely dispersed at the beginning of the period, but by its end there were only large, fortified sites around sources of water. A linguist and an ethnohistorian (someone trained to look for cultural information in documents) collaborate to translate stone tablets found at one of the fortified sites; they are prayers to deities asking that the population be spared from war and pestilence. Thus, by integrating evidence from the natural and social sciences and the humanities, we can trace long-term changes in climate, resources, population distribution, human health, and warfare as they pertain to a particular region.

AN EXCITING NEW TOOL OF ANALYSIS

While the conclusions of such research might appear seamless, these understandings are hard-won. Not only are they labor-intensive (just think about identifying and counting hundreds of thousands of burned seeds!), but it takes effort for people trained in very different disciplines to learn to share their findings in less technical language. Fortunately, the biggest practical problem has been solved.

Geographic Information Systems (GIS) manages the huge amount of data generated in regional-scale research, storing spatial information in such a way that it can be supplemented and compared with ease.[22] Before the past decade, when the availability of both powerful computer hardware and complex software made GIS possible, the archaeologist who wondered if early Neolithic farming communities in Belgium were significantly correlated with sandy soils would run a statistical analysis based on geomorphological (sediment) studies conducted in association with excavations. If, after finding that 75 percent of the sites were on sandy soil, she wondered just where the other 25 percent were located, she would have to mark the locations of all the early Neolithic sites onto a soils map by hand. If her colleague, a geologist, wondered what percentage of the distribution of sites could be explained by the correlation among soils, elevation, and distance from the sea, he would have to start a new map, duplicating some of the long hours at the light table his archaeologist colleague had already spent.

A GIS allows the assemblage of a spatial database all team members can use and encourages "what if?" questions. Each layer of information (elevation, stream courses, administrative boundaries, site and artifact locations, etc.) is entered separately into the GIS either manually (with digitizers) or electronically (by scanners). Although this too takes time, it need only be done once. Cultural data (such as roads and river fords) and environmental data can be entered, and researchers can display any combination of layers on a monitor. Color maps of the combined layers can be printed and the combinations stored for future use.

Even old maps and aerial photographs can be georeferenced (that is, made to match a standard scale) and added to the database. Thus, forests marked on 1759 and 1854 maps in Burgundy, France, can be compared with forest cover in the same area as photographed by military reconnaissance in 1944 and satellite imagery from last month. In addition, the location and percentage of change in forest cover can be calculated for just the area indicated on the 1759 map or for the entire *scene* (the area covered by a single "snapshot" satellite image).

This new tool not only saves time but is also beginning to reconfigure the questions we can ask. We may know that several of a region's Iron Age sites are fortified hilltops, but with a particular GIS display (called view-shed analysis) we can see that several of these sites together offer an unrestricted view of all major routes through the area. We can devise ways of testing the hypothesis that these particular sites were critical to the region's defense: Are they permanently or sporadically occupied? Are they more heavily fortified than other contemporary hillforts? When we have the configuration of defensive sites, the direction from which enemies were expected can be hypothesized. The next round of questions would then concern relations with other groups, terrain, and resources in the region.

Perhaps of most importance, the GIS enables us to use actual site and artifact locations and other data that do not need to be compared with situations the researcher might postulate as "ideal"; instead the physical evidence of social, political, and economic circumstances that formed the landscape of past populations can be read and queried.

Although GIS has great potential, there are some things it cannot be used to do. We cannot search for sites in front of a computer screen, because we can never be sure we know everything about the settlement and land use of the population being studied. It must always be considered possible that deeply buried sites went undetected or that particular methods of site survey biased the sample of sites found.

In fact, GIS analysis and fieldwork must be pursued together for two reasons. The first is that, in order for the computer to recognize the variations in reflectivity in remotely sensed data, the elements must always be verified. To classify all the wheat fields or lakes in an image, a sample of the very cells or polygons representing a wheat field or lake must be found in order to "train" the program to read similar cell or polygon values elsewhere in the imagery. The second reason is that working back and forth from the real world to the model should remind us that it is the model that is subject to critique, not past human behavior.

EXAMINING A FOURTH DIMENSION

In the past century archaeologists have added many important concepts, methods, and techniques to explore past human-environment relationships. Formal (typological) studies, which served as a basis for comparative dating, were joined mid-century by absolute dating techniques (e.g., C^{14}, potassium-argon); in the last half of the century, Spaulding's suggestion that all three dimensions of archaeology (form, time, space) deserved equal attention helped transform site-based archaeology to global historical ecology.[23] With this transition has come the realization that we must now turn our attention to a fourth dimension—perception.

People modify their environment according to their values. For example, a grove of oaks in first century B.C. France was sacred to Celtic peoples, and beneath their branches rites were performed and pigs were fattened on the acorn mast. The Celts' Roman conquerors unsentimentally clearcut the grove, considering the trees an economic resource. To the former, each tree was the living embodiment of deity; to the latter, all were candidates for strong ships' timber. Today, a French farmer might selectively harvest for sale some oaks in such a grove, culling sick and damaged trees and leaving room for new growth. While he follows for the moment his grandfather's management strategy, financial circumstances might force him to contemplate other uses for the land. One option, planting a quick-growing North American species of fir, is lucrative but reduces soil nutrients and is said to change the local microclimate. All three perceptions of the grove are the result of historical, environmental, economic, social, and political conditions that shape, and are shaped by, religious and philosophical values.

Although there are limits to the understandings material remains can give us, they can nonetheless reflect habits of thought and action for which we may have no other source of information. If we have documentary or ethnographic data in addition to archaeological remains, it is possible to construct a rich account of the way humans adapted to and modified their immediate environs. Even where other information is lacking, the archaeological and environmental record offer, for every part of the world, a remarkably complete picture of past landscapes and, implicitly, past mindscapes.

For example, the Imperial Chinese city of Chang An (near the modern city of Xi'an, in the province of Shaanxi) was laid out in the pattern of the cosmic forces that governed Chinese life; this not only rendered the whole city a huge icon, but also reinforced the right of the elite to rule, since their home was synonymous with the structure of heaven.[24] Similarly, the modest sanctuaries of the early Christians bespoke a vastly different attitude toward society, wealth, and the importance of the individual than was transmitted by the cathedrals of Western Christendom's High Middle Ages. The former was meant to comfort, the latter to awe.

We still, both intentionally and unintentionally, transmit such messages in architecture and in the modification of the landscape. Organizers of historical theme parks such as the Civil War battleground at Gettysburg (PA) or the colonial town of Williamsburg (VA) employ the powerful mixture of politics and meaning when they re-create those landscapes for contemporary visitors. Yet they too have been forced to recognize others' perceptions. Contemporary groups of Civil War re-enactors have complained about the inauthenticity of mown grass and the irreverence of concession stands at Gettysburg; scholars of African-American archaeology (among others) have criticized colonial Williamsburg's park management for "beautifying" a slaveholding past by excavating and reconstructing owners' homes but not slave quarters. Students of garbology (the study of trash, a truly ubiquitous artifact) have noted another false beautification: Reconstructed Williamsburg's tidiness bears no resemblance to the muddy, garbage-strewn townscape revealed by archaeological excavations.[25]

Thus past landscapes are as much contested ground as are today's issues, such as whether to allow timber companies concessions in federal parks, or Native Americans access to sacred spots on military reserves. Who owns them? To whom are they accessible? Whose version of history triumphs? Archaeologists have great responsibility in that they must provide thoughtful criticism of all reconstructions of the past, rather like the master sleuth in a mystery tale. How closely does the reconstruction fit the material evidence? What sources were used to document the reconstruction? How reliable are they? What other interpretations are possible? Who benefits from the interpretation chosen as a basis for the reconstruction? Here broad anthropological training pays off, because contemporary archaeologists must be ethnographers, archivists, ecologists, and, more often than not, cultural brokers between factions in dispute.

EMPLOYING PAST LANDSCAPES IN PLANNING CHANGE

Of course, if everyone waited until there was complete unanimity on a subject, considerably fewer aspects of the world around us would change for the better. Rather than allowing things to change willy-nilly, most of us would like to benefit from a modicum of planning as regards the landscapes of our daily lives.

For example, a spatial pattern of urban blight, suburban sprawl, and rural abandonment characterizes more and more of the world. Under-employed urban populations sink into poverty, while the well-to-do seek carefully managed "rural" vistas far from the concrete jungle. As a result of mechanization in agribusiness, fewer and fewer people grow their own or anyone else's food. How old is this pattern? When were the first cities, the first suburbs, the first ghettos? Under what conditions did the shift from an agrarian to an industrial population occur? Must this be the future everywhere, or are there historic or contemporary societies in which the population is distributed differently and that could offer ideas for planning a different landscape?

My graduate students and I have been conducting research on the history of rural settlement and land use in Burgundy (east-central France) since 1975.[26] Our collective goal is to trace three thousand years of changes in the region, as they are manifest in the landscape, from the period before the Roman conquest, when Celtic peoples ruled Western Europe, to the present. Our research methods include archaeology, ethnography, the analysis of documents and maps, satellite imagery, and a variety of paleoenvironmental studies (e.g., geomorphology, climatology, ethnobotany). We integrate the spatial components of these data in a GIS. Each of us has several specialties and particular research goals, and we share information and ideas.

My current research on behalf of the project is to learn how vegetable gardens help people maintain the food supply in times of harsh climate or political upheaval. I have begun studying gardens and interviewing gardeners in the commune of Uxeau (an administrative division like a county); as a test of my understanding of what they tell me, I plant my own garden and solicit their advice.

I collect documentary evidence on plants and gardening practices from almanacs; from leather-bound volumes holding records of baptisms, marriages, and deaths in Uxeau (which are complete from 1670 to the present) I am reconstructing the community's population profile. Each person had two (birth, death) or three (marriage) life-events that were written in the volumes by the village priest, who also noted the person's address (by farm name) and the names and occupations of attending family and friends. Detailed maps of the area dating to the 1500s still exist and, in conjunction with the population data and new excavations of the medieval town center, figuratively enable us to repopulate the landscape of nearly five centuries ago.

Archaeological evidence from a nearby hilltop site called Mont Dardon (which has a 2,400-year-long chronological sequence) includes carbonized seeds excavated from levels dating from the Iron Age (1000 B.C.) through Roman (52 B.C.–ca. A.D. 400) to late medieval times (fourteenth century A.D.) and overlaps with the documentary information. Local and regional environmental evidence, including a massive synopsis of Swiss weather by ten-day periods since 1528, allows a relatively confident reconstruction of climatic conditions during the past three thousand years. The spatial component of all these data has been added to our GIS database.

There are several advantages to the use of ethnography and archival research in conjunction with archaeology and paleoenvironmental studies; in the foregoing example, documents and people's memories can bring alive a period before harsh local conditions were ameliorated by rail transport from more fortunate areas. These insights then serve as links to the even more distant past, accessible only through archaeology. Households had to have a garden then, before long-distance transport of domestic supplies; now, despite the ready availability of produce in stores and at markets, most rural households still do. This tradition appears to be unbroken as far back as at least the first millennium B.C., and offers a remarkable opportunity to study the role gardens have played in allowing households a means of autonomous adaptation to Burgundy's sometimes freakish weather.

Gardens play a critical role in reducing risks associated with inclement weather all over the world. Unlike field crops, gardens shelter numerous species in special soils and under controlled microclimatic conditions. Plants receive individual attention and enable the gardener to develop an intimate understanding of soils, winds, and seasons as they relate to the garden plot. Gardens both conserve traditional species and are filled with small experiments that yield new information as well as abundant produce.

How gardens have been used during periods of environmental stress can be a valuable source of information in buttressing world food resources and fostering domestic economic autonomy. In urbanized countries where a gardening tradition continues, gardeners are usually older (in their fifties or sixties) and remember when gardens enabled their families to survive hard economic times and periods of severe weather. In most parts of the world, techniques of successful gardening are transmitted intergenerationally, from one individual to another.

Today, most citizens of urbanized nations buy internationally-grown produce at the grocery store and know little about the practical art of gardening. Agreements governing international trade (e.g., the GATT accord, hotly protested by French farmers who used their tractors to block the streets of Paris), revealed the extent of urban ignorance of rural risk reduction strategies. Western attempts to foster third world industrial centralization and the support of high yields with complex technology (the "Green Revolution") ignored intricate lessons of rural ecology.

With its long history of climatic instability and an educated and activist rural population, Burgundy offers valuable lessons to policymakers about the role gardens play in buffering extreme weather events. Furthermore, Burgundian gardens provide a strong argument for maintaining the genetic diversity of domesticated species; by growing several varieties of every species of plant, gardeners make sure that unseasonable weather or pests destroy only part of the harvest. The varieties are maintained through trade (among gardeners whose gardens are located in slightly different microclimatic conditions), are passed down from generation to generation, and are purchased from catalogues.

Next I will write about my findings and ask the people I interviewed to review the manuscript until most agree that I have everything right. I will continue to search for information about the history of these practices, especially through archaeological excavation that will yield material for paleoenvironmental analyses. Bit by bit, we will be able to determine the species and practices that enable temperate-latitude rural populations to protect themselves from unpleasant climatic or political surprises without dependence on long-distance trade. Fortunately for the people of the former Soviet Union these lessons had not, despite forced collectivization, been lost; their government's collapse and the suspension of long-distance transport did not result in widespread famine.

Researchers will need to engage in similar activities for each region of the world, because the effects of global environmental changes on regions are now understood to be characterized by frequent periods of unseasonable weather. Everywhere, as dependence on grocery stores (and the governmental infrastructure of roads, ports, bridges, and airports necessary to stock them) replaces more self-reliant domestic patterns, intricate and important local knowledge is being lost. Although it is doubtful that urbanized, industrialized societies will ever return to strategies of independent gardening, it is nonetheless important to understand gardens as a strategy for reducing risk that could yield important lessons for development worldwide.

We hope to demonstrate to policymakers that available and plentiful data about how societies in the past have adapted (or failed to adapt) to major climate shifts can be used to buffer future global- and regional-scale environmental change. Such information can avoid loss of life, help predict future migration, and offer many ideas for buffering "at risk" populations from hardship.

These are enormous issues. So far, physical and natural scientists have been asked to answer questions about the future of the planet with only part of the picture at their disposal. There exists an as yet untapped body of data awaiting application: the record of some three million years of human-environment dialogue. Historical ecology, practiced at local (landscape), regional, and global scales and integrated through GIS, can complete the picture and offer sound planning principles for both the neighborhoods and the planet we all call home. Global ecology is global housekeeping.

NOTES

1. Janet Levy, "An Early but Enduring Monument: Prehistoric Remains on the Landscape" (paper presented at the 87th annual meeting of the American Anthropological Association, 1988).
2. Don D. Fowler, "Uses of the Past: Archaeology in the Service of the State," *American Antiquity* 52 (1987): 229–248; Thomas C. Patterson, *Toward a Social History of Archaeology in the United States* (Fort Worth, TX: Harcourt-Brace College Publications, 1995).
3. Cyril Fox, *The Personality of Britain* (Cardiff: University of Wales, 1932).
4. Gordon R. Willey, "Prehistoric Settlement Patterns in the Viru Valley, Peru," *Bureau of American Ethnology*, no. 155 (1953).
5. J. G. D. Clarke, *Excavations at Starr Carr* (Cambridge: Cambridge University Press, 1954).
6. Richard S. MacNeish, "Ancient Mesoamerican Civilization," *Science* 143 (1964): 531–537.
7. Don Brothwell, and Eric Higgs, eds., *Science in Archaeology*, 2nd ed. (London: Thames and Hudson, 1963).

8. Karl Polanyi, Conrad M. Arensberg, and Harry W. Pearson, *Trade and Market in the Early Empires: Economies in History and Theory* (New York: The Free Press, 1957); Colin Renfrew, "Trade and Culture Process in European Prehistory," *Current Anthropology* 10 (1969): 151–160.

9. Albert C. Spaulding, "The Dimensions of Archaeology," in Gertrude E. Dole and Robert L. Carneiro, eds., *Essays in the Science of Culture* (New York: Crowell, 1960), pp. 437–456.

10. James N. Hill, "Broken K Pueblo: Patterns of Form and Function," in Lewis R. Binford and S. R. Binford, eds., *New Perspectives in Archaeology* (New York: Aldine, 1968); James N. Hill and Joel Gunn, *The Individual in Prehistory* (New York: Academic Press, 1977); Lewis R. Binford, "Willow Smoke and Dogs' Tails: Hunter-Gatherer Settlement Systems and Archaeological Site Formation," *American Antiquity* 45 (1980): 4–20; Lewis R. Binford, *Bones: Ancient Men and Modern Myths* (New York: Academic Press, 1981).

11. J. R. Cann and Colin Renfrew, "The Characterization of Obsidian and Its Application to the Mediterranean Region," *Proceedings of the Prehistoric Society* 30 (1964): 111–133.

12. Willey, "Prehistoric Settlement Patterns in the Viru Valley, Peru"; Kent Flannery, "The Cultural Evolution of Civilizations," *Annual Review of Ecology and Systematic* 3 (1972): 399–426.

13. Carol A. Smith, ed., *Regional Analysis* (New York: Academic Press, 1976); Carole L. Crumley, "Toward a Locational Definition of State Systems of Settlement," *American Anthropologist* 78 (1976): 59–73; Carole L. Crumley, "Reply to Smith," *American Anthropologist* 79 (1977): 903–908.

14. Walter W. Taylor, "A Study of Archaeology," *Memoirs of the American Anthropological Association*, no. 69 (1948).

15. Marc Bloch, *The Historian's Craft* (New York: Vintage, 1953).

16. Peter Burke, *The French Historical Revolution: The Annales School, 1929–1989* (Stanford: Stanford University Press, 1990).

17. Lewis R. Binford, "Archaeology as Anthropology," *American Antiquity 28*, no. 2 (1962): 217–225.

18. David L. Clarke, ed., *Spatial Archaeology* (London: Academic Press, 1977), p. 9.

19. Hill, "Broken K Pueblo: Patterns of Form and Function"; James Deetz and E. S. Dethlefsen, "Death's Heads, Cherubs, and Willow Trees: Experimental Archaeology at Colonial Cemeteries," *American Antiquity* 31, no. 4 (1966): 502–510.

20. Carole L. Crumley and William H. Marquardt, "Landscape: A Unifying Concept in Regional Analysis," in Kathleen M. Allen, Stanton W. Green, and Ezra B. W. Zubrow, eds., *Interpreting Space: GIS and Archaeology* (London: Taylor and Francis, 1990), pp. 73–79.

21. Don Stephen Rice, *The Historical Ecology of Lakes Yaxha and Sacnab, El Peten, Guatemala* (Ph.D. diss., The Pennsylvania State University, 1976); Lester J. Bilsky, *Historical Ecology: Essays on Environment and Social Change* (Port Washington, NY: Kennikat Press, 1980); Carole L. Crumley, ed., *Historical Ecology: Cultural Knowledge and Changing Landscapes* (Santa Fe, NM: School of American Research Press, 1994).

22. Allen, Green, and Zubrow, *Interpreting Space: GIS and Archaeology*.

23. Spaulding, "The Dimensions of Archaeology."

24. Paul Wheatley, *The Pivot of the Four Corners* (Edinburgh: Edinburgh University Press, 1970).

25. W. H. Rathje, "The Garbage Project: A New Way of Looking at the Problems of Archaeology," *Archaeology* 27 (1974): 236–241.
26. Carole L. Crumley and William H. Marquardt, eds., *Regional Dynamics: Burgundian Landscapes in Historical Perspective* (San Diego: Academic Press, 1987).

SUGGESTED READINGS

Allen, Kathleen M. S., Stanton W. Green, and Ezra B. W. Zubrow, eds. *Interpreting Space: GIS and Archaeology*. New York: Taylor and Francis, 1990. A comprehensive introduction to the interface of GIS and archaeology.

Clarke, David L., ed. *Spatial Archaeology*. London: Academic Press, 1977. A collection of articles important to the understanding of early approaches to spatial issues in archaeology.

Crumley, Carole L., ed. *Historical Ecology: Cultural Knowledge and Changing Landscapes*. Santa Fe, NM: School of American Research Press, 1994. A good introduction to historical ecology.

Ucko, Peter J., George W. Dimbleby, and Ruth Tringham, eds. *Man, Settlement, and Urbanism*. London: Duckworth, 1972. A seminal compilation.

ARCHAEOLOGICAL SURVEY IN THE MIXTEC SIERRA[1]

LAURA FINSTEN

In 1990 Steve Kowalewski and I, with a crew of six to eight other archaeologists, carried out a regional survey in the rugged Mixtec Sierra in Oaxaca, Mexico (see Figure 20-1 on page 318).[2] For five months we climbed up, down, and along mountain ridges and walked steep-sided, narrow river valleys looking for pre-Columbian settlements and recording information about what we found. People have asked why we would survey mountains, both while Steve and I were preparing this exciting but daunting project, and since we completed the field work. The answer lies in the development of our thinking during and after earlier surveys in the Valley of Oaxaca. Our goal then had been to understand long-term change in the ancient urban society of the Valley, and to shed light on the development of complex societies, or civilizations, as they are often called.

BACKGROUND

The Mixtec Sierra forms the western border of the Valley of Oaxaca in southern Mesoamerica (see Figure 20-2 on page 319).[3] Monte Albán, center (or capitol) of the largest Oaxacan state, lies jewel-like atop a hill four hundred meters above the valley floor. The pale stone buildings of its Main Plaza, the downtown core, glisten in the brilliant sun of highland Mexico. From the tallest building, probably a temple pyramid unimaginatively (but accurately) named the "South Platform," the vistas are panoramic. North lies the Main Plaza, an area equivalent to three football fields levelled out of a rocky hilltop, and defined by temples, palaces, stairways, a massive columned portico, and a ballcourt, all of carefully hewn rock. Carved stone monuments, embedded in the walls of buildings, or freestanding, tell stories that remain largely undeciphered.[4] What tales do they tell? Why was a city built

FIGURE 20-1   AERIAL VIEW OF THE MIXTEC SIERRA

in such an out-of-the-way spot? How far did the rule of its aristocracy reach? How did the *system*, the political, economic, and social networks of which Monte Albán was a part, change over the city's 1,200 year history? Most ancient cities were parts of complex societies with states.[5] Monte Albán was first settled in about 500 B.C., a thousand years after the first agricultural villages appeared in the Valley of Oaxaca. After A.D. 700, eight hundred years before the Spanish conquest, its magnificent Main Plaza was allowed to fall into ruin as buildings were no longer maintained and new construction ceased. Why did cities arise at all in the Valley of Oaxaca, or anywhere in Mesoamerica? Why did Monte Albán decline more than a millennium later?

Prior to the 1960s, specialists in ancient complex societies everywhere tended to focus on the relationships between major cities in different regions to answer questions about their rise and fall, the emergence of social stratification (social classes), and other social processes.[6] These links were generally seen in terms of trade over distances of hundreds or thousands of kilometers, in objects crafted from rare, exotic materials such as jade, magnetite, or the best made and most elaborate pottery.[7] Other explanations focused on colonizing

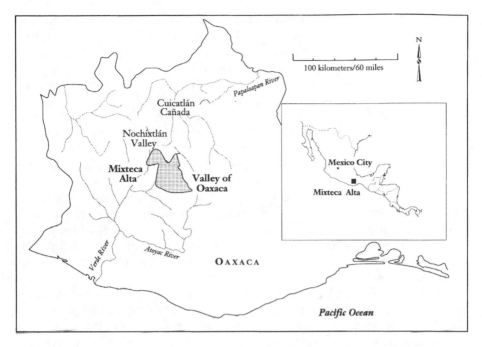

FIGURE 20-2 LOCATION OF THE MIXTEC SIERRA SURVEY AREA IN OAXACA

migrations from distant, already developed areas.[8] Monte Albán's rise was attributed to influence from (through the mechanism of trade in exotics) or migrations by other Mesoamerican peoples—the Maya, according to some early scholars (although it soon became clear that Maya cities were actually younger than Monte Albán), or the Olmec on the Gulf of Mexico coast. Dissatisfied with answers that seemed only to shuffle the question off to another locale and that were unable to tell us just how trade in rare materials resulted in social transformations, many scholars in the 1960s and 1970s adopted a regional approach that focused on the larger regional societies of which ancient cities were a part.[9] This strategy recognized that urban centers were parts of networks of communities, ranging from hamlets of a few families to cities rivaling the "center" in population size. The communities of these networks were linked in complex, changing relationships of political control (e.g., taxation, warfare), specialized economic production (including agricultural production), trade and exchange, and social ties, especially among the families of different local elites (or aristocracies). A regional approach takes a broader perspective, looking not just at a specific urban center but at change over time in the system of different communities of which a particular city was a part.

Seen from atop the lofty South Platform at Monte Albán, beyond the ancient city's terraced slopes where its thousands of residents lived, the Valley of Oaxaca stretches north, south, and east in three broad "arms," carved like a massive sunken oasis in the seemingly infinite mountain ranges of the highlands. Although only a small part of the modern state, the Valley is its only considerable expanse of flat land, so it is not surprising that it has the highest density of people in the southern highlands. Scores of modern villages and towns dot the landscape. On the virtually frost-free alluvium and gentle foothills, farmers grow corn, beans, and squash much as their pre-Columbian ancestors did, although ox-drawn ploughs and the occasional tractor are clear post-conquest additions. Even in the relative haven of the Valley, though, periodic drought in this semi-arid climate means that farming is, and always has been, a risky business except where permanent streams and other rare, year-round water sources can be tapped for irrigation. Still, the Valley has been a magnet attracting people, providing a relatively benign setting for agricultural societies to flourish, for more than 5000 years.

In 1977, I joined a long-term project whose goal was to undertake a regional study by carrying out a large-scale archaeological survey of the Valley of Oaxaca.[10] Richard Blanton had already conducted an intensive study at Monte Albán.[11] Excavations between 1931 and 1958, mostly under the direction of Alfonso Caso, had produced the reconstruction of the Main Plaza visible to visitors today, a host of artifacts housed in museums in both Oaxaca and Mexico City, and a solid history of the construction and development of Monte Albán's Main Plaza between about 500 B.C. and A.D. 700.[12] Before Rich Blanton's research, no one knew how large the ancient city was, how many people lived there at different times throughout its history, or what sorts of economic activities the commoner population had engaged in.

The surveys in which I participated continued this work, locating and recording all visible pre-Columbian sites in the Valley of Oaxaca. We walked every field, hilltop, ridge, and modern town street, mapping and describing archaeological remains wherever we found them, and collecting pottery for closer study in the field lab. When the field work was completed in 1980, we had surveyed 2,150 square kilometers (830 square miles) and located and collected information from about 2,700 pre-Columbian sites.[13]

We learned a great deal. Over eleven phases covering 3,000 years of settled life before the Spanish conquest, the population of the whole Valley of Oaxaca waxed and waned several times.[14] Dramatic changes in the settlement hierarchy reflect shifting political, administrative, and economic arrangements.[15] The population's distribution across the landscape changed, too.[16] At times, large numbers of new settlements were founded and older communities thrived in parts of the Valley, while elsewhere old towns were abandoned or shrank dramatically. Over time the areas of growth and decline changed. Potential agricultural production was not the only factor, often not even a significant factor, determining where settlements were established and whether their populations grew or dwindled. Clearly, during all pre-Hispanic time periods some communities were dependent on the productivity of others for their very survival, especially during the frequent drought years. Complex networks involving productive specialization, trade, and tribute (a form of taxation) integrated towns and villages, although these links were not static. Changes in the distribution and sizes of settlements also point to the dynamic nature of the regional society's boundaries. During some phases many sites, some of considerable size, were located on high hills on the Valley's perimeter. In others, few settlements were situated on the Valley's edges, while in yet others, the distribution of sites is continuous across the Valley floor and into the hills, suggesting that the system of settlement extended beyond the border of the Valley of Oaxaca, beyond the limits of our survey.

Regional archaeological surveys, like ours in the Valley of Oaxaca, have led to a new understanding of the complex, dynamic relationships between population growth, the development of site hierarchies, and the mechanisms integrating cities, towns, and villages in a regional society. But as is true with most research, our efforts led us to formulate new questions—ones that, in a sense, were unthinkable before this earlier work. How did interactions, not limited to long-distance trade, among the regional states of the ancient Mesoamerican world (or macroregion) contribute to long-term change in their structure and operation?[17] What roles did boundaries and frontiers play, as some ancient societies expanded their territories at the expense of others? Were the vast, mountainous peripheries merely inconvenient, largely vacant places to be traversed while journeying from one highland valley to another? New questions demand renewed efforts and new strategies.

THE GOALS OF ARCHAEOLOGICAL SURVEY IN THE MIXTEC MOUNTAINS

From atop the South Platform at Monte Albán's Main Plaza, beyond the Valley floor, the piedmont rises gently at first, then more abruptly, to craggy, pine-covered mountain peaks towering 3,000 meters (9,750 feet) above sea level. The mountains seem distant but ever present, always a part of one's consciousness when in the Valley of Oaxaca. Mountains are visible in most directions from nearly everywhere. Leaving the Valley by highway, whether north, south, or east, means a torturous, seemingly interminable drive along tight, hairpin curves at dizzying elevations, underscoring the Valley's physical isolation despite modern land transportation technology. The 100–120 kilometer (60–70 mile) trip to either coast takes 8 to 10 hours, unless a landslide or washed out road segment slows you down.

Looking west from the South Platform is the Mixtec Sierra. About thirty-five kilometers (twenty miles) beyond as the crow flies is the Mixteca Alta, a series of small, interconnected highland valleys. The easternmost is the Nochixtlán Valley. Devastating erosion since the Spanish conquest, due in part to the introduction of grazing animals (especially sheep and goats), has made it one of the most impoverished parts of modern Mexico. But in pre-Columbian times cities, towns, and villages abounded, and kings of the Mixteca in the centuries before conquest recorded their family histories and military exploits in brilliantly painted books.[18] Several valleys of the Mixteca Alta, as well as areas in the central highlands of Mexico, have been surveyed.[19] Our survey connects these surveys with those in the Valley of Oaxaca to produce a massive block of well-studied territory. This is key to establishing a systematic body of comparable information about settlement hierarchies, demography and other aspects of a Mesoamerican macroregion of different ancient societies.

The Mixtec Sierra is ideal for studying boundaries and frontier zones. Today the native language spoken in virtually all of the Mixteca Alta is Mixtec, while in the Valley of Oaxaca, Zapotec is the language of most native speakers.[20] The ancient Zapotec and Mixtec cultures, while sharing many features, had distinctive characteristics at the time of the Spanish conquest. The Zapotec-Mixtec linguistic and cultural boundary fell within the Mixtec Sierra during much of the pre-Columbian era. Ancient states in either adjacent valley, expanding their territories or endeavoring to maintain control over lands (and people) already ruled, would have had an interest in the Sierra's fortifiable ridgetops and important transportation routes. Traders, diplomats, soldiers, pilgrims, and *tlamemes*, or human beasts of burden, travelled ancient roadways in the mountains linking the Valley of Oaxaca to the Mixteca Alta and to more distant parts of Mesoamerica. Prior to the Spanish conquest, there were no horses, oxen, cattle, donkeys, or other beasts of burden in Mesoamerica. Except where canoe traffic was possible (generally limited to the shallow lakes of the Basin of Mexico, the coastlines, and the broad rivers of the southern Maya lowlands), all travel and transportation was by foot.

The mountainous regions of Mexico are marginal today, but may have been less so before the advent of modern methods of transportation and cultivation. The times needed to traverse mountainous versus flatter terrain on foot probably differ less than they do travelling by car.[21] Compared to the oases of highland valleys, agricultural productivity is lower in the mountains and perhaps less reliable, since irrigation is more limited and damaging frosts occur periodically.[22] A more important difference may be long-term instability because of steep slopes that are more easily eroded. More abundant resources include orchard fruits, wood for charcoal and construction beams, and plentiful deer and other game.[23]

Virtually all archaeological research in highland Mesoamerica has focused on major sites or highland valleys.[24] Peripheral societies in environmentally marginal areas have been largely neglected. How did the complex interrelationships between the state societies of highland valleys and their poorer neighbors in the mountains affect each other's development? Did peripheral societies develop only in response to pressures from their larger, more powerful neighbors, or did they have an internal dynamic that also led to change?

SURVEYING MOUNTAINS

To answer these questions, Steve and I decided to carry out a large-scale survey in an area of about 1,200 square kilometers (465 square miles) in the Mixtec Sierra, to link the previously surveyed Valleys of Oaxaca and Nochixtlán (in the Mixteca Alta), to begin building a macroregional data set for the central and south Mexican highlands, and to cover the crucial boundary zone between these areas. We modified the survey techniques we had employed in the Valley of Oaxaca for use in the mountains to produce information as comparable as possible. This was essential for constructing a systematic macroregional data set. Following the logic that had led to the large-scale survey of the Valley of Oaxaca in the first place, we also decided that systematic coverage (i.e., coverage intended to recover as near 100 percent of sites as humanly possible) was crucial. Because a major interest was change in the integration of communities in the periphery, we had to find as many of the settlements that had been parts of the network as possible in order to understand it. Our goals in the field were to locate, map, describe, and collect artifacts at every visible pre-Columbian site.

In the relatively flat Valley of Oaxaca, we had surveyed by fanning out in crews of three or four to survey land one aerial photograph at a time until the entire Valley was covered and all sites had been recorded. In the mountains, such a strategy would have been an absurd waste of time, and physically next to impossible. We assumed that in the past people did not live in places that today are too steep to stand on, and concentrated our efforts on the crests of ridges and the gentler slopes leading to them and, at first, on the river valleys between ridges. Pairs of surveyors seemed more practical for the terrain and the smaller, less numerous sites we anticipated finding. Pairs would afford a measure of safety in the event of a sprained ankle or other unforeseeable misfortune, while ensuring that there were enough hands to map, write notes, and collect artifacts when sites were encountered.

DEALING WITH THE UNEXPECTED: MODIFYING METHODS TO ACHIEVE GOALS

A truism of virtually all research is that, despite the best planning, things never work out exactly as you expect them to. Unforeseen problems emerged within days of starting in the field. First was a series of problems related to accessibility. The round trip from Oaxaca City where we lived and had set up a field lab was four to five hours, a good-sized chunk of the work day. Not much surveying can happen when crews spend half the day getting to and from work. Because many of the roads into the mountain towns follow river courses (and most modern towns are located low, near rivers, rather than up on the ridges), it took an additional hour or two to climb to the ridgetops from the town and another hour or two to get down. We were just getting to the high places where we needed to start surveying when it was time to turn around and go back. The second problem arose from more interesting circumstances. In the area where we began to work, on the heights above the modern town of Santa María Peñoles, all the ridgetops were littered with the remnants of ancient settlements. Peñoles is mentioned in sixteenth-century documents so we were not surprised to find a site there. We were unprepared, though, for the possibility that every ridgetop in our survey area would have artifacts to be collected and architecture to be mapped. The objective of a survey is to find sites, of course, but sites slow down the work, making it much more difficult to cover large areas. It also became apparent that, because many ridgetops had never been disturbed by ploughing, much more architecture had survived to be mapped than was usually the case at sites in the Valley of Oaxaca, where centuries of ploughing have obliterated all but traces of anything less substantial than mounds.

We decided to change the way we were doing things to see if we could work more efficiently without wasting most of our precious time in travel. We packed sleeping and cooking gear and food and water for four days, and we hired men with burros to haul it up to a suitable place where we could camp at night. From there we could access ridgelines for several days of surveying without having to come down a thousand meters or so every night. This proved to be remarkably efficient since we could begin surveying early in the morning and work far later in the day. (But not everyone liked the suppers of tuna soup made with burro-ripened vegetables.)

Having resolved our logistical problems, we began to survey other parts of the study area, away from Peñoles, to determine whether the extremely high density of sites there was the pattern for the whole projected survey area, or if site densities were more variable (and lower elsewhere). The alternative was to reduce our intended study area size, but we were extremely reluctant to do this until it was proven absolutely necessary. Achieving our goals depended on collecting systematic data from a large area. Our initial forays into areas distant from Peñoles were promising. We found sites, but the density was indeed variable. With this knowledge, we were confident that a large-scale survey was achievable.

The final change in our field methods was the decision to sharply limit our efforts in the river valleys. During the first weeks of the project, we combed the banks of two major rivers and the lower portions of several tributaries. Not only did we not find any trace of significant sites, it was apparent that we were unlikely to. Flat areas are extremely limited along the rivers of the Mixtec Sierra so large settlements are highly improbable in these lower locations, and fast-moving water during the rainy season scours the river banks, obliterating any archaeological remains that may have existed. As our understanding of the mountain zone improved we realized that, in contrast to the flat Valleys of Oaxaca and Nochixtlán where hills are seen as impediments to travel and communication, in the Sierra the mountain ridges form the basis of most physical integration. On foot, it is far easier to follow ridgelines since this means a single major ascent and/or descent (800–1,000 meters [2,500–3,250 feet] in elevation only), and it minimizes the need to skip back and forth across water courses.[25] Eliminating river valleys from the survey made sense because of the improbability of finding ancient settlements, and because of our understanding of the favored locations for pre-Hispanic settlements.

In five months, we surveyed 1,000 square kilometers (385 square miles), mapping more than 500 sites over a broad region linking the Valley of Oaxaca and Nochixtlán Valley surveys.

PRE-HISPANIC SETTLEMENT IN THE MIXTEC SIERRA

The number of sites in the Mixtec Sierra was a surprise (see Figure 20-3 on page 326). Site densities in the Valley of Oaxaca, where on average a site is located in every square kilometer, are only about twice as great. While none of the Mixtec Sierra settlements is as big as the largest ones in the Valley of Oaxaca or the Nochixtlán Valley, several dozen are considerable in size, strung along the crests of ridges for several kilometers. Each would have housed several thousand people.

Parts of the Mixtec Sierra apparently were never inhabited, other areas were occupied only during part of the pre-Hispanic era, and still others were the scene of continuous although perhaps interrupted settlement for as long as 2,300 years. Physically, the survey area consists of two parts, defined by the divide separating the river drainages of the Valley of Oaxaca from those in the Mixteca Alta. The smaller part, east of the divide and overlooking the Valley of Oaxaca, has fewer sites and was probably part of the Valley of Oaxaca regional system. West of the divide, sites number in the hundreds and are found nearly everywhere. Many are large with abundant and complex architecture. The divide itself, a long ridge 2,600–3,000 meters (8,500–9,750 feet) above sea level, had very few traces of ancient settlement.

Like most regional settlement patterns studies, our survey in the Mixtec Sierra dated sites using ceramic styles of known age in the Valley of Oaxaca or in the Nochixtlán Valley.[26] As we walked over sites, measuring and mapping architectural features, we carefully combed the ground surface looking for pottery vessel fragments that would be useful for dating, as well as other

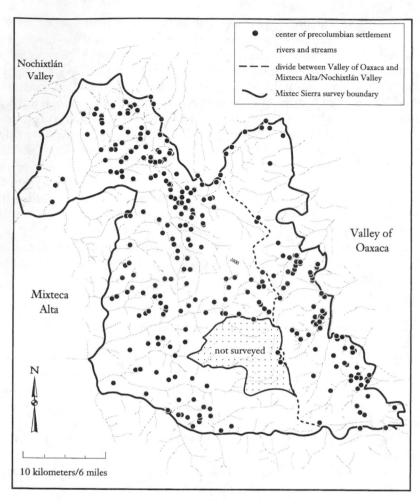

FIGURE 20-3   DISTRIBUTION OF LATE PRE-COLUMBIAN SITES
IN THE MIXTEC SIERRA SURVEY AREA

artifacts. Wherever possible, the age of ceramics was recorded for each architectural feature. Collections of sherds from most sites were taken back to the field lab for closer inspection. Generally though, pottery was rarer on the surface at mountain sites than is true for most Valley settlements because there was less disturbance from ploughing or other recent activities. Thus the conditions that promote excellent architectural preservation are a double-edged sword, making it more difficult to date sites. Highly decorated vessels, which are the most chronologically sensitive markers, also tended to be less abundant. As a result, our chronological placement of many mountain sites is limited to assignment to the broad Mesoamerican periods (Archaic or Pre-ceramic (9000–2000 B.C.), Formative (1500 B.C.–A.D. 300), Classic (A.D. 300–900), and Postclassic (A.D. 900–1521).

EARLY SETTLEMENT

Our survey located a half-dozen probable Archaic period sites, all closer to the Mixteca Alta than the Valley of Oaxaca. One, situated at an outcropping of chert, was a quarry site where raw material for stone tool manufacture was collected and processed.

A few mountain sites have traces of occupation in the Middle Formative period (after 800 B.C.), seen in pottery very similar in style and manufacture to vessels of this age from Monte Albán and other Valley of Oaxaca sites. All of these sites have much larger, later occupations. The few Middle Formative pottery sherds make it impossible to know just how large these early occu-pations were, or whether any of the presently visible architecture dates to this time. These early settlements are concentrated most heavily in the south-ern part of the survey area.

By the Late Formative period (ca. 300 B.C.–A.D. 200), the number of set-tlements had increased substantially and sites may have been larger, although ceramic markers are still very few in number. Diagnostic pottery is identical to contemporary Valley of Oaxaca styles; some vessels probably were im-ported while others were local imitations. The regional distribution of Late Formative sites reveals two processes. First is the continued growth and de-velopment of settlements in the southern part of the survey area. Pottery types suggest that these sites were neither outlying mountainous areas of the Monte Albán state nor founded by directed emigration from the Valley of Oaxaca. Although links with the Valley of Oaxaca are clear, these southern set-tlements retained a degree of independence from Valley of Oaxaca influences.

Second is establishment of a string or corridor of sites along the conti-nental divide, reflecting Monte Albán's concern with controlling routes of access to and from the Valley of Oaxaca.[27] Pottery at these corridor sites is virtually identical to that found at contemporary Valley of Oaxaca sites. The continental divide was one of several strategic transportation corridors controlled by Monte Albán rather than the rival cities of the Mixteca Alta in the Late Formative. The corridor sites all were abandoned at the end of this period.[28]

THE CLASSIC PERIOD (CA. A.D. 300–800)

In the Classic Period, settlement was intensified—there are more sites, and large sites as well as small ones—and site distributions changed. New ar-chitectural forms appeared. We can better associate architecture with occu-pations in later time periods because more recent buildings were modified less by subsequent occupations. But clearly, major construction projects were undertaken at many sites that continued to be occupied from Late Formative times as well as at sites that were first settled during the Classic period.

Many sites occupied in the Late Formative in the southern Mixtec Sierra continued and grew in the Classic period. Other large ones arose anew, especially on the ridges in the center of the survey area. Strings of smaller sites, generally less architecturally complex and impressive, are located on the ridgetops at the western boundary of our survey area and on hilltops well into the northwest. Except for a vacant area at the divide, Classic period occupation in the Mixtec Sierra is continuous with the Valley of Oaxaca settlement.[29]

Strong connections to Monte Albán are apparent in the pottery, which is often identical in style to ceramics at contemporary Valley of Oaxaca sites, although much of it clearly was made locally rather than imported. The distinctive vessel styles of the Nochixtlán Valley are rare, indicating weaker links to the west. Formal mound groups similar to those at Valley of Oaxaca Classic period administrative centers also point to strong ties to the east. While architecture cannot be dated definitively without excavation at sites where more than one period is present, pottery associations suggest a Classic period date for many formal building complexes.[30]

More than twenty sites extend a kilometer or more along the ridgetops. Excellent architectural preservation at many of these sites permits an unparalleled glimpse of their physical layouts, which both reflected and actively formed internal social and other divisions. Larger towns had over a hundred residential terraces carved into the upper slopes of ridges, massive encircling walls, gateways, large platforms, stairways, temples, tombs, and elaborate strings of patio groups. Smaller sites had fewer architectural features but still boasted dozens of terraces, mounds and plazas, patio groups, and often gateways or other wall features to control access.

Site distributions, the predominance of Valley of Oaxaca-style pottery, and formal mound groups like those from Valley administrative centers at larger mountain sites all point to close links to the Monte Albán state. Were Mixtec Sierra settlements mere outposts populated by immigrants from among Monte Albán's faithful subjects? Continuity from Late Formative occupations, at least in the south, suggests more complex processes at work. Monte Albán's boundary concerns may be reflected in new Classic settlements, including fortified ones near the western limit of its territory and others controlling the mountainous frontier. But clearly these towns were not founded in an uninhabited wilderness. How the pre-existing society both affected and was affected by Valley of Oaxaca state interests in the Mixtec Sierra is an important question for which we do not yet have ready answers. However it is apparent that in the Classic period Monte Albán, not the smaller states of the Mixteca Alta, held dominion over the mountainous domain between the highland valleys. Our survey area did not extend far enough west to escape the grasp of Monte Albán's power.

THE POSTCLASSIC PERIOD (CA. A.D. 800–1521)

By the Postclassic period, settlement was dense and nearly continuous almost everywhere except in the limited areas that seem never to have been inhabited. Throughout highland Mesoamerica, at the end of the Classic period, large regional states like the one centered on Monte Albán broke up into smaller political units known as "petty kingdoms."[31] The political world of Postclassic Mesoamerica was a fluid, constantly shifting landscape of alliances, some forged by strategic marriages among noble families, others by conquest or acquiescence to the threat of war. Integration across political boundaries occurred through regional market centers, religious shrines that attracted pilgrims from afar, and perhaps the movement of landless laborers who left their native territories to work foreign lands acquired by their lords.

Forty sites extend a kilometer (360 yards) or more along the ridgetops, and there are hundreds of smaller ones. Itzcuintepec (Nahuatl for "Dog Hill"), above the modern town of Santa María Peñoles in the heart of the survey area, is the largest settlement at more than 3,600 meters (3,900 yards) long. Within two kilometers (1.2 miles) are a half-dozen other large sites. This must have been the center of the Peñoles petty kingdom described in early Spanish accounts.[32] It was similar in population size, internal structure, and organization to the smallest ones archaeologically identifiable in the Valley of Oaxaca.[33]

Other smaller concentrations of settlements may have been under the dominion of different polities. Sites in the east, on the slopes above the Valley of Oaxaca, likely belonged to Valley kingdoms, a number of which had fortified hilltop retreats for the nobility during times of war.[34] A second polity mentioned in early-sixteenth century chronicles is Tamazola, whose modern counterpart lies to the southwest, just outside our survey boundary.[35] Archaeological sites in the southwest sector of the study area may have belonged to the Tamazola kingdom, at least during part of the Postclassic period. The distribution across the region of unusual, circular architectural features may be an important clue to the presence of a boundary between these political units.[36] Future research in the Mixtec Sierra, including an expanded survey to the southwest and more intensive study at sites already mapped, will enhance our understanding of the emergence and historical development of this pan-Mesoamerican political form and the processes by which territories were defined and controlled.

In the Postclassic period, external relationships as they are indicated by pottery were far less monolithic than in earlier periods.[37] Neither of the adjacent Valley's ceramic styles dominate the entire Mixtec Sierra survey area. Instead, the distinctive styles of both occur at mountain sites, but in declining numbers as distance from the Valley of origin increases. Nochixtlán Valley pottery forms are common in the mountains at sites close to the Nochixtlán Valley, and rare at settlements nearer the Valley of Oaxaca. The distinctive bowl forms prevalent at Postclassic sites in the northern and western Valley of Oaxaca occur in great numbers at mountain settlements adjacent to the Valley but drop off in frequency at sites progressively farther west. The spheres of Nochixtlán and Valley of Oaxaca styles overlap. There is no clear "ceramic boundary" permitting us to associate settlements (or the entire system of settlements) with one adjacent valley or the other. This observation, based on pottery, illustrates and underscores the earlier point about the importance of markets as integrative mechanisms linking communities across political boundaries. The spheres of Postclassic market exchanges were larger than political territories and, like many modern markets, overlapped one another.

ANSWERS TO QUESTIONS

The large-scale survey in the Mixtec Sierra was intended to provide information that could be analyzed to answer three broad, related research questions. We can address macroregional processes through broad comparisons between Mixtec Sierra settlement patterns and those of the "core" areas of southern Mesoamerica. Like the better known parts of central and southern Mesoamerica, in the Classic period the Mixtec Sierra tends more toward centralized organization around a pyramidal hierarchy (one that has a few large, powerful places and many more small towns and villages). In fact, its fortified towns may have been directly under the control of Monte Albán itself, or indirectly administered by a big, walled settlement on the eastern slope of the divide just west of Monte Albán. Our present evidence, though, suggests that this characteristic of its organization was a result of its strong ties to the centralized state ruled by Monte Albán. Still, the degree of centralization seems less than is found in core areas, since we cannot identify an obvious regional "capital" in the Classic period. In the Postclassic period, Mixtec Sierra settlement patterns differ little from those of other parts of Mesoamerica, especially in the Valley of Oaxaca and the Nochixtlán Valley. Its territory and population were about the same size as those of petty kingdoms throughout Mesoamerica. The entire Mesoamerican world was made up of small segments just like the Peñoles-Itzcuintepec kingdom, tied together not into massive, centralized states but knit loosely and fluidly into shifting political alliances and integrated across political boundaries by economic and other forces.

A second research question sought to understand long-term change in an environmentally marginal area on the periphery of a core regional state. Perhaps as early as 800 B.C. a society only loosely linked to the "outside" had begun to develop in the southern part of our Mixtec Sierra survey area. Settlement continued up to the Spanish conquest more than two thousand years later. New sites appeared and grew, most of them occupied early on. The high degree of settlement continuity in the region over such a long time suggests that past systems of agriculture and adaptation in the mountains differed substantially from the present ones and were better-suited to long-term survival. Both internal and external factors bear on the history of human settlement in the Mixtec Sierra. Some areas, like the corridor along the continental divide in the Late Formative period, clearly were settled as part of Monte Albán's strategic external interests. In the Classic period, however, a combination of internal developments and superimposition of Monte Albán's control over an expanded western frontier was at work. In the Late Postclassic, the Peñoles region was a small part like most others of the mosaic of petty kingdoms that formed the political fabric of Mesoamerica. Its ties through alliance or conquest undoubtedly shifted,[38] but more stable economic and other links provided integration to both the Valley of Oaxaca and valleys of the Mixteca Alta.

Our third interest was the boundary between the Valley of Oaxaca and Mixteca Alta regional systems. As we can identify them archaeologically, boundaries shifted considerably over time and were defined differently as these regional systems changed. The western limit of the Valley of Oaxaca's Classic period state included our survey area and, in the southwest, apparently extended beyond it. We cannot say whether the Classic period inhabitants of the Mixtec Sierra identified themselves as Zapotec, or spoke Zapotec languages (archaeological data do not speak directly to such matters). But when pottery was imported or received as gifts and "foreign" styles were imitated, Valley of Oaxaca settlements were the source. The Classic period was a time of large state consolidation and military expansion elsewhere in highland Mesoamerica.[39] Heavy fortifications at many mountain sites in this period indicate a major concern with the integrity of the Monte Albán state's boundaries, although this may not have been an interest (or in the interests) of most of the area's inhabitants. In contrast, pottery from Mixtec Sierra sites affirms that political and other (especially, perhaps, economic) boundaries did not coincide in the Late Postclassic period.[40] Late Postclassic system boundaries, then, were more diffuse.

MORE QUESTIONS

Better answers to all of these questions require more analysis of the existing data from the Mixtec Sierra, compilation of all existing settlement pattern data from the southern Mesoamerica highlands for analysis as a single data set and, alas, more fieldwork to collect additional information. These first two steps are underway, although the second will take years to complete. Our ability to understand long-term change in the Mixtec Sierra as a peripheral society is hampered by the paucity of artifacts attributable to the earliest occupations and the present impossibility of associating architecture with them. More intensive study at sites that yielded Formative pottery, including excavations, may be the only solution. Further surveys to the southwest, to determine the reach of Monte Albán's power in the Classic period and to locate and delimit the sixteenth-century Tamazola kingdom in the Postclassic period, will improve our present understanding of boundaries and inter-polity relationships in the ancient urban societies of Mesoamerica.

NOTES

1. The Mixtec Sierra survey was funded by the Social Sciences and Humanities Research Council of Canada, the National Science Foundation, the National Geographic Society, and the Arts Research Board at McMaster University. Permission to carry out the fieldwork was granted by the Instituto Nacional de Antropología e Historia in Mexico.

2. Large-scale, or regional, archaeological surveys are designed to cover lots of ground (hundreds or, if possible, thousands of square kilometers) systematically. Resulting data include the location and number of archaeological sites in the area during each definable time period, the size of each settlement, the nature and approximate abundance of different kinds of artifacts and buildings visible on the surface at every one, and the contemporary environmental setting and land use patterns in the immediate area of every site.

3. The term *Mesoamerica* refers to the southern two-thirds of modern Mexico, Guatemala, Belize, and parts of Honduras and El Salvador. In ancient times, the nobility of Mesoamerica participated in a common system of exchanges and interactions that produced a high degree of similarity in many material aspects of elite culture, such as art, sculpture, architecture, and systems of writing and notation.

4. Joyce Marcus, *Mesoamerican Writing Systems: Propaganda, Myth, and History in Four Ancient Civilizations* (Princeton, NJ: Princeton University Press, 1992), pp. 71–76.

5. A state is a special social institution that serves as the dominant political authority over the territory it governs. See Richard E. Blanton, Stephen A. Kowalewski, Gary M. Feinman, and Laura M. Finsten, *Ancient Mesoamerica: A Comparison of Change in Three Regions*, 2nd ed. rev. (Cambridge: Cambridge University Press, 1993), p. 203.

6. Gordon R. Willey and Jeremy A. Sabloff, *A History of Mesoamerican Archaeology* (San Francisco, CA: Freeman, 1980).

7. Kent V. Flannery, "The Olmec and the Valley of Oaxaca: A Model for Inter-Regional Interaction in Formative Times," in Elizabeth P. Benson, ed., *Dumbarton Oaks Conference on the Olmec* (Washington D.C.: Dumbarton Oaks, 1968), pp. 79–110.

8. Robert J. Sharer and David C. Grove, eds., *Regional Perspectives on the Olmec* (Cambridge: Cambridge University Press/School of American Research, 1989).

9. Richard E. Blanton, "Anthropological Studies of Cities," *Annual Review of Anthropology* 5 (1976): 249–264.

10. Richard E. Blanton, Stephen A. Kowalewski, Gary Feinman, and Jill Appel, *Monte Albán's Hinterland, Part I* (Museum of Anthropology, University of Michigan,

Memoir 15, 1982); Stephen A. Kowalewski, Gary M. Feinman, Laura Finsten, Richard E. Blanton, and Linda M. Nicholas, *Monte Albán's Hinterland, Part II* (Museum of Anthropology, University of Michigan, Memoir 23, 1989).

11. Richard E. Blanton, *Monte Albán: Settlement Patterns at the Ancient Zapotec Capital* (New York: Academic Press, 1978).

12. Ibid., p. 6.

13. Blanton, Kowalewski, Feinman, and Appel, *Monte Albán's Hinterland, Part I.*

14. Phases are subdivisions of time segments called periods and, in the Valley of Oaxaca, range in duration from a century to five hundred years. See Gary M. Feinman, Stephen A. Kowalewski, Laura Finsten, Richard E. Blanton, and Linda Nicholas, "Long-Term Demographic Change: A Perspective from the Valley of Oaxaca, Mexico," *Journal of Field Archaeology* 12 (1986): 333–362.

15. In a settlement hierarchy, progressively more numerous and generally smaller sites are politically and/or economically dominated by the larger, more powerful (and less numerous) settlements at higher levels in the hierarchy. For example, during the Classic period Monte Albán, the regional capital, delegated many administrative tasks to two large "provincial" capitals fifteen to twenty kilometers (nine to twelve miles) away, in different Valley arms. These cities, in turn, oversaw a variety of state functions carried out in other towns, some situated in the higher hills on the Valley edge to control movement of goods and people across the Valley's boundaries, others located to produce agricultural surpluses, and so on. The larger sites at higher levels in the settlement hierarchy attracted people from surrounding towns and villages for kilometers to trade their own craft items or surplus farm products for materials, tools or other things they were unable to produce themselves. See Blanton, Kowalewski, Feinman, and Appel, *Monte Albán's Hinterland, Part I.*

16. Feinman, Kowalewski, Finsten, Blanton, and Nicholas, "Long-Term Demographic Change."

17. A macroregion is a multistate social system, although there may be no formal political or other official recognition of the interrelationships among the component states. Another term, world-system, is suggestive of either empires (which are bound by relationships of political dominance between formerly independent states, or world economies (which are dominated by massive exchanges of both bulk and luxury goods). A good example of the former is Imperial China; see G. William Skinner, ed., *The City in Late Imperial China* (Stanford: Stanford University Press, 1977). The modern world is an obvious example of the latter; see Immanuel Wallerstein, *The Modern World-System: Capitalist Agriculture and the Origins of the European World-Economy in the Sixteenth Century* (New York: Academic Press, 1974). The multistate systems, or macroregions, of ancient Mesoamerica consisted of independent political entities linked through social and other mechanisms to promote the shared interests of nobility; see Blanton, Kowalewski, Feinman, and Finsten, *Ancient Mesoamerica*, pp. 220–221.

18. Alfonso Caso, *Reyes y Reinos de la Mixteca*, 2 vols. (Mexico, DF: Fondo de Cultura Económica, 1977); Mary Elizabeth Smith, *Picture Writing from Ancient Southern Mexico: Mixtec Place Signs and Maps* (Norman: University of Oklahoma Press, 1973); Ronald Spores, *The Mixtec Kings and Their People* (Norman: University of Oklahoma Press, 1967); Ronald Spores, *The Mixtecs in Ancient and Colonial Times* (Norman: University of Oklahoma Press, 1984).

19. Bruce E. Byland, "Political and Economic Evolution in the Tamazulapan Valley, Mixteca Alta, Oaxaca, Mexico" (unpublished Ph.D. diss., Pennsylvania State University, 1980); Bruce E. Byland and John M. D. Pohl, "The Marriage of Twelve-Wind and Three-Flint at White Hill: Pictures, Ruins, and Folklore Reveal a Tenth-Century Mexican Alliance," *Thesis: The Magazine of the Graduate School and University Center, CUNY* 2 (1987): 10–17; Angel García Cook, "The Historical Importance of Tlaxcala in the Cultural Development of the Central Highlands," in Jeremy A. Sabloff, ed., *Supplement to the Handbook of Middle American Indians, Volume 1, Archaeology* (Austin: University of Texas Press, 1981), pp. 244–276; Robert D. Drennan, "The Mountains North of the Valley," in Blanton, Kowalewski, Feinman, and Appel, *Monte Albán's Hinterland, Part I*, pp. 367–384; Elsa M. Redmond, *A Fuego y Sangre: Early Zapotec Imperialism in the Cuicatlán Cañada* (Museum of Anthropology, University of Michigan, Memoir 16); William T. Sanders, Jeffrey R. Parsons, and Robert S. Santley, *The Basin of Mexico: Ecological Processes in the Evolution of a Civilization* (New York: Academic Press, 1979); Ronald Spores, *An Archaeological Settlement Survey of the Nochixtlan Valley, Oaxaca* (Nashville: Vanderbilt University Publications in Anthropology 1, 1972).

20. Closely related, the Zapotec and Mixtec languages diverged from a common ancestral language perhaps five thousand years ago. See Joyce Marcus, "The Genetic Model and the Linguistic Divergence of the Otomangueans," in Kent V. Flannery and Joyce Marcus, eds., *The Cloud People: Divergent Evolution of the Zapotec and Mixtec Civilizations* (New York: Academic Press, 1983), pp. 4–9.

21. A number of people have studied foot travel times in ancient Mesoamerica; there is no persuasive evidence that travel times were significantly longer in mountainous terrain. For a recent discussion and summary of earlier work, see George L. Cowgill, "Comments on Andrew Sluyter: Long-Distance Staple Transport in Western Mesoamerica: Insights through Quantitative Modeling," *Ancient Mesoamerica* 4 (1993): 201–203.

22. Richard D. Garvin, "Modern and Prehispanic Agriculture in the Sierra Mixteca, Oaxaca, Mexico" (unpublished Ph.D. diss., University of Calgary, 1994).

23. Drennan, "The Mountains North of the Valley"; Kent V. Flannery, "Empirical Determination of Site Catchments in Oaxaca and Tehuacán," in Kent V. Flannery, ed., *The Early Mesoamerican Village* (New York: Academic Press, 1976), pp. 103–117.

24. This concentration of archaeological research on major valleys in highland areas, or on the territories immediately surrounding large urban centers, also characterizes research in other areas of the world where ancient complex societies arose, such as Andean South America and the Middle East. See Henry T. Wright, "The Evolution of Civilizations," in David Meltzer, Don Fowler, and Jeremy Sabloff, eds., *American Archaeology: Past and Future* (Washington D.C.: Smithsonian Institution Press, 1986), pp. 323–365.

25. On a trip by foot to Oaxaca in the seventeenth century, Friar Ajofrín complained of having to cross the river sixty times in a day or two. See Francisco Ajofrín, *Diario del Viaje*, vol. 2, ed. P. Buenaventura de Carrocera (Madrid: Real Academia de la Historia, 1959).

26. In stratigraphic excavations where deposits are undisturbed by later activity, earlier pottery is found under more recent pottery. Thus the relative age of different ceramic styles can be determined, and when absolute (or calendric) dates

for layers of the archaeological cake are known, this age can be assigned to all pottery styles found in the dated layer. When vessel fragments of the same types are found on the surface at other sites, we can safely assume that they share the same date as the material dated in stratigraphic contexts.

27. Joyce Marcus, "The Iconography of Militarism at Monte Albán and Neighboring Sites in the Valley of Oaxaca," in Henry B. Nicholson, ed., *The Origins of Religious Art and Iconography in Preclassic Mesoamerica* (Los Angeles: University of California at Los Angeles, Latin American Center, 1976), pp. 123–139; Joyce Marcus, "The Conquest Slabs of Building J, Monte Albán," in Flannery and Marcus, eds., *The Cloud People*, pp. 106–108; Marcus, *Mesoamerican Writing Systems*, pp. 175–177, 394–400; Redmond, *A Fuego y Sangre*; Charles S. Spencer, *The Cuicatlán Cañada and Monte Albán: A Study of Primary State Formation* (New York: Academic Press, 1982).

28. Widespread site abandonments at this time also occurred in the Cuicatlán Cañada, a transportation corridor through the mountains north of the Valley of Oaxaca. See Redmond, *A Fuego y Sangre*.

29. Stephen A. Kowalewski, "Prehispanic Settlement Patterns of the Central Part of the Valley of Oaxaca, Mexico" (unpublished Ph.D. diss., University of Arizona, 1976); Blanton, Kowalewski, Feinman, and Appel, *Monte Albán's Hinterland, Part I*.

30. Laura M. Finsten, "Cultural Frontiers and System Boundaries in Prehispanic Oaxaca," in *Proceedings of the Chacmool 1992 Conference on Cultures In Contact*, 1995.

31. Mary G. Hodge, *Aztec City-States* (Museum of Anthropology, University of Michigan, Memoir 18, 1984); Blanton, Kowalewski, Feinman, and Appel, *Monte Albán's Hinterland, Part I*, pp. 307–366; Spores, *The Mixtec Kings and Their People*; Spores, *The Mixtecs in Ancient and Colonial Times*.

32. Antonio de Herrera y Tordesillas, *Historia General de los Hechos de los Castellanos en las Islas y Tierrafirme del Mar Oceano*, 15 vol. (Madrid: Academia de la Historia, 1947; original 1601–1615).

33. Blanton, Kowalewski, Feinman, and Appel, *Monte Albán's Hinterland, Part I*, pp. 345–348.

34. J. Michael Elam, "Defensible and Fortified Sites," in Blanton, Kowalewski, Feinman, and Appel, *Monte Albán's Hinterland, Part I*, pp. 385–408.

35. Peter Gerhard, *A Guide to the Historical Geography of New Spain*, 2nd ed. rev. (Norman: University of Oklahoma Press, 1993), pp. 199–200.

36. Laura Finsten, Stephen A. Kowelewski, Charlotte A. Smith, Richard D. Garvin, and Mark D. Borland, "Circular Architecture and Symbolic Boundaries in the Mixtec Sierra, Oaxaca," *Ancient Mesoamerica* 7 (1996): 19–27.

37. Laura Finsten, "Frontier and Periphery in Southern Mexico: The Mixtec Sierra in Highland Oaxaca," in Peter N. Peregrine and Gary M. Feinman, eds., *Pre-Columbian World Systems* (Madison, WI: Prehistory Press, 1996).

38. Gerhard, *A Guide to the Historical Geography of New Spain*, p. 203.

39. Blanton, Kowalewski, Feinman, and Finsten, *Ancient Mesoamerica*, pp. 129–135.

40. Mary G. Hodge, "Aztec Market Systems," *National Geographic Research and Exploration* 8 (1992): 428–445; Michael E. Smith, "Long-Distance Trade under the Aztec Empire: The Archaeological Evidence," *Ancient Mesoamerica* 1 (1990): 153–169.

SUGGESTED READINGS

✶ Blanton, Richard E., Stephen A. Kowalewski, Gary M. Feinman, and Laura M. Finsten. *Ancient Mesoamerica: A Comparison of Change in Three Regions*, 2nd ed. rev. Cambridge: Cambridge University Press, 1993. A good introduction to the prehistory of three key regions of Mesoamerica and to major issues in Mesoamerican archaeology, including the value of regional and larger-scale approaches.

Marcus, Joyce. "Zapotec Writing." *Scientific American* 242 (1980): 50–64. A clear introduction to early Oaxacan hieroglyphic writing.

Marcus, Joyce. "Political Fluctuations in Mesoamerica." *National Geographic Research and Exploration* 8 (1992): 392–411. Illustrates shifts in the size of political units over time for several Mesoamerican regions.

Renfrew, Colin, and Paul Bahn. *Archaeology: Theories, Methods, and Practice*. New York: Thames and Hudson, 1991. Although lengthy and tough sledding in places, this excellent introduction to archaeology is particularly strong in relating research methods and problems. Pages 446–454 summarize the results of research in Oaxaca.

Sabloff, Jeremy A. *The Cities of Ancient Mexico: Reconstructing a Lost World*. New York: Thames and Hudson, 1989. Chapter 3 deals specifically with Oaxaca; see the chapters on Teotihuacán and the Aztecs for comparison.

Exploring Aztalan and Its Role in Mississippian Societies

Lynne Goldstein

Aztalan is the name of an archaeological site located on the west bank of the Crawfish River in Jefferson County, Wisconsin (see Figure 21-1 on page 338). Aztalan is probably the most famous archaeological site in Wisconsin, as well as a National Landmark; the site is now also a state park. Aztalan dates to the Mississippian time period, approximately A.D. 1000–1300. Mississippian cultures were among the most complex and geographically extensive ancient cultures in what is now the United States. The organization of villages reflects that complexity with distinct areas in which houses were laid out in organized rows and groupings, flat-topped mounds (often called platform or temple mounds because many of them were used for public buildings and ceremonies), plazas, and stockades. There were a number of different levels of social status within Mississippian society, with a ruling elite at the top of the organizational structure. The Mississippian economy was based on agriculture.

Aztalan can be classified as a Mississippian site on the basis of several criteria. Artifacts found at the site are those associated with Mississippian cultures, and a number of radiocarbon dates from the site indicate a Mississippian time period. The main part of the Aztalan site is about twenty-one acres in size, and this area was enclosed within a wooden stockade with bastions or watchtowers along its walls (see Figure 21-2 on page 339). Archaeologists generally consider Aztalan to be the most northerly large Mississippian village.

When I moved to Wisconsin, I decided to examine Aztalan more closely to see if I could provide a clearer view of the site and its role in the larger Mississippian cultural system. Before I explain my research strategy, however, some additional background information is needed.

There has been some question about how Aztalan got its name. The name sounds vaguely Aztec and it has been reported that the Aztecs spoke of a

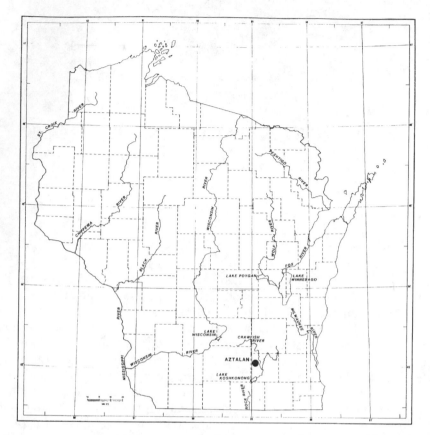

FIGURE 21-1   LOCATION OF THE AZTALAN SITE WITHIN THE STATE OF WISCONSIN

land to the north called "Aztlan." Does this site represent that place and, if so, is it related to the Aztecs? The simple answer is no. Aztalan got its name in the mid-1800s when some local European settlers came across the site and wrote a description of it for a Milwaukee newspaper. Judge Nathaniel Hyer first tagged the site with the name "Aztalan"; apparently he got this idea from the writings of a German naturalist and traveler named Baron Friedrich Heinrich Alexander von Humboldt (1769–1859).[1] Von Humboldt wrote about his travels in Middle America and about the history of the Indians of the Valley of Mexico. He talked about the legend of the Aztecs coming from a place in the north called Aztlan. Judge Hyer, who first drew a map of the Aztalan site for publication, decided that this site must be the place the Aztecs mentioned.

There is no evidence for a relationship between the Aztecs and the people at Aztalan, and even though archaeologists have long discussed the possibility of interactions between Mississippian people and people in Mexico, those interactions were probably limited to indirect contact through trade

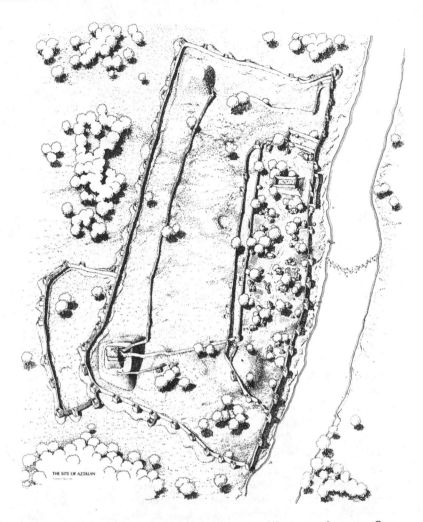

THE SITE OF AZTALAN

Figure 21-2 Artist's Reconstruction of What the Aztalan Site Might Have Looked Like When Occupied

Note that the inner and outer stockade walls were used.

with intermediary groups. No archaeologist today thinks the people at Aztalan were related to the Aztecs.

Another necessary piece of background information relates to other groups that were around when Mississippian people were living at Aztalan. The group that came before the Mississippian people, but who were also in part contemporaneous with them, are called Late Woodland. There are a variety of Late Woodland groups, but in general Late Woodland society was less complex than Mississippian society. These groups had smaller villages *[handwritten annotations: "(2) 5 WISCONSIN", "LATE WOODLAND → ONEOTA → ONEOTA", "↘ MISSISSIPPIAN AZTALAN"]*

without the elite hierarchy and organization present at Mississippian sites. Artifacts were less elaborate and they did not use temple mounds or have plazas within their villages. They rarely created walled villages. Nonetheless, these Late Woodland people lived in permanent or semi-permanent villages, made distinctive pottery and other artifacts, used the bow and arrow, and built mounds. Some of them were gardeners and farmers, although none practiced agriculture to the extent that Mississippian people did. The Mississippian period itself is commonly subdivided into Mississippian and Oneota, with the distinction representing time, geography, and organization. Like Late Woodland groups, Oneota people lived in villages and some of them farmed, but they farmed more intensively and had a more complex organization than Late Woodland peoples, though not as complex as Mississippian people. In Wisconsin, Oneota culture is found in several areas across the state.[2] Mississippian sites, however, are rare in Wisconsin and Aztalan is the clearest example of a Mississippian village in the state. Although Late Woodland began before Mississippian and Oneota apparently continued after Mississippian, there appears to have been some contemporaneity among the groups for a period of time.

Archaeologists have considered Aztalan an unusual or puzzling Mississippian site for the following reasons:

[handwritten annotation: "PUZZLES"]

1. Aztalan is farther north than other Mississippian villages, and there do not seem to be Mississippian villages between Aztalan and comparably sized villages in central and southern Illinois.

2. The banks of the Crawfish River seem to be an odd location for the site since the Crawfish is not a large river, does not have rich floodplains, and does not have direct links to the Mississippi or Illinois rivers, both famous rivers for Mississippian settlements.

3. In other areas, there is a consistent Mississippian settlement pattern, consisting of a settlement hierarchy with a large village and mound complex, a series of smaller sites around this center, and small farmsteads around the smaller sites. For Aztalan, however, we know of no other Mississippian sites in the immediate vicinity and the site seems to have existed as a single entity.

4. As noted earlier, Mississippian pottery and artifacts have been found at Aztalan but earlier Late Woodland period pottery has also been found. There has been considerable speculation as to whether the site was used by different peoples at different times, or by two different groups at the same time.

RESEARCH QUESTIONS

My first task in designing a research strategy focusing on Aztalan and its unusual characteristics was to read all the literature I could find on the site and the area. The most famous research on Aztalan was conducted by Samuel A.

Barrett of the Milwaukee Public Museum in the early 1900s, and a group of archaeologists in the 1950s and 1960s who were helping to create interpretive exhibits at the site just after it was made a state park.[3] A variety of amateur and professional archaeologists had speculated about the site, but relatively few people had worked there or in the general area. It is significant that no one had ever looked systematically around Aztalan to see whether there were related sites. A number of sites had been reported for the general area and no one had reported any Mississippian sites, but the argument that Aztalan was isolated seemed tenuous if no one had actually looked for associated sites.

In order to understand why someone would settle at Aztalan, we have to first understand what the landscape and setting looked like at the time. Even if Aztalan is an isolated outpost, one has to know more about the setting to understand why that location may have been desirable.

Finally, the confusing situation of pottery and artifacts found at Aztalan—the apparent concurrent association of both Mississippian and earlier Late Woodland groups—needs to be resolved.

How do these observations lead to a research design? The general and specific research questions that arise from these observations are fairly obvious and include the following question sets:

1. What was the landscape and natural setting at the time of Aztalan's occupation? What did the topography look like? What grew where? What could you eat? What could you hunt? Where could you find water? Where could you plant?

2. What was the human occupation in the area surrounding Aztalan? Who lived where? Who was local, and who came here to settle from elsewhere?

3. How do we tease apart the temporal sequence of Aztalan's occupation? Was there an earlier Late Woodland occupation, followed by an independent Mississippian occupation? Were they concurrent? Overlapping? Or did one become the other?

The remainder of this chapter will examine how we found the answers to these questions and the conclusions that we reached about the nature of Aztalan.

THE LANDSCAPE AND SETTING: ANSWERING QUESTION SET 1

Answering question set 1 is a problem because things today obviously do not look not the way they looked around A.D. 1000. In fact, with the present roads, houses, and farms, it is difficult to imagine the landscape before the arrival of European settlers.

Landscape Evidence

In most places, and especially within the United States, there are <u>historic documents and other maps and data</u> that can be used to determine what the landscape was like before it was totally altered by modern settlement. In Wisconsin, one critical part of that information is provided by the General Land Office surveys that were conducted in the 1830s and 1840s. Wisconsin was located in what was called the Northwest Territories, and just before this land was opened and sold to homesteaders and settlers, surveyors went over the land to lay out the land description system that is still in use today. That system divided the land into "townships," which are six miles on a side. The individual thirty-six square-mile chunks within each township are called "sections." A section is a square mile, or 640 acres. However, people often did not want to buy a whole section or they wanted to describe a portion of a section, so the system divides sections into smaller pieces. Since sections are square, one of the simplest ways to divide them is into smaller squares. Thus, sections are divided into four smaller, equal-sized squares called quarter-sections (or 1/4-sections), and each of these quarter sections includes 160 acres (640/4 = 160). A quarter section is one-half mile on each side. Each of these quarter sections can be similarly divided into four equal-sized squares called quarter-quarter sections, with each quarter-quarter section including 40 acres of land (160/4 = 40). A quarter-quarter section is 1/4 mile on each side. By keeping the system consistent and in squares, it was easier to locate a place on the ground and on the map.

In implementing this system on the ground, the land surveyors relied on careful notes of what they did and what they saw. The surveyors tried to mark what they called "<u>witness trees</u>" at every section corner, to better flag and identify the corners and edges of the new land units. They noted the <u>type</u> of each witness tree, and they also noted the <u>kinds of trees and terrain they traversed</u> as they set in their lines and mapped out the land divisions. Since a surveyor often conducted the survey for a large area, the individual notes are fairly consistent and a researcher can get a good idea of problems and biases in the data by reading a surveyor's notes. Surveyors would even occasionally note mounds or other archaeological or historic Indian sites.

Botanists discovered that one could use the surveyors' notes to recreate the pre-European settlement vegetation for an area. A variety of specific techniques to create such reconstructions have been developed by botanists and others, and botanists have suggested that these vegetation reconstructions for the Aztalan area are probably fair representations of what the area was like for the last five thousand years prior to European settlement. When these data are combined with information on soils and on topography, one can begin to get a more accurate idea of what the landscape may have looked like at that time. Figure 21-3 represents the vegetation reconstruction for the Aztalan area.

When the vegetation information has been gathered, one can reconstruct what plants and animals might have been available to those who settled at

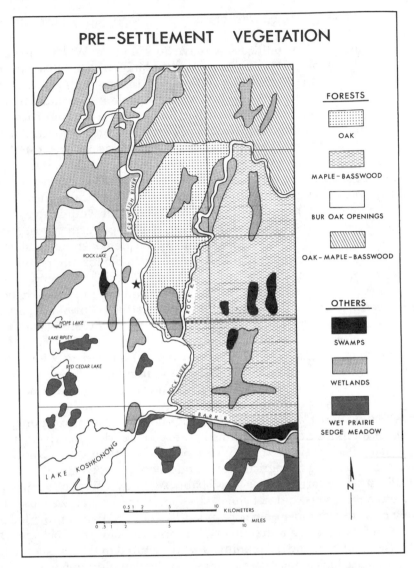

FIGURE 21-3 RECONSTRUCTION OF THE NINETEENTH-CENTURY VEGETATION IN THE AZTALAN AREA

The star denotes the location of the Aztalan site.

Aztalan; knowing the vegetation and the distribution and natural history of animals allows one to deduce the resources that were likely present in each vegetation zone. Knowing how plants and animals were used by different Native American groups can help to determine which zones were most productive, and in which seasons they might be most important. This information is then combined with information on topography, physiography, and water resources.

There is one problem with what we have done thus far: We have assumed that prehistoric people had no real impact on the landscape and that what the surveyors found in the 1840s was a close approximation to the way things were for thousands of years before. Is this a reasonable assumption? Yes and no. Although aboriginal people clearly had an impact on the landscape, it is generally thought that their impact was not major according to the scale at which we have created reconstructions. However, it has also been suggested that the landscape the surveyors saw was partially a result of burning by prehistoric peoples. Some botanists have suggested that the way early farmers (like the people at Aztalan) cleared land was to periodically burn off the trees and other vegetation. Obviously, if this were so it would have a dramatic impact on the landscape—we know this happened further west on the plains. More recently, however, other botanists have demonstrated that lightning strikes could just as easily have been responsible for any patterns of large scale burning. For cultures prior to Aztalan it might be important to work this out more carefully, but for this period and our purposes we need only be reasonably certain that the pattern reconstructed from the surveyor's notes resembles the landscape that the Aztalan folks would have used. And we are reasonably certain that it does.

For Aztalan, the analysis of the site's setting yields a variety of important information. First, we know that Aztalan's location on the Crawfish River provided easy access to transportation and to a variety of aquatic resources. Further, we discovered that the Crawfish River has a number of artesian springs feeding into it, and since these springs flow all year the river does not freeze over for as long a period of time in the winter as do other rivers in the area. Aztalan itself is situated in an oak opening, a setting that would have allowed easy clearing for agriculture. In addition, the soils at this spot are especially good for farming. This is probably significant since other groups, who were not farmers, did not choose this location. Aztalan was also reasonably close to a number of major wetlands. These wetlands provided access to a variety of different resources, including trees for the stockade wall and houses, and deer and other animals who pastured in the marshes in the winter. A careful look at the map indicates that Aztalan's location would have afforded those who lived there easy access to every available vegetation zone in the region, meaning that all plant and animal resources were accessible. This was a good place to live, especially as a farmer. Finally, Aztalan's setting gave the people who lived there a good view of the surrounding countryside but was not so high or exposed that people would have been battered by winds and other elements.

This research on the early vegetation and setting provided most of the answers to the first set of research questions and suggested that there were better and worse areas in which to live within the region. However, the people who settled at Aztalan needed a place that also provided access to fertile and easily workable farm land.

In order to see whether other Mississippian people settled in the Aztalan area, we would have to look in landscape zones throughout the region. Why? Because even though we might be able to guess at some of the best places to live, Mississippian people may have had a variety of types of settlements, including special purpose settlements (like hunting camps). If we did not look in every zone, we would never be able to make confident statements about where people did and did not settle.

THE SURVEY: ANSWERING QUESTION SET 2

Site Locations

SURVEY DESIGN

The second set of questions is related to the first but requires field work rather than working with archival sources. How do you find out where people lived? You go out and look. The technical term for going out and looking is archaeological survey. The region surrounding Aztalan, depending on your ambition, is no less than 20 square miles and could conceivably be 1,200 square miles. Clearly we cannot walk or look at every square inch even of the smaller number, so we use the same statistical technique that political pollsters use: the stratified random sample. The difference is that instead of stratifying a population of people based on such characteristics as income, party affiliation, and so on, we stratify units of land area based on elevation and side of river. What we are trying to figure out is whether and how people may have used the land, so we have to sample the land. What land unit do we use? I chose the quarter quarter section as a sampling unit (the quarter-quarter section was described in an earlier portion of this chapter and corresponds to one voter in the political poll). This choice was made largely for practical reasons: As discussed earlier, modern farming land in the area is divided into sections and portions thereof; the political system in the rural portions of the Midwestern United States divides the land by section, quarter-section, and quarter-quarter section, thus making it simple to sort the area into sample units and keep track of them. People often own parcels of land in quarter-quarter section chunks, and these units are easy to locate on the ground, on topographic maps, and on aerial photographs.

Figure 21-4 on page 346 outlines the areas eventually encompassed by what I call the Crawfish-Rock Archaeological Project (the labeled areas on the map will be discussed later). This area was chosen because it included a major portion of the Rock and Crawfish rivers, and the region represents all of the major landform zones documented in southeastern Wisconsin. A systematic survey here should provide a reasonable idea of which environmental settings were preferred by different groups. Based on what was known about Mississippian settlement patterns elsewhere, if Aztalan had a typical Mississippian pattern, we should be able to find such sites within this region.

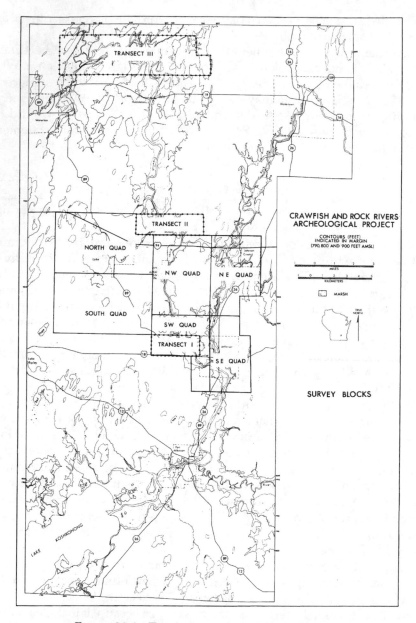

FIGURE 21-4   THE AZTALAN AREA SURVEY REGION,
WITH THE BROAD SURVEY BLOCKS AND TRANSECTS OUTLINED

Only one systematic archaeological survey had ever been conducted in the Aztalan area, and this work was limited to a small area in the immediate vicinity of the site.[4] Because so little of the overall area was known, my other decision was to make the project multistage in design—the results of each phase were used to plan the next phase. Rather than design a strategy and be bound by it, I designed a series of steps that were by their nature open to modification. This approach meant that I could use what I had learned from the previous stage to refine the next stage of work—whatever I learned could be immediately put to use, and if I had made a major mistake in designing the survey, it could be fixed.

For each year of the survey, the majority of the survey work was done by the University of Wisconsin-Milwaukee Archaeology Field School. Students sign up for the field school as they would for any other course, but they spend their "class time" living in tents and working out in the field looking for and excavating archaeological sites. Specifically, students spent the first weeks of their field school surveying, then spent a week mapping and preparing to excavate, and finally spent the last four weeks of the field school excavating the site or sites chosen for that summer. While in the field, all students also participate in washing, labeling, and inventorying the materials they collect.

For all parts of the survey, both pedestrian survey and shovel probing techniques were employed. Pedestrian survey refers to the process of systematically walking plowed fields looking for artifacts, chipping debris, or other evidence of human habitation. Shovel probing is a technique used when one cannot see the ground surface, as in a woods or pasture. A shovel is used to excavate a hole at specified intervals. The hole is approximately thirty to forty centimeters in diameter, and is usually excavated to a depth of approximately thirty to forty centimeters. The excavator carefully examines the soil to look for evidence of cultural occupation and for evidence of artifacts or debris. Shovel probing is time consuming but provides a systematic and simple way to carefully examine unplowed areas; it is often the only way archaeologists can find undisturbed archaeological sites. Pedestrian survey was done in plowed and/or planted fields at intervals reaching a maximum of three meters (although generally one to two meter intervals were used), and shovel probing was done in areas of dense ground cover or woods at ten-meter intervals. When material was found, flags were placed in the ground to note the location (if possible). Site areas were paced off and estimated, then located on an aerial photo. All areas walked were mapped on air photos and U.S. Geological Survey topographic maps (these are standard maps that archaeologists and geologists, as well as hikers and backpackers, often use).

The survey took a total of eight years to complete. The survey's multiphase design can be outlined as follows:

Phase 1   The primary purpose of this initial phase was to familiarize us with the general area. An east-west transect, approximately three-and-a-half miles long by one-and-a-half miles wide, was surveyed as intensively as possible. The transect was located at the northern end of the research area. In

Figure 21-4 (on page 346), this transect is in the center portion of the area labeled "Transect III." Because nearly all physiographic zones in the region were represented in this relatively small area, this transect provided a good introduction to the potential environmental variability of the region. I was particularly interested in the extent to which different kinds of occupations were associated with certain landscape types. In addition to finding a number of sites, we learned that many of the important distinctions we saw in the landscape analysis could be translated on the ground by examining differences in elevation: Areas below 790 feet in elevation are generally wetlands, the area between 790 and 800 feet seems to be a distinct terrace that yields many sites, and the areas above 800 feet were upland zones.

Phase 2   This phase included sampling three transects cross-cutting the Crawfish River (labeled Transects I, II, III in Figure 21-4 on page 346). The northernmost transect (III) was an expansion of the Phase 1 transect to include more of the associated upland areas and a greater portion of the Crawfish Valley width. The center transect (II) represented the southern edge of the region's major swamps and marshes and the point where a major secondary stream (Rock Creek) enters the Crawfish. The southern transect (I) was near the confluence of the Crawfish and Rock Rivers. The three transects represent the north, south, and center of the research area. Based on knowledge gained from Phase 1, each transect was stratified in two ways: first by side of river and second by three strata based on elevation, topography, vegetation, and soils. The three strata included the following: *lowlands*—areas that are relatively flat, subject to flooding, and adjacent to rivers, lakes, and wetlands; *terraces*—visually distinct, relatively flat and wide segments of land often adjacent to lowlands but above flood stage; and *uplands*—lands that are higher in elevation than the lowlands and terraces, not necessarily flat, and generally at some distance from rivers, wetlands, and lakes.

Phase 3   Prior to the third season, the similarity in the kinds of sites and settings we were finding suggested that my strategy should probably change: (1) Focus should shift to the Rock River as well as the Crawfish for comparative purposes, and (2) a broader area must be surveyed. The area I had originally defined was not large enough to include all of the diversity in the region and there were enough differences between the Rock and Crawfish rivers to enable us to compare the two. The Phase 3 survey represents the southern portion of the research area, from below the major swamps and marshes on the Crawfish to just south of the Crawfish and Rock River confluence. The east-west boundaries were drawn to approximate the major drainage limits.

Phase 4   During the next two summers work focused on finishing the Phase 3 sample and beginning a 15 percent stratified proportional sample of the Rock Lake area to the west of Aztalan. As in Phases 2 and 3, the Rock

Lake area was stratified geographically (into a North and South quad; see Figure 21-4 on page 346) as well as physiographically. The Rock Lake area is physiographically somewhat different from the river valleys but the three strata used previously have analogs in this area. Vegetation and topographic differences in this area were expected to have had an impact on prehistoric site location; in general, fewer types of resources would be accessible, and we thought we would find fewer archaeological sites.

SURVEY RESULTS

A 15 percent stratified random sample of a 70-square-mile area meant that we had to survey a total of 170 sample units (that is, 170 40-acre plots of land). Multiplying this, we might have had to cover 6,800 acres of land. Of course, 100 percent of each unit was not surveyable. In fact, only 84 percent, or 5,711 acres, could theoretically be surveyed due to a variety of obstacles, and we actually surveyed 4,398 acres, or 77 percent of what could theoretically be surveyed, or 65 percent of the ideal total. We had set a requirement of covering at least 50 percent of what was theoretically coverable, and the acres not surveyed were skipped because of ground cover conditions or lack of permission. In addition, even though we surveyed 4,398 acres, we have actually accounted for 5,487 acres, or 96 percent of the amount surveyable. These additional acres were primarily wetlands and were treated as part of a special "survey strategy."

These wetlands can be counted as part of the surveyed area because, early in the project, we carefully and systematically surveyed a variety of wetland units. Some had been drained, some were still wet. In each case we found nothing and concluded that if there was something there, it was buried too deeply to locate with standard survey techniques. We therefore developed a strategy for such wetland units, and we employed the strategy throughout the survey. Any unit with wetlands was examined for low rises; these rises would then be surveyed. While many rises can be determined from USGS topographic maps, others can only be seen from an on-site inspection. Since these low rises often had archaeological sites on them, we inspected each wetland unit in the sample for such rises. If there was doubt about a rise, we surveyed it.

Tables 21-1 and 21-2 (on page 350) provide a general survey summary; the strata listed (lowland, terrace, upland; see earlier description of these categories) were delineated and sampled within each of the broad survey blocks or quads outlined in Figure 21-4 (on page 346). It must be noted that sometimes we surveyed areas that were not selected as part of our sampling procedure; this was done for a variety of reasons, ranging from curiosity to a specific invitation from a landowner. These non-sample units are called "out of sample." Figure 21-5 (on page 351) shows the units surveyed, differentiating between those surveyed in and out of sample. In conducting

TABLE 21-1   SURVEY SUMMARY

	IN SAMPLE	OUT OF SAMPLE	TOTALS
# of Units Surveyed	170	107	277
Acres Surveyed	4398	1134	5532
(Total Acreage Accounted for)	(5487)		(6621)
# of Sites Discovered	261	140	401

TABLE 21-2   SURVEY SUMMARY BY STRATA

	LOWLAND	TERRACE	UPLAND	TOTALS
# of Units/Stratum	34	32	104	170
# of Sites/Stratum	32	55	174	261
# of Units with Sites/Stratum	17	25	80	122
Ratio: Units with Sites to Units/Stratum	0.50	0.78	0.77	0.72

certain kinds of statistical analysis, we cannot include the results of surveys in out-of-sample units when making generalizations about the whole area. We do not ignore what we found, but since the areas were not selected as part of the sampling scheme, we cannot use these units to make reliable generalizations about the distribution or density of sites in the region. We can, however, use the data for other kinds of analysis.

The tables indicate the density of archaeological sites in the region—401 sites were recorded in 277 units, an average of 1.45 sites per unit. Table 21-2 suggests that the sites are differentially distributed within the region—the relative proportions of units with sites are highest in the terrace and upland strata. Overall, 72 percent of the sample units yielded at least one archaeological site.

The survey, along with what we had already learned from the landscape analysis, told us a variety of things about sites in the region. Not surprisingly, sites are not randomly distributed throughout the region but are clustered. Site clusters tend to occur in seasonally high productivity areas that are located at the juncture of prime resource zones and wetlands. Similarly, units that yield no prehistoric sites are generally found in "extreme" conditions: very wet (e.g., the middle of a swamp), very dry, at a great distance from water, or in an area with highly irregular land surfaces. While

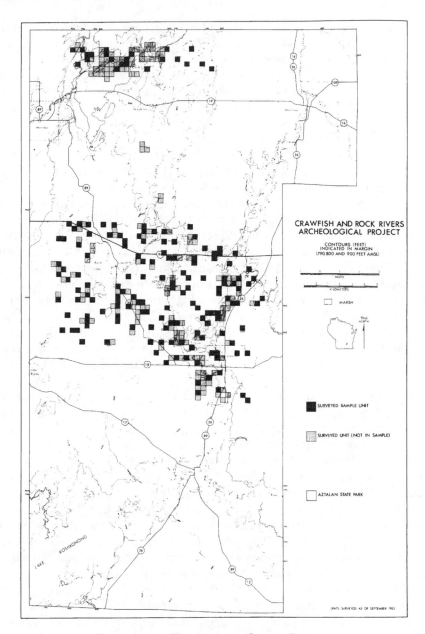

CRAWFISH AND ROCK RIVERS
ARCHEOLOGICAL PROJECT

CONTOURS (FEET)
INDICATED IN MARGIN
(790, 800 AND 900 FEET AMSL)

MARSH

SURVEYED SAMPLE UNIT

SURVEYED UNIT (NOT IN SAMPLE)

AZTALAN STATE PARK

**FIGURE 21-5   THE AZTALAN SURVEY REGION,
WITH INDIVIDUAL SAMPLE UNITS INDICATED**

people don't like living *in* swamps or marshes, they certainly prefer to be
near them; many sites in the sample are located on high ground very near
or in major wetlands.

Large dense sites tend to be within the terrace stratum, especially along the Crawfish and near major wetlands. Many are at or near stream junctures or confluences, or at the juncture of a stream with an intermittent stream. These sites are all within prime resource zones. Another characteristic of large dense sites is that pottery is found almost exclusively in these locations. Sites with pottery are always within prime resource zones and usually occur on the river bank or terrace. These sites tend to be on the east side of the Crawfish on interior river bends, near major wetlands.

Although sites of all time periods were found, there were very few sites specifically dating to the Mississippian period, and those sites with Mississippian components had a very sparse Mississippian presence.

Landscape choices are often made because of the presence of particular plant and/or animal resources. We analyzed the different vegetation zones in the region and found that wetlands were potentially the most productive zone. Wetlands provide a source for food year-round, especially in the winter when food elsewhere may be more difficult to find. However, since it was also clear that people generally would not choose to live *in* a wetland, we had to determine a method to examine whether or not this kind of selection was in operation. We inspected a 0.5 kilometer (0.31 mile) circle around each site, as a way to measure the site environment. Using vegetation reconstructions for the area, we then recorded both the primary and secondary vegetation types in that circle. Our results demonstrated that oak forest, oak openings, and marsh are the preferred zones, and the concurrence of marsh and oak openings is particularly strong. Oak forests may coincide with either oak openings or marsh. By a series of other tests we determined that this pattern is not merely a reflection of the natural landscape, so we assume that these concurrences had cultural significance.

For people in all time periods, proximity to marsh is critical—with a few notable exceptions, over 50 percent of the sites assignable to a time period have marsh as a primary or secondary vegetation type within 0.5 kilometers of the site. However, examining those sites that do not fit this pattern, we find sites with Mississippian components nearly all in oak forests and/or oak openings. Placement near marshes seems not to be as critical. Because it is easier to clear an oak opening for agriculture, it is possible that this shift is due to the importance of agriculture in Mississippian times.

What do these observations tell us about Aztalan? After completing the survey I concluded that many of the conclusions drawn by previous archaeologists were true: Aztalan is an isolated outpost that does not have a settlement system immediately associated with it. It is significant that there are almost no Mississippian sites of any type in the region, suggesting that this area was not attractive to Mississippian or Oneota groups. (The significance of these observations will be discussed later.) Completion of the survey allowed us to move to the third question set and focus on the Aztalan site itself.

At this point, readers might be asking: Weren't you embarrassed after spending eight years proving that earlier archaeologists were right in their guesses about the almost nonexistent Mississippian occupation in the area? The answer is no, because those speculations were just that, and were not based on data. We not only can demonstrate that the Mississippian occupation was minimal, we also can do so with a high degree of certainty. Further, we learned much about the occupation of the region that no one else had ever known, including the fact that there were at least a few small, scattered Mississippian sites. Providing evidence that an earlier hypothesis or speculation is probably right does not show that we did more work than was necessary—it demonstrates that earlier archaeologists made a lucky guess. In other parts of the state, similar guesses have proved to be wrong.

THE OCCUPATION(S) OF AZTALAN: ANSWERING QUESTION SET 3

To address the third question set, which asks about the nature and number of occupations at Aztalan, it was necessary to work at the site. Looking over maps and notes from Barrett's excavations in the early 1900s and some later excavations in the 1950s and 1960s, it was apparent that pottery and other diagnostic artifacts dating to both Late Woodland and Mississippian cultures had been found at the site. The only way to determine the relationship between the two cultures was to find an area of the site that both had used, where their "garbage" might be found in relationship to each other, that is, with the older stuff on the bottom and the more recent stuff above.

The notions of superposition and stratigraphic relationship are important ones in archaeology. An example is probably the best way to explain the ideas. Let us say that every day when you came home you took off the clothes you were wearing and dumped them in a corner of your room. By the end of the week, assuming nothing had happened that would cause you to disturb your pile, the clothes you had worn earlier in the week would be lower in the pile than the clothes you wore more recently. This notion represents the principle of superposition: The older stuff is below, or deeper than, the more recent stuff. This same idea applies to soils and archaeological sites. In the area in which people live, they deposit garbage and go about other tasks in their daily lives. At the same time, winds blow, floods happen, and other events cause the evidence of this activity to be gradually covered over by a layer of soil. We can see evidence of this happening today (think about windstorms, floods, or even dust), but it is particularly apparent when a place is abandoned. Over a long period of time, enough soil can build up so that you cannot tell that other people were living there. Another culture comes along later, likes the same spot, settles there, produces their own garbage, builds their houses, and so on. When an archaeologist comes along at a later time, he or she will first find the most recent culture (it is going to be closer to the ground surface), then find other cultures in order below it. If there is not much soil development, these different occupations can be right on top of each other, and it can be quite difficult to figure out which is which since each may have inadvertently dug into an earlier occupation in building houses and hearths. The principle of ordering is superposition; the actual strata, layers, or ordered culture sequences are known as the stratigraphy.

One of the best places to find a stratigraphic sequence or segment is in a garbage dump, or what archaeologists call a midden. Middens are especially good places to find stratigraphy because they are places where people dump garbage and where they are unlikely to later return and dig things up.

At Aztalan, Barrett had excavated what he called a midden along the river bank. The different strata had been clear and distinct, and although he excavated a portion of the midden, we thought much of it should be left. Excavating in the midden would allow us to examine a stratigraphic sequence to determine the superposition of cultures and would allow us to compare what we found with what Barrett had found earlier; we might be better able to apply some of what we learned to what Barrett had discovered fifty years ago.

Excavations in the midden were important for another reason: There has been some debate among archaeologists as to whether the midden deposit actually reflects a dump, or if it is the result of sheet erosion or slope wash from the upslope or higher areas of the site. When archaeologists excavated at Aztalan in the 1960s, they discovered that in the plaza area of the site, pits and other features were very shallow while those found under a mound were quite deep. The archaeologist directing the project thought the plaza area features might be shallow because of erosion caused by all the farming that had been done in this area of the site. The answer to this question is critical for site interpretation: If the dump is the result of erosion, then the so-called plaza area of the site (see Figure 21-6) may actually be nothing more than an eroded surface, and the midden may be the result of living debris washed downhill from the plaza. In other words, the high degree of structure described for the site may be nothing more than an artifact of nature. Given the significance of resolving this question, we proposed putting test pits in both the river bank and plaza areas of the site.

Our fieldwork at Aztalan demonstrated several important factors concerning the nature of the site. First, midden area excavations suggest a stratigraphic separation between Late Woodland and Mississippian ceramic types. This means there was some time difference between the occupation of the site by the two cultures. Further, the Late Woodland ceramics (as well as the Mississippian ceramics) were generally different from those found elsewhere in the general region, suggesting that Aztalan might represent a location settled by people from outside the region at two separate times.

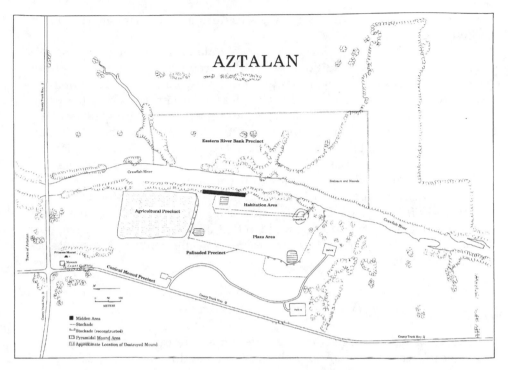

FIGURE 21-6   MAP OF THE AZTALAN SITE,
WITH LOCATIONS OF MAJOR SITE FEATURES NOTED

Second, although large portions of the river bank midden are clearly the result of erosion and slope wash from higher elevations, purposeful aboriginal activity is responsible for a significant degree of midden accumulation. Features encountered during midden excavations suggest aboriginal dumping of kitchen garbage, hearth cleanings, and broken pottery. We were actually able to separate different episodes of dumping.

Third, archaeological deposits in the river bank area exhibit a high degree of stratigraphic integrity. In fact, this area of the site may constitute the only remaining undisturbed deposits within the site proper.

Finally, plaza area excavations demonstrated that remnants of subsurface features do exist in this part of the site, and the structures found were Late Woodland in origin. Although integrity of plaza deposits has been seriously compromised by agricultural practices in the first half of the twentieth century, a substantial amount of information is probably still recoverable. Identification of the nature and extent of these remains could significantly alter current notions of the formation and structure of Aztalan. It appears as though the plaza area of the site may have been used as a plaza in Mississippian times, but as a living area during the earlier Late Woodland occupation.

Radiocarbon dating of a site such as Aztalan is an ongoing process. We were able to have an additional five radiocarbon samples processed from our excavations at the site. From these samples, we can conclude that the Late Woodland materials found in the plaza area represent an earlier occupation, and the midden seems to represent a fairly tightly grouped set of occupations, ranging from Late Woodland to Mississippian times. Although there are some strata in which both Late Woodland and Mississippian ceramics occur, there are earlier strata with only Late Woodland ceramics and more recent strata with only Mississippian ceramics.

The answer to the important questions about Aztalan's site structure is thus "all of the above": The plaza area served as both a living area and a plaza, slope wash did add to a midden that had been created as a result of aboriginal dumping of garbage, and there were apparently two separate occupations of the site.

HAVE WE ANSWERED OUR QUESTIONS?

Here I will take the answers to the different question sets and pull them together to create a general story about Aztalan and its place in southeastern Wisconsin's past. In doing so, I will also address various methodological issues that were important in what we did.

Examination of the landscape made it clear that the Crawfish-Rock Valley region was an area that would have provided a rich variety of food and other resources to people who settled here over the past five thousand years. However, the analysis also demonstrated what was not obvious when we began the project—the importance of wetlands in landscape use. Biologists and ecologists have recently rediscovered the importance of wetlands in maintaining our ecosystem but this was something that people from long ago already knew. Wetlands provide resources regularly, they provide storable resources, and they provide resources at times of year when other locations are less reliable. You can get food in a wetland in the winter, and it will be the last place to dry up in a drought. The extensive pattern of wetlands across southeastern Wisconsin is unusual and makes this area attractive for settlement.

Combining the information on landscapes with the data from our survey, it is not surprising to have found that the region is rich in archaeological sites. What is surprising, however, is that we found few sites that can be classified as Mississippian, or as the type of Late Woodland found at Aztalan. What is also surprising is that Aztalan is not in the same kind of location as other sites in the region; people can access all the different resources in the area, but the site is not adjacent to wetlands as so many other aboriginal village sites are.

Because we conducted a stratified random sample, we can make statements about the relative distribution of different kinds of sites in the region with some certainty. We can use the survey data as evidence that the two occupations at Aztalan—the Late Woodland and the Mississippian—apparently represent people coming from outside the region. We have found few other sites that have the same characteristic artifacts or structure. There are a number of sites with similar artifacts in northern and central Illinois, and it seems likely that Aztalan was settled by two groups who moved to this part of Wisconsin from northern Illinois at different times. This information may help explain why Aztalan is located where it is.

If Aztalan represents a Mississippian occupation populated at least in part from points south, then it might be in a competitive position with surrounding Late Woodland and Oneota groups. The village would not be set up in a location that was clearly claimed by another group (e.g., the Oneota around Lake Koshkonong to the south), nor one that would interfere with another group's activities. Location on the Crawfish makes sense because the oak openings allow easy farming, and aquatic resources are still readily available. From Aztalan's location, the extensive marshes are exploitable. Indeed, Aztalan's more riverine location would be most similar to environments further south. The few Mississippian sites found in the survey may represent seasonal camps for those living at Aztalan.

The earlier Late Woodland pottery found at Aztalan represents an earlier occupation, one whose presence elsewhere in the region is minimal. Such pottery is, however, found at other locations in Wisconsin, and is also found in portions of northern and central Illinois. These Late Woodland groups are more focused on farming than are the local Late Woodland groups, and it seems likely that they also moved to this region from the south.[5] This portion of the Crawfish River is similar to locations in northern Illinois, and this location may have been selected because it "looked like home." When Mississippian people later moved into these same areas of Illinois, they might have been told about a similar location "up north" in Wisconsin. Speculation about this aspect of our discoveries is beyond the scope of this chapter, but the idea of two separate occupations at Aztalan raises a number of questions for future research. Another topic for future research is the question of why people expanded their settlements into new territories.

The question of why people decided to build the Aztalan site *in* southeastern Wisconsin may be beyond the scope of this chapter, but we have been able to address a number of issues that help us to understand Aztalan's location *within* southeastern Wisconsin. We can address the question of why Aztalan is located on the Crawfish River, and why Aztalan is at that specific location along the Crawfish. As mentioned at the beginning of this chapter, archaeologists have viewed Aztalan's location as unusual; it is farther north than any other Mississippian site, and the Crawfish River does not appear to be a likely location for a Mississippian outpost. However, the location is quite reasonable in view of the ecological and cultural context. The Crawfish River can be used as a means of transportation to locations further north and west as well as further south and west, and the specific location of the site allows relatively easy access to all vegetation and resource zones present in the region.

Although the Rock River is a larger river than the Crawfish, the wetland resources available from Aztalan's position on the Crawfish are significantly richer than those available from a comparable position along the Rock. Soils along the west bank of the Crawfish are better drained than those east of the river and are thus more suitable for maize agriculture. The west bank of the Crawfish is characterized by oak openings or savannahs that are easier to clear for farming. These oak openings do not occur along the east bank of the Crawfish or along the Rock. Finally, the Crawfish River, although smaller than the Rock River, is apparently not as susceptible to long freezes in the winter because of concentrations of springs; both the river and its resources would be accessible for greater portions of the year.

With a difference in emphasis or degree of dependence upon agricultural food resources between Mississippian and Oneota people, it is possible that Mississippians would prefer the river bank location with its easier exploitation of the oak openings for intensive agriculture. Given that Lake Koshkonong (to the southwest of the Crawfish-Rock area) was probably occupied by Oneota people at the time of Aztalan's development, that occupation is perhaps one more reason to settle at the Aztalan locality.

This chapter has outlined a multi-stage research program, designed to focus on the nature of ancient land use in general, and the choices and adaptations made by the people at one specific location. How we went about finding the answers to our research questions resulted in a number of new questions, but also allowed us to learn something new about Aztalan itself and the larger Mississippian cultural system.

NOTES

1. Robert L. Hall, "Upper Mississippi and Middle Mississippi Relationships," *Wisconsin Archaeologist* 67 (1986): 365–369.
2. Guy Gibbon, "The Mississippian Tradition: Oneota Culture," *Wisconsin Archaeologist* 67 (1986): 314–338.
3. Samuel A. Barrett, "Ancient Aztalan," *Bulletin of the Public Museum of the City of Milwaukee*, vol. XIII (1933); David A. Baerreis, ed., "Aztalan," *Wisconsin Archaeologist*, special issue, 39 (1958).
4. Fred K. Steube, "Site Survey and Test Excavations in the Aztalan Area," *Wisconsin Archaeologist* 57 (1976): 198–259.
5. Philip H. Salkin, "The Late Woodland Stage in Southeastern Wisconsin," *Wisconsin Academy Review* 33 (1987): 75–79.

SUGGESTED READINGS

Emerson, Thomas E., and Barry L. Lewis, eds. *Cahokia and the Hinterlands: Middle Mississippian Cultures of the Midwest.* Urbana, IL: University of Illinois Press, 1991. The series of articles in this book document a series of Mississippian sites that have been investigated in the Midwest.

Goldstein, Lynne. "The Mysteries of Aztalan." *Wisconsin Academy Review* (Summer 1991): 28–34. An outline of Aztalan and its structure, written for the interested public.

Green, William A., Alice B. Kehoe, and James B. Stoltman, eds. "An Introduction to Wisconsin Archaeology: Background for Cultural Resource Planning." *Wisconsin Archaeologist*, special issue 67 (1986). This special issue provides individual articles on each of the major time periods in Wisconsin.

Ritzenthaler, Robert, *Prehistoric Indians of Wisconsin.* Milwaukee, WI: Milwaukee Public Museum, 1985. (Third revised edition by Lynne Goldstein.) This book is an outline of Wisconsin's prehistoric past, written for a general audience.

Stoltman, James B., ed. *New Perspectives on Cahokia: Views from the Periphery.* Madison, WI: Prehistory Press, 1991. The articles in this book provide a view of Cahokia, an important Mississippian site near present-day St. Louis, as seen from sites at a considerable distance. The idea is that we may better understand Cahokia if we look at it from sites like Aztalan.

Ancestor Veneration in Lowland Maya Society: A Case Study from K'axob, Belize

Patricia McAnany

Crystallization of a Research Question

Archaeologists often argue over "facts"—whether they actually exist and, if they do, how they should be interpreted.[1] One thing is clear, however—facts do not speak for themselves; they exist within an explanatory framework. Some archaeologists specify their research framework by building models of the past or posing specific questions. Others deny that they have a theoretical orientation and claim that they are "objective" scientists simply collecting data. When questioned further, most non-theoretical archaeologists, indeed, have an agenda but are unwilling to engage in the rigors of theory and problem specification. Posing questions and creating an approach to archaeological fieldwork is an extremely important and creative part of the research process. By framing questions, we not only focus our investigation but we also specify our perspective and our biases.

My style of research is to begin by examining ethnographic materials pertinent to the topic at hand—in this case, ancestor veneration. In ethnographic accounts, the richness of human behavior is described (albeit with the biases of the ethnographer). Archaeologists do not collect evidence of ancient behavior but the material residue or "fall out" of behavior; in fact, one of the great challenges within archaeology stems from the fact that archaeologists study physical materials (broken pottery, building ruins, and so forth) in order to evaluate abstract ideas about the past, such as why and how a social institution such as ancestor veneration developed. I find it easier to pose research questions about human behavior and to imagine the different types of archaeological patterns that might result by first reading ethnographic works. Contemporary Maya of the Yucatán Peninsula and the highlands of Chiapas, México, and Guatemala have been studied extensively, particularly their cosmology and ritual—two topics that are highly pertinent to an archaeological investigation of ancestor veneration. In Maya studies there is another rich source of ideas about the past that comes from the past itself—Maya hieroglyphic writing and elite iconography. Over the past three decades we have made tremendous strides in hieroglyphic decipherment; currently in Maya archaeology there is a strong and positive feedback between epigraphy and archaeology "from the earth" as the famous British archaeologist Sir Mortimer Wheeler put it. In short, our research questions can be better informed because we have a richer base of information from which to form them. With these thoughts in mind, I turn to the work of forging a research question.

ANCESTORS AND LAND

In a ritual called *K'in Krus*, contemporary Maya of Zinacantan, Chiapas, México, walk a circuit around their land. At designated shrine locations, they stop and give reverence to their ancestors, who are thought to dwell in the mountains and safeguard their land-holdings, their homes, and their water holes. Anthropologist Evon Vogt, who spent much of his career studying Zinacantan society (see Figure 22-1 on page 362), emphasizes the tremendous power and presence of ancestors in Chiapas Maya villages.[2] The bodies of ancestors may disintegrate but their spirits live and continue to inhabit the landscape around the village. Elsewhere in the highland Guatemalan town of Chichicastenango, anthropologist Ruth Bunzel studied the ways of Quiché Maya, who informed her that their homes belonged to their ancestors—the living were just passing through. Their lands also belonged to the ancestors and they could not sell their fields or houses but passed them on to children and heirs.[3] Reading accounts such as these, I became intrigued by both the similarities and differences in the treatment of the dead between Maya society and western European-derived society. Both societies conceive of an afterlife but in Maya society ancestors stay close to home and exert an influence that is generally beneficial and protective. In our society, when the dead come back it is usually as a poltergeist or some quasi-evil being. Moreover, we rely solely on wills and other legal documents to transmit lands and homes through the generations. Once dead, our ancestors do not continue to guide the course of things. But in traditional societies like that of the Maya, legal documents are amplified by the ancestors themselves who seem to exert a guiding force within society long after they cease to have a corporeal presence in this realm. Frequently invoked to reinforce the strength of precedent or the status quo, ancestors can provide powerful allies in disputes among descendants over resources.

Once I understood something of the link between ancestors and land in contemporary Maya society, I began to read widely on the institution of ancestor veneration. From China to the Andean cultures of South America, ancestors—specifically named individuals—seem to play a pivotal role in the transmission of land and wealth between generations. From classic

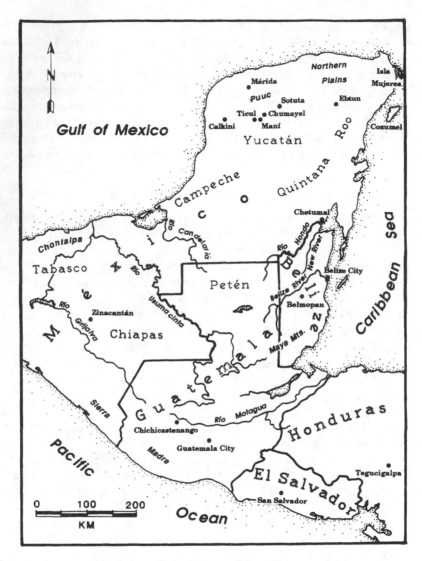

FIGURE 22-1   MODERN MAYA PLACES

ethnographic texts on Chinese and African ancestor veneration by anthropologists such as Meyer Fortes, Maurice Freedman, and Jack Goody, I gleaned
a definitive notion of this institution as the rituals and practices associated
with the commemoration, by name, of deceased individuals.[4] Through commemoration of an ancestor, whether at a shrine or an actual place of burial,
the legitimacy of an inheritance is reinforced. I learned that ancestor veneration is a highly selective practice and not all deceased individuals assume

the status of revered ancestors; it is reserved primarily for those through whom material inheritance or privilege pass. Furthermore, while many societies give general attention to "those who came before," the commemoration of an ancestor by name occurs primarily in societies in which families control well-delineated fields, orchards, or herds of animals, and rarely among groups with a communal ethic of land use or herd management. Thus it seems that counting sheep and measuring land boundaries or otherwise partitioning resources along the lines of individual family interests is part and parcel of reverence for the ancestors.

ROYAL ANCESTOR VENERATION

Although ethnographic accounts link ancestors to homes and fields, a large corpus of archaeological material from the Maya lowlands and elsewhere reveals an equally strong link between ancestors and royal rule. In the first millennium A.D., royal ancestors of Maya rulers were interred in tombs within pyramid shrines at Classic cities as far-flung as Copán, Honduras, and Palenque, Chiapas, México (see Figure 22-2 on page 364). At the latter, Pakal the Great, who ruled from A.D. 616 to A.D. 683, built his own burial pyramid—a structure now called the Temple of the Inscriptions because of the long hieroglyphic text (later commissioned by the son of Pakal) that was carved into the inner walls of the temple. On the sides of his beautifully carved sarcophagus, Pakal instructed sculptors to chisel the profiles of his father, mother, grandmother, and other significant progenitors. Shown from the waist up, the ancestors of Pakal exhibit lifelike detail, and behind each figure is a fruit-bearing orchard species. For instance, Lady Kan-Ik, grandmother to Pakal, is posed with an avocado tree bearing ripe, pear-shaped fruit. Other relatives are shown with a fruit-bearing *cacao* (chocolate bean) tree or the sweet fruit trees of *chico-zapote, nance,* and *guayaba.* Orchards are transgenerational plants; that is, they are planted by one generation and those who follow inherit them and continue to care for them and harvest their fruits. In associating his ancestors with orchard species, Pakal used an agrarian metaphor to express his inheritance of the throne. This metaphor suggested to me that royal ancestor veneration may have been distilled from an earlier institution that was linked to subsistence resources much as is the case today. Regardless, royal ancestor veneration of the Classic Period Maya (circa A.D. 250–900/1000) expressed political power, dynastic lines, and the central importance of the place where royal progenitors were interred.

Images of royal ancestors are not restricted to burial tombs. On Maya stelae (free-standing monoliths) and wall panels, which often commemorate the accession of a ruler or a victory in war over a neighboring city, ancestors are commonly shown at the top of a composition above a central protagonist. Sometimes named hieroglyphically and wrapped either in cloud scrolls or

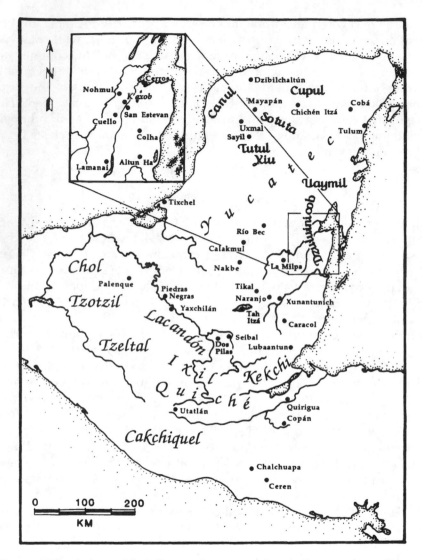

FIGURE 22-2   ANCIENT MAYA PLACES, INCLUDING COPAN, PALENQUE, AND K'AXOB

cartouches to indicate their corporeal removal from the present, such depictions are particularly common at Yaxchilán. Linda Schele and David Freidel have referred to this pattern as "the principle of the anchoring ancestor."[5] By depicting parents as ancestral guardians, a descendant links his or her rule to those who came before and uses the strength of precedent to cement allegiances and to legitimize power and authority.

Occasionally there are hieroglyphic or iconographic references to the physical remains themselves. Shown on Altar 5 from Tikal, for instance, are the long bones and skull of a royal woman who is identified as originally from a nearby place called Topoxte. Two men wearing elaborate costumes perform a ritual over the stack of ancestor bones. David Stuart has translated the hieroglyph at position 26 as "pas-ah" or "was opened."[6] Two dates on the inscriptions, a death date and a later "opening" date, suggest that her primary burial place was a temporary one to be followed by a later exhumation of her remains accompanied by ritual performance. This continued attention to the physical remains of the dead and protracted treatment (including exhumation) of ancestors is a common characteristic of ancestor veneration worldwide.

As a consequence, perhaps, of these rich Maya materials relating to royal ancestor veneration—hieroglyphic texts detailing genealogies, carved portraits on stelae, and nine-tiered, temple-topped pyramid shrines that house the physical remains of deceased royalty—some scholars have gone so far as to suggest that ancestor veneration was solely the prerogative of elites.[7] This perspective assumes privileged institutions of the elite sector and projects a view of ancient Maya society as one of cultured elites and ignoble peasantry. Ethnographic accounts, on the contrary, indicate that a family does not need to be elite in order to venerate named ancestors. Moreover, modern archaeological surveys of broad areas around the central core of monumental architecture at ancient Maya cities are documenting tremendous variation in residential form, size, and elaboration among the nonelite sector of society. Clearly, we are not dealing simply with kings and peasants but with a continuum of wealth and status in both elite and nonelite parts of society. Finally, if ancestor veneration was a creation of Classic period elites, then it was a social practice with very shallow time depth and an anomalous institution since most Classic Period practices—such as divine kingship and pyramid-building—have recognizable Formative-period antecedents.

GENESIS OF ANCESTOR VENERATION: A WORKING THESIS

When I was in graduate school, a professor once told me to investigate a topic until I reached the limits of our knowledge and the scholarly thinking became fuzzy. "When you reach that point," he said, "then and only then will you have a research topic." Well, I thought I now had a research topic—the genesis of ancestor veneration in lowland Maya society. It was a critical institution among Classic Maya elites—indeed a central prop of divine rulership—yet its origins were poorly understood. I also had identified paradoxes within the topic. While there existed a strong bond between ancestors and land in contemporary Maya society, the portrayal of ancestors in elite, Classic-Maya society was overtly political, emphasizing dynastic succession. Clearly, different forces were at work and needed to be pulled apart and examined in order to generate a holistic view of this focal institution.

In addition to the multiple purposes of this practice, ancestor veneration seemed to be an indicator of social inequality. After all, revering ancestral relatives was a selective social practice and had the effect of concentrating wealth and influence within family lines across generational boundaries. Viewed in this way, this social institution promoted the unequal distribution of wealth and power. Archaeologists have long been interested in isolating the mechanisms and development of social inequality but no one had closely examined ancestor veneration—a social practice in which ideology and the material basis of life uniquely converge. Furthermore—and most exciting—the ritual panoply of ancestor veneration in both burial interments and commemoration should leave visible archaeological traces that could be followed by careful excavation, recording, and analysis.

Using a model derived from ethnography, I decided to tackle the genesis of this social practice. I reasoned as follows: If ancestor veneration initially was linked to family consolidation of control over resources, such as land and orchards, then the creation of ancestors should coincide with changes in ancient patterns of land use. If not, then change in one category of archaeological materials should not be contemporary with change in another. Of course, coincident change would not prove my thesis since correlation does not equal causation but it certainly would lend support to it. In archaeological research it is one thing to state a thesis and quite another to figure out how an idea may be evaluated in an unambiguous manner with archaeological data. In truth, our data are often insufficient to allow even a falsification of our research premise. Many archaeologists have addressed this challenge to archaeological research— Lewis R. Binford in particular. He has used the term "middle range theory" in reference to the underdeveloped methodological realm in which ideas and data collide, most often in the absence of robust logical sinew.[8]

In order to be able to evaluate my thesis in light of anticipated field data, I needed to generate expectations regarding how archaeological deposits might change as ancestor veneration and more restrictive forms of land tenure became the norm. I planned to investigate archaeological materials from the Formative Period (1000 B.C. to A.D. 250) of the Maya lowlands. This period spanned the time from the initial establishment of agrarian villages to the emergence of rulers. I anticipated that the creation of ancestors would entail a formalization of burial practices as to locale and number, age, and sex of individuals interred, possible reuse of certain burial locales, and protracted treatment of physical remains that would result in secondary interments. Excavations at other Formative sites such as Cuello, Belize, indicated that, from the early days of the Middle Formative (circa 800 B.C.), individuals were buried under the floors of houses.[9] If I excavated several different Formative houses, I might be able to detect not only temporal trends that would suggest the selective creation of ancestors (as opposed to the burial of a deceased family member) but also emergent differences in the size and elaboration of houses that may indicate an unequal distribution of wealth.

Changes in land use would be more difficult to detect. The Yucatán Peninsula, home to the lowland Maya, originally was a mosaic of tropical rain forest and wetland vegetation. Core samples retrieved from drilling into the interior lakes of the Peninsula indicate widespread disturbance of the forest between 2000 and 1000 B.C.[10] Such disturbance is likely the signature of a colonizing population for which we have scant artifactual remains. As the population grew, more of the rain forest was removed as forests were converted to fields, and lumber and thatching supplies were needed for house construction as well as fuel for cooking and pottery production. In the tropics, there is a predictable succession of tree species; as climax species such as mahogany are removed, early stage "weedy" species replace them. If there is ample land, a field may be left fallow for as long as twenty years, allowing mature tree species to regenerate. From the sixteenth to the nineteenth century, this long-fallow rotation was the practice in much of the Yucatán since forced servitude and disease had caused a catastrophic reduction in the size of the Maya population. If land is in short supply, on the other hand, the cycle of fallow is shortened considerably or even eliminated and mature species do not develop. When this latter scenario is played out, lands are generally partitioned into family holdings much as Paula Brown and Aaron Podolefsky have documented in the highlands of New Guinea.[11] Following this stream of logic, I reasoned that a pronounced decrease or absence of climax forest species in the burned wood samples collected from our archaeological excavations might signal the partitioning of the landscape into permanent family holdings. Of course, a large sample of wood charcoal would have to be carefully collected from a wide range of archaeological deposits using a labor-intensive technique called water flotation. Fortunately, we would be working in the heat of the tropics and few of my staff members or students would object to an afternoon at the float tank.

ARCHAEOLOGICAL FIELDWORK

Archaeological projects don't just happen. There is a tremendous amount of preparation, both in research formulation and in the logistics of fielding a crew and conducting field work, especially when one is working in a host country. Rarely does an archaeologist design a piece of research and then find a site compatible with a research design. More probable is the following scenario: As part of a formal survey or casual reconnaissance, an archaeologist finds a site or an area that is compatible with a researcher's range of interests. If preliminary investigations are fruitful, then the archaeologist sits down and formulates a full-blown research design with specific questions or a formal model, expectations for patterns in archaeological data, and a detailed outline of the scope and timetable of fieldwork to be accomplished. In the first part of this chapter I introduced you to the germination of a research design. Before that occurred, however, my interest in the genesis of ancestor veneration had been piqued by specific archaeological deposits encountered during 1990 while running an archaeological field school for Boston University at the site of K'axob in Belize, Central America, and earlier still while a graduate student on a National Science Foundation-sponsored project called "The Pulltrouser Swamp Project." With K'axob in mind, therefore, this research was formulated and, having secured National Science Foundation support for my project, I assembled a crew for the 1992 field season.

K'AXOB, BELIZE—A FORMATIVE MAYA VILLAGE

Located in northern Belize between the New River and the southern arm of Pulltrouser Swamp, K'axob is proximate not only to a diversified aquatic resource base but also to one of the premier water transport routes into the Petén. For these reasons, small villages sprang up at many locales in this portion of the Maya lowlands by 800 B.C. I first surveyed K'axob in 1981 when, as a graduate student on a project directed by Peter D. Harrison and B. L. Turner II, I was instructed to build a bridge across the swamp in order to see what was over there. Hazarding the "denizens of the deep" so notorious in tropical latitudes, we constructed a spongy bridge of perishable *palmetto* poles. When we reached the other side, we were not alone. The rich soils of K'axob had not escaped the notice of Maya farmers from the nearby village of San Estevan, who had been paddling their dugouts across the New River to cultivate small field plots at K'axob for several decades. As I mapped and dug test excavations at K'axob in 1981, I realized that it was a patchwork of fields in various stages of deforestation and regrowth. For this reason, we decided to call the site *K'axob*, loosely translated from Yucatec Maya as "place of many fallow fields" and actually a double entendre since the surname of the Maya landowner is *Campos* or "field" in Spanish. The western margin of K'axob is a lattice work of canals that drain an ancient system of wetland fields. Local Maya had constructed fish weirs across these canals in order to harvest the bountiful, aquatic resources of this wetland; one of the favorite pastimes of villagers from nearby San José was to sneak into K'axob to poach fish from the swamp.

Altogether the area covered by pyramids, house-mounds, and wetland fields is about 1.5 square kilometers or 0.93 square miles. Within this area, there are two large, focal plaza groups with pyramids as high as 13 meters and substantial platform constructions. Smaller patio groups of residential structures are configured as satellite units around these two focal constructions. At K'axob, construction activity commenced in the Middle Formative (ca. 800–400 B.C.) and continued through the Late Classic (ca. A.D. 600–800); there is an elusive Late Postclassic (ca. A.D. 1250–1500) presence at K'axob indicated by fragments of Maya pan-style incense burners recovered from the base of virtually all pyramidal structures, but there does not seem to be any architecture dating to this late time period.

PROGRAM OF EXCAVATION

During three field seasons (1990, 1992, and 1993), I concentrated our excavation effort in and around the southern group—the area we knew to be the ancestral core of K'axob based on the 1981 test excavations. In the end, we excavated seven large, deep horizontal exposures in structures and plazas (Operations I, VII, VIII, X, XI, XII, and XIII; Figure 22-3). Of the large-scale, deep exposures, by far the biggest is Operation I, which was sunk into the basal platform of the large southern plaza. This unit revealed the earliest part

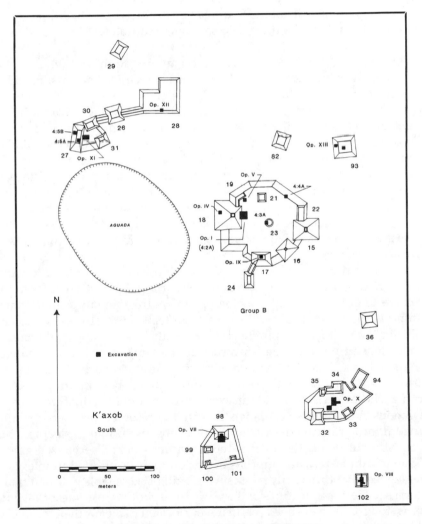

FIGURE 22-3   K'AXOB, SOUTHERN SECTOR

of K'axob—a Middle Formative village. Our "window" to this early time period is a 6 x 8 m excavation expanded from an initial 1.5 x 3 m test trench excavated during the 1981 season. Operation I is located in front of pyramidal Structure 18, which defines the western side of Plaza B. Early Classic (ca. A.D. 250–600) in construction, this pyramid rises four meters from the plaza floor on its eastern face while the western side rises nine meters from the edge of a low-lying *aguada* (seasonal lake) that is most likely a pit created when soil was needed for the construction of the platforms and pyramids of southern K'axob. This excavation unit yielded a series of stratified house floors, middens (refuse deposits), platforms, burials, and pyramid debris. By itself, the excavation sheds considerable light on changes in Formative Maya lifeways and, for this reason, I detail the findings of this finely stratified three-meter-deep excavation that took three field seasons to complete.

Operation 1   By the third field season, getting to the bottom of Operation I seemed analogous to the search for the Holy Grail—engrossing and exciting but impossible. During the 1993 season, however, we did reach the earliest Middle Formative structures that were built around 700 B.C. The first inhabitants of K'axob built right on top of the ancient ground surface, which itself was rich with cultural remains. Postholes sunk into this buried black humus indicated the presence of a simple earthen floor structure during this period. Two deceased individuals were interred in this ground surface: (1) an adult female buried with no associated offerings and (2) an adult male who was interred with over two thousand small, marine shell beads (arranged as bracelets and upper arm bands) and two ceramic vessels. Thus, the earliest burials at K'axob exhibit a marked degree of differentiation in grave accouterments.

Soon after these interments, a series of white plaster floors and low platforms were constructed at this location. The earliest residential configuration is composed of a low, round-to-oblong platform (retained by a single course of stones). The position of this low platform (called Structure 1) was maintained for the next five hundred years as was the midden zone to the north. Immediately adjacent to the main structure is an ephemeral structure that is represented by a series of thin floor surfaces. These floors are located to the southwest (downwind) of the platform and each one bore multiple traces of burning. These deposits provide an example of the familiar, dual structures of Maya households, with a cooking structure (represented by a series of thin, burned floor surfaces) adjacent to a more substantial living, sleeping, and storage structure. Only the floors of the structures were preserved. Fragments of daub (mud plaster with imprints of upright poles) collected from excavations suggest that these early houses were built of perishable pole and thatch materials. Ubiquitous features of this early time period are domestic facilities such as stone- and sherd-lined pits that were located to the north of the kitchen and main structure. Four radiocarbon accelerator dates on charcoal from dark lenses packed between the sequential "kitchen" surfaces indicate a relatively rapid sequence of construction: a time range of 770–520 B.C. for these early structures of K'axob.[12]

There are at least three sequences of structure expansion and floor-raising during later Middle Formative times. The lowest structure (1-G) contained two interments. Stratigraphically above this structure is another house (1-E) with a double burial. (This burial contains two vessels that bear the first observation of what was to become a common motif at K'axob—the red painted cross.) The final Middle Formative structure is a small circular platform (1-D) into which two burials were inserted, one with a deep, red dish inverted over a spouted vessel. Sherd- and stone-lined pits continued to occur off the northern and western sides of Structure 1.

The first construction of a platform with a sufficient height to necessitate a multiple-course, stone retaining wall (called Structure 1-C) occurs during the Late Formative. At this time, the "toss" zone to the north of the platform is still in use and we see new construction of cooking features such as hearths, which suggests a continued residential function for this locale. Burials in this platform and the floor above it (Structure 1-B) maintain the pattern of the Middle Formative (i.e., primary) extended burials. During this period, a cache of four vessels arranged in a cross pattern is deposited into the plaza fill on the western edge of the excavation trench.

Burial patterns change dramatically, however, in the later part of the Late Formative. A series of circular pits (into which tightly wrapped, seated individuals were placed) were inserted into a low platform structure that lacked a plastered surface (Structure 1-A). A thick plastered floor covered the rest of the excavation area. Just short of the western limit of our excavation trench, two extremely deep burial pits had been prepared—an oblong trench and a circular pit. The trench extended down through the Middle Formative floor lenses to terminate on the soft, limestone bedrock. Judging from the condition of the collar lining of the trench and the stratified nature of the interred deposits, the trench was reopened several times and secondary burials were placed within (see Figure 22-4 on page 372). Altogether eleven individuals were interred at this location; they included children, adolescents, and adults of both sexes. The deceased were sent off with their marine shell jewelry (a shell amulet and shell anklets among other pieces), carved bone handles, jadeite beads, and five ceramic vessels. The vessels represent a variety of forms, from a miniature red spouted jar to a large bowl with a flamboyant out-flaring rim over which a streaky slip had been painted. A large cross was painted on the interior of the vessel base. In fact, two of the five vessels from the burial trench were painted with this motif. The small circular pit immediately adjacent to this secondary burial context contained six individuals; two of the three vessels from this circular pit also were painted with the red cross motif. These two burial locales, containing a wealth of burial goods and a concentration of vessels bearing the cross motif, were then sealed over with

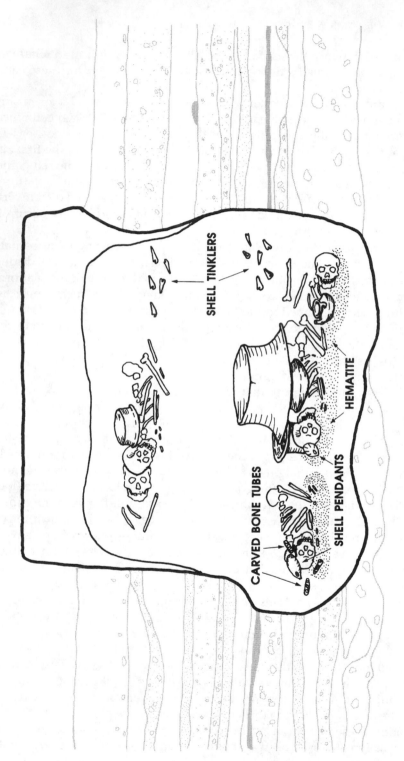

FIGURE 22-4 CROSS-SECTION OF ZONE 18 BURIAL TRENCH

a low platform, creating what was probably the first, formalized shrine at K'axob. At the end of the Formative period, the shrine complex was buried and two caches of ceramic vessels were deposited into the fill—a practice that archaeologists call a "termination cache" because it marks the end of the use of a structure, in this case of the shrine complex. The first cache consisted of a simple flaring-rimmed bowl; the second deposit was much more complex and included three vessels and seven pecked-and-shaped limestone spheres. The lowest vessel was filled with a collection of jadeite and shell carvings.

During the succeeding Early Classic period (ca. A.D. 250–600), pyramidal Structure 18 was built. This pyramid capped the earlier domestic structures, sub-floor ancestor burials, and the Late Formative burial shrine. Although only the basal course of the staircase risers was still intact, fragments of painted plaster excavated amidst the rubble revealed that the pyramid had been painted red. Through the Late Classic and Postclassic (ca. A.D. 600–1500) periods there is no known construction at this locale, but Structure 18 receives ritual attention during the Late Postclassic as evidenced by diagnostic fragments of ceramic, anthropomorphic incense burners (leg and arm parts, in particular) found at the base of the pyramid. The presence of Postclassic projectile points in association with these censers suggests that in addition to ritual practices, defensive or hunting activities were also coordinated from this locale.

Excavations in "Satellite" Residences Operation I clearly appears to be the focal area of ancestral K'axob. But we can only say this because we also excavated most of the residential mounds around Plaza B. Large-scale excavations in six "satellite" residential units within two hundred meters of Operation I revealed no additional Middle Formative construction units, thus confirming the pattern of small, nucleated Middle Formative settlements described elsewhere in the Maya lowlands. Late Formative-to-Early Classic construction units and burials, however, occur in most satellite contexts indicating pronounced settlement growth and internal differentiation at this time. In all units, excavators report a close sequencing between burials and structure refurbishing events. These findings indicate the crucial role of ancestor interments in structure renovation, even at the "household" level—a relationship that has larger implications for social practices such as the intergenerational transmission of resources.

ANALYSIS AND SYNTHESIS

ARCHITECTURAL PATTERNS

Careful stratigraphic excavation at K'axob has resulted in the documentation of over 554 discrete depositional and construction units, the bulk of which date to the Middle and Late Formative periods. In Operation I alone, there are fifteen construction phases with multiple refurbishing events within each phase. Excavations in satellite residences have yielded shorter construction sequences but total over thirty-five phases of Formative construction. Preliminary results of architectural, burial, and ceramic studies indicate that significant changes occurred during the middle of the Late Formative, probably about 200 B.C. At this juncture in Operation I, the first ritual deposit of ceramic vessels (cache) occurred and the first multi-course stone-faced platform was built to replace the thin, plaster floors of earlier times. Soon thereafter, the first identified burial shrine was constructed in Operation I. Excavations in satellite residences indicate a thriving population during Late Formative and Early Classic times albeit living in simpler structures. In addition to evidence of emergent status differentiation in both life and death, excavations have yielded a wealth of information on Formative domestic site structure such as sherd-lined pits that were employed, often sequentially, for soaking, steaming, and roasting vegetal and molluscan foods.

BURIAL PRACTICES AND THE CREATION OF ANCESTORS

Nearly all construction units contained intrusive pits in which burials were interred. Conservatively, a total of one hundred individuals have been recorded from all excavations combined. We have collected detailed stratigraphic records of the construction units into which individuals were interred; thus changes in burial practices can be analyzed with reference to architectural changes. Study of burial data has revealed a pattern of change in interments during the Late Formative. Noted especially in Operation I, an earlier tradition of single interments of fully extended individuals was replaced by multiple interments of individuals who were flexed, seated, or clearly secondarily deposited. These family interments contained individuals of all ages and both sexes and were well-supplied with burial offerings. One burial pit in particular, Zone 18 of Operation I, was re-opened several times in order to add additional individuals and was capped by a low platform or shrine. This evidence suggests that the emergence of a kinship elite and the attendant commemoration of ancestors was a hallmark of the Late Formative at K'axob.[13] Large-scale excavation, as opposed to "test-pitting for chronology," has allowed us to document these complex and interrelated sequences of interment and structure modification. Our results suggest that subfloor burial was not simply an ancient Maya custom; rather it was a selective social practice that (1) created ancestors, (2) stressed continuity between the generations through the ritual observance of the places of the ancestors, and (3) facilitated the transgenerational conveyance of resources.

In a more general sense, these stratigraphic and burial data from three seasons of excavation demonstrate the crucial and determinative role of ancestor interments in the transformation of Operation I, in particular, from the locus of a nucleated Middle Formative village to a Classic period focus of ritual as represented by a pyramidal structure. Following the thoughts of Jack Goody and others, I suggest that this ritual elaboration of an ancestral place was a means of reckoning genealogy, and naming and claiming a place as well as associated resources.[14]

EVIDENCE FOR CHANGING LAND USE

Due to the domestic quality of the Formative deposits, middens as well as infilled sherd-lined pits have yielded a wealth of macrobotanical, faunal, and molluscan data. Plant remains, consisting primarily of burned wood, were retrieved through a comprehensive program of sediment sampling from excavation contexts. Organic remains were then separated from the sediment by means of a technique called water flotation. A total of 330 samples, primarily from Middle and Late Formative contexts, has been amassed through this recovery program. Analysis of these materials is now underway and preliminary results indicate that wholesale removal of the climax rain forest did not occur until the end of the Middle Formative; that is, climax and successive tree species were present throughout Middle Formative times. On the other hand, firewood collected from the swamp, savannas, and economic tree species became dominant during Late Formative times. This analysis can be used to evaluate the original thesis that the genesis of ancestor veneration was linked to profound changes in the use of the agricultural landscape. As mentioned earlier, burial practices changed significantly during the middle part of the Late Formative as evidenced by the construction of a burial shrine. During this period, wood charcoal data indicated that climax rain forest species were no longer easily obtainable for firewood. The landscape around K'axob was most likely a mosaic of regrowth plants as it had been for a few hundred years. The practice of ancestor veneration, therefore, could have been a response to a restructuring of the landscape into carefully delineated and inherited field plots.

CONTRIBUTION OF RESEARCH TO OUR UNDERSTANDING OF MAYA SOCIETY

I hope this chapter has demonstrated how a program of focused research can yield insights to the past that were previously unthinkable. One can also legitimately ask whether this research has changed our understanding of Maya society

As I have written elsewhere, ancestor veneration as it was practiced in Maya and other societies is not really about the deceased but rather how the living make use of the dead to chart a course for the future.[15] It is not an esoteric cult of the dead but rather a means by which a link is maintained between ancestors and their material legacy to future generations. Through attention to ancestors, there is continuity between the generations. While the very conservative nature of this practice reinforces social inequality, it also provides a charter for survival when a people are confronting overwhelming forces of cultural genocide and extinction. Recent history provides a lesson here. Throughout the past five hundred years, Maya living in México and Guatemala have continued to venerate their ancestors through rituals such as the K'in Krus. Labeled "traditional" by anthropologists and other outside observers, these practices, nevertheless, have held together the distinctive fabric of Maya society.

More specifically, this program of research posits a link between ancestor veneration as social practice and human alteration of the environment. It should come as no surprise that preliminary results of our research indicate that landscape modification precedes human organizational change by as much as two hundred to three hundred years. In our own place and time, we are only beginning to modify our behavior and our social and education systems in order to deal with the aftermath of landscape and water degradation incurred over the past one hundred years by the Industrial Revolution and rapid population expansion. In this regard, this research helps to demystify Maya society and to revise the traditional notion that the ancient Maya were unique and mysterious.

NOTES

1. Jeremy A. Sabloff, Lewis R. Binford, and Patricia A. McAnany, "Understanding the Archaeological Record," Antiquity 61 (1987): 203.
2. Evon Z. Vogt, Tortillas for the Gods: A Symbolic Analysis of Zinacanteco Rituals (Cambridge, MA and London, England: Harvard University Press, 1976).
3. Ruth Bunzel, Chichicastenango: A Guatemalan Village (Seattle: American Ethnological Society, 1952).
4. Meyer Fortes, "Some Reflections on Ancestor Worship," in Meyer Fortes and G. Dieterlen, eds., African Systems of Thought (London: Oxford University Press, 1965), pp. 122–144; Meyer Fortes, "An Introductory Commentary," in William H. Newell, ed., Ancestors (Paris: Mouton Publishers, 1976), pp. 1–16; Maurice Freedman, Chinese Lineage and Society: Fukien and Kwangtung (New York: The Athlone Press, London School of Economics, Monographs on Social Anthropology no. 33, 1966); Maurice Freedman, "Ritual Aspects of Chinese Kinship and Marriage," in Maurice Freedman, ed., Family and Kinship in Chinese Society (Stanford: Stanford University Press, 1970), pp. 163–188; Jack Goody, Death, Property, and the Ancestors: A Study of the Mortuary Customs of the LoDagaa of West Africa (London: Tavistock Publications, 1962).
5. Linda Schele and David Freidel, A Forest of Kings: The Untold Story of the Ancient Maya (New York: William Morrow and Company, 1990).
6. Personal communication, 1992.
7. John B. Carlson, "A Geomantic Model for the Interpretation of Mesoamerican Sites: An Essay in Cross-Cultural Comparison," in Elizabeth P. Benson, ed., Mesoamerican Sites and World-Views (Washington, D.C.: Dumbarton Oaks, 1981), pp. 143–215; Clemency C. Coggins, "Classic Maya Metaphors of Death and Life," RES 16 (1988): 64.

8. Lewis R. Binford, *Bones: Ancient Men and Modern Myths* (New York: Academic Press, 1981).

9. Cynthia Robin and Norman Hammond, "Burial Practices," in Norman Hammond, ed., *Cuello: an Early Maya Community in Belize* (Cambridge: Cambridge University Press, 1991), pp. 204–225.

10. Michael W. Binford, Mark Brenner, Thomas J. Whitmore, Antonia Higuera-Gundy, and Edward S. Deevey, "Ecosystems, Paleoecology, and Human Disturbance in Subtropical and Tropical America," *Quaternary Science Review* 6 (1987): 115; Edward S. Deevey, Don S. Rice, Prudence M. Rice, Hague H. Vaughn, Mark Brenner, and Michael S. Flannery, "Maya Urbanism: Impact on a Tropical Karst Environment," *Science* 206 (1979): 298; John S. Jacobs, *The Agroecological Evolution of Cobweb Swamp, Belize* (Ph.D. diss., Texas A & M University, 1992; Ann Arbor: University Microfilms).

11. Paula Brown and Aaron Podolefsky, "Population Density, Agricultural Intensity, Land Tenure, and Group Size in the New Guinea Highlands," *Ethnology* 15 (1976): 211.

12. Radiocarbon sample numbers OxA 2721 to 2724; see *Archaeometry* 34 (1992): 337.

13. Aidan Southall, "The Segmentary State in Africa and Asia," *Comparative Studies in Society and History* 30 (1988): 52.

14. Jack Goody, *Death, Property, and the Ancestors: A Study of the Mortuary Customs of the LoDagaa of West Africa* (London: Tavistock Publications, 1962).

15. Patricia A. McAnany, *Living with the Ancestors: Kinship and Kingship in Ancient Maya Society* (Austin: University of Texas Press, 1995).

SUGGESTED READINGS

Fash, William L. *Scribes, Warriors, and Kings*. London: Thames and Hudson, 1991. A synthesis of recent work at Copán with emphasis on combining hieroglyphic texts and archaeological research to reconstruct ancient political structure.

Houston, Stephen D. *Hieroglyphs and History at Dos Pilas: Dynastic Politics of the Classic Maya*. Austin: University of Texas Press, 1993. Details the dynastic history of a Late Classic Maya capital and synthesizes archaeological work with epigraphy.

✳ Marcus, Joyce. *Mesoamerican Writing Systems: Propaganda, Myth, and History in Four Ancient Civilizations*. Princeton: Princeton University Press, 1992. Provides the only overall view of the ancient writing systems of both the highland and lowland civilizations of Mesoamerica.

Sharer, Robert J. *The Ancient Maya*. Stanford: Stanford University Press, 1994. A thorough and general reference book on Maya archaeology.

Schele, Linda, and Mary E. Miller. *Blood of Kings: Dynasty and Ritual in Maya Art*. Fort Worth, TX: George Braziller, Inc., and the Kimball Art Museum, 1986. A good introduction to elite Maya iconography with a section on royal ancestor veneration.

Turner, B. L., II, and Peter D. Harrison, eds. *Pulltrouser Swamp: Ancient Maya Habitat, Agriculture, and Settlement in Northern Belize*. Austin: University of Texas Press, 1983. An interdisciplinary study of the wetlands around K'axob.

De-Mystifying the Past:
The Great Zimbabwe, King Solomon's
Mines, and Other Tales of Old Africa

Joseph O. Vogel

On the high granite plateau between the Zambezi and Limpopo rivers, in southeast Africa, there stretches a broad plain of semiarid savanna woodlands. This is the homeland of the Shona-speaking people and the site of some two hundred zimbabwes. These stone-built structures range in size from low circular walls enclosing small farming hamlets to multiroomed family compounds and large complexly constructed towns. Great Zimbabwe is the largest of these southeast African towns—a spacious complex of granite-blocked freestone masonry buildings spread out over a broad patch of hilltop and valley in southeast Zimbabwe.

The site of Great Zimbabwe was first occupied sometime in the sixth century by a subsistence farming community. In the thirteenth century its residents raised the first simple stone-walling and sun-dried clay platforms for their pole-and-sun-dried clay walled houses. Soon thereafter construction started on the finest, most elaborate buildings built there. By this time it was a large, populous town of eighteen thousand inhabitants, with a great many pole-and-sun-dried clay-walled houses and elaborate stone-walled buildings. A large multiroomed compound on the steep-sided rocky hilltop used well-coursed freestone masonry to link the natural boulders into a series of enclosures. Two narrow, high-walled freestone masonry passages with sections of sun-dried clay stairs formed the ascent from the valley. In the valley below were large free-standing enclosures built open to the sky, around pole-and-sun-dried-clay houses joined by short lengths of walling. Each of the enclosures was divided into a maze of individual family compounds.

Though Great Zimbabwe was the best known and largest of the southeast African towns, it was only one of many important civic centers. There were magnificent towns in southwest Zimbabwe at Khami, Naletale, and Dhlo Dhlo. The rocky hills of Zimbabwe rise in stark contrast to the surrounding plain. Elite Shona families chose to exalt their social prominence by building family compounds atop these hills, which they decorated with massive, elaborately decorated terracing and narrow masonry ascents. These towns present an impressive panorama of finely coursed stone-walling decorated with bands of inset blocks set in chevron patterns. In northeast Zimbabwe, on the other hand, there are hundreds of miles of stone-built agricultural terraces, the foundations of semisubterranean houses and channels designed to move water from place to place.

It seems hard to believe that for a long time the authorship of these monumental sites was in doubt. Given the profusion of stone-built structures, why was there ever a doubt that monumental architecture was the product of local African cultures? Archaeology spent more than a century caught up in cultural politics associated with interpreting the past in southeast Africa. The first European travelers into southeast Africa believed the stone-walling and evidence of mining to be relics of Near Eastern civilization. In fanciful reconstructions of life in Great Zimbabwe, writers of fiction depicted the people there as mining gold to export to the great markets of the Near East, while farming East Africa to support a vast colonial enterprise.[1]

Why did such a story take hold of the popular imagination? Why were the sites not seen as the product of African ingenuity? Though Great Zimbabwe was well known, along with many other stone-built sites, analysis of the problem of the monumental architecture of southeast Africa started with armchair speculation and the assumption that Africans did not build in stone. In the 1890s, when the era of archaeological investigation at the monumental sites began, it did not start with the same attitudes that a modern archaeologist brings to the study of African culture. The first investigators asked, "Which ancient Near Eastern civilization migrated to southern Africa and left these fabulous lost cities?"[2]

These places became generally known to Europeans in the mid-nineteenth century, when a self-taught geologist, Carl Mauch, prospecting the interior of South Africa in 1871, reached Great Zimbabwe. Excited by Mauch's good luck, European geographers posited a connection between this site in southeast Africa and the lost biblical city of Ophir—the site of King Solomon's mines. The history of archaeology in southeast Africa is one of supplanting such "fanciful" ideas about the history of Africa with the results of objective science.

Because of their lack of scientific method and their racial prejudices, many Europeans at the time saw ample reason to doubt the African genesis of monumental architecture. They had no regard for the antiquity or subtlety of African culture, believing that the local African people were latecomers to the territory. An Nguni army escaping the reach of Shaka had recently ravaged the country, and as a result of the general disruption of settled life in southern Africa following the Zulu wars early in the nineteenth century, Great Zimbabwe was deserted.

FIGURE 23-1   GREAT ZIMBABWE

Great Zimbabwe as it looked to Carl Mauch in 1871, emphasizing the hilltop structures and the Great Enclosure in the lower right. The sketch plan locates the enclosures upon the central hill and the clutter of compounds around the Great Enclosure.

A trader and hunter, Willy Posselt, visited Great Zimbabwe in 1889 and
discovered its first important artifacts: carved soapstone bird figures atop
tall granite pillars. Commentators in Europe compared these figures to sculpture from the Near East. Modern archaeologists, transcending naive comparisons, defining cultural contexts, and utilizing more objective and scientific

studies of African culture, now know that the carvings are African icons symbolizing the mediation of chiefs. Earlier observers only recognized the figures as birds, which they then compared to exotic birds they already knew, with no regard for a proper cultural setting to validate their debate.

The next year, adventurers sponsored by Cecil Rhodes entered and seized Mashonaland, taking time on their ride north to stop and play tourist at Great Zimbabwe. The newspapers headlined the discovery of ruins in a wild land, fostering the myth of King Solomon's mines, not because of an interest in archaeology but to support the stock of the company then developing the colony of Rhodesia.

Early Archaeological Investigations

In 1891 the English archaeologist J. Theodore Bent made the first field investigations at Great Zimbabwe. Bent incorrectly decided, based on reference to ancient cultures already known to nineteenth-century archaeology, that the zimbabwes were three-thousand-year-old fortifications, remnants of a mining colony from Southern Arabia. Having travelled to southeast Africa to locate a lost Near Eastern civilization, he satisfied himself that he had discovered one.

Bent's methods were typical of the time in that they ignored the logical implications of objective observations. In contrast, as early as the mid-1870s an anthropologist and advocate of a more scientific method, Robert Hartmann, correctly attributed the monumental sites to African builders. In his travels in northeast Africa he had observed many examples of African stone-built architecture; it was therefore reasonable to assume that the abandoned towns in southeast Africa were also of African origin.[3] Unlike Bent, he did not attempt to make his observations fit some preconceived explanation. As we shall see, anthropological archaeology goes beyond a description of objects and naive kinds of explanation; it uses cogent models of cultural behavior to give meaning to our investigations of the past.

The first research of a modern kind, using both stratigraphic methods and an understanding of typological analysis, took place in 1905. An archaeologist trained in the stringent methods of Egyptology, David Randall-MacIver, excavated at Great Zimbabwe and some other stone-built sites. He questioned the idea that these buildings were built by non-Africans. Unlike Bent with his vague kinds of comparison, Randall-MacIver excavated beneath the foundations of the stone buildings in order to determine the construction sequence and closely studied potsherds to fix the sequence of pottery and other artifacts associated with their construction. He found nothing that could be associated with the ancient Near East and much that was paralleled in African culture. Because the trade items located by Randall-MacIver could be dated to the fourteenth or fifteenth century, he posited a medieval date for the occupation rather than one of great antiquity.[4] Further research by Gertrude Caton-Thompson in the late 1920s confirmed Randall-MacIver's conclusions that the sites were African and less than a thousand years old.[5]

MORE RECENT ARCHAEOLOGICAL INVESTIGATIONS

Though the archaeology was clear and the major sites were investigated, a tendency to deny the African origins of these sites remained an active part of popular discussions of African history. As a result, archaeologists in the 1950s and 1960s labored to evaluate the sites as parts of African history. They surveyed, mapped, and recorded many sites in the countries now called Zimbabwe and Mozambique, describing them in detail. At the same time, historians collected information about them and the generations of Shona-speaking Karanga who built them. In the 1960s and 1970s archaeologists discovered the 1,600-year-old hamlets of the first farming communities to settle the southern savanna.

With the discovery of the ancient roots of African society, old ideas about the local Africans as latecomers were cast aside. New strategies for interpreting the history of the monumental sites were devised, using a wide-ranging body of anthropological, historical, and archaeological data, as well as information found elsewhere. This was necessary because many early excavations at the major sites were treasure-hunting expeditions or misguided efforts to remove cultural deposits to clear passages for tourists. When I first visited the Khami site outside Bulawayo, K. R. Robinson, who had recently conducted first-class investigations there, pointed out mounds of earth created by treasure seekers in the 1890s. Here and there bits of pottery were eroding out of the soil, all context lost. The very heart of an archaeological investigation, the accumulated trash and sweepings of human activity, was dug up, found wanting in value and cast away. Even worse, the integrity of the deposits was compromised. It was no longer possible to discern context or assign provenance (the location as well as the associations) of things found buried in these spoil heaps.

Some investigators early in the twentieth century had misconstrued the stratigraphy at Great Zimbabwe and its allied towns in order to portray a sequence that began with the most polished of building methods. They wished to imply that the building techniques were imported into southeast Africa in an advanced stage. They argued that there was no evidence of the local development of fine building techniques, but a gradual decay associated with a civilization degenerating from contact with people native to the region. The building sequence and a proper application of stratigraphy was first dealt with in the late 1920s and later by Roger Summers and his colleagues in the 1950s.[6] But there is a lesson to be learned: Explanation in archaeology is a slippery process. Any preconceived idea of the meaning of archaeological remains or the failure to adhere to proper procedure seriously undermines the validity of judgments.

Nevertheless, there were many questions to be asked about the people who had once lived at places like Great Zimbabwe. If the major sites were disturbed, how could archaeology find answers? As archaeology progressed in southern Africa, researchers pursued the problem of the rise of complex society in novel ways, investigating when the first farmers arrived in southeast Africa, how they managed crop production, the nature of their political life, and how they managed the economics of trade. This was necessary in order to reconstruct the lifeways of the societies that once dominated life on the plateau.

The apologists of the colonial period described Africans as simple tribal folk who, having progressed to hoe-agriculture and iron working, failed to achieve any higher level of cultural achievement. To those of us living and working in southeast Africa, it was apparent that the basis of African society was more involved and intricate than this. We began a process of reconstructing the true history of Africa—a history that colonial governments said did not exist. Africa ceased to be a continent without history as archaeologists discovered a new world transcending politics and prejudice.

FIELD ARCHAEOLOGY AND INQUIRY IN SOUTHEASTERN AFRICA

How does one go about reconstructing the history of people who leave no written record? I explored old farming settlements in the Victoria Falls region of the Zambezi valley for over ten years. My intention was not to study a few sites, but to coordinate a wide-ranging areal survey that would permit me to understand when African farmers first came into this part of the Zambezi valley and how they adapted to living there. My field work was designed to produce a long sequence of sites, ranging in time from the first farmers of the sixth century to settlements of the nineteenth century. The development of such a sequence required extensive field surveys and investigations at a variety of sites. Southern Zambia is unique in southeast Africa for its stratified middens. That is, many village sites were reoccupied over long periods of time, leaving a deposit layered into levels, each of which represents an episode of occupation at that location. As a result, I separated the different village horizons and associated changes in the pottery and iron tools into a time-series. Having determined the sequence at one midden, I compared it with the sequence observed elsewhere at another stratified site. Levels missing at one site could be found elsewhere and placed into proper sequence.[7]

But what if we want to go beyond patterns of change and explore the social life of an ancient hamlet? To this end, I investigated single component sites, which showed only a single occupation, in order to determine the layout of hamlets. In many places in southern Africa, settlements are laid out around a central cattle enclosure. This is a place where men gather to discuss matters of common interest and therefore is a place of political prominence. While claims on land are held in mutual trust within lineages, cattle are the private property of men, used to underwrite political alliances with men of other lineages and mark personal prestige. Because cattle-ownership is important to the structure of many southern African societies, locating a cattle enclosure suggests the significance of cattle in the local economy and the owner's adherence to a set of notions about the social importance of cattle-herding and the political prominence of cattle-owning men.[8]

What else can the analysis of settlements tell us about how people organized their society? As I just suggested, people create settlements in Africa, as elsewhere, according to culturally determined formulas, embodying in places ideas of social sanction and political validity. Places achieve special status as the locus of decision-making, ritual propriety, or domestic activity. In our culture we understand the social differences invested in mansions, tract-houses, or mobile homes. We spend our lives distinguishing the cultural values inherent in churches, courts, or pool halls. We regulate our behavior and expectations as we move between art galleries, movie theaters, and ball parks. Traces of these cultural prescriptions remain in the layout and structures found in old settlements.

Having determined which villages were occupied at the same time, I identified groups of associated settlements, determining the relative size of villages in each grouping in order to locate political centers or places engaged in iron or salt production. In the Victoria Falls region, in all time periods, settlements were of near-equal size, suggesting that there was little social differentiation. An important commodity like iron was produced at only one village at any one time. Because the economies of African villagers are usually dependent upon social obligation rather than capital wealth, and because iron objects were found in all the villages examined, it would appear, from our experience of modern Africa, that social mechanisms disseminated metal among villagers of near-equal social standing. Copper was highly valued and traded long distances for the manufacture of objects of bodily adornment; but it too was evenly distributed throughout the different villages, suggesting that everyone had equal access to status items. Later we shall see that differences in the size of villages and location of houses and unequal distributions of status items reflect the social standing of a town or its inhabitants.

FIRST FARMERS IN SUB-SAHARAN AFRICA

The research produced the first sequence of its kind in Africa, answering many questions about the history of culture in the Zambezi valley. But what of the larger problem of the monumental sites? How did this research illuminate the problem of studying Great Zimbabwe? Archaeology is an exercise in problem solving. In a perfect world the investigatory challenges archaeology sets would be solved with some strategic excavations in a narrowly specified study area. Unfortunately, investigation of the complexity of emergent society in southeast Africa requires collation of many kinds of information from many different parts of the continent. As a result, we need to go back to the start of self-sustaining food production in subsaharan Africa in order to understand how the social-ecological arrangements of small-scale savanna farmers underlie the precolonial states of southeast Africa.[9]

Who were the first farmers in subsaharan Africa, and how did they come to rely on agriculture? For a long time it was supposed that subsaharan African agriculture had diffused from southwest Asia. We now know that more than four thousand years ago people living along a broad swath of subsaharan savanna experimented with managing local food plants, notably the cereals finger millet, bulrush millet, fonio, and various kinds of sorghum. People long engaged in the hunting of game apparently found an advantage in transhumant pastoralism, managing domesticated herds rather than being wholly dependent upon the bounty of nature. Consequently, people came to grow plants they had already gathered, whose character they already knew, first as fodder for their stock and later as food plants they ate themselves.[10]

In time, feasible agricultural systems were established and eventually food production based on the cultivation of native cereals like the millets and sorghum was carried south. Cultivated cereals were drought-resistant enough to do well in the chancy climates of the southern savanna, but the nutrient-poor soils could be tilled only by clearing and burning vegetation for their nutrient-filled ash. These fields were profitably cropped for three to five years before they were rested while others were cropped. Thus, shifting subsistence farmers required access to many garden plots and a total acreage three to four times that needed to sustain the village. Shifting slash-and-burn cultivation produced adequate yields, but it forced thin population densities and little latitude to increase production.

SLASH-AND-BURN FARMERS ADAPT TO THE SOUTHERN SAVANNA

Research over the past thirty years suggests that slash-and-burn cultivators first came to the southern savanna 1,600 years ago as small-scale farmers searching out arable land and adequate pasturage for their cattle. Their settlements of a few sun-dried clay-walled houses, set in forest openings created by their gardens, transformed the landscape into a mosaic of gardens on freshly cut fields amidst spent clearings regenerating under secondary growth.

This is very much the pattern you find today traveling in the rural areas of Africa. We can observe that present-day farmers do not uniformly carpet the savanna with their compact villages, nor did their forefathers. I suggest that in the search for arable soil, grass cover, a water source, iron, and other related needs, they dispersed into small hamlets on small tracts of land.

The seventh- and eighth-century settlements at Kumadzulo and Kabondo Kumbo in the Victoria Falls region are typical early farming hamlets. Each is a group of small houses arranged in concentric circles around a central open area. At Kabondo Kumbo, the central area is filled with pits once used to smelt iron, the remnants of clay tubes used to pump fresh air into the heart of the furnace, and slag. The square post-hole wall houses were nearly three meters to a side, with floors prepared from sun-dried clay. Wall posts sunk into the ground were woven together with withies and grass, covered with puddled clay and topped with a thatched roof. Gardens, fallowing fields, and a grassy clearing for their cattle were outside the settlement.

In addition to the usual material culture of iron hoes, axes, spearheads, and arrowheads, these hamlets had copper, glass, and cowrie shells, probably obtained through long-distance trade. Because there was no local copper, it probably came from the same place as ostrich eggshell beads. The closest source of ostrich eggshell was south of the Zambezi, in Zimbabwe or Botswana. In addition, an analysis of the early pottery in the region suggests ethnic ties to people living further south, who used similar designs to decorate their pots. I surmised, based on affinities in pottery design, that the early cultivators had cultural ties to people living south of the Zambezi. The glass and cowrie shells probably came from indirect trade with Indian Ocean traders, and I surmised from ethnographic accounts that this trade was organized along social networks critical to the life of savanna farmers.

We can observe many social networks among the settled people of Africa. And we can surmise their importance to the maintenance of settled life in the past. How are social networks organized? African society may be seen as a mechanism conjoining people into networks of mutual obligation, minimizing the inherent risks of savanna farming. As a result, distant communities are woven into social networks designed to mediate risk by transferring produce from one place to another. The most critical social relationships derived from ties of kinship. In southern Africa descent is most frequently described by the female line (matrilineal descent). But whether governed by matrilineal or patrilineal descent, the group holds title to produce from land inherited from ancestors; the owners of the land, who cleared it, lie buried in it and retain an interest in the fortunes of their descendants. Authority is always held by males important in their descent group, who act as chiefs or stewards overseeing the well-being of their adherents.

As chiefs distribute land to their kin, they retain title to natural resources—minerals or game—but they delegate authority, while retaining the right to veto their kin's decisions, creating a differentiated ranking from paramount chiefs down to local headmen and common village folk. Living on tribal lands, I, too, sought consent for my field investigations from my local chief. Often my wife and I sat in a chiefly court discussing my fieldwork, exchanging small gifts and favors while supplicating villagers on hands and knees petitioned a claim to land or the settlement of a domestic dispute, which our chief granted or not, as he deemed proper.

There are two other significant social networks as well: one formed from contracting strategic marriages and the other by alliances of cattle-owning men. Gifts of cattle from the groom's family to the bride's family create strong bonds between extended families, and the interaction of cattle-owners creates political bonds between men. The different social contracts grant access to production and labor as a means of minimizing the risks inherent to savanna farming. In a broad sense, they create an infrastructure of families and individuals united by mutual self-interest and a command of resources such as ivory, copper, and gold.

THE FIRST TOWNS APPEAR IN THE LIMPOPO VALLEY

What were the conditions that caused the emergence of towns and social complexity among established cattle-keeping farmers of the savanna? Were the various social alliances designed to ease exchanges, minimize environmental risk, and distribute strategic goods suited to new entrepreneurial roles in long-distance trade? I have argued that the roots of the southeast African kingdoms lay in the customary politics of savanna farmers, gathering complexity and energy from value created in commerce with Indian Ocean traders. From the earliest times, Asian and Arab traders plied the coasts of East Africa. In the ninth century, as the Arabs founded towns such as Chibuene on the Mozambique coast, they offered new markets for raw materials.[11] By the ninth century their caravan routes penetrated deep into southeast Africa, bringing exotic luxuries from the Orient to exchange for ivory, gold, copper, and slaves.[12] As a result, customary leaders on the plateau enhanced their personal and corporate status with towns of their own. How can we determine this archaeologically? We can locate trade items, of course, but as we saw in the Zambezi valley these things can be received indirectly as part of small-scale exchanges. The more important changes in societies of the plateau reflecting the influence of intensive long-distance trade are found not only in the volume of foreign goods but also in alterations to the layout and arrangement of settlements.

Archaeologists analyze settlement variety as one way of discerning the social prominence of the inhabitants. Hierarchies are determined by ranking settlements by size. In a typical hierarchical arrangement, a single large site will be surrounded by a number of smaller sites. The settlement pattern suggests that the large town represents a center managing the affairs of adherents in its vicinity. As societies become more complex, new levels of management may be introduced, represented by sites of intermediate size at some distance from the center, surrounded by smaller hamlets. This settlement arrangement permits economical management of a district and convenient means for distributing its produce.

Before the establishment of the trading networks on the plateau, settlements of nearly equal size dotted the countryside, much as we saw in the Victoria Falls region. Now there appeared a ranking of towns and hamlets of varying sizes. Before the rise of Great Zimbabwe, Bambandyanalo and Mapungubwe were the largest towns on the plateau and the homes of the socially elite. Elsewhere, smaller villages located on hilltops probably housed district administrators managing the affairs of the hamlets built on level ground. As the Shona confederacy grew more prosperous, its growing social complexity was reflected in the elaboration of its settlements, as we shall see.

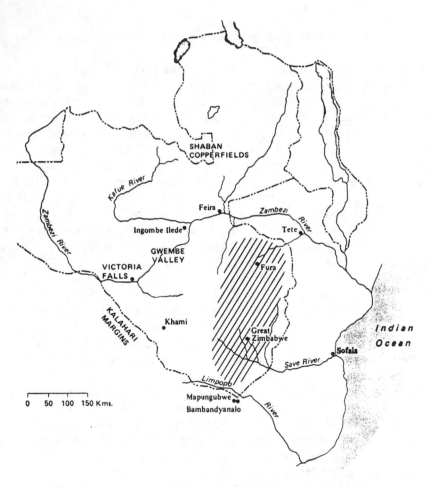

FIGURE 23-2   MAP OF SOUTHEAST AFRICA, LOCATING THE EXTENT
OF THE ZIMBABWEAN TRADING EMPIRE (SHADED) AND ADJACENT AREAS

Although archaeology can describe the growth of complexity from the variety of settlements, a critical problem remains: How did the early entrepreneurs underwrite both long-distance trade and their aspirations of elite status? Obviously, control of trade and raw materials was important. But how could they attract trade routes and how could they command the exploitation of the minerals and other commodities sought by foreign traders? We have seen that economies can command labor as part of wide-ranging social networks and that entrepreneurs can accumulate wealth in cattle or metal. Therefore, archaeologists seek signs of the prevalence of one or the other. In the Victoria Falls region, the earliest hamlets were organized around iron production, but these early settlers were later replaced by ones who organized their lives around the accumulation of cattle. Elsewhere, early evidence of the precedence of cattle-herders is attested to at Toutswe and allied sites in northeastern Botswana. There, a hierarchical pattern of settlements laid out around central cattle enclosures suggests the accumulation of wealth and status in cattle and the political importance of cattle-owning men.[13] Because the same kind of settlement pattern is found at Bambandyanalo, archaeologists have surmised that the chiefly elite used their status as cattle-owners and their customary command of resources to achieve an enhanced political control of their community.

By the tenth century, as indicated by the volume of imported goods and the growth of the town, customary authorities based at Bambandyanalo coalesced their control of production, resources, and foreign commerce into a framework of prestige-affirming activities regulating material transactions throughout the Limpopo drainage. The prevalence of ivory objects suggests that Bambandyanalo's entrepreneurs had an active interest in the harvesting and trafficking of elephant ivory. At the same time, because there is alluvial gold in the vicinity they may have commissioned the panning of gold, but there is little to confirm this.

Ivory may have been important in the beginning and attractive to Arab merchants, but as markets for copper and gold grew the local producers adjusted accordingly. They left few ore sources unexploited. When the first European miners came into southeast Africa in the nineteenth century they found themselves preceded in every instance by long-standing African mining operations. The gold mines, probably the property of chiefs, were worked by young women small enough to crawl into narrow mine shafts. The occasional finds of skeletons of young women, as well as the ethnographic observation of later mining operations, attest to this. In the 1920s some sought to prove that the miners were people from India imported by ancient Near Eastern mine owners. Forensic studies of skeletons found in the shafts settled the question in favor of Bantu-speaking owners and miners.

Archaeology can detect the growth of important places. But how do we infer change in the political life of the plateau at this time? As we have seen, early settlements were arranged around a central cattle enclosure. The cattle

pen is more than the place to keep cattle safe at night. It is also the heart of village life, the place where men gather to tend their animals and debate affairs
critical to the operation of the village. Just as courts or legislative chambers in
our culture give a sanction to the decisions made within them, cattle pens
among the cattle-owning people of southern Africa give a similar sanction. In
the eleventh century, however, a different kind of decision-sanctioning body
developed at Mapungubwe. This was marked by an open area, showing
no signs of building. Even at Great Zimbabwe, where space was at a pre-
mium and houses were built so close together that the roofs touched, the
place where men gathered to hear legal cases is clearly discernible as an
open area near the king's residence. This exclusive men's assembly area su-
perseded the central cattle enclosure as the site of governance. The new
kind of governing assembly also suggests the emergence of a new, more
exclusive class of decision-makers. The surging economy and the emergence of gold as a trading commodity caused control of the trading enterprise to slip away from the low-lying Bambandyanalo to the nearby hilltop
location at Mapungubwe. The beginnings of gold working and the reduced
importance of ivory are suggested by the gold and copper ornaments found
with Mapungubwe burials.

Short of conflict, of which there is no evidence, why did the control of
the trading enterprise shift from one location to another? The circumstance
of changing status may perhaps be explained with reference to my own experiences. Occasionally, while travelling in the bush, you come across satisfied people administered by a capable leader. The benefits achieved may
be psychological—the prospect of good rains or crops gained through the
chief's mediation—or material—the prospect of participation in valuable
distributions of bridewealth or access to good farmland. Nearby are others
less satisfied with the benefits from their alliance. The clients of the lesser
chief feel compelled by family ties or proximity to maintain their loyalty,
but given the opportunity they would shift to a more powerful combine, or
attempt to gain access to more beneficial allies. Apparently the Mapungubwe leadership, by organizing the gold trade, could attract more wealth to itself, underwrite more substantial distributions, and command the allegiance
of a larger force.

The customary leaders at Mapungubwe not only commanded the wealth
created through long-distance trade but also began to adopt the trappings
of class privilege. Free-stone-walling (stone courses laid without mortar) de-
marcated parts of the hilltop for the first time, with elite houses erected farther up the hill, away from the town, displaying precedence of social rank by
their choice of an elevated house site. In the twelfth century the intraregion-
al trading system instituted midlevel managers in smaller hilltop zimbabwes. The common folk lived in farming hamlets arranged around a central
cattle pen. During the thirteenth century, command of the Shona confederacy shifted away from the Limpopo valley to Great Zimbabwe.

THE ASCENDANCY OF THE GREAT ZIMBABWE

Once Great Zimbabwe was a district headquarters within the orbit of Mapungubwe, but when the Save River trade routes generated a more economically managed flow of imports Great Zimbabwe dominated exchanges over a broader area than that overseen from the Limpopo valley. With the ascendance of Great Zimbabwe, the population and importance of the Limpopo valley declined.

The reasons for Mapungubwe's decline may be surmised. We know from ethnological observations noted earlier that political alliances are often created among those seeking the benefits of allegiance to elite individuals. The flow of benefits returned assures support to the leader's assertion of privilege. At the same time, clients are drawn to those leaders assuring the best returns. The rulers of Great Zimbabwe derived savings from its compact interior lines of communication, enabling them to forge alliances throughout a broad territory ranging from the Limpopo drainage to the Zambezi valley. As a result, their distributions probably increased at lower cost, enabling them to expand their investment in distributions to clients and dampening the ability of others to challenge their command of goods or services.

Great Zimbabwe was the most prestigious center in southeast Africa for the next two hundred years; with a population of more than eighteen thousand it was the equal of many contemporary towns throughout the medieval world. It organized mining, and the export of minerals on the plateau and overland trade routes brought it copper from southern Zaire. All was traded toward Arab towns on the Sofala coast. Its elite underwrote new construction, and new art styles and architecture came to the fore. Community resources were also invested in monumental public works allied to the expanded role of its governors.

Monumental construction gave the elite a way to display their organizational ability, investing in symbols of the established order and their custody of it. Social distinction, evident in the emergent architectural styles at the Limpopo valley towns, was firmly consolidated at Great Zimbabwe. Stone was used to join the natural boulders of the steep central hill and free-standing walls encircled and divided its houses. At the same time, a territorial rainmaking shrine was erected near the Paramount's dwelling at Great Zimbabwe, probably to affirm his interest in the affairs of the common folk. This affirmation derives from the fact that the role of rainmaker is a way that village headmen display their value as purveyors of benefit. In drought-prone southeast Africa, rainfall is haphazard. Storms unleash torrents of water capable of washing away young plants, or the sun bakes them into straw. Coordinating planting with the first rains of the season determines success. Therefore, great importance is given to the ritual attending rainmaking and the mediating role of chiefs in producing it within their district. Probably as an extension of this role, the territorial rainmaking shrine at Great Zimbabwe drew attention to its stewardship over the whole region.

On the local level the validity of descent claims to authority are reenforced by adherence to ancestor cults honoring the owners of the land. As the sphere of authority claimed by the rulers expanded, the appearance of new kinds of ritual items suggests that at this time the parochial role of local ancestor cults was supplemented by the institution of an ecumenical rite revolving around a senior god, Mwari, administered by the leadership at Great Zimbabwe.

Why did the customary leaders at Great Zimbabwe feel the need to involve themselves in managing the ritual affairs of their community? I have suggested that this activity was an expansion of an activity already expected of chiefs. Our understanding of the politics of precolonial African societies suggests that customary leaders had few opportunities to use force to coerce their subjects, therefore they sought other means to sanction their authority. Mystification and control of ritual is a subtle yet effective agency of political control. In their control of rainmaking for the Zimbabwean state and the institution of the rites of the supreme Shona god, Mwari, at Great Zimbabwe, Great Zimbabwe's leadership re-emphasized their interest in benevolent mediation and the common good on behalf of their clients.

The network administered by Great Zimbabwe was more extensive than that attached to Mapungubwe, yet its internal organization was very much the same. Great Zimbabwe was the largest center. Smaller zimbabwes with freestone-walling and a men's assembly area were sited atop hills, while the more frequent farming hamlets, without stone-walling, were laid out as cattle-herding villages. The persistence of these settlement variants and the probable managerial structure suggests a cultural continuity as well. This accords well with accounts retained in local historical tradition that describe a succession of Karanga clans dominating the economic and political life on the plateau.

SOME ARCHAEOLOGICAL REFLECTIONS

Randall-MacIver, at the British Association meeting at Bulawayo, Rhodesia, in 1905, argued that the reality of the southeast African towns was as fabulous as the fiction they once inspired. He told his audience that archaeology would not subtract from this wonder but would instead replace one mystery with another equally fantastic romance. Recently, archaeology transformed our understanding of the African past, fulfilling Randall-MacIver's prediction that science would discover the true romance of Africa.

The role of the archaeologist as anthropologist and historian treading the mine fields of cultural politics is a difficult one. More is involved than field explorations and excavation because our efforts describe a history of which we have no other record. The idea that King Solomon's mines were located in southeast Africa, though challenged by science, stayed an active part of the politics of southern Africa throughout the colonial period. To this day the origins of the Great Zimbabwe are challenged by many who prefer to describe the monumental southeast African towns as evidence of exotic interlopers—Persians, Indians, ancient Israelites, or even fictional European-derived black folk, the Hamites—rather than attribute the monumental towns to African achievement.

Cultural politics aside, there is much satisfaction in the performance of a successful reconnaissance or the completion of a large-scale excavation. In southeast Africa field excursions can be long, arduous, and time-consuming propositions. They often require travel on foot trails through rural areas, reconnaissance of river banks from dugout canoes, interviews with local people, and an intense scrutiny of the ground for faint traces of small settlements abandoned many years ago. Excavations take you far from the support of towns or colleagues. In the field you must be prepared to improvise and adapt field methods to the problem at hand while maintaining proper control over the investigation and all of its records. Though a well-conducted excavation develops a rhythm of its own, its success depends on the archaeologist's ability to train and organize novice field crews while arranging living quarters and other necessities deep in the bush.

Is it possible to comprehend an extinct culture solely from the remains of an excavated settlement? My field experience suggests that an archaeologist is required to be an anthropologist as well. Sampling a variety of sites by intensive field survey and selective excavation, I could reconstruct a great deal of the daily life in the old villages. In order to understand how they lived in the past, I first had to gain an idea of how people live today. Therefore, I spent time living among subsistence farmers, discussing the mechanics of crop production or cattle management. I sought insight into how small-scale subsistence farmers managed their social and economic life and speculated on how such people underwrote the complex stratified societies that so mystified archaeology in the nineteenth and early twentieth centuries.

These conversations were particularly useful during my surveys. The linchpin of good field archaeology is the areal field survey, discovering the loci of old occupations. Large-scale surveys can be very time-consuming and frustrating, except that the bush is littered with clues—patches of discolored soil, disturbed vegetation, particular grass cover, and the like—that indicate to an observant archaeologist the research value of one location over another. When I learned how to read the bush and to think like an African farmer, I could sit atop my vehicle, scanning the wooded edges of a broad grassy opening, and suggest the direction of a walking survey with some assurance that my effort would bear fruit. Small settlements of sun-dried clay houses leave little trace of their passing, though the signs are there. Sometimes I would see the stained soil washing on the trail from an abandoned village. The eighth-century Zambezi farm site was found this way, during a drive across a high terrace above the Zambezi river. I found the Kumadzulo site by noticing that the tree cover was less dense on one edge of a clearing than on the other. A trial cutting, just over a meter deep, uncovered a well-preserved sixth-century village buried under the Kalahari sand.

Popular interest has always centered on the supposed mystery of Great Zimbabwe, but many other threads run through the history of society on the southern savanna and tantalize us, drawing us to the wide-ranging problems posed by the past. When archaeology asks the right questions, mystery is swept away. The current practice of archaeology transcends the description of material objects in order to define the byways of an extinct culture, finding in the basic qualities of contemporary or recent African society enough to explain long past events, achieving a level of explanation not available to nineteenth-century archaeology. As a result, we exorcise the phantoms of the lost civilizations with a clear understanding of the African roots of these remarkable places.

The first archaeologists in southern Africa construed a world in which the zimbabwes were the relics of Near Eastern antiquity. As a result, they failed to recognize the African origins of these buildings. They wove fictions of mythical cities, peopled by the long dead of antiquity, lost gold fields, and romantic interludes between Solomon and the Queen of Sheba in the middle of Africa. Other commentators sought evidence of a superior race of African, like the Galla of Ethiopia, as the builders of zimbabwes. Some sought in the chevron patterns on some stone-walling a connection with the Berbers of north Africa. But a generation of more scientific archaeologists sifted the myriad leavings of the past, exploring the byways of subsistence farmers to construe a very different world, in which traditional African culture was capable of epic achievement.

Modern archaeologists at one time or another have suggested that the origins of the monumental towns lay in the prestige-yielding activities associated with cattle-ownership, control of trade, or the propagation of a unifying religion. It is apparent that all three causes plus the influence of massive inflows of foreign goods effected the social changes we have examined here. Science never unearthed the mysterious "lost cities" envisioned by nineteenth-century antiquarians, and it failed to resolve questions that teased earlier archaeologists. It did better; it restored to the people of Zimbabwe their history.

CHRONOLOGY OF EVENTS PERTAINING TO GREAT ZIMBABWE

1891	First archaeological investigations at Great Zimbabwe.
September, 1871	First eye-witness description of the Great Zimbabwe published in Europe, fueling speculation that the monumental sites of southeast Africa were the ruins of King Solomon's Ophir.
1700–present	Great Zimbabwe area reoccupied by various Shona-speaking people.
1498–1506	Portuguese take over East Coast trade from the Arabs. Portuguese chronicles recount tales of an abandoned city in the African interior and European maps mark the Empire of Monomatapa in southern Africa.
1450	Great Zimbabwe area declines in importance as competing centers arise in southwest Zimbabwe at Khami and at Fura Mt., the capital of Mwene Mutapa in northern Zimbabwe.
1270–1450	Great Zimbabwe prospers by its control of long-distance and foreign trade. New art and architectural styles develop as Great Zimbabwe becomes a major urban center.
c. 1270	The Mapungubwe area depopulated as Great Zimbabwe becomes the new capital of the Shona trading confederacy.
1100–1270	Great Zimbabwe under the influence of Mapungubwe; the first walled enclosures built.
by 1200	Mapungubwe becomes the capital of the trading confederacy, superseding the leadership of Bambandyanalo.
by 1100	Bambandyanalo, in the Limpopo Valley, establishes links between producers on the plateau and trading towns on the East Coast.
by 1000	Arab towns spread down the Indian Ocean coast to the delta of the Limpopo River. Ivory and gold trade develops between the interior of southeast Africa and the East Coast.
1000–1100	Shona-speakers settle the central portions of the Great Zimbabwe site.
c. 950	The ancestors of the modern Shona move north of the Limpopo.
900–1000	Hierarchically arranged chiefdoms appear among the cattle-owning pastoralists on the margin of Kalahari in eastern Botswana.
500–900	Settlements of subsistence farmers established throughout southern Africa and farmers settle the Great Zimbabwe region for the first time.
c. 400	Bantu-speaking farmers cross the Zambezi into southern Africa.

NOTES

1. Classic examples of this fiction are by the English author H. Rider Haggard, whose *King Solomon's Mines*, modeled after an earlier novel, H. M. Walmsley's *The Lost Cities of Zululand*, describes the search for the source of Solomon's wealth among the ruins of a lost ancient city. Haggard's novel *Elissa: The Doom of Zimbabwe* describes life in ancient times at Great Zimbabwe.

2. The best history of opinion on Great Zimbabwe is Peter Garlake's *Great Zimbabwe*. Comprehensive coverage of the history of research and literature on Great Zimbabwe and southeast African archaeology in general is available in Joseph O. Vogel, *Great Zimbabwe: The Iron Age in South Central Africa* (New York and London: Garland Publishing, Inc., 1994).

3. James Theodore Bent, *The Ruined Cities of Mashonaland: Being a Record of Explorations and Excavations in 1891* (London: Longmans, Green and Company, 1892); Robert Hartmann, *Die Nigritier: Eine Anthropologisch-Ethnologische Monograph. Erste Theil* (Berlin: Verlag von Wiegandt, Hempel und Farey, 1876), pp. 36–41.

4. David Randall-MacIver, *Mediaeval Rhodesia* (London: MacMillan and Co., 1906).

5. Gertrude Caton-Thompson, *Zimbabwe Culture: Ruins and Reactions* (Oxford: Clarendon Press, 1931).

6. Keith R. Robinson, Roger F. H. Summers, and Anthony Whitty, *Zimbabwe Excavations, 1958* (Bulawayo: Occasional Papers of the National Museums of Rhodesia, 1958), pp. 157–332.

7. Joseph O. Vogel, "The Mosioatunya Sequence," *Zambia Museums Journal* 1 (1973): 103–152.

8. Adam Kuper, "Symbolic Dimensions of the Southern Bantu Homestead," *Africa* 50 (1980): 8–23; Thomas N. Huffman, "Snakes and Birds: Expressive Space at Great Zimbabwe," *African Studies* 40 (1981): 131–150.

9. The suggestion that the social-ecological arrangements of small-scale savanna farmers underlie the precolonial states of southeast Africa can be found in Joseph O. Vogel, "The Cultural Basis, Development, and Influence of a Socially Mediated Trading Corporation in Southern Zambezia," *Journal of Anthropological Archaeology* 9 (1990): 105–147; a similar concept of socially mediated exchange systems is found in Ricardo T. Duarte, *Northern Mozambique in the Swahili World* (Uppsala: Central Board of National Antiquities, Sweden Studies in African Archaeology 4, 1993).

10. Susan K. McIntosh and Roderick McIntosh, "Current Directions in West African Archaeology," *Annual Review of Anthropology* 12 (1983): 215–258.

11. Paul L. L. Sinclair, "Chibuene: An Early Trading Site in Mozambique," *Paideuma* 28 (1982): 150–164

12. The basic information underlying the following discussion of the development of customary states in southeast Africa may be found in these excellent surveys of the precolonial history of southern Africa: Martin L. Hall, *Farmers, Kings, and Traders: The People of Southern Africa 200–1860* (Chicago: University of Chicago Press, 1987); Thomas N. Huffman, "The Rise and Fall of Zimbabwe," *Journal of African History* 13 (1973): 353–366; and Paul L. L. Sinclair, *Space, Time, and State Formation* (Uppsala: Societas Archaeologicas Upsaliensis, 1987).

13. James R. Denbow, "A New Look at the Later Prehistory of the Kalahari," *Journal of African History* 27 (1986): 3–28.

SUGGESTED READINGS

Connah, Graham. *African Civilizations*. Cambridge: Cambridge University Press, 1987. An excellent survey of a wide range of African states.

Garlake, Peter S. *Great Zimbabwe*. London: Thames and Hudson, 1973. The most complete survey of the history of research on the monumental sites of southeast Africa.

Hibbert, Christopher. *Africa Explored: European Travellers in the Dark Continent*. New York: Viking Penguin, 1982. A useful source of information on early European travels in Africa.

Phillipson, David W. *African Archaeology*, 2nd ed. Cambridge: Cambridge University Press, 1994. A useful and extensive survey of all aspects of African prehistory.

Summers, Roger F. H. *Zimbabwe: A Rhodesian Mystery*. Johannesburg: Nelson, 1963. An excellent introduction to the Great Zimbabwe and its interpretation.

Trigger, Bruce G. *A History of Archaeological Thought*. New York: Cambridge University Press, 1989. A general history of archaeology containing a discussion of the politics of archaeological research in southern Africa.

ARCHAEOLOGIST AT WORK

RICHARD E. BLANTON

THINKING ABOUT THE EVOLUTION OF SOCIETY AND CULTURE

My curiosity about other cultures and how they change slowly germinated until it eventually led me away from my early interests in physics, astronomy, and chemistry, to an undergraduate major in anthropology at the University of Michigan. There, stimulated by courses I took from Professor Leslie White, notably his famous "The Evolution of Culture," and by other courses from the distinguished faculty of that institution, my interests deepened. In particular, I was attracted to questions surrounding the evolution of complex human societies. Why, and how, had our species developed densely populated, technologically advanced complex societies of large scale—at least in some places—out of the simple, small-scale foraging groups of the Pleistocene?

During the 1960s, at the same time I was doing my undergraduate studies, a new environmental awareness swept through this country, bringing with it many concerns related to overpopulation, the negative environmental consequences of modern agriculture, and the long-term sustainability of our industrial way of life.[1] Some of the questions raised by the environmental movement overlapped with questions asked by sociocultural evolutionary theorists. For example, what were the past patterns of human population growth, and why had human populations grown? Had overpopulation and environmental deterioration brought the decline of ancient civilizations? Could learning about past societies contribute to our ability to devise sustainable human-environment relationships and stable population size in today's world? It was already apparent that supposedly scientifically based population and agricultural policies had failed because they were built on faulty assumptions about human behavior and the nature of social change.[2] Clearly, new knowledge was needed about the human past and its relation to present developmental trends, and it seemed to me that sociocultural evolutionary inquiry in anthropology had the potential to contribute to an expanded environmental awareness as well as to problem-solving in today's world.[3] My interests were further intensified as I came to realize that understanding the human past is more than just a fascinating intellectual challenge. Anthropological inquiry can also provide knowledge relevant to many of the social and environmental concerns we face in the modern world.

ARCHAEOLOGICAL INQUIRY WITHIN ANTHROPOLOGY

Continuing progress in anthropological method and theory enhances the discipline's ability to enrich our understanding of human social change over long time periods, and to draw useful conclusions from this knowledge. To some degree, this progress results from the application of new technologies, ranging from isotopic dating methods to satellite imagery and computerization, to mention a few examples. More importantly, however, it is based on an elaboration of interdisciplinary cooperation in which the research of various kinds of specialists is linked together in a creative synthesis.

The growth of an integrated approach is facilitated by the fact that anthropology, as it is taught in most departments in the United States, is a unified discipline including sociocultural, archaeological, human biological, and linguistic subdisciplines. My interest in change in human societies over time spans counted in thousands of years meant that I would make use of archaeological methods, but the kind of archaeology I was aiming for had to allow me to address the broad questions posed by sociocultural theory and environmental concerns. Fortunately, I was in a department where a strong sense of disciplinary unity was cultivated, and where it was commonly accepted that archaeological research would contribute importantly to the study of sociocultural evolution in a general sense.

Traditionally, from the middle nineteenth century to the present, most of our understanding of long-term change in human societies came not from direct archaeological evidence from the past, but from the use of a "comparative method." This method involves the placement of ethnographically known societies along a continuum from small-scale and simple, to larger-scale and more complex. This continuum is then divided into evolutionary categories (e.g., band, tribe, chiefdom, state), and is interpreted as a proxy for "stages" of sociocultural evolution that have succeeded one another over thousands of years.[4] The comparative method has been productive in anthropological inquiry, especially so in recent decades, owing to methodological improvements,[5] but it will always suffer from an inability to directly study sociocultural evolution where it actually took place. Ideally, comparative inquiry should complement direct archaeological investigation, but it was not until after World War II that the potential synergism of comparative and archaeological approaches could be fully realized. Anthropological archaeology advanced in its analytical concepts and field research methods, including the development of carbon-14 dating and other chronometric techniques.[6] These developments, coupled with a greater availability of research funding for substantial multidisciplinary, long-term field projects (especially from the U.S. National Science Foundation), made it possible to acquire an unprecedented quantity and quality of new information about the human past.

We can add to these developments in archaeological method and funding levels the fact that, beginning around 1950, a "cultural ecological" theoretical orientation began to influence archaeological field research, contributing greatly to its ability to address broad evolutionary issues. Archaeologists were urged to use their data to address questions relating sociocultural change to ecological processes in a way that engaged the interests of a wide spectrum of natural and social scientists. Putting all of these elements together, it was evident that anthropology was on the verge of realizing a greatly expanded understanding of sociocultural evolution, a new synthesis that would be built on the combined efforts of researchers representing its various subdisciplines, including archaeology, as well as researchers from other disciplines.

THE RISE OF CULTURAL ECOLOGY

Anthropologists, including Leslie White, Julian Steward, Elman Service, Karl Wittfogel, and Marvin Harris, and the economist Esther Boserup, among others,[7] proposed theories that connected various aspects of the material conditions of existence—environment, technology, exchange, production, population growth, and competition for resources—to sociocultural evolutionary change. An admirable feature of this materialist theoretical orientation was that its ideas could be evaluated through anthropological field investigations, including archaeological research. Past environmental conditions can be inferred from archaeological plant and animal remains (by ethnobotanists and ethnozoologists), including remains of pollen (palynology), and through the study of ancient landforms (geomorphology), among other sources of information. Population change could be measured through detailed archaeological surveys of large regions. Ancient production technologies could be reconstructed from the archaeological excavation of activity areas. Testing ecological theories through archaeological field studies is never easy. Problems abound, ranging from difficult working conditions to poor preservation of archaeological sites in some environments. Modern agriculture and construction destroy remains of past societies. And, the new theories placed stringent new demands on the quality and quantity of information that have to be collected by anthropological archaeologists and their colleagues. In spite of these challenges, much progress toward understanding the past can be and has been made within the framework of the long-term, multidisciplinary projects carried out in a cultural ecological theoretical framework.[8]

Most archaeological field research that drew from the cultural ecological theoretical orientation focused on "behavioral regions." Behavioral regions are naturally or culturally bounded territories, such as river floodplains, mountain valleys, or islands. Presumably, within such a region a human population adapted over an extended period to local environmental circumstances. A region-focused approach asks questions like: How have humans adjusted to the environmental features of a region, over time, through technological, social, and cultural changes? What local environmental factors were most important in determining aspects of change in social organization and culture? Has the environment (for example, climate) remained stable over time, or has it changed, and what have been the social consequences of environmental change? What has been the long-term history of population growth in the region? Has population stayed below carrying capacity (the number of people that could be sustained, as calculated from the availability of resources like cultivable soil and water), or has population exceeded carrying capacity? If population levels exceeded capacity, what were the social and environmental consequences?

One of the most stimulating suggestions was made by Julian Steward (Karl Wittfogel had a similar idea). He suggested that irrigation agriculture in major river floodplains in arid or semi-arid environments would entail the development of centralized social controls, bringing in their wake the evolution of complex society. Ideas like his spurred research efforts in important riverine regions, including the Nile Valley and Mesopotamia, and influenced the aims of archaeological research in the semi-arid highlands of Mesoamerica.[9]

RESEARCH PROJECTS IN THE VALLEYS OF MEXICO AND OAXACA, MEXICO

One of the most important region-centered cultural ecological projects ever carried out by anthropologists was already underway by the time I started my graduate studies at the University of Michigan. Eric Wolf, William Sanders, Angel Palerm, and René Millon, among others, proposed and initiated a long-term study of an important Mesoamerican region, the Valley of Mexico.[10] There, a succession of powerful states had developed, including one centered at the famous archaeological site of Teotihuacan, and later the Aztec empire, conquered by the Spanish in 1521. These states had been among the most influential social formations in prehispanic Mesoamerican civilization, making the valley an obvious choice for a major long-term research project. Many specialists contributed to the project, but the main research focus was a systematic archaeological settlement pattern survey of the entire region. In semi-arid environments like the Valley of Mexico, remains of ancient habitation sites and other ancient features (defensive walls, irrigation canals, agricultural terraces, public buildings, etc.) are usually visible on the ground surface except where obliterated by subsequent natural geological processes and human activity (especially, in this case, the massive growth of modern Mexico City). Numerous archaeological sites were located and recorded using surface survey methods. The sites ranged from the earliest small farming villages after about 1500 B.C. to the great prehispanic cities of the Classic period and the later Aztec empire. Ancient human communities show up as scatters of pot sherds, building stone, stone tools, plaster wall fragments, and sometimes more massive features such as pyramid platforms. In the best-preserved situations, even house foundations can be mapped. By analyzing settlement patterns (the spatial distribution of habitation sites), information from stratigraphic excavations, and environmental data, archaeologists can make inferences about many aspects of past social change through three thousand years of settled agriculture life prior to the Spanish conquest, as well as for periods subsequent to the conquest.[11] I spent three valuable, and enjoyable field seasons on the Valley of Mexico archaeological survey, which provided material for my Ph.D. dissertation and helped prepare me for my future research.

The regional study methods developed in the course of the Valley of Mexico project proved gratifyingly productive, and potentially applicable to similar regions elsewhere. Although much work remained to be done in the Valley of Mexico, I decided after three field seasons to apply a similar approach in another important Mesoamerican highland region, the Valley of Oaxaca in the southern highlands of Mexico. This region saw the growth of the Zapotec state, one of the most influential societies of ancient Mesoamerican civilization. There, another long-term, multidisciplinary regional project, Kent Flannery's Oaxaca Human Ecology Project, was in full swing, and clearly would stand to benefit from a systematic archaeological survey like the one I had helped to complete in the Valley of Mexico. Over a period of ten years and six field seasons, my colleagues and I were able to carry out the regional archaeological survey of the core region of Zapotec society, and extensions of the core-zone surveys continue to this day. To date we have located, described, and analyzed the data from more than six thousand archaeological sites in a 2,500 square kilometer area.[12]

ECOLOGICAL THEORY CHALLENGED

The Valley of Mexico Project and the Oaxaca Human Ecology Project have proven to be among the most successful large-scale regional archaeological studies anywhere, providing an unparalleled record of past human occupation of two of Mesoamerica's most socioculturally significant regions. The results of decades of work are important to anthropological archaeology in many respects, but most importantly, from my point of view, in illustrating the complex causal interactions that obtain between political and economic structure, on the one hand, and patterns of population growth and agricultural intensification, on the other. For example, the massive social system of Teotihuacan (roughly 100 B.C. to A.D. 700) concentrated political, economic, and ritual functions of the entire Valley of Mexico, and beyond, primarily in one large capital center. This strongly centered regional structure—called a "primate" system—resulted in the growth of a massive city of more than 150,000 people, but a comparatively underpopulated and disadvantaged rural hinterland. Once this system was established, there was little further overall population growth or agricultural intensification over many centuries. By nearly the end of the prehispanic sequence, however (roughly A.D. 1200 to A.D. 1521), a new arrangement emerged, that we call "Aztec" society, characterized by the growth of a complex system of numerous cities and towns, each providing a variable mix of commercial, political, cultural, and ritual functions.[13] This complex social formation saw a rapid growth in population, to the highest levels of the prehispanic sequence (over one million in the valley alone), and the development of many new agricultural strategies, including sophisticated water-control facilities for large-scale irrigation projects.

How could systems so unlike one another evolve in the same region? I infer from discoveries like these that in our earlier cultural ecological theorizing, we had paid too much attention to how humans cope with the environment of their local region, thinking that the process of environmental adaptation alone would lead us to a better understanding of the nature of sociocultural change. While it is evident that environmental factors provide important constraints and opportunities for human actors, we still need to be attentive to the fact that contrastive social arrangements, such as Teotihuacan and Aztec, themselves generate distinct modes of population distribution, natural resource utilization, and technological development. Further, it is evident from these data that population growth was not a steady, constant factor in human affairs, driving the development of new productive technologies, or bringing about competition for resources, as cultural ecological theory had led us to expect. Differing social structures resulted in differing demographic patterns; some structural arrangements encouraged growth, while others retarded it.

What would explain the evolution of such distinct social systems? One of the most important aspects of society and culture largely ignored by the environmental adaptation theories was the role played by the population of a region in a larger system of interconnected regional populations. Mesoamerican civilization, a social system that extended all the way from what is now Central America to northern Mexico, was as much a part of the environment of an important city like Teotihuacan as was its local agricultural hinterland. While cultural ecological research had produced a vast quantity of useful information, by the late 1970s it was becoming clear to me and other researchers that a fuller explication of sociocultural change would develop out of a more complete and encompassing theory. A new approach would incorporate the most useful insights and findings of cultural ecology, but go beyond its adaptational and region-centered biases. A more robust theory would have to have the ability to explain how processes of change at the local level (including those found in households, and villages, and regions), influence, and are influenced by, processes of change taking place at larger spatial scales, including intersocietal interactions over long distances at the scale of whole civilizations (e.g., Mesoamerican, Central Andean, Greater Mesopotamian, Chinese). This more ambitious research agenda implies a need for a more broadly conceived method and theory, not to mention new kinds of field research.[14]

NEW DIRECTIONS FOR RESEARCH

Anthropology has tended to see its subject matter as local culturally-defined groups that are relatively isolated, bounded, static, and adapted to their local environmental circumstances. But closer investigation shows that people migrate; groups coalesce or split up; local leaders manipulate concepts of ethnic identity to firm up control of a faction and outside powers create named cultural groups where none existed previously to manage a chaotic periphery.[15] To understand processes of change in a dynamic world, one must know more about the behavior of social actors as they respond to changing circumstances both locally and at larger spatial scales. One of the weak points of the cultural ecological approach, and of anthropological inquiry in general, is the failure to account fully for household behavior.[16] And yet, many fundamental processes of social, cultural, and environmental change in the evolution of early complex societies, as well as in the modern world, are outcomes of household choices concerning such things as migration, fertility, production intensity, passing on of wealth between generations, education, market participation, and consumption, among many others.

In our research in the Valley of Oaxaca, my colleagues and I noted what appeared to be substantial changes over time in household behavior related to fertility, craft production, food (including production, processing, and consumption), housing (and other aspects of consumer behavior), market participation, and migration. For example, at about the same time as the development of the region's first urban center (about 500 B.C.), households, even in rural communities, intensified agricultural production, built more substantial houses, engaged in more commercial transactions, and even invented the tortilla, indicating a change in everyday habits of food processing and consumption. We thought that changing household activity in this and other periods had important consequences for change in the larger social systems of the valley, and for those beyond its boundaries, and it seemed natural to pursue this line of investigation as a next step to learning more about Zapotec civilization and its transformations. An excavation program concentrating on houses would allow me to investigate change over time in household behavior, but I realized that little in the way of methodological or comparative data were available to aid me in the analysis and interpretation of this class of data. Given this, I decided to make a temporary career detour in order to make use of the possibilities of a comparative and cross-cultural approach. My goal was to gain a broader perspective on household issues before pursuing further research in Oaxaca. While I realized a change in research approach would ultimately benefit my archaeological investigations, I made the change with some reluctance, because I find archaeological fieldwork to be one of the most enjoyable kinds of research. It combines intellectual stimulation with physical challenge, while at the same time allowing me to enjoy the beauty and pleasure of living in Mexico.

Effective interpretation of archaeological remains is dependent on a well-developed understanding of the relationships between human social behavior and material culture. In the case of households, this issue revolves in part around the house itself. What social factors influence household decisions regarding, for example, house size, building materials, and space use? The aim of my comparative project is to relate the formal properties of houses described in published ethnographic reports to household form and function, including household composition (nuclear family, extended household, etc.) and economic strategies of household members. Formal properties of the house include the use of space (such as gender-specific areas and activity specialization by room), size of the house, spatial arrangements of rooms, costliness and durability of building materials, decorative elaboration of the facade, and internal symbolic aspects of the house (to what degree is the house a cosmological metaphor?). To get at variation, I coded ethnographically and architecturally described rural houses from several localities where peasant houses and households are described in ethnographic works of high quality, including Japan, Java, Thailand, China, Nepal, India, Iran, Iraq, Syria, Turkey, Lebanon, Egypt, Yemen, Mexico, and Guatemala.[17]

There were definitely times when, sitting in my office in West Lafayette, coding data from published reports, I wished I could be back in Oaxaca doing archaeology. Still, I have been very gratified with what came out of this comparative work, and I am even planning to do more in the future. It accomplished exactly what I was hoping for, in that it provided me with a large and varied sample that I can use to better contextualize prehispanic Zapotec households and their changes. I was able to propose hypotheses to explain some aspects of the observed variation in households and their houses by placing the ethnographically-described cases within the contexts of community type and regional market structure.

For example, I found that in certain economic situations, senior generation members of households control the labor and marriages of their children in order to attain desired levels of social status in the community. In these cases, house forms reflect cosmological themes, with potent cultural symbols manifested in shrines and other features in the domestic built environment. Raising children in a house that is a cosmological metaphor evidently conditions them to more readily accept hierarchical social relations, by linking the activities of everyday home life to powerful symbols legitimizing inequality. Now I want to know (among many other questions): To what degree were ancient Zapotec houses cosmological metaphors, and how did this change over time? Although my comparative household research is a small step toward the larger goal of comprehending the evolution of a civilization, this foray into a new methodology has aided me in a pursuit of knowledge about sociocultural evolution, the origins of which can be traced back to Leslie White's courses.

Earlier, I alluded to anthropology's potential to develop a new synthesis that would combine the power of sociocultural and ecological theory with sophisticated archaeological methods. Has this come about? Not yet. But, by and large, we have moved in a direction that allows us to realize that potential. The most important outcome of the synthesis to date, besides an abundance of useful new data, is that we are able to see clearly the shortcomings of the excessively reductionist cultural materialist and population determinist ecological theories. Our data have opened our eyes to the need for more sophisticated approaches that better account for economic, political, and ideational factors in the growth of complex societies.

NOTES

1. For example, Paul R. Ehrlich, *The Population Bomb* (New York: Ballantine, 1968); Garrett Hardin, *Population, Evolution, and Birth Control* (San Francisco: Freeman, 1964); Donella and Dennis Meadows, *The Limits to Growth* (New York: Universe Books, 1972); Taghi Farvar and John Milton, eds., *The Careless Technology: Ecology and International Development* (New York: Natural History Press, 1972).
2. Richard W. Franke, "Miracle Seeds and Shattered Dreams," *Natural History* 83 (1974); Mahmood Mamdani, *The Myth of Population Control: Family, Caste, and Class in an Indian Village* (New York: Monthly Review Press, 1973).
3. My training and interests have enabled me to participate in a Purdue University undergraduate program, funded by the Kellogg Foundation, designed to introduce social and humanistic perspectives to agronomic education, so that students develop an awareness of the social, moral, and environmental consequences of industrialized food systems.
4. Kent V. Flannery, "The Cultural Evolution of Civilizations," *Annual Review of Ecology and Systematics* 3 (1972): 399–426; Elman R. Service, *Origins of the State and Civilization: The Process of Cultural Evolution* (New York: W. W. Norton, 1975).
5. For example, the special issue titled "Cross-Cultural and Comparative Research: Theory and Method," *Behavior Science Research* 25 (1991).
6. Described, for example, in Colin Renfrew and Paul Bahn, *Archaeology: Theories, Methods, and Practice* (New York: Thames and Hudson, 1991).
7. Leslie A. White, *The Evolution of Culture* (New York: McGraw-Hill, 1959); Julian H. Steward, *Theory of Culture Change: The Methodology of Multilinear Evolution* (Urbana, IL: University of Illinois Press, 1955); Karl A. Wittfogel, *Oriental Despotism* (New Haven, CT: Yale University Press, 1957); Marvin Harris, *Cultural Materialism: The*

Struggle for a Science of Culture (New York: Vintage Books, 1979); Esther Boserup, *The Conditions of Agricultural Growth* (Chicago: Aldine Atherton, 1965).

8. For example, Frank Hole, Kent V. Flannery, and James A. Neely, *Prehistory and Human Ecology of the Deh Luran Plain: An Early Village Sequence from Khuzistan, Iran* (Ann Arbor: University of Michigan Museum of Anthropology Memoirs 1, 1969); Douglas Byers, ed., *The Prehistory of the Tehuacan Valley, Volume One: Environment and Subsistence* (Austin: University of Texas Press, 1967), and subsequent volumes of the Tehuacan project reports.

9. Karl W. Butzer, *Early Hydraulic Civilization in Egypt: A Study in Cultural Ecology* (Chicago: University of Chicago Press, 1976); Robert McAdams, *Heartland of Cities: Surveys of Ancient Settlement and Land Use on the Central Floodplain of the Euphrates* (Chicago: University of Chicago Press, 1981); Angel Palerm and Eric R. Wolf, "Ecological Potential and Cultural Development in Mesoamerica," *Pan American Union Social Science Monograph* 3: 1–37; William T. Sanders, Jeffrey R. Parsons, and Robert S. Santley, *The Basin of Mexico: Ecological Processes in the Evolution of a Civilization* (New York: Academic Press, 1979).

10. Eric R. Wolf, "Introduction," in Eric R. Wolf, ed., *The Valley of Mexico: Studies in Pre-Hispanic Ecology and Society* (Albuquerque: University of New Mexico Press, 1976).

11. Wolf, "Introduction"; Sanders, Parsons, and Santley, *The Basin of Mexico;* René Millon, *Urbanization at Teotihuacan, Mexico, Volume One: The Teotihuacan Map, Part One: Text* (Austin: University of Texas Press, 1973). Sites of the "archaic" period previous to about 1500 B.C. have been found and studied but present difficult methodological problems for reconstruction of human social systems.

12. Richard E. Blanton, *Monte Albán: Settlement Patterns at the Ancient Zapotec Capital* (New York: Academic Press, 1978); Richard Blanton, Stephen A. Kowalewski, Gary M. Feinman, and Jill Appel, *Monte Albán's Hinterland, Part I: The Prehispanic Settlement Patterns of the Central and Southern Parts of the Valley of Oaxaca, Mexico* (Ann Arbor: University of Michigan Museum of Anthropology, Memoirs 15, 1982); Stephen A. Kowalewski, Gary M. Feinman, Laura Finsten, Richard E. Blanton, and Linda Nicholas, *Monte Albán's Hinterland, Part II: Prehispanic Settlement Patterns in Tlacolula, Etla, and Ocotlán, The Valley of Oaxaca, Mexico* (Ann Arbor: University of Michigan, Museum of Anthropology Memoirs 23, 1989).

13. Richard E. Blanton, Stephen A. Kowalewski, Gary M. Feinman, and Laura M. Finsten, *Ancient Mesoamerica: A Comparison of Change in Three Regions*, 2nd rev. ed. (Cambridge: Cambridge University Press, 1993), Chapter 4; Frances F. Berdan, Richard E. Blanton, Elizabeth Boone, Mary Hodge, Michael E. Smith, and Emily Umberger, *Aztec Imperial Strategies* (Washington, D.C.: Dumbarton Oaks, 1996).

14. The degree to which new theory is needed is currently an issue of contention, as some researchers are unwilling to accept the critiques of cultural ecology; this is discussed in Richard E. Blanton, "Theory and Practice in Mesoamerican Archaeology: A Comparison of Two Modes of Scientific Inquiry," in Joyce Marcus, ed., *Debating Oaxaca Archaeology* (Ann Arbor: University of Michigan, Museum of Anthropology, Anthropological Papers 84, 1990); cf. Blanton et al., *Ancient Mesoamerica,* Chapter 1. In a study combining the Valley of Mexico archaeological data with early colonial Spanish descriptions of the region, I was able to show that the distribution of cities of the last two prehispanic periods is strongly predicted by market location theory, not environmental factors or carrying capacity. See Richard E.

Blanton, "The Basin of Mexico Market System and the Growth of Empire," in Frances F. Berdan et al., *Aztec Imperial Strategies*.

15. Eric R. Wolf, *Europe and the People without History* (Berkeley: University of California Press, 1982).

16. Robert M. Netting, Richard R. Wilk, and Eric J. Arnould, "Introduction," in Robert M. Netting, Richard R. Wilk, and Eric J. Arnould, eds., *Households: Comparative and Historical Studies of the Domestic Group* (Berkeley: University of California Press, 1984).

17. Richard E. Blanton, *Households and Houses: A Comparative Perspective* (New York: Plenum, 1994).

SUGGESTED READINGS

Blanton, Richard E., Stephen A. Kowalewski, Gary M. Feinman, and Laura Finsten. *Ancient Mesoamerica: A Comparison of Change in Three Regions,* 2nd ed. Cambridge: Cambridge University Press, 1993. Compares the evolution of prehispanic Mesoamerican societies in three major regions, the Valleys of Mexico and Oaxaca, and the lowland Maya.

Harris, Marvin. *Our Kind: Who We Are, Where We Came From, Where We Are Going.* New York: Harper & Row, 1989. Broad-ranging overview of human social evolution from a cultural ecological perspective.

Netting, Robert M., Richard R. Wilk, and Eric J. Arnould, eds. *House-holds: Comparative and Historical Studies of the Domestic Group* Berkeley: University of California Press, 1984. A large collection of papers indicating the range of household studies in anthropology.

Renfrew, Colin, and Paul Bahn. *Archaeology: Theories, Methods, and Practice.* New York: Thames and Hudson, 1991. Recent review of developments in archaeological method and theory.

Wenke, Robert J. *Patterns in Prehistory: Humankind's First Three Million Years,* 3rd ed. Oxford: Oxford University Press, 1990. Summarizes archaeological sequences for all major world areas.

ORIGINS OF SOCIAL INEQUALITY

ELIZABETH M. BRUMFIEL

I became an archaeologist because I began to wonder about the origins of social inequality. As an undergraduate anthropology major, I learned about people such as the Mbuti and the !Kung, and I was told that at one time in the past all humans had lived in such small, egalitarian groups. What events had led from societies where people lived as equals (or, at least, with only minor differences) to the opulent empires of the ancient world? How could a small group of elites seize and maintain control over a much larger group of people, the mass of commoners? How were these early systems of social inequality related to the divisions of rich and poor that characterize the modern world?

When I began graduate school in 1970 I found that many of my questions had already been answered. Many archaeologists believed that social inequality developed because it was beneficial: It helped humans adapt to environmental problems. In a system of social inequality, wealthy, powerful leaders could oversee the construction of large-scale irrigation projects and maintain stores of surplus food to feed the population in years of bad harvests. Rulers could sponsor trading expeditions to procure raw materials that were not locally available and repress warfare so that people could meet in markets to exchange their different wares. This was the theory, but I didn't buy it.

My knowledge of ancient civilizations was not extensive. At that point it came mostly from watching Cecil B. DeMille movies about the Biblical Near East and reading *The Good Earth*. But it did appear to me that the peasants of ancient Egypt or imperial China had to work a lot harder to survive than the Mbuti or the !Kung and lived a more precarious existence. So how could archaeologists say that social inequality was beneficial?[1] My doubts made me want to test the theory. Testing the theory became the focus of my doctoral research in Mexico.

I chose to work in Mexico for a number of reasons. First, I had been to Mexico working on other archaeological projects, and I liked it a lot. In highland Mexico, the days are bright and warm, and the nights are cool. The patios of Mexican houses are filled with brilliant flowers and songbirds. The Mexican people are hard working, generous, and somehow manage to keep a sense of humor despite their poverty. Mexican markets are fascinating; Mexican food is wonderful; the Mexican landscape is breathtaking. Mexico is filled with street life and animal life, and it is *never*, ever boring.

Second, I wanted to use the extensive historical descriptions of the Aztecs of Mexico to supplement my archaeological research. Some of these descriptions were written by the European soldiers, priests, and administrators who ruled the Aztecs after Cortés's victory in 1521. Others were written by the Aztec nobility who, having learned to write Nahuatl (the Aztec language), Spanish, or Latin (the language of the Catholic Church), recorded the native histories that had been passed down to them in memorized oral narratives and pictorial documents. These native histories have all the elements of good soap opera: vivid tales of heroism, betrayal, triumphs, and defeats by members of the ruling class. They also supply information that can be used to interpret archaeological sites and artifacts.

Third, William T. Sanders and Barbara J. Price had just published *Mesoamerica: The Evolution of a Civilization*.[2] This book used adaptationist theory to explain prehistoric Mexican cultures.[3] Drawing upon eyewitness descriptions of the bustling, well-stocked market in Tlatelolco, at the Aztec capital, Sanders and Price argued that the Aztec state developed to prevent the disruption of the complex, highly efficient Aztec market system. The state mediated conflicts between buyers and sellers and prevented the outbreak of warfare within the marketing region. Thus, it promoted the exchange of goods among peasants growing different kinds of crops and craft specialists who produced knives, pots, mats, salt, and the other necessities of daily life. According to Sanders and Price, the intensification of specialization and exchange in the expanding Aztec empire enabled growing numbers of people to live in comfort and security.

DISSERTATION RESEARCH: THE AZTEC ECONOMY

Working with Jeffrey R. Parsons, my dissertation advisor at the University of Michigan, I developed a research proposal to test Sanders and Price's model of the Aztec economy. I planned work at a site where people had at one time lived independent of the Aztecs but had later become part of the Aztec empire. I would determine if there was evidence for greater specialization and exchange at the site once it joined the Aztec empire so that its economic system was no longer subject to disruption.

Parsons recommended that I work at Huexotla (Way-sho'-tla), a small village in the eastern Valley of Mexico. The native histories suggested that Huexotla had once been the most important town in the eastern Valley, a town with its own ruler, its own palace and temples, and presumably its own marketplace. In 1430 Huexotla became part of the Aztec empire. How had this affected Huexotla's economy?

Parsons had visited Huexotla during his site survey of the eastern Valley of Mexico.[4] He observed that while the center of ancient Huexotla lay under the modern village, the remains of much of the old town were exposed in the open fields south of the modern settlement. Here, the ground was littered with prehistoric debris: potsherds, obsidian tools and waste flakes, grinding stones, clay figurines, and occasional stone beads. In addition, isolated clusters of artifacts, marking individual houses, were scattered up the slopes east of Huexotla for a distance of five kilometers. While these artifacts had been disturbed somewhat by plowing and erosion, most had simply lain on the surface of the ground for the past five hundred years, a source of interest to local farmers, but otherwise left alone.

I planned to pick up surface artifacts in all areas of the site. Then artifacts from the areas of the site occupied when Huexotla was an independent center could be compared with artifacts from the areas of the site occupied when Huexotla was part of the Aztec empire. If Sanders and Price were correct, there should be more evidence of craft specialization and exchange in the parts of the site occupied when Huexotla was part of the Aztec empire.

Parsons informed local representatives of the Mexican National Institute of Anthropology and History that I would be working at the site. Then he delivered my husband and me to the nearby town of Texcoco. We took a room at the local Hotel Castillo, and Parsons drove off, leaving us on our own.

A word about my husband, Vince. Vince is a high school math teacher who has always supported my work in Mexico. The first summer we worked at Huexotla, Vince volunteered to be half my crew (I was the other half, except for weekends when we were joined by Jill Appel, who worked the rest of the week at another dig in the valley). Later in my career, Vince stayed home with our son while I went off to supervise other projects. I've tried to pay him back. One year, I quit smoking. Another year, I didn't object when he got rid of the TV. But I've always felt incredibly lucky to have a husband who cared enough about me to promote my career instead of obstructing it.

The first problem we ran into was getting to Huexotla. We knew that a bus ran from Texcoco to Huexotla, and the Hotel Castillo was right next to the bus station (as we were constantly reminded by the exhaust fumes, the roar of unmuffled engines, and the loud buzz of the dispatcher's button that filtered into our room). But *which* bus was headed for Huexotla? Each bus had a destination named on its banner, but we soon discovered that the named destination was not necessarily where the bus was going. It was best always to ask the driver, we learned, and to stop each bus until the right one came along.

The second problem was organizing the work. Huexotla was big. The first five days, we did nothing but walk the site, trying to find out where it ended and what its artifact distributions looked like. I was completely overwhelmed. But slowly, I began to devise a plan for taking collections in a systematic way. First, I traced an aerophoto of the site, showing the boundaries of modern fields, onto a piece of graph paper. Then, because the site was too big to collect in its entirety, I chose one randomly selected square out of each block of one hundred squares on the graph paper to serve as my sample. Then, guided by the graph paper map and the boundaries of modern fields, I located my sample collection units on the ground.

When we finally got started the work was a lot of fun. It consisted of picking up artifacts from five-meter-square collection areas and taking the collections back to Texcoco to be washed (in our hotel room) and stored for further analysis. The days were bright and sunny (until the rains began in the mid-afternoon). The Mexican countryside was rich and green because it was summer. We worked in cornfields and bean fields studded with large, drooping Pirú trees. Usually a donkey, staked out to pasture, was braying in the distance, and we could hear roosters crowing in the village. Some mornings we could look all the way across the Valley of Mexico and see Mexico City nestled at the foot of steep, dark volcanic cones.

The artifacts were interesting. Almost half of the pottery at Huexotla was decorated. The most common type had black designs painted on the smooth, natural orange surface of the dish or bowl. Highly complex curvilinear designs typified vessels from the period of Huexotla's independence; simple series of lines and dots following the circumference of the vessel wall distinguished pots dating to the time of the Aztec empire.[5] Red wares were also common. These were simple rounded bowls covered with highly polished, cherry-red paint. The red paint might be covered with designs in black and white (from the period of independence), or black only (usually dating to the Aztec empire).

Some artifacts could clearly be linked to specific economic activities. For example, cylindrical chunks of obsidian (volcanic glass) with vertical flake scars were the cores from which sharp, parallel-sided blades had been removed (an obsidian blade was the Swiss army knife of Aztec peasant households). Perforated ceramic disks were the weights for spindles used in spinning thread (for weaving cloth). Trapezoidal slabs of basalt posed something of a puzzle until further library research suggested that they were the blades of scrapers used to clean the fibers of maguey leaves (the maguey is a long leafed cactus similar to yucca). These fibers were woven into cloth or twisted into rope. Turtle-shaped chunks of obsidian were scrapers used to hollow out the stalks of maguey plants so that their sweet sap could be drawn off for processing into syrup, sugar, or beer (*pulque*).

Vince and I worked for two summers in the field, making 1,380 collections (a grant from the National Science Foundation enabled the size of the

field crew to grow to four during the second summer). We spent a third summer recording the contents of each collection—counting the artifacts of each
particular type. At the end of this analysis, some aspects of Huexotla's economy had become fairly clear.

The data suggested that there hadn't been many full-time specialists in ancient Huexotla. Obsidian cores were evenly dispersed around the site, as were
spindle whorls. Evidently, peasant households made their own tools and wove
their own cloth rather than depending on outside specialists. Scrapers to clean
maguey fibers and scrapers to hollow out maguey stalks were most frequent
on the eastern slopes of Huexotla where soils were thin and maize cultivation was somewhat difficult. But both kinds of scrapers were found in other
parts of the settlement as well, suggesting that most of Huexotla's peasants cultivated some maguey plants. There were no large dumps of misfired pots that
would have indicated specialized ceramic producers. There were no concentrations of figurine molds resulting from specialized figurine workshops.
Thus, the internal economy of Huexotla seemed fairly simple, not a situation
that seemed to require the presence of a ruling elite.

The ancient Huexotlans had obtained goods from outsiders. Many of the
tools were made from obsidian, but there are no obsidian outcrops at Huexotla. Thus, obsidian had to come from elsewhere. Also, some spindle whorls
were made in a style that seemed foreign to the Huexotla region. And salt,
indicated by the presence of Fabric-Marked pottery (a rough-surfaced, porous
ceramic type associated with salt-producing facilities at other sites), must have
come from elsewhere in the valley. Some of these goods were present in parts
of the site that were occupied when Huexotla was independent, suggesting
that a regional market system operated reasonably well even without a regional state to prevent its disruption.

Some kinds of imported goods, but not all of them, were more common
in parts of the site occupied when Huexotla was part of the Aztec empire, and
this seemed to support Sanders and Price's theory that the Aztec state promoted regional exchange. For example, the frequency of salt and green obsidian from Pachuca increased at Huexotla during the period of Aztec rule.
However, the frequency of other imported goods, such as gray obsidian from
Otumba, declined. According to historical documents, salt was produced near
Tenochtitlan, and obsidian from Pachuca (but not Otumba) was collected by
the Aztecs as tribute. Thus, products that were in some way connected with
the Aztec capital became more available at Huexotla while products that had
no such connection did not. This suggested that Aztec rule was associated
only with the intensification of exchange between the Aztec capital and hinterland communities and *not* with the intensification of the exchange among
all hinterland communities, as Sanders and Price had predicted.

Production at Huexotla also changed under Aztec rule. People at Huexotla produced more maguey-sap by-products (there were more obsidian
scrapers and more jars for boiling sap in the areas of the site occupied when

Huexotla was part of the empire) and less cloth (fewer spindle whorls were used during imperial times). In my view, both of these changes could be understood as consequences of expanded urban-rural exchange.

The Aztec capital, Tenochtitlan, had a population of 250,000 at the time of Spanish conquest (in its time, it was one of the ten largest cities in the world). It contained a large number of non-food-producing specialists who assisted the ruler in governing the empire. This group included high-ranking lords and nobles, army officers, tribute stewards, religious functionaries, skilled artisans, palace guards, entertainers, and domestics. Support of this population depended upon the collection and distribution of tribute cloth. According to Aztec tribute lists, cloth was an item of tribute paid to the Aztec ruler by all subject provinces, and according to historical documents, the ruler distributed this cloth to reward all those who served him. The individuals who received this cloth took at least a part of it to the urban market to exchange for food, such as the maguey syrup, sugar, and beer produced by Huexotla's peasants. This gave peasants the opportunity to acquire cloth for their own clothing and for their tribute payments without having to weave it (a very laborious task). This would explain why people at Huexotla began to produce more maguey sap products and less cloth.

I concluded from my dissertation research that the Aztec state did not arise to facilitate exchange between specialists of diverse types. Some exchange between specialists had occurred prior to Aztec rule, without the presence of a unifying state. Under the Aztecs, only the exchange of tribute for food between urban and rural populations increased significantly; other exchanges, between groups of rural specialists, were not much affected. Thus, the growth of the Aztec state did stimulate market exchange, but this exchange was geared to providing food to the political elites who lived in the city, not to enhancing the rural producers' standard of living.

The published results of my dissertation research drew mixed reactions.[6] Archaeologists who firmly believed that social inequality was a form of human adaptation to the problems of survival thought that there were errors in my research methods. They were critical of my having used surface collections (as opposed to less disturbed excavation data), and they thought that I had taken too small a sample (only 1 percent of some parts of the site). Some regarded Huexotla as an atypical or inappropriate research site. Archaeologists who had their own doubts about the contribution of social inequality to human survival were intrigued by my results, especially the suggestion that political organization had influenced Aztec economic structure.

Since my dissertation, I have carried out field work at two other sites: Xico (She'-co) in the southern Valley of Mexico and Xaltocan (Shal-to'-can) in the northern Valley. Surface collecting these two sites confirmed much of what I had found at Huexotla: little evidence of full-time craft specialization, a modest increase in the use of goods procured at the Tenochtitlan market coinciding with the expansion of the Aztec empire, and some indications of intensified food production. These results have helped to confirm the results of the Huex-otla research. At the same time, there are important differences among these sites. Xico was located in a prime agricultural area, and yet, with less decorated pottery and less obsidian, it was impoverished compared to Huexotla. Xalto-can, on an island surrounded by a shallow lake and swamp, relied more on aquatic resources such as birds and fish and less on agriculture. Differences among Valley of Mexico settlements during the Aztec period are also evident when Huexotla, Xico, and Xaltocan are compared with other sites investigat-ed by my colleagues Tom Charlton, Susan Evans, Deborah Nichols, and Michael Smith.[7]

My most exciting "discoveries" have not been rich tombs or extraordi-nary artifacts that I uncovered in the field. Instead, my "discoveries" have been detecting patterns in the artifact data that suggest *what* people were doing during Aztec times and *why* they did what they did. The questions that have most concerned me are how Aztec rulers constructed their power and how women's lives changed as they became part of the Aztec empire. I have also tried to discover the best way for archaeologists to communicate with the general public. The first two questions grew from my interaction with other archaeologists. The last question resulted from my confrontation with the modern inhabitants of Xaltocan.

POLITICAL PROCESSES IN AZTEC MEXICO

In 1983 Timothy Earle, an Andean archaeologist at UCLA, invited me to join a group that was examining the relationship of specialization and exchange to the development of complex societies. Obviously, my work at Huexotla had given me some expertise in this area. But at Huexotla, I had studied only utilitarian crafts; Earle was interested in both utilitarian and elite crafts. He pro-posed that the two had played different roles in the development of social in-equality.

The historical descriptions of Aztec culture indicated that Earle's proposal was correct. Aztec rulers had very little direct influence on utilitarian craft production. But they did commission many works of art, to serve as furnish-ings for state-sponsored ceremonial activity and to distribute as gifts to loyal allies and subjects. These pieces of art communicated a world view that in-fused Aztec warfare and conquest with cosmic significance; they also enabled the Aztec ruler to maintain his image as an able and generous leader. The his-torical documents suggested that elite craft goods played an ideological role in Aztec culture: They provided an assessment of people (the ruler as an able and generous leader) and events (warfare and conquest as a part of the cos-mic order) that solidified the Aztec king's political power.[8]

I was able to use aspects of the Huexotla data to test the idea that art and ritual were used to construct political power in the Valley of Mexico. In late pre-Hispanic Mexico, art and ritual were tied to feasting, and feasting can be gauged archaeologically using the decorated bowls, dishes, and plates that I had collected at Huexotla. When I was working on my dissertation, I had used these vessels simply as time markers; that is, their decorations helped me to separate areas of the site occupied before Huexotla became part of the Aztec empire from areas occupied later.

Now I returned to this pottery with a new perspective. If art, ritual, and feasting had helped to win political support, there should be more evidence of feasting during Huexotla's era of political autonomy when Huexotla's rulers were free to expand their power. Later, under Aztec rule, there should have been less feasting and coalition building because the political aspirations of Huexotla's lords were more constrained (they were limited to carrying out the commands of the reigning Aztec ruler). This prediction turned out to be accurate. Collections from the earlier areas of Huexotla had more decorated pottery (more feasting, more alliance-building) than areas occupied later, when Huexotla was part of the empire.[9]

Investigating the role of art in Aztec society and documenting the relationship of feast-giving to political alliance building moved me closer to understanding the central mystery of emerging social inequality. I now think that social inequality develops as an ambitious leader implements strategies for building a coalition of followers larger than the following of any other individual or institution in society. In this way, a single, privileged minority can rule because it is the largest organized group in society. People excluded from rule may outnumber those in control, but because they are not organized, they cannot oppose those who are in control under ordinary circumstances. My interest in political organization and alliance-building continues.[10]

WOMEN'S LIVES IN AZTEC MEXICO

My interest in women's lives developed from a conference organized by Joan Gero, an Andean archaeologist at the University of South Carolina, and Margaret Conkey, a paleolithic archaeologist at the University of California at Berkeley. The subject of this conference was "Women's Production in Prehistory." Again, my field work at Huexotla, Xico, and Xaltocan gave me some basis for addressing the topic. The surface collections from Huexotla, Xico, and Xaltocan contained evidence of both spinning and cooking; according to the historical documents, these were the primary occupations of Aztec women. Spindle whorls provided evidence of spinning; tortilla griddles (comals) and jars represented two different cooking techniques (toasting and boiling).

First, I looked to see if women had had to weave more cloth once their towns fell subject to the Aztec empire and its tribute collectors. As noted previously, at Valley of Mexico sites, spindle whorl frequencies actually declined; cloth production decreased as the production of food for market sale intensified. However, at sites outside the Valley of Mexico (in Morelos), spindle whorl frequencies were dramatically higher during the period of imperial domination.[11] Since distance prevented access to the market at the Aztec capital, women did not have the option of purchasing tribute cloth. So they, themselves, wove cloth to meet the Aztec demand for tribute.

Then, I looked to see if the different patterns of cloth procurement (market purchase versus local production) were paralleled by differences in food preparation techniques as women sought to adjust household labor to the demands of the state. Differences in food preparation were evident. At sites within the Valley of Mexico, there was a higher frequency of tortilla griddles, which is surprising since tortillas have to be shaped individually and therefore require more labor than one-pot gruels and stews cooked in jars. But tortillas have the advantage of being a dry, more portable food. Tortillas provided meals that could be carried off and eaten by family members who were tending fields, gathering raw materials, and marketing produce away from home. In Morelos, where there was less opportunity to market produce and where women wove cloth for tribute instead of purchasing it, women saved time and energy by preparing less labor-intensive, one-pot meals, such as the maize gruel *atole*. Sites in Morelos have a lower frequency of tortilla griddles and a higher frequency of jars.[12]

There was, then, a great deal of variation in women's activities in Central Mexico. Although most women were weavers and cooks, some wove more and some less, some cooked one way and some another. Women did not always engage in the same activities; they responded flexibly and strategically to the new circumstances created by Aztec domination. Archaeologists have tended to regard activities such as child care, fuel gathering, food preparation, and cleaning (activities we regard as women's work) as very routinized and uninteresting. But these tasks can be organized in many different ways, depending upon ecological and political variables. Examining the organizational basis of "women's work" is a new and exciting area of archaeological research.[13]

Having studied one aspect of women's lives in Aztec Mexico, I was asked to examine another aspect. I was invited to contribute to a session on gender representation in Mesoamerica organized by Veronica Kahn of the University of Illinois at Urbana and Geoffrey McCafferty of Brown University for the American Anthropological Association meeting in 1990. Previous studies of women's status in Aztec Mexico had suggested that as the Aztec empire grew, the Aztec state increasingly glorified militarism and masculinity.[14] As a result, women lost status and power. I wanted to know how far this Aztec male-dominant ideology had spread. Had it been confined to the Aztec capital, or had it influenced hinterland communities such as Huexotla, Xico, and Xaltocan?

Again, I turned to the surface collections, this time to compare the depiction of women in the ceramic figurines from Huexotla, Xico, and Xaltocan with the depiction of women in the sculptures and manuscripts produced in Tenochtitlan. I found that the images of women in figurines and the art of Tenochtitlan showed almost no similarities.

For example, in Tenochtitlan, a monumental carving from the foot of the Aztec Great Temple presented an image of a goddess, Coyolxauhqui, cut to pieces by her brother, the war god Huitzilopochtli. In smaller sculptures, Aztec women were depicted in a kneeling pose, which emphasized women's roles in weaving and food preparation (weaving and grinding corn were both performed in a kneeling position). In Aztec manuscripts, goddesses were sometimes depicted holding shields and staffs, as if power for women could only be obtained by assuming a male warrior role. In contrast, most ceramic figurines from Huexotla, Xico, and Xaltocan show women in a standing position. Often, the female figurines held one or two children, as if to emphasize women's roles in reproduction.

Images of women with children are unknown in official Aztec art, and mutilated or masculinized women do not appear as figurines. Figurines in kneeling positions do occur, but they are rare. These differences in art are evidence of different views concerning women. Evidently, people in hinterland communities did not share the Aztec state's ideas regarding women. The peasants in hinterland communities maintained their ability to formulate their own views and to communicate these views to others.

This study shows how archaeology can help reconstruct the ideas of common people whose thoughts and activities are rarely included in historical documents produced by the upper class.

MEXICAN ARCHAEOLOGY FOR MEXICANS

This final facet of my research developed from my relations with the people of Xaltocan. On the first day of my work there in 1987, about sixty people gathered to ask me who I was and what I was doing in their town. Why should they let me gather their artifacts? It would clearly benefit me, but what would it do for them? I replied that Xaltocan had an illustrious history and that if I worked in Xaltocan, I could find out more about its history. Then I would tell them, and they could tell their children. The people of Xaltocan agreed to let me work, but they emphasized that I was to tell them what I found out from my studies.

Communicating my results to the community turned out to be very difficult. At first, I tried to meet my obligation by passing out translated copies of my professional papers. But people didn't read them; the papers seemed to disappear without a trace. The papers weren't really too technical, but they were too general. They dealt with theoretical issues like the relationship of craft specialization to social complexity, or the role of feasting in political coalition building. My papers were not unusual in this regard;

most archaeologists study particular sites and prehistoric periods in order to formulate general theories about the factors that produced culture change in the human past.

In contrast, the people of Xaltocan wanted specific information about what had happened in their town. And they were hoping for information that would enhance their self-esteem. Although writing this kind of prehistory was just as difficult as any professional writing, I did manage to organize an exhibit and a twenty-four-page report on my research specifically aimed at the people of Xaltocan.

The exhibit emphasized the success of Xaltocan's people in occupying their town continuously for nearly 1,200 years. It showed how the people of Xaltocan had created an artificial "island" for their town by bringing in soil to build foundation platforms for their houses, generation after generation. It showed how the people of Xaltocan had learned to rely on the fish and waterfowl from the shallow lake and swamp that surrounded the town and how they had constructed a system of raised field agriculture in order to grow crops in the normally water-logged soil.[15] The exhibit described the crafts, trade patterns, and religion of prehistoric Xaltocan using photographs and drawings of the artifacts and structures we had excavated.

This encounter changed my ideas about my obligations as an archaeologist. Prior to my encounter in Xaltocan, I believed that my obligations consisted of publishing my data and theories fully and accurately so that they could be used by other archaeologists and social scientists. My encounter in Xaltocan made me realize that I also have an obligation to make my research results available and relevant to the people whose past I study. Anything less would be an exercise in archaeological imperialism, that is, using a people's artifacts and history to serve the needs and interests of a foreigner (me) instead of the local population.[16]

The exhibit was very well received by the people of Xaltocan. Adding new information to the store of local history was as rewarding as any professional work I've done in archaeology. Instead of being a remote outsider, I found a place in the community.

SUMMARY

Over the years, the satisfactions I gain from archaeology have multiplied. Starting out, I was intensely interested in the artifacts themselves, and in the adventure of living and working in Mexico. More recently, I have been able to move away from topics of traditional interest in archaeology, such as craft specialization and exchange patterns, to deal with topics that are more central to my interests: the construction of social power and the status of women. As my research continues, I see more and more connections among my interests.

For example, the changes that I detected in women's work and women's status under the Aztec state seem closely related to the strategies implemented by Aztec rulers to build and maintain their power. Also, the design of my exhibit of archaeological research for the people of Xaltocan was related to what I had learned about political power. I designed the exhibit to emphasize self-help and problem-solving in Xaltocan's past because I thought that this would encourage the people of Xaltocan to organize themselves to pursue their current political goals. As the connections among my research interests seem to grow, so too does my sense of connection to people. I have more of a sense of place in Xaltocan than I did at Xico or Huexotla, and I have begun to collaborate with Mexican archaeologists on several projects.

I never could have predicted how my career would turn out. In the beginning, I just liked archaeology, and I found it intensely interesting. I advanced in my career by taking on small-scale problems that seemed related to my central problem, the emergence of social inequality. A lifetime in Mexican archaeology has been the result.

I have benefitted tremendously from the generosity of other archaeologists who have shared their ideas and data with me and encouraged me to pursue my interests. I have also benefitted from the generosity, hard work, and trust of people in the Mexican towns where I have worked.

My next project is to write a general overview of the development of social inequality in Mexico. Of course, I hope that everything in the book turns out to be right. But it amuses me to think of the skeptical student out there who will read my book, and just know that I've gotten it wrong, and will set out on a lifetime of archaeological research to find her own answers.

NOTES

1. My skepticism was also rooted in my opposition to the Vietnam war. How could people say that states were beneficial when the government of South Vietnam seemed to have little interest in improving the lives of Vietnamese peasants? How could people say that states were beneficial when our own government seemed bent on supporting the corrupt South Vietnamese government no matter what the cost in American and Vietnamese lives?

2. William T. Sanders and Barbara J. Price, *Mesoamerica: The Evolution of a Civilization* (New York: Random House, 1968).

3. The adaptationist theory proposes that humans use culture to adapt to their environments. It regards social institutions such as states and empires as the product of population-environment interaction. It suggests that social inequality helps human populations solve their problems of survival.

4. Jeffrey R. Parsons, *Prehistoric Settlement Patterns in the Texcoco Region, Mexico* (Ann Arbor: The University of Michigan Museum of Anthropology, Memoirs 3, 1971).

5. The dates of the various ceramic designs were established in previous excavations of other sites in the region.

6. Elizabeth M. Brumfiel, "Specialization, Market Exchange, and the Aztec State: A View from Huexotla," *Current Anthropology* 21 (1980): 459–478.

7. Thomas H. Charlton, Deborah L. Nichols, and Cynthia O. Charlton, "Aztec Craft Production and Specialization: Archaeological Evidence from the City-State of Otumba," *World Archaeology* 23 (1991): 98–114; Susan T. Evans, ed., *Excavations at Cihuatecpan* (Nashville, TN: Vanderbilt University, Publications in Anthropology 36, 1988); Michael E. Smith, *Archaeological Research at Aztec-Period Rural Sites in Morelos, Mexico, Volume 1: Excavations and Architecture* (Pittsburgh, PA: University of Pittsburgh, Department of Anthropology, Memoirs in Latin American Archaeology 4, 1992).

8. Elizabeth M. Brumfiel, "Elite and Utilitarian Crafts in the Aztec State," in Elizabeth M. Brumfiel and Timothy K. Earle, eds., *Specialization, Exchange, and Complex Societies* (Cambridge: Cambridge University Press, 1987), pp. 102–118.

9. Elizabeth M. Brumfiel, "Consumption and Politics at Aztec Huexotla," *American Anthropologist* 89 (1987): 676–686.

10. These coalition-building processes were the subject of a conference, which resulted in a book: Elizabeth M. Brumfiel and John W. Fox, eds., *Factional Competition and Political Development in the New World* (Cambridge: Cambridge University Press, 1994). My current thinking on the emergence of social inequality is summarized in Elizabeth M. Brumfiel, "Distinguished Lecture in Archeology: Breaking and Entering the Ecosystem—Gender, Class, and Faction Steal the Show," *American Anthropologist* 94 (1992): 551–567.

11. Roger D. Mason, *Economic and Social Organization of an Aztec Provincial Center: Archaeological Research at Coatlan Viejo, Morelos, Mexico* (Ann Arbor: University Microfilms, 1980); Michael E. Smith and Kenneth G. Hirth, "The Development of Prehispanic Cotton-Spinning Technology in Western Morelos, Mexico," *Journal of Field Archaeology* 15 (1988): 349–358.

12. Ibid.

13. Elizabeth M. Brumfiel, "Weaving and Cooking: Women's Production in Aztec Mexico," in Joan M. Gero and Margaret W. Conkey, eds., *Engendering Archaeology: Women and Prehistory* (Oxford: Basil Blackwell, 1991), pp. 224–251.

14. June Nash, "The Aztecs and the Ideology of Male Dominance," *Signs* 4 (1978): 349–362; María J. Rodríguez, *La Mujer Azteca* (Toluca: Universidad Autónoma del Estado de México, 1989).

15. Deborah L. Nichols and Charles D. Frederick, "Irrigation Canals and Chinampas: Recent Research in the Northern Basin of Mexico," in B. Isaac and V. Scarborough, eds., *Research in Economic Anthropology,* Supplement 7 (Greenwich, CT: JAI Press, 1993).

16. This issue is explored at greater length in Bruce G. Trigger, "Archaeology and the Image of the American Indian," *American Antiquity* 45 (1980): 662–676; see also Robert Layton, ed., *Conflict in the Archaeology of Living Traditions* (London: Unwin Hyman, 1989).

SUGGESTED READINGS

Berdan, Frances F. *The Aztecs of Central Mexico: An Imperial Society.* New York: Holt, Rinehart & Winston, 1982. An interesting and comprehensive summary of Aztec culture based upon historical documents.

Brumfiel, Elizabeth M., and Timothy K. Earle, eds. *Specialization, Exchange, and Complex Societies*. Cambridge: Cambridge University Press, 1987. Examines the role of elite and utilitarian production in the emergence of social inequality.

Gero, Joan M., and Margaret W. Conkey, eds. *Engendering Archaeology: Women and Prehistory*. Oxford: Basil Blackwell, 1991. Discusses the presence of gender bias in the archaeological literature and investigates the role of women in a number of different prehistoric societies.

Matos Moctezuma, Eduardo. *The Great Temple of the Aztecs: Treasures of Tenochtitlan*. London: Thames and Hudson, 1988. A presentation of spectacular archaeological finds from recent excavations in Mexico City of the Aztecs' principal temple.

Sanders, William T., and Barbara J. Price. *Mesoamerica: The Evolution of a Civilization*. New York: Random House, 1968. Out of print, but still a stimulating introduction to the causes of cultural complexity in ancient Mexico and Guatemala.